Conestoga wagon and ox-team in the 1938 Caravan, reproducing trek of 1788 of the Northwest Territory

The Official Roster

of the

Soldiers of the
American Revolution

who lived in the

STATE OF OHIO

VOLUME TWO

PUBLISHED BY THE STATE SOCIETY
DAUGHTERS *of the* AMERICAN REVOLUTION
of OHIO

Collected under the Regimes of:

1929-32, Mrs. WALTER L. TOBEY, Hamilton, O. *State Regent.*
    Mrs. ORVILLE D. DAILEY, *State Chairman of Revolutionary Soldiers Graves.*
1932-35, Mrs. ASA CLAY MESSENGER, Xenia, O., *State Regent.*
    Mrs. ORVILLE D. DAILEY, *State Chairman Revolutionary Soldiers Graves.*
1935-38, Mrs. JOHN S. HEAUME, Springfield, O., *State Regent.*
    Mrs. ROBERT P. HAYNES, Ashland, O., *Historian.*
    Mrs. JOHN M. MARKLEY, Georgtown, O., *State Vice-Chairman of Revolutionary Soldiers Graves.*

COMPILED BY

Mrs. ORVILLE D. DAILEY, Albany, Ohio, *S. E. Director.*

This volume was reproduced
from a personal copy located in
the Publishers private library

Please direct allcorrespondence and book orders to:
SOUTHERN HISTORICAL PRESS, Inc.
PO Box 1267
Greenville, SC   29602-1267

Originally printed 1938
Reprinted By: Southern Historical Press, Inc.
              Greenville, SC   2022
ISBN #978-1-63914-047-3
Printed in the United Sattes of America

NORTHWEST TERRITORY
1787-88 CELEBRATION 1937-38

ORDINANCE OF 1787

AMERICA'S START TO THE OTHER SEA
AND TO HER UNIQUE EMINENCE AMONG
THE GOVERNMENTS OF MANKIND

"Hail to the men who made us free!
Hail to the stainless swords they drew!
A thousand years will never see
Forgetfulness of men so true;
Their deeds will live while grandly waves
The flag of a united land
Above their scattered sacred graves
From mountain height to ocean strand."

— CURRY.

FOREWORD

THE RESEARCH for Revolutionary soldiers in Ohio, which covered a period of twenty-five years, enabled the National Society Daughters of the American Revolution of Ohio to present the material to the Ohio State Legislature for publication of volume one in 1929.

Nine years of continued research has secured sufficient new material for the publication of a second volume. Although a Bill to publish volume two was passed by the State Legislature, continued delay in financing the project has led to its publication by the Ohio National Society Daughters of the American Revolution.

Volume one was largely the result of definite research by the chapters, who have also made valuable contributions to volume II; but this book contains, in greater part, data from some fifteen hundred applications for pensions, from the Pension Claim department, Washington D. C., for which the State D. A. R. is financially responsible. Such authentic, though brief facts were copied as will lead to the identity of an Ohio ancestor, enabling a descendant to continue research for himself. Other hundreds were contributed by Sons and Daughters who gave patriotic service through personal research.

In addition to these, the absence of a name from volume one has led to the filing of hitherto unknown soldiers by their descendants. As an expression of their appreciation, many genealogists have also contributed valuable material. For all the assistance given, Ohio expresses its grateful thanks.

Contained in this volume is addenda to the first volume, furnishing new facts which clarify previous statements, giving newly found clues; or correcting errors reported by those who hold authentic records. No doubt other errors have crept in, unavoidable in preparing material handed down through various agencies over a period of one hundred and fifty years. Included in this group, are records for your investigation, containing authentic material, but not sufficient proof to permit it to be listed definitely as a Revolutionary soldier of Ohio.

The signing of a record by a chapter or individual indicates responsibility for authenticity of the data contained therein. In justice to all who have searched so diligently for both volumes, may we beg your indulgence in asking for additional facts, for as a rule, all known data is contained in each volume, and is given as a clue for your personal investigation, or by a genealogist. Ohio Daughters have ever been willing to respond to reasonable requests.

New Counties in Ohio were formed by combining townships from several adjoining counties. Hence, in research for ancestral lines, one is advised to seek historical data in the counties which contributed to the formation of newer counties; but search for the burial place could be in the new county formed. Such statistics we have given you in the county lists.

The widespread appreciation with which volume one was received was gratifying to the Daughters, and has inspired them to gather together in volume two, authentic history of other Pioneers of Ohio, that such may be preserved in their honor, with the hope that some interested descendant may find a connecting link and give additional honor to the heroic ancestors who have made America great!

> JANE DOWD DAILEY, (Mrs. O. D.) *Compiler*
> (1923-1938)
> Albany, Ohio

MRS. JOHN S. HEAUME, *State Regent*
Springfield, Ohio
February 1, 1938

vi

Pensions for Revolutionary Soldiers

IN 1789 the first session of the first Congress authorized the payment by the United States of the pensions previously granted and paid by the respective States.

Previous to the year 1818 only those soldiers who were invalids as a result of actual service, or on whose behalf Congress took special action, received compensation.

The Act of 1818 provided that all officers, musicians, privates in every department, who served to the end of the war, or for nine months or longer were to receive a pension according to the rank and stated specifications. It related to the Continental Army and Navy alone, which consisted of those forces raised by Congress or those who were in the Regular U S Army.

The Act of Congress 1820 was made necessary because an alarming number of 8000 applications had accumulated. Congress then required a court statement of the estate and income of the applicant in order to prove his need of assistance. Many soldiers were now dropped from the lists, some not desiring to expose their meager possessions, others because they were not in indigent circumstances.

The facts which brought about the Rejected Pensions should be understood, namely, when evidence of service, or length of service, or property eligibility was not according to the law; or the service was not in the Continental (Federal) Army or Navy no pension was allowed. Many states pensioned their own "Militia," "State Troops," or "Line," which accounts for many pensioners listed in the Census of 1840, perhaps, whose applications are not found in the U. S. Pensions Claim department. A pension claim rejected, however, should have no bearing on the use of such service for eligibility to Revolutionary societies, if positive proof is evidenced.

As a reaction to the requirement of 1820 many transferred their property and others squandered their income in order to come under the law. But many needed assistance. It was an Act of Congress of 1823 which restored pensions to the needy, and to those who had not disposed of their property. A study of later Acts indicates a greater liberality for the soldier, extending even to his wife and children.

The letter S preceding the number of a pension claim indicates the soldier (survivor) himself, applied; W BL Wt 12569-160-55 indicates the widow's application with Bounty Land Warrant, number of file, issued for 160 acres, in 1855, which Act of Congress allowed the children of a soldier to obtain land; R is for rejected claim. Of interest, perhaps, is the following data, that there were 52,504 survivors of the War of the Revolution pensioned; that 22,644 widows received pensions; that Esther S. Damon, Plymouth Union, Vt. the last woman pensioner of the Revolution, died November 11, 1906 æ 92; that Daniel F. Bakeman, of New York, died in 1869, aged 109, the LAST SURVIVOR of the WAR OF THE REVOLUTION; (ref: exhibit of Pension department at Philadelphia Sesquicentennial, 1926, installed under supervision of Hon Winfield Scott, Commissioner of Pensions (p 355, May 1927 D. A. R. Magazine)); and that Ohio, Noble county, claims the LAST SURVIVING PENSIONER, John Gray, who died March 29 1868, at Hiramsburg, Ohio aged 104. (Ref: p 162, Ohio Roster Revolutionary Soldiers, Vol 1).

By JANE DOWD DAILEY
Ref: Acts of Congress.

D. A. R. Chapters of Ohio

A

Aaron Olmstead	Kent
Akron	Akron
Amanda Barker Devin	McConnelsville
Anna Asbury Stone	Cambridge
Ann Rucker	Woodsfield
Ann Simpson Davis	Columbus

B

Bellefontaine	Bellefontaine
Bethia Southwick	Wellsville
Beech Forest	Bethel
Black Swamp	Bowling Green

C

Canton	Canton
Captain James Lawrence	Ironton
Captain James Riley	Celina
Captain John James	Jackson
Captain William Hendricks	Marion
Catharine Greene	Xenia
Cedar Cliff	Cedarville
Childs Taylor	Chardon
Cincinnati	Cincinnati
Colonel George Croghan	Fremont
Colonel Jonathan Bayard Smith	Middletown
Colonel William Crawford	Upper Sandusky
Columbus	Columbus
Commodore Preble	Eaton
Coshocton	Coshocton
Cuyahoga Falls	Cuyahoga Falls
Cuyahoga Portage	Akron

D

Delaware City	Delaware
De Lery Portage	Port Clinton
Dolly Todd Madison	Tiffin

E

Elizabeth Sherman Reese	Lancaster
Elizabeth Zane Dew	Nelsonville
Elyria	Elyria
Eunice Grant	Jefferson

F

Firelands	Willard
Fort Avery	Milan
Fort Defiance	Defiance
Fort Findlay	Findlay
Fort Greenville	Greenville
Fort Industry	Toledo
Fort Laurens	New Philadelphia
Fort McArthur	Kenton
French Colony	Gallipolis

G

George Clinton	Wilmington
George Slagle	Jamestown
Governor Worthington	Logan
Granville	Granville

H

Hannah Crawford	Bucyrus
Hannah Dowd Vanderford	McArthur
Hannah Emerson Dustin	Marysville
Hetuck	Newark

I

Isaac Van Wart	Van Wert

J

Jacobus Westervelt	Westerville
James Fowler	Le Roy
Jane Bain	Alliance
Jane Washington	Fostoria
Jared Mansfield	Mansfield
John Reily	Hamilton
Jonathan Dayton	Dayton
Joseph Spencer	Portsmouth
Juliana White	Greenfield

K

Kokosing	Mt. Vernon

L

Lagonda	Springfield
Lakewood	Lakewood
Lewis Boyer	Sidney
Lieutenant Byrd	Decatur
Lima	Lima
London	London

M

Mahoning	Youngstown
Marietta	Marietta
Mariemont	Mariemont
Martha Pitkin	Sandusky
Mary Chesney	Warren
Mary Redmond	Conneaut
Mary Stanley	Ashtabula
Mary Washington	Mansfield
Massillon	Massillon
Miami	Troy
Michael Myers	Toronto
Molly Chittenden	Chagrin Falls
Moravian Trail	Cadiz
Moses Cleaveland	Cleveland
Mt. Gilead	Mt. Gilead
Mt. Sterling	Mt. Sterling
Muskingum	Zanesville

N

Nabby Lee Ames	Athens
Nancy Wolcott Squire	Oberlin
Nathaniel Massie	Chillicothe
Nathan Perry	Lorain
New Connecticut	Painesville

ALPHABETICAL LIST OF COUNTIES AND THEIR CHAPTERS

ADAMS COUNTY

Established 1797 by proclamation being fourth county formed from N W Territory

SYCAMORE CHAPTER

Alexander, John
Bagley, Azor
Breedlove, John
Brewer, Henry
Brewer, John
Brower, Hendricks
Brown, John
Callahan, Dennis
Corner, William
Crawford, John
Cross, Samuel
Daily, John
David, Zebediah
Edgington, George
Edgington, Isaac
Fields, Simon
Flood, William
Gates, William
Gordon, John

Grimes, Richard
Grooms, John
Hamilton, Charles
Harper, John
Heddleson, William
Jack, Thomas
Lawrence, Jacob
McMahon, Joseph
McCormick, John
McDaniel, Patrick
McPike, John
Magin, Charles
Marlott, Thomas
Mason, Thomas
Matheny, ——
Miller, James
Ogle, William
Reynolds, Nathaniel

Richardson, James
Rogers, William
Simpson, Robert
Smith, William
Stevens, Joseph
Stout, Obadiah
Strickling, Alexander
Symonds, John
Thompson, John
Toland, John
Trotter, Christopher
Trotter, John
Usman, Charles
Vandaman, Frederick
Waite, Jonathan
Walker, James
Walker, Peter
Walsh, James
Wickerham, Peter

ALLEN COUNTY

Formed 1820 from Indian Territory.

LIMA CHAPTER

Turner, James

ASHLAND COUNTY

Formed 1820 from Indian Territory.

SARAH COPUS CHAPTER

Castor, Noah
Church, Henry
Cornell, ——
Crapo, Jonathan
Hassinger, Abraham
Hill, Solomon
Luck, Adam
Marsh, Abijah

Mason, Martin Sr
Metcalf, Vachel
Mowdy, John
Oliver, Allen
Ostrand, Peter Van Sr
Palmer, Joura
Scott, John

Sheffer, Philip
Sheller, Henry
Snyder, ——
Snyder, George
Tannehill, Melzar
Weyman, Andrew
Whitington, Edward
Young, Mathias

ASHTABULA COUNTY

Formed 1805 from Trumbull and Geauga counties.

CHAPTERS: MARY REDMOND, MARY STANLEY, EUNICE GRANT

Allen, Elihu
Amsden, Abraham
Andrus, Clement
Baker, Eli
Barnard, Moses

Heath, Isaac
Hendry, David
Hillyer, Seth
Huntley, Daniel
Inman, Edward

Parker, Joel
Parker, Jonathan
Partridge, Sheffield
Pratt, Elnathan
Ritter, Timothy

Bernerd, Jesse
Bartholomew, Theobald
Barlett, Isaac
Bebee, Samuel
Belknap, Calvin
Benham, Thomas Sr
Brown, James 1st
Brown, John
Burril, Zachariah
Collins, Ebenezer
Crissey, John
De Marianville, Charles
Dickinson, Waitstill
Eaton, Samuel
Fenn, John
Ford, Christopher
Giddings, Joshua
Goodsell, Isaac
Gould, William
Griffin, Ezra
Griswold, Solomon
Gunn, Noble
Hall, Moses

Jenks, Jacob
Johnston, Samuel
Judd, Arumah
Kent, Apollus
Larned, Abijah
Lee, Lemuel
Lee, Samuel
Loomis, Giles
Lyman, Francis
McIntosh, Duncan
McManners, John
Macumber, John
Martin, Thomas
Mastin, Thomas
Mastin, Thomas
Moe, Jacob
Montgomery, Robert
Morris, John
Morse, Elijah
Niks, David
Noble, Caleb
Parker, Ashel

Rogers, Joseph
Sackett, David
Schermerhorn, Richard
Simons, Frederick
Smith, George
Smith, Hazadiah
Stevens, Paul
Straight, Henry
Sweet, Pheleg (Peleg)
Taft, Matthew
Thayer, Joseph
Thomas, Caleb
Thompson, Rufus
Thompson, Seth
Tinker, Silas
Tombleson, Michael
Tyler, Ebenezer
Wade, James
Ward, Obadiah
Webster, Michael
Whitney, William
Wilder, Reuben
Woodworth, Ezra

ATHENS COUNTY

Formed 1805 from Washington.

CHAPTERS: NABBY LEE AMES, ELIZABETH ZANE DEW.

Anderson, Daniel
Bodwell, William
Burnham, Jeremiah
Camp, Dr Jesse
Colombe, Louis de la
Cooley, Asahel
Davis, Nehemiah
Dunlap, Samuel

Ewing, George
Hammond, Thomas
Hudnall, Thomas
Hull, Aaron
McEver, James
Manley, Jesse
Martin, John
Means, Robert
Mingus, Joseph

Mosier, Daniel
Munn, Francis
Rider, John
Rowell, Daniel
Sampson, Samuel
Shepard, Charles
Thompson, John
Woodberry, Nathan

AUGLAIZE COUNTY

Formed 1848 from: Allen, Logan, Darke, Shelby, Mercer and Van Wert.
Ridlin, John

BELMONT COUNTY

Established 1801 by proclamation being ninth county formed from N W Territory.

ZANE'S TRACE CHAPTER

Acton, Henry
Armstrong, Robert
Beach, Roswell
Boyd, John
Campbell, Charles
Chambers, William
Craig, William
Cunningham, James
Curtis, Jonathan
Danford, Peter
Davis, Levi
Dovenberger, Jacob
Duvall, Col
Edge, John
Farnsworth, David

Grey, James
Hardesty, Obadiah
Howell, Jonathan
Iams, James
Iiams, Thomas
Israel, John
James, Thomas
Jones, Thomas
Kinnison, William
Knight, Jacob
Lama, William
McConnell, Thomas
McKnight, Eli
McGhogen, Alexander
Martin, Absolom

Musgrove, William
Paine, William
Pierce, Belmont
Price, Nathaniel 1st
Reed, Amos
Reneson, William
Smith, John N
Smith, Joseph
Starkey, Joseph
Tallman, Peter
Thompson, Joseph
Ware, Robert
White, Thomas
William, David
Williams, John

Forman, Lewis
Gillis, Arthur
Gray, Amos

Mitchell, Robert
Morgan, George

Wilson, Robert Sr
Windom, George
Zane, Jonathan

BROWN COUNTY

Formed 1817 from Adams and Clermont.

CHAPTERS: LIEUTENANT BYRD, RIPLEY, TALIAFERRO.

Alexander, John
Barr, Samuel
Bales, Jesse
Black, John
Blair, John
Bonwell, James
Clark, John
Clinger, John
Conley, Michael
Cordery, James
Cotteril, Thomas
Cowley, Michael
Creekbaum, Philip
Crosley, William
Cunningham, Thomas
Eakins, (Acron), Gabriel
Erwin, James
Fritts, Valentine
Gardner, Benjamin
Gould, Joseph
Grogan, Patrick
Gunsauld, John

Henderson, Jonathan
Hetherly, Thomas
Hodgkins, Samuel
Hopkins, John
Lecroy, Job
Leeton, Benjamin
Lemrick, Patrick
Leonard, James
Liming, Joseph
McCall, James
McClean, Fergus
McDaniel, Edward
Middaugh, Abonijah
Middleswart, Jacob
Monford, Daniel
Newberry, William
Parke, John
Printy, William
Rains, William
Rattan, Thomas
Reeves, William

Reynolds, Joseph
Rice, James
Rilea, Richard
Riggs, John
Rollison, Robert
Rounds, James
Rounds, Lemuel
Sams, Jonas
Sheperd, John
Sherburne, Andrew
Spyers, Benjamin
Spyers, Richard
Stoegel, James
Thompson, John Jr
Waites, James
White, William
Wiles, Christian Sr
Wills, Benjamin
Wood, Thomas
Woods, James
Woods, John
Wright, Robert

BUTLER COUNTY

Formed 1803 from Hamilton.

CHAPTERS: COL JONATHAN BAYARD SMITH, JOHN REILY, OXFORD CAROLINE SCOTT

Adams, Hedman (Heman)
Applegate, Benjamin
Ayres, John
Baird, Joseph
Barns, Elijah
Blackburn, ——
Boone, Thomas
Brann, Jeremiah
Buckley, Joshua
Carns, John
Colyer, Thomas
Cooley, William
Curry, James
Davis, William
DeCamp, Moses
Deneen, James
Dickerson, Walter
Elliott, William
Francis, George
Gregory, Samuel
Griffith, David
Griffith, Nathan
Grooms, John
Handlin, Matthias
Hardon, Samuel
Hazeltine, John
Heaton, David

Higgins, Daniel
Hoff, Isaac
Howe, Ebenezer
Hutchings, Gabriel
Hutchings, William
Irwin, James
Israel, John
Julick, Judiah
Kyle, Thomas
Lane, Hendrick
Leach, Joshua
Line, Benjamin
Line, John
Lintner, Peter
List, John
Logan, Patrick
Lucas, John
Lytle, Robert (Judge)
McCarroll, John
McGuire, Charles
Miller, Henry
Miller, Ichabod
Montgomery, Hugh
Pearce, Michael
Potter, Joseph
Rager, Leonard
Randall, Joseph

Richardson, Matthew
Rickey, Robert
Richart, Leonard
Rienhart, Martin
Sheperd, William
Simmonds, Robert
Simpson, James
Simpson, Josiah
Sinclair, George
Smith, William
Starks, Pardon T
Stine, Martin
Stout, Elisha
Symmonds, Henry
Thompson, John
Vanansdaller, Garrett
Vannostran, George
Voorhees, Stephen
Walker, John Sr
Waller, Ashbel
Wardwell, William
Whitaker, Jonathan 3rd
White, Thomas
Wilkinson, Ichabod
Wilkinson, John
Wilson, John
Wilson, Monroe

CARROLL COUNTY

Formed 1832-33 from Columbiana, Starke, Tuscarawas, Harrison and Jefferson.

Amos, Mordecai
Castleman, Henry
English, William
Gribbon, John

Martin, Henry
Miller, John
Rainsburg, John

Robins, William
Swinehart, Adam
West, Robert
White, Thomas

CHAMPAIGN COUNTY

Formed 1805 from Greene and Franklin.

URBANA CHAPTER

Balits, George
Bareth, John
Barnse, Robert
Bay, David
Beall, Obadiah
Brown, Rans
Clippinger, Anthony
Colgan, William
Cranston, John
Davis, John
Dawson, John
Edwards, Thomas
Fithian, George
Hatton, William

Hazel, Henry
Haus (Hout), ——
Hullinger, Daniel
Irwin, James
Jones, Henry
Kenton, Simon
Kirckwood, David
Legg, John
Lindsey, James
McAdams, John
McIntire, John
Martin, Benjamin
Moses, Ezekiel
Mungee, William

Rhodes, William
Richards, Jacob
Rump, Frederick
Runyan, John
Rutherford, Robert
Spencer, Beverly
Tipton, Thomas
Turner, James
Ward, William Jr
Willard, James
Witty, James
Woods, William
Wooley, Stephen
Wooley, William

CLARK COUNTY

Formed 1817 from Champaign, Madison, Greene

LAGONDA CHAPTER

Anderson, John
Ayers, John
Bagley, Timothy
Blair, James
Brandenburg, William
Butler, Asaph
Chance, John
Craig, James
Davis, William

Davison, Isaac
Hopkins, James
Hunt, James
Liming, Joseph
Loomis, Uriah
Milkollin, Jonathan
Moore, Daniel
Moreland, John
Morris, Cornelius

Mott, Josiah
Nagley, George
Poole, Chester
Ream, Andrew
Smith, Dr Pete
Waggoner, Jacob
Wallen, Daniel
Webb, Barruck
Wilson, William

CLERMONT COUNTY

Formed 1800 by proclamation being the eighth county from the N W Territory.

BEECH FOREST CHAPTER

Aldridge, John
Alexander, Joseph
Bicker, Adam
Brannon, David
Burns, Lawrence
Chalmers, Andrew
Coen, Edward
Davice, John
Davis, Benjamin
Day, Jeremiah
Dennis, John
English, Robert
Ford, Morgan
Gregg, John
Hall, Richard
Huber, John
Irwin, John

Johnson, James
Kinnan, Edward
Knott, Ignatius
Lane, Mordecai
Law, Barton
Leeds, Robert
Lightfoot, Jeptha
McCollum, Cornelius
Mikle, John
Naylor, Ralph
Nelson, John
Owen, Amasa
Owen, William
Penn, Benjamin
Pompelly, John
Porter, Eli

Rathben, Jonothan C
Reddick, William
Richardson, Joshua
Riggs, Gideon
Sargent, James
Sergeant, Elijah
Sherwin, Elnathan
Short, John
Smith, Obadiah
Sprague, Timothy
Stoner, Philip
Thomas, Jonathan
Weaver, John
Webster, Samuel
Whidden (Whiten) Solomon
Wilson, Samuel
Wullem, Samuel

CLINTON COUNTY
Organized 1810

CHAPTERS: WARRIORS' TRAIL, GEORGE CLINTON.

Allen, John
Armstrong, George
Beard, Jacob
Biggs, William
Dalyrymple, David
Dillon, Jesse
Disbrow, Asa

Hall, John
Hallam, Thomas
Howard, Gordon
Jones, John
Jones, Samuel
Laughhead, Benjamin
Leim, Samuel
Lieurance, George

McDaniel, William
Nixon, George
O'Laughlin, Dennis
Spencer, Williams
Wakle, Thomas
Wolf, Michael
Woolard, John

COLUMBIANA COUNTY
1803, formed from Jefferson and Washington.

BETHIA SOUTHWICK CHAPTER

Anderson, Robert
Arter, John
Augustine, George
Ball, Nathan
Berger, Nicholas
Blecker, Frederick Sr
Bothman, Barnhart
Bowker, Isaiah
Boyd, James
Bricker, John
Bunton, Samuel
Bushong, Jacob
Caldwell, William
Campbell, Obadiah
Carmody, John
Carnagey, William
Chamberlanin, Stout
Chamberland, William
Clapsaddle, Daniel
Clark, James
Coburn, John
Cook, James
Cook, Job R Sr
Cope, John
Cope, Nathan
Craig, William
Crain, William
Crow, Abraham
Crow, William
Davidson, James
Davis, Ichabod
Davis, William
Dayhoof, George P
Dennis, James
Dickson, George
Dild, Richard
Duck, George Sr
Ehrhardt, Phillip
Esterly, Michael
Eyster, Peter

Fife, John
Figgins, James
Forney, Henry
Foultz, William
Frederick, John Sr
Frederick, Thomas
George, William
Glass, Henry
Harris, Isaiah
Hawley, Caleb
Heald (Hale), Nathan
Helman, Martin
Hight, John
Hise, Jacob
Hole, Jacob
Howell, Reuben
Huston, Daniel
Huston, William
Johnston, Jacob
Jackson, Isaac
Lee, William
Lessier, Henry
Liggins, William
Lodge, Jonathan
McCalla, Thomas
McClain, Abijah
McClane, William
McCook, George
McCoy, Alexander
McKensie, James
McKinnon, Joseph
McKinsley, David
McNutt, Alexander
Manal, William
Marrs, William
Meek, Samuel
Might, John
Milburn, Andrew
Miller, Nicholas

Moncrief, John
Montgomery, John
Moore, John
Moore, Thomas
Muriel, William
Myers, Henry
Nold, Jacob
Nolf, George
Painter, Jacob Sr
Palmer, Stephen
Pancake, Benjamin
Queen, John
Quigley, Samuel
Ream, Nicholas
Rogers, Thorne
Schaak, Jacob
Scheenam, William
Seabrist, Jacob
Sharp, Amos
Shawke, Jacob
Sheehan, Cornelius
Sheets, Frederick
Sherman, William
Smith, James
Smith, Lorentz
Snider, John
Snook, John
Spence, David
Springer, E
Stock, Michael
Swartswelder, Christian
Swartswelder, Jacob
Test, Zacharias
Thomas, Owen
True, Ephriam
Walter, Matthias
Wellington, Jonathan
Wilkison, Amos
Williamson, Peter
Wilyard, Philip

COSHOCTON COUNTY
Organized 1811

COSHOCTON CHAPTER

Bautham, John
Beatty, James
Bradford, John
Brown, Alex Crawford

Draught, Richard
Fickle, Benjamin
Thayer, Bartholomew
Vail, Solomon

Wiley, Samuel
Williams, James Jr
Williams, William
Wilson, Monroe

CRAWFORD COUNTY
Formed 1820 from old Indian Territory.
CHAPTERS: HANNAH CRAWFORD, OLENTANGY.

Bergerhoff, Nicholas

Canfield, Daniel
Doud, Chandler

Knapp, Samuel
Myers, Henry

CUYAHOGA COUNTY
Formed 1807 from Geauga
CHAPTERS: LAKEWOOD, MOSES CLEAVELAND, WESTERN RESERVE

Abbott, Ebenezer
Aiken, Thomas
Andrews, Nathaniel
Beckworth, Rice
Brown, Levi
Burman, Isaac
Cochran, Abner
Cooper, Richard
Coply, Samuel
Cummins, Nathan
Dike, Colvin
Diller, David
Edwards, Rudolphus

Ferrand, Jared
Gaudinier, Jacob
Hamblin, Levi
Hardey, Pary
Harmon, Joseph
Hollister, Appleton
Hull, Abner
Humphrey, Roswell
Hutchins, Jacob
Jackson, James
Jones, Asa
Jones, Richard
Johnson, William

Morrison, John
O'Brien, Daniel
Peck, Isaac
Pelton, Jonathan
Perkins, David
Powers, Simeon
Ratleton, Edmund
Richardson, Daniel
Saddler, Christopher
Skysard, John
Squires, Asa
Upson, Joseph
Whitney, Benjamin

DARKE COUNTY
Formed 1809 from Miami.
FORT GREENVILLE CHAPTER

Borders, Christopher
Byers, William
Douglass, David
Dugan, William

Fountain, Stephen
Satterly, Samuel
Smith, William
Stoner, Caspar

Tucker, John
Walker, William
Winegardner, Josiah
Wood, James

DEFIANCE COUNTY
Formed 1845 from Williams, Henry, Paulding
FORT DEFIANCE CHAPTER

DELAWARE COUNTY
Formed 1808 from Franklin.
DELAWARE CITY CHAPTER

Budd, John
Case, George
Cronkleton, Joseph
Darst, Peter
De Ford, Thomas
Ely, Michael
Fancher, William
Finley, John
Forman, Aaron
Ford, John Morrison
Gregory, James

Hamlin, John
Hawlen, Nathaniel
Himrod, Andrew
Hoadley, Philo
Hoff, John
Jones, Crocker
Knapp, Edward
Knapp, Obadiah
Landon, James
Lindsley, Simeon
McNett, Adam
McNitt, Adam

Minter, John
Munroe, Leonard
Place, Peleg
Porterfield, Robert
Reed, William
Rose, Jacob
Shaw, John
Smith, David
Smith, Silas
Welch, Ebenezer
Young, Christian

ERIE COUNTY
Formed 1838 from Huron and Sandusky.
CHAPTERS: MARTHA PITKIN, FORT AVERY

Barrett, Oliver
Brailey, Gideon
Burdue, Nathaniel
Dunbar, John
Harrington, Seth
Harris, Luther
Harrison, Thomas

Harvey, George
Heath, Richard (Robert)
Hoak, Henry
Lee, Ezra
Loop, Peter Jr
Ninis, Asa

Parker, Ashael
Paynter, Nathaniel
Ramsdell, Joseph
Randall, Joshua
Sprague, Jonathan
Thorp, Augustus
Washburn, Anson

FAIRFIELD COUNTY

Established 1800 by Proclamation of Gov St Clair.

ELIZABETH SHERMAN REESE CHAPTER

Anderson, Thomas
Bowling, Charles
Bowling, William
Cook, Johnson
Courts, Low
Crawford, Samuel
Ebright, Philip
Elsey, Thomas
Embick, Christopher
Fisher, John
Fitzgerald, Henry
Fry, John
Garey, Killyan
Hedges, Elijah
Hill, James
Hopwood, William
Hubbert, Ephraim

Hunter, Joseph
Hunter, Robert
Irwin, Edward
Johnson, William
Karmmerer, Philip
Kiger, George
King, John G
Lamb, James
Lambrecht, Daniel
McClelland, Robert
Manley, Jesse
Manley, John
Montgomery, John
Morris, James
Peters, Philip
Preston, Samuel
Priest, William

Radabach, Nicholas
Ream, Abraham
Ream, Jacob
Reynolds, John
Ricketts, Edmund
Ricketts, Edward
Ruffner, Emanuel
Russel, Elijah
Shlife, John
Stevenson, Daniel II
Sturgeon, Peter
Torrence, Thomas
Valentine, George
Woodring, Peter
Wright, David
Young, Christopher
Zwier, Thomas

FAYETTE COUNTY

Formed 1810 from Ross and Highland

CHAPTERS: WASHINGTON COURT HOUSE, WILLIAM HORNEY.

Allen, Ananias
Bainter (Painter), Henry
Binegar, George
Bloomer, Joseph
Boon, Ralph
Boyd, Francis
Briley, John
Buck, John
Burnett, Robert

Carder, Sanford
Clevenger, Eben
Christy, John
Crawford, Thomas
DeValon, Francis
Hays, James
Legore, John
McClure, Hugh

McElhaney, Felix
Mark, Joseph
Meason, John
Newman, Jacob
Payne, Abram
Rankin, William
Salmons, Soloman
Tracy, John
Tway, John

FRANKLIN COUNTY

Formed from Ross in 1803

CHAPTERS: ANN SIMPSON DAVIS, COLUMBUS, JACOBUS WESTERVELT

Anderson, John
Armstrong, James
Babcock, Nathaniel
Ballard, William
Baumgarten, Henry
Butterfield, James
Case, Israel
Casey, Jacob
Center, Jonathan
Chapman, Benjamin
Chenoweth, Thomas Jr
Cheneweth, Elijah
Chester, Simeon Sr
Corson, Robert
Earhart, John
Fisher, Isaac
Fix, Henry
Franklin, Samuel
Gale, Richard
Geer, Jedediah
Gray, Littleton

Grubb, Peter
Harrison, Alexander Sr
Hill, Henry
Holton, John
Hungerford, Lemuel
Hunter, Joseph
Justice, Robert
Lewis, Joseph
Lack, Philip
Lord, Abner
McBurney, James
McElvain, Samuel
McGown, John
McKee, Samuel
McNinch, Archibald
Mahon, Neil
Manely, Jesse
Manning, William
Mapes, Joseph
Menely, Jesse
Miller, Henry
Miller, Josias

Montgomery, John
Moore, William L
Nickens, Moses
Patterson, William
Phillips, William
Price, Joseph
Sibliss, Thomas
Slote, Peter G
Smith, Thomas
Stewart, John
Thompkins, Phineas
Thompson, John
Tipton, Sylvester
Trusler, John
Turney, John
Vorys, Isaiah
Weatherholt, John
Weightman, George
Whaley, Edward
Whaley, Nathan
White, John

FULTON COUNTY

Formed 1850 from Lucas, Henry, Williams

WAUSEON CHAPTER

Capps, Dempsey

Gunn, Elijah Sr

GALLIA COUNTY

Formed 1803 from Washington

FRENCH COLONY CHAPTER

Allison, Benjamin
Buck, Charles
Butler, William
Campbell, Samuel
Carroll, William
Clark, John
Cress, George
Freehold, William
Fulton, James
Gee, Moses
Graham, John

Hailey (Harley), Anthony
Haptonstall, Abraham
Hughes, Jonathan
Jones, Richard L
Knight, Elijah
Lasley, Abraham
Martindale, James
Niles, Gaius
Polley, Daniel
Prows, Thomas
Rhiner, George
Rickabaugh, Adam

Russell, Charles
Safford, Dr James
Sheets, George
Smith, Johnston
Sprouse, David
Switzer, Philip
Viah, Gideon
Viers, Benjamin
Wasson, William
Wigner, Daniel
Williams, Benjamin

GEAUGA COUNTY

Formed 1805 from Trumbull

CHAPTERS: MOLLY CHITTENDEN, CHILDS TAYLOR.

Benty, Francis
Carter, Jason
Cheesman, Isaac
Donaldson, Samuel

Doty, Asa
Durand, Andrew
Gardner, Jonathan

Peydor, Benjamin
Phelps, Laving
Root, Daniel
Wetherill, David

GREENE COUNTY

Formed 1803 from Hamilton and Ross

CHAPTERS: CATHARINE GREENE, CEDAR CLIFF, GEORGE SLAGLE

Allen, Burgess
Bain, James
Beeks, Christopher
Beeson, Mercer
Beniger, George
Bryan, Andrew Morrison
Davis, Owen

Ferguson, Samuel
Fields, John
Gibson, John
Gowdy, James
Holmes, John
Huston, David

January, James
Laughead, David
McFarland, William
Mills, Jacob
Sheley, John
Sterrett, Joseph
Wolfe, George Sr

GUERNSEY COUNTY

Organized 1810

ANNA ASBURY STONE CHAPTER

Ader, Morris
Cockley, John
Cummins, John
Eaton, Joseph
Hawkins, Philip
Lawrence, William
Lieuzader, Abraham
Linn, Adam

Matthew, Garrett
Montgomery, Mitchell L K
Morgan, George
Newlin, William
Porter, Hugh
Schoff, Philip
Sharrock, James
Stackhouse, Amos

Tobin, Isaac
Turner, John
Waller, William
Waterhouse, William
Webster, John
Wherry, David
White, Samuel
Wyrick, Peter

HAMILTON COUNTY

Second county established from N W Territory in 1790 by Gov St Clair

CHAPTERS: CINCINNATI, MARIEMONT

Babbs, John
Bach, Judah
Berry, James
Bigham, William
Bonnell, Samuel
Broacher, Henry
Burniham, John
Campbell, Jonathan
Campbell, William
Childers, Mosby
Clark, James
Connor, Philip
Delzell, William
Dickinson, Zebulon
Douglas, John R
Drake, Joseph
Engart, Benjamin
Faulkner, Robert
French, Feremiah
Gannon, William
Gray, James 2nd
Greene, Charles
Hamilton, John
Hamond, John
Hardin, James
Harthorn, James
Harvey, Asa

Harvey, Edward
Hawley, Ebenezer R
Hicks, Durfee
Hodgson, Joseph
Hosbrook, John
Huddleston, Thomas
Ingalls, Israel
Isham, George
Kelly, William
Kitchell, Samuel
Kitley, John
Leonard, Patrick
Logan, John
Looker, Othniel
Love, Henry
Ludlow, John
Lyon, John
McCollough, Robert
McCormick, Rev Francis
Mercer, Aaron
Middock, Moses
Mitchell, Amasa
Norris, Bethuel
Parmetter, Abraham
Peck, William
Preston, Abiah
Preston, Robert
Preston, William

Purviance, Samuel
Reynolds, Justus
Ricketts, William
Roll, Abraham
Ross, Reuben
Rowley, Abigail
Sayre, Ezekiel
Silver, John
Sloate, Philip
Smiley, John
Snow, Lemuel
St Clair, James
Stephen, Nicholas
St John, John
Sumner, Samuel
Tolman, Robert
Tucker, William
Tullis, Michael
Turner, George
Vatter, Charles
Voorhees, Stephen
Voorhees, Minue
White, Jacob
Williamson, Joseph
Wilson, William
Worthington, William
Wright, Robert

HANCOCK COUNTY

Formed 1820

FORT FINDLAY CHAPTER

Fuchs, John

Kowns, Christian

HARDIN COUNTY

Formed 1820 from Indian Territory

FORT McARTHUR CHAPTER

HARRISON COUNTY

Formed 1814 from Jefferson and Tuscarawas

MORAVIAN TRAIL CHAPTER

Cole, Samuel
Harper, William

Pugh, John
Parker, John

Parker, John II
Robinson, John 2nd

HENRY COUNTY

Formed 1820 from old Indian Territory

HIGHLAND COUNTY

Formed 1805 from Ross, Adams and Clermont

CHAPTERS: JULIANA WHITE, WAW-WIL-A-WAY

Adkins, Samuel
Beard, John
Boatman, William

Hatter, John
Horn, Joseph
Johnson, Benjamin

Nicely, Jacob
Pegan, Andrew
Pugh, John

Brady, Thomas
Dickey, Thomas
Emery, John
Fishback, Jacob
Godwin, William
Halter, John
Hand, Edward

Manker, William
Middleton, John
Miller, Philip
Milner, Beverly
Moler, Joseph
Morris, William Sr

Reeson, Benjamin
Rickey, Joshua
Serbor, Jacob
Smith, John
Stoops, Philip
Strange, John
Wilson, Matthew

HOCKING COUNTY
Formed 1818 from Ross, Adams, Fairfield

GOVERNOR WORTHINGTON CHAPTER

Smith, Robert

Steel, James

Wartleman, Matthias

HOLMES COUNTY
Formed in 1824

Booth, Edwin
Carter, Anold
Chase, Aaron
Corbin, John

Casper, John
Davis, John
Dutcher, Henry
Hites, John

Miller, Matthew
Perry, Josiah
Tipton, Luke
Wheaton, Jonathan

HURON COUNTY
Formed 1809, organized 1815

CHAPTERS: SALLY DE FOREST, FIRELANDS

Ashley, James
Bemiss, Jonas
Barton, Josiah
Benschoter, Orley
Brooks, Lemuel
Buckingham, Thomas
Carpenter, David
Carter, David
Cartright, Solomon
Cherry, Reuben
Courtright, Solomon
Eastman, Charles
Fanning, William
Johnson, William
Kingsbury, Lemuel

McKelvey, William
Mason, Michael
Mins, or Nims, Asa
Moore, Joseph
Myers, Adam
Nessle (Nestle), Conrad
Palmer, Alva
Parker, Thomas
Parks, Michael
Parsons, Rev Justin
Parsons, Solomon
Phillips, Spencer
Pigsley, Paul
Pollack, Elijah
Randall, Charles

Raymond, Thadeus
Reed, Benjamin
Reed, Talcott
Rowe, John
Rowland, Hezekiah
Rowland, Luke
Shaefer, Lambert C
Skinner, Micah
Smith, William
Sutton, Philip
Swartz, Phineas
Taylor, John
Wheeler, Samuel
Winslow, Kenelin
Young, Morgan

JACKSON COUNTY
Organized 1816

CAPT JOHN JAMES CHAPTER

Brown, Nathan

Dailey, Samuel

JEFFERSON COUNTY

Fifth county established from the N W Territory by proclamation of Gov St Clair, west of Pa., east and north of a line fr mouth of Cuyahoga river, south of Muskingum river and east to Ohio river, 1797

CHAPTERS: STEUBENVILLE, MICHAEL MYERS

Brooks, Charles
Bryan, Thomas
Calhoun, Thomas
Carpenter, John
Chamber, Joseph
Clancy, John

Gordon, Barnardus
Gray, John
Greenelsh, Edward
Grove, Jonas
Hanna, Henry
Humphrey, George

Moore, Abraham
Moore, Elijah
Myers, Matthew
Myers, Michael
Norton, Thomas
Ong, Jacob

Clark, Benjamin
Clark, Jacob
Cole, Ezekiel
Crawford, David
Davis, John
DeHuff, John
Edginton, Thomas
Elkins, William
Evans, George
Evans, John
Folkner, Absolem
Glenn, James

Humphrey, John
Jackson, Richard
Jackman, William
Kerr, Joseph
Lock (Starr), William
Lowther, William
Minor, Thomas
McComas, William
McDowell, John
McElroy, John
McElroy, William

Palmer, John
Pennell, Hugh
Ripley, Jacob
Roach, William
Rouse, Thomas
Shouse, Christian
Slutts, John Sr
Starr, (Locke), William
Vance, David
Van Lilburgs, Henry
Vantilburg, Henry
Williams, Joseph

KNOX COUNTY

Formed 1808 from Fairfield

KOKOSING CHAPTER

Ball, Valentine
Beebe, William
Bower, Ellis
Bryant, David
Bryant, David
Chadwick, Levi
Clutter, Casper
Critchfield, Benjamin
Daggett, Gideon
Davis, Jonathan
Davis, Thomas
Dowd, Samuel
Dunham, Jacob
Elwell, Thomas
Fine, Peter

Folkner, Absolem
Fratt, Henry
Hess, David
Hoffmire, Samuel
Holcomb, James
Holt, John
Hunt, Jonathan
Karakin, John
Kennedy, Andrew
Kinny, John
Kirkpatrick, John Robert
Kline, Jacob
Laster, Thomas
Lewis, Henry
Lewis, Jacob

McFarland, Walter
Myers, Christopher
Northrup, Joseph
Price, Nathaniel
Riney, John
Stephenson, George
Stewart, William
Terrill, Nathan
Thornhill, Reuben
Vanansdall, Cornelius
Vantresse, Joseph
Welsh, David
Woodruff, Philo
Young, H H
Young, Jacob

LAKE COUNTY

Formed 1840 from Geauga, Cuyahoga

NEW CONNECTICUT CHAPTER

Call, Asa
Fowler, Jonathan

Morton, Solomon
Nicholas, Jonas
Parish, Cyprian

Pepoon, Joseph
Sperry, Elijah

LAWRENCE COUNTY

Organized 1816

Adams, Robert
Anderson, Henry
Ballard, Micajah
Bowen, Michael
Brumfield, Humphrey
Clark, Anthony

Davidson, William
Davis, Zachariah
Ellison, John
Lanebaugh, Joseph
Layne, Samuel

Mannon, Henry
Overstreet, John
Prichard, Comford
Prichard, Nathaniel
Riall, Isaac
Rowley, Joseph L

LICKING COUNTY

Formed 1808 from Fairfield

CHAPTERS: GRANVILLE, HETUCK

Avery, George
Beaumont, Isaiah
Bower, John
Boyer, Daniel
Brown, Owen
Burnet, Squire

Feazle, John
French, Jonathan
Green, Benjamin
Haas, John
Hartwell, Nathan
Hayes, Levi

Ranstead, James
Richardson, Jeremiah
Robinson, Maximilian
Scovill, Thomas
Searl, Aaron
Shadley, Daniel

Burnside, Jonathan
Butler, David
Caldwell, Hugh
Carp, Samuel
Carson, Samuel
Chamberlin, Freegift
Colville, John
Cooper, Albert
Critchard, Benjamin
Cunningham, Patrick
Danforth, Peter
Denman, Mathias
Devaun, James
Dove, Richard
Dunlap, Samuel
Emmitt, John

Herron, John
Hickey, Edward
Hill, Simon
Hoskinson, Isaiah
Hull, Samuel
Humphreys, Jacob ?
Jackson, Joseph
Kemp, John
Lacey, Samuel
Laws, John
McQuown, John
Mantzer, Japat
Miles, John
Newman, Walter
Pratt, Phineas
Priest, John

Shaver, Nicholas
Smith, Henry
Southard, Abraham Jr
Stephens, Peter
Stump, Jacob
Stump, Lewis
Sturges, Lewis
Sutton, Zebulon
Van Buskirk, John
Waters, Jacob
Wells, Israel
Wheeler, Samuel
White, Thomas
Williams, Richard
Wilson, Obadiah
Wright, Eliphas

LOGAN COUNTY
Formed 1817

BELLEFONTAINE CHAPTER

Chamberland, Judah
Coffel, James
Crawford, William
Griffey, Zachariah
Hanks, Thomas

Harrison, William
Hites, John
Lee, James
Marquis, Thomas
McIlhany, Felix

Moore, Joseph
Newell, Robert
Reams, William
Stannage, Thomas
Vanaker, George H

LORAIN COUNTY
Formed 1822 from Huron, Cuyahoga, Medina

CHAPTERS: ELYRIA, NANCY WOLCOTT, NATHAN PERRY

Bates, William
Battle, Justus
Beers, Zachariah
Beldon, Bildad
Bender, Jacob
Buck, Jonathan
Campbell, Joshua
Clark, Adna S
Crawford, Eleazer
Dyke, Calvin
Fauver, George

Ferguson, Samuel
Fox, David
Gibson, Daniel Jr
Gilbert, Thaddeus
Griffith, Samuel
Howard, John
Hulet, Asa
Kingsbury, Joseph
Laboni, Peter
Meeker, Robert

Morgan, Jesse
Pember, Eli
Richerdson, Gersham
Rising, Benjamin
Smith, John
Terrill, Joel
Terrill, Ichabod
Wallace, Isaac H
Ward, Josiah
Williams, Thomas
Young, William

LUCAS COUNTY
Formed 1835

CHAPTERS: FORT INDUSTRY, URSULA WOLCOTT
Dyer, Stephen

MADISON COUNTY
Organized 1824

CAPT WILLIAM HENDRICKS CHAPTER

Allen, Isaac
Beach, Obil
Brittenham, Solomon
Cary, Calvin
Coleman, Joel
Colver, David
Dine, John
Dockum, James

Gregory, Jehiel
Helphenstone, Peter
Hobaugh, Philip
Kehr, Kavid
Langham, Elias
McIntyre, Thomas
Minchell, William
Morris, Stephen
Powers, Walter

Ross, Robert
Shields, Tobias
Stroup, John
Tucker, Isaac
Van Ness, George
Wale, Thomas
Weaver, John
Wilcox, Joel

MAHONING COUNTY

Formed 1846 from Trumbull and Columbiana

MAHONING CHAPTER

Armitage, Benjamin
Arnold, Levi
Austin, William
Bates, Joseph
Bell, William
Bellard, John
Black, Thomas
Blosser, Jacob
Bradford, James
Britton, Nathan
Brooks, James
Brown, John
Brown, William
Buck, William Sr
Bull, Samuel
Burnet, Henry
Burnet, Samuel
Bush, Philip
Caldwell, James
Callahan, James
Callahan, William
Carr, John
Carr, Joseph
Christ, Jacob
Chubb, Henry
Church, Nathaniel
Clay, David
Clemmons, Nicholas
Cochran, John
Comyns, Joseph
Cooper, David
Cooper, Henry
Cooper, James
Cory, Ebenezer
Coy, David
Craig, James
Crawford, William
Cray, John
Crosby, David
Crumrine, Michael
Davis, Samuel
Dawson, Jacob
De Pew, Benjamin
Dickinson, Jacob
Dickson, John
Diehl, Philip
Dobbins, Hugh Sr
Douglass, John
Duncan, James
Durr, Michael
Elser, George
Fasnacht, John
Fink, George
Fitch, Andrew
Flickner, Christian
Foster, James
Fowler, Jonathan
Frank, Jacob
Frankfuerter, Philip
Frazee, Barnhart
French, Alexander
French, Elijah

Harness, John
Hannah, William
Harroff, John
Hemenway, James
Hill, John
Hill, Robert
Hinman, John
Hoover, Jacob
Hoyl, John
Hull, Andrew
Hull, George
Hull, Isaac
Hunt, William
Hunter, John
Inman, John
Irwin, John
Irwin, William
Jackson, John
Jones, Thomas
Johnson, David
Johnson, Thomas
Johnston, James
Johnston, John
Keck, Michael
Kerns, George
Lamborn, David
Lane, John
Lanterman, William
Leonard, John
Linn, James
McDonald, James
McGill, James
McGuffey, William
McKinnie, Henry
McKean, Robert
McKean, Thomas
McLane, John
McClelland, John
McCombs, John
McCullick, William
McCullough, Thomas
McNutt, Alexander
McNutt, Benjamin
Madam, John
Martin, Simeon
Martin, William
Masten, Peter
Matthews, Thomas
Mellinger, Jacob
Messerly, Peter
Metz, Jacob
Miller, Abraham
Miller, John
Minard, Joshua
Monteith, John
Moore, James
Morris, Joseph
Morrison, John
Moyer, John
Musser, Samuel
Myer, Daniel
Mygatt, Comfort

Paulley, James
Pennell, John
Phillips, James
Phillips, Samuel
Pierce, Joseph
Piper, William
Platt, Joseph
Pollack, William
Porter, Aaron
Porter, William
Powers, Abram
Ramsey, James
Rapp, John
Ratcliffe, John Sr
Raub, Peter
Reagle, Jacob
Reed, James Jr
Reed, Noah
Rhoads, George
Ritter, Jacob
Roberts, Joseph
Robinson, John
Rudisill, Jacob
Rummell, Peter
Russell, John
Scott, Samuel
Sell, Samuel
Shaffer, Samuel
Shoaf, Peter
Simons, Adam
Slater, William
Slaughter, William
Smith, Hugh
Smith, James
Smith, Jonathan
Smith, William 2nd
Snead, Samuel
Snyder, George
Sprague, Simeon
Squier, Benjamin
Squier, John
Stanley, James C
Stanley, Thomas
Starnford, Oliver
Stauffer, Jacob
Stauffer, John
Stephens, Robert
Stephenson, Robert
Stevens, John
Stewart, James
Stoddard, Eliakim
Strain, Hugh
Strock, Joseph
Thompson, John
Thompson, Thomas
Thornton, John
Townsend, John
Townsend, Joseph
Tupper, Reuben
Walker, William
Wayne, William
Webb, John

French, Thomas
Fullerton, Andrew
Gibson, Eleazer
Gilbert, Jacob
Glasgow, Robert
Goodwill, David
Goucher, Henry
Hahn, Jacob
Haines, Nathan

Neal, John
Nisbet, Francis
Osborn, Abraham
Osborn, John
Packard, John
Painter, John Adam
Palm, Adam
Palmer, William
Parker, James
Parkhurst, John

Welch, James
White, James
Whittenberger, Adam
Wilson, David
Wilson, James
Wilson, William
Witterecht, Peter
Wolfcale, John
Wright, Joseph

MARION COUNTY
Organized 1824
CAPT WILLIAM HENDRICKS CHAPTER

Britton, William Sr

Lewis, Ebenezer
Powell, Joseph

Stayner (Stainer), William

MEDINA COUNTY
Formed 1812 from Western Reserve
JAMES FOWLER CHAPTER

Alsbrough, Foster
Armstrong, Ebenezer
Bronson, Phineas
Brown, Ezra
Brown, Josiah
Clark, Clement
Deacon, Joseph
Deming, Solomon
Eastman, Deliverance
Goff, Solomon

Green, Jehiel
Hickox, Giles
Hogeboom, John
Hubbard, Asa
Jennings, Esbon
Keyes, Daniel
Marsh, Eleazer
McCloud, Samuel
McClung, Robert
Munson, Herman
Palmer, Ephraim

Phillips, Philip
Rhoades, Samuel
Riley, Joseph
Rogers, Edward
Sharon, Foster
Smith, Aaron
Smith, Timothy
Towsley, Matthew
Waite, Peter
Watt, Michael

MEIGS COUNTY
Formed 1819 from Gallia and Athens
RETURN JONATHAN MEIGS CHAPTER

Anderson, John
Benedict, Felix
Campbell, William
Castle, Joel
Cooper, David
Everton, Thomas
Gilleland, Daniel
Griffin, Joseph
Grow, Peter
Guthrie, Joseph

Harper, Daniel
Harrell, George
Hecox, Truman
Kent, Samuel
Kimball, Andrew
Knowlton, Robert
Lindsay, Samuel
Love, Thomas
McBride, Roger

Oakley, Miles
Pickens, John
Rice, Charles
Sayre, David
Sayers, Ephraim
Shreve, Godfrey
Sims, Francis
Smith, Thaddeus
Strong, Horatio
Van Duyn, John

MERCER COUNTY
Formed 1820 from Indian Territory
CAPT JAMES RILEY CHAPTER

Berry, William
Buck, William

Curts, Michael
Lattimer, John
McCumsey, Robert

Spear, Edward
Wilson, Peter

MIAMI COUNTY

Formed 1807 from Montgomery

CHAPTERS: MIAMI, PIQUA

Bailey, William C
Boltenhouse, John
Broderick, Absalom
Byrne, John
Campbell, John
Farmer, Ezekiel
Fulles, Aaron

Huston, William
Jackson, Alexander
Julian, Isaac
Kelsey, Thomas
Lloyd, David
Martin, Levi
Morris, Benjamin
Parsons, Harmon

Pawling, Albert
Prilliman, Jacob
Severns, Edward
Spencer, Amos
Taylor, Isaac
Tilford, Alexxander
Wilson, James

MONROE COUNTY

Formed 1813, Belmont, Washington, Guernsey

ANN RUCKER CHAPTER

Carmicheal, John
Craig, James
Crum, Adam
Derrough, John
Evans, Anthony
Fulherson, James
Hazzard, Arthur
Headly, Carey
Hendershot, John

Hicks, John
Hixson, Elijah
Hupp, Phillip
Liske, John
McClain, William
McVay, Benjamin
Morris, Basil
Okey, Levin
Pearsall, Benjamin

Pensall, Benjamin
Pratt, John
Sands, Alexander
Smith, Anthony
Smith, Henry
Stackhouse, Isaac
Tingley, Ebenezer
Turner, John
Walters, John

MONTGOMERY COUNTY

1803 from Hamilton and Ross

JONATHAN DAYTON CHAPTER

Alexander, George
Arnold, Jacob
Bailey, John
Bates, Issacher
Baum, Jacob
Becker, Jacob
Bigger, Joseph
Bowen, John
Bowman, David
Bradford, John
Brandt, Abraham
Burkhard, Jehu
Campbell, John
Cilney, George
Clayton, David
Cloney, George
Coble, Nicholas
Cunias, John
Darrough, John
Davis, Lewis
Dille, Samuel
DuBois, Benjamin
Flory, Abraham
Flory, Joseph
Gebhart, George
Gebhart, John

Harris, John
Heber, Jacob
Heeter, Sebastian
Hole, Daniel
Hole, Zachariah
Hoover, Felix
Hosier, Abraham
Howard, John
Hubler, Michael
Huston, Alexander
King, William
Lichty, Conrad
Long, Michael
Lowery, David
Luce, Benjamin
Lusk, Samuel
McCandless, John
McLlanahan, Mordecai
Manlove, William
Meyers, Henry
Miller, Daniel
Miller, David
Miller, Jacob
Miller, James
Mills, Elijah
Mills, Menan
Minturn, John

Moore, Samuel
Morgan, Evan
Morris, James
Morris, William
Moyer, Michael
Myers, Nicholas
Nicholas, John
Oblinger, John
Ollinger, John
Porter, James
Richeard, Peter
Roaff, Peter
Roseboom, John
Rudolph, John
Rumbarger, George
Stetler, Christian
Stetler, George
Stetler, Henry
Strain, Robert
Tibbals, Samuel
Troxell, Abraham
Warner, Henry
Weber, Jacob
Weber, Philip
Weidner, David
Weimer, George

MORGAN COUNTY
Organized 1818

AMANDA BARKER DEVIN CHAPTER

Allen, Asher
Beckwith, William
Coburn, Phineas
Dean, Benjamin
Fall, Aaron
Hoyt, Nicholas
Jacobs, William
Mahana, John

Moler, Gasper
Mumy, Charles
Nott, Thomas
Offing, Patrick
Osbourne, Hugh
Russell, Ashur
Sailor, Philip
Shacklee, Peter
Smith, Edward

Smith, William
Springum, John
Walter, Peter
Wickham, John Sr
Widdess, Robert
Wiley, Thomas
Wilson, Matthew
Worral, Benjamin

MORROW COUNTY
Formed 1848 from Richland, Knox, Marion, Delaware

MT GILEAD CHAPTER

Baskin, George Washington
Brendlinger, Frederick
Brochway, Martin

Jackson, Daniel
Sayers, Josiah

Steward, William
Van Norman, Isaac
Wallace, ——

MUSKINGUM COUNTY
Formed 1804 from Washington, Fairfield

CHAPTERS: MUSKINGUM, TOMEPOMEHALA

Adams, George
Addison, Jacob
Alford, John
Baird, John
Bean, Daniel
Bell, William
Berry, James
Blunt, William
Buker, Israel
Campbell, John
Clark, John
Culing, John
Cullens, John
Curtis, Joel
Fleming, Robert
Forshey, Thomas
Grady, Younger
Green, John
Grover, Isaiah

Harmon, Conrad
Hawbeard, Thomas
Holcomb, Elijah
Holcomb, John
Jemison, David
Johnson, Philemon
Johnson, Silas
Kent, John
King, Charles
Leedom, Thomas
Lyon, Abraham
McHenry, Robert
McMillen, James
McQueen, Alexander
Mayberry, William
Mayberry, William Sr
Miller, John
Mingus, Moses
Moody, Alexander
Morris, William

Newton, Hananiah
Pelham, William
Ramey, John
Reddick, John
Reynolds, George
Reynolds, James
Richardson, David
Shaffer, Jacob
Simpson, Thomas
Sims, Jeremiah
Sockman, John
Thomas, Josiah
Walker, Benjamin
Walker, Meshec
Walker, Samuel
Waltemyer, George
Williams, Lewis
Wilson, James
Wood, Jeremiah

NOBLE COUNTY
Organized 1851; last county of 88 counties

Bryan, Cornelius
Bryan, William

Crum, Adam

McCann, James M
Thorla, Thomas

OTTAWA COUNTY
Organized 1840, Sandusky, Erie, Lucas

DE LERY PORTAGE CHAPTER
Wolcott, Benajah

PAULDING COUNTY
Formed 1820 from Indian Territory

PERRY COUNTY

Formed 1817 from Washington, Muskingum, Fairfield

Allwin (Allwine) Lawrence
Barron, Robert
Brown, John G
Butler, John
Crist, W P C
Crosby, James
Deits, Adam
Everett, Abel
Hitchock, Isaac
Irwin, Francis
Kennard, John

Kent, Isaac
Latimer, James
Lewis, Charles
Lewis, Samuel
Magee, Peter
Martin, Jacob
Melick, John
Meyers, John
Moore, Thomas
Myers, John
Owens, Stephens

Parsons, Enoch
Parrett, Samuel
Randolph, Christian
Rudolph, Christian
Sayres, Ruel
Simms, Jeremiah
Spohn, Philip
Walker, William Jr
Wards, Edward
Winner, John
Winner, Israel

PICKAWAY COUNTY

Formed 1810, Ross, Fairfield, Franklin

PICKAWAY PLAINS CHAPTER

Bowsher, Anthony
Brown, John
Bown, William
Burton, Joshua
Burwell, Zachariah
Champ, William
Clark, John
Clark, Joseph
Cline, Conrad
Crow, Thomas
Davis, John
Davison, Edward
Dingman, Peter
Downey, Thomas
Duryea, Charles
Fisher, John Sr
Fleming, Lieut Archibald
Foreman, Alexander
Funk, Abraham
Gay, John Sr
George, Parnick
Gibson, Thomas

Glenn, George
Grim, Jacob
Hampton, John
Harman, George
Herbert, Thomas
Hill, George
Hill, William
Holman, Samuel
Hunter, Benjamin
Huston, Hugh
Judy, John
Kepner, Benjamin
Knapp, John
Kuder, Elias
Leigh, Daniel
Ludwig, Daniel
Martin, Robert
Miller, Joash (Joas)
Miller, William
Moore, Fergus
Morris, Ezekiel

Perry, Jacob
Peter, Jacob
Peters, Tunis
Phebus, George
Reeves, Josiah
Reeves, Josias Sr
Rout, (Routt), William
Sandy, William
Saylor, Jacob
Schamehorn, ——
Simpson, John
Smith, John O C
Stump, Conrad
Sudduth, William
Swisher, Abraham
Tallman, Benjamin
Teegardin, Aaron
Try, Jacob
West, George
Williams, James
Williams, William
Wolfley, John

PIKE COUNTY

Formed 1815 from Ross, Highland, Adams, Scioto, Jackson

SCIOTO VALLEY CHAPTER

Barker, Charles
Beekman, William
Black, (Blackwell) Hugh
Bristol, Reuben
Brooks, Joshua
Cissna, Charles

Dike, Henry
Halladay, John
Holam, Samuel
Penniston, George
Peril, John

Ridgeway, Samuel
Satterfield, John
Sewall, Thomas
Stewart, John
Stewart, John
Walcott, John

PORTAGE COUNTY

Formed 1807 from Trumbull co

CHAPTERS: AARON OLMSTEAD, OLD NORTHWEST

Allen, George
Anderson, James Arthur
Austin, Samuel
Bacon, Nehemiah
Baldwin, Stephen

Garrison, Benjamin
Goodrich, John H
Goodsard, Valentine
Hall. Asa
Hardesty, Francis

Pike, Jonathan
Pitkin, Stephen
Preston, David
Redden, Christopher
Remington, Anthony

Bixby, Benjamin
Blair, John
Blair, Reuben
Burroughs, Daniel
Burrows, Elijah
Cackler, Christian
Chapman, Lemuel
Coe, David
Crittenden, Gideon
Crocker, Charles
Downing, Phineas
Elliott, Samuel
Ettinger, Jacob
Furman, Nowell

Hardy, Nathaniel
Harrington, John
Hawley, Ozias
Heart, Reuben
Horn-Baker, Philip
Hulet, Sylvanus
Judd, Reuben
Loomis, Asa
Loveland, Elisha
Mason, Elijah
Meeds, Cato
Mott, Ezekiel
Mott, Samuel
Nicholas, James

Richards, Thomas
Ridden, Christopher
Robinson, Daniel
Seward, John
Shepard, Joseph
Smith, Noah
Spencer, John
Starr, Josiah
Tuffs, William
Waite, Jonathan
Walker, Jonathan
Wallace, Joseph
Wallace, Joseph
White, William

PREBLE COUNTY
Formed 1808 from Montgomery and Butler

COMMODORE PREBLE CHAPTER

Aikman, John
Armontrout, Charles
Beall, Thomas
Beard, Francis
Black, John
Bridge, John
Bruce, William
Bunger, John
Cailes, John
Campbell, John
Carter, John
Caughey, John
Clinger, (K), Philip
Cowgill, Daniel
Craigs, Robert
Curry, William
Dailey, Dennis
Dalrymple, John
Davisson, Josiah

DeCoursey, William
Farber, Daniel
Frame, Jeremiah
Hamile, Ebenezer
Haraman, David
Harbison, Robert
Herron, Samuel
Homan, Eber
Jaqua, Gamaliel
Kesler, Jacob
Lanier, James
Lesh, Jacob
Lock, Capt John
McChukin, Matthew
McCohan, Thomas B
McClung, Matthew
McNutt, Alexander
Magaw, William
McWhinney, Thomas
Miller, Frederick

Mitchell, Elijah
Mitchell, Samuel
Moore, James
Ozias, John
Parker, Jacob
Patterson, John
Piles, Jeremiah
Ramsey, William
Rape, John
Runyan, John
Sherer, John Jacob
Sheuerdecker, Michael
Simonton, John
Taylor, Richard
Tillman, Tobias
Toney, Carey
Thatcher, Amos
Vandevender, Barnabas
Woolverton, Col Thomas

PUTNAM COUNTY
Formed 1820 from Indian Territory

Otis, Edward

RICHLAND COUNTY
Organized 1813

CHAPTERS: JARED MANSFIELD, MARY WASHINGTON

Allen, Luke
Ames, Ephraim
Arnot, Samuel
Bachelder, William
Baggs, James
Bennett, Abraham
Bumpus, Frederick
Camp, John
Cline, Jonas
Clive, James
Collins, John
Cook, Jacob
Decker, Abraham
Edgington, Jesse
Evarts, Timothy

Freed, Jacob
Gibbney, George
Hadley, Moses
Harrison, Stephen
Hendrickson, William
Herbert, Thomas
Holmes, Seth
Hydecker, Jacob
Johnston, William
King, George
Lee, William C
McCormick, John
McDougal, Alexander
Marshall, John

Mellot, Benjamin
Nail, Henry
Oyster, John
Phipps, Samuel
Pierce, James
Pope, Ezra
Prosser, Daniel
Selser, Frederick
Smith, Ebenezer
Snell, David
Snyder, Peter
Strickland, Joseph
Thompson, James
Ulrick, Jacob
Young, Charles

ROSS COUNTY
Organized 1798 by proclamation. Sixth county formed from N W Territory
NATHANIEL MASSIE CHAPTER

Arrohood, Thomas
Beach, Capt John
Beaumont, Samuel
Betz, Adam
Bodine, John
Cisna, Stephen
Claypool, Abraham
Clifton, Thomas
Coldon, Richard
Conner, Isaac
Cook, Joel
Costigan, Francis
Dukes, Isaac
Evans, Col John
Finley, Samuel
Fleming, Alexander Capt
Francis, John
Frew, James
Gale, Nicholas
Gates, William
Gillfillan, Thomas
Glover, William
Hardin, Richard
Hendrick, Charles
Hobday, Richard
Howard, Adam

Hull, John
Hurley, Cornelius
Jamison, Francis
Jamison, (Jemison), William
Johnson, Alexander
Johnson, Caleb
Klelogg, Jason
Kerner, Philip
Lackey, John
Leby, Christian
Liggett, William
Lingan, James Macubbin
McBride, Alexander
McCartney, James
McDonald, Col John
McMahon, Cornelius
McMahon, John
McMillen, Daniel
Mallow, Adam
Miller, Thomas
Moore, John
Murphy, John
Murray, Neal
Nice, William
Norris, Arnold

Orchard, Thomas
Orchead, Thomas
Parker, Joseph
Price, Sampson
Prough, Peter
Raymer, Philip
Records, Josiah
Reeves, Nathan
Rider, Adam
Roberts, William
Robinson, Peter
Sheets, Mathias
Sherlock, Edward
Siprill, Nicholas
Smith, William
Somerset, Thomas
Sperry, Peter
Terney, James
Timmons, Robert
Thompson, Abraham
Vandervert, Charles
Van Gundy, Christian Sr
Warren, Peter
Wentworth, John
Wroten, Shredrick
Young, Christopher

SANDUSKY COUNTY
Formed 1820 from Indian Territory. Seventh county formed from N W Territory
COL GEORGE CROGHAN CHAPTER

Bates, David
Crow, Christian
Daggett, Jacob

Davenport, John
Dunbar, William
Fenstermacker, John
Gehret, Jacob

Green, Dana
Loop, Peter
Waters, Allen

SCIOTO COUNTY
Formed 1803
JOSEPH SPENCER CHAPTER

Brady, William
Canady, Meredith
Canter, John
Chapman, James
Concklin, Joseph
Connor, William
Copes, Southey
Crumb, Christopher

Deaver, William
Foster, Job
Harbert, William
Hull, Isaac
Hutton, George
McClurg, Robert
McDougal, Joseph

Moore, Jacob
Salter, James
Salter, Samuel
Thompson, James
Wheeler, Amos
Wheeler, Isaac
Wheeler, Nathan
Williamson, Henry

SENECA COUNTY
Formed 1820 from Indian Territory; organized 1824
CHAPTERS: DOLLY TODD MADISON, JANE WASHINGTON

Campbell, Francis
Campbell, William
Lane, Ezekial

SHELBY COUNTY
Formed 1819 from Miami
LEWIS BOYER CHAPTER

Blankenship, Benjamin,
Botkin, Charles

Curtz, Thomas
Davis, William

Hall, Peter
Pixley, Elijah

STARK COUNTY
Established 1808; formed 1809
CHAPTERS: CANTON, JANE BAIN, MASSILLON

Albert, John
Bagum, Henry
Bower, Jacob
Copes, William
Drury, Leonard
Edgington, John
Elliott, John
France, Peter
Groninger, Joseph
Hahn, Michael
Henning, Conrad
Henry, John D
Hildebrand, Michael

Houser, Ludwick
Houser, Martin
Kephart, Martin
Knapp, Joshua
Krichbaum, John William
Kroninger, Joseph
McClelland, Hugh
McGinnes, James
Masters, Stephen
Maxwell, John
Miller, Abraham
Nagle, Jacob

Nelson, Moses
Rickey, Cornelius
Shaffer, Andrew
Simonton, Thomas
Simmons, William
Stanbury, Samuel
Sweigert, Jacob
Watson, William
White, Ebenezer
Wise, Peter
Winter, Jonathan
Wood, Jonathan
Zeignfuss, Jacob

SUMMIT COUNTY
Formed 1840 from Portage, Medina, and Stark
CHAPTERS: AKRON, CUYAHOGA FALLS, CUYAHOGA-PORTAGE

Markham, Daniel

Nesbit, William
Rice, Lewis

Sackett, Salmon

TRUMBULL COUNTY
Formed 1800; comprised whole of Connecticut Reserve
MARY CHESNEY CHAPTER

Ackley, Ahira
Alderman, Timothy
Allen, James
Allen, Joseph
Allen, Rufus
Andrews, Asa
Annis, Benjamin
Barns, John
Bates, Aaron
Beach, Ezekiel
Beckwith, Samuel
Belden, Benjamin
Belden, David
Beman, Thomas
Bentley, Benjamin
Brill, Michael
Brink, Benjamin
Burlingame, Wanton
Burrell, Jedediah
Burrows, Moses
Carns, Zophar
Chapman, William
Cline, Gasper
Cole, Jacob
Cossett, Silas
Crosby, Timothy
Curtis, David
Dailey, Elias
Davis, Joshua
DeCoursey, Peter
DePue, Nicholas
DeWolf, Peter
Dickinson, Friend
Doughton, Stephen
Edgecomb, John
Folsom, Thomas
Foot, Levi D
Gardner, John
Gerrills, John

Gildersleeve, Obadiah
Godden, John
Green, Daniel
Green, Jared
Guild, Otis
Hamman, Jacob
Hammond, John
Harper, Joseph
Harris, Moses
Hickock, David
Hine, Nathan
Hinsdale, Jacob Jr
Holt, Thomas
Horton, Henry
Hover, Henry
Huff, Peter
Jacobs, John
Jaqua, Simon
Kelly, Nathaniel
Key, Stewart
Lane, John
Linscutt, Samuel
Loveless, George
Lyons, Barnabas
McElroy, John
McLene, Jeremiah
McMahon, Abner
Malone, John
Mann, Isaiah
Mansfield, Jonathan
Maybee, Jasper
Meeker, A C
Melony, John
Mitchell, David
Moore, William
Moses, Abner
Morley, John
Mowrey, Reuben
Netterfield, William

Newcomb, Ethan
Newcomb, John
Norton, Jacob
Percy, Joseph
Perry, Abijah
Porterfield, William
Price, Samuel
Reily, James
Scott, Isaac
Scott, Nehemiah
Scovill, Amasa
Scoville, Michael
Shaw, Richard
Sheffleton, George
Sheldon, Jonathan
Shipman, Abraham
Stewart, John
Stow, Samuel
Streeter, Napthali
Sullinger, John
Sutliff, David
Sutliff, Samuel Jr
Talcott, Joseph
Taylor, Henry
Taylor, John
Thompson, John
Tidd, William
Trescoat, Jonathan
Tucker, James
Tulley, John P
Vanaker, Gideon
Van Gorder, Abraham
Westbrook, Leonard
Wheeler, Simeon
Whipple, Elijah
Wick, Lemuel
William, (s), Daniel
Williams, John
Wilson, William

TUSCARAWAS COUNTY
Formed 1808 from Muskingum

FORT LAURENS CHAPTER

Biner, George
Barnet, George
Barr, John

Gibbs, William
Lock, Ayres
Organ, Matthew
Palmer, George M

Shears, Peter
Stark, Caleb
Walker, Asher

UNION COUNTY
Formed 1820 from Delaware, Franklin, Madison, Logan

CHAPTERS: HANNAH EMERSON DUSTIN, PLAIN CITY

Curry, James
Davis, James

Judy, John
Sager, Dr John
Tignor, Thomas

Weiselake, George
Woodruff, Cornelius

VAN WERT COUNTY
Formed 1820 from Indian Territory

ISAAC VAN WART CHAPTER

VINTON COUNTY
Formed 1850 from Gallia, Athens, Hocking, Ross, and Jackson

HANNAH DOWD VANDERFORD CHAPTER

Fuller, Thaddeus

Lotz, Jacob

Wyman, John Jr

WARREN COUNTY
Formed 1803 from Hamilton

TURTLE CREEK CHAPTER

Baldwin, Benjamin
Ballard, Wyatt
Bedle, Francis
Bennett, Richard
Blackburn, James
Boal, Robert
Bodine, John
Bond, Nathaniel
Borden, Job
Bowers, John
Brant, John
Brooks, Charles
Brown, Thomas
Carter, Uzzial
Clarke, John
Connelly, Patrick
Coovert, Burgum
Cox, Benjamin
Cummins, William
Davis, Jonathan 2nd
Death, John C

Dougherty, William
Drullinger, Frederick
Dunlevy, Anthony
Earinfight, Jacob
Easton, Moses
Foote, John
Green, Joseph
Houston, John
Howe, James
Hubbell, John
Hunter, Robert
Huxson, Matthew
Johnson, James
Karr, Andrew
Kenney, Stephen
Kesling, Peter
Kinder, George
King, Gerard
Lake, John
Leonard, James
Long, James

McDonough, Robert
McMeen, John
Moore, Jonathan
Morris, Reuben
Murphy, James
Osborn, Joseph
Parks, Joseph
Pearson, Mahlon
Piper, James
Reddington, Daniel
Richardson, Samuel
Riggs, Eleazer
Ross, John
Rue, Benjamin
Shawan, Darby
Sidle, Peter
Simpson, William
Van Voorhis, Daniel
Venard, Thomas
Wilkerson, James
Wilson, James

WASHINGTON COUNTY
Formed 1788 by proclamation. 1st county formed from N W Territory

MARIETTA CHAPTER

Allison, Lieut Hugh
Allison, Robert
Bailey, James
Ballard, Jesse
Bivins, John
Bosworth, Joseph
Broome, John

French, William
Gales, Timothy
Gates, Capt David
Gilman, Joseph
Gossett, John
Greenman, Jeremiah
Harmar, Joseph

Morley, Daniel
Morse, Isaac
Nantz, Frederick
Nestler, John
Norman, Bazabeel
Olds, Gilbert
Olney, Cogswell

Burch, Eddy
Carroll, George
Chandler, Joseph
Chandler, Zebulon
Chapman, Samuel
Childs, Isaac
Clapp, Caleb
Clay, Daniel
Cline, George
Clough, Aaron
Cogswell, Eli
Converse, Benjamin
Corns, Joseph
Cory, Thomas
Davis, Dudley
Davis, William
Delano, Cornelius
Dennis, Andrew
Dodge, Oliver
Dunbar, William
Dunham, Daniel Sr
Dunham, Daniel Jr
Dutton, James
Eastman, Peasley
Ellis, Ephraim
Emerson, Ephraim
Flake, George
Floyd, John

Hart, Jonathan
Haskell, Elnathan
Haskell, Moses
Hatch, James
Hawkins, Thomas
Hayward, Henry
Heywood, Benjamin
Hilderbrand, George
Hildreth, Samuel
Hill, John
Hinkley, Nathaniel
Hobby, John
Holden, John
Holdren, Levi
Hoskins, Cornelius
Inman, Rufus
Kelly, John
Koon, Philip
Lake, Archibald
Lake, Mrs Mary Bird
Lake, Thomas
Lankton, Levi
Lewis, Benoni
McClunie, Michael
McClure, James
McGee, William
Medley, William G
Mills, John
Mitchell, Nathaniel

Pain, John
Paine, Benjamin
Perry, Thomas
Porter, Ebenezer
Ray, John McRush
Riggs, James
Roach, William
Rouse, John
Scammel, Leslie
Sharp, Spencer
Sherman, Timothy
Smith, David
Smith, Nicholas
Spacht, Anthony
Sprague, William
Springer, Jacob
Stephens, Moses
Stephenson, Peter
Thomas, Jeremiah
Thomas, Jonathan
Tice, Solomon, Sr
Trible, Joseph F
Tucker, William
Van Clief, Peter
Waterman, Ignatius
Waterman, John
Webster, Andrew
Woodbridge, Dudley

WAYNE COUNTY

Was 3rd county formed 1796 from N W Territory with very extensive limits

WOOSTER-WAYNE CHAPTER

Anderson, Andrew
At, Peter
Blew, Frederick
Burns, John
Campbell, William
Cockerell, Robert
Coe, Ebenezer
Davis, John 2nd
Denman, Samuel
Ewing, William
Foster, Benjamin
Fox, Stephen
Givin, Thomas
Goodspeed, Sympson

Grant, Jonathan
Gray, James
Hagerman, Barnett
Hutchison, James
Isbel, Joel
Jeffrey, John
Lash, Peter
Luke, John
McCurdy, Robert
McKaig, Patrick
Miller, William
Nixon, William
Patterson, James

Piper, Frederick
Powell, David
Richards, Jesse
Skinner, John
Slimer, John
Smith, Peter
Smith, Philip
Stanford, William
Starkey, Isaac
Taylor, Edward
Thompson, James
Underwood, Isaac
West, Clement
Wonder, Andrew

WILLIAMS COUNTY

Formed 1820; organized 1824 from Indian Territory

Hagerman, Abraham

WOOD COUNTY

Formed 1820 from Indian Territory

BLACK SWAMP CHAPTER

Hall, John
Hendricks, Elijah

McNealy, James

Morrison, A——
Rice, Daniel

WYANDOT COUNTY
Formed 1845 from Crawford, Marion, Hardin, Hancock

COL WILLIAM CRAWFORD CHAPTER

Knapp, Samuel

McKinley, John

SOLDIERS FOUND IN OHIO BUT COUNTY UNKNOWN

Ackright, Isaac
Allen, Eliphalet
Allen, William Jr
Armstrong, Benjamin
Armstrong, James
Ashley, William
Atset, Joseph
Bailey, Seth
Baker, Michael
Ball, Davis
Bareth, Robert
Barngrover, George
Barnum, Enoch
Batterson, William
Beirce, William
Bennett, Joshua
Bennett, Richard
Bennett, Thomas
Bidwell, Samuel
Birney, Henry
Black, Charles
Black, Samuel
Blackman, Nehemiah
Bloomfield, Moses
Blount, Adam
Bolten, Lemuel
Boswell, Joseph
Bowyer, William
Boyles, Absalom
Breck, William
Brees, Timothy
Brinton, William
Brooks, Hananiah
Brown, Benjamin
Brown, Samuel
Brown, Samuel
Brown, Samuel
Buell, Joseph
Burk, Robert
Burnham, John
Burns, John
Burton, Selah
Burwell, Jonathan
Bushnell, Andrew
Butler, Stephen
Campbell, John
Carter, Daniel C
Cary, Christopher
Cary, Luther
Cassidy, George
Chance, James
Chandler, Joseph
Chinaworth, Elijah
Chrichton, James
Clymer, Henry
Combs, Robert

Dowler, Thomas
Eddy, Livens
Eldred, Moses
England, Joseph
Enos, Joseph
Elwell, James
Evans, Edward Rev
Fay, John
Felt, Joshua
Ferree, John
Fielding, Daniel
Follett, Frederick
Foster, Jacob
Forsyth, Elijah
Frost, Samuel
Frothingham, Ebenezer
Fry, Jacob
Frye, Frederick
Gadd, William
Gallespie, James
Gatchel, John
Gates, Nathan
George, William
Gibson, Thomas
Goodale, Silas
Green, Elisha B
Green, Isaac
Green, Nehemiah
Grosvenor, Thomas
Guthrie, Truman
Hallman, Stephen
Holden, Joseph
Hough, William
Hubbard, John
Hull, Uriah
Ingersoll, George
James, John
James, William
Johnson, James
Johnson, Thomas
Jones, Asa
Jones, George
Kerr, John
Kinney, John
Kirk, John
Knowles, Charles
Lewis, Isaac
Lincoln, Rufus
Line, Joseph
Lisk, James
Lisle, Jacob
Loomis, Jonathan
Lunt, Daniel
Lusher, John
McClung, Thomas
McCoy, Daniel

Nassey, Ezekiel
Neblet, Aaron
Nixon, Thomas
Norris, Richard
Oliver, David
Paisley, John
Palmer, Sylvanus
Pearce, Benjamin
Phelps, Capt David
Phillips, Peter
Pierce, Ebenezer
Pierce, James
Pike, Zebulon
Plumer, William
Potter, John
Pratt, Joel
Putnam, Jethro Capt
Rawlings, Moses
Rice, Benjamin
Ringland, John
Roads, (Reed), John
Rogers, Nathaniel
Rogers, William
Roll, John Jr
Root, Elijah
Ross, Matthias
Sargeant, Winthrop
Scott, John
Scull, James
Seward, James
Shaeffer, Philip
Shayer, Bartholomew
Shields, David
Shoff, Philip
Shuman, Timothy
Smith, Adam
Smith, Jonathan
Smith, Robert
Spaulding, Sampson
Spelman, Timothy
Sprague, Joseph
Sproat, Earl
Staur, Abijah
Stiver, Casper 3rd
Story, Andrew
Story, William
Stothard, Thomas
Straden, George
Strain, David
Strait, John
Summers, William
Teerman, John
Teter, Samuel
Thayer, Elias
Thompson, Samuel
Tison, Mathias

Cook, Johnson
Corliss, William
Craig, James
Crary, Archibald
Cross, David
Crow, Israel
Cuddington, Benjamin
Cue, Robert
Cyprus, Andrew
Dana, Benjamin
Davis, James
Davis, William
Delong, Solomon
Demina, Powall
Devol, Allen
Doane, Benjamin
Dodge, John
Dolaw, William
Dovenberger, David

McCullock, Robert
McDermot, Michael
McGaffey, Neal
McGowan, Charles
M'Leroy, James
McMinnis, James
McMullen, James
Mallory, Gills
Malt, Moses
Matthews, Abel
Mills, John
Mills, William
Mitchell, James
Mitchell, Joseph
Mooney, John
Moore, Ephraim
Moore, George
Mosey, John
Moss, Isaac

Tuman, Peter
Wartman, Peter
Webster, Joseph B
West, John
Wheeler, Walter
White, George
White, John
White, Joseph
Wilkins, Gabriel
Williams, David
Williams, Robert
Williams, William
Willis, Nathaniel
Wilson, David
Wilson, Jonathan
Wingard, James C
Wolf, George
Wolf, John
Wood, Joseph

INDEX

LIST OF ABBREVIATIONS

Months, States and Titles as usual.

abt .... *about*
aft .... *after*
ae .... *age*
appl .... *application*
appld .... *applied*
appt .... *appointed*
bk .... *book*
b .... *born*
B L Wt .... *Bounty Land Warrant*
B R ....*Blanche Rings, Col. O.*
bur .... *buried*
cem .... *cemetery*
cert .... *certificate*
chldr .... *children*
chpt .... *chapter*
Co .... *Company*
contl .... *Continental*
co .... *county*
da .... *day*
dau .... *daughter*
desc .... *descendant*
d .... *died*
disch .... *discharge*
drftd .... *drafted*
enl .... *enlisted*
fr .... *from*
gr yd .... *grave yard*
Hist .... *History*
J D .... *Jane Dailey*
Libry .... *Library*
Lin .... *Lineage*
livd .... *lived*
mar .... *married*

ment .... *mentioned*
mkd .... *marked*
milit .... *militia*
mo .... *month*
mvd .... *moved*
nat .... *native*
Natl .... *National*
O. .... *Ohio*
Pa Arch .... *Pa Archives*
pd .... *paid*
p .... *page*
pp .... *pages*
pens .... *pension*
pensd .... *pensioned*
pvt .... *private*
recd .... *record*
ref .... *reference*
Regt .... *regiment*
res .... *resided*
Rev .... *Revolution*
S .... *Series*
serv .... *service*
soldr .... *soldier*
srvd .... *served*
St Ch .... *State Chairman*
twp .... *township*
Vol or V .... *Volume*
w .... *with*
wf .... *wife*
whl .... *while*
whn .... *when*
whr .... *where*

Records of Revolutionary Soldiers

ABBOT (or Abbott), EBENEZER, Cuyahoga co

Pvt Mass St Trps. Enl Apr 1775, Mass. Served 8 Mo. Appl for pens 8-4-1832, in Cuyahoga Co., states was b 10-14-1753, Worcester co Mass. Movd to Chester in Hampshire co Mass 1780. After thirty years moved to Worthington Hampshire co Mass and in 1826 to Cuyahoga co O. Ref Mass S 2027. Rept by Ohio State D A R.

ACKLEY, AHIRA, Trumbull co

Pvt Conn St Mil pens 25-3-1833. Servd over a period from 1776 to 1782. B in East Haddam Conn on 4-22-1761. Mar Mary Holmes 7-6-1783 in Middlesex co Conn. Chldr: Anna, Elizabeth, William, Daniel, Asa, Pliny. Soldier died 4-19-1846, Fowler O. Bur Fowler Ridge cem Trumbull co. Ref: pens Cl W 4872. Cop by Jane Dailey. Rept by Mary Chesney D A R

ACKRIGHT, ISAAC, ? co

Pvt listed Doc 31 1-6-1831 but rejected a pens as did not srv 9 mo. Rept by Blanche Rings Columbus O

ADAMS, GEORGE, Muskingum co

Cop fr "Past and Present of Muskingum Co" p 504; George Adams came to O 1808 and settld Madison twp Muskingum co. Came fr Fauquier co Va whr he freed all his slaves. Was son of Littleton Adams (p 324 in War of 1812) who came to O abt 1797-8 w wf and nine chldr; settled on land secured fr Govt. The youngest child of George, the soldr was George W Adams. Attempts to secure more data locally failed. Suggest No 214307 D A R for ref. Soldr bur nr Dresden O. Rept by Jane Dailey on the name fr suggestion of Mrs Frank, Marietta.

ACTON, HENRY, Belmont co

Ref Pens Cl S 2337 and E J Tillett, Armstrong Mills O. Pvt Conn Contl. Enl 1776 Flying Camp under Col Addison, Capt Lowe Pens 1819 in Belmont co. In 1832 said he was 77 yrs old. mar Lucy (a widow) in 1843. He livd in Prince George's Co nr Piscataway, Md at enl. Cop by Jane Dailey Wash D C

ADAMS, HEDMAN (or Heman), Butler co

Pvt Mass Contl. Pens 5-31-1820. B 1761 Sandwich Mass. Mar Lucy ?. D 1845 Butler co O. Ref V 33 p 12 D A R Lin. Thro dau Asenath No. 32035 D A R. Cop by Jane Dailey

ADAMS, ROBERT, Lawrence co

Pvt Va Contl. Pens 1-10-1819. Enl Albermarle co Va 1776; served two yrs. Appld for pens in Lawrence co 8-3-1819 and 1820. Stated he was b 1757; mentions "wife" and grand-dau 11 yrs old (1820). Was disch at Valley Forge 1778. Ref: Pens Cl S 45175 Va. Rept by State D A R.

ADDISON, JACOB, Muskingum co

Pens 8-8-1833 and 1840, age 79. Liv in Springfield twp Muskingum Co O. In 1832 res of Putnam twp same Co. Pens S16029 Del. Enl May 1780 in Sussex Co Del. Servd 6 mo Pvt Del St Tr. B 1750 Oct 11 in Sussex Co Del. Rept by State D A R.

ADER, MORRIS, Guernsey co

Appl pens 1-27-1819. Res Guernsey Co O Madison twp farmer. Pens 9-7-1819 there. Pens S 44289 N J. Enl 1-1-1778. Pvt N J Cont srvd 3 yrs. B 3-12-1757. Mar Rebecca, mentions gr-chl William Ader, ae 5 (in 1820 appl). Rept. by State D A R.

ADKINS, SAMUEL, Highland co

Appl pens 2-8-1819 Highland Co O. Enl 1776, Mass cont as Pvt. Servd 3 yrs. Ref: S44288, Mass Cont. Rept by State D A R.

AIKEN, THOMAS, Cuyahoga co

Appl for Pens Cuyahoga Co O 11-9-1832, stating he resided in Chatham Co Conn till abt 18 yrs ago, came to Brooklyn twp Cuyahoga Co O Pens 4-27-1833 'stating: Enl Chatham Co Conn. Srvd 14 mo. B Chatham Co Conn 1748. Rept by State D A R.

AIKMAN, JOHN, Preble co   12

Pvt b in N J 1760 Srvd under Capt Brady. Mar Mary Dysert in Pa. Came from Cumberland co Pa with family to O in 1809. Bur Harrison twp. Rept Commodore Preble chpt.

AIKMAN, JOHN B, Preble co

Pv. Was b 1760 N J; mar Mary Dysert of Pa. Soldr d Harrison twp and bur there. Came to O 1808-9. Rept by Commodore Preble chpt. Research in N J Wills found no John B but one John Aikman of Pa Arch Vol 4 S 5 p 257 Northumberland co; also p 672 and S V 6 pp 8-418 Pa Arch. (Mrs A C Moore Col O and Edith Rathburn State Libr).

ALBERT, JOHN, Stark co

Appl for pens Franklin Co Ky 4-13-1818 and in Stark Co O 11-23-1821. A tailor. Pens S44293 Pa Cont. Enl Philadelphia 1775 srvd 3 yrs as pvt. Disch 6-25-1781. Mentions wf ae 62 and dau pensr also Stark Co O 3-22-1819. Rept by State D A R.

ALDERMAN, TIMOTHY, Trumbull co

Pvt in Capt Amasa Mills Co 1778. Re-enlisted short terms. B 1754 Avon Conn. Mar Ruth Hart 10-7-1784. Chld Timothy, Phoebe, Chauncey, Sally, Arunah, Clarissa, Dorcas, Eliza, Riley. D 12-28-1815 Brookfield O Trumbull Co. Prob bur Brookfield cem by wife. Ref: V 40 D A R Lin 39841 thro dau Phoebe. Rept by Nathan Perry & Mary Chesney chaps.

ALDRIDGE, JOHN, Clermont co and Ind.

Pens 11-4-1819 Clermont co O. Pens No. 15676. Widows Cl 9698 Va. Enl 1777 for 3 mos term. Srvd 3 yrs pvt Va line. B 2-9-1761. Mar Mary Lakin 11-18-1783. Cldr Nathan, Eramus, Drucila, Layton, and Elizabeth Stiens. D 11-17-1842 Rush co Ind whr widow appld for pens 7-24-1843. She died 11-28-1843. Rept by State D A R.

ALEXANDER, JOHN, Brown co

Bur cem 2 mi NE of Fincastle Brown co. Family Stone: "In memory of John Alexander who departed this life March 3 1832 in 77 yr." Sergt Va Line. Wounded at Guilford C H 1781 taken prisoner. Started a Sandy Riv expedition it failed. B Augusta co Va Long Meadow Run parents James Alexander and Jerusha mar Jennet Alexander (of no kin) 3-10-1790. Chld: Francis; William; Andrew; John Jr; 2 daus. Came to O from Staunton Va founded Fincastle O a cooper and cabinet maker. Ref 18 rept N S D A R p 156; Beer's Hist Brown co 576-586; Mrs. H M Chaney Wash D C 2115 F St N. W. Rept by Taliaferro chap.

ALEXANDER, JOSEPH, Clermont co

Pvt and Lt volunteered 1779 S C Milit servd 2 yr. B 1759. Pens appl in Clermont co O May 1833. Ref S 15355 S C. Rept by State D A R.

ALEXANDER, JOHN, Adams co

Pvt Pa Contl enl for 3 yr in Spring of 1777 Hannahtown Pa servd in Regt commanded by Col Brodhead Pa for 3 yr. B 1753 mar Polly abt 45 yr old in 1820. Pens appl in Adams co 4-15-1818 again 8-20-1819. A stone mason. Ref S 44294 Del and Pa. Rept by State D A R.

ALFORD, JOHN, Muskingum co

Appld for pens Muskingum co O 5-1-1818 and again in 1822. Pens No. S 44290 Pa Line pvt 1 yr. B 1749. Mar Margaret mentions "grnd chld;" John Conaway ae 12 (in 1822). Enl 2-14-1776 Pa. Rept by State D A R.

ALLEN, ANANIAS, Fayette co

D 1825 Bloomingburg Fayette co O. Capt of 2nd Sussex co N J Regt. B 1742 Sussex co N J mar Rachel Harker 1772 one son was Daniel wh married Hannah Litton 1797. Ref V 107 p 105 D A R Lin No. 106348. Cop by Jane Dailey. Died Oct 2 1825 bur Bloomingburg cem. Cldr: John; Mary; Daniel; George; Margaret; Rachel; Elijah; David; Ananias Jr; Elizabeth; Jeremiah. Reported by Washington C H chpt.

ALLEN, ASHER, Morgan co

Appl pens 5-11-1818 Washington co O (now Morgan where he bur). Pens No. W 9325 Conn Pvt Conn Cont srvd 10 mo then 14 mo Corp Enl abt 5-3-1777 disch 1-8-1780 mar Elizabeth Palmer 4-29-1777 names Asher Allen jr in appl as child. Hired a substitute to finish his time. Rept by State D A R.

ALLEN, BURGESS, Green co

Cousin of Ethan Allen. Buried Silver Creek twp. Information given by old resident. Ref. Catherine Green Chapter.

ALLEN, ELIHU, Ashtabula co

Appl pens Wayne twp Ashtabula co O 4-2-1822. Had pens 7-9-1819 same co. Enl 5-1-1776 Mass Cont Pvt srvd 1 yr. B 1762 Litchfield co Conn. Mar Triphena Smith 9-19-1811 (Fr widow appl) mentions son Milton; dau Eliza; son Harvey. D 6-8-1835 Wayne twp Ashtabula co O. Pens Cl W 2511 Mass Cont & B L Wt 16279-160-55. By State D A R. See p 14 Ohio Roster Rev Sold V 1.

ALLEN, ELIPHALET, ? co

A pvt listed Dec 31 1-6-1831. Refused a pens as he deserted the service. Rept by Blanche Rings, Columbus.

ALLEN, GEORGE, Portage co

Pensr in Portage co O 11-21-1833. Had appld for pens in Beaver co Pa 3-6-1833. Enl abt June 1776 whl liv in Harwick N J. Srvd 5 mo as pvt 4 mo as sergt was ae 76 in 1833. Pens No. S 2488 N J death date not known. By State D A R.

ALLEN, ISAAC, Madison co

Memb Capt Francis Burn's Co Ulster co Milit N Y 3rd Regt under Col Levi Pawling & Col John Cantine. See N Y in Rev as Colony & State V 1 p 195. Enl July 9 1776 & marched Aug 3 1776 (Adjt Gen Office). B 12-1753 Cumberland R I. Parents

Daniel Allen & wf Sarah Sprague Allen. Mar 9-8-1745 Smithfield R I. Isaac mar Betsy Miller, North Pa Wyoming Valley. Chld: Abigail mar Daniel Fox; Sarah Allen Whitney; Rev Samuel Allen; Solomon and Isaac a farmer. D 1-16-1825 Madison co O (Bible recd). Bur on farm of Vern Phellis E of Rosedale Madison co O. Daniel and Abigail were circuit riders and bur here. Her father, Isaac came to O with them; first to Champaign co; thence to Madison over the border. Cem overgrown. Isaac and bros Stephen and David S were at Wyoming Massacre. They mvd to Towanda crk 1796 blt gristmill at Franklindale. Ref Annals Bradford co Pa Hist Soc 1906 1910 No. 3 p 16. C F Beverly's Hist & Georg same co p 384 & v 1 p 274. Pioneer & Patriot Fam same co by same author. Rept by Taliafero chpt.

ALLEN, JAMES, Trumbull co

Pens 9-24-1833 Trumbull co O Newton twp whr he came 1803. Pens Cl S 2489 Pa. Pvt in Capt Isaac Lewis Co Pa fr May to Nov 1776. Drftd 1776 Chester co Pa. B 1737 Down co Ireland. After Rev resided in Chester co Pa 4 or 5 yrs then Huntington co Pa 10 or 12 yr then Trumbull co O for 30 yrs. By State D A R.

ALLEN, JOHN, Clinton co

Appl Pens 9-5-1832 Clinton co O. Was pensr there 4-25-1833. Enl Culpeper Co Va 11-29-1779 srvd 3 yrs Va St Trps. B 1762. Pens Cl No. S 4259 Va. By State D A R.

ALLEN, JOSEPH, Trumbull co

Pens applied for 1833 there. Married "Mary" lived at Braceville O. Rept by Mary Chesney Chap.

ALLEN, LUKE, Richland co

Where he appld pens 6-6-1833. Enl Hartford Conn 1777 whl a res Windsor co srvd 6 mo Infantry; 2 mo Cavalry. B 2-6-1757. Pens Cl No. S 16030 Conn. By State D A R

ALLEN, RUFUS, Trumbull co

Appl for pens Trumbull co. Servd in Mass Trps from Berkshire Co. B 2-6-1762. D 8-17-1829 Braceville Trumbull co O. Mar Lydia Brooks had nine chldr only known name is "Hannah." Ref Mass Soldr & S in Rev p 183 Vol 1. Rept by Mary Chesney chap.

ALLEN, WILLIAM JR, ? co

Listed as pvt Dec 31 1-6-1831 but refused a pens as servd in Regt not on Contl establishment. Rept by Blanche Rings Columbus.

ALEXANDER, GEORGE, Montgomery co

Pa. 5th Ser Pa Arch Vol 4 p 820. Pvt in infantry Capt Park Shawdr Major Moore 1783. Bedford Co Vol 4 787 enl Oct 8 1783. Bur in Spanker Lutheran Church cem Bohlander farm. Was b 1761; d 1838. Rept by Wm Pettit S A R.

ALLISON, BENJAMIN, Gallia co

Died 1807 Gallia co O. Bur country cem Green twp. Srvd pvt in Capt Richard Balys Co of Orange co Milit (Florida & Warwick precinct) com by Col John Hathorn & Lt Col Henry Wisner. Cl No. 35646. Recd fr State Histor Soc Albany N Y. Mar Rachel chld John, Thomas, Benjamin, Jessee, Raumy & Polly, Samuel, Jemima & James. Lvd in Warwick twp Orange co N Y. Thence to Greenbrier Co Va in 1792. Thence to Gallia co O in late 1790's. Rept by French Colony Chpt.

ALLISON, LIEUT HUGH, Washington co

Came to Marietta abt 1790. In Campus Martius dur Indian War. Movd to his farm at Lowell abt 1798. B 1747 Va son of Robert Allison. B N Ireland, d in Va 1800-1810, ae 104. Soldr mar Sallie Scott, b 1757, d Oct 18 1823 Lowell O whr he d 1824, Aug 18 and bur in Greenlawn cem. Chldr Robert, William, Hugh, Charles, Betsy, Polly, Andrew, Hannah. Grave markd 1930 by Marietta chpt who rept this record. Ref Hildreth's and Williams Hists. Washington co.

ALLISON, ROBERT, Washington co

Pvt 2nd trp 1st Regt. Light Dragoons, Theodoric Bland. Enl for 3 yrs. Name 1st appears on Co pay rolls Apr 1778. B 1755 Aug 31 Va son of "Short" Robert Allison, b N Ireland d Va ae 104. Mar Elizabeth Phillips, of Md abt 1781. Chldr Charles Nov 11 1782, Nancy, William, Polly, Josiah, Stephen, Sally, Sophis, Hugh, Napolean, Joseph Allison. A weaver in Va moving 1782-84 to Fayette co Pa whr settld on Youghiogheny Riv, thence in 1789 to Pittsburg Pa, and to Marietta O 1789. In Campus Martius dur Indian War; in 1795, livd in Kinne's Garrison Lowell O later settling on his farm. Ref No. 12942 and 13020 D A R. V M Allison 79 Park Ave Col O. County Hists War Dept (Bridges). Rept by Marietta chpt.

ALLWIN (or Allwine), LAWRENCE, Perry and Muskingum co

Appld for pens 2-19-1819 in Muskingum co. Appld on 10-9-1832 fr Perry co O whr receiving one 6-22-1833 ae 78 yrs. Enl May or June 1776 in Pa line srvd 6 yrs also N J Milit. B 7-15-1756. Widows Cl W 511. B L Wt 11273-160-55 states he mar Phebe Worley 9-2-1821. He d 10-1-1833 Perry co O. Rept by State D A R.

ALSBROUGH, FOSTER, Medina co

A veteran of the Rev. Early arrival in Sharon twp Medina co O. Cop fr "Pioneer Women of Western Reserve" by Mrs. T R Oehlke.

AMES, EPHRAIM, Richland co

D 9-10-1824. Richland co whr he mvd in 1822 fr Delaware co O whither he came fr Pa in 1820. Appl for pens in Bradford co Pa 4-29-1818 and on 10-2-20, for trnsfr to Delaware co O. Srvd Pvt Mass Cont fr Bradford co Pa term 4 yr. Enl 1778 in Cherry Valley N Y. Mar Margaret 4-19-1789, names Elias, the 4th chld. Pens Cl W 9704 Mass. B L Wt 2069-100. By State D A R.

AMOS, MORDECAI, Carroll co

Pens Perry twp Carroll co O ae 94 living w Henry Amos (fr Cens 1840) Cl No. S 2034 Md. States Pvt Md Milit 2 yrs fr 1777 Pensd. 12-20-1832 Harford co Md whr he resided. Enl Sept or Oct 1777 b 1753 Harford co Md. Mvd to Harrison co O to reside with his children. This name appears in Vol 1, Roster of Rev soldiers Bur in O as "Ames." Liv in North twp Harrison co ae 90. Likely the same. Rept by State D A R.

AMSDEN, ABRAHAM, Ashtabula co

Not "Armsden" as sometimes found. Appld for trnsfr 12-18-1828 to Ashtabula co O fr Washington co Ver whr pensd 4-11-1818 Cl No. 4115 Mass Cont Pvt B 1752 Southboro, Mass. Mar Submit Morse 4-28-1773. Appl names Samuel ae 21 in 1820 (youngest) has 5 chldr in Ashtabula co O. D 1833 Ashtabula co. Mar 28. (This is addit data to p 16 V 1 Ohio Roster Rev Soldiers, which is filed here to avoid continued research on "Armsden"). By State D A R.

ANDERSON, ANDREW, Wayne co

Appld for pens Wayne co O 4-30-1834. Enl York co Pa. Pvt Pa Milit; Cl No. 8026 Pa. B Hopewell twp York co Pa 5-12-1761. States "Father kept record of his age." Was drftd & srvd 3 yr during 1777-1778 & 1781. Since Rev livd in York co Pa; Brooke co Va; & Wayne co O Perry twp. By State D A R.

ANDERSON, DANIEL, Athens co

Appld pens 7-9-1822. Athens co ae 68. Cl No. S 44302 Pa Line 1st Lieut; Col Hartley Capt. William Scott, 7th Regt for 2 yrs. In appl 1822, mentions wf, 65 and dau Rachel (15 yr). D Aug 6 1822, grave not located. Cop by Jane Dailey.

ANDERSON, HENRY, Lawrence co

Appld for Pens Lawrence co July 1819. Cl No. S 44301 Va. Srvd 3 yrs Va Cont. Enl Rumney Va. Mentions "wife" in appl. Rept by State D A R.

ANDERSON, JAMES ARTHUR, Portage co

Rev soldr; grave located Rootstown. By Mrs J M Owen. Old Northwest chpt.

ANDERSON, JOHN, Franklin co

Pvt Va Cont Pensr 1819 in Franklin co O. Trnsfrd fr Ky. In 1819 aged 86. D 7-7-1826. Rept by Columbus chpt.

ANDERSON, JOHN, Clarke co

Appld for pens Clark co 7-28-1832. Cl No. S 2036. Mass & N H. Pvt N H Cont. Enl 1775 Rockingham co N H. Srvd 15 Mo. M 1759. By State D A R.

ANDERSON, JOHN, Meigs co

Pensioner Meigs co. Bur Anderson cem 2 mi east of Dexter, Meigs co. On stone is data: Died 2-24-1847, ae 84 yr 3 mo 27 das. "Farewell my wife, my children, friends. This is the way that Jesus sends to take us to that Heavenly shore, Where we shall meet to part no more." Data secured by J D from C F Anderson, Dexter O a gr-gr-grand-son.

ANDERSON, ROBERT, Columbiana co

Cumberland co Pa Rangers and same in Milit. Wm Huston's Co 5 of 4th Battl. 1780-81. B 1758. Mar Rebecca, b 1774 d 10-5-1856. He d Feb 13 1853. Bur W Beaver twp cem. Ref Pa Arch 3 vol 23 pp 278, 701, 757 and Columbiana co Recds. Rept by Wilma M Molsberry Youngstown O.

ANDERSON, THOMAS, Fairfield co

Enl 1776 for 3 yr as pvt Va. Milit Capt John Gillison. B 1733, Hampshire co Va. Mar Mary Bruce, one son was called James, he d 1806 Fairfield co O. Ref Vol 116 p 101 D A R Lin No. 115319 also Vol 113. Cop by Nathan Perry chpt.

ANDREWS, ASA, Trumbull co

Conn Histor Coll Vol 12 p 369, lists him in Sold fr Hartland Conn; also listed in Hartland persons exempt fr taxes because of Contl service 1775. (Conn State Libr). Born 10-25-1736 East Haddam Ct. Mar Lucy Ackley (b 3-1-1763 — d 9-11-1828 at Hartford O) on Nov 27 1783. Chldr: Chester, Wells, Thurman, Schuyler, Asa, Nelson, Lucy-Fidelia. He d 2-25-1813 Hartford O. Bur Center cem. A resident of Hartland Ct 1758 whence he came to Hartford O Trumbull co. Rept by Mary Chesney and Mahoning. Wm Pettit repts ref 50889 S A R.

ANDREW, NATHANIEL, Cuyahoga co

Enl Nov 1779 pvt Ct Milit for 8 mo while residing at Berlin Ct whr b in 1762. Son of Moses and Lydia Andrews. 1st wife was Mary Lewis, mar 5-12-1785. Chldr were Polly, Orpaha, George, Phillip, Clarissa, Samuel, Sally, Lydia, Mary Ann, and Edward W. Birth dates given in Appl. Mar Jerusha Sage 10-3-1790. in 1805 movd to Whitestown twp. Oneida co N Y whr pensd 5-11-1833, thence to Cuyahoga co O 1834, whr in 1840 was receiving pens in Cleveland, ae 77. Ref Conn W 4117, B L Wt 19753-160-55. He d 8-27-1845 Flint Mich. Wf appld pens in Genessee co Mich 4-22-1848. Rept by State D A R.

ANDRUS, CLEMENT, Ashtabula co

Enl 1781 in Va Contl. Servd also in Conn Contl. Pvt 2 yrs. Son of Ichabod Andrus. Chldr Rebecca ae 10, Lydia 7, Amy 4, Seth 2, Sally 28 da (in yr 1820). He d 5-2-1837. Bur at Austinburg O. He was pensr in Kingsville twp Pike co O and in 4-24-

1818 appld for pens Ashtabula co O. Was wounded in leg by timber. Ref Conn and Mass S 44304, and 3rd rept N S D A R p 229. Rept by State D A R.

ANNIS, BENJAMIN, Trumbull co

Wf Eunice d Nov 26 1844 ae 78. Both buried in old cem at Gustavus Center Trumbull co O. By Western Reserve Chpt.

APPLEGATE, BENJAMIN, Butler co and Ind.

Pvt N J Contl. Enl Apr 1779 Northampton Co Pa. Servd 4 yrs. B 1763. Mar Phebe Grimes Feb 10 1785. Chldr Hannah ae 13, John 10, James 7 (appl of 1820). In affidavit of a witness gives oldest dau Catherine, oldest son, Richard. He appld for pens Butler co O July 20 1819 and again in 1820. He d Apr 4 1832, Shelby co Ind as stated in widow's appl there 8-10-1840 (ae 72). Ref W 9706 N J Contl. Rept by State D A R.

ARMITAGE, BENJAMIN, Mahoning co

Pvt. Ref Pa Arch. Ser 5 vol 2 pp 51 and 127. Mar Mary Drake, 1773—5-31-1854. Chldr: Elizabeth 1792-1869 mar Daniel Wick; Ephram mar Margaret Ramsey dau of James a Rev soldier. Grave not located, tho he d in Jackson Mahoning co. Came fr Huntingdon co Pa. Ref Henry Baldwin S A R List and Republican Sentinel of 5-31-1854.Rept by Mahoning chpt.

ARMONTROUT (various spellings), CHARLES, Preble co

Pvt Mass Contl enl 1-16-1781, Rockingham co Va. Servd 6 mo. He was b there May 1763. Mar Christina Gray 6-23-1807. He d 5-6-1836 Preble co O states the widow in her appl made 5-30-1853 in Monroe twp Preble co. Ref W 5641 B L Wt 26823-160-55 Va and H Z Williams County History Preble co. Rept by State D A R and Commodore Preble chpt.

ARMSTRONG, BENJAMIN, ? co

Pvt listed p 172 Pens 1818 as Invalid pensr U S belonging to Ohio. Pd $96 annually at Chillicothe O. Cop by J D.

ARMSTRONG, EBENEZER, Medina co

Appld for pens 9-11-1819 Chatauqua co N Y. Appld 12-27-1837 in Worthington Franklin co O. Appld for trnsfr 3-27-1840 to Medina co O. States he was b 1756 servd 5 yrs. No names but "children" mentioned. Ref S 44298 Conn Contl. Rept by State D A R.

ARMSTRONG, GEORGE, Clinton co

Rept by George Clinton D A R Chpt. Ref 13. Rept N S D A R p 121, as bur in York twp Clinton co O. Cop by Nathan Perry chpt.

ARMSTRONG, JAMES, Franklin co

Pvt Pa. State Tr enl Bucks co Pa 1776 servd 7 mo. B July 1761, Bucks co. Appld for pens Franklin co O 9-25-1832 Franklinton twp. Ref Pens cl S 2916 Pa. Rept by State D A R.

ARMSTRONG, JAMES, ? co

Order bk 6-133. Made declaration for pens under the act of June 7 1832 and the clerk is directed by the War dept to issue certf. Rept by Blanche Rings.

ARMSTRONG, ROBERT, Belmont co

Service in York and Cumberland Pa milit; b 1755 Ireland; d 1846; mar Rosanna McGowan. Ref 52201 S A R. Rept by Wm Pettit.

ARNOLD, ARNOLD, Holmes co

Ref Va Militia in Rev p 262. Cens of 1840 O pensr in Holmes co aged 75. Cop by Jane Dailey, St Ch.

ARNOLD, JACOB, Montgomery co

Appld for pens 1832 rejected because his service less than 6 mo. Lived in Wayne twp. Rept by W M Pettit State Sec S A R.

ARNOLD, LEVI, Mahoning co

Pvt Ref Ct Men in Rev p 277. Mar Hannah 1775 (4-24-1853 b in N J). Chldr: Samuel, Edwin mar Ann, John W. Soldr d abt 1843 in Goshen twp. Came to Poland O in 1804. Ref Will Bk 12 p 70 Columbiana co Recds. Rept by Mahoning chap.

ARNOTT, SAMUEL, Richland co

Exec Doc 37 of 1852. Refused a pens; was a wagoner. Rept by Wm Pettit.

ARROWHEAD, THOMAS, Ross co

Was a pensr liv in Ross co O Concord twp in 1840. Cop fr H C Pemberton's bk of Obituary notices fr pens recds etc and rept by Mrs Orion King Circleville O.

ARTER, JOHN, Columbiana co

Rev soldier record not found. B 1768, d 1808 bur Center twp Columbiana co. Cop fr cem records, by Wilma Molsberry Youngstown O.

ASHLEY, JAMES, Huron co

Was b Taunton Mass; mar Middleborough Mass Feb 17 1767 to Annett Caswell. Minute Man Capt Isaac Woods and Capt John Burrows Co Col Ebenezer Sprout's Regt 6 das 1778 and Alarm of Dartmouth. Bur Steuben cem; no mrkr. Record of his family consult Mrs Ross Cherry Sandusky O.

ASHLEY, WILLIAM, ? co

Listed Doc 31 1-6-1831 as Pvt but refused a fed pens as servd in a Regt not on Contl Establishment. Rept by Blanche Rings Columbus. (Cf: p 20 Vol 1 Ohio Rev Roster).

AT, PETER, Wayne co

Cop from stone in Mt. Eaton cem, Wayne co O was the following: "Peter At War of 1776." Rept by Wooster Wayne chpt.

ATSET, JOSEPH, ? co

Pvt but because he servd in Regt not on Contl Estab was rejected a pens. Ref listed Dec 31 1-6-1831. Rept by Blanche Rings, Columbus O.

AUGUSTINE, GEORGE, Columbiana co

Rev soldier recd not found. B 1753 d 1826 Dec 11 ae 72. Bur Unity twp Forney cem. Estate settled in Unity twp 1826. Ref Columb co recds and Ohio Patriot. Rept by Wilma Molsberry Youngstown.

AUSTIN, SAMUEL, Portage co

Pvt Conn Contl Enl Mar 1776 at Litchfield Ct. Dischgd at Farmingford Ct. Appld for pens Portage co O 2-23-1829 giving ae as 80 said wf not living no chldr under his care. Pensr 12-10-1833 same co. Ref Pens cl S 2931 Conn Contl. Rept by State D A R. (N B One Samuel Austin in rejected list of Ohio, as did not serv in Regt on Contl Estab. Ref Doc 31 1-6-1831. Rept by Blanche Rings, Columbus).

AVERY, GEORGE, Licking co

Servd under Wayne at Stony Point. Came to Granville O fr Westfield Mass. B Norwich Conn. Mar Mary Allen of Croton Conn. Chldr George, Christopher, Simeon, Mary, Alfred, Cynthia. Soldr d 9-29-1806. Bur Old Cemetery Granville O. Ref Hill's Hist Licking co pp 613-618. Rept by Hetuck chpt.

AUSTIN, WILLIAM, Mahoning co

Servd R I in Capt Amos Green's Co Col Joseph Noyes Regt enl 2-6-1777. Dischgd 3-6-1777. Servd 29 da at South Kingston also in list of men who recd wages etc fr Capt Green at Charlestown. He was b at Exeter R I 1752. D Clark twp Coshocton O. Mar first Mary Rogers at Exeter R I she b 1746-1790 had 10 or more chldr. Mar second Lucy Austin abt 1805 at Pittstown Rensselaer co N Y. Dau Lucy b abt 1800 mar Ed-Ward Potter of Trumbull co O. Rept by Eva Scott Mahoning chpt.

AYERS, JOHN, Clark co

Pvt Md Contl. Servd 3 yrs fr Mar 1777 to Mar 1781. Born 1754. Appld for pens Clark co O Mar 24-1824. D 3-16-1833 also a pensr in Clark co 4-18-1825. Ref Pens cl S 45226 Del and Md. Rept by State D A R.

AYRES, JOHN, Butler co

Enl Somerset co N J Sept 1776 as pvt under Lieut Thos Collyer Capt McCoy Major James Linn Cols Ten Eick Winds Freylinghuysen and Dickinson. In battles Eliza-bethtown Piscataway and Monmouth. B 1760 wf Sarah d May 20 1835 ae 77. Soldr d 2-5-1839 bur on Princeton Pike Whitehead farm Butler co O. Family stone. Ref S 14983 N J and family data. Rept by Meryl Markley State Vice-Ch. (Think this is same as "Ayres ———" Clermont co p 22 Vol 1 Roster O .J D)

BABBS, JOHN, Hamilton co

Enl 1776 in Col Smallwood's Regt of the Md Line; b abt 1752 aged 68 yrs in 1820 (appl); resides with "son" (appl); pensd 9-25-1818 Hamilton co.   Ref Md S 45241. Rept by State D A R.

BABCOCK, NATHANIEL, Franklin co

Eenl Coventry Conn June 1778 pvt in Capt Squire Hill's Co Col McLellan Conn Regt. Disch Sept 1778; enl in Oct 1778; servd 3 mo under same officers; stationed at New London. In Nov 1779 movd to Middlefield N H co Mass. Here enl the following May as subs for his bro Rodolphus Babcock; servd as pvt in Capt Levi Ely's Co Col John Brown's Mass Regt. Went to Stone Arabia; also in small engage wh Col Brown was killed; b 3-26-1765 at Coventry Conn; mar Rachel Rodgers d 1857; chldr: Jacob; Ira; Erastus; Roswell; Elizabeth; Olive; Welthy; Cynthia; Rosemanly and son-in-law Noah Smith; soldr d Dublin 7-4-1839; bur fam cem; movd to Mass 1798; thence to Luzerne co Pa and 9-19-1814 to Ohio; pensd 1832 Franklin co. Ref S 2367 Conn; D A R No 75260 and No 78603 Mrs Kate Abegg Blakesburg Ia. Rept by Columbus D A R.

BACH, JUDAH, Hamilton co

B 1738 in Conn; d 1821; mar Priscilla Gates; Ref 46951 S A R. Rept by Wm Pettit.

BACHELDER, WILLIAM, Richland co

Enl 1777 at Kingston N H pvt N H Contl. Served 3 yrs; lived Oxford co Mass; Lincoln co Me June 11 1818; and Richland co Ohio; Pens appl Lincoln co Me June 11 1818 and Richland co Ohio 1825. Ref Pen Cl S 45236 N H. Jared Mansfield chpt rept mention of him in Graham's Hist Richland co in Lexington O and one in Mifflin. Rept by State D A R.

BACON, NEHEMIAH, Portage co

Enl Pomfert Conn in Capt Abner Bacon's Co Col John Durkee's Regt. Disch West Point N Y Serv in Conn Cont Line. Previous to this in 1775 servd 8 mo in Capt Israel Putnam's Co and was disch at Cambridge Mass. B 1736 Pomfret Conn. Mar 1756 Ruth Adams d Nov 1832 in Gustavus Trumbull co Lived Portage co O 1818; pensd appl 1818. Ref Pens Cl S 45239 and D A R Lin vol 110 p 264. Rept by Jane Dailey and Mary Chesney chpt.

BAGGS, JAMES, Richland co

Enl Jan 22 1776 Chester co Pa. Served till May 1777 when disch at Philadelphia Pa. B 1743; mar Nov 30 1780 to Susannah ——; soldr d Feb 1 1827; Appl for pens Brooke co Va Nov 29 1819 pens 5-24-1820; appl for transfer of pens to Fichland co Ohio Nov 8 1822. Wid had letter written from Richland co June 24 1837 for pension as wid of James Baggs. Ref Pens Cl S 44346 Penn. Rept by State D A R.

BAGLEY, AZOR, Adams co

Enl Sept 1778 on Hudson River at Fishkiln N Y. Servd 3 yrs pvt N Y Contl. B June 20 1757. Left discharge with "father" N Y. Appl for pens Adams co Ohio July 16 1830. Ref Pens Cl S 44341 Cont N Y. Rept by State D A R.

BAGLEY, TIMOTHY, Clark co

Listed as such but is incorrect spelling for Bayley Timothy which see Vol 1 Ohio Roster p 32. (J D).

BAGUM, HENRY, Stark co

Enl 1777 Md Militia. Served 1 yr 5 mo as pvt. B Jan 27 1761 Dauphin co Pa; bur Stark co. Res at time of enlistment in Washington co Md. In 1788 or '89 removed to Huntington co Pa; 1801 to Fayette co Pa; 1806 to Westmoreland co Pa 1811 to Wayne co Ohio; 1822 to Stark co Ohio. Appl for pens Stark co Tuscarawas twp. Pens 8-1-1833. Ref Pens Cl S 5269 Md. Rept by State D A R.

BAILEY, JAMES, Washington co

Enl 1776 at Dumphries Prince Wm co Va 1st Regt of Va State Troops. Disch Feb 9 1780 pvt. b Dumphries Prince Wm co Oct 1751. Res 4 yr Fairfax co Va; 9 yrs Prince Wm co; 10 yrs Fredericksburg Va. Removed to Ohio and lived in Marietta twp Warren co and Washington co for 29 yrs (appl 1832). Appld for pens Roxburry twp Washington co O Oct 25 1832. Drew 100 A bounty land for 3 yrs service (appl). Pension Cl office states he is only one of that name in Ohio. However Mahoning co reports a James Bailey as d at Poland Mahoning co. No data on death so may have been same man. Ref S 2945 and Mass S & S Vol 1 p 453. Rept by State D A R.

BAILEY, JOHN, Montgomery co

First Pa Contl Line 5th S Vol 2 p 670, 1777-78, James Ross' Co; Vol 3 p 463, 9th Pa Contl Line 1783 trnsfr fr 5th Capt Van Lear's Co. Recd depreciation pay. Bur in Old Baptist cem at Centerville. Rept by Wm Pettit.

BAILEY, SETH, ? co

Served in the Militia and on the Committee of Safety of Scituate Mass. B Scituate Mass 1747 son of Adams and Sarah (Howard) Bailey who were mar 1746; chld Sarah Howard; mar 1770 Deborah Packard (b 1750); soldr d 1810 in Ohio. Ref D A R Lin Bk Vol 36 p 198. Rept by Nathan Perry chpt. Ref 2276 S A R.

BAILEY, WILLIAM C, Miami co

Enl Feb 4 1777 Alexandria Va. Last discharge July 2 1808 6 yrs as Corp 16 yrs as Non commissioned officer. B abt 1753; aged 55 in 1808; chld: Mrs. Gates (widow) with whom he and his wife resided (appl). Soldr d Sept 2 1837. Was paralytic invalid and almost blind when appl for pens 1-1-1821. Ref S 44342; Rept by State D A R.

BAIN, JAMES, Greene co

Reputed soldier. Wife Mary d Feb 14th 1848. He d July 2 1828. Bur Old Pioneer Cemetery Bellbrook. Rept by Catherine Green chpt.

BAINTER (or Painter), HENRY, Fayette co

B Apr 8 1759; mar Elizabeth (b June 3 1704; d June 7 1840); chldr: John; Peter; Henry; Sally; Jonathan; and Jacob. Soldr d Sept 19 1845; bur Painter, Stuckey Cem nr Good Hope Fayette co. Ref Pa Arch 3rd S Vol 22 p 344. Rept by Washington C H chpt.

BAIRD, JOHN, Muskingum co

Enl 7-20-1776 Philadelphia Pa while residing in Lancaster co Pa Pvt Pa Line 6 mo. B Feb 1760 Bucks co Pa; mar Susan —— (d 12-20-1841). Chldr: Jane; Moses; James; John; and Sarah. Soldr d Dec 24 1843 dau Jane made declaration for arrears of father's pens Muskingum co 3-7-1855; appld Pens Jefferson twp Guernsey co Ohio 3-25-1833; Census 1840 pensr in Monroe twp Muskingum co æ 82. Ref Pens Cl 2058. Rept by State D A R.

BAIRD, JOSEPH, Butler co

Pvt N J Militia; pens'r 1832 Butler co. Enl 1778 Monmouth co. N J. Served 2 yrs; b Monmouth co N J Feb 1762; mar Mar 9 1785 Jane Van Cleave. Chldr: John; Benjamin Anna; Mary; Zebulon; Cornelius; Arthur; Andrew; James; and Jane. Soldr d Mar 27 1835 Butler co. Appl for pens Butler co Aug 1 1832. Aft Rev removed to N Y; thence to Butler co 1805. Ref Pen Cl W 5759 N J. Rept by Jane Dailey.

BAKER, ABNER, Huron co

Pvt Capt John Kirkland's Co Col Ruggles Woodbridge Regt 3 mo 22 da to reinforce the northern army. Capt Edward Hammond's Co Col Theophilus Cotton's Regt; Capt Isaac Ward's Co Col Thomas Capets Plymouth Co; Lieutenant Abner Baker in John Doty 2nd Co Col Ebenezer Sprout's Regt. Also to Dartmouth; soldr b 1754; d 1845; bur Norwalk cem Huron co. Rept by Marjorie Cherry; and Sally DeForest chpt p 24 Vol 1 Ohio Roster Rev.

BAKER, ELI, Ashtabula co

Pvt Mass State Trps; pensd 20-7-1833. Enl Sept 1776; served 14 mo. B Woodbury twp Conn 1750. Appl for pens in Ashtabula co 10-2-1832. Resided in Williamstown twp Berkshire Co Mass at the time of the Rev. About one yr aft war moved to Charleston Vermont. In 1831 moved to Ashtabula co O. Ref Mass S 18304. Rept by State D A R.

BAKER, MICHAEL, Illinois

Sergt Pa. Enl 1779 in 8th Regt Pa line. Not pensd. B London Eng 3-27-1753; mar 2-14-1791 Mary Crage; chldr in 1820; William æ 23; John æ 18; Michael æ 14; Nancy æ 25; two gr chldr: a boy æ 6 and girl æ 11. Soldr d 9-13-1831 Greene co Ill. Though bur in Ill name taken from Ohio Pens list. Ref Penn S 46,700 and B L Wt 616-100. Rept by State D A R.

BAKER (or Hornbaker), PHILIP, Portage co

Is filed under "Hornbaker." (J D).

BAKER, THOMAS, Greene co

Pa Service; b Chester co Pa; mar Sarah Woodward 1785 Chester co; chldr; Richard; Thomas; Joshua b 1788; Nayl b 1796 mar Huldah Mills; Phebe; George b ?; bur

Clifton cem Greene co O on Barker lot; came to Greene co 1812; had saw mill; was Trustee; Robinson's co Hist; and Chapman's co Hist. Rept by Catherine Greene chpt.

BALDWIN, BENJAMIN, Warren co

Sergt Va Line. Pens 14-2-1829. Letter filed by W H Baldwin Blanchester Clinton co for heirs 9-11-1854. Ref R 19355. Rept by State D A R.

BALDWIN, STEPHEN, Portage co

Enl Jan 1776 served till last 1776 whn a pass was given him to go home because of illness. Served 1 yr as pvt. B abt 1760; æ 58 in 1818. Appl pens June 18 1818 pens 6-9-1819 as resd Nelson twp Portage co. Ref S 45235 Cont (Mass). Rept by State D A R.

BALDWIN, THOMAS, ? co

Invalid pensr of U S belonging to state of Ohio. Pd at Chillicothe. Annual allowance $96. Ref p 172 Pensr 1818. Rept by Jane Dailey.

BALES (or Bayles), JESSE, Brown co

Enl Oct 2 1776 Winchester Va. Pvt Va Cont. Servd 3 yrs. B 1760 mar 1787-'88 Jane ——. She had son Moses Lunchford by a former mar. Soldr d Apr 27 1830 Brown co. Appl pens Mason co Ky Nov 16 1819; pens 14-12-1819; Appl pens to be paid Brown co Apr 4 1821. Wid appl pens Mason co Ky Aug 24 1838. Ref W 8345 Va. Rept by State D A R.

BALTZ (or Balizts), GERGE, Champaign co

Enl May 1777 Baltimore. Disch 1783 Lancaster Pa. B 1737; d 7-19-1825. Pens Urbana O 17-3-1819. Appl pens Champaign co 7-18-1820. Ref S 44349 Cont Md; B L Wt 1843-100 and B L Wt 2379-100. Rept by State D A R. Hetuck chpt reports b 1738; d July 19 1825 æ 87.

BALL, DAVIS, ? co

Served as minute man Essex co N J mil. B 1759 Essex co N J. Mar Mary Hatfield (b 1764; d 1835); Child one son was Abner. Soldr drowned in the Miami River O. Ref D A R Lin Vol 115 p 188; Rept by Nathan Perry chpt.

BALL, NATHAN, Columbiana co

Pvt Capt Wm Kirk's Co Upper Darby Chester co Militia. B 1763; d Apr 26 1842. Ref Pa Arch. 5 S Vol 5 p 758. Rept by Wilma M Molsberry Youngstown.

BALL, VALENTINE, Knox co

Enl in early part of Rev in Chesterfield co Va whr he then resd. Pvt N J Cont 12 mo Inf 3 mo. Cav. B abt 1754; æ 78 yr 1832. Pens 2-21-1833 Campbell co Ky. Soldr d Feb 23 1833. Ref S 16317 Va; O Pens Roll 1835; III: O-136. Rept by State D A R.

BALLARD, JESSE, Washington co

Enl Aug 17 1777 R I; disch Stillwater N Y; Capt R I Contl. Appl pens Washington co 5-5-1818; pensd 8-15-1818. Was later dropped from pens roll on charge perjury. That he had uncle by same name who performed alleged service but the one who made appl was only a waiter to his uncle; b abt 1763 æ 55 in 1818. Pensr under act of 1818 but not under 1820 as not considered in indigent circumstances. Ref S 44325 R I & Doc 31 Jan 6 1831. Rept by State D A R & Blanche Rings Columbus O.

BALLARD, MICAJAH, Lawrence co

Enl Bedford co Va Sept 1780 pvt Va Cont. Servd 18 mo. B 1736. Appl mentions "wife" and "one dau æ 50" (in 1820). Appl pens 12-6-1819 Lawrence co. Pensd 9-29-1820. Ref S 44,326 Va. Rept by State D A R.

BALLARD, WILLIAM, Franklin co

Enl Apr 4 1779 pvt Capt Thomas Madisons & James Bartons Cos Col Francis Taylors Va regt. Disch May 22 1781. B Mar 18 1760 mar 2nd wf Franklin co 11-7-1830 Cathern Troxell. Had 7 chldr; one dau mar John Stinson. Came to Ohio 1800. Soldr d Mar 13 1841-2 Franklin co. Said to be bur Press Peters farm; cem now destroyed. Will filed Franklin co resd Jackson twp. Pensd 7-21-1832 Scioto twp Pickaway co. Wid pens Feb 2 1853 Madison co. She lvd S Charleston Clark co 1855 æ 72. Ref W 25220 Va. Rept by Pickaway Plains and Columbus D A R.

BALLARD, WYATT, Warren co

Enl Warrentown Warren co N C. Feb 1781 pvt Capt Carter Col Dixon 2nd N C Contl. Servd 1 yr. Ae 59 in Feb 1819. Had wife and child Susan æ abt 17. Appl pens 3-3-1819 and 7-4-1820. Pensd 7-8-1819. Ins Rolls Knox co Tenn. Appl for transfer 5-4-1822 to Ohio. Payable at Chillicothe letter to be sent Waynesville Warren co O. Trnsfrd grant June 19 1822. Ref S 44327 N C. Rept by State D A R.

BARETH (Barrett), JOHN, Champaign co

Enl Winchester Va 1781. Servd Va line 1 yr. Dischrgd Little York Penn. B 1755 mar Jan 8 1783 Elizabeth ——. Soldr d Mar 21 1837. Appl pens Champaign co 5-2-1818. Pens 11-26-1819. Removed from rolls under act of 1820 as not in indigent circumstances. Wid appl pens 10-15-1838 and 11-5-1844. Ref W 5213 Contl Va B L Wt 1660-100. Rept by State D A R.

BARETH, ROBERT, ? co

Pensr under Act of 1818 taken fr Rolls, Act of 1820, as not considered in indigent circumstances accd to Act. Cop fr Doc 31, 1-6-1831 by Blanche Rings Col O.

BARKER, CHARLES, Pike co

Enl 9-7-1777 in Va. Pvt Va Contl. Servd 3 yrs. Ae 71 in 1822. Appl pens Pike co 3-5-1822. Pens 10-24-1822. Had resd Pike co 13 yrs. Ref S 45238 Contl Va. Rept by State D A R.

BARKER, JOSEPH COL, ? co

Listed in news clipping found in old scrap book no date by "L A A" as Rev who participated or interested in settlement of Marietta; with but few exceptions these (who have desc here) are bur Washington co. Rept by Marietta chpt.

BARKS, MICHAEL, Huron co

In list of deaths of Rev Soldr in Adler's (Pa) Journal Dec 23 1845. "D in Huron co O Nov 22 1845 Michael Barks æ 86 yrs." Rept by Mary Owen Steinmetz Reading Pa.

BARLOW, AARON, ? co

Listed in scrapbook clipping as Rev soldr-Capt connected with settlement Marietta, and filed here for future research.

BARLOW, JOEL, ? co

Marietta scrap book list of Rev soldr interested there, 1788 with descendants bur in co. Was Capt.

BARNARD (car sp), MOSES, Ashtabula co

3rd Battl 6th Co Conn St Trp. Served 2 yr. Mar 5-27-1784 Reliance Norris. Soldr d 10-15-1830 Windsor twp Ashtabula co; bur Windsor O. Grave located Mary Stanley D A R. Wid appl pens Ashtabula co 4-19-1839. Ref 18 Rep N S D A R p 162; 21 Rep N S D A R p 84 & W 4634 Conn. Rept by Nathan Perry chpt & State D A R.

BARLOW, WILLIAM, ? co

Capt in Rev listed in Marietta clipping as interested in settlement many had descendants bur in co. Filed here for research.

BARNARD (var sp), JESSE, Ashtabula co

Monument Windsor O. Located Luther Reeve D A R. Ref 15 Rep N S D A R p 164. Rept by Nathan Perry chpt.

BARNES, CAPT JOHN, Hamilton co

N Y services; b Ireland 1735; d 1804; mar —— Hamilton; Ref 27745 S A R. Rept by Wm Pettit.

BARNET, GEORGE, Tuscarawas co

Enl June 1777 Penn. Servd 6 yrs pvt Penn Contl. B 1760. Appl mentions "ch." Appl pens Allegheny co Penn Aug 1818 as resd Steubenville Jefferson co July 1819 pensd 9-15-1819 Tuscarawas co 45243 Wt No 9004 Issued Aug 29 1793 Pa Arch S 3 vol 23 p 582. Rept by State D A R.

BARNGROVER, GEORGE, ? co

Pvt. Pens $96 yr. Invalid list of U S belonging to Ohio. Pd at Chillicothe. Pens 1817 p 172. Rept by State D A R.

BARNS, JOHN, Trumbull co

Enl 6-1-1776 Watertown twp Conn. Pvt in Conn and Contl lines. Ae 59 in 1818. mar Fanny Chalker; mar 2nd Nancy Dutton. Soldr d 6-12-1834 Trumbull co. Pensd 9-6-1819. Ref S 2047 Conn Contl. Rept by State D A R.

BARNS, ELIJAH, Butler co

Enl July 1776 Ann Arundel co Md. Pvt Pa Contl. Servd 7 mo. B 1755; mar Aug 17 1784 Catherine Shipley (b abt 1767 æ 76 in 1843). Soldr d Aug 13 1840. Pens 1-4-1819. Appl pens Butler co O Oct 16 1832. Wid appl pens May 27 1843 Decatur co Ind. Ref W 9717 Md. Rept by State D A R.

BARNSE, ROBERT, Champaign co

Enl June 24 1770 Little York Penn. Servd 1 yr Penn Contl. B 1744. Appl pens 5-5-1818 Champaign co. Pens 2-2-1819 Champaign co. Ref S 45240 Cont Penn. Rept by State D A R.

BARNUM, ENOCH, ? co

Listed in Invalid Pensr of U S belonging to Ohio. Pd at Chillicothe. Annual allowance $96. Ref Pensr 1818 p 172. Rept by State D A R.

BARR, JOHN, Tuscarawas co

Pvt Penn Contl line 6 yr. Was b 1750; mar Margaret ——. Chldr: James æ 15; Mary Ann æ 13 in 1820. Pens 2-2-1819. Taken from rolls by act 1820 as not in indigent circumstances. Appl pens 10-4-1820 Tuscarawas co. Ref S 45244 Continental Penn. Rept by State D A R.

BARR, SAMUEL, Brown co

Enl May 1775 in Washington co Penn. Servd 19 mo as pvt and Sergt. B Jan 5 1759 Elktown Md. Lvd Washington co Pa several years aft Rev. Had lvd in Ohio 35 yrs and Brown co 14 yrs at time of appl. Supposed bur Mt Carmel cem nr Sardinia. Appl pens 5-3-1833; pens 6-6-1833 Brown co Ohio. Ref S 2366 Penn. Rept by State D A R.

BARRETT, OLIVER, Erie co

Enl Nov 14-1776 Cumberland Conn Brattleboro; Return of Col Seth Ware's Regt; Oliver Barrett Sergt Jan 1 1777 to Nov 14 1778; Ensign 11-14-1778; payable 6-5-1781; d 1820 bur Oak Grove cem Venice-Gov mrkr. Ref Vt recds 107:109:110:623:668; Fire-lands Pio. O S 8 p 91; co Hists p 498. By Marjorie Cherry.

BARRON, ROBERT, Perry co

Sergt Rev Army. Pens 10-12-1792 (not under any act of Congress). In Ohio list 1818 invalid pensr recd pens Chillicothe $96 per annum. Listed in Perry co. Also O Pens Roll 1835; III O — 23. Ref Pens Dept repts this record was burned but is on 1835 list of Pensr. Rept by State D A R.

BARTHOLOMEW, THEOBOLD, Ashtabula co

Family taken prisoners night before attack on Fort Charlotte 1778. Servd with distinction during border warfare. First settler Geneva twp Ashtabula co. Came from Charlotte Schoharie co N Y 1805; located on South Ridge. Ref Pioneer Women of West Reserve p 9210. Rept by Nathan Perry chpt and Jane Dailey. 3rd Rept N S D A R p 229.

BARTLETT, ISAAC, Ashtabula co

Enl 3-20-1777 Lebanon twp Conn. Pvt R I line 2 yr. B 7-9-1759; d 2-14-1845 Andover twp Ashtabula co; mar Sibbil Cants ? had 3 daus. Pens Rensselaer co N Y 8-2-1819. Transfd to Ashtabula co Jan 21 1836. Pensr Andover Ashtabula co æ 81 in 1840. Occup weaver. Wid appl pens Trumbull co 10-30-1851 and Allegany co N Y 3-16-1853. Ref Cont (Conn). W 517; B L Wt 33570-160-55. Rept by State D A R.

BARTON, JOSIAH, Huron co

Enl 1779 at Albany N Y. Discharged June 8 1783. Pvt N Y Contl. B Long Island N Y abt 1761 æ 58 in 1819. Appl pens Norwalk Ohio 1818. Pensd 11-20-1819. Ref S 45245 N Y. Rept by State D A R.

BASKIN, GEORGE WASHINGTON, Monrrow co

B 1760; mar 1797 Rachel Braddock (b 1759; d 1844); a son was George W who mar Elizabeth Morgan. Soldr d 1858 Iberia Ohio. Ref D A R Lineage Book V 113 p 8. Rept by Jane Dailey.

BATES, AARON, Trumbull co

Prob Aaron Bates who served with Hampshire co Mass forces at Ticonderoga. B Jan 20 1753; mar Sarah King. Chldr: Sally; Orilla; Sabina; Horace; James; (possibly others). Soldr d Feb 19 1821 Vernon Trumbull co; bur Old cemetery Vernon. Came to Vernon from Hartland Conn. Ref Mass Soldrs & Sailors vol 1 p 779. Rept by Mary Chesney chpt.

BATES, DAVID, Sandusky co

Research at Pens Dept indicates there was no "David Bates of Ohio." Papers found for Daniel Bates (see v 1 Ohio Roster). (J D).

BATES, ISSACHAR, Montgomery co

Enl abt 1775 Boston Mass 16 mo as fifer and 9 mo as fife major Mass state trp. Servd in Capt Ichabod Dexter's Co June 1775. Enl May 1 1775; servd 3 mo 8 days at Cambridge; was in Bennington Vt and Burgoyne Campaign. 1st servd in Col Wood-throps Regt. B Jan 29 1758 Hingham Mass. Resd Worcester co with father at enl. Appl pens Montgomery co O 9-11-1832. Pens 4-9-1833. Ref Mass S 2360 and Mass Soldrs and Sailors V 1 p 788. Rept by State D A R.

BATES, JOSEPH, Mahoning co

Pvt N Y Men in Rev p 41; also Conn Men and Mass Men. D abt 1811 Green twp Mahoning co. Ref Ohio Patriot April 5 1811 est Joseph Bates. Rept by Mahoning chpt.

BATES, WILLIAM, Lorain co

Soldr of Rev War commended for gallantry and bravery in battle Sacket's Harbor. B abt 1764 Conn. Mar 1st —— (5 chldr); mar 2nd Mrs Sarah Wood b abt 1777; d abt 1861 (10 chldr). Resd Lowville N Y most of life. Moved to Ohio 1836. Soldr d 1848. Among chldr were Francis; Ottis; Bennett; Hannah; Moses; Lyman; Thaxter; Norton; Charles. Ref Commemorative and Biograph Rec of Co of Huron and Lorain p 1104. Rept by Nathan Perry D A R.

BATTERSON, WILLIAM, ? co

Pensd act 1818 but denied a pens under act 1820 as servd in a Regt not on Contl Estab. Ref Doc 31 Jan 6 1831. Rept by Blanche Rings Cols O.

BATTLE, JUSTUS, Lorain co

Marched from Tyringham Berkshire co Mass as a minute man aft battle Lexington to Roxbury where he enl May 1 1775 and servd 8 mo in Capt Samuel Warren's Co Col Joseph Reeds' Mass Regt. Reenl; servd 1 yr in same Co; was in battle White Plains. Marched to Lake George; at evac of Ticonderoga and in retreat to Stillwater; servd abt 4 mo. mar Esther Taylor who survived him. Soldr d July 17 1840 Brighton Lorain co. Appl pens Brighton Lorain co Aug 2 1832. Ref S 4939 Contl Mass Gen Accounting Office; Pioneer Women of W R p 463. Rept by Nathan Perry chpt and State D A R.

BAUM, JACOB, Montgomery co

5th S Pa Arch Vol 4 p 278; vol 6 p 650, 561; Contl Line; Cumberland Milit 1782, Col Lamb, Vol 6 p 649. Muster roll 1783 Capt Wm Lamb. Bur St John's Lutheran Ch cem east of Miamisburg. Rept by Wm Pettit.

BAUMGARTEN, HENRY, Franklin co

Enl Oct 1780 in Va Line. Pvt in Armands Corps 15 mo serv. B abt 1757 æ 65 in 1822. Wife æ 54 in 1822; one son æ 18 and 2 daus æ 16 and 9 in 1822. Pens 9-27-1819 Franklin co O. Ref S 45246 Contl Va; B L Wt 1567-100. Rept by State D A R. (Many various spellings) Ref Order bk 2-273 of June 17 1820 at Col O rept by B R.

BAUTHAM, JOHN, Coshocton co

Enl 6-18-1777 Georgetown twp Kent co Md. Pvt Md Contl. B abt 1758 æ 72 in 1820. Mar Rachel ——. Appl pens Coshocton co O 4-22-1818; pens 9-22-1819. Ref S 44344 Md; B L Wt 434-100. Rept by State D A R.

BAY, DAVID, Champaign co

Enl 1777. Pvt Va Contl. Servd 3 yr. B 1756. In 1820 had 2 sons æ 17 & 19 yrs. Pens Champaign co O 1818. Appl Pens Champaign co 1820. Was Pensd 1818 but removed in 1820 as not in indigent circumstances. Ref S 45237 Va & Doc 31 Jan 6 1831. Rept by Blanche Rings Cols O and State D A R.

BEACH, EZEKIEL, Trumbull co

Enl Litchfield Conn. Pvt Conn State Trps. B March 24 1751 Litchfield Conn son Samuel and Rachel (Strong) Beach. Mar Feb 24 1774 Azuba Courlery. Chldr: Ezekiel S; Ezra; Abiel; Diadema. Soldr d Hartford twp Trumbull co May 5 1836. Lived Litchfield till abt 1826; then moved to Vernon twp Trumbull co where pensd 1833. Wid app pens 7-7-1837. Ref W 4130 Conn and Family Bible. Rept by Mary Chesney chpt & State D A R.

BEACH, CAPT JOHN, Ross co

"D at the Watson's Hotel in Chillicothe O yesterday morning (Thursday Jan 14 1819) aft a short illness. Capt John Beach was in his 71st year of his age. His late place of residence was at Glouster Cape Ann Mass where he has left a wife and several children to regret his decease. His remains were committed to the grave the following afternoon attended by the citizens generally and the brothers of Scioto Lodge No 6 who performed the customary honors." Ref Scioto Gazette 1-15-1819. By Mrs Nellie Beach Conway 1629 Memorial Dr Dormont Pittsburg Pa. Rept by Pickaway Plains chpt.

BEACH, ROSWELL, Belmont co

Enl 1778 for 3 yr as pvt in Capt Jos Mansfield's Co Col Meigs Regt. Later trans to others. Rec Hon Disch fr Lieut Col Ebenezer Gray. B 1761-2; æ 55. Dec 1817 æ 94. Apr 10 1855 mar Elizabeth ——; one child Lucas æ 7 in 1820. Pensd 1818 Belmont co. Living Mead twp Belmont co 1847 and Armstrong Mills Belmont co April 10 1855; Rec 160 A B L Wt 15412 Act 1855. Ref S 45315 Conn. Rept by Jane Dailey.

BEALL, OBADIAH, Champaign co

Enl Jan 29 1780 Mass. Dischrgd Oct 28 1783 West Point N Y. Corpl Mass Contl. B 1761 mar Feb 25 1787 Rebekah. Soldr d Sept 11 1822. Appl pens Champaign co Apr 28 1818; pens 1819. Wid appl for pens Franklin co O May 23 1839. Resd Perry twp in Cens 1840 Rebecca Beal a wid rec pens in Washington twp Franklin co æ 73. Ref W 5216 Mass. Rept by State D A R.

BEALL, THOMAS, Preble co

Serv 7-3-1778 to 4-3-1779 as pvt in Md Contl. B Md July 1761. Came fr Md 1816 to Somers twp Preble co with wf Fanny and 4 chldr. Prob bur on farm or in Camden Cem'y. Pensd Preble co 1819. Ref Pens Record. Rept by State D A R and Commodore Preble chpt.

BEAN, DANIEL, Muskingum co

Enl spring 1781 Washington co Penn; servd 18 mo. pvt Penn militia. B nr Winchester Va Mar 1763 or 4. Mar Sept 20 1832 Susannah Elson. Her chldr by previous mar were Henry; Michael; and David Elson and Mary Whitley. Soldr d Nov 1 1840 Burlington Ia. Appl pens Muskingum co July 30 1833. Appl for trns fr Marion co Ind Apr 20 1837. Appl for trns fr Sangamon Ill Aug 22 1839. Wid appl pens Jackson co Ia Mar 21 1854. Wid d Jackson co Ia Sept 27 1867. Ref W 8124 Penn and B L Wt 67968-160-55. Rept by State D A R.

BEARD, CHRISTOPHER, Franklin co

Cop fr news item: Christopher Beard d in Perry twp May 19 1839 aged 91 yr; was father of Mrs Margaret Pierce, (consort of Harding Pierce) who d May 5 1839 age 32 yr in Clinton twp; she left husband and four chldr. Order bk 6-133 soldr made declaration for pens Franklin co Crt House, June 6 1832 Act of Cong on Sept 29 1832. Rept by Blanche Rings.

BEARD, FRANCIS, Preble co

Drafted Sept or Oct 1777 York co Penn where then resd. Resd Rockingham co Va at time he was drafted for last two terms. Servd 8 mo. B Apr 15 1753 York co Pa. Appl pens Preble co O 7-13-1833. Ref S 2978 Penn Va. Rept by State D A R.

BEARD, JACOB, Clinton co

Enl Apr 15 1781 pvt Va Militia. Serv 6 mo. Shenandoah co Va. Resd there till 1802; then to Frederick co Va whr he resd 12 or 13 yrs. Then to Shenandoah co Va till Dec 2 1831 whn moved to Clinton co. B Aug 29 1762 Shenandoah co. Mar May 15 1819 Rosanna Windle. Soldr d Mar 27 1839 Clinton co. Appl pens Nov 12 1833 Clinton co. Wid appl pens Clinton co 3-3-1855. Ref W 25224 Va and B L Wt 29042-160-55. Rept by State D A R.

BEARD, JOHN, Highland co

Enl Westmoreland co Pa. Serv 9 mo pvt Penn militia. B Apr 4 1766 Franklin co Pa; mar Aug 24 1815 Maty Graves. Had "Several ch." Soldr d Aug 28 1835 Highland co O. In 1798 moved to Nicholas co Ky and abt 1804 to Highland co. Appl pens Jackson twp Highland co Oct 28 1833. Wid appl pens Liberty twp Highland co June 13 1853. Soldr also servd in Indian Wars 1790-1-2. Ref W 25,224 Va and B L Wt 24949-160-55. Rept by State D A R.

BEARD, WILLIAM, Knox co

Pvt N C Militia. Pensr 1833 Knox co O is believed to be "William Beard Sr" of Ross co p 33 Ohio Roster vol 1 accd to comparison of data at Pen Cl dept S 2370 Md & N C. Rept by State D A R.

BEATTY, JAMES, Coshocton co

Enl spring 1776 in Lancaster Pa Pvt in Pa Militia 2 yr. B 10-15-1762 York co Pa. Moved to Sussex co N J when he entered the service and livd there till 1800 whn he moved to Fayette co Pa. Appl pens Fayette co Pa 3-21-1833. Pensr 1840 cens Jefferson twp Coshocton co æ 80 liv with Sam'l Mad——. Ref S 23540 N J & Penn. Rept by State D A R.

BEAUMONT, ISAIAH, Licking co

Enl 12-1-1775 Capt Robinson's Co Col John Durkee's Regt. Wounded in arm at Princeton for wch pensd Mar 4-1795. Dischrgd 2-1-1777 Morristown N J. Later servd in Capt Ridd's Co Gen Sullivan's R I Exped 2 mo. There were 5 bro in service: William; Oliver; Dan'l; Isaiah and Samuel. Pens 1785 & 1832. In 1827 referred to "chldr." One was A Beaumont a son of Wilkesbarre Pa in 1835. B 1758 Lebanon (now New London) Conn. Lived Johnstown Licking co 1836. Soldr d 1837 St Albans twp Licking co. Ref S 9099; Hill's Licking co Hist p 590. Rept by Jane Dailey and Hetuck chpt.

BEAUMONT, SAMUEL, Ross co

Enl April 1776 Saybrook Conn Pvt Conn militia 5 yr. b abt 1755 æ 63 in 1818. Pensd Marietta 10-21-1819. Lvd with mother and daughter in Chillicothe O 1821. Trans Va 9-27 1836 whr lived with wf and chldr whr prob is bur. Ref S 37,736 Conn Continental. Rept by State D A R.

BECKER, JACOB, Montgomery co

Pa. Pensr d 1850; bur Ellerton Cem Montgomery co; Grave mrk S A R Dayton 1933. Ref Penn Arch vol 4 p 312; vol 5 p 188, 603, 636 etc. Rept by Wm Pettit (S A R) Dayton O.

BECKER, JOHN, Montgomery co

Lancaster co Pa; ref Pa Arch S 5 V 7 p 904 Milit 7th Class 1779 Capt Smuller's Co. In 1782 V 7 p 169 Capt Holderbaum. D 1824 æ 66. Bur Minnich cem by side of Patrick Heagen, a Rev Soldr. Rept by Wm Pettit.

BECKWITH, SAMUEL, Trumbull co

Pvt. 1st call for trps. Pvt Capt Samuel H Parson's Co May 1775. M Lois Winchel. Chldr: Lurinda; Ira; Lois; Almira; Lydia; and Samuel. Bur Braceville Trumbull co. Ref Conn in Rev p 72. Rept by Mary Chesney chpt.

BECKWITH, WILLIAM, Morgan co

Enl spring 1776 until close of Rev Serv 2 yr and 3 mo. Pvt Md State Trps. Was in a number of short terms. B Frederick co Md. Chldr: Rebecca; Richard; and Gobias. Soldr d Oct 27 1836 Morgan co. Appl pens Morgan co 7-21-1832 pens 1832. Ref S 2071 Md. Rept by State D A R.

BECKWORTH, RICE, Cuyahoga co

Enl New Lebanon Springs N Y in Feb 1776 while residing Manchester Vt. Pvt Vt Militia 2 yr. B 11-20 1757 at Lynne Conn. In pens appl states "resd with chldr." Movd to Plattsburgh N Y abt 1800 pens 5-4-1833 Clinton co N Y; trnsfr Cuyahoga co 12-16-1836. Pensr 1840 Cleveland æ 85 liv with Joseph Wyley. Ref S 15321 N Y. Rept by State D A R.

BEDLE (Bedla), FRANCIS, Warren co

Pvt in Penn St Trp. In 1775 movd with father to Washington co Penn. Srv summer 1777 as sub for Nathan Hathaway in Co of Rangers Capt Graycraft. Also srvd as a volunteer in Capt Crass's Co Col Evans Regt Pa mil for 7 mo et al. B Nov 13 1758 N J. In 1788 moved to Mason co Ky. In 1789 to Columbiana O. In 1790 to Cowall's Stat on Little Miami. In fall to Round Bottom July 14 1792 captured by Indians and taken to Detroit whr sold to Col English an English officer who freed him and gave him a pass to Niagara from whence he returned to Round Bottom Hamilton co. Then moved to Warren co whr resd "ever since." Appl pens 10-13-1832 Warren co æ 74. Pens 3-26-1833. Soldr d abt 1837. Rhoda Mills a wid dau appl for arrear of Father's pens 1-18-1858. Ref S 2375 Pa & Va. Rept by Jane Dailey.

BEEBE, SAMUEL, Madison or Ashtabula co

Fifer Mass Contl line 3 yrs. Resd Mass Feb 20 1778 whn enl and 7 yrs aft war. Moved to N Y; then to Canaan twp Madison co. Pensd 6-6-1820 to 2-3-1835. In 1834 was in Ashtabula co. Ae 55 and wife æ 56 in 1820. Chldr "crippled boy" and girl æ 13 in 1820. Ref S 8069 Contl Mass. Rept by State D A R.

BEEBE, WILLIAM, Knox co

Exec Doc 37 of yr 1852 refused a pens as servd less than 6 mo. Rept by Wm Pettit.

BEEKMAN, WILLIAM, Pike co

Enl abt middle March 1775 in N C militia. Enl in N J militia about 1788. Srvd 11 mo pvt and 13 mo as Capt. B 8-27-1755 nr Germantown N J. M 8-10-1781 Sarah. Chldr: Gabriel b 1782; Christopher b 1784; William b 1788; Abraham b 1790; Aaron b 1793; Mary; John; and Elizabeth. Soldr d 6-13-1834. Abt 1784 movd frm Princetown N J to Landon co Va. 3 yrs later to Hampshire co Va in 1797 to Mason co Ky. Then to Ross (now Pike) co. Appl pens Mar 28 1833 Pike co. Wid appl pens Pike co 4-10-1843 æ 81. Ref W 24644 N J & N C. Rept by State D A R.

BEEKS, CHRISTOPHER, Greene co

Fr Mrs R Winnagle, Warren comes ref to D A R Magz V 64 No 7 July 1930 whc was copd by Jane Dailey as follows: Servd in Rev fr Va; mar Catherine Barnes perhaps in Va; was in Greene co O nr Xenia whr he d before 1818. Chldr: Elizabeth mar Eli Adams; Nancy mar George May; Sarah mar Wm Powers; Catherine mar George Smith; George; Thomas mar Nancy Beall; Wames mar Katherine; Henry; Samuel mar Elizabeth Lambden; John. Widow mar 2nd Samuel Ewing.

BEERS, ZACHARIAH, Lorain co

Enl 1774 Litchfield co Conn. Srvd various enls. B Woodburry Conn June 23 1758; d 1843 Tully N Y as stated No 49397 D A R. Chldr: Edwin; Philo and Ira. Rsd Litchfield co Conn till movd to Onondaga co N Y 2 yr and 7 mo ago (Appl July 1833). Appl for pens Onondaga co N Y 7-2-1833. Appl for tans to Lorain co June 17 1839 to be "near his children." Pensr 1840 in Carisle twp Lorain co living with Abiram Drakely. Ref S 4946 Conn and 6762, 1036 & 1037 D A R. Rept by Nathan Perry chpt and State D A R.

BEESON, MERCER, Greene co

Was b aft 1730 possibly in Berkley co Va son of Richard Beeson Jr and Ann Brown Beeson. Mar Katie Rains; chldr: Henry; John; Mary mar Jonah Turner; Betsey mar Joseph Cole. Soldr d Greene co O; bur Old Baptist cem Baptist Ch-yd New Jasper pike abt one mile east of New Jasper. Descendants vouch for grave located on Beeson lot. A bro of Henry Beeson founder of Uniontown Pa. Livd at Boone and Kenton Stations Ky. Noted scout and pioneer of those sections. Mentioned in Kentucky and Ohio Hists. Ref Beeson Genealogy by Jasper Luther Beeson. "Mercer Beeson Covington Ky Quartermaster under Col William Crawford in Indian campaign; also in Rev. Pack Horse master under Col Crawford." Rept by Catherine Greene chpt.

BEIRCE, WILLIAM, ? co

Pvt. Pensr under act 1818 but refused under act of 1820 as not in indigent circumstances. Ref Doc 31 Jan 6 1831. Rept by Blanche Rings Cols O. See P 39 Ohio Roster Vol 1 on Bierce, William (J D).

BELDEN, BENJAMIN, Trumbull co

Drafted Hartford co Conn 1776. Serv 13 mo as pvt in Conn Militia. B Hartford Conn Oct 25 1757; mar Jan 1785 Sylvia Culver. Chldr: Owen; Frances; Webster; "son-in-law." Soldr d Feb 5 1839 Cherry Valley Ashtabula co. Appl pens Apr 28 1834. Wid appl for pens Ashtabula co June 27 1843. Ref W 5819 Conn. Rept by Mary Chesney chpt and State D A R.

BELDEN, DAVID, Trumbull co

Enl Apr 1777 Hartford co Conn; 4th Conn Regt 1780. B Hartford co Conn. 1758; mar Lois Wolcott. Chldr: Daniel; Selah; Burrage; Milly; Asa; Asahel; Harvey; Rosanna; Calvin; Lois; David; Josiah Wolcott; Jona. Soldr d 1839 æ 84 Trumbull co. Lvd Hartford co Conn abt 14 yrs after Rev and in Trumbull co for past 20 yrs. Appl pens June 28 1834 Trumbull co. Ref Conn Men Rev and R 714 Conn. Rept by Mary Chesney and State D A R.

BELDON, BILDAD, Lorain co

Enl 1775 in Capt Ozias Bissell's Co Col Jedeiah Huntington's Conn Regt; dischrgd Oct 1776; enl at Wethersfield Conn whr was b 1742 (stone record); d Aug 4 1824 Brownhelm Lorain co O whr bur in neglected cem on R No 2 but the above data on white marble slab in good condition. Nathan Perry chpt mrkd grave also. Pens appl 1818 æ 73 fr Griswold Conn; arrears pd to Clifford Belden Adm at Hartford Conn 8-13-1825. (Data fr Bur of Pens and Genl Acct Office D C). Ref Bureau of Pens General Acct office Washington D C. Rept by Mrs Oehlke.

BELKNAP, CALVIN, Ashtabula co

Enl Apr 1781 Windham co Vt whr he was resd. Pvt Vt Trps 9 mo. B abt 1766 æ 66 in 1832; mar 11-1-1786 or 7 Bathsheba Laraba? Soldr d 3-17-1848. Appl pens Ashtabula co 8-17-1832; pens 7-24-1833. Wid appl pens Ashtabula co 8-26-1850. Ref W 5215 Vt. Rept by State D A R.

BELL, WILLIAM, Mahoning co

Servd in Va. B 1761; mar Mary Orrick (b 1769 d 10-24-1866). Chldr: John M; William mar Catherine; James mar Nancy; Elizabeth mar James Orr; Sarah mar Cramer Marsteller; Thomas. Soldr d Dec 7 1854 Coitsville Mahoning co. Pensr act 1818. Ref Will Book I p 502; Republican Sentinel 12-15-1854. Pens Book 1818. Rept by Mahoning chpt.

BELL, WILLIAM, Muskingum co

Pvt Va Contl. Serv 3 yrs. B 1732; weaver. Appl pens Muskingum co May 1 1818. Pensr 1819. Ref S 42,617 Va. Rept by State D A R.

BELLARD (Ballard), JOHN, Mahoning co

Serv Mass. Mar 1768; bur Old Market St Cemetery. Stones and many bodies removed 1870-75. Rept Mass Men (many enl) V I p 598. Rept by Mahoning chpt.

BELLIS, NATHANIEL, ? co

Ensign Mass. This is thought to be another spelling of "Bettes or Bettis, Nathaniel" Ohio Roster Rev Sold V I p 38. (J D).

BEMAN, THOMAS, Trumbull co

Lieut. Capt Hutchins Co; Mar Ann Fuller. Chldr: Bethael; Rufus; Erastus; Elisha; Thomas. Soldr d Gustavus. Prob bur with wf in old cem Gustavus Center. Ref Conn in Rev p 472. Rept by Mary Chesney chpt.

BEMISS, JONAS, Huron co

Enl Granville N Y Apr 1 1782. Disch Schenectady N Y. Pvt N Y St Trps. Serv 10 mo. B abt 1765 Washington co N Y æ 53 in 1818. Since Rev lvd 2 or 3 yrs in Hand co Vt and in Addison co and now lvs Milan twp Huron co. (Appl) Res Cato Cayuga co Apr 29 1818. Appl pens July 28 1832 Huron co. Pensd July 24 1833. Grave located Sandusky ? D A R. Ref 18 Rep N S D A R and S 18, 310 N Y. Rept by Nathan Perry chpt and State D A R.

BENDER, JACOB, Lorain co

Exec Doc 37 of yr 1852 objections to his pens were obviated by Act of Cong 1848. Rept by Wm Pettit.

BENEDICT, FELIX, Meigs co

With father Capt Elisha was taken prisoner Oct 1780 by British and Indians under Major Monroe. Was kept prisoner two and a half years. B May 13 1767 Norwalk Conn; mar Clarissa (dau Jabez and Sarah Hubbell) b April 21 1767; d July 9 1849. Chldr: Sarah; Polly; Enretta; Elisha H; Hariet; Jabez b Otsego co N Y 1802; Felix S; William S. Movd to Ohio 1803. Soldr d Oct 29 1829 Rutland Meigs co. Bur near Rutland. Inscrip "In Memory of Felix Benedict who departed this life Oct 29 A D 1829 æ 61 yr 5 mo 16 da." Ref Journal of Prov Cong of N Y vol 1 p 184; vol 2 p 56, 58; Forces Am Arch vol I p 776 Hist Meigs co by James Evans p 6. Secured fr Eldo B Lane, 1334 Cypress St Pueblo Colo by Jane Dailey, who visited the cem and secured inscript at Rutland; and from gr-dau of Felix Benedict, Mariam Benedict Grapes æ 89 liv there (July 30 1934) "thot he mar Clarissa Hubbell of N Y."

BENHAM, THOMAS SR, Ashtabula co

Pvt. Enl 1776. Srvd 8 mos and 2 das in Conn Line. (records corrected as to serv fr N Y). Was b 5-28-1759 Cheshire twp Conn. Two chldr were: Samuel; Thomas Jr. Soldr d Sept 4 1841. Res in New Haven co Conn until 1783-84; movd to Waterbury Conn. In 1811 he movd to Ashtabula co O whr appl for pens 4-18-1834. Ref Conn S 8068. Rept by State D A R.

BENIGER, GEORGE, Greene co

Exec Doc 37 of yr 1852 refused a pens as served only 4 mo. Rept by Wm Pettit.

BENNETT (or Bennitt), ABRAHAM (or Abram), Huron co

Pvt N Y Contl. Enl Apr 1780 Orange co N Y whr he was b 1764. Appl of 1845 mentions chldr. Soldr d May 12 1852. Since Rev resd in Pa 5 or 6 yrs. Then Steuben co N Y; thence to Seneca N Y and from there to Seneca co O whr appl for pens July 22 1833. Pens appl Jackson co Michigan Mar 22 1845 stated he wished to reside with his chldr in Mich. Appl again Aug 15 1848 for trnsfr to Huron co O whr he res with chldr who livd there. Ref S 2987 N Y. Rept by State D A R.

BENNETT, JOSHUA, ? co

Listed in Invalid Pensr of U S Belonging to O pd at Chillicothe p 172 Pensrs of 1818. He recd annual allowance of $96.00. Cop by Jane Dailey.

BENNET, RICHARD, ? co

Refused a pension as servd in Regt not on Contl Estab. Ref Doc No 31 Jan 6 1831 O S Libry. Rept by Blanche Rings Col O.

BENNETT, RICHARD, Warren co

Pvt St Trps. Enl Richmond V 3-1781. Srvd 18 mos. Was æ 63 in 1826. 1st wf d 1813; mar Margaret Turney Warren co O 1826. Appl mentions 7 chldr: One son was Abraham. Soldr d Warren co O 1835. Wid Margaret Bennett appl for pens in Lawrence co O June 29 1857. Wm Bennett "nephew of Richard Bennett" made deposition for widow's appl for pens in Warren co O Dec 11 1857. He was nephew by a child of Richard's 1st mar. Soldr livd with chldr by 1st wf in Warren co O till remarried in 1826. Ref W 9350 B L Wt 73540-160-55. Appld for pens in Warren co O Oct 2 1832; æ 96 yrs. Appl for his original pension claim in Warren co O Apr 10 1826 then æ 63. Rept by State D A R.

BENNETT, THOMAS, Ohio

3 yr in 5th Md Regt. Mar Ann Tillett; had one dau Margaret. Soldr d Ohio co O. Ref p 52 D A R Lin No 31146. (Tho there is no "Ohio co" O we include this thinking there may be an error in statement only. No further data found). Rept by Nathan Perry chpt.

BENSCHOTER, ORLEY, Huron or Erie co

Listed as Rev soldr by Berlin "in defense of the country" p 487 Hist Huron and Erie cos O. Rept by Mrs Rathburn O S Librarian.

BENTLEY, BENJAMIN, Trumbull co

Associates and milit of Wash co Pa under Capt James Carven Lieut Leonard. B in Conn Aug 14 1756; mar Mary Baldwin; chldr: Robert; Elizabeth; Adamson; George; Hannah; Benjamin; Mary; Ahiolab; Shesbazzer. Came to Brookfield Trumbull co in 1808 and d there 1818. Ref S 6 Pa Arch Vol 2 p 201. Rept by Mary Chesney chpt. Compare p 37 Roster of O Vol 1 (J D).

BENTY, FRANCIS, Geauga co

Exec Doc 37 of yr 1852 refused a pens as service was in French army. Rept by Wm Pettit.

BERGER, NICHOLAS, Columbiana co

Servd Northampton Co Milit. B 1736 Switzerland; d 1828; mar Ann Marie ———— 1781. Rept by Wm Pettit.

BERGERHOFF, NICHOLAS, Crawford co

Pvt Va Contl. Enl 1777 Elizabethtown N J. Servd 3 yrs. Was æ 64 in 1820. Mar Elizabeth; chldr: Catharine æ 26; Susanne 22; Mary 18; Sally 15; Lydia (from Appl 1820). Pens Pendleton co Va 7-31-1819. Trnsfrd to Crawford co O 4-24-1832. Ref Contl Pa S 42087; O Pens Rolls 1818. Rept by State D A R.

BERRY, JAMES, Hamilton co

Rev Patriot. Was b Smyrna Del Oct 14 1759; d Cincinnati Mar 27 1847. Was a pvt and srvd under Capt Skillington. From "Cists (Cincinnati) Advertiser" Mar 29 1847. Cop fr notes of Alice Boardman D A R St Libr by J D.

BERRY, JAMES, Muskingum co

Was a soldr in Capt William Lusk's Co of light infantry 7th Pa regt. Born in Westmoreland co Pa 1764; d Zanesville O 1825. Mar 1793 Hannah Williams (1769-1865). One dau was Emily. Ref Nat No 111241; Nat No 111994; and Nat No 58246 D A R. Rept by Nathan Perry chpt.

BERRY, WILLIAM, Mercer co

Pvt Va Vol 1781 Rockbridge co Va Capt Alex Telford 3 mo Saml McDowell Regt Major Alex Steward. Was b abt 1763. Appld Nov 1832 in St Marys Mercer co O æ 69. Last pens pd to Atty Saml McKee Cin O 9-19-1836 covering per fr 9-4-1834 to 9-4-1836. Ref Certf No 13309 O Agency; S 2371 — V A p 25 O bk E Vol 8 p 2 Act 6-7-1832. Rept by Jane Dailey.

BETZ, ADAM, Ross co

Commis May 10 1780 Lieut 1st Co 3rd Battl Berks Co Milit. Ref Pa Arch 5th S Vol 5 p 194. Was b 1745 native of Pa Spring Forge nr Reading. One son was Henry; sheriff of Reading Pa many yrs. A Reading Pa Newspaper of Dec 31 1839 has: "Adam Betz d Nov 17 1839 in 95th yr at Chillicothe O; formerly fr Amity twp Berks co Pa and father of Henry Betz Esq of Reading Pa." Had personal acquaintance w Indian chiefs of Scioto valley; was doorkeeper to Territory Legislature; frank; bold; honest; generous. Ref: Obituary fr Chillicothe Advertiser Nov 23 1839. Rept by Pickaway Plains chpt and Mary Steinmetz Reading Pa.

BICKER (or Bricker), ADAM, Clermont co

Pvt Pa Milit. Enl Mar 1776 Westmoreland co Pa. Srvd 9 mos. Was b 1755 Pa nr Philadelphia. Mar Rebecca Nov 1792; chldr: John; Mary; Elizabeth; Thomas; Christopher; Samuel; Robert; Wm; Rachel and Isabel. Soldr d Aug 31 1843 Clermont co O. Pens appl Clermont co O Nov 8 1832. Wid appl for pens Clermont co O Aug 28 1844. Ref W 2714 Pa. Rept by State D A R.

BIDWELL, SAMUEL, ? co

Pvt refused a pens as did not serve 9 mo in Contl Army. Ref Doc No 31 Jan 6 1831. Rept by Blanche Rings Col O.

BIGGER (Biggart), JOSEPH, Montgomery co

Lancaster co Pa S 5 Vol 7 p 1059 Capt Reland's Co Associators 1775. Soldr d 1804; bur Beavertown Montgomery co O. Ref Estate Adm Montgomery co. Rept by Wm Pettit Dayton O.

BIGGS, WILLIAM, Clinton co

Srvd 2nd Lieut Capt David Platt's Co Cumberland co N J milit. Was b N J; d 1828 Cuba O; bur Clinton co; mar Nancy Russel. Ref Vol 27 p 276 D A R Lin bk Nat No 26747 through son Alfred (1821-76). Rept by Nathan Perry chpt by Mrs T R Oehlke.

BIGHAM, WILLIAM, Hamilton co

Ensign Capt Patrick Marshall's 7th Co 2nd Battl Lancaster co Pa 1777. Was b 1752 Williamsburg Va; mar 1779 Mary Reed; one son was William; soldr d Hamilton O. Ref Vol 123 p 297 D A R Lin. Rept by State D A R.

BINEGAR, GEORGE, Fayette co

Enl Frederick co Va 1781 Mar 1. Srvd 2 mo in Capts Crookshank and Jenkins Co. Enl again in Capt Marquis Calmes Co Col Drakes Regt. Was b Lancaster co Pa 8-28-1763; mar Mary Matlock, Martinsburg W Va 1816; chldr: George; Samuel; Sarah; Gregory; Mary Simpson. Soldr d 3-27-1837. Rept by Washington C H chpt. Compare Beniger, George this vol. (J D).

BINER, GEORGE, Tuscarawas co

Enl Loudon co Va Dec 1 1780. Srvd 1 yr and 24 das. Was b Mar 15 1765 Philadelphia Pa. Res in Loudon co Va aft Rev for abt 12 yrs. Then movd to Belmont co O; thence to Harrison co O. Pens appl July 23 1833 Harrison co O res of Washington twp. Ref S 4266 Va. Rept by State D A R.

BIRNEY, HENRY, ? co

Was sergt in a Co of milit organized aft the Wyoming massacre with Capt John Franklin in command serving in Sullivan expedition; b in Ireland; d in Ohio. Mar Rachel Shears; one dau was Mary. Ref D A R Nat no 56682 and Nat No 57531. Rept by Nathan Perry chpt.

BIVINS, JOHN, Washington co

Pvt and fifer Mass St Trps. Enl 1775. Dischrgd N Y 1779. Srvd Mass Line 2 yrs. Was b 1760 Middletown Conn. Mar Hannah Owens Sept 18 1779. Wid appl mentions 11 chldr oldest abt 61: Lorenzo; Milton; Benjamin O; Mary; John; Fanny; Ira; Henry; Harriet surviving. Soldr d Feb 24 1839 (No 121106 states bur at Marietta O). Pens appl Wayne co O Mar 21 1833. Livd at Northampton Mass when ent service. At close of war livd at New Lebanon N Y. Movd from N Y to Middletown Conn; livd there 1 yr then movd to N Y state for 2 yrs in Millertown. Livd abt 30 yrs in Milford N Y; then to Clarence ? nr Buffalo N Y for abt 2 yrs. Then to Wayne co O. Hannah Bivins wid appl for pens McDonough co Ill on Oct 6 1840 then res Fulton co Ill. She d Nov 9 1843 Lorain O. Ref R 875 Contl Mass N Y; No 118189; No 121806 D A R. Rept by State D A R.

BIXBY, BENJAMIN, Portage co

Pvt Conn Contl. Enl latter part of 1778 or early part 1779 at Reading Conn. Reenl Boston Mass June 1782. Srvd 3 yr. Was æ 70 in 1818. B Windham co Conn. Srvd part time in Conn and part time in Mass lines. Occupation a Miller. Ref Conn Contl and Mass S 42618. Rept by State D A R.

BLACK, CHARLES, ? co

Pvt Invalid pens of $48 yrly belong to O pd at Chillicothe. Ref p 172 Pensr 1818. Cop by Jane Dailey.

BLACK (or Blackwell), HUGH, Pike co

Pvt Md Contl. Enl Baltimore Md in 1776. Srvd 3 yrs. Was æ 81 in 1818. Chldr: William C of Van Buren Ark and Mrs Lucy Hill of O. Soldr d 11-7-1835. Pens appl Pike co P 7-7-1818. Ref Md R 893. Rept by State D A R.

BLACK, JOHN, Brown co

Enl Washington co Md 1778. Was b 3-13-1763 Lancaster co Pa. When abt 15 yrs of æ his father movd from Lancaster co Pa to Washington co Md. Aft war livd 5 yrs in Berkley co Va; then movd to Fayette co Pa for 13 yrs; then to Adams co O for abt 10 yrs; then to Brown co O for 4 yrs then to Clermont co O whr appl for pens 1839. Pens appl Highland co O Mar 13 1834; Brown co O May 4 1852. Pens claim was rejected on grounds that he did not serve 6 mos. Ref R 887 Md Va. Rept by State D A R.

BLACK, JOHN, Preble co

Enl at the age of 17 srvd through the entire Rev. Was b Dec 13 1756 Rockingham co Va. Chldr: Catharine the youngest; Sarah; John Jr; Joseph; Mary Ann; the other four names unknown. Soldr d 1826 on farm just outside of West Alexandria Preble co O. Bur East end of West Alexandria; grave covered up. Was pensr in West Alexander 1840. With his family came from Rockingham co Va to O in 1812 and settled in Lanier twp Preble co on a large tract of land a short distance south of W Alex. Some of this land has always been in possession of the family. The wf d in 1853. Ref Hist of Preble co by H Z Williams and bro 1881. Rept by Commodore Preble chpt.

BLACK, THOMAS, Mahoning co

Ranger Northumberland co Pa. Pa Arch S 3 V 23 p 243. Was b 1764; d May 14 1838 Coitsville O. Bur Deer Creek Pulaski Lawrence co Pa. Many Coitsville early settlers attended church just over line in Pa and were bur in ch cem on Deer Creek as no cem in Coitsville before 1835. Ref List of late Henry R Baldwin. Rept by Mahoning chpt.

BLACK, SAMUEL, ? co

Boatman. Refused a pension as case not provided for by law. Ref Doc No 31 Jan 6 1831. Rept by Blanche Rings Col O.

BLACKBURN, ——, Butler co

Pens No 1654. Pvt pens Contl "Flying Camp". Srvd 8 mo. Enl June 1776 in Co commanded by John Paxton. Pensr 11-8-1832 Butler co O. Was b 6-11-1758 York co Pa. Movd from York co Pa to Butler co O whr he had resided abt 28 yrs. Ref Pa S 2078. Rept by State D A R.

BLACKBURN, JAMES, Warren co

Pvt Pa Contl. Srvd in Va line 1 yr. Enl in Md for 6 mos in 1776. Dischrgd in Phila Pa. Was b Nov 12 1752. Mar Martha; she d since 1818. Had a dau Rebecca 17 yrs of æ; son James æ 19. 2 chldr dead. Pens appl May 14 1818 Ridgeville O; appl Warren co May 29 1823. Ref S 42619 Contl Md and Va. Rept by State D A R.

BLACKMAN, NEHEMIAH, ? co

Pvt. Refused a pension, as no satisfactory evidence of service exhibited. Ref Doc 31 Jan 6 1831. Rept by Blanche Rings Col O.

BLAIN, ALEXANDER

Erroneously listed for Blount, Adam which see, this vol. (J D).

BLAIR, JAMES, Clark co

Pvt N H Contl. Enl Feb 1781 in 2nd N H Regt. Was æ 57 in 1820. Mar Molly; one girl Mary æ 13 in 1820. Soldr d 1848; maybe in Erie Pa. Movd from Vt to Erie co Pa in 1816. Appl pens Waterford twp Erie co Pa Feb 7 1818. Appl for trnsfr to Geauga co 6-16-1833; appl for new certficate Clark co Mar 11 1846; appl for trnsfr from O in Erie co Pa 2-28-1848. Ref Contl N H S 42621. Rept by State D A R.

BLAIR, JOHN, Portage co

Mass. Arch V 2 p 119; was in O 1810; ref No 1359 S A R. Rept by Wm Pettit.

BLAIR, JOHN, Brown co

Pvt N J Milit. Pvt in Capt Alex Peekes Co 1st Battl Cumberland co Pa Milit James Dunlap Colonel. Was b 1737 Ireland; mar 1757 Martha Laird. Chldr Lieut John; Ann; Robert; Brice; Richard; William; Joseph; Martha. Livd in Huntington twp Brown co at an early date. He his wf and family are listed as members of the Ebenezer M E Church in 1834. Was high sheriff Washington co Tenn. Ref Blair data compiled by Dr Elinore M Hiestlad Moore of Phila now deceased; (Mrs Levi) Will Jenks Jamestown O; Mrs (O P) Maud Haggerty Hillsboro O; Mrs (Warren) Bessie L Robinson Jamestown O. Rept by Taliaferro chpt.

BLAIR, REUBEN, Portage co

Srvd in Mass 1779-80; dischg 1-6-1780; ref 27778 S A R; livd in Amora Portage co O. Rept by Wm Pettit.

BLANKENSHIP, BENJAMIN, Shelby co

Pvt of artillery Va Contl. Enl 9-16 or 17-1777 at Hampton Va; Pensr 1832 Shelby co O. Was æ 72 or 73 in 1832. May have d in McClean co Ill. Appl for pens Montgomery co O 9-5-1819 whl res Shelby co O. Movd from Shelby co O to McClean co Ill in 1836. Ref Contl (Va) S 30870. Rept by State D A R.

BLECKER, FREDERICK SR, Columbiana co

Rev soldr. Rec not yet found. Was b 1753; d 6-22-1832 æ 79; estate settl 1832. Ref "Ohio Patriot." Rept by Mrs Wilma M Molsberry.

BLEW, FREDERICK, Wayne co

Exec Doc 37 of yr 1852 refused pens as servd less than 6 mo. Rept by Wm Pettit.

BLOOMER, JOSEPH, Fayette co

Name listed in Rev soldr bur in Washington C H cem which has been destroyed. Rept by Washington C H chpt.

BLOOMFIELD, MOSES, ? co

Pvt in Capt Asher F Randolph's Regt Middlesex co N J Milit. Was b 1755 N J; mar Mary Moss (1770-1837); a son Isaac mar Mary Hahn. Soldr d 1807 Ohio. Ref Vol M D A R Lin No 110352. Rept by Jane Dailey.

BLOSSER, JACOB, Mahoning co

Pvt in Capt McIsaac's Co York co Pa. Pa Milit. Was b York co Pa; mar Barbara Beery (1764-1840) mar 1788. One son Joseph 1795 mar Sarah J Basye. Soldr d 1842 Mahoning co O. Ref Lineage bk C X L p 75; Desc Mrs Sarah (Blosser) Anderson. Rept by Mabel S Askue Mahoning chpt.

BLOUNT, ADAM, Franklin co

(Also spelled Blont) Cop from Order bk 6-401 dated June 7 1834. This day came Adam Blont and exhibited his declaration for a pens to this court with the testimony and the court is of the opinion that the applicant was a Rev soldr and srvd as he states and do order the same to be admitted of record. Rept by Blanche Rings. On list of pens in St Libry is given as Alexander Blain.

BLUNT, WILLIAM, Muskingum co

Pvt Va Contl. Enl Aug 15 1775 in Va. Was b 1756. Appl for pens Muskingum co O May 1818. Ref S 42088 Va. Rept by State D A R.

BOAL, ROBERT, Warren co

Service in Lancaster co Pa milit as Ensign 1777. B 1747; d 1830. Was a ruling Elder in the Dick's Creek Presbyterian Church 1814 to 1830. Bur Dicks Creek Pres Ch-yd Warren co. Mrkd and rept by Richard Montgomery S A R. Dayton O.

BOATMAN, WILLIAM, Highland co

Pvt in Capt Swearengen Co; Col Hiatt Regt Va Milit 6 mo. Was b Fauquier co Va Dec 1757. Liv at Redstonefort Pa when enl; movd to Washington Pa. Thence to Ky resided in co of Fayette or Bourbon; to Highland co abt 1800. Unclaimed pens pd July 9 1839 from March 4 1838 to Sept 4 1838. Srvd also a subs for another man. Ref S 8085. Rept by Jane Dailey.

BODINE, JOHN, Warren co

Pvt Va Cont. Enl 1782 Regt of Col Armand. Pvt in Va line 1 yr under Capts

Lee and Bart. Was æ 61 in 1825 (b 1764); mar Jane Marlott. "Abraham Marlott, my wf's father" mentioned in appl. Abraham Marlott made will on Apr 6 1799 in which he bequeathed his property to his sons Abraham and Richard Marlott; his dau Jane Bodine and grdau Elizabeth dau of Jane and John Bodine. 10 chldr: Abraham; Hannah; Ann; Jno; Wm; Catharine; Margaret; Polly; Peter; Lydia. Pens appl Warren co O Dec 5 1825 æ 61. Formerly resided in Bartley co Va. Ref S 42628 Contl Va. Rept by State D A R.

BODINE, JOHN, Ross co

Was one of Washington's life guards. B 1744; d Sept 2 1822. On pens roll June 9 1820. Pens began Nov 9 1819 æ 78 yrs Ross co O. Rept by Pickaway Plains chpt.

BODWELL, WILLIAM, Athens co

Pvt Mass Contl. Pensr Mar 24 1819 Athens co O. Act March 18 1818 in Col H Jackson's Regt 6 for term of Rev war. Was æ 59 in 1818; appl mentions "wf" and 7 chldr; the eldest a dau 14 yrs old; 2nd a dau 11 yr; one 7 yr and invalid for 5 yr; 2 sons 9 and 2 yrs old." Formerly of Methuen Essex co Mass. Livd Alexander twp July 4 1820 æ 58. Ref S 42629 Mass. Rept by Jane Dailey.

BOLTEN, LEMUEL, ? co

Pvt Mass. Pens 9-24-1825 Act of 1818. Trnfrd to Mich and filed here to avoid further research. Cop by J D.

BOLTENHOUSE, JOHN, Miami co

Often misspelled "Bottehouse." Pvt Va Contl. Enl abt the 1st of Sept 1777 in Morris ? co N J. Was taken prisoner at Rocky Ford sometime in Aug 1780. Sons were Abraham and Henry. Pens appl Aug 7 1820 in Miami co O. Ref Contl (NJ) S 42630. Rept by State D A R.

BOND, NATHANIEL, Warren co

Was b Essex co N J 1762; d 1855; mar Rachel Potter 1793; srvd N J Contl. Grave mrkd by S A R. Ref S A R 44934. Rept by Wm Pettit.

BONNELL, SAMUEL, Hamilton co

Pvt; srvd seven yrs. Was b 2-10-1755 N J. Son of Benjamin Bonnell and Rachel Van Winkle; mar Elizabeth Crane; chldr: Louis; Benjamin; Abbie Frazee; Phoebe Marsh; Lydia who mar Maxwell Frazee was b 7-20-1791. Soldr d Hamilton co; bur beside wf in lot of his son Louis Pleasant Ridge; family lot of Bonnell. Soldr was one of six bros who all srvd in Rev War from N J. One of the men at Whites Station nr present site of Carthage O. Had forfeit Corner of Sec 6 in 1805. On tax list in 1809. Ref Oxford chpt D A R. Rept by Cincinnati chpt Mrs E P Whallon.

BONWELL, JAMES, Brown co

Pvt Va Contl. Enl Va Feb 10 1776; dischrgd at Valley Forge Pa Feb 1778. Srvd 2 yrs. Was b 1750. Pens appl Brown co O Sept 12 1818. (A pioneer family of this name in Pleasant twp. Thot to have had a son Arthur member of Hillman M E Church) Ref S 42626 Va. Rept by State D A R and Meryl B Markley.

BOON, RALPH, Fayette co

Pvt Pa Contl. Enl Dec 1776 in Pa. Appl for pens Muskingum co O Aug 12 1826. Srvd 1 yr. Was b 1760. Appl for pens Fayette co Pa Feb 14 1822. In 1840 a pensr æ 95 residing in Union twp Fayette co O. Ref S 3026 Pa. Rept by State D A R.

BOONE, THOMAS, Butler co

A pvt in 10th battl Lancaster co Pa milit 1781. Was b Reading Pa 1759; d in Oxford

O 1831; mar Susanna Brumfield. One son was Brumfield. Ref D A R Nat No 56240; and Nat No 59741. Rept by Nathan Perry chpt.

BOOTH, EDWIN (Edward), Holmes co

Enl in Md in Fall of 1777; srvd Capt Harris' Co Colonel Otho H William's 6th Md Regt was in battles of Monmouth; Camden; Cowpens; Eutaw Springs and srvd 3 yrs. Was b March 26 1753 England; mar Rachel Reynolds in Cecil co Md 1780. Chldr: Eli; Jacob; Prudence Edwards; Henry; Jane Hays; Edwin; Rachel Stanley; Caleb Booth. A son William d prior to 1853. (One Eli Booth of Rome Richland co O made oath as to eleven chldr). Soldr d Oct 11 1836 Holmes co O. Occupation was a stocking weaver. Ref Edwin or Edward Booth (No explanation is given to the use of two names on pens appl.) was allowed pens on his application executed May 6 1818 at which time was residing in Belmont co. Then there is a pens claim R 1021 of later date (which was rejected as indicated by "R"). Rept by Jane Dailey and Mississinewa chpt of Portland Ind.

BORDEN, JOB, Warren co

Pvt N J Milit. Co commanded by Gen Perkins. When called into service livd in Burlington N J whr was b 1760. Soldr d June 20 1842. Pens agt was notified of his death by letter. Since Rev livd in N J till last 15 yrs which he spent in O in Warren co whr appl for pens Oct 4 1832 æ 72. Ref S 2050 N J. Rept by State D A R.

BORDERS, CHRISTOPHER, Darke co

Pvt Va Milit. Enl Spring of 1779 or 80 in Va Milit. Srvd 6 mo. Was b 8-15-1763 School Kill ? river. Whn he was very young his father movd to Md; then to North Carolina. Abt 5 yrs aft the war he movd to Rockingham co N C 2 yrs later he movd to Greenbriar co Va whr resd abt 22 yrs and movd to Green co O. 6 yrs later movd to Darke co O. Pens appl Darke co O 5-12-1834. Ref Va S 9104. Rept by State D A R.

BOSWELL, JOSEPH CAPT, ? co

Listed in news clipping by L A A found in old scrap bk no date as "Rev soldr who participated or interested in settlement of Marietta and with few exceptions are bur in Washington co." Filed here for cont research. Listed by Marietta chpt.

BOSWORTH, JOSEPH, Washington co

Son of Deacon Jos Bosworth and his second wf Sarah Cobb. B Halifax Mass Nov 15 1756; d Marietta Apr 30 or May 6 1830. Mar Mary Winslow dau of Wm Winslow of Wareham Mass June 11 1766. Settled in Marietta with their dau Mary who mar Jos Babcock. Ref Bosworth Genealogy by Mary B Clark Part 5 p 638. Rept by Mrs Winnagle Mary Chesney chpt.

BOTHMAN, BARNHART, Columbiana co

Va Line as pvt 1 yr. Was æ 78 in 1832; mar Catharine 10-16-1783; soldr d 1-12-1843 Columbiana co. Came to America in the Services of a Frenchman. Became waiter for Capt Parker. Pensd 1-21-1833 Columbiana co P; wid pensd 6-12-1847. Ref N J; Va W 5861. Rept by State D A R.

BOTKIN, CHARLES, Shelby co

Va Trps under Capt David Scott. Was b 1738 Ireland; mar 1st 1782 Jemima Kahrl (d 1807); soldr d 1820 Shelby co O. Ref V 125 p 74 D A R Lin. Cop by Jane Dailey.

BOWEN, JOHN, Montgomery co

N J "Men of Rev" p 152. Place of burial unidentified. Soldr d 3-22-1845 Lebanon O. Pens paper is John D Bowers. Rept by William Pettit.

BOWEN, MICHAEL, Lawrence co

Pvt Pa Contl. Enl Mar or Apr 1776 Pa. Srvd 3 yrs. Was b 1756. Mar Anna (2nd wf) June 7 1829; 1 son living with him. Soldr d Oct 15 1830. Pens appl Lawrence co O June 16 1818; wid appl June 2 1853 Gentry co Mo æ 83. Ref W 4136; B L Wt 30614-160-55 Pa. Rept by State D A R.

BOWER, ELLIS, Knox co

Pvt N J S Trps. Enl June 1776. Was b 1756 east end of Long Island. Mar Martha Bowers 11-7-1779; chldr: Molly; Jeremiah; Calap; Mehitable ?; Stephen; Sarah; George; Susannah; Anny and Elias. Soldr d 9-22-1839. Resd in Morris co N J at time of enl. Sometime aft the war he movd to Washington co Pa and res abt 15 yrs. Then movd to Brook co Va and res abt 3 yrs and movd to Knox co O abt 1812. Pens appl 9-8-1832 Knox co O. Ref N J S 5850; O Pens Roll 1835; III; 0-136. Rept by State D A R.

BOWER, JACOB, Stark co

Md and Pa service; b 1754 Lancaster co Pa; d 1825; mar Anna Rohrer 1782. Ref S A R qualification. Rept by Wm Pettit.

BOWER, JOHN, Licking co

Pvt N J Milit. Enl as substitute Burlington N J. Was b 1762 or 63 Monmouth co N J. Mar Sarah Benjamin 1-30-1826; soldr d 8-24-1833 Brownsville O Licking co. Residing in Monmouth during the Rev; abt 1785 he movd to Fayette co Pa; abt 1789 he movd to St Clairsville O and movd to Muskingum co O in 1805. In 1816 movd to Licking co O. Ref N J W 8379; B L Wt 26007-160-55. Rept by State D A R.

BOWER (Bouser or Bowers), **JACOB,** Stark co

Pvt Pa Contl. Enl 1775 Md; dischrgd 1776. Srvd 5 yrs. Was b Lancaster co Pa 1754 (see Vol 109 p 162 D A R Lineage), Mar Anna Rohrer Feb 14 1782; chldr Jacob; Anna; Susannah; John; Catherine; Frederick; Barbara; Elizabeth; Sarah. (Family Bible as evidence for wid). Soldr d 1824 Uniontown O. Pens appl Stark co O Apr 13 1818; appl again 1823; wid appl Sept 13 1839 res of Lake twp. Occupation was a mill-wright. Ref W 5227 Md Pa. Rept by State D A R and Jane Dailey.

BOWERS, JOHN, Warren co

Pens No 1187. Drummer. N J Line 6 yrs. Enl 1777 in 1st Regt of the Jersey Line. Was æ 61 in 1820. Mar Rebecca Murphy 6-22-1822; soldr d 3-22-1845 Lebanon twp Warren co O. Pensd 6-30-1818 Warren co O; wid appl Floyd co Ind 4-26-1853. Ref N J W 1216; B L Wt 23-60-55; "Men of Rev" p 152. Rept by State D A R and Wm Pettit Dayton O.

BOWKER, ISAIAH, Columbiana co

Rev soldr. Rec not yet found. Was b 1766; soldr d 1845; bur Madison twp. Ref Col co Cem Recs. Rept by Mrs Wilma M Molsberry.

BOWLING (Bawling), **CHARLES,** Fairfield co

Pvt Va Milit. Srvd 7 mos and 26 das. Was b Apr 13 1763 Westmoreland co Va. Pens appl Fairfield co O Mar 11 1833. Ref S 16041 Va. Rept by State D A R.

BOWLING (Bawling), **WILLIAM,** Fairfield co

Pvt Va Milit. Enl 1775 Westmoreland co Va whr was b July 13 1758. Srvd 7 mos and 18 das. Pens appl Fairfield co O Mar 11 1833. Ref S 16040 Va. Rept by State D A R.

BOWMAN, DAVID, Montgomery co

Pa. Ref Fifth Ser Pa Arch Vol VII p 443. Bur at Trissel's cem Jackson twp. Has monument. Rept by W M Pettit S A R of Dayton O.

BOWSHER, ANTHONY, Pickaway co

Pvt Pa St Trps. Chldr: Anthony Jr; Peter; Henry; Jacob; David; Uni; Cathrine; wf of Jesse Justice; Barbara wf of John Buch; Elizabeth Harpster. Soldr said to be bur in old Bowsher cem on Island Road Circleville twp. Ref Will probated Feb 2 1835; desc Miss Mariam Blacher Chillicothe O. Rept by Pickaway Plains chpt.

BOWYER, WILLIAM, ? co

Listed in Invalid Pensrs of U S belonging to Ohio pd at Chillicothe; annual allowance $96. Ref p 172 Pensr 1818 at S of R Libry L A. Cop by Jane Dailey.

BOYD, FRANCIS, Fayette co

Pvt Va Contl. Pensr 1819 Fayette co O; pensr Ross co O act of June 24 1788 as pvt 7th Va Regt. Was b 1758; mar Nancy Ann Wosnum; soldr d 1824. Ref No 24882 D A R thro son George. Rept by Washington C H.

BOYD, JAMES, Columbiana co

Pens No 19857. Pvt Pa Milit 8 mos. Enl May or June 1780 York co Pa. Pensd 9-21-1833 in Columbiana co O æ 74. Wid pens No 3868. Was b 1759 Lancaster co Pa. Mar Lydia 10-13-1825; soldr d 7-17-1848 Butler twp Columbiana co. Res at time of enl in York co Pa. Since the Rev he has res in York; Cumberland; Somerset; and Fayette co's in Pa and movd from there to Columbiana co O. Ref Pa W 9362; B L Wt 26496-160-55. Rept by State D A R and Mahoning chpt.

BOYD, JOHN, Belmont co

Pvt Md State Trps. Pensd Act of 1832 issued Belmont co O Co of Capt Moffet Col Rumsey Regt for 6 mo fr 1777. Was b Cecil co Md 1756 (Bible). Res Union twp 1832 Belmont co O. Ref S 2088 Md. Rept by Jane Dailey.

BOYER, DANIEL, Licking co

Exec Doc 37 of 1852 objections to his suspended pens were obviated by resolutions of 1848. Rept by Wm Pettit Dayton O. State D A R repts; Pvt Del St Trps. Enl Kent co Del June 1 1776. Srvd 6 mo as sergt; 6 mo as Lieut. Was b 3-9-1756 Kent co Del; mar Sarah Williams 1785; chldr: John; Margaret; William; Caleb; Rachel. Soldr d 9-18-1835 Licking co O. Movd from Kent co Del to Allegheny abt 1790. In abt 1805 or 6 they movd to Muskingum co O. Later movd to Licking co O. Pens appl 10-30-1832 Licking co O. Ref Del R 1103.

BOYLES, ABSALOM COL, ? co

Listed in news clipping found in old scrap bk no date by L A A "as Rev who participated or interested in settlement of Marietta; most of whom are bur in Washington co". Filed here for cont research by Marietta chpt.

BRADFORD, JAMES, Mahoning co

Pvt Ser 5 Vol 7 p 223 Lancaster co Pa Arch; ser 5 Vol 4 pp 392, 701 Contl Army; also Conn Men p 89; N Y men 98; N J Men p 515; Mass Vol 2 p 403. Mar Betsey; livd Coitsville. Built 1st saw mill in Coitsville. Possibly bro-in-law of Mary (Bradford) wf Jonathan Frezee. Rev soldrs in Roster. Ref Tax list 1826 Poland James Bradford; Deed by I p 44 to James Bradford Coitsville 1807; Deed bk C p 247 from James and Betsey Bradford Coitsville 1811; Hist Trumbull and Mahoning co Vol I pp 48, 168; Mahoning co p 197 by Sanderson; Mahoning Register Jan 6 1865 List Early Settlers Coitsville 1811. Rept by Mahoning chpt.

BRADFORD, JOHN, Montgomery co

Washington co Pa Milit. Soldr d 1821; bur Beavertown cem Montgomery co O. Grave mrkd by S A R Dayton O. Ref Emigr to O 1800; will record Dayton O Mrs Fannie Lynch (D A R). Rept by Mr Wm Pettit S A R.

BRADFORD, JOHN, Coshocton co

Pvt Capt Thos Berry's Co 8th Va Regt fr May 25 1776 to Apr 13 1777. Was b abt 1745 England. Mar Miss Strouse 1778; chldr Joseph; Nancy; George; Peter; John Jr; Elizabeth; William; Hannah; Gasper; James; Mary. Soldr d Coshocton O 1830. Res dur Rev War Hampshire Co Va. Ref Rev soldr of Va p 41 Vol 9; Mrs W W Woodrum 1309 Lake Ave Pueblo Colo No 271276 on this line. Accepting this information Jane Dailey.

BRADY, THOMAS, Highland co

Pvt Va Contl. Enl Nov 3 1780 Halifax co Va. Recd land dischge Jan 3 1782. Srvd 6 mos and 15 das. Was b Oct 17 1762 Halifax co Va. Pens appl Highland co O Apr 7 1829. Ref S 4271 Va. Rept by State D A R. Fr Blanche Rings comes data: Brady, Thomas: Pvt refused a pens as servd in Regt not on Contl estab. Ref: Doc No 31 Jan 6 1831 O S Libry.

BRADY, WILLIAM, Scioto co

Pvt Pa Milit. Volunteered Washington co Pa 1776. Srvd 2 yrs in Pa Milit. Was b May 4 1760 Sussex co N J. Movd from Sussex co N J to Washington co Pa whn abt 14 yrs of æ. Movd from there 1799 to Scioto co O. Pens appl Scioto co Sept 26 1833. Ref S 8103 Va. Rept by State D A R.

BRAID, JOSEPH, Butler co

Listed often in Butler co, is incorrect spelling for Baird Joseph which see. Rept by Jane Dailey.

BRAILEY, GIDEON, Erie co

1776-79 Mass trps. Was b Dartmouth Mass 1758; mar 1791 Anna McCloud (d 1834); Gideon Jr was one son. Soldr d Milan O 1840 Erie co. Ref Vol 121 p 130 D A R Lin No 120417. Rept by Nathan Perry and Jacobus Westervelt chpts.

BRANDENBURG, WILLIAM, Clark co

Pvt Va Milit. Enl June 1781 Frederick co Md. Srvd 6 mos. Was b Oct 8 1758 Middleton co N J. In 1812 movd from there to Fayette co Pa; 1818 to Montgomery co O and in following fall to Clark co O. Pens appl Clark co O Oct 2 1832 res of Bethel twp. Ref S 2495 Md. Rept by State D A R.

BRANDT, ABRAHAM, Montgomery co

Lancaster co Pa Milit. Ser 5 Vol 7 p 135. Active duty: tour of Bucks co with 2nd battl. Bur in Landis cem. Was b 1763 and d 1838. Rept by W M Pettit.

BRANN, JEREMIAH, Butler co

Pvt Va Milit. Enl 1778 Westmoreland co Va. Srvd 2 yrs. Mar Sarah Reeder Mar 20 1789. Pens appl Oct 11 1832 Butler co O. Wid appl for pens Apr 18 1840 æ 77. Ref W 5933 Va. Rept by Jane Dailey. (Not spelled Braun). Oxford Caroline Scott repts d 7-27-1834 æ 70 bur Layhigh cem.

BRANNON, DAVID, Clermont co

Pvt Pa Milit. Volunteered 1776 Chester co Pa. Srvd 11 mos. Was b 1751 Antrim co Ireland. Emigrated to America 1771. Aft Rev livd in Chester co Pa and Bedford co Pa till abt 1790; then migrated to Mason co Ky; then to Bracken co Ky and abt 9 yrs ago to Clermont co O (Appl). Appl for pens Aug 24 1832 Clermont co O res of Franklin twp. Ref S 2094 Pa. Rept by State D A R.

BRANT, JOHN, Warren co

Pvt N J Cont. Enl Mt Holly N J 1778. Srvd in Regt Commanded by Col Ogdens N J line for 9 mos. Was in battles of Monmouth and Springfield besides several skirmishes. Was æ 67 in 1822; b Lancaster co Pa. Appl states "wf been dead yrs (in 1822); 5 chldr who have livd with other people since wf's death." Soldr d 1830; bur Dick's Crk Pres ch-yd. Grave mrkd by Richard Montgomery chpt S A R. Soldr made appl for pens in Warren co O June 10 1822 æ 67. Ref S 42635 N J; Pa Arch Vol 7 p 818; S 5. Rept by State D A R and Wm Pettit.

BRECK, WILLIAM CAPT, ? co

Listed in news clipping found in old scrap bk by L A A as "Rev soldr interested or participating in settlement of Marietta." Probably bur in Washington co. Filed here for cont research by Marietta chpt.

BREEDLOVE, JOHN, Adams co

Pvt Va Milit. Was drafted in Culpepper co Va whr he then resided. First entered service Oct or Nov 1780. Srvd in Co commanded by Capt Lillard; of Regt commanded by Col Glenn for 7 mos. Was b Apr 5 1752. Appl for trnsfr of pens on Dec 11 1833 from Va whr he lately removd to Adams co O. Pens appl Madison co Va Aug 2 1832. Ref S 2192 Va. Rept by State D A R.

BREES, TIMOTHY, Springfield twp ? co

Enl Basking Ridge Somerset co N J in 1776 or 7 as pvt in Capt Mead's Co Col Ogden's First N J Regt. Was in Battle of Monmouth and with General Sullivan in Indian country. Srvd to close of war. Allowed pens on his appl executed May 14 1818 whl a res of Springfield twp O æ 60 yrs. In 1821 he referred to his wf and 12 chldr. Samuel 20; Timothy 12; William 10 were the only names stated. Ref Pens No S 42632 N J. Rept by Ind Historical Commission.

BRENDLINGER, FREDERICK, Morrow co

Bur Harmony twp Blackbird cem Morrow co. Rept by Mt Gilead chpt.

BREWER, HENRY, Adams co

Pvt Congress Regt. Enl latter part of Dec 1779 Martinsburg Berkley co Va. Srvd in legion commd by Col Armond for 2 yrs on Va Contl. Was b 1765; soldr d 1829 or 30 Adams co O. Appl for pens in Adams co O June 13 1818. Made appl some place Nov 1 1820. Ref S 42093; B L Wt 1631-100 Va Contl. Rept by State D A R.

BREWER, JOHN, Adams co

Srvd as soldr in Tryon co N Y milit. B in N Y; d Adams co O; mar Elsie; one son was Edward. Ref Vol 113 p 285 D A R Lin Nat No 112875. Rept by Nathan Perry chpt.

BRICKER, JOHN, Columbiana co

Pvt 4th Co 3rd Battl 1781 Lancaster co Milit under Capt Frederick Cerper. Pvt 4th co 3rd Battl 1781 Lanc Co Milit Capt Joe Gehr; Pvt 4 Co 3rd Battl 1782 Capt Jos Gehr; Pvt 6 Battl Nov 1783 Capt Jos Gehr; Pvt 4th Co 9th Battl Nov 1779 Capt Jos Gehr. Soldr b Switzerland. Mar Md 1775 Nancy Boyer also of Swiss birth. She d March 1828. Chldr: Henry; Sally; Nancy; Elizabeth; Catherine; John; Rebecca; Susannah; Jacob; David (12th child b 1800); Lidia; Solomon. Soldr d Oct 1818 Salem twp Columbiana co O. Came to Am 1770 from Switzerland. Settled Frederick co Md. Came to Salem twp 1808 with 14 chldr. Ref Henry Baldwins Records; Pa Arch 5 VII pp 263,270, 295, 297, 614, 879. Rept by Mrs Wilma Molsberry.

BRIDGE, JOHN, Preble co

Srvd throughout the war. Was b N J; d nr Eaton O; bur Mound Hill cem Preble co. One of the earliest settlers in Preble co. Rept by Commodore Preble chpt.

BRILEY, JOHN, Fayette co

Pvt Md Contl. Enl Aug 6 1781 Annapolis Md. Srvd 2 yrs. Mar Sally; chldr: John Jefferson æ 14 in 1820; Samuel æ 12; Wilson æ 10; Gete æ 7. Pens in Madison co O 1818; trnsfr to Fayette co O Nov 1831. Ref Md S 42631; B L Wt 1790-100. Rept by State D A R.

BRILL, MICHAEL, Trumbull co

Exec Doc 37 of 1852 refused a pens as servd less than 6 mo. Rept by Wm Pettit.

BRINK, BENJAMIN, Trumbull co

Enl December 1777 under Capt Dathic Hewit; was in battle at Wyoming but escaped and joined a Co of volunteers stationed nr the Del river in Northumberland co Pa and cont therein until a force was sent on to take part at Wyoming which force he joined and on arrival at Wyoming was attached to Capt Spaulding Co. Was b 1750; d March 1813 in Weathersfield Trumbull co O. Rept by Mary Chesney chpt.

BRINTON, WILLIAM, ? co

Listed in Invalid Pensrs of U S belonging to O pd at Chillicothe; annual allowance $72. Ref p 172 Pensrs of 1818 S of R Libry L A. Cop by Jane Dailey.

BRISTOL, REUBEN, Pike co

Pvt Conn Milit. Enl June 1775 in Cres ? Conn. 1 yr as pvt and 3 yr as teamster. Was b 10-23-1755 New Haven co Conn. Soldr d 12-24-1851 Pike co O. Livd in Chesire twp Conn until abt 35 yrs of age then movd to Westmoreland co Pa; livd here 5 or 6 yrs and movd to Bourbon co Ky 4 or 5 yrs. Later movd to Ross co O now the co of Pike. Appld for pens Pike co 3-5-1833. Ref Conn Contl S 12316. Rept by State D A R.

BRITTENHAM, SOLOMON, Madison co

Pvt 2nd Regt Md line. Pensd Apr 25 1832 Act of 1828 O Pens Roll. Cop by Jane Dailey.

BRITTON, NATHAN, Mahoning co

Pvt pensd. Mar Rachel; soldr d Austintown O. Ref Tax list Trumbull co 1826; Deed bk C p 5; Old pens bk 1808 Trumbull co; Hist Trumbull and Mahoning co Vol F p 49. Rept by Mahoning co.

BRITTON, WILLIAM SR, Marion co

Pvt in Capt John Cole's Co Col Ashley's Regt and Capt Kimball Carleton's Co Col Moses Nicol's Regt Gen Stark's Brigade of New Hampshire also Col Stichney's Regt. Was b Oct 15 1757 Concord N H. One son was William Jr. Soldr d Feb 5 1840 Marion co O; bur Pleasant Hill cem nr Big Island Marion co nr west side of cem. Inscript on M "William Britton Sr b in Concord N H. Srvd 7 yrs 6 mo in Rev War. Emigrated to Marion co O in 1835. D Feb 5 1840 æ 83 yrs 3 mo 20 das". Grave mrkd by Capt Wm Hendricks chpt with bronze D A R mrkr on June 1 1933. Ref New Hampshire Arch. Rept by Capt Wm Hendricks chpt Marion O.

BROACHER, HENRY, Hamilton co

Capt; ref Pen cl of John Brasher N Y service. Rept by Wm Pettit.

BROCKWAY, MARTIN, Morrow co

Bur Cardington twp; Bethel cem Morrow co O. Rept by Mt Gilead chpt

BRODERICK, ABSALOM, Miami co

Alleged he srvd in Sussex co N J. Enl Dec 1776 at Newton that co and srvd as pvt in Capt Jonathan Pitman's Co Col Black's N J Regt etc and srvd 6 to 9 mo. No pens allowed as he "failed to furnish proof of said service accd to law." (from D C Vet Adm). Son of Thomas and Berthenia. At one time livd in Miami co (bur place unknown). Ref R (Rejected) 1236 Pens Cl; Hist Monmouth and Ocean co N J by Edwin Salter p 136; Stryker's list of old Monmouth. Rept by Mary M Hoge St Clairsville O.

BRONSON (or Brunson), PHINEAS, Medina co

Pvt Conn Milit. Enl Hartford co Conn. Srvd 6 mos. Was b Nov 9 1764 Oblong Conn. Appl mentions chldr. Aft Rev res in Hartford co Conn 8 or 9 yrs. 1817 movd to Medina co. Soldr appl for pens Medina co O Apr 9 1833; Wayne co Ind July 21 1838; appl for trnsfr of pens to Peoria co Ill Mar 4 1839. Ref S 32137 Conn. Rept by State D A R.

BROOKS, CHARLES, Warren co

Pvt Pa State Trps; Capt Boyd co Gen Way Brigade 7 mo resd York co Pa when enl. Ref S 2404. Rept by Jane Dailey.

BROOKS, CHARLES, Jefferson co

Pvt Va Contl. Enl 9th Va Regt Spring of 1775. Srvd 4 yrs. Was æ 61 in 1819. Mar Malinda; one dau Christina æ 19. (1820) Soldr d May 25 1845 Allegheny co Pa. Pens appl Jefferson co O Sept 2 1819 Res Knox twp. Appl also 1820. Wid appl for pens Allegheny co Pa June 17 1845 res Sewicklyville twp. Soldr made dec in Allegheny co Pa July 15 1826 that he resd in said co having removd from O. Ref R 1256 (pens rejected) Va. Rept by State D A R.

BROOKS, HANANIAH, ? co

Pvt. Refused a pens as did not serve 9 mo under one engagement. Ref Doc 31 Jan 6 1831 O S Libry. Rept by Blanche Rings.

BROOKS (or Brook), JAMES, Mahoning co

Many enlist. N Y Men p 270 prob Va Men p 46. Pvt in Rev War. Mar Ann (1766-1-10-1859); chldr: James b 1791 mar Hester; dau mar Dr Hughes; dau mar Daniel Boone. Soldr d 1837 Poland Mahoning co O. Ref Will bk 8 p 525 1817 Mahoning co (then Trumbull co O); Hist Collections Mahoning co p 293. Rept by Mahoning chpt.

BROOKS, JOSHUA, Pike co

Pvt 9th Regt. Enl Jan 1780 Mass Line. Was æ 66 in 1831. Pens appl in Pike co O 11-22-1831. Ref Mass S 17865; B L Wt 1787-100. Rept by State D A R.

BROOKS, LEMUEL, Huron co

Was b 1741; d 1831; mar Esther Sprague (2 minor chldr when he d). Mrs Cecil Newberry of Greenfield Huron co a dau. He was in battle of Quebec. Soldr bur Steuben cem. Has family mrkr. Ref Pioneer Women of Western Reserve p 729; Firelands Pioneers O S Vol 1 p 17 and Vol 4 p 3. Rept by Marjorie Cherry.

BROOME, JOHN, Washington co

Sergt Va Contl. Enl at Romney Va; dischrgd at Philadelphia Pa. Srvd 3 yrs. Was b 1749; mar Mary æ 51; had dau Ruth æ 15 (appl 1820). Appl for pens Washington co O July 24 1820 res of Flaring twp. Stated property value $82.50. Ref S 42095 Va. Rept by State D A R and Helen Sloane.

BROWER, HENDRICKS, Adams co

Minute men, Dutchess co N Y Milit. Also in 1812 war. Was b 1755 N Y. Mar Anne Hawk; Sarah was one dau. Soldr d Adams co O. Ref No 123173 Vol 124 D A R Lin. Cop by Jane Dailey.

BROWN, ALEX CRAWFORD, Coshocton co

Pvt Del Contl. Enl Newark Del Feb 1776. Srvd 2 yrs. Was æ 63 in 1818. Resided on son's land. Pens appl Coshocton co O 5-1-1818. Occupation was a weaver. Ref Del S 42634. Rept by State D A R.

BROWN, BENJAMIN CAPT, ? co

Listed in news clipping in old scrapbk. Rev soldr probably bur in Washington co. Filed here for cont research by Marietta chpt.

BROWN, EZRA, Medina co

Pvt Conn Milit. Enl Hartford co Conn 1780. Srvd 1 yr and 6 mos. Was b 1763 Hartford co Conn. Soldr d Dec 28 1843. Since Rev livd in Johnstown; Verona and Sweden ? cos N Y. Livd in York Medina co O whn appld for pens Oct 24 1832. Ref S 2391 Conn. Rept by State D A R.

BROWN, JAMES 1ST, Ashtabula co

Pvt Mass Contl. Enl June 27 1780 Mass trps. Srvd 3 yrs. Was æ 58 in 1818. Had wf Merriam who was very infirm and 2 sons with whom they livd. Movd from Niagara co N Y abt 1826. Appl for pens 5-6-1818 in Niagara co N Y. Appl for trnsfr 1826. Ref Mass S 42096. Rept by State D A R.

BROWN, JOHN, Adams co

Proven S A R record No 2437; b 1734; d 1821; ref Mass Arch 13-154. Rept by Wm Pettit.

BROWN, JOHN, Ashtabula co

Pvt Conn Contl. Enl 1777 Tolland co Conn. Pvt under Capt Thos Abbe; Col Samuel Wylly's Regt Conn Trps. Dischrged Westfield N J May 1780. Was b Coventry Conn 1760. Mar Elizabeth Dorman Oct 14 1784 (b 1766-d 1839); Had son Nelson æ 20 in 1820. No 119911 D A R names a son Jesse. Soldr d Jan 6 1837 Windsor O. Grave located by Mary Stanley chpt (21st Rept D A R). Pens appl Ottega co N Y Apr 18 1818; appl again 1820; appl Trumbull co Mar 14 1826; Wid appl Ashtabula co O Apr 19 1839. Ref W 5871 Conn. Rept by State D A R and Mary Chesney chpt.

BROWN, JOHN, Mahoning co

Pensd Aug 6 1818. Mar Mary (b 1781-d 3-17-1851 bur Canfield O). Soldr d June 1 1827 Poland O. Ref Republican Sentinel 3-17-1851. Rept by Mahoning chpt.

BROWN, JOHN G, Perry co

Pvt Va Contl. Enl in Va. Srvd 3 yrs. Was b 1747 in Va. Mar Mary Spillman Apr 3 1825. Chldr: dau and wf has some chldr of her own. One son was Geo Washington Brown; daus of John Brown by 1st wf; Betsy Johnson and Sally Gale. Soldr d Feb 6 1832 Perry co O. Pens Muskingum co O Feb 4 1818. Wid appl for pens Athens co O May 16 1853. Ref W 25276; B L Wt 21828-160-55 Va. Rept by State D A R.

BROWN, JOHN, Pickaway co

Exec Doc 37 of 1852 in suspended list his service was admitted. Rept by Wm Pettit.

BROWN, JOSIAH, Medina co

Pvt N Y Milit. Enl as a substitute for his father spring of 1778 Westchester co N Y. Srvd 10 mos and 14 days. Was b 1764 Westchester co N Y. Father was in Rev. Soldr d Feb 25 1843. Res at Westchester and Dutchess Cos N Y during the Rev. Aft Rev res in Albany co N Y. Movd 1826 to Hinkley Medina co O whr appl for pens Apr 9 1833. Ref S 2101 Mass N C N Y and Va. Rept by State D A R.

BROWN, LEVI, Cuyahoga co

Pvt Mass Contl. Enl Worcester co Mass May 15 1780. Srvd 3 yrs. Was b 1763. Pens appl Tompkins co N Y Apr 14 1818. Appl for trnsfr to Cuyahoga co O July 5 1824 res of Brooklyn twp. Ref S 42633 Mass. Rept by State D A R.

BROWN, NATHAN, Jackson co

Enl 1781 Vt Milit. Capt Charles Nelson Col Benjamin Wait's Regt. Was b Vermont. One son was Zephania; soldr d Jackson co O. Ref No 59212 and 50193 D A R. Rept by Nathan Perry chpt.

BROWN, OWEN, Licking co

Was b Simsbury Conn. Father of John Brown the Abolitionist. J H Galbraith Historian "Ohio High Spots." Rept by Hetuck chpt.

BROWN, RANS, Champaign co

Soldr bur Williams farm below Aberdeen O. Ref S A R list. Rept by Jane Dailey.

BROWN, SAMUEL, ? co

A lieut was a pensr under Act of 1818 but taken fr rolls under Act of 1820 as not considered in indigent circumstances accd to that act. Ref Doc 31 Jan 6 1831 O S Libry. Rept by Blanche Rings Col O.

BROWN, SAMUEL, ? co

Pvt refused a pens as srvd in Regt not on Contl Estab. Ref Doc No 31 Jan 6 1831 O S Libry. Rept by Blanche Rings Col O.

BROWN, SAMUEL, ? co

Was b 1745 Anne Arundle co Md. Son of Benjamin and Susannah Rondal. Mar Achsah Riggs (b 1746 d 1817) dau of John and Mary (Davis) Riggs. Chldr: Elisha; John; Mary; Susannah; Samuel; Vachel. Soldr d 1833 Southeastern Ohio. Was First Lieut in Capt Charles Hammond Co Elk Ridge Battl milit 1776 Conn. A Capt in 1778 under General Smallwood Md. Was too old to take an active part in war of 1812 but signed the Commission for three of his sons John; Samuel and Vachel all officers in war of 1812 and all were wounded. John d of wounds 1814. Elisha was a doctor. Elisha Brown b 1774 Maryland d 1-1-1863 Minnesota Jct Wisconsin. Soldr ancestors came fr Dumfries Ayrshire Scotland and settled in Anne Arundle co Md prior to 1665. Samuel was given a military funeral a negro servant led his horse, with saddle reversed, behind the corpse. A rifle salute was fired over his grave. The family livd nr Athens O abt 1833 to 35 but another relative thinks a Brown was bur in old Mounds cem Marietta. (This is not same data as Samuel Brown Athens co p 55 Ohio Roster Vol 1. J D). Received fr S W Wallace 304 Lincoln St Denver Colo.

BROWN, THOMAS, Warren co

Srvd in Prince George's co Md Milit. Mar Ruth Brashear; chldr: Elizabeth; Eleanor; Ignatius; Thomas; Levi; Beal; Zacharius; Nancy Ann; Simon; Ruth. Soldr d abt 1797; bur Lebanon O. Rept by Joseph Spencer chpt.

BROWN, WILLIAM, Pickaway co

Res in Pickaway co 1833 æ 75. Ref Pa Arch. Rept by Mary Steinmetz.

BROWN, WILLIAM, Mahoning co

Pvt. Pensd. Was b 1760; mar Martha (1760-1846); William a son (1788-1833) mar Ann Porter. Soldr d 1833 Poland O. Ref Will bk 11 Martha Brown prob 1841; Old Pension Bks; News letter establishes son William Brown. Rept by Mahoning chpt.

BRUCE, WILLIAM, Preble co

Srvd thro Rev fr Va. Was b 9-20-1762 Va; mar Frances Lewis b 1771 in Ky; soldr d 1832 bur Mound Hill cem Preble co. Had a family. Came to O; was founder of Eaton Preble co O and a great man of co. Rept by Commodore Preble chpt.

BRUMFIELD, HUMPHREY, Lawrence co

Pvt Va Milit. Was b June 22 1752 Amelia co Va. Movd to Halifax co Va whn abt 10 yrs of æ; then to Pittsylvania; then Montgomery co till 1816 when movd to Gallia co O whr appl for pens Nov 28 1833. Pensd 4-3-1834 in Lawrence co O. Ref S 8105 Va. Rept by State D A R.

BRYAN, ANDREW MORRISON, Greene co

Bur nr Jamestown Greene co. Mrs Lindsay M Brein Dayton states record is estab Rept by Catharine Green chpt.

BRYAN, THOMAS, Jefferson co

Pvt Md Milit. Enl in Md whl living Baltimore co. Srvd 1 yr. Was æ 92 in 1833; b Mar 17 1741 Waterford Ireland. Res for abt 4 yrs aft Rev in Baltimore co Md and from there movd to Berkley co Va and livd abt 4 yrs; then to Green co Pa for abt 6 yrs; from there to Jefferson co O whr appl for pens Aug 27 1833 res Steubenville twp. Ref S 3050 Md. Rept by State D A R.

BRYAN, WILLIAM, Noble co

Pvt in the Rev 5th Md Regt. Was b Berks co Pa 1728. (C C Danford Lewisville O rept he was b in Fayette co Pa). Mar Mary Ann 1750; chldr: James; Cornelius; (both Rev soldrs); Josias; Rebecca. Soldr d 1795 Monroe now Noble co. Bur Beaver twp Noble co O. Ref Bryantown Hundred 1775-78; Md Arch Vol 18 p 186; Census of Charles co Md recd p 310. Rept by J D and Columbus chpt.

BRYAN, CORNELIUS, Noble co

Enl Bryantown Hundred. Srvd in Jefferson co W Va Milit fr 5-31-1781 to 6-22-1781 under Capt Aquilla Whitaker. Was b Charles co Md 1760. Son of William Bryan and Mary Ann; mar (1st wf unknown) 2nd Sarah Danford. Chldr: James; John; Ann; Thomas; Peter; Cornelius Jr. Soldr d 1830 what is now Noble co; bur Watson cem nr Summerfield O. Inscript "C B — 1760-1830." He came to O 1795 fr Jefferson co W Va. Grave mrkd with small square stone even with the ground. Ref Md Arch; cens Charles co Md; Bryantown Hundred 1775-8. Was a farmer; mill wright; J Peace and postmaster. Rept by Columbus chpt.

BRYANT, DAVID, Knox co

Capt Major Lieut-Col of N H Milit 1776-80 b Haverhill Mass; d Mt Vernon O; mar Mary Gilman (1763-99); David was one son; ref V 115 p 112 No 114361 D A R.

BRYANT, DAVID, Knox co and Ind

Ref Bryant Genealogy by Clara Vaile Braden gives military recd p 34 of this soldr; b 1756 Springfield N J; removd to Pa 1791; thence to Knox co O in 1816 whr was pensd 1833. At advanced age went to Indiana w son Elias who bot Gov land 15 mi N W of Fort Wayne in summer of 1835. Both parents d in Aug 1835 and bur on East bnk of Eel Riv. Mar Catherine Wooley. Cop fr book of Jane Daileys gift of Jeanette Bryant, D A R Hebron Ind.

BUCK, CHARLES, Gallia co

Exec Doc 37 of 1852 refused a pens as servd less than 6 mo. Rept by Wm Pettit.

BUCK, EBENEZER, Ashtabula co

Pvt Mass Contl. Mary Redmond chpt repts he is bur in city cem Conneaut O Ashtabula co d 11-2-1837 æ 73. He enl Mar 1781 in Cheshire twp New Hampshire whr he then resided. Enl Apr 1782 Wilmington twp Mass. Pens appl Ashtabula co 8-19-1832. Was a cooper. Ref Mass N H S 16963. Rept by State D A R.

BUCK, JOHN, Fayette co

Pvt Pa Contl. Was æ 64 yrs in 1819. Pens appl Fayette co O 7-15-1819. Pens discontinued aft 1820. Ref Pa S 42103. Rept by State D A R. One "Buck, John" (no co stated) was a Lieut and refused a pens as srvd in a Regt not on the Contl Estab. Ref Doc No 31 Jan 6 1831 O S Libry. Rept by Blanche Rings Col O.

BUCK, JONATHAN, Lorain co

Pvt Conn Milit. Enl 1777 Sharon Conn. Srvd 6 mos and 7 das. Last payment of pens covered from 3-4-1840 to 9-4-1840. Was made to P R Friend Pittsburg Pa (Atty). On 9-30-1840 pensr certified he livd in Russia O for 20 yrs and previously in Henrietta O. Aft Rev res in Vermont; N Y; and O. Pens appl Apr 15 1833 Lorain co. Ref S 3108 Conn. Rept by State D A R and Nathan Perry chpt.

BUCK, WILLIAM SR, Mahoning co

Accd to an address of Compatriot Lynn he is a Rev soldr bur in Poland cem Mahoning co. Rept by W M Pettit S A R Secy.

BUCK, WILLIAM, Mercer co

Enl in 8th Pa in Westmoreland co Pa. Pensd Athens co as pvt Conn Milit 7-14-1819 fr Dept Inter "pvt Capt Sam'l Miller's Co 8th Pa Regt Col David McCoy." In battle of Yorktown and many others. Ae 73 4-3-1818; b therefore 1745. Mar 1806 to Phebe (whose 2nd husband was Nicholas Christian; she mar him in Whitehall Greene co Ill). Enoch was the 2nd son b 1810 (he livd at Cass co Pokagon Mich. Later went to Ill). Bur St Marys Mercer co 1838. In his appl of 1820 says "wf is 40; has 7 chldr; oldest 19; son mentioned as 17 yrs old." Ref Pa Arch Ohio list; above data cop from Dept Int W 25411 by Jane Dailey.

BUCKINGHAM, THOMAS, Huron co

Exec Doc 37 of 1852 refused a pens as srvd less than 6 mo. Rept by Wm Pettit.

BUCKLEY, JOSHUA, Butler co

Pvt Va Contl. Enl Aug 1779 Winchester Va. Srvd 4 yrs. Was b 1760. Pens appl Butler co O Nov 27 1819. Ref S 42104 Va. Rept by State D A R.

BUDD, JOHN, Delaware co

Pvt Va St Trps. Enl 1776 or 7 Wyoming Pa. Srvd 11 mos. Was b 10-23-1750 Long Island N Y. Res with father before war. (Poss bur Harlem twp repts Delaware chpt). was res in Wyoming Pa at time of enl. Res there until 1810 and movd to Delaware co O. Pens appl Delaware co O 11-19-1832. Ref Pa S 2090. Rept by State D A R.

BUELL, GEN JOSEPH, ? co

Listed in news clipping by L A A found in old scrapbk "as Rev soldrs participating or interested in settlement of Marietta." Filed here for further research. Listed by Marietta chpt.

BUKER, ISRAEL, Muskingum co

Sergt Mass. Enl Apr 1775 in Capt Jacob Allen's Co. Srvd 8 yrs and one mo. Mar Sally Black Aug 24 1816. Soldr d Nov 4 or 5 1848 in Otsego Muskingum co O. Pens appl Coshocton co O 4-22-1818. Wid appld 11-24-1857 same co. Ref Contl (Mass) W 25566; B L Wt 890-100; B L W 342-60-55. Rept by State D A R.

BULL, SAMUEL, Mahoning co

Pvt. N Y State. N Y Men in Rev p 162. Chldr: Thomas mar Hannah; Isaac; Samuel mar Catherine —— d in Portage co. Soldr d before 1828-29 Green twp. Ref Deed bk S p 170-2 p 446 Heirs of Samuel Bull and W p 346. Rept by Mahoning chpt.

BUMPUS (or Bunpus), FREDERICK, Richland co

Pvt N Y St Trps. Enl N Y State 1782. Srvd 10 mos from 1781. Was b 1764; appl for pens Ontario co N Y May 7 1818. Ref S 2045 N Y. Rept by State D A R.

BUNGER, JOHN, Preble co

Srvd in Rev. Was b 1760 Va; mar Eva House (b in Va); had large family. Soldr d 1831; bur Roselawn cem at Lewisburg O Preble co. Came to O 1817; bur Roselawn cem at Lewisburg O Preble co. Came to O 1817; settld in Harrison twp. Rept by Commodore Preble chpt.

BUNTING, RAMOTH, Clermont co

Found listed in Clermont as Rev soldr. Is another spelling for "Bunton, Ramoth" filed p 59 Vol 1 Ohio Roster Rev soldr and in additional data this vol. (Jane Dailey).

BUNTON, SAMUEL, Columbiana co

N J St Trps. Enl in N J abt 2 mos before battle of Trenton. Was b 1759 Oxford twp Chester co Pa; mar Martha d 8-13-1847; chldr: Mary Williamson; Margaret Prior; Martha Cunningham; Nancy Bunton; Samuel; Alexander. (appl of Alexander). Soldr d 6-18-1838. Whn enl was residing in Oxford twp Chester co Pa. Afterwards he movd to Bowen co Pa and from there to Brook co Va. From there to Yellow Creek twp Columbiana co O. Pensd 1-3-1833 in Columbiana co pension no 3838. Wid pens no 1435. Ref Pa R 1435. Rept by State D A R.

BURCH, EDDY (Edy), Washington co

Enl 1776; srvd various enls in Vt co and dischrgd Oct 29 1777; returning to Hartford Vt whr he had enl. Aft 20 yrs here livd 4 yrs in Canada; returned to Hartford; aft 3 yrs to Cayuga co N Y; then 1817 with family movd to Washington co O. Was b 1760 Stonington Conn son of Benjamin Burch. Chldr of Soldr: Diantha Burch b 1779 (Mrs Justus Hall); Elesta Burch (Mrs Eli Vaughn); Eliza Burch (Mrs Enoch Davis). Soldr d Oct 15 1848; bur Liberty Hill cem Aurelius twp Washington co which is situated in west half of S W 1-4 of Sec 30. Inscript on monument "In Memory of Edy Burch d Oct 15 1848 in 89 yr of his æ." Also "In Memory of Elizabeth Burch consort of Edy Burch who d July 19 1848 in 85th yr of her æ." Grave mrkd by old slab sandstone by family and Rev mrkr. Mrkd by Marietta chpt 1934. Ref Mrs Nathan R Park East Walnut Hills Cincinnati O No 285999 on this lineage. Rept by Jane Dailey and Marietta chpt.

BURDUE, NATHANIEL, Erie co

Enl Westmoreland co Pa 1775 2 mos Capt Richard Williams co Pa Milit Capt Delap's Co until Delap killed by Indians then Capt Adams took command. Burdue srvd from May 1 until Nov 1 each yr for a period of 4-5 yrs. During winter livd at his home which was 8 mi from Bedford. He then went to Washington co Pa and srvd abt 3 weeks under Wm Hudson. Amounted to 2 yrs and 6 mos in all. Was b 1748 Woodbridge N J; d Mar 2 1837 Berlin twp; bur family lot Baptist cem Berlin Heights; grave mrkd by govt mrkr. Wf's name was Margaret. Aft Rev livd part of time in Bedford co Pa; in Washington co Pa; and in Erie co Pa. Res Huron co O June 11 1833 Berlin twp whr pensd Sept 21 1833. Ref S 3104 Pa. Rept by State D A R and Marjorie Cherry. Ref Pa Arch S 3 Vol 23 p 588; Williams Hist p 477; Firelands Pioneers O S Vol 1 p 31.

BURK, ROBERT, ? co

Pvt refused a pens as srvd in Regt not on Contl Estab. Ref Doc No 31 Jan 6 1831 O S Libry. Rept by Blanche Rings Col O.

BURKHARD (Burkett), JEHU, Montgomery co

N C Milit Rowan co; recd depreciation pay proving long service. Henry was one son. Soldr d 1823; bur Fort McKinley on farm of son Henry at Stringtown Montgomery co O. Ref J M Burkett 1838 Ontario Place Washington D C and Wm Pettit Dayton S A R.

BURLINGAME, WANTON, Trumbull co

Ae 76 pensd in Gustavus twp. Srvd from Apr 1779 to Apr 1781 with the Vermont trps. Chldr: Wanton; Simon; Betsey; Diantha; Amy; Lucinda; Juliann; Polly. Soldr d Sept 9 1853 Attica N Y whr res for 12 yrs before his death and previous thereto he res in Trumbull co O. (Auditors dept U S A). Rept by Mary Chesney chpt.

BURMAN, ISAAC, Cuyahoga co

Pvt 2 yr Conn Line. Enl Apr 1781 Northampton twp Mass. Appl for pens mentions a son with whom he lvd. Pens N Y 9-30-1818. Appl for trnsfr to Cuyahoga co 1-15-1838. Pensr 1840 Parma twp Cuyahoga co æ 75. Ref Contl (Mass) S 42638. Rept by State D A R.

BURNET, HENRY, Mahoning co

Pvt Pa. Pa Arch Ser 5 p 589 Chester co Pa; also Mass Men Vol 2 p 872. Mar Sarah dau Benj Ross R S. Chldr Henry b 1801 Nancy Jones; Sophia b 1808 mar William Lanterman; probably others. Soldr d abt 1830 Austintown. First in Connecticut; then Westmoreland co Pa; later still in Austintown Mahoning co O. Ref Tax list 1826 to 1837 Trumbull co O; Hist Trumbull and Mahoning co Vol 2 pp 165 & 167; Hist Mahoning co p 725 Sanderson; Deed bk J p 13. Rept by Mahoning chpt.

BURNETT, ROBERT, Fayette co

Pvt in Capt Alex Lockhart's Co 4th Co of Concord and Bethel twps Chester co Milit. Ref Pa Arch S 5 Vol 5 p 197. Was with Washington at crossing of Delaware. Was b 1755 Pa son of John S Burnett one of Washington's Va Buckskins at Braddock Defeat. Mar Susannah —— (d 1824 æ 66); chldr: Samuel; Amor; Mary Friend; Robert Jr mar Susanna Bush; Thomas mar Rachel Bush; Susan; Henry mar Magdalene Bush; John S. Soldr d 2-2-1820 Fayette co O; bur on farm now owned by Charles Bush nr Jasper C C C Hiway. Wf bur by his side. Soldr was at battl Brandywine hauled baggage dur retreat. Ref Clara G Mark Columbus O. Rept by Washington C H chpt.

BURNET, SAMUEL, Mahoning co

Appl for pens 1832 in Circuit Ct Warren O; also N J Men in Rev p 526. Was b 1763; mar Nancy. Ref Deed bk G p 228 Samuel and Nancy Burnet of Austintown 1840. Rept by Mahoning chpt.

BURNET, SQUIRE, Licking co

Pvt at Mt Holly N J Capt Isaac Morrison 1 Regt commanded by Col Matthias Ogden N J Line. Srvd 9 mo. In battle of Monmouth. Was b 1749 Elizabethtown N J;

mar Rhoda 1760. Was a shoemaker; Enl June 1778 at Mt Holly N J. Ref Pens S 42113 and S 42110. Rept by M S Askue Mahoning chpt and State D A R.

BURNHAM, JEREMIAH, Athens co

Pvt Mass Contl. Enl Apr 15 1777 for 3 yrs; cont service. Srvd under Capt Whipple Mass Trps Col Rufus Putnam. Mar Mehetable Sanborn at Bridgeton Cumberland co Dist of Me (a part of Mass) on June 8 1791 by Nathan Church a Congreg minister. (Copy of church recd filed). Bohemia was one son æ 53 in 1846 b Mar 21 1793; a bro Ira in Ill. Soldr d June 23 1839 Athens co O. Ref W 5970; B L Wt 3832-160 A; Wid pens iss June 6 1846 to begin 1853; in 1855 was a res of Athens twp; "Mar 20 1855 Mehetable wid of Jeremiah Burnham of Lodi twp." A sons deposition said he understood his father was a widower whn he mar his mother. Cop by Jane Dailey.

BURNHAM, JOHN MAJOR, ? co

Listed in news clipping by L A A found in old scrap bk "as Rev soldr who participated or interested in settlement of Marietta." Filed here for cont research by Marietta chpt.

BURNHAM, JOHN, Hamilton co

Enl April 1775 Glouster Mass. Was æ 73 yrs in 1818. Wf æ 64 in 1820. He and his wf were liv in Ind in 1820 with their oldest son but moved to Hamilton co O in 1821. Was a boot and shoemaker but crippled in his right arm and unable to work. Pensd 9-6-1819 Susquehanna co Pa; trnsfrd to Hamilton co O 10-10-21. Ref Mass S 42107. Rept by State D A R.

BURNS, JOHN, ? co

Pvt refused a pens as deserted the service. Ref Doc 31 Jan 6 1831 O S Libry. Rept by Blanche Rings Col O.

BURNS (or Burne), JOHN, Wayne co

Enl Middlebrook Va 1778. Srvd in Va line 6 yrs. Was b June 1739. Mar Rosanna. Pens appl Wayne co O June 25 1818. In deed for sale of land filed 1828 Wayne co O wf is named. This appl was sent to Judge of Warren co O in Ridgeville on July 18 1818 for his certf of the truthfulness of the statement. Ref S 42108 Va. Rept by State D A R and Wooster-Wayne chpt.

BURNS, LAWRENCE, Clermont co

Pa Rev Soldr. Enl 1776 Philadelphia Pa. Srvd 6 yrs. Was b 1753; mar Elizabeth 1794; chldr: Sarah æ 17; Nancy Fisher wf of David Fisher; Margaret Hobbs wf of James Hobbs; Wm K Byrne; George S. Soldr d Clermont co 7-15-1832 æ 78. Pens appl Clermont co May 27 1819; appl again 1820. Wid appl Clermont co Sept 13 1818. Wid d Dec 13 1838. Ref Pa Arch Vol 23 S 3; R 1576 Pa. Rept by State D A R. Byrn or Byrne also spelled.

BURNSIDE, JONATHAN, Licking co

Pvt Va Contl. Enl Loudon co Va Spring of 1779. Dischrgd fall of yr 1782 Philadelphia. Srvd 18 mos. Was b 1764 or 61. Had wf æ 57 in 1820 and chldr: Jno æ 13; Charlotte æ 11 (appl 1820); Only 2 surviving chldr Andrew and Ellen Smith whn appl for arrears of pens Apr 6 1851 Greene co. Soldr d Jan 19 1835 Licking co O. Pens appl Fairfield co O June 1 1818; Licking co Oct 28 1820. Ref p 406 name appears in list Wiseman's Hist Fairfield co as pioneer; S 42112 Contl Va; B L Wt 2471-100 Issued July 2 1852. Rept by State D A R and Jane Dailey.

BURRELL, JEDEDIAH, Trumbull co

Pvt N J Cont. Enl Mar 1776 Wareham N J. Was in battles of Brandywine; Germantown; Springfield; Monmouth. Was wounded; also with Gen Montgomery at Quebec. Srvd 7 yrs. Was b 1746. (Mary Chesney chpt states b 2-2-1748 in N Y City).

Pens appl Trumbull co O Oct 3 1820 living in Weathersfield. Ref S 42106 N J. Rept by State D A R and Mary Chesney chpt.

BURRIL, ZACHARIAH, Ashtabula co

Pvt N J Contl. Enl N J in Feb 1776. Was æ 63 in 1818. Mar Martha; chldr: Elizabeth æ 17 in 1820; son and 2 more daus. Soldr d 7-19-1835. Pens in Ontario co N Y 4-28-1819; appl for trnsfr Ashtabula co '-19-1821. Was a blacksmith. Martha Burril his wid appl for a pens in Huron co in 1838. Ref N J W 5235. Rept by State D A R.

BURROUGHS, DANIEL, Portage co

Pvt N H Contl. Volunteered 1775. Srvd 1 yr. Was æ 77 in 1833; b 1755 Hartford co Conn. Res in Alstead N H when enl. Since war has res 17 yrs in Williamstown Vt and 23 years Shalvesville Portage co O whr now lives. Res Portage co O Apr 2 1833 res Shalersville twp. Ref S 32144 N H. Rept by State D A R.

BURROWS, ELIJAH, Portage co

Pvt N H Contl. Enl in Feb 1776 Cheshire co N H. Pvt for 1 yr. Ae 61 in 1820. Pens appl Feb 22 1820 in Portage co O. Ref N H S 42105. Rept by State D A R.

BURROWS, MOSES, Trumbull co

Ae 95 Ensign in Farmington liv with Lorenzo D Wilbur. Cens of 1840. Ref Pens Bureau repts recd not found. Rept by Mary Chesney chpt.

BURTON, SELAH, (alias Othneil Selah Burton), ? co

Pvt refused a pens as srvd in Regt not on Contl Estab. Ref No 31 Doc Jan 6 1831 O S Libry. Rept by Blanche Rings Col O.

BURTON, JOSHUA, Pickaway co

Pvt Md Contl. Enl in Md first yr of Rev. Dischrgd at Ft Pitt Pa 1779. Was b Oct 24 1746. Pens appl Pickaway co O Aug 1821. Ref S 42111 Md Pa and Va. Rept by State D A R.

BURWELL, JOHNATHAN, ? co

Pvt refused a pens as srvd in a Regt not on Contl Estab. Ref No 31 Doc Jan 6 1831 O S Libry. Rept by Blanche Rings.

BURWELL, ZACHARIAH, Pickaway co

Srvd as pvt in Capt Andrew Billings Co Col James Clinton 3rd N Y Regt. Was in Battle of St Johns and Canada. Was dischrgd Jan 1776; returned home to Elizabethtown; enl 1776 in Capt Joseph Meeker's Co Col Sterlings 1st N J Regt. Was dischrgd Dec 1776 at Elizabethtown N J. Enl Aug 1777 in Capt Cooper Co Col DuPois N Y Regt. Was b July 1753; d July 19 1835; grave not located. Was allowed a pens Apr 8 1823 whl living in Pickaway co O. Aft Rev servd under Gen Wayne in campaign against Indians. Ref S 42109 N Y or N J. Nathan Perry chpt repts "Burwell ——" listed p 142 in Hist of North Central O by Wm Duff as a Rev soldr bur McFall cem Ashland co O. Rept by Pickaway Plains chpt.

BUSH, PHILIP, Mahoning co

Pvt. Ser 5 Vol 8 p 24 Pa Arch. Capt John Arndt's Co 1776. Mar Maud; one son was John. Soldr d Green. Was among early settlers. Ref Hist Trumbull and Mahoning co Vol 2 p 196-7; Hist Mahoning co p 208 Sanderson; Deed bk P from Philip and Maud Bush. Rept by Mahoning chpt.

BUSHNELL, ANDREW, ? co

2nd Lieut. Listed in invalid pensrs of U S belonging to Ohio pd at Chillicothe; annual allowance $45.00. Ref p 172 Pensr of 1818. Cop by Jane Dailey.

BUSHONG, JACOB, Columbiana co

Pens no 4268. Pvt Va 18 mos. Enl in 1780. Pensd 11-15-1818 Columbiana co O. Was æ 64 in 1818. Dropped fr Pens Roll May 1 1820. Ref Va S 9297. Rept by State D A R and Wilma Molsberry.

BUTLER, ASAPH, Clark co

Pvt N H Cont. Enl Claramont N H Mar 1778. Srvd 5 yrs. Was b 1752. Mar Jane McFarland Dec 1790; daus Amanda; Lucinda; Sally; Fanny; sons Anson; Charles; Ira; Joel; Wm McGuire ?; Levi; Jno; Benjamin; Charles. Soldr d 9-x-1825 Springfield. Soldr appl for pens Clark co O May 29 1819. Ref Act Cong 1818 (Col O) æ 63; W 21716; B L Wt 18378-160-55. N C. Rept by State D A R.

BUTLER, DAVID, Licking co

Corp. Enl as pvt May 10 1775 Middletown under Major Jonathan Meigs —— Dec 30 1775 to Aug 19 1776 in Co of Lieut Bidwell. Made Corp Apr 5 1781. Was b in Conn 1764 (Upper Houses); son of George Butler (1st wf Ann Plum 4-10-1755; 2nd wf Desire Dimmick). Mar Olive Henry 1792 (b Mass 1777 d Ohio 1830). Chldr: Leverett 1793; Ann 1796; Henry 1800; Charles 1804 d Aug 9 1886. Soldr d nr Granville O Apr 5 1815; bur old burying ground Granville O N W corner just inside nr the gate. Inscript on mrkr "David Butler d Apr 5 1815 æ 51" 1905 and now badly chipped. Copied from records. Grave not mrkd by D A R. Ref Paymaster Records Conn Minutes Rev War p 61. Was a charter member Masonic Order Granville O co Deeds. David Butler was son of 2nd wf. Rept by Luella B Faut Newark O Public Library. Accepting this information Mrs O D Dailey.

BUTLER, JOHN, Williams co

Pvt 2nd Regt Pa Line. Soldr Williams co 11-22-1830. Ref Pa Arch Vol 23 p 3. Rept by Mary Steinmetz Reading Pa.

BUTLER, STEPHEN, ? co

A pensr under act of 1818 but taken fr Rolls Act of 1820 as not considered in indigent circumstances accd to the act. Ref Doc 31 Jan 7 1831 O S Libry. Rept by Blanche Rings Col O. Cf same p 62 Vol 1 O Roster Rev Soldr J D.

BUTLER, WILLIAM, Gallia co

Pvt Rev Army. Mar Tasy —— (mentioned in Will); chldr (mentioned in Will Record C p 545) John; Isaac; Symmes; Mary Glassburn; William Henry Jr; Ealy; Thomas G. Soldr probably d June 1830; bur Huntington twp Gallia co O. Pens in Gallia co Act of June 1795. Will dated Feb 13 1830 probated July 1 1830. He gave a tract of land called "Soldrs rite of land" to his sons John; Isaac and Symmes. No records of pens at D C. Rept by French Colony chpt.

BUTTERFIELD, JAMES, Franklin co

In Columbus Gazette issue of Apr 25 1819 is the following: John R Parish says "I have recd from the War dept a certficate for Moses Rugg that he is placed on the pension list. The application of James Butterfield and James Crawford are rejected." Rept and cop by Blanche Rings.

BYERS (also spelled Boyers), WILLIAM, Darke co

Pvt Va Milit. Enl 1781 Va Milit. Srvd 7 mos and 15 das. Was b July 1764. Abt 2 yrs aft war he movd to Montgomery co Va and resided abt 10 yrs; movd to Powel Valley Va and 8 or 9 yrs later he movd to Gallia co O. 2 yrs later movd to Ross co and resided abt 2 yrs and movd to Phoebe co O (?) and resided abt 25 yrs from there to Darke co O whr appl for pens 11-18-1833. Ref Va S 8130. Rept by State D A R.

BYRNE, JOHN, Miami co

Pvt Pa St Trps. Enl Spring of 1776 and for 4 mos. Was b May 27 1753 Philadelphia Pa. Movd from Pa to Miami co O and res there since. Pens appl Sept 25 1832 Miami co O. Ref Pa S 2408. Rept by State D A R.

CACKLER, CHRISTIAN, Portage co

Pvt in Capt Wm Rippey's Co Col Irvin's Pa Reg in Battle of Three Rivers. Pensd 1818 living in Portage co Mar Jan 29 1780; died Sept 28 1830. Buried in small family lot in Streetsboro twp. A gr-son age 94 now living (1830) 123 Brady St Kent O. Ref Aaron Olmstead chpt W H Farley of Boise Idaho S A R is a descendant.

CAILES, JOHN, Preble co

Pvt in Va Milit; pensd Dec 27 1833 in Preble co; served 10 mos. Drafted from Augusta co Va. Has lived in Preble co for last 3 yrs. Previously lived in Nicholas co Va. Appld for pens Preble co O Nov 19 1833 lived in Wash twp. Ref S 8165 Va. State D A R chpt.

CALDWELL, HUGH, Licking co

Servd in Pa line. Had ten chldr. D shortly aft 1814 whn he came from Pa. Ref Brister's Hist Licking co Vol 2 p 876. Rept by Hetuck chpt.

CALDWELL, JAMES, Mahoning co

Pvt. Many enlistments. Pa Arch Ser 2 vol 13 p 30. B Mch 20 1760. Mar Esther Pierce Oct 11 1786 ?. Chldr were: Betsey b 1790; James b 1791; Margaret b 1802; Lovina b 1804; Fidelia b 1807 mar Horace Rowland. Soldr d Youngstown. Ref Hist Trumbull & Mahoning Cos Vol 2 p 124 Upper Ohio Valley p 377 Mahoning chpt.

CALDWELL, WILLIAM, Columbiana co

Pensr living in Wash co N Y in 1819 Ranger Westmoreland co Pa Lt Pa Line. B 1728; d June 20 1820 in 82nd yr (Some discrepancy); bur Westfield Cem Columbiana co. Ref Baldwin's Records. Pa Arch Vol 3 XXIII p 178, 224, 239, 324, 329, 472, 816. Rept by Mrs Wilma M Molsberry Youngstown O.

CALHOUN, THOMAS, Jefferson co

Pvt in Westmoreland Milit; Pa Arch 5th Ser Vol 4 p 737 Same ser p 453 listed as receiving Depreciation Pay. Certificate no 2687. B 1735; d Jan 17 1823. Bur in an abandoned cem at East Springfield. Stone reads "In memory of Thomas Calhoun who departed this life Jan 17 A D 1823 in the 88th yr of his age." The stones no doubt placed by son Adley. A flag on the grave was placed by Dr John C Calhoun of Pittsburg Pa. Was a farmer in Rostraver twp Westmoreland co Pa first as renter then owner; after death of wife and daughter made his home with son Adley of Jefferson co O. There he d. Data fr Dr Calhoun.

CALL, ASA, Lake co

Enl 1778 in Capt Jos Taylor's Co Col Timothy Bedel's N H Regt. B 1752 in N H; mar 1782 Phebe White; had a dau Eunice who mar Horace Tubbs. D 1806 nr Painesville O. D A R No 106154 Vol 107 D A R.

CALLAHAN, DENNIS, Adams co

Served in Maryland Cont 5th Regt 9 mo; b 1748; pensd 1820 Adams co. Ref Evans & Stivers Hist of Adams co p 330; Rept by Meryl B Markley; S 42118 Md. Rept by State D A R.

CALLAHAN, JAMES, Mahoning co

Pvt; Ser 5 vol 3 p 721 Pa Arch. Was son of John and Eleanor Callahan; mar Martha ———. D abt 1840 Green twp. Ref Hist Mahoning co p 602; Sanderson's List of Henry R Baldwin S A R. Rept by Mahoning chpt.

CALLAHAN, WILLIAM, Mahoning co

Pvt. Pa Arch Ser 5 Vol 4 p 281, 22, 647. Chldr were: Elias; Nathan; Elizabeth; Matilda; Nancy; Maria; Rachel; Keziah. Soldr d abt 1842. Came fr Redstone Pa with brothers Jeremiah, James and Jesse in 1804. Ref Hist of Mahoning co p 967; Sanderson's Hist of Columbiana co Green twp; Will Book II p 347 Columbiana co. Rept by D A R and Mahoning chpt.

CAMP, DR JESSE, Athens co

Surgeon Contl Line fr Conn; wounded at Bemis Hgts; b Conn; d 1830 nr Albany, Athens co O; bur in orchard on his farm; autobiography by a grson Horace Wilson; proven S A R recd rept by Wm Pettit.

CAMP, JOHN, Richland co

Pvt Pa Contl. Enl Pa. Dischrg Trenton N J. Appld for pens Stark co Ohio June 4 1818. Served 4 yrs. B 1755. Named 3 children; George; Elizabeth Arnett. Rec'd arrears of pens from Sept 1743 (wrong). Appld for pens Richland co Sept 7 1832. Livd in Richland co 1833 age 79. Ref Pa Arch Vol 23 p 63. S 2418 Pa. Rept by State D A R.

CAMPBELL, CHARLES, Belmont co

Ref 5th Ser V 4 p 226 Pa Arch; b York co Pa; mar Abbie Rankin. Ref S A R 52201. Rept by Wm Pettit.

CAMPBELL, FRANCIS, Seneca co

Pa. Contl in Col Wm Irvine's Regt Capt Wm Rippey from Shippensburg Pa. D in Cumberland co Pa Oct 2 1834. Copied by Jane Dailey at Nat Regstr Gen office.

CAMPBELL, JOHN, ? co

Pvt. Refused a pens as served in a Regt not a Contl Estab. Ref Doc No. 31 Jan 6 1831 O S Library. Rept by Blanche Rings Cols O.

CAMPBELL, JOHN, Montgomery co

Lancaster Co 5th Ser Pa Arch Vol 2 p 33 with Col Miles' riflemen, Capt John Marshal 1776. Was fifer Vol 7 p 643 8th class Capt Whithill. Bur at Pyrmont Perry twp. B 1764; d 1842. Rept by Wm Pettit.

CAMPBELL, JOHN, Miami co

Pvt Pa Milita part time and part time Sergt. Drafted in to service July 1777 in Pa. B Apr 1757 in Ireland. Mar June 10 1816 Mary Bigger. D July 4 1838, Piqua O. Appld for pens May 2 1833 in Miami co O. Ref W 9772 B L Wt 32235-160-55. Emigrated to the U S from Ireland 1773 and was residing in Cumberland co Pa at the time of his first enlistment. He resided here until 1814 and then moved to Miami co O. Rept by State D A R.

CAMPBELL, JOHN, Muskingum co

Pvt V Contl Troops. Enl May 1777. Srvd 4 yrs. Pensr 1819 Muskingum co. B 1752; mar Eleanor (æ) 45; chldr: dau Polly age 15 at time of pens. Pensr 1840 æ 79 living in Zanesville O. Ref S 42640 Va. Rept by State D A R.

CAMPBELL, JOHN, Preble co

Pvt Va State Troops. Enl June 1778 Bedford co Va. Ser 6 mos 12 days. B 1761 Bedford co. Mar Sarah Vance Dec 1796. Chldr were: Samuel; Jane; Elizabeth; Arch; Mary; James; Ansen; Andrew; Robert; Joshua; Alexander and Nancy. He d Mch 4 1847 in Preble co. Since Rev he lived in Knox co Tenn and from there came to Preble co. Appld for pens Preble co Sept 21 1832 res Jackson twp where he was a pens and in 1840 census. Ref W 1713; B L Wt 26821-160-55; William's Bros Hist of Preble co. Rept by State D A R.

CAMPBELL, JONATHAN, Hamilton co

Listed p 265 "Va Mil in Rev" living in Hamilton co æ 77. Cop by Jane Dailey.

CAMPBELL, JOSHUA, Lorain co

Enl 1778 Brimfield Mass. Served 8 mos. Pensd 1840 Russia twp Lorain co age 78. B Mch 8 1762 Cumberland R I. Mar Hannah Sheperd Dec 5 1793 Rutland co Vt. Chldr: Alpha; Miranda; Jonathan; Ralph; Orin; James; Philena; Ebenezer; Alice M; and Stephen; Artemas; Osinia; and Lawrence Simpson Campbell .Family record submitted by widow. Appld for pens Medina co O Jan 13 1834 res of Wadsworth O; widow apld for pens at Lorain co O May 3 1851 age 80 yrs. Ref W 6622 B L Wt 31 441-160-55; B L Wt 36, 659-160-55 Mass. Rept by State D A R and Nathan Perry chpt.

CAMPBELL, OBADIAH, Columbiana co

Rev war veteran; record not yet found; b 1752; d 5-18-1822 æ 70; Estate settld 1822 Center twp Columbiana co; Ref Ohio Patriot. Rept by Wilma Molsberry.

CAMPBELL, SAMUEL, Gallia co

Pens No 12939; pvt Chester co Pa. Vol Nov 1777 Capt Hector McNeal's co Lt Col John Bartholomew's Battl of Penn Mil. B 1761 Chester co Pa. Was the son of Samuel Campbell (also a Rev Soldr). Mar Sarah Coulter abt 1781; bur Hulbert Cem. Sarah Coulter was b 1761, d Mch 12 1834. Chldr were: John; James, 3rd son; Rev Samuel; Elisha; Elijah; Nancy (Graham Vol 1 p '95). D Mch 8 1841 Gallia co. Bur in Perry twp. Ref Mrs C P Nagley (Mary Campbell) Delaware O; also Mr Jack Nida Columbus O S A R No 50112. French Colony chpt Gallipolis O.

CAMPBELL, WILLIAM, Meigs co

Sept 25 1832 appeared Wm Campbell in Yates co N Y a resident of Benton co 73 yrs old. B in Orange co N Y 1759. (His father killed in French War). He resided in Ulster co during the Rev War. In 1776 he was called out in the milit of Orange co a pvt under Capt Tuttle sent to Clarkstown and was there dischrgd. He removed from Orange co to Benton co 25 yrs ago. Only survivor Sarah Green Campbell did not receive his pens in Sept 1834 on account of being transfered to Meigs co O. He d early in 1835. Rept by D A R chpt Patterson N J.

CAMPBELL, WILLIAM, Seneca co

Pvt in Pa Militia. Pens no 22482. Pensd Mch 12 1834 while living in Seneca co. Served more than two yrs as pvt. B 1762 in Shippinsburg Pa. Mar Sarah ——. Soldr d Apr 13 1833 Seneca co. Ref S 3130 Pa. Rept by State D A R.

CAMPBELL, WILLIAM, Hamilton co

Pvt Pa Contl; pensd 1819 Hamilton co Ohio. Served 1 yr. Enl York co Pa Mch 1776. B 1750. Appld for pens Hamilton co May 19 1818. Ref S 42177 Pa. Rept by State D A R.

CAMPBELL WILLIAM, Wayne co

Pvt Pa Militia pensr Wayne co O. Served 1 yr. Enl 1776 in Westmoreland co. Lived in Westm and Huntingdon cos Pa for 36 yrs. Aft War lived in Westm co 17 yrs.

Has lived in Wayne and Stark cos Ohio and now lives in Wayne co. B 1761 in Cumberland co Pa. Mar 1792 Martha Beard; chldr: Mary; Jane; Floranda; Martha; Peggy; James; Wm; M C; Hannah; and Sarah. (Record from family bible). D 1836 Mary made appl for pens in Wayne co O July 23 1852. Stated that she was a daughter; named other heirs. He is bur on R R ground that was formerly the Willford farm about a mile S W of Orville accd to data from W H Long Orville O who is 85 yrs old. Appld for pens in Wayne co Feb 22 1834 Martha Campbell widow d Dec 7 1847. Ref R 1638 Pa.

CANADY, MEREDITH, Scioto co

Exec Doc 37 refused a pens as servd less than 6 mo. Rept by Wm Pettit.

CANFIELD, DANIEL, Crawford co

Pvt in N Y Contl; pensr in 1828 Crawford co O. B 1757; d Oct 1832. Mar Dec 1778 Elizabeth; chldr were: Nathan; Mary; Titus; Zachariah; Sarah; Daniel; Amos; Moses; Pedediah; Henry; and Margaret. Wid appld for pens Jennings co Ind Aug 1841. He had appld Orange co N Y for pens Randolph co Va June 24 1828 and in Crawford co 1828. Rept by State D A R.

CANTER, JOHN, Scioto co

Pvt in Va lines. Pensr Aug 1826 Jackson co Ohio. Was in Co of Capt Finley Col Dask Reg Va line for 2 yrs. B 1750 mentions wife about 60 (in 1824 appl); daughter Mary 15; Hiram 27; John 39; Henry 26; James 30; Daniel 23; all living abroad and not able to help him. Was living as late as June 21 1841 Census of 1840 shows was a pensr in Madison twp Scioto co æ 94. S 42642. Rept by State D A R.

CAPPS, DEMPSEY, Fulton co

D in Fulton co O in 1839. McEnder Capps mentioned Vol 1 p 306 of Reighard's History is thought to have been son of Dempsey Capps. Ref Wauseon chpt by Miss Read and Mrs Maddox. Pensd 1825 in Highland co O for service as pvt in N Car line. B 1760 in N Car. Mar 1784 Sarah Overman. One daughter Rhoda mar Elijah Harbour 1807. D 1839 Fulton co. Ref D A R Lineage Vol 107 No 106611. Rept by Mrs Dailey.

CARDER, SANFORD, Fayette co

Enl Sept 1780 resident of Hampshire co Va; served 6 mos as pvt in Capt Dan'l Richardson's Va Co. Enlisted Apr 1781; served 18 mos in Capt Gunn's Co Col Anthony White's Regt of Cont'l Dragoons. B Sept 16 1760 Culpeper Va. Mar 1st Nancy Hoffman 1789 Hampshire Va. Chldr: Rebecca mar —— Hoover; Mary mar Isaac Cooper; Nancy mar Jacob Thompson; Armistead; Elizabeth mar Sam'l Herrod; Phebe mar —— Herrod; Sanford mar 1st Susan Pendergraf; Sarah mar —— McGowan; Peter mar Catherine Mouser; Charith mar Jacob Power. Soldr d Aug 7 1845 Union twp Fayette co. In 1794 moved to Bourbon co Ky from Va and in 1800 moved to Fayette co O where he was pensd in 1832. Ref Mrs C S Passmore of Butte Mont. By Washington C H chpt.

CARMICHAEL, JOHN, Monroe co

Pvt in Va Line. Enl in 1775 and served till almost close of war. Pensd 1840 Franklin twp Monroe co. Was 96 in 1838 "wife lately deceased." He then came to Ohio to res with his son (appl Nov 22 1833). Had son John. Res Monroe co Dec 22 1831. Ref S 26989 Pa. Rept by State D A R.

CARMODY, JOHN, Columbiana co

Pvt in Pa State troops Robinson's Rangers Northumberland Co Pa Serg Capt Thos Kemplin's Co of Rangers. B York co Pa was 83 in 1832. In receipt of certificate of pay signs name as John Carmedy and dates it June 24 1784 as of Robinsons Rangers. Pa Arch 3 XXIII p 584 Ser 5 Vol IV p 361 Vol 8 687. Census 1840 Pa Sea Service S 2108 Pens Dept. Rept by State D A R.

CARNAGEY, WILLIAM, Columbiana co

Pvt Mt Bethel Co Col Jacob Stroud's Batt Northampton Co Pa Milit. Out in service in summer of 1776. Pvt Milit Wash Co Pa. B 1754. Altho d in Liverpool twp is thot to be buried in Pa. Came from Wash co Pa. Living 1840 a pens in Ohio aged 86 own home. Ref Henry Baldwin's Records Pa Arch Ser 5 Vol VIII p 537; 5 IV p 394. Census of Pensr 1841. Rept by Mrs Wilma M Molsberry Youngstown O.

CARNS, ZOPHAR, Trumbull co

Also spelled Karns; Karnes; Carnes. Capt Western Battl Morris Co N J of Heard's Brigade June 14 1776. Also Lieut in Contl Army. Was a resident of Warren co in 1802 and d before 1810. His wife Jemima was possibly his second. Grave not located. Ref Officers and Men of N J in Rev p 394. Rept by Mary Chesney chpt.

CARNS, JOHN, Butler co

Pvt N J Contl. Enl July 1 1780 Basking Ridge Som Co.

CARP, SAMUEL, Licking co

Ref Vol 103 D A R Lin No 102897. Cop by Jane Dailey.

CARPENTER, DAVID, Huron co

Listed pp 142 & 143 in "Hist of North Central Ohio" by Wm A Duff as Rev soldier bur Houfstatter Cem Ripley twp or in New Haven Huron co O. Rept by Nathan Perry chpt.

CARPENTER, JOHN, Jefferson co

John Carpenter was one of Washington's servants in 1753 when he made his trip of remonstrance to the French Forts. He was a Va rifleman in Braddock's War and was made captain of one of the garrisons along the Va border by Washington. About 1780 Carpenter and his family came from the eastern side of the Ohio and settled in the bottom land near where Warrenton now is. The following summer he and his neighbors erected a log house which was known afterwards as Carpenter's Fort. This was the first fortification of this kind erected within the boundaries of Jefferson co. Carpenter took part in Crawford's retreat and also in St Clairs expedition in 1791. Ref Hist of Upper Ohio Valley Vol 2 p 32; Hist of Belmont co p 452; Hist of the Valley by Kercheval p 290.

CARR, JOHN, Mahoning co

Pvt 5th Class Washington co Mil. Pa Arch Ser 6 Vol 2 p 174; Ser 5 Vol 6 pp 527, 547. D in Green twp Mahoning co. Came in 1804 from Adams co Pa with Peter Weikert. Ref Hist Trumbull & Mahoning cos Vol 2 p 190; Hist of Mahoning co 208; Hist of North Central Ohio by Wm A Duff p 142 lists one John Carr as Rev Sold in Ashland co. Rept by Nathan Perry chpt.

CARR, JOSEPH, Mahoning co

Pvt Va Men p 59. Mar Jane ——; mar 2nd Dr Eve Brainard. Had son William mar Jane ——; D before 1826 in Youngstown O. Ref Tax List early settlers 1803; Deed Bk F p 490 Joseph Carr heirs 1831; Hist Trumbull & Mahoning cos Vol 1 p 48. Rept by Mahoning chpt.

CARREL, GEORGE, Washington co

Pvt Md Contl. Pensr 1819 Washington co O. Servd 3 yrs. Enl Dec 6 1776 Phila Pa in appl states had wife and 2 chldr. Appld for pens Wash co May 5 1818 and 1821 res in Waterford twp. Ref S 42138 Md. Rept by State D A R.

CARROLL, WILLIAM, Gallia co

Pvt. Refused a pens as served in a Reg not on Contl Estab. Doc No 31 Jan 6 1831 Ohio State Lib. Rept by Blanche Rings. Name listed as pvt in Md troops. Pensr 1832 in Gallia co.

CARSON, SAMUEL, Licking co

Pvt 7 yrs. Enl aft Battle of Bunker Hill 1775 in Capt James Taylors Co at Fogg's Manor Pa 4th Reg com by Col Anthony Wayne. Joined co on Long Island. Went to Albany to Ticonderoga for nearly 2 yrs. Re-enl in Co of Capt Thos Bond 5th Reg Pa for 3 yrs aft war. Discharged at Phil. D in Licking co O Nov 5 1830. Appld for pens Apr 28 1818. Pens No S 42113; B L Wt 9086-100 issued Mch 31 1790. Rept by State D A R. Hetuck chpt sends d Nov 3 1830.

CARTER, ARNOLD, Holmes co

Pvt Va Mil; served 6 mos. Pensr Holmes co 1832. Enl in Aug or Sept 1778 in the Milit Rockingham twp Rockingham co where he resided at the time. Was 74 in 1833. Appld for pens in Holmes co Mch 6 1833. Rept by State D A R.

CARTER, DANIEL C, Ross co

Pvt Invalid Reg; pensr of U S belonging to Ohio. Paid at Chillicothe $48 annually; pensr 1818. Cop by Jane Dailey.

CARTER, JASON, Geauga co

Troy. Ref 5th Rept of N S D A R p 387. Grave located by New Connecticut Chpt Painesville.

CARTER, JOHN, Preble co

Pensd in Preble co on Pens Rolls; also listed page 266 "Va Militia in Rev" as living in Preble co. J D.

CARTER, UZZIAL (Usial), Warren co

Pvt in Militia under Col Seeley. Pensr Sept 17 1833 Warren co age 70. Enlisted Essex co N J. B Morris co N J 1764. Appld for pens 1832 age 68 Act of June 7 1832. Aft the Rev lived in Luzerne co Pa till came to Ohio. Ref S 16069. Cop by State D A R.

CARTWRIGHT, DAVID, Huron co

4th Rept N S D A R p 299. In 1900 a gr grand-daughter. Mrs C E Humer was living at Perrysburg Ohio. Rept by Mrs Winnagle Mary Chesney chpt.

CARTWRIGHT, SOLOMON, Huron co

Served in N J Trps from Mch 1st 1776 1 mo in Capt Jos Harkers Co Col Ephraim Martins Regt. Served in various Cos to 1781. Livd in Wantage N J. Mar Hannah Ayres 1774; chldr: Elizabeth; Hannah; William; Rachel; Osey; Phebe; 2 sons and one dau not listed. D in Peru twp Huron co 1847. Rept by State D A R.

CARY, CALVIN, Madison co

Was b 1739 Morris co N J; son of Ezra and Mary Holman Cary; movd to west Pa; thence to O in 1801; had a son Calvin and 3 dau; one Hannah b 1775 mar Stephen Winget. Service: (Certif fr Pa) pvt in James Craven Co Washington co Pa Milit. (P 201 V 2 Pa Arch S 6). Livd in Plain City O; laid out Caryville, Champaign co. Recd fr Mrs R J Warner, Osborn O. (Authenticity of service not yet investigated Apr 1936. Jane Dailey).

CARY, CHRISTOPHER, ? co

Pvt. Refused a pens as served in a Reg not on Contl Estab. Ref No 31 Doc Jan 6 1831 Ohio State Lb by Blanche Rings.

CARY, LUTHER, ? co

30th Report N S D A R p 62. B 1759; d Oct 8 1830 in O. Cop by Nathan Perry chpt.

CASE, GEORGE, Delaware co

Pvt Conn Militia. Enl June 1776 in Conn. State Trps. Pensr Delaware co 1833. Served 12 mos. B Mch 4 1759 Simsbury Conn. D Feb 19 1834. Left Conn in 1806 and came to Delaware co. Appld for pens Nov 12, 1833. Ref S 3115. Rept by State D A R. Delaware chpt repts bur in field East of Powell O.

CASE, ISRAEL, Franklin co

Served from Simsbury Conn in Capt Jonathan Humphries Co Col. Samuel Mc-Clellan Reg which marched to Providence 1777; b Simsbury Conn Nov 11 1757; par: Isaac and Bathsheba (Humphries) Case; mar Joanna Case (dau of Job and Joanna (Wilcox) Case) on Mch 12 1778; chldr: Joanna mar Butler Andrews; Israel Putnam mar Laurinda ——; Abiel b 1784; Violet mar Samuel Beach Jr; Oren mar Mira Andrews; Emily mar William Webster Jr; Esther; Ursula mar Alpheus Bigelow; Laura b 1799; and Aseneth b 1802; soldr d from obit "Capt Israel Case died at Worthington formerly of Simsbury Conn. A soldier of the Revolution" Iss of Apr 30 1818; grave has not been found nor that of his wife. Ref Old North West Quarterly Vol 7 p 49; D A R Lin 56 p 38 No 55079 (says he d 1815 but will is dated 1815 and prob 1818); Will Bk A; Obit from newspapers of above date. Sent by Blanche Rings.

CASEY, JACOB, Franklin co

Pvt Va Contl. Pensr 1819 Franklin co Ohio. Enl May 1776 in Va State Troops and again in the Cavalry of Va. Was 67 yrs in 1832. Wife aged about 60 in 1822. Had one son age 20; one daughter age 30 and a daughter aged about 24 in 1832. Appld for pens continuance in Franklin co July 3 1822. Contl Pa Va S 42 114. Rept by State D A R.

CASSIDY, GEORGE, ? co

Pvt Invalid pensr of U S belonging to Ohio. Paid at Chillicothe $96 annually. Copied from p 172 pensr 1818. S of R Lib Los A Cal by Jane Dailey.

CASTEEL, ZADOC, Monroe co

Exec Doc 37 yr 1852 good for pens cl under Act 1838. Wm Pettit.

CASTLE, JOEL, Meigs co

Pvt Conn Contl pensr in Meigs co 1834. Appld Aug 1 1832. B Jan 1 1750 Waterbury Conn. Ref S 8143 by Bertha B Chase. Return Jonathan Meigs chpt.

CASTLEMAN, HENRY SR, Carroll co

Died at his res in Harrison twp Carroll co O Feb 26 1845 in his 92 yr was one of the Revolutionary fathers who fought and bled in defense of his country's liberty. (Iss of Mch 20 1845 Weekly State Journal) "Carroll Free Press" Cop by Blanche Rings.

CASTOR, NOAH, Ashland co

Listed page 142 in "Hist of North Central Ohio" by Wm A Duff as a Rev Soldier. Rept by Nathan Perry Chpt.

CAUGHEY, JOHN, Preble co

Pvt enl Cumberland co Pa Jan 1776 Capt Adams and McDonalds Co Col William Irwins Pa Regt. Dischgd Feb 1777. Pvt 6th Class Capt William Moores Co 2nd Bttl Cumberland co Milit Ensign Sept 22 1781 in Capt John Neepers Co 6th Battl Lancaster co Milit Ensign Capt Ramseys Lancaster Milit 1781. Allowed pens on Appl June 29 1819 while res in Nicholas co Ky. Certif 16725 issued Apr 1820. Came to O 1821; b in Pa 1747. Soldr d Preble co 1833. Rept by Commodore Preble chpt.

CENTER, JONATHAN, Franklin co

Pvt Pa Contl. Pensr 1819 July 24 Franklin co 1820 appl for pens transfer to Fairfield co served Pa Line for 3 yrs. B 1744 Oct 18. Wf was 74 in 1820. Had one dau named Lucy Book living with them. Appd for pens Fairfield Co Oct 23 1820 now res of Fairfield co. Trnsfrd to Franklin co Apr 11 1818 res of Franklin co Ohio. Ref S 42119 Contl Penn. Rept by Mary Chesney and Mahoning chpts.

CHADWICK, LEVI, Knox co

Pvt N J Contl. Pensd Knox co 1824. Enl in Morris co N J in Oct or Nov 1775. Ae 71 yrs in Aug 2 1823. Mar Sarah ——. Had Sally æ 21 yrs in 1824. At age of 88, was living in Monroe twp Knox co. (census 1840). Ohio pens Roll 1835 S 42643 B L Wt 716-100. Rept by State D A R.

CHALMERS, ANDREW, Clermont co

Pvt Pa Contl. Pensr 1824 Clermont co. Enl Westmoreland co 1776. Dischrgd at Pittsburg 1783. Served 7 yrs. B 1754. Mar Alice —— June 20 1785. Chldr: Isaac and James; Rebecca; and Hannah. Appld for pens Clermont co June 5 1818. Wid appld aft his death in Nov 25 1833. Ref W 4152 Pa. Rept by State D A R.

CHAMBERLAIN, FREEGIFT, Licking co

Pvt pensd Mch 28 1833. B 1757. Rept by Hetuck chpt. Pa State Troops served 6 mos 23 days as pvt Indian spy for 3 mos 14 days. Enl Sept 1776. Resided in Wash co Pa during the war. B Oct 20 1758. Appld for pens in Licking co O Oct 29 1832. Ref S 151. Rept by State D A R.

CHAMBERLAND, JUDAH, Logan co

Pvt in Capt Spencer's Co Col Fayne Regt N Y for 6 mos. At time of enlistment resided in Albany co N Y in Spencertown 30 miles S E of Albany. B Apr 21 1761 in Colchester twp Hartford co. Married Phebe Mead about Feb 15 1801 Shenango co N Y. "Raised a large family." D at Logan co O abt May 29 1847. 1806 came to Hamilton co O 1 yr. then to Clark co O lived till 1834; thence to Logan co while a resident of Union Logan co O (late res of Harmony Clark co) as "better known in Clark co" his papers say. Widow Phebe appl in Logan co for bounty land June 2 1855. Ref S 9314. Cop by Jane Dailey.

CHAMBERLAIN, STOUT, Columbiana co

Pvt Pa State Troops. Pens granted Jan 3 1833 aged 77 res. Columbiana co O. Was in Capt Peter Kidd's co Militia Wash co Pa. B May 1 1758 in N J as by his papers. Enl in Washington co Pa. June 20 1777 and came to Columbiana co abt 1817. Ref Henry Baldwin's Records Pa Arch Ser 3 Vol 23 p 584; Ser 6 Vol 2 p 153-5. Vol 4 p 393. S 2119 Pa Pens Dept Wash D. C. Rept by State D A R.

CHAMBERLAND, WILLIAM, Columbiana co

Pvt and ensign; served from Birmingham twp West Chester co Pa.. Pa Arch 5th Ser Vol 5 pp 469, 494, 495, 557, 585. p 495 Apr 21 1783. A return of the male inhabitants of the twp of Birmingham between the ages of 18 and 23. Entered service June 27 1777; returned Apr 21 1783. B Birmingham twp Chester co Pa 1760 to 1765. Parents were Robert Chamberland and Ann Painter. Second wife was Jane Darlington. Chldr were: Isaac by 1st wife; Samuel; Binsh; Mary; Orpha mar Richard Baker; Robert; Aaron and Joseph. D between June 28 1836 and Nov 16 1836 at East Fairfield Columbiana co. Member of a prominent Quaker family of Chester co Pa but aft the death of his 2nd wife 1818 he followed his elder sons to Ohio bringing the rest of his family buying and also receiving by patent from the U S govt a vast tract of land in Columbiana co. Most of which he deeded to his children on June 28 1836. His death occurred soon after this date and on Nov 16 1836 his sons Robert and Samuel were appointed Adms of the balance of his estate. At the final settlement of same on Aug 16 1845 all his children signed off. He made no will. Ref Columbiana co Hist pp 130-131-132; court records of deeds Vol 5 p 536; vol 8 174; vol 21 p 46; vol 24 p 404; vol 24 p 451, 479, 480; vol 25 p 121 Probate Court Records; Common Pleas Rec. Rept by Etta M Kyle Youngstown O. Late rept comes fr Mrs R S Baker 148 Willis Ave Youngstown O (to the rept of Etta Kyle) states: he mar for his second wf Ann Beale, which fact is found in court records (no page ref given). She suggests that Jane Darlington ment may have been a first wf. Authenticity for each statement open for proof. (J D).

CHAMBERS, JOSEPH, Jefferson co

Serg in Pa Milita. Served 6 mos; was pensr Jefferson co 1833. B Oct 4 1751. Enl May 1776; then res Derry twp Lancaster co Pa. In 1780 removed from Lan co to Monongahela R about 20 miles above Pittsburg where he lived until last 27 yrs during which time he resided in Jefferson co O. Appl for pens Jefferson co May 13 1833 Res Crosswick twp. Ref S 2120 Pa. Rept by State D A R.

CHAMBERS, WILLIAM, Belmont co

Pvt Conn Line. Served 3 yrs under Capt Watson co; Col Swift Regt. Pensd 1818 age 78. Ref S 42644. Cop by Jane Dailey.

CHAMP, WILLIAM, Pickaway co

Pvt Vir Contl; enlisted at Paddytown So Branch Potomac Va Feb 1778 Pvt Capt John Savage's Co. Col Abraham Hite's Regt guarded prisoners at Winchester Va. Also in Capt Andrew Wallace's Co Col Abraham Buford's Regt. In 1820 he referred to wife age 66 but did not give her name or marriage. Mentions a daughter Elizabeth age 17 in 1820. He was b in 1754. Pens papers S 42120 Penn allowed July 14 1819 age 65 yrs and lived in Pickaway co. Rept by Pickaway Plains chpt.

CHANCE, JOHN, Clark co ?

Servd fr Md; b Ellicott Cy Md abt 1761; mar Martha Watkins; came to Catawba Clark co O abt 1821; both d of fever abt 1824 and bur one grave in Old Vernon cem; data fr Dr P S Chance London O to Urbana chpt.

CHANCE, JAMES, ? co

Servd in Battl Bladensburg; b Ellicott Cy Md; bro of John a Rev Soldr (above). Rept by Urbana chpt.

CHANDLER, JOSEPH, ? co

Pvt. Refused a pens as deserted the service. Ref Doc 31 Jan 6 1831. Rept by Blanche Rings.

CHANDLER, JOSEPH, Washington co

Pvt Conn Contl. Pensd Oct 16 1819 in Washington co O. Servd 1 yr & 5 mos. B Sept 10 1753. In appl speaks of wife; had dau Sally age 30. Had son Henry æ 21 in appl of 1820; had son Hiram res Jersey co Ill 1842. Enl in Conn 1776. Appld for pens Wash co Apr 20 1818 res of Wooster twp. Appld for pens at Madison co Ill July 7 1842 then a res of Jersey co Ill where he may have d. Ref S 35206 Conn. Rept by State D A R.

CHANDLER, ZEBULON, Washington co

Pvt Capt Samuel Canfield's Co Col Benj Bellow's Regt N H Mil under command of Genl Gates. Enl Sept 21 1777; went with N Ham Mil to reenforce northern Contl Army at Saratoga. Disch Oct 29 1777. B Nov 23 1754 Enfield N H. Parents Jonathan Nehemiah Chandler and Mary Burroughs. Mar Miriam Simrods 1776. Chldr Stephen; Margaret (Mrs. Wm Cady). Elizabeth (Mrs James Cady) (Wm & James were brothers). D at Archer's Fork aft 1843. Bur Cady family Cem Wash co O. Ref William's Hist of Wash co p 697. Pay Roll of N Ham "Chandler Gen" by George Chandler. Family papers of his gr-dau Diana Ellis Cady Cline (b 1821 d 1918) at whose home Zebulon Chandler died. Rept by Helen Sloan Marietta Ohio.

CHAPMAN, BENJAMIN, Franklin co

Servd in a Co of Levies under Capt Theophilus Monson Lt Col Isaac Sherman 8th Conn Regt; b Feb 26 1763 at Southington Conn; Son of Rev Benjamin and Abigail (Riggs) Chapman; his father was a Chaplain in Rev; mar 2nd wf Sylvia Upson in 1793 (she b 1773); chldr: Roswell Riggs; Albert; Mary; Sally; Lucinda; Sylvia; Harriet; Henry; and Lucius (the last 4 minors at fathers d); soldr d abt June 1823 (by date of prob of will); wid d and bur at Worthington; soldr grave not found but is in locality of Worthington O; livd at Southington Conn; Blandford and Russell, Mass; and Worthington Franklin co O; was pensd. Ref Chapman Gen p 322; Will Bk Franklin co O; William Bros Hist of Franklin and Pickaway co p 421; deeds and settl of Est in this co. No. 73555 Vol 74 p 205; Vol 125 p 246 D A R Lin Bks. Sent by Blanche Rings. Later research believes only his sons came to O. Rept by Mrs John Titus Col chpt.

CHAPMAN, JAMES, Scioto co

Pvt Va Militia. Enl 1775 in Va. B Amelia co Va 1757; mar 1782 Phoebe —— had one son Josiah. D in Scioto co. Appld for pens Scioto co Sept 8 1830. Ref Vol 125 page 169 D A R Lin. Book R 1871 Vo. Rept by State D A R, Nathan Perry chpt.

CHAPMAN, LEMUEL, Portage co

Pvt Conn Mil. B 1753 Tolland co. Mar Chloe Pinney Aug 20 1822. Had son Lemuel Jr who mar Cynthia Burgess. D Edinburg O 1824 Portage co. Appld for pens at Knox co O July 20 1818-9 per application. Ref Vol 44 p 332. Mass W 1144 D A R Lin. Rept by State D A R.

CHAPMAN, SAMUEL, Washington co

Lt listed in news clipping signed L A A found in old scrap book Washington co O as "soldiers who participated in or interested in authorized Settlement of Marietta"; who have descendants in this section; and w with few exception are bur in Wash co cem were active in Indian war at own expense never reimbursed by U S Rank may have been changed. This name is not among those verified by Marietta chpt which reports it for further investigation.

CHAPMAN, WILLIAM, Trumbull co

Corp in Capt Hutchin's Co 1776; Sergt in Capt Watson's Co. Col Webb's Regt 1777-1781. Conn in Rev page 472. Came to Hartland Conn in 1776. Land record shows that he left there in 1797. Said to have d in West Brook but his estate was settled in Trumbull co June 1813 when he is called of Vernon O. He d intestate and Wm Chapman his son was appointed adm. This soldier must not be confused with the Wm Chapman of Canfield who d the same year testate his will being proved Apr 1813 nor with Wm Chapman Jr son of the soldier who also died testate his will being proved July 1821. In 1823 Thos Giddings giving testimony in a law suit says "In 1804 I sold the farm I had taken up to Wm Chapman the grand father of Erastus Chapman who with his wife and their family had come from Conn." Widow Mary survived her husband and was living in July 1814. Rept by Mary Chesney chpt.

CHASE, AARON, Holmes co

Mass S and S V 3 p 342; b 1760 Swansey Mass; d 1839; mar Susanna Comel 1784. Rept by Wm Pettit.

CHEESEMAN, ISAAC, Geauga co ?

Located by Taylor chpt Chardon. Ref 16th. Rept of N S D A R p 146. Rept by Nathan Perry chpt.

CHENOWETH, ELIJAH, Franklin co

Page 443 Vol 1 O Roster instead of Pike co. Of 5 bro who came to Pike co Arthur and Abraham (b 1770) remained; Elijah Sr and Thomas moved to Franklin co; John went west; John's son Elijah may be bur in Pike co. Soldr w Col Crawford in campaign vs Sandusky 1782; b June 12 1762 in Md or Va; son of Mary (Prickett) and Thomas Chenoweth; mar abt 1785 Rachel Foster (1769-1825; chldr Thomas mar Rachel Morgan; Elizabeth mar John Carr; Lewis (d young); John Foster mar Margaret Ferguson; Sarah mar John Haines; Joseph mar Margaret Heath; Cassandra mar John Morgan; Rachel mar Jesse Wood; Elijah Jr mar Nancy Chenoweth; Ruth mar —— Davidson. Soldr d 12-5-1828; bur on farm as was his wf. Movd to S W Franklin co 1799 to fertile land cleared by Indians and secured title; ref Williams Bros Hist Franklin and Pickaway p p 433, 435, 438, 439; Chenoweth General; History Acct Sandusky Exp by C W Butterfield p 78; Mrs Mabel C Brown Col O. Rept by Clara G Mark, Jacobus Westervelt chpt. (There being no data in Vol 1, filed here as new record).

CHENOWETH, THOMAS JR, Franklin co

Pvt from Md under Capt Bell and Major Coulter in the frontier service. 1782 was a member of Col Crawford's arm in his expedition against the British and Indians at Upper Sandusky. B Md Sept 10 1753; Son of Thomas Chenoweth Sr and wife Mary Prickett. Married Mch 17 1785 in Alleghany co Md. Cassandra Foster dau of John Foster 1st. Chldr: John mar Betsey Foster; Ruth mar —— Parish; Ann mar —— Clark; Benj; Richard Thomas mar Ruth Perin; Joseph mar Rosa Mitchell. Aft the Rev War Thomas Chenoweth and his family went to Ken from which state they came to Pike co O in 1796. In 1799 he and his brother Elijah located in Pleasant twp. Franklin co O. He d in Pleasant twp Aug 17 1814 and is bur in the Chenoweth Cem the oldest in the twp. This is on the farm belonging to Elijah Chenoweth now (Jan 1931) the property of Prof Samuel J Kiehl. Exact location of the grave is uncertain. Aft the death of Thomas Chenoweth his widow and at least part of his children went west. Ref Pens Claim R 1906 (widow's claim executed in 1843). William's Bros Hist of Franklin & Pickaway Cos p 433 Chenoweth Gen. Rept by Mrs C S Hibben Columbus Ohio.

CHERRY, REUBEN, Huron co

Exec Doc 37 of 1852 in suspended list of pensrs as under the age to be recognized for service for pens. Rept by Wm Pettit.

CHESTER, SIMEON, SR, Franklin co

Granted half section twp 12, Range 21, in Franklin co for Rev service. Deed bk 182 p 227. Nat No D A R 50352 and 76058. Rept by Hetuck chpt.

CHILDS, ISAAC, Washington co

Appld for pens July 25 1820 in Com Pleas Court Marietta Ohio stating value of property $20. Ref V 3 419. Rept by Helen Sloan.

CHILDERS, MOSBY, Hamilton co

Pvt Va Contl. Enl Albemarle co Va. Served 3 yrs. Pensr 1819 Hamilton co O. Appl mentions wife and 7 children. App for pens in Gallia co June 26 1818. Ref S 42121 Va. Rept by State D A R.

CHINAWORTH, ELIJAH, ? co

Pvt. Invalid pensr of U S belonging to Ohio. Pd at Chillicothe O $48 annually. Ref p 172 Pens 1818. Rept by Jane Dailey.

CHRICHTON, JAMES, ? co

Pvt. Invalid Pensr of U S belonging to Ohio pd at Chillicothe O $96 annually. Ref p 72 Pensr 1818 by Mrs Dailey.

CHRIST, JACOB, Mahoning co

Pvt Penn Ser 5 Vol 8 p 120-152-199. Pa Arch;Ser 3 Vol 26 pp 55-345. Chldr: Abraham mar Mary; Andrew; Christian a dau mar Samuel Frye; grand dau Mary mar a Shultz. D before 1824 Springfield twp. Ref Will Book 3 p 544; probated 1824. Deed Bk R p 634. Heirs Jacob to Mary Shultz 1825. Deed Bk P p 636. Andrew and Catherine to George Seidner land from father Jacob Christ; Hist Trumbull and Mahoning cos Vol 2 209-228. Rept by Mahoning chpt.

CHRISTY, JOHN, Fayette co

Gun maker in arsenal Harpers Ferry; Md service also; ref Heitman's Reg p 154; 2nd Lieut in 2nd Md Battl Flying Camp July 1776; b Va 1756; d Washington C H 4-13-1856; 100 yrs old; mar Mary 1-6-1794; (Nov 30 1874). 9 chldr: Robert; David Dawson; Andrew; John; Marshall; Sarah Ann West; Martha; Mary Rachel (mar 1 Uriah Goldsberry; 2 Uriah W Paxton; 3 Ebenezer Christy; had 5 or 6 chldr by each husband); unable to find name of 9th chld. Ref co courthouse; cem data. (the name is erroneously filed as Robert p 77 Vol 1 accd to later research. Rept by Jean Howatt (1931) Washington C H chpt.

CHUBB, HENRY, Mahoning co

Pvt. 4th class Pa Ser 5 Vol 7 p 1036 Pa Arch. Had a son Henry b 1788 in Pa; mar Catherine ——. D Canfield Mahoning co. Ref Deed Bk D p 35 Henry Chubb Canfield 1822. On Tax Lists 1826 and 1837; Hist of Mahoning co O p 950 and 954 Sanderson. Rept by Mahoning chpt.

CHURCH, HENRY, Ashland co

Listed page 142 in "Hist of North Central Ohio" by Wm A Duff as Rev Soldier Milton twp. Rept by Nathan Perry chpt.

CHURCH, NATHANIEL, Mahoning co

Bur in Canfield Ohio. Ref 3rd Report of N S D A R p 229. Reported by Nathan Perry chpt.

CILNEY (or Clency), GEORGE, Montgomery co

Pvt in Va Contl. Served 3 yrs 6 mos. Enl at Staunton Va in Spring of 1776. Was 85 in 1832 accd to Application. Appld for pens Sept 11 1832 in Montgomery co Ohio. Ref S 3164 Va. Rept by State D A R.

CISNA, STEPHEN, Ross co

Pvt. Pa Contl. Pensr 1819 Ross co Ohio. B in Bedford Pa. D Chillicothe; bur in Old Presby Cem; then movd to Greenlown. Bronze marker furnished by co Commissioners 1930. Son of a farmer mchd from Bedford to Bunker Hill and was one of the first riflemen A family pamphlet states that his father was captured by the Indians near Carlisle in 1756; his fr fa was Capt in 1690. His brother Jonathan built the first house in Louisville. Was killed while fighting Indians with Boone; Brothers Maj John; Col Charles; and James are buried at Ada Ohio all in Rev. Ref Mrs Peter J Blosser. Cop fr p 172 Invalid Pensr of 1818 pd at Chillicothe. J D.

CISSNA, CHARLES, Pike co

2nd Lieut. Invalid Pensr U S belonging to Ohio pd at Chillicothe. Cop at S R Lib Los An by Jane Dailey Name filed by Scioto Valley chpt as bur in Pike co.

CLANCY, JOHN, Jefferson co

Pvt in Md Line for 3 yrs. Pensd in Steubenville twp Apr 7 1819. Enl Mch 23 1777 in Logtown Md. Was 65 yrs old in 1819. Ref S 42126 Md. Rept by State D A R. See p 77 Vol 1 Roster of O.

CLAPP, CALEB, Washington co

Listed in news clipping signed L A A found in an old scrap book Washington co O as "soldiers who participated in or interested in authorized settlement of Marietta. O. Who have descendants in this section and with few exceptions are bur in Washington co cem. Were active in Indian War at own expense never reimbursed by the U S Rank may have been changed; this name not among those verified by Marietta chpt which repts it for further investigation.

CLAPSADDLE, DANIEL, Columbiana co

Capt of Rangers of the Frontiers Cumberland co Pa. B 1756; d 1813 in Center twp Columbiana co. Ref Columbiana co Cem Records. Pa Arch Ser 3 Vol 23 p 274. Mrs Wilma Molsberry Youngstown Ohio.

CLARK (Clarke), ADNA S, Lorain co

Pensd Mch 4 1831 (certf). Pensr 1840 Elyria Lorain co age 77 living with A S Clark. Served 1 yr and 1 mo. B Sept 19 1760 Middlesex co Conn. Enl Middlesex co Conn. Since Rev has resided in Green co N Y and then in Lorain co O. Appld for pens July 12 1833 Lorain co. Ref S 8209 Conn. Rept by State D A R; Nathan Perry chpt. The last payment of pension to Adna Clark covering the period from Sept 4 1842 to Mch 4 1843 was made to T J Laughlin at Pittsburg Pa on Mch 13 1843 as Atty for the pensioner. On Mch 4 1843, the pensioner certified that he had resided in the State of Ohio for a period of 3 yrs and previous there to he had resided in Brown co N Y. Ref General Accounting Office Washington D C.

CLARK, ANTHONY, Lawrence co

Pvt and Sergt in Vir State Troops. Served 7 mos. B in Ireland. Enl Oct 1777 at Baltimore co Md. Came to Baltimore co 1774 (appl). Appld for pens at Lawrence co O Aug 28 1832. Ref S 3156 Md & Va. Rept by State D A R.

CLARK, BENJAMIN, Jefferson co

Res Steubenville O 1815 Pa Arch. Rept by Mary Steinmetz Reading Pa. (genealogist).

CLARK, CLEMENT, Medina co

Pvt. N H Contl. Pensd Sept 1819 Medina co Ohio. Served 3 yrs. Enl in Rutland Vt 1776; pvt under Capts Grant and Lee Col Warner's Vert Reg; In appl he was 68 in 1819 "wife aged 62 she was Chloe Andrews; had one daughter Lucy." D in Norton O 1852. Res Wadsworth twp Medina co Sept 3 1819 Ref S 42130 Vt. D A R Lin Vol 115 p 268 and 114853. Rept by State D A R and Nathan Perry chpt.

CLARK, JACOB, Jefferson co

Pvt. Md Contl. Pens Aug 1st 1833 Jefferson co. Served 11 mos. Enl Md Jan 1776 in City of Baltimore. B Oct 13 1754. Appld for pens May 13 1833. Ref S 15379 Md. Rept by State D A R.

CLARK, JAMES, Columbiana co

Pvt Pa State Troops 6 mos 14 days. Pens Dec 20 1832 Col co. B Feb 4 1743 Ireland (appl). D Dec 28 1836. Was residing in Lan co Pa at time of enlistment. Resided about 9 yrs in Baltimore co Md previous to coming to Columbiana co Aug 25 1829 (appl). Ref S 2125 Pa. Reported by Wilma Molsberry Mahoning chpt is "one James

Clark" pvt Va State Troops pensr 1832 age 91 living in Columbiana co O may be same soldier. Rept by State D A R.

CLARK, JAMES, Hamilton co

Tradition says he served as drummer boy at Battle of Yorktown he was then 16 yrs old. Likely is son of John Clark who served in Rev for Va. B Va Sept 3 1765, Cf p 78 Ohio Roster Hamilton co. May be same. D Sept 4 1852 age 87. Bur in church yard on Clough Rd near Bogart Rd Clough Hamilton co O. Ref Mariemont.

CLARK, JOHN, Warren co

Served in 1st Md Rifles July 1 1775 to June 30 1776 under Capt Michael Cresap. B 1754. D 1841 Waynesville Warren co O. Rept by John Martin Burkett 1838 Ontario Place Washington D C to St Ch.

CLARK, JOHN, Pickaway co

Pvt Va Contl. Pensr 1819 Pickaway co. Enlisted in Balt Md Oct 16 1775 and was pvt in Capt Nathaniel Smith's and Richard Dorsey's Co Col Harrison's Reg of Contl Artillery. Disch at Annapolis Aug 15 1783. B Aug 13 1747. Mar Sarah Louden Aug 1794 in Berkley co Va. She was b 1774; d Oct 15 1853. Chldr; Joseph b June 20 1795; Nancy b Feb 19 1797; John b Mch 7 1799; Catherine b June 19 1801; Sarah b Aug 9 1804; Elizabeth b Jan 2 1807; Jane b Aug 20 1811 and James b Aug 1st 1813. D July 27 1822; his widow mar Simon Cochran, who d 1845. Proof of a John Clark Va found in Columbiana co 1832 pensr age 72 is not found. After Rev followed seafaring business for 5 yrs and was pilot at Balt for 2 yrs after which he lived in Md and Pa. In 1840 was a pensr aged 86. Pens No W 6741 allowed June 4 1818 then having lived in Pickaway co about 18 yrs. Rept by Pickaway Plains chpt.

CLARK, JOHN, Gallia co

Pvt N Car Contl. Enl 1776 in Bates co N Car. Pensr 1825 in Gallia Co. Served 2½ yrs. Age 66 in 1818 (appl). Has 7 sons from 15 to 20 yrs of age and 3 daughters age from 12 to 28. Appld for pens in Gallia co June 24 1818. Ref S 42124 N C. Rept by State D A R.

CLARK, JOHN, Brown co

Pvt Pa Contl. Served 1 yr. Enl Mch 1779 in Pa. B 1748; Had a son Thomas; d June 12 1825 age 77. Pa Arch Vol 23 S 3. Probably bur Ebenezer Cem Lewis twp reports Mrs Markley. Appld for pens Brown co O Oct 25 1721. Ref S 42127 Pa. Rept by State D A R. Mrs. G. C. Schoolfield Charleston W Va rept Capt John Clark, father of Joseph Clark (who w wf is bur at Felicity O Smyrna cem), is bur Lewis cem Northumberland co Pa and grave marked.

CLARK, JOHN, Muskingum co

Pvt Pa. Enl June 15 1775 Pa. Served 2 yrs. Pensr 1818 Musk co. B 1743; mar Agnes —— July 21 1787. From widow's pens she says he d Nov 14 1819. He appld for pens Apr 4 1818. Wid appld for pens Jan 25 1839 in Muskingum co. Ref Pa Arch Ser 3 Vol 23. W 4654 Pa. B L Wt 9128-100 pvt Issued Dec 13 1791 to Gideon Merckle assignee. Rept by State D A R.

CLARK, JOSEPH, Pickaway co

Pvt in Capt Irvin's Co Col Richard Butler Reg. Aft 16 mos was wounded at Battle of Monmouth; aft leaving hospital drove a team till end of war. Pensd 1828 in Pickaway co. B Dec 21 1760; d Sept 4 1848 age 87-10-15. Pens papers say born Jan 11 1760. Had 3 wives, 1st and 2nd names not given. 1st d about 1803, 2nd about 1825; 3rd wife was Mary Lofland mar Aug 16 1827, both living in Pickaway co. He stated he had no children by his 2nd or 3rd wife, 3rd wife allowed pens July 26 1852 age 74. Bur old family cem on Walter Leist's farm. Ref Pens No W 25418 appld Oct 24 1827 then living in Pickaway co. Having moved to O about 1807. Rept by Pickaway Plains chpt.

CLAY, DANIEL, Washington co

Pvt N Ham. Enl 1781 Rockingham Co N Ham also 1783. Disch at West Point N Y Dec 17 1783. Served 2 yrs. B 1765. Mentions wife in appl. Ch: Sarah; Eunice; Daniel; Timothy; and Jonathan. Appld for pens Washington co July 13 1819 and 1820, stating had $122.75 propty, res of Salem twp. Ref S 42128 N H. Rept by State D A R.

CLAY, DAVID, Mahoning co

Pvt. Ser 5 Vol 6 pp 488 & 499 Pa. Childr: Isaac; David; George; John; Mary; Alice mar Rogers. D before 1813 Beaver twp. Ref Will Bk 1 p 387 prob May 1813. Rept by Mahoning chpt.

CLAYPOOL, ABRAHAM, Ross co

"A Rev soldier d at his residence at High Banks Liberty twp Ross co May 5 1845, age 83-1-3. He was b in Va Apr 2 1762; he early enl as a border pioneer and served in repeated campaigns against the savages; he served under 'Mad' Anthony Wayne. While yet a young man he served 4 yrs in the Legislature of Va. Emigrated to Ross co Ohio 1799 and settled in Liberty twp." From the Scioto Gazette May 22 1845. Also Ross co History which states that he came from Randolph co Va. He had 9 children: Solomon; Jacob; Newton; Wilson; Able; Isaac; Ann; Sarah; Maria. His wife Elizabeth Claypool d at her res at High Banks Mar 20 1849 age 83-3-22 whose obit was recorded in this same paper May 1845. She was born in Va July 2 1766. From Scioto Gazette Mar 26 1849. Rept by Mrs Orion King.

CLAYTON, DAVID, Montgomery co

Pa Arch Ser 5 Vol 6 p 248; served 1778 in Lieut James Duncan's Co Cumberland co. Enl in Capt Clelan's Co p 479. Bur Beavertown Ohio. Rept by Wm Pettit S A R.

CLEMMONS, NICHOLAS, Mahoning co

Pvt. Served as cook for Genl Washington; Pa Arch Ser 3 Vol 23 p 217 Ranger. B before 1750 in Germany. Brought wife from Ger 1775. Had children Daniel mar Barbara Stambaugh; Elizabeth; Nicholas; Phillip; George; Susanna. D about 1837 Boardman twp Mahoning co. Aft the Rev lived in Washington co Pa for 30 yrs then came to Boardman O. Hist Mahoning co p 878 — Sanderson; Hist Trumbull co Vol 2 p 127 Upton; Hist Mahoning co Butler — Vol 2 p 361; Tax Lists 1826 not on 1837. Rept by Mahoning chpt.

CLEVENGER, EBEN, Fayette co

Pvt Va Contl. Served 3 yrs. Enl Dec 1775 in Va. Aged 66 in 1820 (appl). Had Elizabeth aged 25 in 1820. Washington C H chpt reports cem probably near Holland and Pick co line but no stone standing. Appld for pens Apr 25 1818 in Court Com Pleas. Ref S 42648 Va. Rept by State D A R.

CLIFTON, THOMAS, Ross co

Honesegger's German Regt. Put in Md line for 3 yrs. Enl abt July 15 1778 or 1779 Hagerstown Md. Aged 74 in 1819 (appl). Had one son aged 15 yrs in 1821. Appld for pens in Ross co July 19 1819. Grave could not be located in Ross co. Ref S 42125 Rept by State D A R.

CLINE, CONRAD, Pickaway co ?

Pvt Pa. Enl in Pa 1776. Pvt in Capt Grubb's Co Col Miles Reg. Disch Jan 4 1778. B 1757; D aft 1834. Grave not found. William's Bros Hist of Pickaway says p 250. "Conrad Kline was one of the earliest settlers in Salt Creek twp and lived in that twp until his death. He was a soldier of the Rev. Allowed a pens Mar 16 1829 age 72 Pa. Paper no S 42123. In 1834 at age of 77 was still living in Pickaway co. Ref Pa Arch Ser 3 Vol 23. Rept by Pickaway Plains chpt. Compare Cline Conrad p 85, Vol 1 Roster O, Delaware co, with name reversed. J D.

CLINE, GASPER, Trumbull co

Known to be Rev soldier served probably with the famous Ger Reg of which no roll has been preserved. B 1746 in Va. Mar Anna Terler and children were: Mar· garet; William; Phillip; Betsey —— family incomplete. D Apr 13 1835 Bristol Trumbull co. Ref Hist Shenandoah Va by Wayland page 204 is the service of this regt. Two companies were made up in the Shenandoah Valley. Rept by Mary Chesney chpt.

CLINE, GEORGE, Washington co

Enlisted Nov 4 1776 for "Duration of War" served as Corp. Pa Reg 12th. Later as Serg in 3rd Reg name on Roll dated Aug 10 1778. Was later at Fort Henry. B abt 1740 in Northern Ger. Mar Susannah Buck June 8 1770 N Y. Had children; Joseph 1771; John 1772; Levi or Lewis killed by the Indians when a lad; George 1787; Catherine 1788 mar John Tice. 1st wife David May 6 1790 in Ft Henry. Rosanna 1793 mar Solomon Tice; Christina 1794 mar John Tice as his 2nd wife. D 1795 in Grandview twp. Bur in a field at mouth of Mill Creek Gr twp. No stone now remains. D A R marker ordered by Marietta chpt. Ref Family history Washington co Hist of Monroe co War Dept Wash D C Mrs C R Sloan Marietta O.

CLINE, JONAS, Richland co

Enl in the Spring of 1780 in Ulster co N Y. In 1805 he moved to Wayne co Pa and then to Beaver co Pa. Abt 1817 he moved to Montgomery co O. Pensr 1833 Richland co O. B June 21 1760 in Rochester co N Y. Mar Caty Roos b Feb 8 1787. Children were: Margaret b Nov 11 1788; Elizabeth Jan 20 1790; Rachael Mch 31 1795; Benj Nov 1 1797; Sarah b Feb 5 1800; Mary Jan 31 1802. Soldr d July 20 1840 (Fulton co Ill). Appld for a trnsfr from Ohio to Fulton co Ill Mch 18 1839. Enl 4 times serving 16 mos as pvt. R 2049 N Y. Erroneously spelled "Clive," James. Rept by State D A R.

CLINGER, JOHN, Brown co

Exec Doc 37 of yr 1852 pens suspended list as term of service questioned. Rept by Wm Pettit.

CLINGER, PHILLIP, Preble co

Served as pvt in Capt Griffin's Co in 1775; in Capt Jacob Hetterling's Co in 1776 was in the Battle of Princeton. B 1754 Chester co Pa. Mar Barbara (b 1759). Had a family of children; came to Ohio in 1810 located in West Alexandria. D in W Alexandria east end. That part of Cem destroyed. In 1833 age 80 living in Preble co. Pa Arch Ser 3 Vol 23. Rept by Commodore Preble chpt. See p 217 Roster of O Vol 1 as Klinger cop fr D A R No 73377. J D.

CLIPPINGER, ANTHONY, Champaign co

Delaware Contl Line; b 1752 Ireland; d 1839; mar Ann Ford; ref S A R 32849. Rept by Wm Pettit.

CLIVE, JAMES, Richland co

Error for Jonas Cline, which see this vol. J D.

CLONEY, GEORGE, Montgomery co

Va Contl line. Pensd Oct 8 1833 Montgomery co Settler. Rept by Wm Pettit S A R.

CLOUGH, AARON, Washington co

B 1765; d 1825; said to be a Rev soldier. Helen Sloan.

CLUTTER, CASPER, Knox co

Pvt in Md. Pensr 1833 age 88. Age 86 in 1832 (appl). Enl Dec 1775 and disch spring of 1781. O Pens Roll 1835 111; 0-137 S 5010. Md. Rept by State D A R.

CLYMER, HENRY,

Pvt Pa. Mar Jane Luder 1762; Joseph was one son who mar Ruth Briggs. D in O (unable to locate). Proven recrd. Cop from Cal S R Bulletin by Jane Dailey. (We refer you to No. 107140 Vol 108 D A R Lin for comparison).

COBLE (or Cobble), NICHOLAS, Montgomery co

Of Pa; emigrated to this co in 1800; settled in Butler twp; bur Iutheran ch cem nr Spanker; d 1827-28. Ref Pa Archives 5th Ser Vol 1 p 480-485 inclusive. History says he had chldr born as early as 1774. Rept by W M Pettit S A R.

COBOURN (or Coburn), JOHN SR, Columbiana co

Pvt 1st class of Capt McCoy's Co for 1781-82 Cumberland Co Pa Mil; same regt in Nov and Dec 1780 in serv in Penn's Valley; b 1754; d Calcutta twp Columbiana co; pensr Pvt Pa Mil while res of Columbiana Co; Pens granted Oct 25 1833 æ 78 yrs. Ref Pa Archives Ser 3 vol 23 p 585; Ser 3 vol 6 p 360; ser 3 vol 6 p 622 and S 3213 Pa. Rept by State D A R and Mahoning chpt.

COBURN, PHINHEAS (or Phineas), Morgan co

Enl Jan 1781 Mass line; disch 1783 in Dec; Sergt Mass Contl; served 2 yrs from 1781 (Certf); mar Polly (May 1 1817 (wid appl)); Chldr: had two (appl of 1818); soldr d Sept 29 1848 Morgan co O (wid appl); res Washington co O May 4 1818 (appl); res Morgan co July 16 1832 (appl); wid appl for pens Jan 11 1854 Morgan co O. She also appl Washington Co O June 26 1855. Ref W 8190 B L Wt 31892-160-55 Mass. Rept by State D A R.

COCHRAN, ABNER, Cuyahoga co

Enl 5-2-1781 in Hampshire co Mass (appl); b 6-6-1758; mar Elizabeth 1-13-1785; chldr: Amous ? 12-20-1785; Submit 2-25-1788; Elizabeth 2-27-1791; Marvin 7-3-1796; and Levi 1-30-1800 (appl); Soldr d 12-17-1819 (appl); 13161 pvt Mass line for 3 yrs; pensd 7-26-1819 Cuyahoga co O; wid pensd 2-19-1840 Cuyahoga co O. Ref W 5248 Mass. Rept by State D A R.

COCHRAN, JOHN, Mahoning co

Appl for pens Warren O Circuit Ct Bk 6 p 301; ch John M. Ref Tax 1 list 1826. Ref Mahoning chpt.

COCKLEY, JOHN, Guernsey co

Pvt 3rd Batl Pa line; b 1741 Pa; mar Elizabeth Whitman; ch: Rachel was one dau; soldr d 1823 Guernsey co O. Ref Vol 122 p 158 D A R Lin Bk. Rept by Nathan Perry chpt.

COCKRELL, ROBERT, Wayne co

Was b 1755; mar "Prudence d May 10 1867 æ 87" on stone. Bur Canaan Bend cem. Inscript on monument "D Nov 3 1841 æ 86 Soldr War 1776." Rept by Wooster-Wayne chpt.

COE, DAVID, Portage co

Srvd as pvt in Mass Milit and in the Contl Army 1777-82. Was b in Granville Mass; d Charleston O; mar 1785 Sarah Pratt (1763-1828). Son Claudius Lucius. Ref Vol 114 p 48 D A R Lin Nat No 113140; also No 105052.

COE, LIEUT EBENEZER, Wayne co

Lieut Capt John Leache's Co Westmoreland Co Mil fr 1778-1779; b Morristown N J 1736; mar Eunice Jagger 1761; chldr: Elder Silas Coe b 1776 mar ——; soldr d

Dalton Wayne co O 1827; bur Dalton O; grave located 1935 by Wooster Wayne chpt; Prob Ct rec show he made no will but Stephen Coe was administrator under bond. Ref Arthur Moler Cincinnati O 49859 S A R Natl 2343 Ohio S A R; also S of R in Los Angles Cal Bulletin Nov 1930 Calif S of R. See vol 122 p 74 D A R Lin No 121225 says b Darham Conn. Rept by Jane Dailey.

COEN, EDWARD, Clermont co

Pvt Pa Mil served 1 yr; b Nov 22 1754 Harford co Md (appl); appl for pens Clermont co O May 22 1832; pensr Clermont co O 1833. Ref S 17356 Pa. Rept by State D A R.

COFFEL, JAMES, Logan co

Enl at Steuben twp York co Pa spring of 1776; pvt Pa mil; servd 1 yr (certf); was æ 89 in 1833 and b Ireland (appl); he appl for pens Logan co Apr 25 1833; 3 or 4 yrs after disch removed to Va nr Winchester and remained 6 or 7 yrs; then to N C; back to Va in Prince William co and about 20 yrs ago to this state (appl). Ref S 2459 Pa. Rept by State D A R.

COGSWELL, ELI, Washington co

Rev Rolls Vt p 7; b 1757 Mass; d in Washington co Waterford O; mar Jean Gilmore 1782; Ref 50113 S A R. Rept by Wm Pettit.

COLDON, RICHARD, Ross co

Richard Coldon a rev soldr d Jan 8 1830 in Ross co O. Ref H C Pemberton's Newspaper recds. Cop by Pickaway Plains chpt.

COLE, EZEKIEL, Jefferson co

Exec Doc 37 refused a pens as servd less than 6 mo. Rept by Wm Pettit.

COLE, JACOB, Trumbull co

Exec Doc 37 of 1852 admits he had 6 mo service. Rept Wm Pettit.

COLE SAMUEL, Harrison co

Exec Doc 37 refused a pens as servd less than 6 mo. Rept by Wm Pettit.

COLEMAN, JOEL, Madison co

Enl 2-14-1780 at Leesburgh Va (appl); pvt in the Va line 18 mo; pensd 1-8-1821 in Union co O; was aged 66 yrs in 1820 and very feeble (appl). Ref Va S 42139. Rept by State D A R.

COLGAN, WILLIAM, Champaign co

Enl Aug 1 1777 Berkley co Va; disch at Halifax N C Aug 1 1780; pvt Va Contl; served 3 yrs (certf); by appl of 1820 he states he had dau æ 18 and son æ 14; appl for pens Champaign co O May 20 1818 and again 1820; reed maker by occupation (appl). Ref S 42652 Va. Rept by State D A R. Fr Blanche Rings comes ref to Ohio State Journal and Political register of 11-24-1837 stating William Colgan d nr Evansport Williams co O Oct 25 1837 at æ 87 yr. "A more upright man has not survived him."

COLLINS, EBENEZER, Ashtabula co

Pvt Mass Contl line; served abt 2 yrs; by appl æ 58 in 1820; mar Anna æ 53 in 1820 has 2 daus aged 17 and 15 yrs in appl of 1820; pens from Oswego co N Y 1818 and appl for transfer to Ashtabula Co O 3-15-1827 (appl). Ref S 42135. Rept by State D A R.

COLLINS, JOHN, Richland co

Enl Apr 1777 Baltimore co Md; Sergt Md St Trps; served 6 mos and 9 da (certf): B 1760 Baltimore co Md (certf); appl for pens Richland co O Nov 1 1832. Ref S 2442 Md. Rept by State D A R.

COLOMBE, LOUIS DE LA, (or Columbia, Lewis), Athens co

Was allowed pay as Lieut Contl army 1st Dec 1776; Capt 15th Nov 1777, and served as Aide de camp to Gen Lafayette or De Kalb to Oct 1779; b France 1750 (Desc say Walker's Hist of Athens co date 1770 b is error); mar Margaret ——; chldr. John b June 24 1795 mar 1819 and Margaret et al; soldr d 1825 Ames twp Athens co O grave not found; came to Ames twp 1815 erected a tannery there; was taken prisoner at Savannah Dec 29 1778. Ref No 205099 of Henry Dawson ch D A R McPherson Kansas. Rept by Helen M Townsend Nabby Lee Ames chpt.

COLVER, DAVID, Madison co

Enl Aug 1 1781 in Columbiana co N Y. (appl); Pens No 19719; Pvt in N Y line for 1 yr 9 mo; pensd 8-24-1833 in Madison co O (certf); b 6-24-1764 Spencertown N Y; soldr d 10-24-1847; resided in Spencer at the time of enlistment and for a number of yrs after the war; then moved to Clinton co N Y and res abt 15 yrs; then movd to Champaign co O; lived there 5 yrs and then to Madison co O (appl). Ref S 17358 N Y. Rept by State D A R.

COLVILLE, JOHN SR, Licking co

Bur Hill Top cem Bowers farm Buena Vista Road. Ref Ben Jones Historical Comm of Licking co Historical and Archaeological Society. Rept by Hetuck chpt.

COLYER, THOMAS, Butler co

Lieut N J Contl, served 2½ yrs (certf); b 1744 (appl); appl for pens Butler co O July 30 1832. Ref S 2134 N J. Rept by State D A R.

COMBS, ROBERT, ? co

Pvt fr Va; b 1753; mar 1st Nancy Sears Mch 1 1806; chldr: a son Joseph Napoleon Combs (1808-1864) mar Nancy Jane Brabham ? Soldr d in Ohio 1846 (place not stated). Ref No 110164 p 53 vol 111 D A R Lin. Cop by Nathan Perry chpt.

COMYNS, JOSEPH, Mahoning co

Ranger Bedford co 1776-1783; chldr: John, another son who mar a Grove and a dau Wendell R S; soldr d Boardman. Ref Ser 3 vol 23 p 235; was on early tax list and Hist of Trumbull and Mahoning co vol 2 p 86. Rept by Mahoning chpt.

CONKLIN (or Concklin), JOSEPH, Scioto co

Enl Salem co N J 1775 N J Contl served 14 mo (certf); b 1752 (appl) mar Hannah and had Sarah Barber and May Conklin daus a son Noble and Abigail Knight formerly Conklin (by aff of heirs); soldr d 1833 Scioto co O; appl for pens from Scioto co O Sept 6 1832. Ref S 3201 N J. Rept by State D A R.

CONLEY, MICHAEL, Brown co

Enl June 1778 Md; pvt Md Contl served 9 mo (certf); b 1750 (appl) mar Rebecca Bradcock Apr 20 1825 and had one son in this country (wid app); soldr d Dec 19 1841; he appl for pens Mch 23 1824; pens 1825 in Brown co O. Wid appl for pens Brown co O May 11 1853. Ref W 1240 Md B L Wt 9443-160-55. Rept by State D A R. Filed Vol 1 Ohio Roster p 85, by Ripley chpt as bur at Sardinia.

CONNELLY, PATRICK, Warren co

A pensr d Warren co O in 1834 aged 80 yrs. Ref Pa Archives 5th Ser Vol 2. Rept by Hetuck chpt and filed by Mary Steinmetz Reading Pa.

CONNER, ISAAC, Ross co

Rev soldr fr N J. Ref Findlay and Putnam Hist Ross co O p 40. Rept by Mrs Edith Rathburn Genealogist Libr Ohio State Office Library.

CONNER, PHILIP, Hamilton co

Enl 1775 Hampton Va (appl); pvt Va Contl line; b 1752; in appl 1828 says wf d 1815; he has 2 sons Lon with whom he lives and a son in Mo; soldr may have d in Indiana where he appl for pens Mch 25 1828 at Jennings co Ind. Ref S 42134 Va. Rept by State D A R.

CONNER, WILLIAM, Adams co

Ensign in Va Contl. Pensd May 11 1819; soldr d July 1819. Ref Evans and Stivers Hist of Adams co p 330. Rept by Meryl B Markley Vice Ch. Note (death date indicates is not same as 'William Conner' Ens of Va data by State D A R which see).

CONNER (or Connor), WILLIAM, Scioto co

Enl Va served 5 yrs (certf); b 1757 (appl); mar Rosannah Mch 13 1782. (wid appl). Chldr: wid says a dau Sarah Stewart b in Allegheny co Pa where she lived with her parents till mard and she has 7 older brothers and sisters; soldr d Mch 14 1827 Scioto co O (appl) he appl for pens Scioto co O Dec 6 1820; wid appl for pens Warren co Ind Sept 11 1830. Ref W 22817 and Va Half Pay. Rept by State D A R.

CONVERSE, CAPT BENJAMIN, Washington co

Listed in news clipping signed by L A A found in old scrap book Washington co O as " soldier participated in or interested in authorized settlement of Marietta; who have descendants in this section;" Marietta chpt repts it for further investigation. Ref p 89 Converse Gen. Rept by Mrs R Winnagle Warren O.

COOK, JACOB, Richland co

Bur Mansfield cem. Stone marked "Revolutionary Soldier." J D.

COOK, JAMES, Columbiana co

Rev sold, rec not yet found; b Ireland 1737; a son James Jr; soldr d 12-28-1836 aged 99 yrs; Warrentee of land Washington co Pa 400 A surveyed Aug 6 1784 and on Chester co Pa tax list 1781. Ref "Ohio Patriot" Pa Archives Ser 3 vol 26 p 542 and Vol 12 p 631. Rept by Mrs Wilma M Molsberry.

COOK, JOB R SR, Columbiana co

Rev soldr, rec not yet found. B England; mar Mary Warack in N J; chldr: Jacob; Thomas; William; Job Jr; Mary mar —— Teeters; soldr d Perry twp æ 117 yrs; came from N J in 1806 and set on 600 A in Perry twp Columbiana co. Ref Hist of Upper Ohio Valley Columbiana co Vol 2 p 205. Rept by Mrs. Wilma M Molsberry. (Cf No 140150 D A R. J D).

COOK, JOEL, Ross co

Enl May 20 1777 in a regt commanded by Jonathan Meigs (appl); pens pvt Conn line 6 yrs; æ 68 yrs in 1818 (appl); mar Rebecca ——; chldr: Jennet æ 16 and Joel W æ 12 yrs in 1820 (appl). Ref Pens Cl Conn S 43392. Data by State D A R (Cf No 74925 D A R). Rept by Jane Dailey.

COOK, JOHNSON, ? co

Sergt. Invalid pensr of U S belonging to O pd at Chillicothe $48 annually. Cop fr p 172. Pensr of 1818 Libry L A. Cop by Jane Dailey.

COOK, JOHNSON, Fairfield co

Sergt Conn Contl. Enl Jan 30 1777 Conn; disch 1783; served fr Jan 1777 5 yrs (certf); b 1760 (appl) mar Mary who was æ 53 in appl of 1820; chldr dau Mary æ 30 yrs; Rachel æ 21; Thomas Jefferson abt 19; Elisha æ 16; Rosannah 15; Meriah æ 14; Justice æ 11 (in 1820); soldr likely d Perry co O; appl for pens Washington co O Nov 9 1814; again Fairfield co O June 19 1820 while res of Richland twp; in census of 1840 gives Johnson Cook æ 80 living in Thorn twp Perry co O. Ref S 42141 B L Wt 5572 Conn issued Dec 6 1791. Rept by State D A R.

COOLEY, ASAHEL, Athens co

Minute man Mass milit 1775 w his father, Jabez Cooley of Springfield Mass. Ref: Mass S and S Rev War Vol 3 pp 959, 960; Copeland's Hist Hampden co Mass Vol 2 P 40; Mason Green's "Springfield 1636-1886" pp 282, 284; No D A R 269269. Soldr b 4-5-1753 Longmeadow (Spr) Mass; came to O fr Fairfield co Conn 1796 settled in Carthage twp nr Coolville Athens co; mar Esther Warriner b 2-19-1755 dau of Benjamin and Persis Willard Warriner of Springfield Mass intention declared 8-11-1778. Soldr d 9-11-1828; Coolville O; has Rev mrkr; wf d there 2-14-1834. Chldr: Zeruiah Cooley b 1779 mar 1801 Benjamin F Stone; Simeon Willard Cooley b 1780 mar Sarah Cranston; Esther b 1782 mar 1802 Stephen Buckingham son of Ebenezer Buckingham Rev soldr and Esther Bradley; Asahel Cooley Jr b 1784 mar Milly ———; Caleb b 1786 Fairfield co Conn mar Matilda Buckingham in 1809; Heman b 1794-5 mar 1816 to Abigail Cowdry. Rept by Mabel L Kutz (desc) Col O Ann Simpson Davis chpt .

COOLEY, WILLIAM, Butler co

Pvt N Y Mil; served 1 yr 2 mo 24 da (certf); mar Nancy Jones Jan 8 1793 (wid appl); soldr d Aug 11 1837 Butler co O (wid appl); he, appl Butler co O July 12 1832; Pensr 1833 Butler co O; wid appl for pens Butler co O Feb 25 1851 æ 77 yrs. Ref W 6744 B L Wt 26376-160-55. Rept by State D A R.

COOPER, ALBERT, Licking co

Lieut Dunmore co Milit; b 1749 Va; d 1814. Ref 2203 S A R. Rept by Wm Pettit.

COOPER, DAVID, Meigs co

Pvt N J Contl pensr 1833 Meigs co O; b 1758; in 1796 or 1797 removed fr Morristown N J to Brownsville Pa; from there to (?) Creek Va and moved to O in 1814; Pens S 3191 N J appl for pens Meigs co Oct 2 1832; pensr of Meigs co O 1833. Rept by Jonathan Meigs chpt by Mertha Bing Chase. Also David Cooper of Meigs co O appeared 1-2-1832 a res of Chester co 74 yrs old. He was drafted in Morris co N J (where he was b) for 9 mo under Capt Mead Col Ogden. Ref P 173 Jerseymen in the Rev War. Rept by Mattie M Bowman of Garret A Hobart D A R Patterson N J.

COOPER, DAVID, Mahoning co

Pvt Pa Ser 3 Vol 23 p 329; also Ser 5 vol 7 p 1016 Pa Archives served in Porter's Battl Lancaster Co Pa; b 1762 Lancaster co Pa; mar Rebecca Armstrong; chldr; 12 — James; Jane; Rebecca; John; Sarah; David; Eliza; Margaret; Polly; William; Robert; Armstrong; soldr d May 23 1855 Coitsville twp; bur Duck Creek Cem Lawrence co Pa; was bro of James Cooper also a Rev soldr who res also in Coitsville twp; was civil engineer. Ref Biog E Ohio p 49 by Summers; Hist Mahoning co p 879 and 740 by Sanderson and Republican Sentinel 5-23-1855 David Cooper, æ 93 yrs. Rept by Mahoning chpt.

COOPER, HENRY, Mahoning co

Pvt; Ser 5 Vol 7 pp 917 942 Pa Archives; also N J Men p 552 and Va Men p

75; d Coitsville; bur Hopewell Presby Ch Cem New Bedford Pa. Rept by Mahoning chpt.

COOPER, RICHARD, Cuyahoga co

Enl in Flaverstraw ? N Y May 14 1778 (appl); pvt N Y Contl; pensr 1819 Cuyahoga co O; served 3 yrs (certf); b 1745 (appl); chldr: James (made aff after d of his father); soldr d Feb 28 1836 Cuyahoga co O (aff of son); appl for pens Bradford co Pa May 27 1818; also appl for transfer of pens to Cuyahoga co O Jan 10 1834. Ref S 42133 N Y. Rept by State D A R.

COOPER, JAMES, Mahoning co

Ranger Ser 3 Vol 23 pp 227, 280, 313, 326, 700 Pa Arch; also Va Men in Rev p 78; Vt men pp 325 829; Md Arch Vol 18 p 98; N H Men in Rev many; soldr d Coitsville; bur on his farm; lived on farm in Coitsville twp bro of David Cooper also a Rev soldr. Ref Biog E Ohio p 49 by Summers; Hist Mahoning co p 879 740 by Sanderson; List of late Henry R Baldwin. Rept by Mahoning chpt.

COOVERT, BURGUM, Warren co

States in appl that he entered serv of Rev 1 mo before he was 16 yrs of age; pvt N J Mil; pensr 1833 Warren co O æ 74 served under Capt Smook and Col Hendrickson N J line 2 yrs; b July 29 1760 Somerset co N J; mentions "decd son and family" of said son who have family Bible with family rec (appl): he lived in Monmouth co N J with his parents when he enl for service (appl); made appl for pens in Warren co O on Nov 2 1833. Ref S 3215 N J. Rept by State D A R.

COPE, JOHN SR, Columbiana co

Pvt in Capt William Brisban's Co 1st Battl Lancaster Co Mil; came 1800 from Redstone Fayette co Pa. Ref Pa Arch Ser 5 Vol 7 p 74. Rept by Mrs Wilma M Molsberry.

COPE, NATHAN, Columbiana co

Pvt East Bedford Chester co Pa ? Mil 1780 (4th Co Col John Hannum). Ref Pa Archives Ser 5 Vol 5 p 851. Rept by Mrs Wilma M Molsberry.

COPES, SOUTHY, Scioto co

Sergt Va Contl; served 2 yrs; Pensr in Scioto co 1818. B Accomac co Va 1761; his son Southy Copes Jr appld for arrears of pens said "wife age 60". Soldier's chldr were Esther Andrews; Annie Lancaster; Parker Copes; and one other son. Resided in Lewis co Ky before going to Scioto co. Appld for pens Scioto co July 31 1818 and again in 1820. "Southy Copes my father left a widow his 3rd wife. She moved to Iowa where she d abt 1847." Rept by State D A R.

COPES (or Copis), WILLIAM, Stark co

Enl 1778; pvt Va Contl served 4 yrs and 6 mo; pensr June 18 1819 Stark co O; appl for pens Stark co O Apr 27 1818. Ref S 42316 Va. Rept by State D A R.

COPLEY, SAMUEL, Cuyahoga co

Enl Feb 1777 New Milford Conn; pvt Conn Mil served 10 mo and 27 da. B New Milford Conn 1758 (appl); in 1782 movd fr New Milford Conn to Clarendon Vt; aft here 6 yrs to Pittsford Vt; then to New Lebanon N Y in 1802; aft 7 yrs to Oneida N Y; in 1816 to Granger co and 1826 to Cuyahoga co O (appl); appl for pens Cuyahoga co O Apr 29 1833; recd pens from same co 1833. Ref S 18362 Conn. Rept by State D A R.

CORBIN, JOHN, Holmes co

Enl in St Trps of Va in the first yr of the Rev (appl); res in Culpepper Culpepper co Va at the time of enlistment; pvt Va Mil served 8 mo and 15 da (certf); was æ 82 in 1833 (appl); mar Sarah æ 70 in 1833 (appl) chldr: Celey æ 43 in 1833 and Fanny æ 46 (appl); he appl for pens in Holmes co O 10-10-1833 (appl); pensr 1833 Holmes co O. Ref S 3202 Va; also listed p 268 "Va Men in Rev." Rept by State D A R.

CORSON, ROBERT, Franklin co

Exec Doc 37 refused a pens as servd less than 6 mo. (Decd) Franklin co O. Rept by Wm Pettit.

CORDERY, JAMES, Brown co

Pvt Capt Walton's Co Col Cholick or Caulick Regt Del for 6 mo; b 1754 Sussex co Delaware; in appl ment a wife not named; lived opp Maysville Ky in Huntington twp Brown co O but moved to Pendleton co Ky where he res in Aug 16 1838; also Sept 1 1838. (We list this soldr to avoid further research since he once lived in Brown co O but may have d in Ky. Ref S 9266. Rept by State D A R.

COREY, THOMAS, Washington co

Pvt R I Contl pensr 1820 Washington co O; b 1763; soldr d 1822; bur Becket farm above Waterford Washington co O; inscr on marker "a native of R I an active aider in the Revolution patiently endured the toils and hazards of the western wilds; underwent many privations and hardships;" grave marked 1930 by Marietta D A R. Appl pens July 30 1822 at Com Pleas Ct Marietta O. Ref vol 4 p 30. Was a pensr under act of 1818 but taken fr rolls Act of 1820 as not considered in indigent circumstances acc to that act. Ref Doc 31 Jan 6 1831 O S Libr. Rept by Mrs. Helen Sloan.

CORLISS, WILLIAM, ? co

Major; listed in news clipping signed by L A A found in old scrap book Washington co O as "Soldier who participated in or interested in the settl of Marietta; who have desc in this sec." This name not among those verified by Marietta chapt which repts it for further investigation.

CORNELL, ——, Ashland co

Listed p 142 in History of North Central Ohio by William A Duff as a Rev soldr bur in Pioneer Cemetery. Rept by Nathan Perry chpt.

CORNS, JOSEPH, Washington co

Appl pens Oct 25 1832 in Com Pleas Court Marietta O. Ref vol 6 p 350. Rept by Helen Sloan.

CORY, EBENEZER, Mahoning co

Capt Ebenezer Allen's Co for defense of U S 1777 and many others; mar Polly Thompson in 1804; she mar 2nd James Crooks; chldr: Elnathan; Mary mar Samuel Harriff; Sarah mar William Bissell and George; soldr d 1812 in Coitsville twp; family all removed. Ref Will Bk I p 310   prob 4-18-1812; Trump of Fame 4-18-1813-Est Ebenezer Cory; Deed Bk K p 615; Bk I p 679 Ebenezer Cory Heirs; Hist of Trumbull and Mahoning Co vol 2 p 168. Rept by Mahoning chpt.

COSPER, JOHN, Holmes co

Exec Doc 37 of yr 1852 of sus.

COSSETT, SILAS, Trumbull co

Hist of Mercer co Pa "Dr Silas Cossett migrated from Granby Conn in spring of 1805 and settled in Trumbull co O. He had served as a captain in the Revolutionary War." He was b June 23 1756 at Granby Conn; son of Rene and Phebe (Hillyar) Cossett; mar May 8 1783 in Salmon Brook Conn to Sarah Shephard; chldr: Epaphroditus; Silas Jr; Eli; John C; Sarah; James; Harlow G; Henry D; and Nancy C; soldr d May

1, 1820. When his est was prob in Trumbull co he is called "late of Vernon." Rep by Mary Chesney chpt.

COSTIGAN, FRANCIS, Ross co

Enl in N J line; dischgd in Philadelphia Pa (appl of 1818); Lieut N J Contl; served in Co Comm'd by Lord Sterling in the N J line (pens certf); b 1750; in appl says 'wife only family at present' (appl); soldr d July 29 1821 (pens certf); likely bur in Ross co; appl for pens in Adams co O on Aug 6 1818; pensr 1819 Adams co O; made declaration Ross co O Ct Aug 2 1820, then resided in Chillicothe Ross co O; was Lieut during Rev (appl of 1820); schoolmaster. Ref S 42653 N J. Rept by State D A R. Ref p 330 Evans & Stivers Adams co Hist. Rept by Meryl Markley.

COTTRILL (or Cotterill ?), THOMAS, Brown co

Va mil pensr 1833 Brown co O; enl Aug 1774 at Shenandoah River Va; b July 16 1750 at Shenandoah co Va (appl); mar Nancy 1775 May 14 (wid appl); had 12 chldr John White was a son-in-law (wid appl); soldr d Mch 27 1836 Brown co O; bur Lewis twp near White Oak Creek on farm now owned by R E Campbell; a limestone marker but inscr gone; grave located by Taliaferro chpt; by appl says has lived in Brown co O abt 5 yrs previously lived in Nicholas co Ky for 38 yrs; wid appl for pens July 6 1836 Brown co O; soldr appl for pens Brown co O July 22 1833; lived in Scott twp in 1829. Ref W 4165 Va. Rept by State D A R. Listed also p 268 in "Va Militia in Rev" d in Brown co O æ 84. (J D).

COTTON, JOHN, Trumbull co

Enl 1776 as Quartermaster in John Bailey's Reg; Lieut Mass; Pens No 11616; pensd 6-30-1819 Trumbull co O (certf); served 2 yrs (certf); was æ 75 yrs in 1821 (appl); wife æ 63 yrs in 1821 (appl). Ref Continental Mass S 42649. Rept by State D A R.

COURTRIGHT, SOLOMON, Huron co

Volunteered to serve in N J troops; many enlistments from 1776 to 1781; b 1752; mar Hannah Ayres 1777; soldr d 1847; bur Peru twp cem Huron co O. Inf by Mabel Steel Taylor.

COURTS, LOW, Fairfield co

Pvt Pa line; pens 1829 Fairfield co O; enl in Contl line of Rev for during war (appl). Appl for pens Fairfield co O Nov 13 1828. Ref P 406 Wisemans hist of Fairfield co O name listed among pioneers and S 46435 Pa. Rept by State D A R and Jane Dailey.

COWGILL, DANIEL, Preble co

Pvt Va St Trps; enl 1779 Culpepper co Va; discharged 1781 (appl); pensr Feb 22 1833 Preble co O; served 3 yrs from 1777 (certf); b Oct 9 1755 Burlington co N J (appl); says "father" kept family rec; appl for pens Preble co O Dec 13 1830; appl again in 1832 and says he res in state of O 17 yrs and Preble co O 3 yrs (appl of 1832). Ref S 3199 Va. Rept by State D A R.

COWLEY, MICHAEL, Brown co

Believed to be misspelling for Michael Conley (which see this roster) Meryl Markley.

COX, BENJAMIN, Warren co

Pvt N Y Mil; res in Orange co N Y when enl; was engaged in battle of the Fall of Ft Montgomery; pensr 3-26-1833 Warren co O æ 74; Co commanded by Capt Hillford N Y Mil 17 mo 5 da; b Orange Co N Y in 1760; æ 72 in 1832 when he appl Oct 3 1832 for pens in Warren co O. Ref S 2463 N Y and Pa. Rept by State D A R.

COY, DAVID, Mahoning co

Pvt pensr N Y; Conn Men in Rev pp 149, 172, 209; names one ch David b 1786 mar Sarah; soldr d bef 1819 in Beaver twp; is listed among early settlrs. Ref Hist Trumbull and Mahoning co vol 2 p 192. Rept by Mahoning chpt.

CRAIG, JAMES, ? co

Appl for pens Nov 12 1821 in Common Pleas Ct Marietta O. Ref Vol 3 p 534. Rept by Helen Sloan.

CRAIG, JAMES, Clark co

Pensr 1819 of Clark co O; pvt N H Contl; enl Concord N H 1777; discharged at West Point 1780 (appl); served 33 yrs (certf); b 1753 (appl); chldr: Robert æ 21; Andrew æ 19; and Alexander æ 15 yrs (wid appl); soldr d 9-10-1823; appl for pens Clark co O May 11 1818 (appl). Ref S 42143 N H. Pensd by act of Congress 1818 æ 65 yrs. Rept by State D A R and Mahoning chpt.

CRAIG, JAMES, Mahoning co

Pvt N J Men p 387; soldr d abt 1840 Milton twp; on list of early setlr Milton twp; Ref Hist Trumbull and Mahoning co vol 2 p 180; Tax list 1826; Adm Bk 1 1840 est; Trumbull co Democrat; Est James Craig 5-16-1840 Milton twp. Rept by Mahoning chpt.

CRAIG, JAMES, Monroe co

Enl 1777 Philadelphia Co pa (appl); pvt Pa Contl pensr 1833 Monroe co O; pensd 3-4-1831 (certf); served 2 yrs from 1777; Mabel Askue Mahoning chpt rept he d in Philadelphia Pa; appl for pens Monroe co O Sept 22 1832; Mary Steinmetz Reading Pa repts liv in Monroe co O in 1833. Ref Pa Arch list and S 2477 Pa. Rept by State D A R.

CRAIGS, ROBERTS, Preble co

Pvt Pa Contl; pensr 1819 in Preble co O; enl Carlisle Pa in the 3rd Reg; enl in July or Aug 1781; (appl); wid pensd 8-24-1854 in Preble co O (certf); soldr was æ abt 60 yrs in 1818; wife was Elizabeth Hood mar 9-20-1820 (wid appl); chldr: Nancy; Rebecca; Melinda; Hannah; Isaac; Jacob and Susannah ages in 1820 the oldest 15 yrs and the youngest 3 yrs (appl); (these are correct dates Elizabeth may have been a second wf); soldr d 5-7-1834 in Preble co O (appl of wid); by occupation a laborer but too infirm to support himself (appl). Ref Pa W 25445 B L Wt 16280-160-55. Rept by State D A R.

CRAIG, WILLIAM, Columbiana co

Rangers of the Frontier Westmoreland co Pa William Love's Co; b 1726; soldr d 1806 Center twp; bur Center twp Columbiana co O; warranted 300 a of land Apr 28 1773 in Westmoreland co Pa. Ref Columbiana co Cem Records; Pa Archives Ser 3 vol 23 p 283. 315 and same ser vol 26 p 405. Rept by Wilma M Molsberry.

CRAIG, WILLIAM, Belmont co

Pvt; Md Mil; pens 1832 in Belmont co O; in Capt Maxwell Co Col McGaw Regt for 6 mo; came to Cecil Co æ 6 lived Cecil co Md when enl; b Hartford co Md June 15 1755; he quotes in appl "Year he was born King George sent to America to know how many male chldr were born in a yr;" on Mch 8 1833 appl for pens in Belmont co O æ 77; at æ 85 yrs was living in Richland twp Belmont co O (1840). Aft Rev war 1781 or 1782 moved to Charston (now Willsburgh) Va lived 7 yr thence to Belmont co O where he always and now resides. Ref S 2479 Md. Rept by Jane Dailey. Zanes Trace chpt Regent Mrs G M McCommon repts he was bur in Morristown. Ref Belmont co Hist of Ohio Valley 1880.

CRAIN, WILLIAM, Columbiana co

Rev soldr rec not yet found; b 1757; soldr d 1829; bur at Salem; lived and taxed in Lancaster co Pa 1779-1782 Colerain twp; estate settled 1830 Salem. Ref Columbiana co Cem Recds Pa Archives 3rd Ser; vol 22 p 620 853; and Ohio Patriot. Rept by Mrs Wilma M Molsberry.

CRANSTON, JOHN, Champaign co

Pvt; b Newport R I; soldr d on farm near Woodstock; bur on this farm in a cemetery which land he gave to the twp for this purpose; farm now owned by John R Wilson north of Woodstock; inscr: "John Cranston d Aug 29 1825 æ 70 yrs" "Phebe A wife of J Cranston d Feb 10 1805 aged 30 yrs" "John and Margaret infant chldr" "This stone though silent calls to mind the virtue of our worthy friends." A dau Phebe Ann d Mch 10 1871 æ 78-8-18. Rept by Helen C Neese.

CRAPO, JONATHAN, Ashland co

Enl 1781 Mass; served 2 yrs 8 1-3 mo (certf); pens 3-4-1831 (certf); mar Celia Clark (b 10-13-1763) in 1786 (wid appl); chldr: Jonathan; Polly; Celia a dau; Asenath; Asa; Carra; Henry C (family rec submitted by wid in appl); soldr d Oct 22 1846 Ashland co O; appl for pens at Henderson Jefferson co N Y Sept 11 1832; moved to Jamestown Mass wh lived 3 mo; thence to Boston; thence to Philipsburgh N Y; appl for transfer of pens to Lorain co O Oct 17 1835; wid appl for pens from Ashland co. Ref W 5254 Mass. Rept by State D A R and Nathan Perry chpt.

CRARY, ARCHIBALD, ? co

Col; listed in news clipping signed by L A A found in old scrap book Washington co O as "Soldier who participated in or interested in the settl of Marietta; who have desc in this sec. This name not among those verified by Marietta chpt which repts it for further investigation.

CRAWFORD, DAVID, Jefferson co

Enl Sept 1780; then res Mingo Creek near town of Williamsport Washington co Pa; pvt in Capt Johnson's Co Pa Mil; pensd May 27 1833 Jefferson co O; served 11 mo and 12 da (certf); æ 69 in 1833; b July 1 1764 (appl); soldr d May 26 1835 (on pens certf); appl for pens Jefferson co O May 13 1833 res of Knox twp. Ref S 2152 Pa. Rept by State D A R.

CRAWFORD, ELEAZER, Lorain co

Enl while a res of Windsor Co Vt; served four 6 mo periods; Dec 1 1777 as pvt under Capt Blandin Col Sergeant Vt; Aug 1 1778; Jan 1 1779 as pvt under Capt Lemuel Blandin Col Sergeant; June 20 1779; Jan 1 1780 as Orderly Sergt under Capt Rosebrooks Col Whitcomb N H; sept 1 1780; Mch 1 1781 as pvt under Capt Lemuel Blandin Col Sergeant Vt; b Sept 8 1760 in Windham Co Conn; soldr d July 28 1843 in Black River twp Lorain co O; in 1853 Temperance Cutler æ 46 yrs and a res of sd Black River twp is mentioned as dau of soldr by his first wife (name not given); mar Sept 1 1813 in Cornwall Vt Mary Phelps; he appl for pens in Lorain co O Nov 30 1833 which appl allowed; wid pens Nov 18 1853 while living in Black River twp æ 74 yrs; after service he lived in Vt and N Y then moved to Ohio. Ref Bur of Pens. Rept by Nathan Perry Chapter and State D A R.

CRAWFORD, JOHN, Adams co

A soldier in the army of Col Wm Crawford in his campaign against the British and Indians at Sandusky (Upper Sandusky) in May and June 1782! only son of Col Wm Crawford; b prob in the Shenandoah Valley Va; date of birth not found but he was a married man with three chldr: William; Moses; and Richard in the spring of 1782; was reported killed in the retreat after the battle but escaped the Indians and later made his way home; in 1782 was living on the Youghiogheny River in what is now Fayette co Pa then a part of Westmoreland co. "John Crawford afterward emigrated to the State of Ohio settling upon land bequeathed to him by his father at the mouth of Brush Creek on the Ohio river bottom in Adams co where he died leaving two sons about the yr 1816." Ref Notes taken from "Crawford's Campaign against Sandusky" by C W Butterfield pp 90, 113, 115, 117, 118, 247, 249, 295, 296. Rept by Clara G Mark Jacobus Westervelt chpt.

CRAWFORD, SAMUEL, Fairfield co

Pvt and Sergt Mass St Trps pens 3-4-1831 in Fairfield co appl pens Fairfield co 10-30-1832. Enl 11-5-1776 in Vol Regt from Mass under Col Eli on exped vs Ft Cumberland. Aft Rev lvd 6 yr in N H thence Cambridge in Washington co N Y later to Pa for 2 yr then to O. B Ireland 4-10-1751. Movd to Nova Scotia in 1763. Mar Martha Dicey (or Riley) 7-4-1776. Wid appl pens 10-31-1839 Fairfield co when dau Mary made aff naming Jane McIntyre; James; Jenet; Matthew; Martha; Margaret; William; David; John; Isaac; Rebecca as chldr. Soldr d 6-14-1838. Grave not located. Ref Wiseman's Hist Fairfield co p 406; Pens W 4164 Mass Sea Service. Navy. A descendant Mrs P B Rumer of Petersburg Ind States soldr bur in Warren co. Rept by State D A R. Refer to correct record as James Crawford (addenda) of Franklin co.

CRAWFORD, THOMAS, Fayette co

Pensioner 1840 æ 87 while residing in Concord twp Fayette co O. Was born then in 1753 (Ref Census 1840). Rept by Washington C H chpt.

CRAWFORD, WILLIAM JR, Logan co

Lieut in Capt John Bigg's Co under Col Wm Crawford in his expedition against the British and Indians at Sandusky in May and June 1782; son of Valentine Crawford and nephew of Col Wm Crawford. He was killed by the Indians June 1782 at Wapatomica (near Zanesfield) at the same time as Col William Harrison and two others whose names are not recorded but one was supposed to have been Major John McClelland fourth in command of the expedition. Ref Notes taken from "Crawford's Campaign against Sandusky" by C W Butterfield pp 118, 138, 311, 333, 346. Rept by Clara G Mark Jacobus Westervelt chpt. Also by Gretchen Miller Dolly Todd Madison chpt who says: A reputed officer in Rev and nephew of Col William Crawford Vol 1; Reference from Cleveland Plain Dealer Issue of Jan 20 1937.

CRAWFORD, WILLIAM, Mahoning co

Pvt; Ser 5 p 345 and 49 Pa Archives; mar Jane; chldr: James; William b 1790; David; Mary; Eleanor; and Nancy; soldr d abt 1816 Coitsville. Ref Will Bk 2 p 388 prob 1816. Rept by Mahoning chpt.

CRAY, JOHN, Mahoning co

Pvt Washington co Mil; Ser 5 vol 4 p 346 Pa Archives; mar Elinor; chldr: John; James; David; Sarah mar James Porter; Mary; and Robert; soldr d abt 1821 Poland O; Ref Will Bk 3 p 266 prob 1821; tax list 1826 John Cray's heirs. Rept by Mahoning chpt.

CREEKBAUM, PHILIP, Brown co

Enl June 1776 and served to July 1779 as pvt under Capt William Keider Col Hansegger German Regt; was in battles of Trenton Princeton Brandywine and Germantown; b 1758 in Hagerstown Md; mar Catherine Jolly in Hagerstown Md; chldr: John; Philip; Catherine; Susan; Nellie; Elizabeth; Marie; and Adam. Appl for pens Sept 1818 and was then living in Fayette co Pa; came to Brown co where he d; bur in old cem at Ripley Ohio. Ref Erie Pa Records Cincinnati Public Libry; Family Bible and Nat'l Nos 111047 and 111542. Rept by Meryl B Markley Vice Chairman.

CRESS, GEORGE, Gallia co

Pvt. Rev army; pens 1810; mar Christiana; Gallia County Will Rec B p 291 mentions wife and chldr: Nicholas; Jacob; John; George; Christiana; Elizabeth Miller; and Henry; soldr d 1823; will dated Mch 1823; prob May 14 1823; in Gallia co Civil Jr 1 p 89 dated May 19 1854. Appl was made for back pens naming Henry Cress and

Christiana Williams as only living heirs; rec show he left farm in Perry twp Sec 1 T 5 R 16 to Henry Cress and Christiana Williams. Rept by French Colony chpt Gallipolis Ohio.

CRISSEY, JOHN, Ashtabula co

Enl 1776 (he thinks) (appl); pensr 1840 Austinberg, Ashtabula co æ 83 lived with Ebenezer A Mills; pvt Conn Mil 6 mo; pensd 5-11-1836 Franklin Co Vt; b 1757 in Stratford Conn (appl); was residing in Farmington twp Conn at the time he enl; abt the close of the war he moved to Landoff N H; 10 yrs later he moved to Franklin Co Vt where he now lives (appl); appl for pens in Franklin Co Vt 7-27-1832 (appl); there is no mention of his records at Pension Bureau of his living in Ohio; however, Census of 1840 lists one John Crissey in Ashtabula co O. Ref Conn S 19265. Rept by State D A R.

CRIST, W P C, Perry co

Enl under Washington and served throughout the war; mar Miss Butts of Pa; one ch Frederick; soldr d in Perry co; was weaver by trade. Ref Brister's Hist of Licking co p 850. Rept by Hetuck chpt.

CRITCHARD, BENJAMIN, Licking co

Enl at Charleston N H Feb 1 1777; pvt N H Contl pensr 1819 in Licking co O; Lieut 2 yrs 9 da (appl) æ 68 yrs in 1820 (appl) pens 5-21-1819 (appl) appl for new certf 10-23-1820 (appl). Ref S 42145 N H. Rept by State D A R.

CRITCHFIELD, BENJAMIN, Knox co

Listed in Cens 1840 as pensr liv in Howard twp Knox co aged 79 yr. He was b then abt 1761 and tho research has found no Rev serv it is listed here for research. Three others of this family name are filed Vol 1 Roster of O in Knox co. J D.

CRITTENDEN (or Chittenden), GIDEON, Portage co

Enl Oct 1777 in N Y State at Fishkill in sd state (appl); pvt Conn Contl; pensr 1819 Portage co O; served 3 yrs from Oct 10 1777 to Oct 1780 (certf). Was æ 66 in 1818 (appl); ch: one son Chauncey æ 17 (appl 1820); res in Portage co O on May 20 1818; res Atwater twp (appl for pens there also) Aug 8 1820. Ref S 42660 Conn. Rept by State D A R.

CROCKER, CHARLES, Portage co

Enl æ 16 yrs; in Campaign of Quebec with Arnold; also under Gen Green and with Washington at Yorktown; was Capt in Conn Mil in 1812; b 1760 Vt; soldr d 1849; bur Old Cem Mantua Portage co O; brought family to Western Reserve 1827 to 5 mi north of Mantua Sta. Ref Charles Crocker 367 Sieber Ave Akron O. Cop fr Akron paper. Rept by Cuyahoga Falls chpt.

CRONKLETON, JOSEPH, Delaware co

Pa Archives 5th Ser vol 6 pp 114, 130; class roll Aug 24 1782; 6th Co 1st Bat of Cumberland Co Mil commanded by Col James Johnson; b July 1760 in Antrim twp Franklin co Pa; son of John and Elizabeth (Gordon) Cronkleton; mar 2nd Mary Craig Apr 27 1794; chldr from his will: Joseph; William; Samuel; John; Elizabeth; Robert; Ann; Margaret; soldr d Oct 17 1824 in Liberty twp Delaware co O; bur on Cronkle-Craig Apr 27 1794; chldr from his will: Joseph; William; Samuel; John; Elizabeth; Robton Farm just south of Stratford Delaware co O in family burying place on farm; inscr on marker "Joseph Cronkleton d Oct 17 1824 æ 64 yrs and 3 mo;" Joseph Cronkleton brought wife and children to Delaware co O from Pa Antrim twp Franklin co Pa in 1808 was owner of large tract of land in Delaware co and in southern O; he called his place a plantation as he and his father both had slaves in Pa; will on file in Delaware co O. Rept by Mrs W J Hadley Toledo.

CROSBY, DAVID, Mahoning co

Corporal. Pensr S 43413 Conn 1818; enl 4-12-1777 Conn; served under Capt Christopher Darrow Col Huntington and in other companies and Regts; was in battles of Germantown Springfield N J and Groton River; disch 6-8-1783 (two b dates rept so omitted each); mar 1780 Catherine; chldr: John 1807; Susannah 1809; Martha 1813; William 1816; and Isaac 1818; soldr d Aug 12 1837 Poland; pens rec does not give date of mar maiden name of wf or res where he d. Ref Old Pens Book Vol 3; pensrs in Ohio Trumbull co æ 78 yrs and Tax list 1826 Poland. Rept by Mahoning chpt.

CROSBY, JAMES, Perry co

Volunteered Apr 1 1777 in Hagerstown Md; pvt and Sergt Md Mil; pensr 1833 in Perry co O æ 92 yrs; served 8 mo (pens certf); b July 25 1741 Westmeath co Ireland; abt 25 yrs of age when he left Ireland (appl); lived in Washington co Md during Rev till 1791; then lived Bedford co Pa 5 yrs has lived in Perry co 16 yrs; appl for pens Perry co O Nov 8 1832. Ref S 17339 Md. Rept by State D A R.

CROSBY, TIMOTHY C, Trumbull co

In Sheldon's Dragoons 1781; mar Eunice Sutliff Feb 26 1787; chldr: 8; among them were Tully; Timothy; Eunice; and Sabrina; soldr d spring of 1811 in Vernon Trumbull co O; went from East Haddam Ct to Hartland Conn where he bought land Feb 11 1784; thence to Farmington Conn 1799; thence to Vernon Ohio about 1805 where he lived the rest of his life. Rept by Mary Chesney chpt.

CROSLEY, WILLIAM, Brown co

Enl Apr 1781 Washington co Md; pvt Md Mil; pensr 1834 in Brown co O; served 6 mo (certf); b 1762 (appl) mar Sarah Apr 27 1785 (wid appl); chldr: Catherine; Mary; Elizabeth; George; Sarah; Rachel; Moses; Cynthia; William; and Anna (wid appl); soldr d Sept 7 1839 (wid appl); appl for pens Brown co O Mch 31 1834; wid appl for pens Shelby co Ind Sept 8 1845. Ref Rejected as pensioner: R 2517 Md. Rept by State D A R.

CROSS, DAVID, ? co

Sergt Pa line; in battles of the Jerseys and Valley Forge; b Ireland came to U S 1767 located in Washington co Pa came to O; mar Margaret Moore; one ch was Thomas 1771-1827; soldr d in Ohio 1801. Ref Vol 30 D A R Lin Bk. Rept by Nathan Perry chpt.

CROSS, SAMUEL, Adams co

Res in Franklin co Pa till July 1 1776 when he entered service of Rev; pvt Pa Mil; pensr 1833 in Adams co; served in Pa line 8 mo (pens certf); b Jan 1 1755 Franklin co Pa; remained in Franklin co Pa till abt 15 yrs aft the war then moved to the Monongahela River co of Fayette and lived there 7 yrs; from thence to Adams co O; appl for pens in Adams co O on Oct 10 1832 res in Wayne twp. Ref S 2475 Pa. Rept by State D A R.

CROW, ABRAHAM (Abram), Columbiana co

Pvt N J Men p 563 Middlesex co; b 1749; had 13 chldr; soldr d Oct 8 1845 Elk Run twp; came with fam to Ohio 1787 leaves 4 ch liv 9 dead 71 gr chldr 24 dead 141 grt gr chldr liv 11 dead 3 gr gr grand chldr in all 219 desc liv and 44 dead. Rept by Mabel S Askue Youngstown O.

CROW, CHRISTIAN, Sandusky co

Enl in Lancaster pa and served 5 yrs (appl); enl on St Patrick's Day 1777 (appl). Pvt Pa Contl; pensr 1819 in Sandusky co O; chldr: Jacob and Jane (twins); Andrew æ 3 and Peggy æ 7 mo; was liv in Sandusky co 1834 æ 72; appl for pens in Pickaway co O 1820 (appl); shoemaker (appl); was farmer when enl (discharge). Ref Pa Arch Ser 3 vol 23; Pa Md War of 1812 U S A; S 43417 B L Wt 9111-100; B L Wt 19704-160-12. Rept by Jane Dailey.

CROW, ISRAEL, ? co

Wagoner; refused a pens as case not provided for by law. Ref Doc 31 Jan 6 1831. Rept by Blanche Rings Columbus O.

CROW, THOMAS, Pickaway co

Born 1746; mar Elizabeth who d Oct 3 1855 æ 81; soldr d Jan 15 1814 æ 65; bur in Mead twp Pickaway co O; grave marked by D A R May 8 1934. Rept by Pickaway Plains chpt.

CROW, WILLIAM, Columbiana co

Pvt in Capt William Skiles Co 1st Battl Lancaster Co Mil May 1781; pvt in Capt William Skiles 4th Co 1st Battl Lancaster Co Mil 1782; furnished a substitute for a tour of duty Lancaster Co Mil; came from Pa; voter in Columbiana co in 1816. Ref Columbiana co Recs; Pa Arch Ser 5 vol 7 p 37 and Ser 5 vol 7 pp 61 925. Rept by Wilma M Molsberry Youngstown O.

CRUM, ADAM, Noble co

Enl July 1775 in Md; pvt Md Contl; pensr 1819 Monroe co O; nat of Germany; wounded at Bunker Hill; settl in Pa; moved to Monroe co 1808; later to Noble co O; b 1750; mar Mary; chldr: David; William; Mary; and Henry (aff of Henry); soldr d Feb 26 1851; wid d July 18 1851 (aff of son Henry) Ref W 2069 Md. Rept by State D A R.

CRUM, ADAM, Monroe co

Data fr the following letter given as evidence: "Woodsfield Monroe co Ohio 7 Aug 1819. Sir: I forwarded to your office the declaration in favor of Adam Crum dated 12 May 1818 for the purpose of obtaining a pension for his service in the Rev War. It was returned to me on the 4 May 1819 with the request to give a certificate as to the reduced circumstances of the claiment which I did freely as he is a poor and distressed man. It appears from the piece attached to the declaration that name was on records or muster rolls of the Maryland trps as stated in the declaration I sent to your office on the 11th day of May 1819. I have not since had any return or a decision. The poor ould much distressed and asks me to rite on to know if he is lible to get relief. Sir I remain your Obed't servant Levin Okey. To Hon John C Calhoun, Sec of Dept of War." Rept by Mrs E M L Indianapolis Ind. (Levin Okey, a Rev Soldr, Monroe co). Letter was found amg papers for another applicant, Benjamin Pearsall, neither one known to the one who rept both recds to Ohio, hence suppresses her name.

CRUM (or Schoonover), CHRISTOPHER, Scioto co

Enl by name of Crumb which was his true name on return from service. His mother told him his name was "Schoonover" and afterwards he went by that name; enl at Minnisink N Y Dec 1 1778; pvt N Y Contl; pensr 1819 in Scioto co O; served 4 yrs; b 1762 (appl); chldr; 3 survive: Isaac Crumb or Schoonover who made appl for arrears of pens 1852 in Scioto co O; and Benjamin and Chandler; soldr d at Tippecanoe co Ind 1830 or 1831; "mother d 2 yrs aft father" (aff of son Isaac); appl for pens Scioto co O Apr 30 1819. Ref 43421 B L Wt 2479-100 N Y. Rept by State D A R.

CRUMRINE, MICHAEL, Mahoning co

Pvt; N J Men p 577; Morris co N J; b 1762 Berks co Pa; mar Elizabeth Canfield; chldr: 4 sons and 3 daus: John b 1795 mar Susan Burgert; and Daniel mar Mary Moherman; soldr d Nov 22 1840 Ellsworth; bur Old German cem; Ref Hist Mahoning co p 199 and 882 Sanderson; Biog E Ohio p 351 Summers and Hist Columbiana co p 596 McCord. Rept by Mahoning chpt.

CUDDINGTON, BENJAMIN, ? co

Appl pens July 29 1822 in Com Pleas Ct in Marietta O. Ref Vol 4-26. Rept by

Helen Sloan. Listed Doc 31 Jan 6 1831 as refused a pens as servd in a Regt not on Contl Estab. Rept by Blanche Rings.

CUE, ROBERT, ? co

Pvt; Invalid pensr of U S belonging to O pd at Chillicothe. Copy fr p 172 Pensrs 1818 by Jane Dailey.

CULING, JOHN, Muskingum co

Cop from a note of late State Librarian Alice Boardman saying he "was a Rev Soldr living in Muskingum co O." (Jane Dailey).

CULLENS, JOHN, Muskingum co

Exec Doc 37 of yr 1852 suspended pens as servd less than 6 mo. Rept by Wm Pettit.

CUMMINS, JOHN, Guernsey co

Enl 1776 N J; pvt N Y St Trps; pensr 1833 in Guernsey co O; servd 2 yrs (certf; b 1751 Jan 24 Hunterdon co N J (appl); lived in Hunterdon co N J til 1795 moved to Frederick co Va; in 1829 moved to Guernsey co O (appl); appl for pens Guernsey co O Sept 19 1832 res of Cambridge twp. Ref S 3240 N J. Rept by State D A R.

CUMMINS (or Commins), NATHAN, Cuyahoga co

Joined Rev 1776; pvt Mass Contl; in 1833 pensr in Cuyahoga co O; served 2 yrs; b 1758 Dunlap co N Y (appl); when 15 yrs of age moved to Stephentown and next year to Honock Mass; aft 16 yrs he removed to Saratoga co; aft 2 yrs to Clinton co then to Champlain; aft 11 yrs to Whitley in Upper Canada; in 2 yrs to Hamburgh co N Y; in 10 yrs back to Upper Canada where he res 8 yrs; then to Cuyahoga co O; appl for pens Cuyahoga co O Nov 5 1832 res of Euclid twp. Ref S 3241 Mass and N Y. Rept by State D A R.

CUMMINS, WILLIAM, Warren co

Pvt and Sergt N J St Trps; pensr 1833 Warren co O æ 72; enl Mch 1778; pvt and Sergt in Co commanded by Capt Parker and Col Alexander in N J line for 6 mo; b Basconridge twp Sommerset co N J May 20 1762 and res there when entered Rev serv; mar Deborah Thompson July 27 1826 in Warren co O (wid appl(; wf æ 85 in 1855; soldr d Nov 8 1833 at Lebanon Warren co O; abt last of Apr 1779 rem to Rowan co N C and set near Saulsberry; made appl for pens in Warren co O on Oct 3 1832 res of Turtle Creek twp; wid filed for pens in Warren co O July 26 1853. Ref W 5253 B L Wt 67676-160-55. Rept by State D A R.

CUNIAS, JOHN, Montgomery co

Enl Mch or Apr 1782 in Pa (appl); Lycoming co Pa; pvt Pa Contl; pensr 1826 in Montgomery co O; rept by S A R Dayton O; Serv 5th Ser vol 2 p 868 vol 14 p 505; disch 11-1-1778; æ 58 in 1823 (appl) in which he says wife is disabled and son is mar; was a tailor; appl for pens in Lycoming co Pa Sept 2 1823 (appl); appl for transfer to Montgomery co O Mch 15 1826 (appl). Grave not located; was living in Montgomery co O 1834 æ 69. Ref 43441 Pa. Rept by State D A R.

CUNNINGHAM, JAMES, Belmont co

Rev soldr bur at Key Belmont co O. Found in co Hist of Ohio Valley (1880) Rept by Mrs G M McCommons Shadyside O. Zanes Trace chpt.

CUNNINGHAM, PATRICK, Licking co

Enl York co Pa spring of 1776 as pvt Capt Moses McClean's Co Col Thomas Hartley's Pa Reg marched to Three Rivers Canada; disch spring 1777; b between Mch 17

1749-1752; mar Isabell b 1746; ch: Polly Gaws b 1780; soldr d Feb 7 1832; grave not located; pensd Apr 27 1818. Rept by Hetuck chpt.

CUNNINGHAM, THOMAS, Brown co

Pvt Pa Contl; pensr 1819 Brown co O; served 4 yrs. Enl 1777 at Pittsburg Pa; disch July 1781; b 3-2-1742; chldr: John; James; and Mary; bur Evans Cem Huntington twp; came to Brown co (then Adams co) in 1803. Ref Beer's Hist Brown co P 496 and S 42664 Va. Rept by State D A R and Mrs Meryl B Markley Taliaferro chpt.

CURRY, JAMES, Butler co

Enl Mch 1776 Westmoreland co Pa to serve as ranger on frontiers against Indians (appl); pvt Pa St Trps; Pensr 1832 in Butler co O; b Apr 7 1756 Lancaster co Pa (appl); mar Martha Crooks 1774 (appl); chldr: had 12 (wid appl) "son James" (aff of wit); soldr d Nov 18 1832 Butler co O (wid appl); appl for pens Aug 3 1832 in Butler co O; wid appl for pens Butler co O Oct 7 1845 æ 89. Ref R 2595 Pa. Rept by State D A R.

CURRY, JAMES SR, Union co

B 1732 Va d 1834 Union co O; Capt of 4th Va Regt 1779 etc; S A R No 2203 who repts also James Curry Jr 1752-1839; see latter this volume in addit data to p 98 Vol 1 Roster Rev soldr Ohio. Rept by Wm Pettit.

CURRY, WILLIAM, Preble co

Pvt Pa Line. B 1750 Lancaster co Pa. Recd pens 1832. D Preble co 1835. Rept by Commodore Preble chpt.

CURTIS, DAVID, Trumbull co

Corporal; endorsed by Capt James Booth's Ration Roll Co of Guards from the 11th Reg Mil Apr 1777 (Collections) Vol 8 p 181 Hist of Harwinton Conn by Manning Chipman p 114; b Jan 8 1744 Waterbury Ct; parents Abel Curtis and Elizabeth (Bishop) Curtis; mar Elizabeth Hill 4-20-1769; chldr: Zenas; Huldah; Freelove; Elizabeth; Ezra; David; Adah; Ruth; Marilla; Richard; Sarah possibly others. Soldr d Oct 30 1823 Farmington Conn. Rept by Mary Chesney chpt.

CURTIS, JOEL, Muskingum co

Pvt Conn Line; pensd Apr 20 1819 Act of Cong 1818. Ref Ohio Pens List. Rept by Jane Dailey.

CURTIS, JONATHAN, Belmont co

B Charlton Mass; mar 1780; chldr: a son Eli was b in Belmont co O June 24 1784; mar Elizabeth Benton. Eli d there 1852. Ref No 1166 vol 23 p 141 S of R Libry. Rept by Ella Tafe Librn Los Angeles.

CURTS, MICHAEL, Mercer co

Pvt Pa Contl; pensr 1819 in Butler co O. Note: A "Michael Curts" d 10-10-1818 Mercer co O æ 66; of Pa serv. Ref Pa Arch 3 Ser vol 23. Rept by Mary Steinmetz Reading Pa and Jane Dailey.

CURTZ, THOMAS, Shelby co

Enl 1780 Cumberland co Pa; pens No 25748 Cumberland co Mil Capt Hay's Regt; pensr 12-30-1833 for 7 mo serv (certf); pensr in Lycoming co Pa (certf); b 1755 Northampton co Pa (appl); soldr d May 28 1842 (certf); bur Curts cem 1 mi so Botkins O Rt 6 T 7 Sec 9; res in Cumberland co Pa at time of enl; after leaving the serv he moved to Dunstable twp Lycoming co Pa where he now res (appl). Ref Pa Arch 5 Ser Vol 6 p 505; 654; Pa Arch vol 4 p 284 490. Ref S 22714 Pa. Rept by State D A R and Lewis Boyer chpt.

CYPRES, ANDREW

Pensr under act of 1818 but taken fr Rolls under Act of 1820 as not considered in indigent circumstances accd to that act. Ref Doc 31 Jan 6 1831 O S Libry. Rept by Blanche Rings Columbus O.

DAGGETT, GIDEON, Knox co

Enl 2-21-1777 Sutton twp Mass. Servd 3 yrs as pvt Mass Contl. Pensr 1819 in Licking co O. Appl of 1823 states his æ as 63. Chldr named are Harvey and Gideon. D 8-27-1838. Pens trnsfrd to Licking co fr Vermont 3-25-1825; to N Y 3-5-1827. Ref Mass S 44025 Bureau Pensions. Rept by State D A R.

DAGGETT, JACOB, Sandusky co

Enl June 1774 Sutton Mass Pvt 13 mo 1 da; teamster one year; Mass Contl. Pensd 1834 Sandusky co O. He resided in Wooster co Mass at time of enl. Later movd to N Y state; thence to Green Creek Sandusky co O where he appld for pens Apr 29 1833 stating his age as 73. Ref Mass S 16098 Pens Bureau. Rept by State D A R.

DAILEY, DENNIS, Preble co

Pvt Va Enl in Milsborough N C Nov 1780 as trumpeter. Va Cavalry 3 yrs. Pensd 2-29-1819 Preble co O. Trnsfrd to Scot co Ky 9-30-1844. In his appl 1818 states age as 57. Ref Contl Va S 30375. Rept by State D A R.

DAILEY, ELIAS, Trumbull co

Enl 1775; served one year Capt Thomas Craig's co Col Hand's Pa Regt Pvt Pa Cont'l; pensd 1819 Trumbull co. Pension Record R 2628. B 3-22-1749 N J mar Polly Bunnel abt 1776. Among chldr were Abraham; Eleanor; Rachel. D 4-16-1820 Bristol Trumbull co Ohio. Rept by Mary Chesney chpt.

DAILY, JOHN, Adams co

Servd as private in Capt Taylor's co Col Wayne's Pa Regt. B 1755 in Germany; mar Rebeckah Frederick in Blair Co Pa. One dau Elizabeth who mar George Swigart. D 1823 in Manchester Ohio Adams co. Ref V 106 D A R Lin 105049. Rept by J D.

DAILEY, SAMUEL, Jackson co

Enl at Killingsley Conn. Appld 8-5-1819 before 2nd Circuit Court æ 60. Issued 9-22-1819 sent to Chillicothe O. Appld 4-18-1821 æ 63 in Ross co Courts. Srvd by sea and land 18 mo. By land Com Capt Curtis belonged to Mass line under Col Leonard and Lieut Col Shepard; in various battles. Ref Conn (or Mass) S 44128. Cop by Jane Dailey.

DALRYMPLE, DAVID, Clinton co

Cop fr 13 Rept N S D A R p 121 .Grave located by George Clinton chpt in York twp Clinton co O. By Mrs Oehlke. (Compare name reversed in Sandusky co O p 101 Vol 1 Roster of Ohio. J D.)

DALRYMPLE, JOHN, Preble co

Exec Doc 37. Refused a pens as servd less than 6 mo. Rept by Wm Pettit.

DANA, BENJAMIN, ? co

Capt. From old scrap bk clipping of Rev soldrs interested in or participating in Marietta settlement descendants of whom are bur in Washington co. Listed here for research by Marietta chpt.

DANFORD, PETER, Belmont co

Enl pvt in Capt Cornelius Neinkirk's Co Col Benj Holm's 2nd Regt Salem co N J Milit 2-4-1778. Srvd at Haddonfield under command Col Joseph Ellis. Recd discharge 3-9-1778. B Chesterfield N J 1739. Parents were Samuel Danford and Mary Groom: Mar (1) Sarah Morris 1764; (2) Mercy Ewing 1783; (3) Margaret Starr DeLancey 1803. Chldr Rebecca; Sarah; Samuel; Peter; William; Ambrose; Nancy; Margaret. Soldr d 8-22-1827 Alledonia Belmont co O; bur Belmont Ridge cem Alledonia O; inscript on monument "Dec 8-22-1827." Grave mrkd by common field stone. Movd from Burlington co N J to Washington co Pa; settled on Patterson Creek 1795. Thence to Section 23 Belmont co P in 1797 whr he entered land on Bend Fork Creek. Ref Adjutant General of N J; Hist of Belmont co O. Rept by Columbus chpt from C C Danford Lewisville R No. 3 O.

DANFORTH, PETER, Licking co

Enl 4-1781. Pvt Mass Cont'l; served 3 yrs. Pens'd 1833 in Licking co Ohio. Appld for pen in 1831 stating age as 70. Resided in Vermont until about 1830; thence to Licking co Ohio. He became almost blind; the wife very infirm; both resided with a son (unnamed). Was a farmer. Ref Mass S 2506. Rept by State D A R.

DARROUGH (Dorough), JOHN, Montgomery co

Washington co Pa 1780. 5th S Pa Arch p 348. Came with Newcon party that settled Dayton 1796. Rept by W M Pettit S A R Dayton Ohio. No pension record located — J D.

DARST, PETER, Delaware co

Ref Exec Doc 37 refused a pens as servd less than 6 mo. Rept by Wm Pettit.

DAVENPORT, JOHN, Sandusky co

Enl in fall of 1778 and served 12 mo (four 3 mo terms). Pvt Mass Milit. Pensd in 1883 in Sandusky co Ohio. B in 1760. Movd from Mass to Vermont when he was about 33 or 34 years old. Moved from Vermont to New York; thence to Sandusky co Ohio. Appl for pens Oct 2 1832 in Sandusky co Ohio. Was blind when he appl for pens. Ref Mass S 3271. Rept by State D A R.

DAVICE, JOHN, Clermont co

Rev soldier Pa service residing in Clermont co. Age 82 in 1834. Rept by Mary Steinmetz Reading Pa. (Research failed to secure more data).

DAVID, ZEBEDIAH, Adams co

Pvt Pa Milit. Servd in the Pa line 6 mos. Pens'd in Adams co O in 1833. B 8-10-1758 at Newark Del. Movd to Philadelphia Pa when about two yrs of æ. When he ent service he resided there. Aft leaving Phila he lived first in Cumberland co N J; then in Red Stone Creek near Brownsville on the Monongahela R in Pa; then in Mason co Ky; then in Clermont co O; and last in Adams co O. Made declaration for pens in Brown co O. Appl for pens Adams co O 4-4-1833 when res of Liberty twp. Ref Pa S 2504. Rept by State D A R.

DAVIDSON, JAMES, Columbiana co

Cumberland co Pa Rangers Pvt Cumberland co Pa Milit 5th Co 4th Batt'n Aug 12 1780. Was a native of Maryland; b in 1765. Mar Mary Johnson. There were 10 chldn. One son (was James?) b Middleton twp Columbiana co O 12-25-1814. Soldr d 1828 aged 63. He was one of 1st settlers on Little Beaver Creek Middleton twp. Came one year after state line was run. Was a shoemaker and farmer. Ref Hist Beaver co Pa. Warner p 638 Pa Arch 3rd 23, 242, 289, 702. Rept by Wilma M Molsberry Youngstown O.

DAVIDSON, WILLIAM, Lawrence co

Pvt Westmoreland co Milit Contl. Ref p 434 Vol 4 Pa Arch. Also p 739 Vol 4 Pa Arch 5th Ser. Was b in Pa 11-20-1747. His father was Wm Davidson b in Ireland of Scotch ancestry. Mar (1) Rosanna Hutchinson 1768; (2) Barbara McDole (McDowell). Chldr by 1st wife: Comfort; John; Lewis; Mary; David. Chldn by 2nd wife: Thomas; Abraham; Margaret; Elizabeth; Sarah; William W; Rose; Jesse; Joseph Wm; Cynthia. D at South Point O 11-16-1811. In Scioto co & Pioneer Record of Southern Ohio by Nelson W Evans is found an article which says that the inscriptions on the tombstones of William and Barbara were easily read in 1911 but did not tell where they were except at South Point O. The article was accurate except it said he was b in Ireland and it was his father, William who was b in Ireland. Our tradition is that he had charge of a pack horse outfit transporting food from Philadelphia to Valley Forge. Was a farmer. Rept by Dora Kellogg (Mrs F G) Omaha Nebraska of the Major Isaac Sadler chpt. Accepted by J D.

DAVIS, BENJAMIN, Clermont co

Enl 1776. Pvt Pa Cont'l served 3 years. Pen appl for 12-13-1820 in Clermont co O. Pen'd in 1821 in Clermont co O. Was b in 1752. There was a wife æ 70 in 1870 also one son grown up. Ref Pa S 44127. Rept by State D A R.

DAVIS, DUDLEY, Washington co

Enl 6-1779 Middlesex co Mass Corp Mass Cont'l. Served 2 yrs and 9 mos. Discharged 12-23-1783 West Point N Y. Appl for pens Washington co O 5-19-1818 Res of Salem twp. Pensd 1819 Washington co O. Was b 1764. In appl of 1820 named a wf Mercy æ 54 and children Sally æ 17 and Betsey æ 15. Was a farmer. Appl also 7-25-1820 there stating property value as $188.19 (Ref Vol 3 p 416) by Helen Sloan. Ref William's Hist p 687 Mass S 44119. Rept by State D A R.

DAVIS, ICHABOD, Columbiana co

Pvt b 1756 Mass; mar Catherine who d 3-1-1844; soldr d 7-9-1844 Wayne twp Columbiana co; ref The Aurora of July 1844; Mass S and S V 4 p 490 Freetown Mass list recd of Jonathan Warner Com fr Col R Putnam. Rept by Mabel Askue, chpt ch.

DAVIS, JAMES, ? co

Pvt refused a pens as servd in Regt not on the Contl Estab. Cop fr Exec Doc 31 1-6-1831 by Blanche Rings Col O.

DAVIS, JAMES, Union co

Enl Stafford co N H Aug 1777. Pvt N H Cont'l. Discharged 1779. Pens'd 1833 in Champaign co O. B in Stafford co N H 9-4-1762. There was a wf Susannah to whom he was mar 11-23-1826. D 10-28-1841 in Union co O. Aft his discharge res in N H for about 20 yrs; then removed to Orange co Vermont for 10 yrs; then to state of N Y (Washington co) and res 4 yrs; then to O. Appl for pens Champaign co O 8-3-1832. Ref R 2725 Mass & N H. Rept by State D A R.

DAVIS, JOHN, 2nd, Wayne co

Enl 5-20-1776 in Pa. Pvt Pa Cont'l 1776. Was pens'd 4-20-1824. Was b 3-25-1762. Appl names a wf Elizabeth. Chldr named: Martha aged 25 in 1823; Eliza 11; George 14; Mary Ann 12; & Margaret 9. Also 3 other chldn: Thomas 19; Sophia 17; & David 16 in 1824. D Aug 21 1856. Appl for pens in Wayne co O 3-22-1824 Wooster twp. Was a boot and shoemaker. Ref Cnt'l Pa S 44126 B L Wt 26-60-55. Rept by State D A R.

DAVIS, JOHN, Jefferson co

Enl 1776 8th Pa Regt Pvt Pa Cont'l; served 3 yrs. Discharged 1779. Pensd 7-20-1822 in Jefferson co O. In 1820 gave æ as 72 also named a son Benjamin æ 20 who has a wf & 2 chldr. D 2-22-1822. Appl for pens Jefferson co O 8-21-1820. Was a skin dryer. Ref Pa S 4417. Rept by State D A R.

DAVIS, JOHN, Champaign co

Enl Stafford co N H 1776. Pvt N H St Trps. Served 6 mos and 15 das. Pensd 1833 in Champaign co O. B in Stafford co N H 8-10-1757. Mar 4-22-1807 wf's name Eleanor. Widow's appl names a son David. Soldr d 9-2-1840. Remvd fr N H to Vt then to lower Canada; then to Washington co N Y; then to Champaign co O twp of Goshen. Appl for pens Champaign co O 8-3-1832. Wid appl for pens 12-31-1858 Champaign co O res of Mechanicksburg twp. Ref W 6972 N H B L Wt 26309-k60-55. Rept by State D A R.

DAVIS (or Davas), JOHN, Pickaway co & Buchanan co Mo

Pvt Va Contl. Enl in spring of 1775 while living in Prince Williams co Va and served 3 mos in Capt Heatter Co Col Levin Powels Va Regt. He reenlisted as wagoner under wagon-master John Morris for 15 mos. He enlisted in 1780 in Rowan co N C. Pensd 1832 in Pickaway co. In fall 1843 moved to Buchanan co Mo where he d 5-31-1847. Pens No S 2155. Allowed a pens 8-10-1832 while living in Perry twp Pickaway co. Rept by Pickaway Plains chpt.

DAVIS, JOHN, Holmes co

Rev service in Pa. D in Holmes co 6-7-1830 æ 64. Was pensr there in 1822. Rept by Mary Steinmetz Reading Pa.

DAVIS, JONATHAN, Knox co

Enl 3-19-1776 in Deerfield twp Cumberland co N J 14519. Pvt N J Milit 9 mos. Pensd 9-21-1819 Knox co O. B 5-9-1755. Pens appl said 5 daus all married. Ref N J S 44122. Rept by State D A R.

DAVIS, JONATHAN 2ND, Warren co

Enl the same spring British left Philadelphia in the Jersey line. Pvt N J Contl 9 mos. Pensd 3-20-1819 in Lebanon twp Warren co O. Appl of 1820 gave age as 70 yrs; named wf Susannah aged about 59 yrs; named chld Hester aged 15 yrs. He may have d in Indiana. Appl for new cerf 8-25-1820 Warren co O. Appl for a transfer to Indiana 5-2-1834. Was a weaver. Ref N J S 35873. O Pens Roll 1835:3:0-71. Rept by State D A R.

DAVIS, JOSEPH, Morris co

Ref Doc 27 Exec under suspended list his Rev service is admitted. Rept by Wm Pettit.

DAVIS, JOSHUA, Trumbull co

Pvt Conn Men pp 123-150; also Pvt Vt Men p 609; also Pvt N H Men p 336 — Bachillor. B in 1764. D 1-29-1847 in Bristol twp. Ref Western Reserve Chronicle Jan 1847. Rept by Mahoning chpt.

DAVIS, LEVI, Belmont co

Pvt Mass Contl Capt Pierson Co Col Tupper Regt 9 mos. Act 32. Pensd 6-20-1833 in Belmont co O. B 10-19-1764. At æ of 76 was living in Somerset twp Belmont co O. Appl for pens stated: ent serv from Newburg-Port Mass; since Rev been in Mass; Me; N H; now Ohio Belmont co Somerset twp. Ref S 2502 Mass. Rept by Jane Dailey.

DAVIS, LEWIS, Montgomery co

Va Lif Rev 1910-11 R W 4 165; War 5-68. Pens 2-1836. (Not a pensr at D C). D 3-11-1809. Buried in Woodland Cem Montgomery co O. Rept by W M Pettit S A R.

DAVIS, NEHEMIAH, Athens co

Mrs. Robert Jones 211 Palmetto St New Smyrna Beach Florida regrets (as we do) the omission of her ancestral line thro Mary Stone Davis dau of 2nd wf Phebe, and sends following data accd to her knowledge but does not state whr proof may be found. Chldr by 1st wf Betty (Merston) mar 1777: Elisha b 1777; Benjamin 1780; Anna 1783; Sarah 1785; Nehemiah 1787. Chldr of 2nd wf Phoebe (Dorr) mar 1793; James Dorr b 1795; Rufus Putnam 1798; Isaiah 1801; Hannah 1803; Judith P 1805; Phoebe 1809; Mary Stone 1811. However we have investigated the mar records of Athens co and find mar of those named by her including a Susan and Reuben (omitted by her but filed Vol 1). Especially found mar of Mary S Davis her line, to Harry Gardner 8-5-1832. Addit ref No 212567 D A R. Rept by Jane Dailey.

DAVIS, OWEN, Greene co

Servd fr Pa; co hist says he is a bro of Thomas Davis Rev soldr (11724 D A R); bur in Clifton cem n e of Clifton very old stone reads "In Memary of Owen Davis b Wales Oct 13-1751 d Clifton Feb 18-1818." Soldr mar Letitia Phillips; chldr: Lewis (unmar); Catherine mar Gen. Benj Whiteman 1793 at Limestone (Maysville) Ky; Owen blt 1st mill Beaver Crk 1798; his home became 1st courthouse; Ref Robinsons and Dills co Hists. Rept Catherine Greene D A R.

DAVIS, SAMUEL, Mahoning co

Ranger on frontier Washington co Pa. Ser 3 V 23 p 207 Pa Arch. B in 1763. Wf's name was Mary (1759-4-27-1842). Names of the chldr are: William; Rachel mar Lewis Townshend; Rebecca mar David Scofield; Mary mar Benj Hawley; Samuel; Joshua. D 4-15-1830 in Goshen twp. He settled in Goshen at an early date. Ref Will Bk 6 Prob 1830 Goshen then Columbiana co; Hist Columbiana co pp 203 & 293. Deed Bk V. Transcribed Records p 429. Rept by Mahoning chpt.

DAVIS, THOMAS, Knox co

Enl in July or Aug 1781 in Charles co Md; then his place of res. Pvt Md Contl 2 yrs. Pensd 5-28-1833 in Perry co O at æ of 84. B 11-8-1753. Appl gives marriage date as 1-2-1786 & wf's name Joanna. D in Knox co O 9-22-1840. Ref O Pens Roll 1835:3: 0-151; 16th Rept N S D A R p 142 Md W 6974. Rept by State D A R.

DAVIS, WILLIAM, Washington co

One of this name appl pens 7-24-1820 in Common Pleas Court Marietta O stating property value of $11.70. Ref V 3-416 (May be any one of others listed). Rept by Helen Sloane.

DAVIS, WILLIAM, ? co

Capt. From old scrap bk clipping of Rev soldrs interested in or participating in Marietta settlement descendants of whom are bur in Washington co. Listed here for research by Marietta chpt.

DAVIS, WILLIAM, Columbiana co

Pvt 1st Regt Inf Regulars Pvt Broadhead's 1st Regt Pa lines. Pens granted to heirs Sept 25 1821 to extend from 8-15-1821 to 8-15-1826. His heirs were William and George Davis. Soldr d 2-15-1821. Pens pd at Pittsburgh agency to heirs William and George Davis 5 yrs. Half pay in lieu of bounty land. Ref 1833-34 Pens Recs U S. American State Papers Vol 5 p 26. Rept by Mrs Wilma M Molsberry Youngstown O.

DAVIS, WILLIAM, Butler co

Pvt Va Contl. Pensd 1832 in Butler co O. Was b in Stafford co Va. Wf's name was Nancy; a dau Nancy was one chld. Soldr d in Butler co O. Ref Vol 115 p 77 D A R Lin No 114249. Rept by Nathan Perry chpt.

DAVIS, WILLIAM, Clark co

Pvt N J Milit. Served 2 yrs. Pensd 1833 in Clark co O. B in Monmouth co N J 3-11-1754. Res in Monmouth co N J at time of enlistment. Moved from there to

Washington co Pa. After 2½ yrs moved to Harrison co Va. Aft 38 yrs moved to Clark co O. Appl for pens in Clark co O 10-4-1832. Ref S 16097 N J. Rept by State D A R. (N B Compare to same p 106 V O Roster fr Pike co O — J D.)

DAVIS, WILLIAM, Shelby co

Enl in Monmouth co N J Pvt N J line 2 yrs. Pensd 8-8-1832. B Middletown N J 3-11-1754. Res in Monmouth co N J at time of enlistment. Moved from ther to Washington co Pa and resided 2 yrs. Movd to Harrison co Va and resided 38 yrs. Then moved to Pike twp Clark co O. In 1840 one was living with one F R Harding Shelby co O. Ref N J S 16097. Rept by State D A R.

DAVIS, ZACHARIAH, Lawrence co

Enl 1780 in Pa Pvt Pa Contl served 8 mos 15 das. Discharged at Valley Forge Va in 1781. Pensd in 1833 Lawrence co O æ 73. B 2-6-1760. Appl of 1839 names wf and chld. He might have d in Tenn where he made appl for transfer of pens to Knox co Tenn 2-16-1839. Since Rev lived in Bedford co Va 12 yrs; then Powell's Valley Va; then Sevier co Tenn; from Tenn to Lawrence co O 8 yrs ago. Appl for pens 3-12-1832. Ref S 1660 Pa & V 23 S 3 Pa Arch O List. Rept by State D A R.

DAVISON, EDWARD, Pickaway co

Ref fr Williams Bros Hist Franklin and Pickaway cos 1880 p 293: Edward Davison came from Bourbon co Ky and settled in Deer Creek twp Pickaway co in 1803. His wife d soon aft Mr Davison d in Pickaway co 8-1827 æ 77 yrs. He was a soldier of the Rev an Indian fighter "on the dark and bloody ground" of Ky and an intrepid hunter in the backwoods of O. He was opposed to slavery and come to O that he might not witness its evil effects. There were seven chldr four now living Robert now living in Darke co; John who lives in Washington co Iowa; Lydia (Cumberford); and William who mar Rachael and lives in Deer Creek twp. (Edward Davison's will p 100 Will Book 1-2 Pickaway co.) Mentions wf Lydia and 5 chldn under æ: John; Katy; Nancy; Lida and Edward. The other chldr were: Robert; Samuel; William; Jonathan; Mary White; Elizabeth Watterman; and Margaret Pierce. Made 7-23-1827. Witness John Twebaugh and Isaac Hornbeck. Probated 10-1-1827. (I find in 12-12-1811 Edward Davidson mar Elizabeth Ikes. Marriage License Book 1.) Rept by Pickaway Plains chpt.

DAVISON, ISAAC, Clarke co

Various spellings. Pvt Va Milit on Sept 4 1846 pensr certified had resided in Clarke co O for 5 yr coming fr Tippecanoe co Ind. Pens appl of 11-12-1832 was a resident of Blue Riv twp Johnson co Ind; came to O 1841 whr he had two sons liv. Last payment pens from Mar 4 to Sept 4 1846 made to John Holmes Cincinnati on Sept 24 1846. Ref Vol 54 p 57 and vol 66 p 282 D A R Lin states b Clarksburg Va 1746; (now W Va); mar Isabella Anderson; son Isaac Jr b 1790 mar Sarah Curl. Ref S 2509 Va. Rept by Indiana Histor com. Mrs Roscoe O'Byrne.

DAVISSON, JOSIAH, Preble co

Services 1 V. R.; W D 2, 1; 6, 6; 287, 1; 2nd Va St R; W D 57, 1. Was fr Rockingham Va; d in Preble co 1825 æ 81; Ref Va Lib Rept 1912 p 88. Rept by Wm Pettit, S A R.

DAWSON, JOHN, Champaign co

Enl 1778 Westmoreland co Pa Pvt N J Milit. Pensd 1833 Champaign co O. B 1747 in Frederick co Md. In appl he mentioned his "father's family." Moved with his father's family from Md to Pa; moved from Westmoreland co Pa to Ky in 1785; aft several yrs moved to O Champaign co abt 30 yrs ago. Appl for pens 4-15-1834 in Champaign co O. Ref S 8296 Pa. Rept by State D A R. (Urbana chpt located grave in Oakdale Cem Urbana O. Inscription: John Dawson d 10-21-1845 æ 97.)

DAWSON, JACOB, Mahoning co

Pvt. Ser 5 V 3 p 175 6th Pa. Contl line Pa Arch. Chldr were: Rachel mar Samuel Miller; William mar Margaret; Joseph; Isaac mar Ruth; Sarah mar John Angell; Homer mar Ruth; Nancy mar Jacob Harmon; Aaron. Soldr d before 1832 at Poland O. Ref Deed Bk F p 566, 567, 561, 562, 563, 564, 565; Tax list 1826; Western Reserve Chronicle 5-7-1832 Est Jacob Dawson of Poland O. Rept by Mahoning chpt.

DAY, JEREMIAH, Clermont co

Enl at Amboy N J 1777. Pvt N J Contl. Served 6 yrs. Discharged at New Windsor N Y 1783. Pensd in 1819 in Clermont co O. Was born in 1752 in England. Appl for pens Clermont co O 6-5-1818. Ref S 42669 N J; and S A R 39894. Rept by State D A R.

DAYHOOF, GEORGE, Columbiana co

Ref Exec Doc 37 refused a pens as servd only 4 mo. Rept by Wm Pettit.

DEACON, JOSEPH, Medina co

Listed pp 144 and 145 in "Hist of North Central O" by Wm A Duff as Rev soldr of Middlebury O. Rept by Nathan Perry chpt.

DEAN (or Deen), BENJAMIN, Morgan co

Enl Feb 1776 Va Line. Pvt Va Contl. Served 3 yrs. Pensd 6-24-1818 in Morgan co O. Appl for transfer of pens to Morgan co O 8-12-1828. Appl stated æ 57 in 1821; named a wf æ 61; also a son. Res Washington co O 3-18-1818. Was a farmer. Ref S 44130 Va. Rept by State D A R.

DEATH, JOHN C, Warren co

Pa early settler of County. Justice of the Peace in 1807. Fifth Ser Pa Arch vol 4 pp 434, 740. Rept by Wm Pettit S A R Dayton O.

DEAVER, WILLIAM, Scioto co

Enl Md line 7-1-1778. Pvt Md line 3 yrs. Pensd 5-14-1819 Scioto co O. Transfrd to Mason co Ky in 1822. B in Hartford co Md in 1764. Appl of 1820 named these chldr: William 17 yrs; Deborah 15; Elizabeth 13; George 10; Rebecca 8; Mecajah ? 7; Della 5; Mary Ann 2. Soldr d in Wayne co Ind 2-9-1832. (Listed here to avoid further research). Ref Md S 12754. Rept by State D A R.

DE CAMP, MOSES, Butler co

Volunteer in Essex co N J Milit. Was b Westfield N J 1735. In 1763 mar Sarah Ross (b 1747 d 1835; chldr:o ne dau Nancy mar Squire Pierson. Soldr d 1827 Millville Butler co O whr bur Bethel cem Hanover twp. Ref D A R Lin V 109 p 210 and V 123 p 159; 4th Rept N S D A R p 295. Cop by Jane Dailey and Nathan Perry chpt.

DECKER, ABRAHAM, Richland co

Sergt N J 3 yrs 6 mos. Enl in 1775 he thinks under Capt Abraham Miller Sussex co N J. Pensd in 1833 in Richland co O. B 10-16-1741. Ref Contl Pa S 15405. Rept by State D A R.

DECOURSEY, PETER, Trumbull co

Enl 1777 under Capt Dathic Hewit; was with his Co at defeat at Wyoming but escaped and reenlisted with a Northumberland co Pa Regt. Was in camp at Morristown with Col Hartley of Va and was discharged at Trenton N J having served 3 yrs. Was a resident of Newton twp. Rept by Mary Chesney chpt. Exec Doc 31 of Jan 6 1831 he is refused a pens as servd in a Regt not on Contl estab. Rept by Blanche Rings.

DECOURSEY (or Decourcy), **WILLIAM**, Preble co

Enl Rowane co N C where then lived. Pvt N C Milit. Pensd 1833 in Preble co O. Served 8½ mos. B in Baltimore co Md 5-24-1756. Mar Elizabeth Irvin 7-15-1776. Family record of chldr: Son William DeCourcy (made appl for mother's pens); Mary; John; Leonard; Jane; Nansey; Joel; Irvin; Elizabeth. Soldr d in Campbell co Ky. (Commodore Preble D A R reports burial in family cemetery in Dixon twp.) Since Rev resided in Campbell co Ky; then moved to Preble co O 16 yrs ago. Appl for pens Preble co O in 1832 res of Dixon twp. Wid appl for pens Campbell co Ky 7-7-1842. Ref W 8665 ½ N C. Rept by State D A R.

DEFORD, **THOMAS**, Delaware co

Enl in Frederick co Md Dec 1776. Pvt Md Milit about 8 mos. Pensd 6-22-1833 in Delaware co O. B on the eastern shore of Md 12-9-1736. Resided in Frederick co Md until some time after the war; then moved to Pickaway co O; and from there to Delaware co O. Appl for pens in Delaware co O 11-19-1832. Ref Md S 2514. Rept by State D A R.

DEHUFF, **JOHN**, Jefferson co

Pvt Pa St Trps. Pensd in 1833 in Jefferson co O. B in 1757. D in 1823. Bur in Island Creek Cem Jefferson co O; the grave was located by Steubenville D A R in 1931. Rept by Mrs Mary Sinclair Steubenville O.

DEITS, **ADAM**, Perry co

Enl in Va Musician in Va Contl. Pensd in 1818 in Butler co O. Mar Wid Mary Stiles who was a former wid of Adam Deits. Appl for pens Perry co O 3-14-1853. They were mar Nov 1825. Adam Deits mentions wf Rachel æ 60 in his appl of 1820. Mary seems to have been Adam's 2nd wf. "D away from home on business" 8-9-1834. Appl for pens at Cincinnati O 4-24-1818. Appl for pens Perry co O 6-5-1820. Ref W 598 Va. Rept by State D A R.

DELANO, **CORNELIUS**, Washington co

Rept by Helen Sloan Marietta O as likely a Rev Soldier in Washington co O. (No data).

DELONG, **SOLOMON**, ? co

Pvt; refused a pens as served in a Regt not on the Contl Estab. Exec Doc 31. Rept by Blanche Rings.

DELZELL, **WILLIAM**, Hamilton co

Enl in 1775 in Bucks co Pa. Pvt Pa Contl. Served 3 yrs. Pensd in 1831 in Hamilton co O. B in 1755. Appl said "wf" not living and "9 chldr grown." Rept "dead" in a letter written Sept 1837. Appl for pens 6-13-1831. Ref S 43478 Pa. Rept by State D A R.

DE MARIANVILLE, **CHARLES**, Ashtabula co

Enl March 1776 Rhode Island. Pvt R I Contl; served 1 yr. Pensd 10-25-1819 in Ashtabula co O. Appl of 1820 gives æ as 74 and names a wf Deborah æ 63. Came to Salem twp Ashtabula co O in 1810. Appl for pens in Ashtabula co 4-27-1818. Ref R I S 42152. Rept by State D A R. (Mary Redmond chpt reports 1931 he lived and owned land in Conneaut O. The family lot is in Center Cem Conneaut O where his son Charles and others are bur. His grave not located.)

DEMING, **POWNALL**, ? co

Capt. From old scrap bk clipping of Rev soldrs interested in or participating in Marietta settlement descendants of whom are bur in Washington co. Listed here for research by Marietta chpt.

DEMING, SOLOMON, Medina co

Enl at Landisfield Mass. Pvt Mass Contl. Pensd in 1833 in Medina co O and 1840 æ 76 liv in Brunswick with Carrol Denning. B in Berkshire co Mass 4-26-1763. Appl for pens 8-31-1832 in Medina co O. Ref S 3275 Mass. Rept by State D A R. (Nathan Perry chpt reports he is bur at Brunswick Center.)

DENMAN, MATHIAS, Licking co

Served from N J for which he received land grant of 4000 A. in Madison twp on March 28th 1800. Married Phebe ——. Children: Philip, Hathaway, Fenas and Mathias. Died near Hanover. Farmer. Sold his Hanover property and went to Woodbridge farm. Ref Brister's History, Family records and Deed book Vol 108 page 36. Rept by Hetuck chpt.

DENMAN, SAMUEL, Wayne co

In Dalton Cem Dalton O is inscription on monument "d 1-1-1852 æ 86 yrs. Soldier of war 1776" Samuel Denman. Rept by Wooster-Wayne chpt. (Sketch of Denman Family Union co N J (no Samuel) Hist Union & Middlesex cos N J Ed by W Woodford Clayton p 9-290.)

DENEEN, JAMES, Butler co

Appl for pen allowed July 30th 1832. Pvt Hunterdon co Milit under Capts Thomas Jones, Hazlett and Bray, Cols Taylor and Maxfield. After engaging in several skirmishes was transferred to making shoes for the Army. B Nov 11th 1756 in Hunterdon co N J. Reared by Peter Roddenbough. Mar Esther Criswell who was b 1756 and d 1844. Had son Alexander. Soldr died Sept 26th in Reily, Butler co. Bur Ward Cem on lot of his son. Inscript "James DeNeen b Nov 11th 1755 d Sept 26th 1841." Family head stone. Ref S 2162 N J; Rept by State D A R and John Reily chpt.

DENNIS, ANDREW, Washington co

Enl 1775 in Pa line. Pvt Pa Contl. Served 7 yrs. Pensd 5-4-1818 in Morgan co O. B in 1766. Appl of 1820 names a wf æ 54; a son Uriah æ 18; a dau Jemima æ 13. Res Roxbury twp Washington co O 5-4-1818. Appl there for pens in 1820. Was a farmer. Ref S 44129 Pa. Rept by State D A R.

DENNIS, JAMES, Columbiana co

Exec Doc 37 refused a pens as served less than 6 mo. Rept by Wm. Pettit.

DENNIS (or Dennie), JOHN, Clermont co

(Incorrectly spelled "Denine"). Enl Glouster co N J 10-30-1760. Pvt N J Milit. Served 10 mos & 4 das. Pensd 1833 in Clermont co O. B in 1760. Wid appl gives wf's name Sarah mar 1-1-1823. Soldr d in Clermont co O 6-8-1850. Appl for pens in Clermont co O 4-22-1833. Wid appl for pens in Clermont co O Mar 12 1853. Ref S W 8196 N J; B L Wt 26790-160-55. Rept by State D A R.

DE PEW, BENJAMIN, Mahoning co

Lieut N J in Rev p 436; d in Milton, Mahoning co; was schoolteacher in twp; Ref H R Baldwin Recds. Rept by Mahoning chpt Research in Pens Claim dept brot back rept no one of this name found in O as pensr. (J D).

DEPUE, NICHOLAS, Trumbull co

On Roll of 5th Battalion, Second class Northampton co Pa Militia. Ref Pa Arch Ser 5 Vol 8 page 397. Resided in Braceville Trumbull Co in 1820. Had a son Marshall. Rept by Mary Chesney Chapter.

DERROUGH, JOHN, Monroe co

Enl in Mar 1779 in Va Pvt Va Contl. Served 4 yrs. Pensd 1819 in Monroe co O. B in 1740. Appl for pens in Monroe co O 6-12-1818. Was a wheelwright or chair maker. Ref S 44137 Va. Rept by State D A R.

DEVALON, FRANCIS, Fayette co

Name in a list of soldiers of 1776 bur in old cem at Washington C H. B in 1723. D 9-22-1819 æ 96 yrs. No further data found. Rept by Washington C H chpt.

DEVAUN (or "Ven," var spellings), JAMES, Licking co

Enl in Prince George co Md in Feb 1776 under Capt James Scott. Pvt Md Contl served 3 yrs. Pensd 1819 in Licking co O. Appl of 1818 gave æ 66. Wf's name was Lydia. Appl also said he and his wf Lydia both very infirm live alone. Was a farmer. Ref S 44132 Md. Rept by State D A R.

DEVOL, ALLEN, ? co

Capt. From old scrap bk clipping of Rev soldrs interested in Marietta settlement descendants of whom are bur in Washington co. Listed here for research by Marietta chpt.

DEWOLF, PETER, Trumbull co

Pensd 1833 for serv in Conn Milit while living in Trumbull co O. (S A R 1897 yr bk). B East Hartford Conn 1753. Mar to Elizabeth Clemmons in 1777. Names of chldr were: Roxanna; William; Horace; Betsey; Clemmons. Soldr d at Fowler Trumbull co O in 1843 where he is bur by side of wf in a cem located in the center of Fowler O. There is marker and inscription on wf's grave but none on husb grave. Ref Am N Y 8-18-1776. Disch 9-25-1776 Capt Brittolph St Joseph Norris Ens Etna Holcomb Regt Mil Conn Men of Rev; Pens Dept Sec War. Rept by Mary Chesney chpt.

DICKENSON, FRIEND, Trumbull co

Enl in Litchfield Conn in 1776 in Capt Beebe's Co Col Bradley's Regt. Other service Pvt Ct St Trps. Pensd in 1832 in Trumbull co O. Pension Record S 44147. Among the chldr were Samuel W and Friend Jr. Soldr d 4-12-1833 in Johnston Trumbull co O. Rept by Mary Chesney chpt.

DICKERSON, WALTER, Butler co & Ind

Enl in July 1780 in Morris co N J. Servd 6 mos in N J St Trps. Pensd in 1832 in Butler co O. B in Morris co N J in 1763. Mar to Sarah 8-26-1850. Mentions "chldr" in appl. Moved from Morris co N J to Washington co Pa; then to O. Appl for pens in Butler co O 7-31-1832 res of Oxford twp. Soldr d 10-8-1855 in Vigo co Ind. Wid appl for pens Vigo co Ind 7-10-1856. Ref W 25543 B L Wt 32324-160-55 N J. Rept by State D A R.

DICKEY, THOMAS, Highland co

Enl in 1777 in Cumberland co Pa. Pvt Contl. Served 9 mos. Pensd in 1832 in Highland co O. B in Ireland in 1758. Aft Rev lived in Rockbridge co Va 23 or 24 yrs; then in Highland co O. Appl for pens 8-25-1832 in Highland co O. Ref S 2175 Pa. Rept by State D A R.

DICKINSON, JACOB, Mahoning co

Pvt. Mass Men in Rev p 575. Was b in Scotland. A son Jacob d in Poland O 1852. Served in War of Rev from Roxbury Mass. Ref Hist Columbiana co 1 p 143. Rept by Mahoning chpt.

DICKINSON, WAITSTILL, Ashtabula co

Sgt 3rd Ct Line. B in 1758; d in 1843 and bur at Kingsville O. Grave was located by Mary Stanley chpt. Ref 18th. Rep N S D A R p 189. Rept by Nathan Perry chpt.

DICKINSON, ZEBULON, Hamilton co & Ind

Pvt & fifer under Capt Woodworth & Thompson N Y line. B in N Y in 1761. D in 1835 at Lawrenceburg Ind. Grave marked by the Cincinnati O D A R. Tho he d across line in Ind his desc are members in O. Rept by Mrs Ed F John 816 N W 41st St Oklahoma City Okla.

DICKSON (Dixon), GEORGE, Columbiana co

Pvt Capt James Poe's Co 8th Battl Cumberland co Milit. B 1763. D 1-18-1844 æ 81; bur Deer Creek cem Columbiana co. Ref Pa Arch 3rd 23 p 451 Columbiana co Cem Recs. Rept by Mrs Wilma M Molsberry Youngstown O.

DICKSON, JOHN, Mahoning co

Pvt Ser 5 V 5 p 520 Pa Arch. B 1756 Ireland. 11 chldr: James mar Martha dau Samuel Galbraith R S; George b 1808 mar Isabella McBride. Soldr d 1826 Poland O. Came from Ireland 1769 with his parents when 13 yrs old; came to Poland in 1801. Ref Hist Trumbull and Mahoning cos V 2 pp 59 & 72 Henry R Baldwin S A R list. Rept by Mahoning chpt.

DIEHL, PHILIP, Mahoning co

Pvt. Ser 5 V 4 pp 172 & 257. B Germany Apr 1766 son of Samuel Diehl. Mar Elizabeth 12-15-1770; also mar 10-27-1848. Chldr: Henry mar Sarah Bort; John b 1791 mar Sarah; Samuel mar Catherine; William; Adam. Soldr d Ellsworth O 7-22-1852; bur on Kager Farm. Ref Memoirs of Pioneer Women of Western Reserve p 866; Hist of Mahoning co V 3 p 547 Butler. Rept by Mahoning chpt.

DIKE, COLVIN, Cuyahoga co

Enl 1778 Woodstock Vt. Pvt Vt St Trps. Served 2 yrs. Pensd 1833 Cuyahoga co O. B 7-7-1761 Springfield Vt. Appl for pens 11-6-1832 Cuyahoga co O. Ref S 15410 N H & Vt. Rept by State D A R.

DIKE (or Dyke), HENRY, Pike co

Enl 1776 Loudon co Va. Pvt Va Contl. Served 2 yrs. Pensd 1819 while living in Gallia co O. B 1754. Appl for pens Pike co O 6-1820. Ref S 44146 Va. Rept by State D A R.

DILD, RICHARD, Columbiana co

Cop fr Cem recds b 1764 d 1824 Unity; Rev soldr but recd not found. Rept by Wilma Molsberry.

DILLE, SAMUEL, Montgomery co

Received depreciated pay Washington co Pa Milit; Pa Arch 5th Ser vol 4 pp 397, 706. Bur Dille cem Valley Pike. Rept by Wm Pettit.

DILLER, DAVID, Cuyahoga co

Listed p 270 in Va Militia in Rev as a trnsfr fr Ky Mrch 4 1834. (Compare David Dille p 114 Vol 1, Ohio Roster for possible error of one). Cop by Jane Dailey.

DILLON, JESSE, Clinton co

Corp Contl line Va. B 10-10-1753 Norfolk Va. Parents were Daniel Dillon and wf Lydia (?). Mar to Hannah Ruckman 4-29-1778 dau of Joseph R & Sarah (White) R of Greensboro N C. Chldr were: Achsah Hodgson; Jonathan; Susannah Starbuck; Martha Fisher; Sarah Dwiggins; Luke; Hannah Wright; Abigail Wright. Soldr d 10-3-1823. Bur Centre Union twp Clinton co O. Moved with his family to Wilmington O from Guilford co Carolina. Will proba 1823 Wilmington O. Ref Seffels List Va Soldiers p 13; Va State Libr. Rept Vol 8 p 138; Va St Libr certif for service as Corp; 1st Fam America V 3 p 162; Mar Ref p 36 No 644 in Dillon Hodson Fisher Leonard Fam Bk. Secured from Mrs Floyd Kimble Tuttle Okla No. 217620 D A R. By Jane Dailey.

DINE, JOHN, Butler co

Exec Doc 37 refused a pens as servd less than 6 mo. Reported by Wm Pettit.

DINGMAN, PETER, Pickaway co

Enl N J Trps 1st in the milit. 4 terms of 1 mo each and 1 of 6 wks; was pvt in Capt Manuel Hovers & Henry Cortwright's Cos in Col John C Symmes & John Rosekranzs Regt from the spring of 1778. Served 9 mos as pvt in Capt Peter West Brooks Co Col John Rosekranzs Regt; in 1781 6 mos as a ranger and Indian spy under Capt Manuel Hover & Col Rosekranz. B 1757 Sussex co N J where he enl. D aft 1832; grave not found. Soon aft Rev movd to Kingston on the Susquehanna River & later moved to Milton N Y; thence to Jackson twp Pickaway co O. Was allowed a pens 11-26-1832 æ 74 yrs 8 mos & living in Pickaway co. Ref Pen No S 16103. Rept by State D A R & Pickaway Plains chpt.

DISBROW, ASA, Clinton co

Pvt Conn St Trps. Pensd 1833 Clinton co O. Served 6 mos. B 6-13-1753 Fairfield co Conn. Enl 1776 Fairfield co Conn where remained till 1819; thence to Clinton co O. Appl for pens Clinton co O 11-4-1833 res of Chester twp. Ref S 9385 Conn. Rept by State D A R.

DIXSON, JOSEPH, Licking co

Ref Exec Doc 37 refused a pens as servd less than six mo. Rept by Wm Petit.

DOANE, BENJAMIN, ? co

Appl pens 4-4-1821 in Common Pleas Court Marietta O stating property value at $69.56. Ref V 3-466. Rept by Helen Sloan.

DOBBINS, HUGH SR, Mahoning co

Pvt. Mass Soldiers V 4 p 808. B 1762. Wf Elizabeth (1772 — 8-13-1827). Chldr were: Matthew mar Elizabeth; Joseph mar Jane; Hugh b 1803 mar Rosannah; David mar Martha; Mary H; Margaret mar James McCullough; Elizabeth mar James Smith; John mar Anna. Soldr d 3-18-1819 Poland O. Ref Will Bk 3 p 4 Prob 1820. Deed Bk 1 p 152 to Hugh Dobbins Poland 1810; Tax List 1826 Hugh Dobbins Heirs. Rept by Mahoning chpt.

DOCKUM, JAMES, Madison co

Pvt N H Milit 6 mos. Pensd 4-9-1833 Madison co O. B 10-20-1761 Rockingham co N H. Mar Polly Barker 11-23-1788. Soldr d 9-15-1833 Madison co. Enl July 1780 in Rockingham co N H where he resided. Some yrs aft the war moved to Maine; then to Vermont; thence to O; lived in various parts previous to moving to Madison co O. Wid appl for pens 6-25-1847 in Madison co O. Ref N H W 7037. Rept by State D A R.

DODGE, JOHN, ? co

Lieut. From old scrap bk clipping of Rev soldrs interested in Marietta settlement descendants of whom are bur in Washington co. Listed here for research by Marietta chpt.

DODGE, OLIVER, Washington co

B 1776 Hampton Falls N H son of Nathaniel (1738-1830) & Sally H (Dodge) Dodge (d 1793). Mar a wid Mrs Nancy (Devol) Manchester 7-4-1800. Only son Richard Hubbard Dodge d 1866 leaving no chld. Only a dau Mary M mar Dr Perley B Johnson (member of congress 1843-1845 from 13th dist O). They left a son Perley Brown Johnson killed at Fort Wagner 7-18-1863. Soldr d 8-26-1817 Marietta O at brother Nathaniel's; bur Schantz Cem 2 mi above Lowell O. Inscription on monument reads, "In memory of Oliver Dodge who departed this life 8-26-1817 in the 52nd year of his age." Was one of the band of "48" who made the 1st settlement at Marietta 4-7-1788. Indian War was in Campus Martius. Was a Mason & bur with full Masonic honors. Ref Hildreth's & Williams Histories of Wash Co p 557; Gen of the Dodge Fam of Essex co Mass 1629-1894 p 121. Rept by Marietta chpt Helen Sloan.

DOLAN, WILLIAM, ? co

Appl pens 7-25-1832 in Common Pleas Court Marietta O. Ref V 6 p 311. Rept by Helen Sloan.

DONALDSON, SAMUEL, Geauga co

Name appears p 943 Pioneer Women of Western Reserve along with his sister Mary (Moore) & bro James & sisters Jane (Inman) & Margaret (Norton). Fam came from Washington co (prob) Pa. Were devout M E's. (Cop by J D). Soldr d at Middlefield O. Grave located by New Connecticut D A R. Ref 5th Rep N S D A R p 387. Rept by Nathan Perry chpt.

DOTY, ASA, Geauga co

Enl in Mass in fall 1781. Pvt 2 yrs 6 mo Contl. Pensd 4-17-1820. Pensr 1840 New Lyle Geauga Ashtabula co æ 77 living with Oliver Brown. B 9-9-1765. Wf's name Lurania. Chldr named: Sophia b 2-12-1805; Asa Jr b 9-13-1807; Mary b 1809; Sally Marcia 1811; Benjamin Horwood b 1814. Soldr d (probably) at Parlsman Geauga co. Appl for pens Geauga co O 12-2-1818. Estate administered 1856 Geauga co. Lived with son Ezra in last days. Ref Contl Mass S 42673 Hist of Geauga co: "A Capt Asa Doty came to Parkman from Aurora Cayuga co N Y 1815. Rept by Mary Chesney chpt & State D A R.

DOUD, CHANDLER, Crawford co

Enl May or June 1781 Tyringham Mass. Pvt Mass Contl. Served 3 yrs. Discharged 12-23-1783 West Point N Y. Pensd 1822 Washington co O. B 1755. Aff of son said "Left a widow who later mar again; she d 2-10-1836." Appl of 1820 said "3 daus all married," a son Elihu. Soldr d 9-29-1824 Crawford co O. Appl for pens Washington co O 3-19-1821. Was a farmer. Son Elihu appl for arrears of pens by letter written 3-28-1855 from state of Wis. Aff of son Elihu said "Mother d in Wisconsin." Ref S 42672 Mass. Rept by State D A R.

DOUGHERTY, WILLIAM, Warren co

Pvt Pa Contl Enl March or April 1778 Northumberland co Pa. Served in Pa line for 3 yrs under Capt Boyd & Col Chamber. Discharged Brunswick N J ? 1780 fall of yr. Pens Warren co O. Appl named a "wf" "Margaret" æ 63 in 1826. Appl mentioned "11 chldr; 9 living 5 males 4 females. Margaret æ 38; James 36; Susan 35; Martha 31; William 29; Franklin 27; Napier 23; George 21; & Washington 21. All mar except George & Washington and have chldr to support." Was formerly a cooper by occupation Made original claim for pens 8-23-1826 Warren co O. Ref S 42674 Pa. Rept by State D A R.

DOUGHTON, STEPHEN, Trumbull co

A gunsmith in Washington's Army. Married Margaret Farran. Children Marmaduke; David; Clarissa and Stephen. Worker in Heaton iron furnace at Niles in 1803. Bought land near Hubbard in 1804 and died in that locality in 1830. Grave not located. Rept by Mary Chesney chpt.

DOUGLAS, DAVID, Darke co

Exec Doc 37 refused a pension as servd less than 6 mo. Rept by Wm Pettit.

DOUGLAS, JOHN R, Hamilton co

Cop fr Cens 1840 a pensr liv in 6th Ward Cincinnati æ 80; was b then 1760. Research at Pen Cl brot no data. Jane Dailey.

DOUGLASS, JOHN, Mahoning co

Pvt. 4th class-Ser 5 V Pa Arch 1st Co 5th Battl Capt Nelson. Other records Mass V 3 p 992 Many Men in Rev. Wife's name Nancy. Children were James and Robert b 1791. Soldr d about 1818 (Springfield twp?). Ref Will Bk 3 p 431 Columbiana co Records probated 1818; Deed Bk p 336 John & Nancy Douglass to 1818. Rept by Mahoning chpt.

DOVE, RICHARD, Licking co

Enl Apr 1776 Prince George's co Md. Served 3 yrs. Pvt Md Milit. Pensd 1833 Licking co O. B 1774 Annarundel co Md. Appl stated: resided until about 4 yrs ago in Md; then moved to Licking co O. Appl for pens 3-13-1833 Licking co O. Ref Md S 17391. Rept by State D A R.

DOVENBERGER, DAVID, ? co

Pvt Pa. In Ohio list of 1818 pensrs. (no recd found at Bur Pens.) Cop by J D.

DOVENBERGER, JACOB, Belmont co

Enl Lancaster Pa Pvt Pa Contl Col Hampton's Regt. Pensd 4-16-1819 Belmont co O. B 4-1-1759. Appl mentions "wf" and 2 chldr Mary æ 6; John æ 2. Appl for pens 6-22-1818 Belmont co O. Ref p 574 S 3 V 23 Pa Arch. Ref S 43511 Pa. Rept by J D.

DOWD, SAMUEL, Knox co

War recd; Enl Watertown Conn; pvt in Capt Samuel Barker's Co 6th Conn Regt Col Return Jonathan Meigs. Name first appears on muster roll May 1778; dischrgd Nov 7 1778. Fr Stone recd Strong cem Middlebury twp Knox co abandoned cem: "Samuel Dowd d Nov 19 1840 æ 83 yr 2 mo and 10 da." (B then in 1757). Kokosing D A R placed Rev mrkr 1937. Fr Centennial Biog Hist Knox co O: "The Strong cem is still in use . . . Among these pioneers laid to rest was Mr Dowd a Rev soldr." Rept by Emma Blair Ewalt Ch of Kokosing chpt. Mary Chesney chpt repts same war service on a Samuel Doud but adds dischrgd June 10 1783 fr Waterbury Conn; gives b Sept 9 1763; res Howland twp Trumbull co. Ref Conn in Rev p 210.

DOWLER, THOMAS, ? co

Listed p 172 Invalid Pensrs of U S 1818 belonging to O and pd at Chillicothe. Pvt. Named for continued research. J D.

DOWNEY, THOMAS, Pickaway co

Enl 2-10-1776 in the 1st Regt Pa line. 4365 Pvt Pa line 1 yr. Pensd 11-12-1818 Pickaway co O. Trnsfrd to Lexington Ky 4-3-1828. (May have d in Ky.) B Frederick co Md. Ref Pa S 35895. Rept by State D A R.

DOWNING, PHINEAS, Portage co

Enl into Conn State Trps 6-25-1776. Pvt Conn Milit. Served 12 mos. Pensd 1833 Portage co O. B 1761 Canterbury Conn. Soldr d 1835. Mar Polly Young. Chld Erastus. Was residing in Canterbury Conn at the time he enl. Aft war moved to N Y; and later to Northfield O. Appl for pens 10-11-1832 Portage co O. res of Northfield O. Ref Conn S 31651. Rept by State D A R.

DRAKE, JOSEPH, Hamilton co

1st Lieut in Capt James Walling Co Col Davis Major Oerndoff Md Milit 6 mos. Enl fr 6 mi of Hagerstown Md Washington co. Aft war removed to Pa; lived 8 yrs; thence to O opposite Columbia 2 or 3 yrs; thence to Warren co O; and to Hamilton co. B Somerset co N J (not recollect yr) in his father's Bible is record. Appls for pens in Warren co O as nearer his res at this time 7-4-1836 was 88 or 89 yrs old. Ref S 9387 Md. Cop by J D.

DRAUGHT (or Drought), RICHARD, Coshocton co

Enl Opsum N H April 1779. Pvt N H Contl. Served 4 yrs. Discharged in N Y at Constitution Island. B 1768. Appl said "7 chldr but none residing with me." Appl for pens Wayne co O 8-26-1818. Appl for pens in Coshocton co O where he resided in 1821 on July 4. Ref S 42675 N C. Rept by State D A R.

DRULLINGER, FREDERICK, Warren co

About 6-17-1776 2 British vessels "The Roebuck" & "The Liverpool" entered Delaware Bay for purpose of battle it was thought & at this time he entered service. Pvt St Trps. Served in Regt commanded by Col Holmes in N J line for 21 mos. Pensd 8-17- 1833 Warren co O æ 80. B 6-20-1754 Upper Alloway's Creek twp Salem co N J. "The chld of Frederick Drullinger dec'd" rec'd the arrears of the pens pay of the dec'd soldier. Record of information of death contained in letter written 3-9-1844. Made appl for pens in Warren co O 5-21-1833 æ 79 on 20th last June. Ref S 16106 N J. Rept by State D A R.

DRURY, LEONARD, Stark co

Enl St Mary's co Md 1777. Pvt Md St Trps. Served 6 mos. Pensd 1-26-1833 Stark co O. B 6-17-1759 St Mary co Md. Since Rev lived Port Tobacco nr Frederick Town; then Leesburg Va; then nr Hagerstown; then Franklin co Pa; then Md; to Stark co O. Appl for pens Stark co O 10-29-1832. Ref S 2183 Md. Rept by State D A R.

DUBOIS, BENJAMIN, (or Daniel Dominie), Montgomery co

N J service. B 1739 Pittsburg Salem co. D 1827; bur Carlisle Cem on Warren co line but lived in Montgomery co. Ref No. 180121. Cop by J D at D C.

DUCK, GEORGE SR, Columbiana co

Lieut in Capt Martin Bowman's Co 10th Battl Lancaster co Milit 12-6-1777. 1st Lieut Capt Martin Bowman's Co as above 1777. 1st Lieut in Capt Martin Bowman's Co 5th Battl Lancaster co Pa Milit. B in Maryland. D at New Lisbon (probably 1811 when estate was settled). Came to Columbiana co 1808; estate settled 1811 New Lisbon. Was 1st sheriff of Columbiana co. Ref Ohio Patriot Pa Arch 3, 23, 433 5, 7, p 978; 512 Hist Columbiana co. Rept by Wilma M Molsberry.

DUGAN, WILLIAM, Darke co

Enl Morris co N J March 1777. Pvt N J Contl 3 yrs service. Pens'r 5-10-1819 Butler co O. Appl for continuance of pens in Darke co April 1821. Appl 1818 gave æ 58. Wf's name was Jane. Appl of 1821 named chldr: James æ 11; one dau æ 11, Rossae 5 or 6 yrs. Ref N J S 42678. Rept by State D A R.

DUKES, ISAAC, Ross co

Enl Warcester co Md. Pvt Md Milit. Served 14 mos & 12 das. Pensd Ross co O 1833. Ae 73 in 1832. Parents d when he was a chld. Mar April 1793 to Elizabeth. Appl of wid names chldr: Mary b 1796; James 1798; Isaac 1800; Elizabeth 1802; Katharine 1806; Spencer 1808; Samuel 1811. Soldr d Clinton co Ind 4-17-1835. Resided in Warcester co Md until 1812; then moved to Ross co O. Appl for pens Ross co O 10-17-1832. Wid appl for pens in Clinton co Ind 2-11-1840. Ref Md Privateer R 3111. Rept by State D A R.

DUNBAR, JOHN, Erie co

Pvt Mass line. Pensd while living in Otsego co N Y. B (prob.) Wallingford Conn 1766. Mar Rebecca Bliss 1788. A son William mar Betsey Pickle in 1811. Soldr d Erie co O 1858. Ref V 110 D A R Lin p 260. Rept by J D.

DUNBAR, WILLIAM, Washington co

Pvt Va Contl. Pensd 1832 Washington co O. B 1742. D 1854 æ 112 yrs; bur Layman Washington co O. Grave marked by D A R Marietta O 1930. Ref V 6 p 326 Court Records Washington co O. Rept by Marietta chpt.

DUNBAR, WILLIAM, Sandusky co

Enl summer 1780 in the Co of Capt Martin. Pvt N Y Line. 11555 Pensd 6-9-1819 Sandusky co O. Trnsferd to Wayne co Mich 4-28-1822. B 6-24-1760. Appl of 1822 mentions wf æ 42 yrs & very feeble; John æ 18 yrs; Benjamin æ 12 yrs; & Jeptha æ 9 yrs. Date of death and where d unknown. Ref N Y S 34770. Rept by State D A R.

DUNCAN, JAMES, Mahoning co

Frontier Ranger 1778-1783 Washington co Pa Rev James Duncan was an early settler on the north side of the Mahoning adjoining the State line. First pastor of church at center of Poland O. Also preached in Pa in 1801. Ref Pens Cl Dept D C. Find none who came to O. Poss he lived over line of Pa in O Pa Arch Ser 3 V 23 p 211. Hist Trumbull & Mahoning co V 2 p 59. Rept by Mahoning chpt.

DUNHAM, DANIEL SR, Washington co

B 1746. D 1791. Said to be Rev soldier. Rept by Helen Sloane.

DUNHAM, DANIEL JR, Washington co

Reported as Rev soldier; for continued research listed here. Rept by Helen Sloane.

DUNHAM, JACOB, Knox co

Enl Woodridge N J fall 1775. Pvt N J Milit. Served 2 yrs. Pensd 1833 Knox co O æ 77. B Middlesex co N J 10-9-1757. Mar Sarah Outcalt 11-27-1790. D 7-6-1838. Has resided in Middlesex co N J & Knox co O since Rev. Appl for pens 9-1-1832 while res in Clinton twp Knox co O. Wid appl for pens Knox co O 10-29-1845. Ref N J W 7055. On O Pens Roll 1835;3;0-137 B L Wt 36558-160-55. Rept by State D A R.

DUNLAP, SAMUEL, Licking co

Enl Fifth Pa Battl under Capt John Bull. Mustered out 1776. Served in Philadelphia Militia as a matross in Artillery. Married Mary Ann Howie (Howey) in 1754. Children: James; John; Joseph; and Samuel. Died Oct 1813. Buried on farm north of Utica. Ref Pa Arch 6 Ser Vol 1 p 808. Muste" Roll Capt John Edwards Philadelphia Militia; Archives 6 Ser. Vol 12 p 615. Sent to Vice Chairman by Mrs O M Sherman Elizabeth Benton Chapter Kansas City Mo. Nat'l No. 170428. Rept by Meryl B Markley Vice Chairman.

DUNLAP, SAMUEL, Athens co

Pvt Mass Contl. Pens 1820 Athens co O. Enl Winter Hill Fort (near Boston Capt Adam Wheeler Co) at Dept Interior. Ref S 42679 Mass gives: Pvt in Col Nixon's 14th Regt Mass line 1 yr. Pens in O $8 a mo fr 5-22-1818. Lived at Hubbardtown Worcester co Mass. On 7-5-1821 he was 63 yrs old therefore b about 1758. Mentions his wf; a son Stephen 17 crippled; Delan (?) a dau 9 yrs; Moses 5 yrs. Resided Alexandria twp Athens co. Cop by J D.

DUNLEVY, ANTHONY, Warren co

See No. 113078 D A R for comparison. (J D).

DURAND, ANDREW, Geauga co

1833 a pensr in Geauga co O; moved to Indiana; Ref File 2528 Vol (?) p 103 Pens Dept. Listed here to avoid continued research. Rept by Florence.

DURR, MICHAEL, Mahoning co

Ranger on frontier Ser 3 V 23 p 297 Pa Arch. B Maryland 1766. Father was George Durr b in Germany. Mar Elizabeth Snider (1797-1889) 1815. Chldr were: George b 1817; Mary 1819; Jacob 1 1820; Magdalena 1822; John 1825; Elizabeth 1827; Michael 1831; David 1833; Josiah 1835. Soldr d 1849 Old Springfield Springfield twp. Ref Will Bk 1 p 146 Mahoning co. Biog E O pp 230-231 Summers. Rept by Mahoning chpt.

DURYEA, CHARLES, Pickaway co

Enl 1776. Served 3 mos as pvt in Capt Wm Hazlett's Co Col John Taylor's N J Regt 1777. Served 2 mos in same Regt. Served 2 mos in Capt John Bell's Regt same Col. Was at Valley Forge & Monmouth. In 1779 was appointed Capt and served as such at various times on short tours. Served 5 yrs and was noted as a terror to the Tories in the neighborhood where he resided. B 5-10-1753 near Brunswick N J. A son Wm mar Nancy Williamson dau of John Williamson early settler in Walnut twp. Soldr d 12-1843 Walnut twp Pickaway co O; bur Reber Hill abt 6 miles N E of Circleville in S W corner with about a hundred other graves that were moved from other cem. Inscript: "Charles Duryea b 5-10-1753 d 12-1843 æ 90 yrs 6 mos 27 das. Grave mrkd by Pickaway Plains chpt bronze marker May 1932. Aft Rev lived in Hampshire co Va about 7 yrs; also Allegany co Md abt 7 yrs 10-24-1832; had lived in Walnut twp Pickaway co more than 20 yrs. Ref William's Hist p 276. Charles Duryea came from Cumberland co Md to Walnut twp in 1812. He never owned any land. Mentions son Thomas. In 1833 his sister Hannah Smith æ 68 resided in Pickaway co. Pens No. S 4278. Rept by Pickaway Plains chpt.

DUTCHER, HENRY, Holmes co

Enl Dec 1775 in N Y line. Pvt N Y Contl. Served abt 2 yrs. Dischgd Feb 1777. Pensd 7-25-1825 Cayuga co N Y. B 7-30-1751. Resided in Dutcher co N Y at time of enlistment; moved to Cayuga co prior to 1824; in 1830 moved to Holmes co O. Pens 1825 in N Y. Appl for transfer to Holmes co O 1-6-1831. Ref N Y S 42683. Rept by State D A R.

DUVALL, COL, Belmont co

Rev soldier in Belmont co at Pleasant Hill York twp cf p 122 Vol 1 O Roster "Jacob Duvall." Rept by Mrs G M McCommon.

DYER, STEPHEN, Lucas co

Enl 1775 as a drummer; servd under Capt Arthur Fenner; was in the battle of White Plains and Long Island. In 1832 allowed pens for service as sergt, R I Line. B Cranston R I 1752; d Toledo O 1847. Mar Sarah Matthewson (1750-1814); son Edmund. Ref Vol 112 p 268 D A R Lin Nat No 11826; also No 40782.

DYKE, CALVIN, Lorain co

Enl spring of 1778 Woodstock Vt Pvt N H. More than 2 yrs. Various enlistments. Pensr 8-1-1833 & in 1840 Amherst twp Lorain co æ 78; and also 1848. B 7-7-1761 Springfield Vt. Parents moved to Woodstock Vt before the war resided here till 1831. Soldr d previous to 1855 Lorain co O. First moved to Madison twp Geauga co. Appl for pens at Rovalton Cuyahoga co O 11-6-1832. Ref N H & Vt Pens Bureau. Rept by Nathan Perry chpt & State D A R.

EAKINS (or Acron), GABRIEL, Brown co

Pvt Va St Trps. Enl July 26 1778 Pa. Servd 7 mo 28 da. b 1759. Pens allowed 5-2-1833 residing in Lewis twp Brown co. Ref Va S 16775 Pens. Taliaferro chpt repts he d Apr 1836. His will v 1 p 317 Pr Court Brown co names a nephew John Pribble as sole heir. Rept State D A R.

EARHART, JOHN, Franklin co

In "Ohio Statesman" issue of Nov 25 1848 was the following: "Another Revolutionary soldier gone John Earhart ae 99 yr 1 mo 10 da d at the home of his grandson John Earhart. Burial will be —— etc." Place of bur not stated. One son was Adam. John came to Franklin co abt 1834. Rept by H. Preston Wolfe Col O. to State Chairman Jane Dailey.

EARIN, JAMES, Brown co

Is inccorrect spelling for Erwin, James, which see, this volume. Listed here to avoid continued research.

EARINFIGHT, JACOB, Warren co

Pvt Pa Contl. Enl Apr 1778. Servd under Col Flowers Pa Line 3 yrs. Pensd in Warren co O 11-24-1818 also 8-7-1821 fr Lebanon O Warren co. Ref S 42691 Contl. Rept by State D A R. Mary Steinmetz Reading Pa repts Ref Pa Arch for Ohio soldiers he was liv in Warren co 1834, ae 90.

EASTMAN, CHARLES, Huron co

Pvt Mass St Trps. Enl in Milit 1776 re-enl 1777. Resided in Greenwich, Huron co O whr pensd 4-9-1833. B 2-10-1762 Ashford Conn. "His father movd with him to Montague co Mass. Had a "Dau livd with her son in N Y." A grnd-son Z Coswell who appld for his pens and for arrears. D 1851 Huron co O. Rept by State D A R. Ref Mass S 2533 and 18th Rept N S D A R p 192 (Rept by Mrs. Oehlke).

EASTMAN, DELIVERANCE, Medina co

Listed pp 144 & 145 in History of North Central Ohio by Wm A Duff as a Rev soldr Friendsville Medina co O. Rept by Nathan Perry chpt.

EASTMAN, PEASLEY (or Peaslee), Washington co

Pvt N H Contl servd 2 yrs. Enl June 1778 N H Milit. Disch at West Point. Mar Mary Graham 11-1-1786. His appl for pens in Washington co 1820 names chld: Mary ae 15; Lucy ae 9; Geo W ae 7. In widows appl 8-9-1839 other chldr named are Hannah, Asicha, Sally, and Polly. On Apr 23 1840 widow appl for pens in Scioto co O. On 1-16-1849 widow appl residing at Quaker Bottom Lawrence co.

EASTON, MOSES, Warren co

Pvt 1st Reg J Line. Enl Cont Line Co commanded by Capt Jno Holmes. Pensd Oct 22 1828. Appl for pens in Warren co on Sept 18 1828 Res of Turtle twp on Sept 27 1799 in Hamilton co Moses Eastman apptd an Atty to secure his pens. S 46356. BL Wt 156-100 N J BL Wt allowed on disccharge certificate which discharge was signed by Geo Washington and Richard Cox on 6-5-1783.

EATON, SAMUEL, Ashtabula co

Exec Doc 37 of 1852. Refused a pens as servd less than 6 mo. Rept by Wm Pettit.

EATON, JOSEPH, ? co

Pvt refused a pens as not in indigent circumstances on acct of the amt of property he had. Ref Doc 31 Jan 6 1831. Rept by Blanche Rings Cols O.

EBRIGHT, PHILIP, Fairfield co

Enlisted 1775 Lancaster Co Pa Res Lebanon in that Co .Remained at Leb Pa for some time then removed to Shafferstown from there to Cumberland Co and from there to Fairfield co O. Served two years from 1775 Mar 1754 Lan Co Pa. Appl for pens Fairfield Co Ohio Nov 25 1829 pensd there 1833 S 3319.

EDDY, LIVENS, ? co

Artificer. Refused a pens because he deserted the service Ref Doc 31 Jan 6 1831. Rept by Blanche Rings.

EDGE, JOHN, Belmont co

Pvt Va Contl pensd 1819 in Belmont co O. Enlist Frederick co Va 1777 for 3 yrs as pvt under Capt Thomas Blackwell's Co Col Edw Stevens 10 w Va Reg Several enlistments. Dischrged in N J B 1753. Mar Jan 8 1781 Nancy Cummins in Farquier co Va. chldr: Molly 1781; Rosannah 1783 mar Dunfee; Israel 1785; John 1786; Levincy 1787; Letice 1791. He died June 11 1832 in Belmont co (widow says July 4 1830. Pens W 4946 Widow app in 1855 ae 99; lived Wash twp. Ref "Commander-in Chief's Guard" by Carlos E. Godfrey M D p 159 Copied from D A R Mag March 1927 p 228.

EDGECOMB, JOHN, Trumbull co

Made appl for pens through Trumbull Court. Lived in Braceville twp in 1831. No further data. Ref Mary Chesney chpt.

EDGINGTON, GEORGE, Adams co

Pvt in Capt James Munn's Co 2nd Batt Washington co Pa militia. B abt 1750 in Va Father's name was George; chldr were Tacy William and others. Said to be buried in Edgington cem near Bentonville Adams co. Pioneer to North West Ter and one of the first settlers in Sprigg twp Adams co. Ref Pa Arch 6th Ser Vol 2 p 41 83 Evan's & Stivers History of Adams co. Rept by Mrs. Ora Leeka Marion O.

EDGINGTON, ISAAC, Adams co

Pvt on Sandusky Exp under Col Wm Crawford in Capt James Munn' Co Washington co Pa Militia. B 1752 in Va. Son of Geo Sr Mar Elizabeth chldrs: Isaac; John; Abraham; Azariah; Jacob. Bur in Bentonville Adams co. D abt 1836. Ref Pa Arch 6th Ser Vol 2 p 51, 72, 84, 396. Evan's & Stivers Hist of Adams co. Draper Mss 19 S 162, 163.

EDGINGTON, JESSE, Richland co

Pvt in Washington co Pa Militia Capt James Munn's Co 1782; Sandusky Exp under Col Wm Crawford. B Hampshire co Va 1759. Son of George Sr. Mar Margaret Parramore, about 1780 (or Palmer). Children: Thomas; John; Levi; Isaac; and Jesse. D July 6 1821 on farm 7 mi west of Mansfield bur near Ontario Rich co removed from Jefferson co near Steubenville to Richland co in 1815. Will probated in Richland co. Ref Pa Arch 6th Ser Vol 2 p 72, 84, 257, 396. Draper Mss 9-No.-44. Data from Mrs R L Erickson Stromsburg Neb Suppl papers Mrs. Ora Leeka Marion O.

EDGINGTON, JOHN, Stark co

Pvt in Capt James Munn's co 2nd Batt Washington Pa Militia ordered to rendevous 18th of Mch 1782. B abt 1757 in Va. Son of Geo Sr. Mar Nancy Bruce chldr: Aaron; John; Sarah; Mary; Rebecca; Noah; Nancy; Margaret; and Isaac. Died 1813 in Stark co bur 1 mi west of Canal Fulton. Moved from Brook co W Va to Stark co in 1811. Ref Pa Arch 6th Ser Vol II p 36, 60, 83. Data by Mrs. Leeka, Marion, O.

EDGINGTON, THOMAS, Jefferson co

Pvt in Capt Kidd's Militia, Col John Marshall, 4th Batt. Washington co Pa. B in Va 1744 Son of Geo Sr. Married Martha chldr: George; John; Thomas Jr; Jesse;

Drusilla; Sarah; Rachel and Mary (possible Asahel). Died Jefferson co 1814. bur Steubenville O Inscr on Monument "Thomas Edgington, died 1814, aged 70 yrs" Settled in Brook co W Va, captured by Indians Apr 1 1782 and taken to Detroit and sold to the British. Ref Pa Arch 6th Ser Vol II p 153. Draper Mss 2 S 292, 293. Reported by Mrs. Ora Leeka Marion, O.

EDWARDS, RUDOLPHUS, Cuyahoga co

Ref p 810 Pioneer Women of Western Reserve (Cleveland). For 2 yrs after her arrival from Tolland Ct. in Cleveland Mrs. Rudolphus Edwards (Anna Merrill) lived in a cabin at foot of Superior St. Had 2 chldr then a step-son and infant. Removed to Woodhill Rd 6 chldr; added: Sally was daughter of 1st wife Rhoda Barnett Edwards; chldr of 2nd wife Anna Merrill were Rhoda Rhodes; Cherry Stewart; Clara Burrough; Anna Olmsted; Lydia Little; two sons Stark and Rudolphus Jr; soldr bur in abandoned cem Doan St Cleveland. Ref 3rd Rep N S D A R. Reported by Nathan Perry.

EDWARDS, THOMAS, Champaign co

Enl 1776 in Md was Sergt in Contl Line Pensd Champaign Co in July 29 1819 served 2 yrs and 5 mos. Dischrg at Phila B 1745 S 42 695 Md. Appld for pens June 3, 1818 ref State D A R.

EHRHARDT (Erhart, Earhart), PHILIP, Columbiana co

Record not yet found.

ELKINS, WILLIAM, Jefferson co

Pvt in Md Line. Enlst 1780 in Fredericktown Md pens May 17 1819 in Mt Pleasant twp Jefferson co O. B 1733 was 87 in 1820. Ref S 42703 Md State D A R.

ELLIOTT, JOHN LT, Stark co

Pens Sept 24 1818 for service in Capt Bird's Co Col. Cadwallader's 4th Pa Reg. Settled in Sharon Pa abt 1798. B 1742 mar Catherine had a daughter Patience who mar John Hall. Died in Stark co. Bur in Westlawn cem. Pensd 1840 while living in Stark co. Copied from Vol 108 D A R lin S A R yr book 1897 by Jane D Dailey.

ELLIOTT, SAMUEL, Portage co

Exec Doc 37 of 1852. Refused a pens as servd less than 6 mo. Rept by Wm Pettit.

ELLIOTT, WILLIAM, Butler co

Pvt from Balt co Md B 1758 in Bal Married Rachel Bosley (b 1760) One son was Arthur. Died Butler co. Ref Vol 114 p 95 D A R Lin. Nat No. 113280. Rept by Nathan Perry.

ELLIS, EPHRAIM, Washington co

Pvt Mass Contl Enlis Apr 5 1781 Mass. Dicharged Dec 1783. Pensd Mch 23 1833 Washington co Ohio served 2 yrs and 8 mos. B June 15 1755 Appld for pens Washington co June 3 1818. Res of Roxbury twp. Mass S&S S 3330 Mass State D A R.

ELLISON, JOHN, Lawrence co

Pvt Va militia served 15 mos. Pensd May 23 1833 in Lawrence co. Enlisted 1777 Bedford co Va. From Burlington co N J he moved to Pa then to Md then Bedford co Va when 9 or 10 yrs old and remained till 1810 when he came to Lawrence co. Appld for pens at Lawrence co Aug 28 1832. Ref S 3334 Va p 270 "Va Militia in Rev" State D A R.

ELSER, GEORGE, Mahoning co

Pvt in Pa militia. Ref Pa Arch Ser 2 Vol 10 p 358 also N Y Men pp 50, 253. B 1765 Hanover twp Lancaster co Pa. Peter Elser came to America 1749 married Catherine Summers Oct 25 1776 died Aug 17 1826. Children: Jacob born 1790, married Margaret Greensmyer. George born 1800 married Mary ——. Died Aug 25 1847 Springfield twp. Bur Kurtz cem. Ref Hist of Mahoning co; Sanderson.

ELSEY, THOMAS, Pickaway co

Pvt Md militia Enlisted in Rev Sept 1 1780 served 2 yrs. Appld for pens Pickaway co Aug 10 1832 Res of Pickaway twp. Appld for pension Fairfield Co Violet twp Oct 10 1829. B Aug 16 1760 Md. "father" kept family record in bible. wife married at close of Rev. Ref p 406 Wiseman's Pioneer People Fairfield co lists name "Elsey Thomas." S 8404 Va. State D A R.

ELWELL, THOMAS, Knox co

Matross, Pa. Contl served 1 yr. Appld for pens in Knox co July 9 1818 Widow appld for pens Sept 4 1848 in Knox co. Aged 67 in 1818. Married Elizabeth — Dec 1786. Ch; Tomas Jr. Mary aged 18, Sarah aged 15, and Elizabeth aged 13 in 1820. Died May 21, 1825. Ohio Pens Roll 1835, III p 0-71 Contl Va W 7096 B L Wt 695-100. State D A R and Clara Mark, Westerville, O.

ELY, MICHAEL, Delaware co

No record other than reference in Delaware co Hist which states he served 7 yrs in Rev Army. Mary S. Williamson, Delaware Chapter.

EMBICK, CHRISTOPHER, Fairfield co

Pvt Pa State troops pens Jan 8 1833 Fairfield co served Pa line 10 mos. Enlisted 1776 while res at Lebanon Pa. Removed from Lebanon Pa to Hagerstown Md and from there to the neighbor of Pittsburg Pa. Widow appld for pens at Fairfield co O Oct 25 1837. B 1756 Conestoga co Pa married Anna Maria —— Jan 20 1779. Ch Jacob, John and Maria. Died July 23 1837. He appld for pens Nov 1832 Fairfield co Ref Wiseman's Hist Fairfield co; W 9427 Pa.

EMERSON, EPHRAIM, Washington co

B 1767 died 1833 Washington co. Said to be a Rev Sold. by Helen Sloan, Marietta Ohio.

EMERY, GEORGE, ? co

Order bk 0-133. Made declaration for pens under act June 7 1832 and the clerk is directed to issue certificates as directed by the War dept. Dated Sept 29 1832. Rept by Blanche Rings.

EMERY, JOHN, Highland co

Pvt in Capt James Moore's Co Col Francis Johnson's 5th Reg Pa. B Pa. Ref 15th Report N S D A R p 165. Nat No. 51488.

EMMITT, JOHN, Licking co

Pvt Md militia served 6 mos and 15 days. Enlisted July 1776. Residing in Cecil co Md when enlst since the Rev he has resided in Pa, Va, O, Ill, Ind, and Ross co O. Pen transferred from Ohio to Ill to Licking co Ohio. Widow appld for pens in Jefferson co Iowa May 25 1855. B Cecil co Md Dec 22 1759 married Margaret —— June 7 1808. Died Licking co Ohio about 1847. Ref Md W 692.

ENGART, BENJAMIN, Hamilton co

Pvt in N Jer militia lived in Middlesex co N J until after the Rev then in Pa. He moved to Ohio in 1798. Enlisted at Woodbridge N J in Apr 1778 pensd May 3 1833 Hamilton co. B 1759 Woodbridge Middlesex co N J. Died 1842. He res in Springfield twp Hamilton co in 1832. Pens Ci N J S 2539 S A R.

ENGLISH, BENJAMIN, Hamilton co

Found listed as "English" should be Engart which see — J D.

ENGLISH, ROBERT, Clermont co

Pvt Va Contl served 8 mos enlst Burlington co N J. Appld for pens at Clermont co O Nov 1832 Res of Batavia twp. Ref S 2540 N J. State D A R.

ENGLISH, WILLIAM, Carroll co

Va militia entered service at 15 yrs of age in 1776 "Wm English of New Lisbon Ohio was on the pens rolls of Ohio. Res in Augusta twp Carroll co where he made appl for pension Apr 18 1833. Ref S 3336 Va p 270." "Va mil. in Rev." State D A R.

ENOS, JOSEPH,

Died in N Y. Research on No. 121 978, D A R. Lin Vol V p 122 finds this soldier did not die in Ohio, as stated in Nassau, N Y. Ref W 16977. B L Wt 27634-160-55, R I. Rept by State D A R (Listed here to avoid further research).

ERWIN (Irwin), JAMES, Brown co

Lt in Col Butler's 3rd Reg Pa Line 3 vrs pens 1818. Dischcarged at end of war at Lancaster Pa. B 1763 married Frances Morford June 29 1820 aged 35 in 1820. Died in Brown co Mch 7 1849. Taliafero Chap. repts burial in Old Arnheim Cem Franklin twp; grave shown to them by Jacob Lindsey, ae 91, who attended funeral of the soldier. Grave 18 ft. N· E of twin cedar trees in center. A sunken grave to south of James Irwin is that of his son. Aug 1820 and Dec 1818 appld for pens from Adams co O 1828 made claims from Brown co which was granted. Widow appld Oct 25 1854 in Brown co. Ref W 7117 Pa. Stated by James Rains that his wife was "only child" by first wife of James Erwin Apr 27 1857 Cop by Jane Dailey.

ESTERLY, MICHAEL, Columbiana co

Service not yet found. B 1761 Wertemberg, Germany. Married Catherine (b 1766, d 1831 aged 65 yrs) Esterly pvt cem. Died Mch 18 1843 aged 82 yrs 10 mos. Came with wife from Ger with Bishop Rapp of Old Mennonites. Mrs. Wilma M Molesberry 143 Broadway Youngstown O.

ETTINGER (Eatinger), JACOB, Portage co

Pvt Pa Contl. Enlisted Mch 1776 in Pa and served till Jan 1778 when discharged. Served 1 yr pens Dec 4 1819 Portage co. Was 82 in 1818 married Mary Ann Apr 2 1782. Ch; son Gottleib age 21 on Dec 21, 1815 George, James, Samuel, Benjamin, Betsy Ward, Margaret Stough. Died Jan 2, 1832 Portage co. Ref W 5269 Pa. Widow died Mch 4 1843 State D A R. Soldier refused a pens as not in indigent circumstances. Ref Doc 31 Jan 6 1831 p 70 Rept by Mrs. Blanche Rings Col O.

EVANS, ANTHONY, Monroe co

Fife Major Pa Contl Pensd Apr 15 1819 Washington co (now Monroe) B 1752 (Pen Claim says 55 yrs in 1820) married Oct 13 1808 Mrs. Susan Buck Cline, widow of Geo Cline aged 76 in 1820. Died Feb 19 1822 in Gerico Monroe co bur Jerico Ch-yard. Rept by Mrs. Mary Steinmetz of Reading Pa. Ref Washington co Mar Records; Family papers on Cline family by Helen Sloan; Pen Claim S 42713 Pa by State D A R.

EVANS, EDWARD REV, unknown

Enlisted from Berkshire co Mass. Mt. Washington. In Apr 1782 was in Capt Jonathan Perry's Co, Col Morehouse and Willet of N Y. Went up the Mohawk River to defend the inhabitants from organized forces of British and Indians, Was at Forts Hunter and Herkemer and suffered terrible hardships from frozen feet and limbs. B Amenia, Dutchess co N Y May 5 1767. May have died in Ind when last known. Was a Presby minister lived at Mt Wash until 1798; Grafton N Hamp 25 yrs Woodstock Vt 3 yrs Orleans co N Y 3 yrs then Trumbull co Ohio. In May 1848 he was living in Lima, Lagrange co Ind. Rept Mary Chesney Chap.

EVANS, EPHRAIM, Franklin co

Cop fr Ohio State Journal Iss Jan 18 1839 is the following: "Evans, Eprhirm d in his 91 yr a native of Philadelphia Pa whr he res during the Rev and took part in the struggle for Independence. A few yrs aft the close of the war he removed to Alexandria D C. In 1828 to Wheeling Va and for the last 18 mos a res of this place. Friends are requested to attend the funeral at the res of Daniel Evans on Water St at 2:00 tomorrow." Evans, Mrs Sarah d May 15 1853 mother of Daniel Evans in her 85th yr. Cop fr Green Lawn cem recds "Evans, Daniel B Sept 8 1793 Alexandria Va d Nov 25 1862 Columbus son of Ephraim and Sarah Evans. Lot 24 S ½ Sec L. Rept by Blanche Rings.

EVANS, GEORGE, Jefferson co

Pvt Pa Contl Enlisted Jan or Feb 1776 in Pa. Served from Jan 1776 to Jan 1777. Was 72 yrs old in 1829. Children mentioned in a letter written Oct 22 1855 for arrears of pens, of George Evans deceased. This letter stated that the children claimed half pay from 1780 to 1825 for which he did not apply while living. Date of death and names of ch. not given. Appl for pens Jefferson co. May 20 1829. Ref S 42715 Pa.

EVANS, JOHN COL, Ross co

B Balt Md May 11 1766 Mary his mother, born 1738, died 1812. Married Miranda G, b Frederick Md Jan 22 1781, died Feb 21 1817. He died Dec 27 1841, bur Springbank cem Ross co. Rept by Nathaniel Massie Chap. Evans, Col. John in Chillicothe Adv. Jan 1 1842: "A Rev soldier died on Mon. eve last at his residence about 10 miles north of Chillicothe, in his 76th yr. He was one of the oldest settlers of Ross co and asssisted in laying out the City of Chillicothe. He moved to the Western country from Baltimore Md. about 1797. He was a surveyor and accumulated a large amount of property. He was elected Representative to the Ohio Leg. and was a volunteer in the last war. He left two daughters to mourn his loss." By Pickaway Plains Chap.

EVANS, JOHN, Jefferson co

Pvt Pa Contl. Enlisted Feb 1776 Lan co Pa. Discharged Jan 1781. Served 4 yrs. Pens 1826 Jefferson co. B 1749. Died May 9 1826 (Record on pens). Appld for pens at Belmont co O Mch 24 1826 Res Jefferson co also for Jeff co Aug 1 1820. Ref S 42714 Pa. State D A R and Hetuck Chap.

EVARTS, TIMOTHY, Richland co

Pvt Vermont Regt. Bur Evarts cem Jefferson twp Richland co O. By C M Garber, Butler O.

EVERETT, ABEL, Perry co

Served in Rev. Buried in Bethel Cem near Bremen, Ohio. Rept by Mrs. Fred Deal of LaGrange, Ind. D A R on this line.

EVERTON, THOMAS, Meigs co

Pvt Mass Contl Line. Appld for pens at Chester, Meigs co Ohio in 1832. Pens No. 4996. Filing envelope No. S 2202 Mass. Born in Dorchester, Suffolk Mass in 1762; moved to Kennebuck, Me and lived there. Moved to Penobscot, Me. and lived there 8 yrs;

movd to Whitestown, N Y. then to Rutland, Meigs co. Ohio in Sept 1795. Ref Return Jonathan Meigs Chap. by Bertha Bing Chase.

EWING, GEORGE, Athens ?

Officer in N J Line. One is listed as lieut in Rev in a news clipping found in an old scrap book. Rept by Marietta D A R. B Salem N J. Was first settler in Ames twp. P 289 Hist Coll of Ohio After the Rev he lived on Frontier near Wheeling W Va 1793; moved to Waterford settlement on Muskingum and 1798 to Ames twp Athens co. No bur place located. Ref Jane D Dailey.

EWING, JOHN, Montgomery co

5th Ser Pa Arch Vol 2 p 228 5th Battl Col Wm Irwin Capt Robt Adams; Vol 4 p 213 Contl Line; 1778 2nd lieut Vol 6 p 161 etc. Burial place unidentified. Rept by Wm Pettit S A R.

EWING, WILLIAM, Wayne co

Pvt and drummer Pa militia Pens 1834 Wayne co. Served 5 mos pvt and 5 mos drummer. At time he entered service he resided at East Line in Lebanon twp Lan co Pa. Since Rev lived in Dauphin co Pa and from there to Wayne co O B Lancaster co Pa 1762. "Mother" kept memo of his age in German Language (Wooster Wayne Chap repts a sale of land; names his wife, Agnes. Unable to locate more). Appld for pens Wayne co O Apr 30 1834 Res in Perry twp. Ref S 8447 Pa. State D A R.

EYSTER, PETER, Columbiana co

Record not yet found. B 1762 married Margaret (b 1769 d 1850 aged 81) Died Feb 19 1836 aged 73 yrs 6 mos 2 days. Bur Unity twp Forney cem. Ref Col co cem records; Hist Col co. Rept by Mrs. Wilma M. Molsberry.

FALL, AARON, Morgan co

Enl Portsmouth N H 2-1-1781 commanded by Capt Deering N H line for 9 mo. B July 12 1761 in Lebanon N H; appl and recd pens in Athens co Oct 13 1832 æ 71 yrs; recd hon disch; ret to home in Lebanon N H whr resided till 1788; then movd to Kennebec Me; resided there till 1816 when he movd to Marietta O; then in same twp to Homer in Athens co where he now resides (appl) (Homer twp is now Morgan co O). Ref S 17410 N H. Rept by State D A R.

FANCHER, WILLIAM, Delaware co

Enl 1781 when 17 yrs old from Pound Ridge Westchester co N Y; pvt Capt Bouton's co Col Crane's Regt; was wounded in both feet on June 10 1781 for which disability the legislature of N Y granted him a pens. B Westchester co N Y July 6 1764; mar Lucy Stark 1789; chldr: Henry; Nancy; Samuel; William Jr; Amy; Polly; Nehemiah; David; Rebecca. Soldr d 1829; bur Fancher cem Harlem twp Delaware co O. Ref Mrs Elma P Valentine of Columbus chpt a desc.

FANNING, WILLIAM, Huron co

Mass Contls. Movd to Yates co N Y aft war. There his dau Fanny mar Stephen Post and all came to Ohio. Ref Pioneer Women of the Western Reserve p 778. Rept by Marjorie Cherry.

FARBER, DANIEL, Preble co

At æ 16 yrs on Mch 15 1781 drafted into army at Morristown Co 1 Bat'l 3 1st Regt N J Mil John Howell Capt; Maj Gowers Col Seely and Gen Wayne; in June 1781 entered Capt Howell's new Co for 3 yrs; wounded twice at Yorktown. B Mch 4 1765 Morris co N J; mar Nancy ——; chldr: Sally Ann æ abt 44 wf of Daniel Goorman; Margaret wf of John G Spade æ 42; Lewis S æ 23; John æ 18; Jane æ 16; Catherine æ 14; and Lucinda æ 12. Soldr d Feb 21 1847 Preble co O; bur New Paris; disch Mch 4 1784; in 1834 went to Jay co Ind bought govt land; his disch filed in 1840 and lost in 1843; appl for pens failed; walked twice to Washington D C to prove service aft 80 yrs old (wore out 2 pr boots on these trips); soldr d Preble co O on way home from Washington and bur there. Securing this information Jane Dailey from Registrar Mrs Oscar Finch of Mississinewa D A R Portland Ind.

FARMER, EZEKIEL, Miami co

Enl 1778. Pvt S C Mil; served in all more than 2 yrs (appl); was aged 69 in 1833; resided in S C until 1800; then moved to Tenn and 3 yrs later moved to Ky; aft a short res there moved back to Tenn; in 1822 moved from Tenn to O; has since res there in Darke co and Miami co where he now res (appl dated Aug 10 1833). Ref S 16112. S C Rept by State D A R.

FARNSWORTH, DANIEL, Belmont co

Pvt N J St Trps Capt Locke's Co Col Beaver's Regt; 21 mos service. B May 3 1763 Bethlehem twp Huntington co N J where he lived when he enl; also lived Loudon co Va abt 9 yrs; part in Brooke co Va; part in Jefferson co O from 1814 to 1826; since in Goshen twp Belmont co. Ref Appl May 28 1833; S 16113 N J. Cop by Jane Dailey.

FASNACHT, JOHN, Mahoning co

Pvt Co Capt David Morgan's Camp in the Jerseys; Ser 5 Vol 7 p 806. Lancaster Co Mil. B 1756; mar Susanna (1766-3-26-1850); soldr d Dec 12 1846 Beaver twp; bur old cem in North Lima. Ref List of cem rec of late H R Baldwin S A R. Rept by Mahoning chpt.

FAULKNER, ROBERT, Hamilton co

Enl Jan 1 1777 Philadelphia Pa; Ensign Pa Cont line, served 3 yrs (certf). B 1758; by appl 1820 states that wife is not living; chldr all support themselves except Thomas æ 18 yrs; appl for pens Genesee co N Y Apr 11 1818 and at Cincinnati O June 16 1820. Ref S 42717 Pa. Rept by State D A R.

FAUVER, GEORGE, Lorain co

Bur Butternut cem Eaton twp. Ref "History of Lorain co" by G Rrederick Wright (1916) p 125. Rept by Mrs T R Oehlke Nathan Perry chpt.

FAY, JOHN, ? co

Pvt listed in Invalid Pensrs of U S belonging to O. Pd at Chillicothe $96 annually. Cop fr p 172 Pensrs of 1818 at S of R Libry L A by Jane Dailey.

FEAZLE, JOHN, Licking co

Enl abt 1777 in Shenandoah co Va (appl); pvt Va Contl line; served 1 yr 9 mo (certf). B 1752 Va. Hetuck chpt repts that Christina was one dau and that soldr d in Franklin twp Licking co; appl for pens 10-29-1832 in Licking co O. Ref Va S 4284. Rept by State D A R and Hetuck chpt Licking co.

FELT, JOSHUA, ? co

Pvt; served 8 mo which was not sufficient time to secure a pens. Therefore in rejected list. Ref Doc 31 Jan 6 1831. Cop and rept by Blanche Rings Columbus chpt.

FENN, JOHN, Ashtabula co

Pvt Conn Contl; pens 1819 Ashtabula co; soldr d 11-30-1831 æ 81 yrs; bur West Andover O. Rept by Mary Redmond chpt.

FENSTERMACKER, JOHN, Sandusky co

Exec Doc 37. Rev Soldr res in O in 1852 or before; refused a pens as did not serve 6 mos. Rept by Wm Pettit.

FERGUSON, SAMUEL, Greene co

Local history states that he recd land warrant and was a pensr; b in Va; mar Mildred Garrison; came to Greene Co in 1824. Rept by Catherine Green chpt.

FERGUSON (or Furgeson), SAMUEL, Lorain co

Enl Litchfield co Conn and lived there till after close of Rev; Sergt Conn Mil (certf); b 1760 Middlesex co Conn (appl); may have d in Michigan where last transferred; appl for pens Lorain co Aug 28 1833 and for transfer of pens to Lenawa co Mich Mch 4 1835; this soldr pens was made payable in Richland co 11-31-1834 but the records show that he resided in Lorain co O; no rec of his having lived in Richland co. Aft Rev lived in Mass and Oneida co N Y and now in Lorain co O. Jared Mansfield chpt reports his death 1863 æ 98 no place stated and that he prob mar in Allegheny co Pa where his children were b; one ch was James (may not be same man) Ref S 29151 Conn. Rept by State D A R.

FERGUSON, SAMUEL, Mahoning co

Pvt; ser 5 Vol 3 p 778 Pa Arch; mar Willimene ——; soldr d 1841 Austintown twp. Ref Hist of Trumbull and Mahoning cos Vol 1 p 49; Hist Washington co Pa p 737 by Crumrine; and Deed Bk B p 147 to Samuel Ferguson Jr and wife Willimene land in Austintown 1808. Rept by Mahoning chpt.

FERRAND, JARED, Cuyahoga co

Pa service. B 1761 Conn; d 1862 Vt. Ref 2228 S A R. Rept by William Pettit.

FERREE, JOHN, ? co

Pvt in Capt John Slaymaker's Co 7th Bat'l Lancaster co Pa Mil. B 1761 Pa; mar 1792 Rebecca Marsh (1771-1844); chldr: Snowden was one son; soldr d in Ohio 1839. Ref No. 123, 281, Vol 124, D A R Lin; no rec of any pens at Pens Claims. Rept by J D.

FICKLE, BENJAMIN, Coshocton co

Lieut Contl Md served 3 yrs 10 mo; res Frederick Co Md; mar Phebe (d before 1857); chldr: one was Isaac in Williams Co O in 1857; left 8 chldr, 3 living in 1857, Rachel Vansky, Catherine Rill, Patrick and Isaac H Fickle; soldr d May 20 1839 leaving wid; in Mch 1822 appeared before J P in Muskingum co O; Dec 27 1833 certfied his serv in Coshocton co Pike twp O for increase pay; pens last pd to Sept 4 1838 Treas. Ref S 8478 Md. Cop by Jane Dailey. Also listed in Invalid pensrs of U S belonging to O, pd at Chillicothe $204 annually. Cop from p 172, Pensrs of 1818 by J D.

FIELDING, DANIEL, ? co

Sergt Mil; invalid pensr of U S belonging to O; pd at Chillicothe $64 annually. Cop fr p 172 Pensrs of 1818 by Jane Dailey.

FIELDS, JOHN, Green or Montgomery co

Pvt in Capt Budd's Co Col Hight Regt N J Mil; many enlistment's, over 2 yr 3 mo; b May 14 1754 Springfield twp Burlington Co N J; lived in Ky; 1st dec of pens for Greene co Nov 1834 where he lived for 5 mo æ 80 yrs; 2nd fr Warren co O as more convenient to his home; lived in Montgomery Co 3 mo. Ref S 8472 N J. Rept by State D A R.

FIELDS, SIMON, Adams co

Enl Hampshire co Va Aug 1776; disch Oct 1778 in N Y (appl); pvt Va Contl; served in Va line for 2 yrs (pens certf); b 1757; appl of 1829 says wf æ 67 yrs and chldr all of age and from under his control; soldr d Nov 9 1832 (pens certf); appl for pens in Adams Co Mch 18 1829. Ref S 42723 Va. Rept by State D A R.

FIFE, JOHN, Columbiana co

Pvt Va Mil; b 1747 Scotland; mar Elizabeth Fife (d 1839); chldr: Son Samuel (1791-1848) mar Elizabeth McCoy; soldr d 1817 Columbiana co. Ref D A R Lin V 138. Rept by Wilma M Molsberry.

FIGGINS, JAMES, Columbiana co

Enl Sept 1780 (appl); member of staff of Gen Baron Von Steuben; pvt reg Va line; nat of Westmoreland co Pa 1761; soldr d at home of son John in Wayne twp Columbiana co O æ 90 yrs; he and wf bur Lebanon Churchyard; was living in 1841 in Wayne twp æ 80 yrs and pens here at that time; pens $8 per mo gr Feb 20, 1830. Ref: Census of Pensioners 1841; S A R Year Book 1912; Census of Pensioners 1833-34; and Hist of Columbiana Co by McCord 1905. Rept by Wilma M Molsberry Youngstown O. Also same; pvt Va line; wid pensd 7-8-1845 Columbiana co O (certf) pens No. 700; Wid Mary states in appl was mar soon after Rev; soldr d 9-20-1844 Columbiana Co O; enl Sept 1780; she appl for pens in Columbiana co 5-28-1845. Ref W 4952 Va and B L Wt 1602-100. Rept by State D A R.

FINE, PETER, Knox co

Enl July or Aug 1776; pvt Md Mil; at time of enl res Frederick Co Md; served 7½ mo (certf); b 1750 Morristown N J; in 1825 moved to Wayne twp Knox co; appl for pens in Knox Co 9-27-1832. Ref Ohio Pens Roll 1835 Vol 3 p 137 and S 2209 Md. Rept by State D A R.

FINK, DANIEL, Mahoning co

Ranger Northampton co Pa; b Northampton co Pa; mar Elizabeth Ann Welzel; chldr: Daniel mar Susan Kentney; Jacob mar Mary Shafer; Barbara mar Matthew Boyer; Katherine mar Samuel Shafer; Molly mar Nathan Klingan; Susanna mar —— Velnagle; and John mar Katherine Sprinkle; soldr d abt 1836 Canfield O. Ref Ser 3 vol 23 p 296; also Ser 5 vol 4 p 320 and 351 Depreciation Pay Pa Arch Hist of Mahoning co by Butler; Hist of Columbiana co p 757 by McCord; Deed Bk D, p 477 to Daniel Fink Canfield 1805 and Tax list of 1826. Rept by Mahoning chpt.

FINLEY, JOHN, Delaware co

Exec Doc 37 appl for pens required a new declaration. Rept by Wm Pettit.

FINLEY, SAMUEL, Ross co

Capt 3 m Major 1 yr and 9 mo Va line; b Pa; mar Polly Brown 5-5-1789. Chldr: John b 3-30-1790, d 7-13-1791; soldr d 4-2-1829; appl for pens in Chillicothe Ross co O 7-3-1828; wid appl for pens in St Joseph co Ind 11-12-1838; she d 12-23-1838. Ref Va W 10026 B L Wt 761-400 Major issued Nov 5 1796 (no papers). Rept by State D A R. We pub also extracts from clipping as follows: Gen Samuel Finley d in Philadelphia Pa at the res of Rev W L McCalla, his son-in-law on Thursday Apr 2 1829 of this place (Chillicothe) in the 77th yr of his age; was a nat of Pa; emigrated to the neighborhood of Martinsburg Va; volunteered in Va; marched to Boston as a member of the 1st co that was raised in the northern neck of Va; in the battle of Bunker Hill; abt this time recd a subalterns commission in the Reg Cont'l army; was taken prisoner at an early period; held captive for nearly four years; was exchanged in time to join the southern army under Gen Green; in battle of Eutaw Springs and other conflicts in the Carolinas; at the close of Rev left the army as Major of the line and returned to Pa where he mar; in 1797 or 98 removed to this town (Chillicothe) and was app in 1800 the 1st receiver of Public Monies here (From Scioto Gazette, Apr 15, 1829).

FISHBACK, JACOB, Highland co

Pvt Va Contl; enl Culpepper co Va Apr 14 1779; served 3 yrs (certf); b 1749; mar Hannah 1787 (aff of son); chldr: son John and grand daughter Mary Ann (aff of John Fishback); soldr d Mch 30 1826 Highland co (aff of son); appl for pens Highland co O Mch 16 1819; Ref Rejected 3562 Va. Rept by State D A R.

FISHER, ISAAC, Franklin co

Enl June 1780; pvt N J Mil; aged abt 66 yrs in 1832 (appl); mar Fanny Jones 7-10-1833; chldr: Thomas H b 1834; Jane 5-14-1836; Gennet 1-16-1838; Isebel 1-7-1840; Peter 4-2-1842; and Flavel 4-16-1844 (fam rec); soldr d abt 1846 in Pike co Ind (appl of wid); wid pensd 11-30-1868 Pike co Ind (certf); in appl of Feb 22 1834 states he a res of Sharon twp Franklin co O; was a wit to will of Benjamin Chapman Sharon twp Mch 6 1823. Ref N J W 10598 B L Wt 105513-160-55. Rept by State D A R. The following data rept by Blanche Rings Col O: Early Franklin co Fishers fr Sharon twp. Fisher, Carlina mar John Clark 1825, consent of her father Isaac Fisher. Fisher, Elizabeth mar Daniel Weeks Jr, both of Worthington 1807. Fisher, Elizabeth mar Wm Stewart 1811. Fisher, Josiah mar Jane White 1814. Fisher, Ruth B of Sharon twp m Timothy Anders (Andrews) 1819 by Isaac Fisher. Isaac Fisher gives consent for his dau Ruth B Fisher to marry Timothy Andrews of Delaware Co. Wit Daniel Week.

FISHER, JOHN SR, Pickaway co

Enl for Serv in 1781; pvt Va. St Trps; served 3 mos under Capt Michael Stump and Major McPherson before 1782; was at battle of Bottbury Bridge under Capt Ward; b Oct 15 1760 near Tulpehaken Creek Berks co Pa; mar Elizabeth —— (d 1844); chldr: Abraham; Absolom; John; Jetro; Washington Dill; Sarah Erih; Eunice Staley; Jamima Lee and Elizabeth; soldr d 1847 Jackson twp; bur on old William Bell farm Jackson twp but grave destroyed by new owner of farm; came from Pendleton co Va in 1815 with son Absolom and family. Ref Pens allowed Aug 10 1832 at that time living in Pickaway co O and will of wife Elizabeth Bk 3 p 108. Rept by Pickaway Plains chpt.

FISHER, JOHN, Fairfield co

Pvt Md St Trps; served 8 mos from 1781 (certf); removed from Reading Pa to Hagerstown Md where he remained till the Rev and volunteered there (appl); in appl states he æ abt 70 yrs in 1832; b Reading Pa; Apr 5 1832 appl for pens while a res of Bloom twp Pickaway co O. Ref Name listed in Wiseman's Pioneer people of Fairfield co p 406 and S 2211 Md. Rept by State D A R.

FITCH, ANDREW, Mahoning co

Clerk of Lebanon Conn; in Lexington Alarm; b New London co Conn; mar Mary Levenwell; chldr: Samuel b 1784; Henry; Joseph; Benjamin; James; Sally; Charles; Polly mar Samuel Stewart; Charlotte mar Stephen Comstock; soldr d 1805 in Coitsville twp; came fr Lebanon New London co Conn in 1801. Ref Conn Men in Rev p 15; Hist of Mahoning co Vol 2 p 216 by Butler; Will bk 1 p 17 of Trumbull co 1805; Deed bk b p 49 to Andrew Fitch of New London Conn 1802; Deed bk C p 382 Andrew Fitch heirs 1814. Rept by Mahoning chpt. Compare same name p 141 of Roster Vol 1.

FITHIAN, GEORGE, Champaign co

N J service. Was b N J 1760; d 1824 at Urbana. Ref 30909 S A R. Rept by Wm Pettit.

FITZGARALD (or Fitzgerald), HENRY, Fairfield co

Enl Westmoreland Co Pa Mch 2 1777; pvt Pa Contl; served 1 yr 9 mo; was discharged at Valley Forge Pa; b Oct 15 1749-50 (appl); soldr d June 18 1824 (Letter from Vet Adm on file in Pens Off); appl for pens Fairfield Co May 2 1818; Ref Name listed p 406 in Wiseman's Pioneer People of Fairfield co O and S 42724 Pa. Rept by State D A R. Hetuck Chapter reports he enl in Hannahstown Pa; came to O in 1804; from Westmoreland Co Pa; mar Joanna dau of John Gradley in 1804 soldr d June 14 1824.

FIX, HENRY, Franklin co

Pvt Pa Mil; mar Annalouis French 1-12-1748; chldr: Samuel; David; Mary; Henry; Jacob; Dolly; and George by 2nd wife; had 4 chldr by 1st wife (appl of wid); soldr d 5-14-1837; pens Franklin co 1832; in Oct 1833 was 83 yrs old; wid pens 4-24-1846 and 9-5-1848 in Delaware co. Ref W 8087 Pa. Rept by State D A R. Ref given by Blanche Rings col chpt order Bk IX Franklin co P Ct affidavit of Elizabeth Fix that Henry Fix Pensr d May 15 1837 leaving widow Anna Lovice Fix date Sept 1838.

FLAKE (Fleck or Flek), GEORGE, Washington co

Enl 1776 Washington co Hagerstown Md and was attached to 1st Pa Regt (appl); pvt Pa Contl; served 4 yrs (certf); b 1760; his appl of 1821 says his wife abt 58 yrs old and he has a child; appl for pens Washington co O May 14 1818 while a res of Union twp; again Nov 26 1819 at Frederick co Md and then again Apr 3 1821 Washington co O. Ref S 42725 Pa Rept by State D A R. Also to George Flake Pa George Fleck appl for pens in Common Pleas Court in Marietta O Apr 3 1821 stating property value at $21.75. Ref Vol 3 p 460. Rept by Helen Sloan Marietta chpt.

FLEMING, CAPT ALEXANDER, Ross co

Chapman Bros Hist of Fayette, Pickaway and Madison cos 1892 p 122 says: Capt Fleming came to Wayne twp Pickaway co with his son John from Berkeley co Va abt 1802 from an old newspaper in Circleville Libr; Alexander Fleming d Sept 12 1821 aged 87 yrs; b May 24 1734 in Lancaster co Pa; was a capt of Milit in battle of Germantown and Brandywine; went to Berkley co Va; from there to O. A desc Mrs. James Strode Swearingen No 246472 D A R thinks he was bur in the Westfall cem Wayne twp; grave of his wife in Ross co; insc reads "Hannah Fleming wife of Alexander Fleming died July 20 1802 aged 64 years;" she bur in Mt Pleasant cem Kingston Ross co abt a mile from Pickaway co line. Rept by Pickaway Plains chpt.

FLEMING, LIEUT ARCHIBALD, Pickaway co

First Lieut of Capt Innis's Co 8th Batl Chester co Pa Mil; b Ireland; mar Jane Speer in 1768; ch-Archibald Jr 1783-1869 mar 1810 Eva Stahl-d 1865; soldr d Circleville O. Ref Nat No. 133361 D A R. Rept by Pickaway Plains chpt.

FLEMING, ROBERT, Muskingum co

Pvt Pa Contl served 3 yrs (certf); b 1743 Ireland; appl of 1820 for pens states that his wife abt 50 yrs of age and he has 1 young son; migrated to this country prev to Rev; appl for pens Muskingum co O Apr 24 1818 also 1820. Ref S 42726 Pa. Mary Steinmetz Reading Pa reports he d Muskingum co O 2-28-1821 aged 78 yrs. Ref Pa Arch. Rept by State D A R. Etta M Kyle Youngstown repts wf's name Ann Kyle dau of Samuel and Jean (Bell) Kyle.

FLICKENER (Flickinger), CHRISTIAN, Mahoning co

Pvt 2nd class Capt Joseph Gear Col Jay Huber 1778 and 1779 Lancaster Co Mil; b Pa; mar Anne; childr: Christian b 1788 mar Elizabeth ——; John; Jacob mar Elizabeth ——; Samuel b 1792 mar 1st Elizabeth Rogers; Benjamin; Jesse mar Nancy Beight; Catherine; Joseph; Elizabeth mar Christian Gross; soldr d abt 1829 Springfield twp. Ref Ser 5 vol 7 p 613, 878, 898, 297 Pa Arch; Will Bk 5 p 689 Columbiana co Pa prob 1828; Deed Bk Q p 159 transcribed from Columbiana co Christian and Anne Flickener to Samuel Flickenger 1826. Rept by Mahoning chpt.

FLOOD (or Flud), WILLIAM, Adams co

Enl May 1775 in Co of Va riflemen; pvt Va Contl; served in Va line 8 yrs (pens certf); b 1740; mar (by appl of 1820) says wf Elizabeth æ 49 yrs; childr: dau only heir (Letter written May 25 1846); soldr d Dec 9 1833 (letter); appl for pens Adams Co Apr 17 1818; made dec same place Aug 11 1820; well digger. Ref S 42728 Va. Rept by State D A R. (This is correct spelling from applications for pension; see p 142 Vol 1 Roster where "William Floyd" is another spelling — J D).

FLORY, ABRAHAM, Montgomery co

Service 5th Ser Pa Arch Vol 7 pp 451,688, 701, 757, 740, 777, 785, Capt Robinson Col Lowry Associator of Lancaster Co Pa Mil; b 1735; soldr d 1827; bur cem Madison twp on Seegly farm which at that time of its establishment was on farm of his son Emanuel Flory; settl 1805 Montgomery co O with his sons Joseph and Emanuel. Hist of Montgomery co by Beers says the Florys came from Somerset co Pa where they had removed to after the war. Ref S A R Dayton O. Rept by W M Pettit.

FLORY (or Florey), JOSEPH, Montgomery co

Of Pa; early settl of co; burial place not identified. Ref 5th Ser Pa Arch Vol 7 p 369, 372. Rept by W M Pettit Dayton.

FLOYD, JOHN, Washington co

Enl spring of 1780 while res near the Shenandoah Berkeley co Va; pvt Va Mil; served 6 mo; b 1747 near Annapolis in Md in appl of 1840 says wife recently d; likely bur where he last appl for pens; says after Rev moved from there and since lived in Hagerstown Md; abt 2 yrs near Harper's Ferry; abt 10 yrs on Cheat River; a short time near Geneva Pa; 15 yrs in Westmoreland co Pa and 14 yrs past in Washington co O; appl for pens Washington co O May 27 1833 a res of Lawrence twp; trnsfd to Wheeling Va from Mch 4 1840; appl for pens Monongahela co Pa Nov 20 1840 now a res in said co and state. Ref S 8493 Va and p 271 Va Mil in Rev. Rept by State D A R.

FOLKNER, ABSOLEM, Jefferson co

Exec Doc 37. Rev Soldr res in O in 1852 or before; refused a pens as he was a privateer. Rept by Wm Pettit.

FOLLETT, FREDERICK, ? co

Served under Capt Simon Spaulding; was wounded and scalped 1779 but survived; b Windham Conn 1761; Mar Giffey Babcock; only 2 chldr found Oron and Nathan; soldr d 1804 in Ohio; in 1796 was granted pens by Congress (no rec of serv found in pens office). Ref Vol 35 p 310 D A R Lin No. 34890 and Vol 38 p 262 No. 37742. Cop by Mrs T R Oehlke, Nathan Perry chpt.

FOLSOM, THOMAS, Trumbull co

Enl in Capt Nathan Brown's Co Col Jacob Gale's Regt of Volunteers in Contl army for serv in R I Aug 7 1778; was at Bunker Hill (appl). B Mch 21 1754 in Epping N H; son of David Folsom; mar Sally dau of Benjamin Watson of Nottingham N H; was a cooper; chldr: David; Noah; Watson; Moses; Polly; Betsey; Hannah; and Abigail. Folsom Gen says soldr d in 1840 Gustavus Trumbull co O; wf also bur there. Ref N H Rev Rolls Vol 2 p 565 and N H Pens papers Vol 13 pp 66-67 says he enl from Epping for 3 mo according to his deposition but has a serv of 23 das according to pens authorities; served under Capt Brown. Aft the Rev moved to Dorchester Grafton co N H; lived there abt 10 yrs; then to Essex Chittenden co Vt in 1800 and in 1809 moved to Gustavus Trumbull co O; in winter of 1838-39 went to Youngstown O to live with his son Moses. Pens rejected because he could not give exact date of serv. Filed by Mrs W B Shuler and Mary Chesney chpt.

FOOT, LEVI D Trumbull co

Bur Fowler (administration) Oct 9 1841. Ref 27th rept N S D A R p 128. Cop by Mrs Oehlke.

FOOTE, JOHN, Warren co

Exec Doc 37. Rev soldr res in O in 1852 or before; refused a pens as he had not srvd 6 mo. Rept by Wm Pettit.

FORD, CHRISTOPHER, Ashtabula co

Pvt and artificer Pa St Trps; pensd 1832 Ashtabula co O. Mary Redman chpt repts he d 7-5-1855 æ 87; bur City cem Conneaut O.

FORD, JOHN, MORRISON, Delaware co

Exec Doc 37. Rev soldr res in O in 1852 or before; refused a pens as he had not served 6 mo. Rept by Wm Pettit.

FORD, MORGAN, Clermont co

Exec Doc 387. Rec soldr res in O in 1852 or before; refused a pens as he had not served 6 mo. Rept by Wm Pettit.

FOREMAN (or Foresman), ALEXANDER, Pickaway co

Capt Rev army; b 1753 in Province of Ulster Ireland; son of Robert Foresman and Jane All—?; mar Sarah Keith abt 1773; she d 6-3-1835 æ 73; chldr: Margaret Miller; Jane Foresman who mar her cousin Henry son of Robert and Catherine Jacoby; Elisa Wilson. Soldr d Dec 25 1831 in Circleville O; bur cem Circleville O on Foresman lot in center of western part; insc on stone: "Alexander Foresman d Dec 25 1831. Was a captain in the Revolutionary War." Marked by Pickaway Plains chpt with bronze marker May 11 1932. He came to Pickaway co 1812; was a weaver; in 1821 was living in Circleville æ 68 and wife æ 64 and 3 mr'd daus; pensd Pickaway co O Jan 1 1803 from Pa agency on account of disability of two wounds — one in right and one in left cheek. Recd while in serv at Allentown Pa Oct 1777. Ref S 26998 Pa. Rept by Pickaway Plains chpt.

FORMAN, AARON, Delaware co

Pvt in Capt Hines co Col Shryhawk's Flying Camp Md for 6 mo. Enl under Col Bowman Capt Harden's Co of Ky; Indian Spy Ky. B Sept 1755 Frederick co Va; in 1776 went to Va from Hagerstown Md; previous to going to Ky in 1777; resided in Martinsburg Va; in 1778 at Falls of the Ohio; aft the Rev settl in Va; then to Pa till 1805; came to Ross co O lived there abt 20 yrs; abt 1834 to Westfield twp, Delaware co O. Pens by act of Congress June 7 1832; on Mch 25 1835 æ 78 yrs. Ref S 8507. Cop by Jane Dailey.

FORMAN, LEWIS, Belmont co

Pvt Va Mil Capt Coleman's Co for 7 mo and Capt Paine's Co. B Winchester Va. Appl pens Nov 16 1832 by guardian Peter Tallman and again Dec 3 1833 by same guardian; he abt 76-78. Res Loudon co Va till 1805; then to Belmont co O where he lives (1832). Ref S 4679. Pensd 1833 Belmont co. Cop by Jane Dailey.

FORNEY, HENRY, Columbiana co

Rev soldr rec not found. B Oct 22 1747; mar Mary —— (b 1743; d 4-1-1817 æ 75 yr 45 da); both bur Unity twp Forney cem. Came from Mt Pleasant twp York co Pa; taxable 1780-1783 inclusive. Ref Columbiana co cem rec and Pa Archives. Ser 3 Vol 21 pp 234, 83, 378, 799. Rept by Mrs Wilma M Molsberry.

FORSHY (or Forshey), THOMAS, Muskingum co

Enl 1775 in Pa; Ensign Pa Mil; served 2 yrs. B 1751. Appl for pens Muskingum co O Oct 20 1832. Ref S 3376 Pa. Rept by State D A R.

FORSYTH, ELIJAH, ? co

Pvt. Pens refused as served in a regt not on Cont estab. Ref Doc 31 Jan 6 1831 O S Libry. Cop by Blanche Tipton Rings Columbus chpt.

FOSTER, BENJAMIN, Mercer co Pa and Wayne co O

Served 15 mos Corpl; 9 mo as Sergt. B 1754 Bristol co Mass; res in Clarendon Vt in 1776 when called into service; lived there till about last 12 yrs; moved to Genessee co N Y where he appl for pens Feb 6 1834 and then again appl Oct 26 1835 for pens in Mercer co Pa and states he lost his wife and wishes to live with his children. Ref S 5421 Vt. Rept by State D A R. Also Wooster-Wayne chpt reports no records found. Notice: (This soldier having applied for pens in Geneva co N Y and Mercer co Pa but not in O). However one Benjamin Foster æ 86 was a pensr in Ohio Milton twp Wayne co. Census 1840 which fact led to the above research.

FOSTER, JACOB, ? co

Made declaration for pens under act of June 7 1832 and the clerk was directed by the War dept to issue certificate. Cop fr Order bk 6-133 by Blanche Rings Columbus chpt.

FOSTER, JAMES, Mahoning co

Pvt in 1st Regt Line; Col Goose Van Schaick. B 1738; one son was Henry. Soldr d 1814; bur prob Boardman cem; cam to Boardman twp with his son Henry bef 1808; Henry Foster was a wheelright. Ref N Y Men in the Rev p 21 and Hist of Trumbull and Mahoning co Vol 2 p 85. Rept by Mahoning chpt. Also found as Sergt in Lists of invalid pensrs of U S belonging to O pd at Chillicothe $48 annually. Cop fr p 172 Pensrs of 1818 by Jane Dailey.

FOSTER, JOB, Scioto co

Enl Va Mch 1781 (appl); pvt Va Contl line; served 18 mo (certf). Appl for pens Scioto co O June 28 1819; pensd 1833 Scioto co O. Ref S 2216 Va. Rept by State D A R.

FOULTZ (or Fouts), WILLIAM, Columbiana co

Rev sold rec not yet found. B 1766; soldr d 1859; bur Madison twp. Ref Columbiana co cem rec. Rept by Mrs. Wilma M Molsberry.

FOUNTAIN, STEPHEN, Darke co

Enl in Aug 1777 in N Y; pvt Mass Contl; æ 66 in 1820 (appl); mar Rodah (by appl says she æ 55 yrs in 1820); also says he has 1 girl 11 and 1 grand child æ 2 yrs in 1820; was pens in Huron co O 6-20-1818 and in 1819 in Darke co O for certf in Darke co 12-15-1820. Ref S 42199 Mass. Rept by State D A R.

FOWLER, JONATHAN, Lake co

Exec Doc 37; Rev soldr res in O in 1852 or before; refused a pens as he had not srvd 6 mos. Rept by Wm Pettit.

FOWLER, JONATHAN, Lake co

Exec Doc 37 of 1852. Refused a pens as servd less than 6 mo. Rept by Wm Pettit.

FOWLER, JONATHAN, Mahoning co

Patriot N Y Men; p 254 Supp and pp 132-252 in Vol 1; another rec pvt Vt Men pp 54, 114 and 369. B Feb 20 1764 Guilford Conn; son of Andrew and Martha (Stone) Fowler; mar Lydia Kirtland abt 1798. Chldr: Lydia 1797; Rachel 2-16-1800 mar Thomas Riley; Chauncey 2-25-1802 mar Mary D Holland; and Jonathan 1804. Soldr drowned in Big Beaver Riv Apr 12 1806; bur Poland O; was 1st white settlr in Poland twp. Built 1st saw mill and grist mill in 1801;also built a stone tav in 1804. the farm of his father in Westchester co N Y was devastated by both armies as his dau had mar a British officer and some of his sons (Andrew Fowler's) had servd in the rebel army. Ref Hist Trumbull and Mahoning co Vol 2 p 59 68 and 9; Will Bk 1 p 56 Trumbull co O prob 1806; Church Rec of St James Prot Episcopal Ch Boardman O. Rept by Mahoning chpt D A R.

FOX, DAVID, Lorain co

Pvt Conn Contl; servd 14 mo various enlistments trom 1775 (certf). B 1751 East Haddam Conn (Appl); soldr d Mch 6 1833 (on back of certf). Appl for pens Lorain co Aug 2 1832. In 1781 moved to Granville Mass thence to Brighton O. Ref S 2217 Conn. Rept by State D A R and Nathan Perry chpt.

FOX, JOHN, Hancock co

See "Fuchs, John," this volume.

FOX, STEPHEN, Wayne co Ind not O

Pvt Conn Contl; enl 3 yrs in Dec 1780 in Conn; discharged at West Point N Y. B 1760; mar Mary —— July 20 1790 (wid appl); chldr: Bates æ 18, Samuel æ 14; Stephen æ 9, Enos æ 7 (appl 1820). Appl of Nov 10 1845 wid left chldr to whom this appl is made: Jemimah Price; Mary Baldridge and Samuel. Soldr d Feb 25 1842 Wayne co Ind (wid appl). Soldr appl for pens Sept 7 1820 Hamilton co O; wid appl for pens Delaware co Indiana Nov 13 1843; wid d Sept 11 1844. Ref W 10031 Conn and Harmer's Indian War (1790). Rept by State D A R. (Listed here to avoid continued research in Wayne co O).

FRAME, JEREMIAH, Preble co

B in Va; mar in Va and had several chldr there; d on farm in Jackson twp; bur Frame cem near Eaton Preble co O; came from Va through Bourbon co Ky to O; settl in Jackson twp 1815. Rept by Grace Runyon Commodore Eaton chpt.

FRANCE, PETER, Stark co

Enl Aug 1776 Md line; discharged Aug 9 1779; pvt Md Mil; served 3 yrs (certf). Was æ 76 in 1827 (appl). Mar Elizabeth S Myers? (1793); chldr: David (made appl for arrears of pens); Henry; Daniel; James (by aff of David); soldr d Apr 26 1836 (aff of son); wid d Feb 19 1851 (aff of son). Appl for pens Sept 17 1827 Stark co O. Ref W 7328 Contl Md. Rept by State D A R.

FRANCIS, GEORGE, Butler co

Enl Phila Pa 1776 (appl); served till close of war 1783 and was disch at Phila Pa; pvt Pa Mil. B 1745; appl for pens Butler co O June 5 1818. Ref S 42204 Continental Pa. Rept by State D A R.

FRANCIS, JOHN, Ross co

Exec Doc 37. Rev soldr res in O in 1852 or before; refused a pens as he did not serve 6 mos. Rept by Wm Pettit.

FRANK, JACOB, Mahoning co

Pvt. N Y Men in Rev pp 21 and 272; mar Elizabeth ——; chldr: Samuel; Andrew; John; Isaac; Jacob; Henry; James; Jones; George; Elizabeth mar Peter Getz. Soldr d 1849 Canfield twp; came to Canfield O 1809. Ref Hist Trumbull and Mahoning co Vol 2 p 84; Will Bk 1 p 141 Mahoning co prob 1849; and deed bk E p 414 Jacob and Elizabeth Frank to —— Canfield 1821. Rept by Mahoning chpt.

FRANKFERTER (or Frankford), JOHN, Mahoning co

Found listed as pensd; served in War of 1812; his father Philip was the Rev soldr which see. Rept by Mahoning chpt.

FRANKFUERTER, PHILIP (John), Mahoning co

Pvt. Pensd as John. B Feb 5 1762; mar Elizabeth (Dec 9 1771-Mch 28 1841); chldr: Elizabeth; John b 1782 mar Mary ——; Margaret mar Jacob Witter; Susanna mar —— Marshall; Sarah mar —— Bennett; Rachel mar —— Mensing; and another dau mar —— Hahn. Soldr d July 11 1828 Springfield twp; bur old cem North Lima; Mahoning chpt reports that only "John Frankfuerter" found is son b 1782; so this Philip is prob John Philip Frankfuerter. Ref Will Bk 6 p 4 Columbiana co prob 1828; Deed Bk R p 8 Columbiana co transcribed Philip and Elizabeth Frankfuerter to John 1822. Rept by Mahoning chpt.

FRANKLIN, SAMUEL, Franklin co

Dragoon Lee's Legion; pend Oct 6 1828 Franklin co O. Is listed here to aid continued research. Jane Dailey.

FRATT, HENRY, Knox co

Exec Doc 37 service as Rev is admitted. Wm Pettit.

FRAZEE, BARNHART, Mahoning co

Rept by W M Pettit. S A R named as a Rev Soldier in Mahoning co; bur in Pleasant Grove cem in address of compatriot Lynn (S A R).

FREDERICK, JOHN SR, Columbiana co

Rev soldr rec not yet found. Came from Pa Northumberland co; taxable as farmer 1772-1788. Ref Pa Arch Ser 3 vol 19 p 20 356. Rept by Mrs Wlima Molsberry.

FREDERICK, THOMAS, Columbiana co

Pvt Rangers Northumberland co Pa. B 1751; a dau Mary mar at New Lisbon O Sept 15 1815 to Matthew Elder. Soldr d 1808 Elk Run twp; came from Lancaster co Pa; prisoner of Indians in 1758; carried off by Indians from home in Eastern Pa in early childhoood; remained with them until languages and customs of whites nearly forgotten when he returned. He only established his identity by scar on back of neck recognized by his mother. Ref Pa Archives Ser 5 Vol 4 p 365 and Ser 3 Vol 23 p 244 Baldwin's Records and Hist of Beaver co Pa by Warner p 648. Rept by Mrs Wilma M Molsberry. See same p 148 O Roster Vol 1.

FREEBORN, THOMAS, Summit co

Rept as Rev Soldr d 1829 bur cem nr Miller Rubber Co Plant. Cuyahoga Portage chpt listed here for further investigation. By Meryl B Markley St Vice-Chairman 1935-38.

FREED, JACOB, Richland co

Pensr Green twp Richland co (now Ashland) 1840 æ 73 living with Frederick Shafer. Report from Pens Dept states he was not a Rev U S pensr. Filed here to avoid continued research by Jane Dailey. Jared Mansfield chpt reports that a Joseph Freed came to Springfield twp in 1833 and d; formerly lived in Pa where he was b 1808; in 1827 he mar Hannah Snider. They had 15 chldr.

FREEHOLD, WILLIAM, Gallia co

Pvt Co of Capt Morgan Regt of Col Campbell Va line for 18 mo. B 1755; in application for pens mentions wife and 2 grandchldr; a boy of 3 yrs and a girl of 6 prs (appl Aug 1820). Appl for pens from Gallia co O Feb 29 1820; was pens here. Soldr d 1829. Ref 42730 Va. Rept by State D A R and French Colony chpt who found no real estate to or from Freehold; no wills; an adm was app on his est on Oct 14 1829 and mention made of his wife who was not named; mention of his farm in Raccoon twp is made in the inventory. Ref is made to Rec of Wills Inventory end etc. No O pp 469 and 492.

FRENCH, ALEXANDER, Mahoning co

Pvt Cumberland co Pa; b 1760. Mar Elizabeth Morrison; (1760-Nov 9 1834). Chldr: William mar Betsey Davidson; Margaret mar John Hannah; Martha Ann mar Robert Russell; Jane mar Capt John Sheffleton; Betsey mar John Shearer; and Sally mar William Moore. Soldr d Dec 10 1832 Newton twp; bur Pricetown cem Newton twp; came to Milton in 1810. Pens appl Circuit Ct Warren Trumbull co O. Ref Pa Arch Vol 4 Ser 3 p 286 and 626; Ser 3 Vol 3 pp 949, 1017; Vol 6 S 3 p 410; Baldwin Gen lists him as a Rev soldr; Hist ofMahoning co pp 741, 985 by Sanderson; Will Bk 7 p 260 Trumbull co O prob 1834; Deed bk L p 108 transcribed Mahoning co and Lin Bk Vol 113 p 56 D A R. Rept by Mahoning chpt.

FRENCH, ELIJAH, Mahoning co

Pvt Mass Men; mar Susanna ——; chldr: Thomas; Rebecca; Eliza Ann; Joseph C; and Elijah. Soldr d 1815 Goshen twp. Thomas; Elijah; and Barzilla French, brothers, came to Goshen twp in 1805. Ref Vol 6 p 70 Mass Men in Rev; also N H Vol 1 p 370 and 378; Hist Columbiana co p 293; Hist Mahoning co p 203 by Sanderson; Will Bk 2 p 200 Columbiana co probated 1815 and Deed Bk R p 142 Columbiana co Rec Elijah French heirs. Rept by Mahoning chpt.

FRENCH, JEREMIAH, Hamilton co

Pvt Hunterdon Co Mil of N J; b 6-12-1762 N J; mar Hannah Williams. Chldr: Nathaniel; Moses; William; Sarah; Elizabeth; Mary; Hannah; Jeremiah Jr. Bur Spring Grove cem Cincinnati O. Ref Adj Gen N J Stryker's N J in Rev St Trps. Rept by Mrs W B Shuler John Reiley chpt.

FRENCH, JONATHAN, Licking co

Enl 5-21-1775 at Cambridge N Y (appl); while a res of Cambridge Washington co N Y he served with the N Y trps as follows: May 21 1775 as pvt in Capt James Wells co; from abt July 20 1775 at various times amounting to 5½ mo in all as pvt in Capt Joseph McCracken's Co; on July 4 1778 was commissioned Capt in Lt Col John Youngblood's Mil of N Y; b Sept 22 1751 Dunstable twp N H; mar Janet (d July 4 1831 in her 75th yr). John B French was a son. Soldr d at his home in Licking co abt 3 mi from Reynoldsburg; both are bur in Seceder Cem located 1½ mi s of Reynoldsburg Franklin co O; inscr "Jonathan French Revolutionary soldier b Sept 22 1751 d May 17 1838 aged about 87 yrs". Ref Veterans Adm Washington D C; Ohio Genealogical Quarterly Vol 1 p 21; S 8516 N Y Pens Claim. Rept by Mrs F A Livingston Columbus chpt and State D A R. (Had several chldr).

FRENCH, THOMAS, Mahoning co

Pvt Mass Soldiers and Sailors Vol 6 pp 94 and 95 (many); chldr: James b 1773; Robert b 1779. Mar Ann ——; Thomas; Barzilla b 1782 mar Mary Yates. Thomas, Elijah and Barzilla French came in 1805 to Goshen twp. Ref Deed Bk P p 197 Thomas and Esther to —— Goshen 1819 and Hist of Columbiana co p 293. Rept by Mahoning chpt.

FRENCH, WILLIAM, Washington co

Pvt Pa Mil; served 1 yr (certf); b Aug 15 1741 Cumberland co Pa (appl); he appl for pens Washington co O Oct 27 1832 while res of Warren twp; pensd July 22 1833 while res Washington co O. Ref S 18411 Pa. Rept by State D A R.

FREW, JAMES, Ross co

"A Rev soldr d on Fri last Nov 26 1830 in Chillicothe in the 87 yr of his age; decd was nat of Ireland and emigrated to Pa before Rev in which struggle he took the side of the Colonists and served as a common soldr under the command of Gen Washington. In 1804 he removed to Chillicothe in which place he res until his death." Ref Scioto Gazette Dec 1 1830. Rept by Pickaway Plains chpt.

FRITTS (Fretts or Frith), VALENTINE, Brown co

Pvt Va Contl; servd 3 yrs (certf); b 1758 (appl); mar Mary——; chldr: Sarah æ 19 son Valentine æ 13; dau Priscilla æ 11 (appl 1820). Soldr appl for pens Brown co Aug 5 1818 and again 1820. Ref S 42732 Va. In addition Taliaferro chpt repts chldr: David; Michael and Henry. Soldr d 1823; bur Fritt's cem bet Fayetteville and St Martin; came to Perry twp in 1817. Will prob July 25 1823 he owned land in Ky and in Clark co. Ref Will Bk 1 p 59 Probate Ct Brown co O. Rept by State D A R.

FROST, SAMUEL (a Captain), ? co

Listed in a news clipping found in an old scrapbook signed L A A in Washington co as "names of soldiers and rank in Rev war who participated in or were interested in the first authorized settlement at Marietta; these soldr who have desc in this section with but few exceptions are bur in Washington co cem; were active in Indian war protecting settlement at own expense never reimbursed by U S. Promotion or retirement may have changed the rank. This name not verified by Marietta chpt who repts it for further investigation.

FROTHINGHAM, EBENEZER LIEUT, ? co

Listed in a news clipping found in an old scrap book signed by L A A in Washington co as "names of soldiers and rank in Rev war who participated in or were interested in the first authorized settlement at Marietta; these soldiers who have descendants in this section with but few exceptions are bur in Washington co cem; were active in Indian War protecting settlement at own expense never reimbursed by U S. Promotion or retirement may have changed the rank. This name not verified by Marietta chpt who repts it for further investigation.

FRY, JACOB, ? co

Found listed as pvt Pa Mil; pensd age 77 Pickaway co may be mispelling for "Jacob Try" which see. (Jane Dailey).

FRY, JOHN, Fairfield co

Rev soldr came fr Va to Lancaster Fairfield co and d there. Ref p 176 Chapman Bros Hist of Madison; Fayette; and Pickaway co. Cop by Pickaway Plains chpt.

FRYE, FREDERICK, ? co

Found in list of Rev soldrs in a news clipping in old scrap book as participated or interested in Marietta settlement most of whom bur in Washington co. This name not among those verified by Marietta D A R and rept here by them for continued investigation.

FUCHS (or Fox), JOHN, Hancock co

Enl in Reading co Pa in 1781; served 1 yr in S C Sea Serv; pens 3-5-1819 Berks co Pa; transferred to Hancock co O 7-9-1832 (certf); lived Alsace twp Berks co Pa; name of dau not given in appl. Soldr d Nov 27 1843 æ 73 yrs 10 mo 27 da. Appl for pens Feb 8 1819 in Berks co Pa (appl); laborer (appl); Marine (certf). Ref In list of Rev Soldrs of Adler's (Pa) Journal Feb 20 1844 is: "D in Union twp Hancock co Nov 27 1843 John Fuchs formerly from Alsace twp Berks co Pa aged 73 yr 10 mo 27 da" and S 2219 S C Sea Service.). Rept by Mary O Steinmetz Reading Pa and State D A R.

FULHERSON, JAMES, Monroe co

Enl in fall of 1775 in N J; pvt 3 yr N J Privateer (certf). B 3-7-1765; chldr: Letitia æ 14 yrs in 1820 (appl); soldr d 7-11-1840. Pens 3-15-1819 Reading N Y; appl for transfer of pens from N Y to Monroe co O 12-6-1838; in 1840 was a pensr in Centre twp Monroe co O whr moved in 1838. Ref S 42207 N J Privateer. Rept by State D A R.

FULLER, THADDEUS, Vinton co

Pvt in Reg commanded by Col Greaton Tupper Mass line for 1 yr in 1776 and 9 mo in 1779. A pensr Aug 12 1818 living in Athens co O. B Oct 14 1758 (vol 4 p 212 Fuller Gen); son of Benjamin and Hannah (Wadsworth) Fuller; mar Susannah (Oliver?); chldr by copy of will 1833: Thaddeus Jr; James; Oliver; Samuel; Selinda Nelson; Fanny Sisson; 2 gr-dau are named (Hussey) indicating another dau (deceased). Soldr d Jan 11 1834 Elk twp Athens co O (now Vinton co O). Grave not yet located. Was a desc of Robert Fuller of Dedham and Dorchester (Fuller Gen vol 3 p 247) was a prisoner of Rev war; removed to Francistown N H; was on tax list there 1793; in 1821 was living in Athens co æ 62, wife æ 57. Ref No. 18732 Ohio and Hist of Francestown N H 1758-1891. Rept by Jane Dailey Regent of D A C this line.

FULLES, AARON, Miami co

Pvt Capt Hugh Stinson's Co Va line; b 1753 N J; mar Sarah Thompson (b 1760); d Miami co. Cop from 10735 vol 108 D A R Lineage bk.

FULLERTON, ANDREW, Mahoning co

Pvt Pa Artillery Capt Thomas Proctor Ser 5 Vol 3 p 949 Pa Archives; mar Margaret ——; chldr: William; Alexander; Cyrus; Robert; Mary; Julian (is a girl) and Margaret. Soldr d abt 1838 Springfield Mahoning co. Ref Will Bk 16 p 260 Columbiana co Rec prob 1838; and Deed Bk V p 498; trnscribed Mahoning co from Andrew and Margaret Fullerton to —— 1831. Rept by Mahoning chpt.

FUNK, ABRAHAM, Pickaway co

Was a nat of Va; came to O in 1810; entered land on the present site of the State Reform School in Fairfield co; afterward moved to Circleville where he d at age of 78 yrs. Altho but a boy he drove a team in the Rev war carrying provisions. His dau Mary mar Isaac Hammel (and several of his desc live in Circleville); inscr "Abraham Funk drove a wagon in the Revolutionary War B 1770 d Mch 1 1848;" wife Catherine b 1768; d Jan 9 1844; bur cem Forest twp Circleville O. Ref Chapman Bros Hist of Fayette Pickaway and Madison co 1892. Rept by Pickaway Plains chpt.

FURMAN, NOWELL, Portage co

Pvt N Y Mil. Was aged 81 yrs in 1832 (appl). Served 18 mo (certf). He appl for pens in Huron co O July 27 1832. Ref S 18412 N Y. Rept by State D A R. Fr Wm Pettit comes date d 1833 Portage co; b in N Y.

FULTON, JAMES, Gallia co

"Dunmore War" Pvt Pt Pleasant W Va Oct 10 1774; b Apr 15 1752; mar 1st —— Matthews, 2nd —— Fowler; chldr: William; John; Thomas; James Jr; Mary Fulton Bing; Margaret Kincade. Soldr d July 15 1839 Addison twp Gallia co O; bur Jones cem Addison twp; inscr: "James Fulton d July 15 1839 aged 87 yrs 3 mo." Ref Roy Rothgeb Addison O. Rept by French Colony chpt.

GADD, WILLIAM, Monroe co

Enl Apr 1779; Pa Milit. Servd one yr 4 mo 13 da. B in Baltimore co Md June 30 1759; pens appl Sept 21 1832 Monroe co O. Ref S 2231 Pa. Rept by State D A R. (cf No. 191, 151) D A R.

GALE, JONATHAN, Lorain co

Refused a pens as did not serve 6 mo. Exec Doc 37. Rept by Wm Pettit.

GALE, NICHOLAS, Ross co

Ref 4th rept N S D A R p 300 cop by Mrs Winnagle Warren O states he d Chillicothe Sept 26 1826; bur Second St site of Old Presbyterian Ch Graveyard. Also see Old N W Genealog Quarterly Apr 1900 p 92 notes and queries; and Hist Ross and Pickaway co p 588 on "Gale" family — (J D).

GALE, RICHARD, Franklin co or Mo

Enl June 1773; served over 2 yr 3 mo as pvt N Y Milit. Was æ 75 in 1833 (appl); Appl for trnsfr to Lemis co Mo 7-4-1838 whr "lived with his son." Was pensr 9-21-1833 in Franklin co O. Ref N Y S 16816. Rept by State D A R. Research by Columbus chpt Franklin co found no data.

GALLESPIE, JAMES, ? co

Pvt. Listed in Invalids Pensr of U S belonging to Ohio and pd at Chillicothe $76-

80 annually. Cop fr Pensrs 1818 by Jane Dailey. Cf "James Gillespie p 157 O Roster Vol 1.

GANNON, WILLIAM, Hamilton co

Pvt N J Contl and N Y Trps. In 1823 gave his æ as 70 wf 67; pensr Hamilton co O 1824; "Chldr all grown;" d March 3 1834 Hamilton co aft his wf d. Listed in 1830 cens in Greene twp Ham co; in 1790 cens and 1800 cens as head of family in Warwick Orange co N Y. Ref S 49219 N Y and Mrs. Carl Schmidt 2612 Piermont Ave Berkley Cal. (Accepted by St Ch.)

GARDNER, BENJAMIN, Brown co

Though reported from several D A R numbers is found to be same data as "Gard, Benjamin" p 152 Brown co which latter is believed to be a misspelling. (Jane Dailey).

GARDNER, JONATHAN, Geauga co

In Geauga co list removd to Coles co Ill. Ref File 31051 Vol 2 P 149 pens dept. Rept by Mrs Presley Geauga co.

GARDNER, JOHN, Trumbull co

Servd as Wagonmaster in N J. Wf's name Elizabeth. Chldr: Andrew; John; and James. Resident of Hubbard Trumbull co whr he d 1828. Ref N J Men in Rev p 848. Rept by Mary Chesney chpt. (1937).

GAREY, KILLYON, Fairfield co

Ref p 400 Roll of Assoc Co of twp of Richland Bucks co Pa Oct 9 1775 at Pa St Libry. He was b Nov 9 1757; mar first Barbara Miller 1780 mother and chld d; mar 2nd Shoalter by whom 3 chldr and she d 1800; mar 3rd Beckie Walters no recd of any chldr; mar 4th Catherine Neff; and had six chldr who were all b nr Lancaster O whr he had come in 1809 fr Lancaster Pa. Fam movd to Bluffton Ind abt 1887; 6 chldr are: Sarah mar Isaac Morgan; Catherine mar Thomas Smith; Louise mar Michael Miller; Eliza mar William Covert; Mary Ann mar Amos Townsend; Jacob mar Elizabeth Turner. Soldr d Aug 31 1833 and bur nr Lancaster on his farm (once owned by Judge Reeves). He was wounded at Battle of Monmouth; left hospital; went to Washington's Hdqrtrs whr he mended shoes. His tools and watch now owned by family was of Swiss-German ancestry spelling name "Gideon" instead of "Killyon" often. Rept by Jane Dailey fr data of Jessie Riley Griest 129 E Main St Portland Ore.

GARRISON, BENJAMIN, Portage co and Muskingum co and Pa

Enl Dec 1776 in Pottsgrave Pa whr livd. Servd 2 yr as pvt Pa Milit. Was b May 15 1738; one chld was named Jacob. Pens appl 1835 and 2-3-1838 Washington co Pa whr he had movd in 1833; he livd in Muskingum co O fr 1823 to 1832; pensr in Portage co O 1833; may be bur in Pa whr last pensd 1838. Ref Pa S 5170. Rept by State D A R.

GATCHEL, JOHN, ? co

Pvt refused a pens as servd in a Regt not on the Contl Establishment. Listed in Ohio pens appl Doc No 31 Jan 6 1831 at O S Libry. Cop by Blanche Rings Col O.

GATES, CAPT DAVID, Washington co

On old stone Righteous Ridge beyond Waterford O found: "In memory of (Nancy ?) Gates dau of Capt David Gates and (Priscilla ?) or (Pamela?) his wife who d Sept 6th 1807 aged 6 yr 2 mo 17 da." This led to research on Capt Gates and fr old people in neighborhood it was found a stone had oft been seen with Capt David Gates Revolutionary soldier on it; one man said he had placed the broken stone against the fence when the field was being plowed up. Rept by Rev Graves com for preservation and research. However see p 153 Vol 1 of Ohio Roster whr one is bur in Athens co — Once a part of Washington co.

GATES, NATHAN, MAJOR

Rev soldr listed in scrap bk item as associated in settlement of Marietta whose descendants likely bur in Washington co. Listed for continued research by Marietta chpt.

GATES, WILLIAM, Ross co

Enl in Contl Line abt 1782 Lancaster co Pa whr he resided. Servd 6 mo. Pens appl 10-17-1832 in Ross co O again in 1832 giving æ as 68; and again in 1833. Ref Pa S 5172. Rept by State D A R. Nathaniel Massie chpt reports "Probate 1840 — Case 2634; no will."

GATES, WILLIAM, Adams co

Enl 1780 for 3 yrs as pvt Md Contl. Was b 1760; mar Sarah McDaniel 1793; had a son William æ 25 in 1820; a dau Mary and son Allen; He appld for pens in Adams co in 1818; his widow appld in Brown co July 7 1838. He d Oct 27 1829. The son Allen stated his parents were mar in Charles co Md. Mary stated she had livd there w her parents till 1817 whn they movd to Ohio. (Affid of 1843) Ref W 5279 Md. Rept by State D A R.

GAUDINIER, JACOB, Cuyahoga co

Enl Montgomery co N Y. Servd one yr pvt Mass Milit. Pens appl Nov 7 1832 in Cuyahoga co O states was b Apr 4-1758 Montg co N Y. Ref S 15583 N Y. Rept by State D A R.

GAY, JOHN SR, Pickaway co

Born London Eng; was at Quebec under Wolf; and Braddock's defeat; d Sept 19 1823 Pickaway twp Pickaway co. Ref Will bk 1-2 p 54 — his will mentions wf Barbara; chldr: John; Peter; Elizabeth; Thomas; Mary; Susannah (wf of George Hitler); Catherine; William; Jacob; Exs. William and Jacob. Made Sept 12 1823-witn Henry Bishop; David Kinnear; and Daniel Stingley. Bur place known and descendants will mark it. Rept by Pickaway Plains chpt.

GEBHART, GEORGE, Montgomery co

Pa service 5th S Vol 7 p 168 Capt Gossert Lancaster. Also Berks co 5 S V 5 p 246 Capt Fulmer 6th Btl U S serv. Bur St John's Luthern ch cem Miami twp Montgomery co. Rept by W M Pettit Dayton S A R.

GEBHART, JOHN, Montgomery co

Drummer boy under Capt John Reinsell or Nichols 6 mo under John Nichols 9 mo Col Murdock Md. At enl livd Georgetown Md. B Aug 15 1760 Tulbehocken Pa; mar Phebe Van Sickle July 1816 (by Andrew Wadkins J P); at Mason co Va nr Pt Pleasant. No names stated of the seven chldr; he d Sept 23 1845 Montgomery co O whr livd in Miami twp. Widow pensd fr Miami co Piqua 1868 æ 69. Ref W 10054 B L Wt 96097-160-55. Cop by Jane Dailey.

GEE, MOSES, Gallia co

Pvt N Y St Trps. Servd under Capt Hombanock Regt of Col. Wisenvelt N Y Line 8 mo; was b 1760 Duchess co N Y. Mar Phebe — Nov 10 1784; chldr: 1st two d; Hannah mar Henry Sager; Joseph; Solomon; Sarah mar Elijah Gleason; John; ninth chld d; Peter; Nancy mar Samuel D Gleason. They (Moses) were mar in Orange co N Y; movd to O 1819 to Gallia co. Pens appl in Huntington twp. Aug 1832. Ref W 5280 N Y. He d Feb 6 1842 Gallia co. Rept by State D A R.

GEER, JEDEDIAH, Franklin co

Enl 1776 pvt Conn Line one yr. Pens appl 9-27-1819 in Franklin co O. In 1820 ments one dau 30 yr old who had three chldr. Ref S 42741 Conn. Rept by State D A R.

GEHRET, JACOB, Sandusky co

In lists of deaths of Rev soldrs in Adler's Journal Pa Sept 19 1848 states: "D in Sandusky co O Aug 5 1848 Jacob Gehret formerly of Richmond twp Berks co Pa." Rept by Mary Steinmetz Reading Pa. (No data found at Rev pens cl dept) (J D).

GEORGE, PARNICK, Pickaway co

Servd his country in Rev and war 1812; he and Catherine (Van Meter dau of Isaac a Rev soldr) said to be bur McLane cem this co; natives of Tenn and Va. Aft their mar livd in Ky; then Chillicothe; then Deer crk twp Pickaway co. Cop fr p 447 co Hist by Pickaway Plains chpt.

GEORGE, WILLIAM, Columbiana co

Pvt 6th class Capt Alex Peeble's co 1 Btl 4 Marching Co 4th Class called Oct 23 1777 Cumberland co Pa Milit. Pvt in Capt John Campbell's Co 1 btl Cumberland co Milit Nov 19 1777. He mar Linney —— b 1777 d 9-11-1852 æ 74-8-22. She is bur East Palestine Columbiana co O. Ref Pa Arch S 3 V 23 p 625, 626. and Cem recds Columb co. Rept by Wilma Molsberry.

GEORGE, WILLIAM, ? co

Many Rev services; also in Navy under Henry Dougherty. From Frankford Pa. Bur place not located. Remarks: Co Treas 1818-19. Rept by W M Pettit Montgomery co S A R.

GERRILS, JOHN, Trumbull co

Enl 1778 Mass. Servd 2 yrs 4 mo Capt King's Co Col Brooks 7th Mass Regt. Appld for pens Apr 1818 Washington co N Y; again 1820 naming wf; one dau Ruth; and "chldr liv in O." Pensd Trumbull co O Mar 8 1826. Rept by State D A R. Mary Chesney chpt adds he livd Salem N Y; Westmoreland N Y; Gustavus O.

GIBBNEY, GEORGE, Richland co

Came fr Ireland 1774. Settld in Chester co Pa. Enl 1776 there. Dischgd fr Schuyl- kill Pa. Pvt and Sergt Pa St Trps. Servd 10 mo 7 da. B 1754. Pens appl in Richland co O Aug 1832. Ref S 2234 Pa. Rept by State D A R.

GIBBS, WILLIAM, Tuscarawas co

Pvt Va Contl. Servd 3 yrs. B 1760; mar Jane —— æ 64 no chldr under æ all grown (appl of 1820). Pens appl Tuscarawas co O Oct 1820 1822. Ref S 42746 Va. Rept by State D A R.

GIBSON, DANIEL JR, Lorain co

Listed p 144 in Hist North Central Ohio by Wm Duff as a Rev Soldr. Said to be markd by Western Reserve chpt. Rept by Nathan Perry. (Mrs. Oehlke).

GIBSON, ELEAZER, Mahoning co

Pvt 5th Contl Regt 1777 to 1780; b 1754; d 1841 bur Canfield O; grave located by Mahoning chpt. Ref 1st rept N S D A R p 93 cop by Mrs Oehlke Nathan Perry chpt. Ref Cens 1840 lists same name as pensr æ 80 liv w Ansel Beaman Canfield Mahon- ing co O. Cop by Jane Dailey.

GIBSON, JOHN, Greene co

Pvt under Capt James Poe 1777; b 1754 Pa; mar Martha Parks 1772; one son was named Thomas; soldr d 1830 Xenia O. Bur Massie Crk cem Greene co. Ref V 40 D A R Lin No. 39911. Rept by Mrs Oehlke Nathan Perry chpt. Rept also by Catherine Greene chpt; and Cedar Cliff chpt which marked the grave May 30 1935.

GIBSON, THOMAS, Pickaway co

Rev soldr; came to Madison twp Pickaway co O w son George abt 1804. Bur Reber Hill Twp Walnut; Inscr on stone: "Thomas Gibson b in Va 1750; d May 3 1814; wf Sarah b in Va; d Nov 28 1781." Rept by Pickaway Plains chpt. Grave markd 1932 by that chpt.

GIBSON, THOMAS, ? co

Cop fr V 115 p 43 D A R Lin by Mrs Oehlke Nathan Perry chpt is following: "pvt in Capt Richard Salter's Co 5th Battl Phila co Pa Milit. B in Scotland 1754; mar —— Buchanon in 1802; had a son named George; no burial place stated."

GIDDINGS, JOSHUA, Ashtabula co

Pvt Capt John Watson's Co 1775-1777 in Capt Asahel Brainard's Co. Pensd 1833 Conn St Trps. Was b 1755 Lyne Conn; mar Submitt Jones; one son was Elisha; Soldr d 1833; bur w Williamsfield O. Cop fr 21 rept N S D A R p 93 w grave located by Mary Stanley chpt V 58 p 168 D A R Lin. Cop by Nathan Perry chpt. Mary Redmond chpt repts: He d 10-21-1833 æ 77 at Williamsfield O.

GILBERT, JACOB, Mahoning co

Pvt. Ref Pa Arch S 6 V 1 p 973; N Y Men in Rev p 214; Mass Men p 412 V 6; Will bk 9; Columbiana co Recds Proba 1836; Deed bk O p 67 trnscrb Mahoning co Jacob and Eliz Gilbert to 1807. Chldr: Jacob mar Phebe ——; John mar Catherine ——; Magdalene. Soldrd abt 1836 at Goshen Mahoning co O. Rept by Mahoning chpt.

GILBERT, THADDEUS, Lorain co

Enl Welton Parish Norwalk Conn 3-4-1777; servd as Sergt in Capt Comstock's Co Col John Chandler's Ct Regt; dischgd at Valley Forge after one yr. Was an armorer; in 1820 pens appl fr Chatauqua co N Y; appld for trnsfr to Genesee co N Y 1841; trnsf to Lorain co O Mar 9 1829 stating wf "was 67 yrs old." Ref S 43596 Conn. Rept by State D A R. Rept by Nathan Perry chpt. Comm additional reference is made to one Ira Gilbert 1822; and George G Gilbert 1829 but no relationship given. Soldier movd back to Genesee co N Y 1841 to live w chldr no names given; Last payment pens fr 1844 to Mar 1845 made to Samuel March at Albany N Y (Atty). In 1845 soldr stated he had livd in St Joseph co Mich for 11 mo and had previously livd in N Y. (Data fr Genl Accounting Off D C). Vol 5 p 160 D A R Lin No. 4448 thro a son Banford states Thaddeus mar Martha Turney; that in 1775 he servd under Capt M Meade; and in 1777 enl for the war in Conn Line.

GILDERSLEEVE, OBADIAH, Trumbull co

One of Refugees fr Long Isl to Conn. D in Gustavus Trumbull co in 1805 æ 50. Mar Chloe Bushnell in Hartland Conn 1786. Chldr: Obed; Sally; Bailey; Polly; Orrel; Annes; Phebe; Chloe; Betsy; came to O in 1804 fr Canton Ct. Rept by Mary Chesney chpt.

GILLELAND, DANIEL, Meigs co

B Middlesex co South Brunswick N J in 1765; on Apr 16 1809 movd to Cuyuga co N Y; thence to Seneca co N Y; aft 7 yrs to Marietta O; aft 7 yrs to Meigs co O whr appld for pens July 26 1833. Was son of John Gilleland an Ensign; he mar Mary —— at Cranbury N J Aug 1786; chldr: Reuben b 1787; Jonothan Owen (1801); Abraham. Soldr d Oct 5 1838; (was he bur in Bedford twp ?). Rept by Return Jonathan Meigs chpt Mrs. Bertha Bing Chase.

GILLFILLAN, THOMAS, Ross co

Cop fr stone inscript: "A Revolutionary Soldier d Mch 28 1816 in 65th yr." Near by is stone "Agnes Gilfillan d Apr 24 1828 in 65th yr." Rept by Nathniel Massie chpt. Wm Pettit rept service in Westmoreland co Pa; b Ireland 1751 d 1816; mar Agnes ——. Ref 27742 S A R.

GILLIS, ARTHUR, Belmont co

Pvt Col Porter's Regt Artill. Enl 1777; servd to end of war. Pa Contl. Appld for pens Belmont co O 27 Apr 1818; pensd 1819 æ 80. Ref Pa Arch S 3 V 23 p 574; and S 42742 Pa. Rept by Jane Dailey.

GIVIN (or Gevin) (not Gwin), THOMAS, Wayne co

Enl nr Greensburg Pa; servd 3 yr in Va Line; was b 1740; pens appl Wayne co O 9-27-1820. Ref S 42208 Va. State D A R.

GLASGOW, ROBERT, Adams co

Refused pens as not serv 6 mo. Exec Doc 37. Rept by Wm Pettit.

GLASS, HENRY, Columbiana co ?

Cop fr Com Pleas Court Marietta V 5 p 132 by Helen Sloan is his appl for pens Washington co O Apr 13 1827. From Wilma Molsberry Youngstown is: A ranger on the frontier; Washington co Pa. B 1763; d 1855; bur Center twp accd to county recds. Ref Pa Arch V 23 S 3 p 215.

GLENN, GEORGE, Pickaway co

Military Aid. Ref Military W Va Rev Ancestor by Anna Waller Reddy p 33 Hampshire co Va. B Jan 10 1748 prob Va. Son of Earhart and Eva Glaze; mar Elizabeth Williams abt 1778. Chldr: George; Susannah and Elizabeth (twins); Mary; Elizabeth and Mary (twins). Soldr d June 25 1826, Pickaway co. Bur in pvt cem Niles farm nr Waterworks. Inscr: "In memory of George Glaze Sr son of Earhart and Eve Glaze who d June 25 1826 A 77-5-5. On stone for wife: "Elizabeth wf of George Glaze and dr of Richard and Susannah Williams d Oct 9 1824 A 62-9 mo. Rept by Pickaway Plains chpt.

GLENN, JAMES, Jefferson co

Pvt Enl Fall of 1776 whl resident of Cumberland co Pa in Pa Milit. Servd one yr. Emigrated to U S 1760; in 1785 movd to Westmorland co Pa; thence to Jefferson co O in 1804; was b Apr 1744 Antrim co Ireland. Pens appl in Jefferson co Ross twp Aug 21 1833. Ref S 4298 Pa. Rept by State D A R.

GLOVER, WILLIAM, Ross co

Listed as pvt Del Contl pensr 1819 in Ross co O (S A R). Fr Nathaniel Massie chpt research ref V A B C D p 232 made will June 30 1826 w Noble Crawford Exec. Son Thomas and dau Jane (Blackstone) named; will probated Mar 29 1827 B 322-case 2601. Land was on Buckskin Crk.

GODDEN, JOHN, Trumbull co

Servd in Contl Army fr Morris co N J. Ref N J Men in Rev p 608. Was one of first settlers of Bazetta twp Trumbull co O; d abt 1810; bur in Orchard on Wm Davis farm this lot being now a part of Hillside cem. Rept by Mary Chesney chpt.

GODWIN, WILLIAM, Highland co

Enl 1776; servd as Corp in Capt Parson's 1st Co N Y Trps. B in 1756 N Y; mar Mary Bowman 1778; one son Nathan mar Elizabeth Wirt. Soldr d 1803. Ref V 107 No 106611 D A R Lin bk. Cop by Jane Dailey.

GOFF, SOLOMON, Medina co

Pvt Conn Contl. Enl 1781; servd 2 yr. B 1763; wf Huldah æ 44 in 1820 whn pens appl made in Bradford co Pa naming chldr: Hannah æ 15; Huldah 12; Nancy one; Oliver 9; Daniel 5. Trnsfr to Medina co 1833. Ref S 42749 Ct. Rept by State D A R.

GOODALE, SILAS

Rev soldr listed in scrap bk item as associated with settlement at Marietta; whose descendants likely bur in Washington co. Listed for continued research by Marietta chpt.

GOODSELL, ISAAC, Ashtabula co

Pvt Conn Line; mar Elizabeth Sullivan 8-18-1808; widow appld for pens in C ——ford? co Pa 7-7-1855. He never appld for a pens. Ref Conn B L Wt 40502-16055. Rept by State D A R. From No. 13188 D A R Lin V 14 states he d 2-29-1844 æ 81 and bur old Monroe twp cem.

GOODRICH, JOHN H, Portage co

Pvt Conn Contl. Enl Mar 1778; dischg 1781 nr West Point. Servd 2 yrs. Pens appl July 4 1818 in Portage co O gives his æ 57; he mar Esther Parmelle (?) June 1784. Aft her death 1785 he mar Eunice Burmiler Feb 28 1788; Chldr: Esther b Aug 1781; Chauncey b July 31 1791. Esther dau d May 28 1808; Eunice wf d June 8 1792. He then mar Mary Read Sept 26 1793. Eunice a dau b Mar 30 1795 and mar Joseph D Wolf Jan 5 1814; John G W Wolfe b July 23 1816; Mary Wolf b July 12 1819. These recds fr the Family Bible. Widow appld Portage co O Sept 11 1840 æ 89 liv in Rootstown twp. Ref W 4682 Conn. Rept by State D A R.

GOODSARD, VALENTINE, Portage co

16th rept N S D A R p 144 cop by Mrs Oehlke states he was b Chambersburg Pa and d Portage co Rootstown twp. (Extended research found no other facts.)

GOODSPEED, SIMON

Found listed in Cens 1840 in Wayne co O æ 76 liv w Simpson Goodspeed is believed to be same as Sympson Goodspeed record below of same age. (J D).

GOODSPEED (or spead), SYMPSON, Wayne co

Pvt R I; Enl Providence 1782; servd 9 mo. Was b 1764 Providence co R I; son of Stephen and Anna Goodspeed; Mar Marcy Hinkley 2-17-1792; chldr: son Simpson æ 16; dau Sally 14; Maria æ 12; Deboraha æ 8 (in Appl of 1821). Soldr d Mar 14 1851 in Wayne co O accd to Widow appl. Aft mar livd in Essex co N Y where 12 chldr were b. He appld for pens 1821 there; in 1836 in Cuyahoga co O. Wid appld Nov 6 1851 Wayne Co O; and in 1855 in Erie co. Other names of chldr: Forest; Anna; Charles; Patty; Orvillia; Marcy; Silas; Salloma. Ref W 2786 B L Wt 26825-160-55 R I. Rept by State D A R.

GOODWILL, DAVID, Mahoning co

Appl for Pens. Ref Circuit court Warren O Bk 6 p 107. He d at Poland Mahoning co O. Was on tax list 1837 Poland twp. Rept by Mahoning chpt.

GORDON, BERNARD (or Barnardus), Jefferson co

Pvt N J Contl. Enl Spring of 1777 N J. Dischgd 1783 Murdney Crk N Y. Pens appl fr Jefferson co O Aug 21 1820 gave his æ 63; a son Peter æ 28 wf and two small chldr. Ref S 42753 N J. Rept by State D A R.

GORDON, JOHN, Adams co

Pvt Pa Contl. Servd 3 yr fr Apr 1780 to 1783; b 1758. In October 1824 appld for pens in Adams co O. Ref S 42751 Pa. Meryl Markley Georgetown State Vice ch repts name listed in Evans and Stivers hist Adams co. (Not same one listed p 160 V 1 Roster). Rept by State D A R.

GOSSETT, JOHN, Washington co

Pvt Va Contl. Enl Oct 1776 Va. Servd 6 yrs. Was b 1753; appld for pens Washington co O May 14 1818; again in 1820 had one chld named Abi; stated property value at $18.00 (Ref V 3 p 430). Rept by State D A R.

GOUCHER, HENRY, Mahoning co

Pvt. (name Gouter). S 6 V 18 p 577 Pa Arch. B April 8 1757; mar Rhoda Rose; chldr: Henry Jr; Robert b 1788 mar Margaret Patterson. Soldr d Jan 14 1842; bur old Goucher farm nr Lowellville Poland twp. Came to Poland O fr Washington co Pa. Member Presb church. Ref Abrdg Compend Amer Gens V 3 p 95 and V 1 p 567; Deed bk 1 p 35 Trnscrbd Trumbull co O. (Mahoning) 1806; Tax list 1826 Poland O. Rept by Mahoning chpt.

GOULD, JOSEPH, Brown co

Mass Pvt. Enl Apr 1775 in Maine; at Leasborough; servd 8 mo. B June 1746 York co Mass. Pensr 1833 Brown co O whr had livd abt 30 yrs. Rept by State D A R. Two sons William and Daniel are rept by Meryl Markley, Taliaferro chpt.

GOULD, WILLIAM, Ashtabula co

Pvt Conn Line; enl Apr 1776 in 5th Regt. Servd 7 yr. In pens appl 1818 gives æ 61; mar Esther; 1819 pensr in Ontario N Y; trnsfr to Ashtabula co O 1838 whr in 1840 liv w Harlow B Seager Pierpont twp in 1840 (census). Ref Conn S 42752 Rept by State D A R.

GOWDY, JAMES, Greene co

Pvt 4th Batl Lancaster co Trps under Capt James Burd; b Newcastle co Delaware Nov 5 1742; son of James Gowdy; (see p 161 V 1 Roster); mar Abigail Ryan abt 1772 in Pa. Chldr: James; Samuel; Robert; Martha mar John Jolly; Jane mar Joseph Kyle; John; Alexander; Ryan; Abigail mar Robert W Stephenson; Sarah mar Peter Jacoby; Mary unmarried. Soldr d 11-7-1814 æ 66 yr 11 mo 28 da. Accd to stone inscr in Assoc. Reformed cem often called Godwy cem E 3rd St Xenia O. Ref Robinson's Hist Greene co O; Dills co hist; Hist Gowdy Fam by Mahlon Gowdy; R I and Pa Arch. Rept by Catherine Greene chpt.

GRADY, YOUNGER, Muskingum co

Pvt listed in Invalid Pensr of U S belonging to Ohio pd at Chillicothe $57-60 annually. Cop fr p 172 Pensrs 1818. Fr List fr War Dept Act 1832 June 7 his name is found in Muskingum co. Cop by Mrs O D Dailey.

GRAHAM, JOHN, Gallia co

Pvt Conn Contl. Servd in Regt commanded by Col Wyllys for 3 yr. Made appl for pens in Eastern Distr of Pa Sept 22 1820; appl for trnsfr Dec 31 1822 to O whr then liv in Gallipolis Gallia co O.

GRANT, JONATHAN, Wayne co

Pvt Va Contl. Enl Feb 1776 Pittsburg Pa. Servd 2 yr. B 1755; mar Sally ——; chldr: four; Rebecca age 16; Peggy 12; Jenny 10; Jno 8 (Accd to appl of 1820). Pens appl 1820-21 in Wayne co O. Ref S 42758 Va. Rept by State D A R Wooster-Wayne chpt repts sale of land in Wayne co 1817 naming wf "Sarah" in deed.

GRAY, AMOS, Mahoning co

Pvt Mass Men V 6 p 792; mar Mary ——; then 2nd Elizabeth Heil; chldr: eleven: Samuel Amos; George b 1802 mar Margaret Early for first wf then Jane Early; David; Jesse; Catherine mar ——Krayl; Mary Ann mar —— Kirkpatrick; Sophie mar Harmon Dunscomb; Stewart; Amos; Margaret. Soldr d abt 1838 Coitsville; came fr N J in 1804; settld in Liberty twp; soon movd to Coitsville twp. Ref Hist Mahoning co by Butler V 3 p 353; co hist by Sander son p 763; Will bk 9 p 175 Trumbull co. Probated 1838. Rept by Mahoning co.

GRAY, JAMES, Wayne co and Ashland co

Pvt Mass Contl. Servd 2 yr. Enl in Pelham co Mass Apr 1782; b Jan 1765; mar Easther; liv w him "two gr-chldr whose parents are both dead — Easther Howe æ 10; and Horace Howe æ 14" (appl 1820). Pens appl in Wayne co O 1818 and 1820. Ref S 42761 Mass. Research by Wooster-Wayne chpt found no records or grave. Cop fr news clipping by Hetuck chpt is "Born Mass 1761; mar Esther Sabins in Mass; d 1845; came to Wayne co 1812. Cop fr p 142 Hist North Central Ohio by Wm A Duff as Rev soldr bur in Pioneer cem Ashland co. (by Nathan Perry chpt).

GRAY, JAMES 2nd, Hamilton co

Pvt in Co of Capt Doudle Col Thompson Pa Line one yr. Enscrb Ohio May 1825 Act 18 Mch 1818 May 1 1820; b 1751; Enl at Little Yourk Pa. Dischg Long Isl in 1824. Pens appl in Hamilton co O æ 73 names "wf upwards of 61 and 2 chldr one grown up." Ref S 42759 Pa. Rept by Jane Dailey.

GRAY, JOHN, Jefferson co

Member Council at Annapolis 1779; b 1721 London; mar Mary Gray (1740-1817); one son was David; d 1817 Steubenville O. Cop fr V 121 p 162 No. 120519 D A R Lin by Nathan Perry chpt.

GRAY, LITTLETON, Franklin co

Cop fr Chapman Bros Hist of Fayette; Pickaway; and Madison cos p 747: "Little-ton Gray was a native of Maryland and a soldier in the Revolutionary war. By trade he was a shoemaker and came to Ohio in 1838; settled in Franklin co O where he d aged 76 years. Rept by Pickaway Plains chpt.

GREEN, BENJAMIN, Licking co

Servd in N J; settled at Pataskala Licking co O; had a son Richard. Ref J H Gal-breath "Stories of the Buckeye State." Rept by Hetuck chapter. Tho this rept states not the same one filed V 1 p 163 O Roster compare. (J D).

GREENE, CHARLES, Hamilton co

Capt of Kentish Guards and pvt in Philip Grafton's Co Col John Tapham's Regt R I Trps. Born East Greenwich R I 1753; d Cincinnati O Sept 15 1816. Cop fr p 54 Calif Sons of Rev yr 1901 by Jane Dailey.

GREEN, DANA, Sandusky co (?)

Cop fr 13 rept N S D A R p 119 as Rev soldier grave marked by Col George Crog-han chpt Green Crk twp by Nathan Perry chpt. (Mrs Oehlke). (No co stated).

GREEN, DANIEL, Trumbull co

Made application for pension from Trumbull co. No date to decide if Rev or 1812 soldier. Rept by Mary Chesney chpt.

GREEN, ELISHA B, ? co

Sergt listed in Invalid Pensr of U S belonging to Ohio pd at Chillicothe $96 annually. Cop fr p 172 Pensr of 1818. By Jane Dailey.

GREEN, ISAAC ? co

Pvt listed in Invalid Pensrs of U S belonging to Ohio pd at Chillicothe $48 annually. Cop fr p 172 Pensrs of 1818. By Jane Dailey.

GREEN, JARED, Trumbull co

Pvt Mass Men V 4 P 810. B 1765; mar Prude —— b 1863 Sterling Mass d 1845; 8 chldr; Jared Jr; Cyril b 1793 mar Polly Sherman; Julia mar Whitcomb; Amelia; Soldr d 3-21-1841 Bloomfield Trumbull co; came from Mass with 8 chldr. 2 of sons were mar. Ref Western Reserve Chronicle Mar 1841; Hist Trumbull and Mahoning co; V 2 p 387. Rept by Mabel S Askue Mahoning Ch Youngstown.

GREEN, JEHIEL, Medina co

Enl Westchester co N Y 1779 pvt; served 2 yrs. B 1762 Nov 27 Westchester co N Y. Mar Esther ——; fr widow's appl Caleb; Catharine; Betsey; Daniel; William; Ezra; Cold?; James; Sarah; Jehannah; Aaron; Thomas, Hiram, Rachel; Joseph; Elsie; Sally; Avery; Deborah; Jane; Benjamin; d Sept 28 1845; appl for pens Steuben co N Y Apr 24 1833; appl for pens Medina co Ohio Jan 8 1834; appl for pens Medina co O Aug 21 1846. Res of Chatham. Ref W 7556; N Y; Mary; Avery; and Jehiel appear to be grchildren. Rept by State D A R.

GREEN (or Greene), JOHN, Muskingum co

Enl Va 1775; in Contl. Servd 8 yrs; b 1744; d Apr 27 1834; mar Johanna —— 1777; "Had a family of chldr" (affidavit of witness). Was dischgd at Pittsburg Pa close of Rev. Soldr appld for pens May 1 1818 Muskingum co O; widow appld there Mar 17 1837. Ref W 4216 Va. Rept by State D A R.

GREENE, JOSEPH, Warren co

Capt in N Y 1776 with other services. B 1762 d 1835; bur Dicks Crk Presb Ch Yd. Marked by Richard Montgomery S A R Dayton. Came to Warren co 1814; was nephew of Gen Nathaniel Greene. Rept by S A R Dayton.

GREEN, NEHEMIAH, ? co

Mariner. Refused a pens as service not on a vessel on the Contl Estab. Ref Doc 31 Jan 6 1831 O S Libr. Rept by Blanche Rings col.

GREENELSH, EDWARD, Jefferson co

Pvt Va Contl. Enl 1779 whl liv in Shenandoah co Va; servd 18 mo. Pens appl in Jefferson co Aug 20 1833 æ 86. Ref S 5209 Va. Rept by State D A R. (name been found spelled "Greenelah).

GREENMAN, JEREMIAH, Washington co

Enl 1775 pvt in Capt Samuel Ward's Co Col Arnold's R I Regt. Pensr B 1758 Newport R I May 7; mar Mary Eddy 1784; chldr: one son (name not legible); wf Mary Eddy are bur on same plot w soldr, in abandoned cem nr Waterford; soldr d at Waterford Nov 15 1828; insc on stone: "Revolutionary soldier — in memory of Jeremiah Greenman Esq an active officer in that army which bid defiance to Britons power and established the independence of the United States." Marked by Marietta chpt 1923 with D A R marker. Soldr org Freemasonry in Waterford twp; Masonic emblems on tombstone. Ref V 105 D A R Lin No. 104756 (cop by J D); and rept by Marietta chpt. A complete account may be found also in "American Friend" and Marietta Gazette Sat Nov 29 1829 rept by Pickaway Plains chpt(See p 164 Vol 1 Ohio Roster — "Jeremiah Greenway").

GREGG, JOHN, Clermont co

Servd in Capt Thomas Gaddis' Co Va Milit 1776; b 1747 Washington Pa; mar Sarah Gregg 1773 (b 1753); soldr d Moscow O 1833. Ref V 124 p 40 No. 123118 D A R Lin. Cop by Nathan Perry chpt.

GREGORY, JAMES, Delaware co

Pvt enl 1780 in Fairfield co Conn. St Trps; servd 3 yrs; b 12-19-1764; came to Delaware co 1808 whr pens appl 11-20-1832. Ref S 17445 Conn Delaware chpt repts he d 2-2-1842; bur Berkshire cem Berkshire twp.

GREGORY, JEHIEL, Athens, Fayette and Madison co

Enl 1775 in Joseph Benedict co Col James Haolmes N Y Line. B Gregory's Pt L I 1755; son of Nehemiah who with his son servd in Westchester co Regt under Gen Thomas Frum. Soldr mar Elizabeth Andrews; one son was Andrews; one dau was Annis wh mar Ozias Strong. Soldr d 1818 bur Yankeytown Fayette co but body of his wf and of him moved to cem at London by Theodore Annette Phelps Lincoln (first state regent of Ohio D A R). Soldr came to O 1801; was a trustee of Coonskin Libry; first postmaster of Athens co; movd to Fayette co 1815; recd title of Col in war of 1812 his militia brigade being the first brigade mustered in Athens co; He with John Haver by special act of Legislature built first dam across the Hock-hocking R 1808; was memb of House Rep fr Washington co 1811-12-14. Data fr Elizabeth Andrews Felton West Bainbridge and co Hists. Ref No. 1921 and No. 93975 D A R.

GREGORY, SAMUEL, Butler co

Refused a pens as did not serve 6 mo. Exec Doc 37. Rept by Wm Pettit.

GREY, JAMES, Belmont co

Pvt in Capt John Underwoods Co Col John Hammon's Regt Chester co Pa Milit; b 1739 Scotland; mar Jane Gass first wf; a dau Mary Grey mar Alexander Cassill 1796; soldr d 1829 Belmont co. Cop fr V 107 No. 106832 D A R lin; S 42759 spells James "Gray" Hamilton co

GRIBBON, JOHN, Carroll co

Pvt Pa Contl under Capt Wilson Col Porter; mar Margaret McIlrain, Gibbon Strasbrough twp Lancaster co Pa Mch 15 1788; soldr d at res of son July 3 1842 Harrison twp Carroll co whr he was listed in Cens 1840 æ 89 liv w William D Gribbon; ref W 4965 B L Wt 26548-160-55 cop by Jane Dailey who also cop (in old Pens. Dept D C): Ohio Agency Cert No. 5350 widow Margaret d 2-4-1858 in Carroll co O; named chldr James; Duffield; and Jane Gribbon Crop Arrears of pens due at death appr 11-5-1859, and pd to James Gribbon and James Crop Admstrs. Soldr certif No. 19774, fr Pittsburg Agency Pa. (where soldr's pens was pd).

GRIFFEY, ZACHARIAH, Logan co

Pvt Va Line enl Fredericksburgh Va; servd 6 yrs; b 7-5-1750; Pens appl 1827, stated "family consists of 2 daus æ 9 and 5; "resides with son-in-law, who has a large family." Ref S 42757 Va. Rept by State D A R.

GRIFFIN, EZRA, Ashtabula co

Pvt enl 1778 Granby twp Conn St Trps; servd 13 mo; b 1761 Hartford co Conn whr livd till after Rev thence to Md Pa and Va the next 4 yrs; and to Ashtabula co O "about 23 yrs ago" as stated in appl for pens there 9-25-1832. Ref S 16136 Conn N J. Rept by State D A R.

GRIFFIN, JOSEPH, Meigs co

Pvt N Y St Trps; b July 16 1760 Duchess co N Y; no record in appl of any marriage; later movd to St Lawrence N Y thence to O in 1819; until 1823 had no fixed residence which time he resided in Meigs co whr was a pensr in 1832. Cop by Mrs John Chase Return Jonathan Meigs chpt fr S 2581 N Y Pens cl.

GRIFFITH, DAVID (or Daniel), Butler co

Pvt enl May 1775 Berkshire co Mass Contl; servd 2 yr; in appl for pens July 13 1832 Butler co O stated he was æ 74 was b Litchfield co Conn 2-7-1758; mar Elizabeth Cowell 8-9-1793; soldr d Apr 1 1839 Butler co O. Ref W 9462 Mass. Compare p 165 Vol 1 Roster of O same county but named Griffis. Rept by State D A R.

GRIFFITH, NATHAN, Butler co

Pvt enl June 1 1776 in Baltimore co Md; servd 9 mo; b Mar 4 1759 in Md. Livd in Butler co O ever since co was organized; here he appld for pens July 30 1832 Ref S 8616 Md. Rept by State D A R.

GRIFFITH, SAMUEL, Lorain co

Enl in state of N Y. Pvt in Capt Nathan Herrick's Co. Col Van Dyck's Regt; Orderly Sergt in Capt John Smith's and other enl to dischg Nov 15 1779. In 1780 was pvt in Capt Johnathan Warner's Co acting as guard for city of Albany. Soldr was b June 13 1755 Dartmouth Mass; after Rev livd in Delaware co Dela 6 yr; thence in Shenango co on Susquehanna R 3 yr; in Montgomery co north of Albany 3 yr; Ontario co N Y abt 7 yr thence to Ohio; pens allowed Mar 27 1833, whl liv in Amherst Lorain co O. Ref S 3427 N Y. Rept by State D A R. Fr Nathan Perry chpt Lorain co comes following: He died Dec 25 1835; in 1834 refers to a son Judah; in 1835 one Duty Griffith made affidavit, Lorain co to soldrs claim no relationship to soldr shown; (Ref: Pens Bureau). Then this statement is made: "Samuel Griffith d Dec 25 1838, in Henry co Ind, leaving no widow, and only one child, Judah; arrears of pens due soldr apprvd Jan 8 1842 in favor of only child. (Note error in death date, of one statement J D).

GRIM, JACOB, Pickaway co

Enl as pvt batl of Brandywine; servd in Capt Jacob Waggoner's Co Col James Dunlap's Pa. Regt enl 1778 servd 2 mo in Capt Kilion Leeby's Pa Co May 10 1780 made Ensign; servd other enlistments; was b 2-22-1754 in Northampton co Pa; mar Deborah ——; soldr d Apr 1837 and bur at Tarlton Salt Crk twp Pickaway co O. Inscr on stone: Jacob Grim d Apr 1837 æ 83-1-28. In 1782 he movd to Dauphin co Pa; in 1783 to Northumberland co Pa; after 20 yr movd to Pickaway co O in 1803; wf is bur in Imler cem-inscr: Deborah wife of Jacob Grim d Sept 15 1815 age 51 yr. Pensr 1832; Ref S 2243 Pa. Rept by State D A R and Pickaway Plains chpt.

GRIMES, RICHARD, Adams co

Pvt in Capt Henry Darby's co of Col Hazlet's Del Regt. Enl Jan 31 1776; dischd 1-31-1777. Ref Evans and Stivers Hist Adams co p 331. Rept by Meryl Markley St. Vice Chairman 1935-38.

GRISWOLD, SOLOMON, Ashtabula co

Enl in Hartford co Conn 1776; in 8th Co 1st Regt Mass Line (not Conn) 22 mo; Qrtr-mastr and Srgt; in appl for pens 1832 Ashtabula co gave age as 75; Ref S 15589 Mass. Rept by State D A R. Mary Stanley chpt repts: he d 1834 Windsor O, and have located the grave. Mary Chesney chpt repts: "cop fr Western Reserve Chronicle May 22 1834. Died in Windsor Ashtabula co on 16 inst Hon Solomon Griswold in 80th yr of his age. Was one of first settlers of Western Reserve and an officer in the Rev War." Nathan Perry chpt sends ref to:Rept N S D A R 21st p 94; and 18th p 204.

GROGAN (or Grogen), PATRICK, Brown co

Pvt enl Loudon co Va 1777 or 8; Dischgd at Pittsburg; Servd one yr Va Contl; was b 1743; pens appl fr Brown co O 12-17-1819 and again in 1823 stating "Children all grown and had left me." Ref S 41593. Rept by State D A R. (This name found misspelled "Grogran" in some lists).

GRONINGER, JOSEPH, Stark co

Service under Col Phil Cole Northumberland co Pa. B Germany 1753 d 1835; mar Elizabeth Hill. Ref S A R 48800. Rept by Wm Pettit.

GROOMS, JOHN, Adams co

Ent service whn liv in Barkley co Va; servd 6 mo in Va Line; was b 1740 Md; whn young his father moved to York co Pa; thence to Barkley co Va; "Came to Adams co abt 34 yrs ago" (appl for pens Oct 1833). Ref S 3419 Va. Rept by State D A R. Also listed p 273 Va Militia in Rev.

GROOMS, JOHN, Butler co

Came fr England to America in 1775; was b there 1754; servd 3 mo as pvt in Artillery; 6 mo in Navy was given no written discharge; has resided in O 37 yr and Butler co 14 yr (appl for pens Butler co 1830). Ref Pa and Pa Sea Service S 2247. Rept by State D A R.

GROSVENOR, THOMAS, MAJOR, ? co

One of list in news clipping fr scrap bk of Rev soldr who were associated w settlement of Marietta whose descendants livd and d in Washington co; many servd in Indian war at own expense never reimbursed by U S. Filed here for continued research by descendants. List fr Marietta chpt.

GROVE, JONAS,, Jefferson co

Enl 1778 Barclay co Va as pvt Contl servd one yr; and dischgd in N J; was a butcher; in pens appl 8-21-1820 Jefferson co O said wf was æ 72; had a dau æ 20; Ref S 41591 Va. Rept by State D A R.

GROW, PETER, Meigs co

Pvt Mass Militia; b 4-30-1763 Oxford Mass; movd to Dudley Mass; thence to Vermont; thence to Washington co O; then to Athens co which part was later Meigs co. Pensr 1833 Meigs co. Ref S 18425 Mass. Rept by Return Jonathan Meigs chpt by Mrs John Chase. (See No. 132596 D A R).

GRUBB, PETER, Franklin co

Ref fr Berks and Schuylkill Journal of Nov 13 1830 rept by Mary Steinmetz Reading Pa states "he d in Columbus O 1830 aged 80 yr; he came to America fr Germany at æ 14 to Lancaster Pa. Took up arms for adopted country. Was a member of M E church and ornament of the church and daily walk an example worthy of imitation." (Research by Columbus chpt found no data). The following was rept by Marietta chpt: On a stone is found "Mary Grub consort of Peter Grub died Aug 7 1815 æ 44 yr." this in old cem nr Waterford O. Washington co nr a Van Clief grave stone. Listed in half-pay Pensr of U S arising fr relinq of bounty land etc p 38 Roll of Capt George Nagel's Co Peter Grubb 3rd Lieut-appl to Miles Rifle Regt; also p 400 see and 30 other ref. Also a Peter Grubb Jr Lancaster co. Capt Appt 3-12-1776 by J D.

GROVER (or Grovier), ISAIAH, Muskingum co

Enl 1777. Servd in Mass Contl for 2 yr; b 1756; mar Elizabeth June 21 1776 in Hartford co Conn whr livd for 25 yrs. Chldr: Samuel; Elizabeth wf of Samuel Parker; Salinda wf of John Wesley; Simon; and Edmund. Soldr d June 12 1829; movd to Bradford co Pa whr appld for pens May 11 1818 and in 1820. Widow appld here also 9-17-1838; she d 1844. Soldr appld for pens transfer 4-23-1821 to Muskingum co O. Ref W 3183 Mass. Rept by State D A R.

GUILD, OTIS, Trumbull co

Pvt Ref Mass Men V 4 p 940 Dedham Mass 1779 service at Tiverton R I. Mar Lois Robinson (b 1766-d 3-7-1842); chldr: Otis (Oliver); Albert Dr in Boston; Jairus;

Jerusha who mar Nathan Hanchett; Charlotte first white chld b in twp; Aurelia died at 18 yr; Oswin. Soldr d 3-29-1830 Mesonotamia Trumbull co O. Came fr Sharon Conn in 1801; dau Jerusha taught school in 1804; Ref Western Reserve Chronicle March & April 1839; cem recds of H R Baoldwin S A R; Pioneer Women of Western Reserve p 145; Trumb and Mahon co Hist Vol 12 p 493. Rept by Mabel S Askue Chapt Ch. Rev Soldrs of Mahoning chpt. Following data is fr Western Reserve Chpt: Soldr b July 7 1763 son of Timothy and Jane Davis Guild of Wrentham Mass. He mar Lois Robinson 1-7-1788;he d Feb 21 1839.

GUNN, ELIJAH SR, Fulton co

Cop fr tombstone: "Elijah Gunn Sr d Sept 22 1855 aged 95 yr 8 mo 8 da. A Pioneer of Ohio July 1796 and of the Maumee Valley 1815." (The G A R Post 66 marker should be on the grave of his grandson, Cyrus Gunn). His son Elijah Jr was in war of 1812 and all three are bur in this Gunn cem. Mamie Hunt Cassety Napoleon No. 257881 Wauseon writes he settld at Girty's Pt a pioneer of 1826 opposite the east end of the Island in what is now Flat Rock twp. He was a Rev Soldr. The house he built is still standing; R W Hartman, of Napoleon, 88 yr old in conversation with the writer said he knew Elijah Gunn Sr and attended his funeral; he remembered the details. Ref p 670 Aldrich Hist. Henry and Fulton co (1888). Rept by Mrs W H Maddox Wauseon O.

GUNN, ELISHA, Lucas co

Refused a pens as servd less than 6 mo. Exec Doc 37 Rept by Wm Pettit.

GUNN, NOBLE, Ashtabula co

Enl May 1777 Mass Contl servd 3 yr; mar Lucy Gleason prior to 1790; chldr: Burrill (?) spelling aged 15; Estill 12; Martha 10; Doris 6 (accd to appl for pens 1820). In 1818 gave his æ 56; he d 10-22-1830 in Ashtabula co O whr had appld for trnsfr 9-28-1821; was a miller. Ref W 3983 Mass. Rept by State D A R.

GUNSAULD (or Gunsaula), JOHN, Brown co

Enl N J 1776 pvt St Trps; servd 16 mo; was b 1754 N Y. Aft Rev livd in Washington co Pa; thence to Ky "abt 40 yrs ago"; thence to Ohio whr appld for pens July 1832 Brown co. Ref S 2254 N J and Pa. Rept by State D A R from Taliaferro chpt Brown co (Meryl B Markley) comes data: He was at Kenton's Station in Ky. Stolen by Indians; rescued at Chillicothe O by Logan; settled in Huntington twp abt 1803. Ref Beer's Hist Brown co p 494; and "Simon Kenton" by Edna Kenton pp 180-185. States it is the opinion he left Brown co late in life and is bur at Attica Ind.

GUTHRIE, JOSEPH, Meigs co

Recd land grant in Washington co for Rev service; native of Conn; settled at Newbury; one son by first wife came fr Conn to Lottridge Orange twp. Was bur either in Orange twp or Athens co in abandoned cem nr Lottridge; a marker placed by 3 grt-grandchildren — one of whom was Josephine Guthrie Tucker. This information fr Mrs Keziah Woodyard Dye Harrisonville O.

GUTHRIE, TRUMAN, CAPT

Listed in news clipping found in old scrap bk as associated w settlement of Marietta a Rev soldr whose descendants likely bur in Washington co. Many servd in Indian war at own expense never reimbursed by U S. Listed here for continued research.

GWIN, THOMAS

Found listed in Wayne co O is misspelling for Givin or Given Thomas which see this volume.

HAAS, JOHN, Licking co

Gave material aid (furnished food). Was b 1756 Va Shenandoah co. Mar Elizabeth Wilkin (b 1758 d 1837 Licking co O); chldr: Simon; John; Catherine; Sarah mar Joseph Parrett. Soldr d 1827; bur Licking co O. Ref 177830. Secured fr Mrs. Paul Minich Springfield O by Mrs Jane Dailey.

HADLEY (or Hadly), MOSES, Richland co

Pvt N J Contl. Servd 4 yrs. B 1745; appld for pens Jan 18 1819 whl residing Austin twp Richland co O. Ref N J S 41626. Trnsfrd fr Trumbull co 1820 to Richland co. Rept by State D A R.

HAGERMAN, ABRAHAM, Williams co

Bur near West Unity Williams co O. On the stone marker are the words "Revolutionary soldier." Rept by Mrs H L Prouty West Union O Wauseon chpt. (Unable to find more data) (J D).

HAGERMAN (or Hageman), BARNETT, Wayne or Ashland co

(This pens clm was rejected as his name did not appear on Pa or O Rolls. To avoid further research it is given here. Enl 1776 or 7 Bucks co Pa. B 1756. Appld for pens Mar 18 1833 resident of Plain twp Wayne co. Edith Ewers Bucks co Pa inquired abt cl 1836 and stated he d in Wayne co abt 1833-4. Ref R 4426 Pa. Rept by State D A R. (D A R in Wayne co found no records).

HAHN, JACOB, Mahoning co

Ref Pa Arch S 5 V 4 p 563. Contl Line Northampton co pp 215 & 324. Depreciation Pay V 8 pp 125-152-172. Chldr: John b 1785 mar Mary Spouseller (possibly); Adam 1790; Isaac 1788; Barbara mar John Stahl; Andrew 1781. "Jacob and Michael Hahn bros both toop part in Rev War — Michael went south" (See Vol 1 p 168 Roster Rev). He d in Springfield twp Mahoning co O. Ref Biog E Ohio p 734 by Summers; Hist Columbiana co p 778 by McCord. Rept by Mahoning chpt.

HAHN, MICHAEL, Stark and Wayne co

Pvt Md Line. Enl 1775 Fredericksburg Md whr he livd. Movd to Northumberland co Pa whr enl 1777. in 1827 went to O liv 1 yr in Jefferson co; 6 yrs in Wayne; about 5 in Starke co Tuscarawas twp whr he appld for pens 8-6-1833; b 8-15-1748 Bucks co Pa; mar Nancy July or Aug 1801; he d Aug 1844; bur West Lebanon cem north at church with "U S Soldier Rev War" on stone as rept by Wooster-Wayne chpt. Widow appld for pens May 20 1853 Wayne co O. Ref Md & Pa R 5109 (meaning he was not allowed a pens for some legal reason). But listed as pensr 1-17-1834 in Stark co æ 95. Rept by State D A R.

HAHN, PAUL, ? co

Capt. Because he servd in Regt not on Contl Estab was rejected a pens. Ref Doc No. 31 Jan 6 1831. Rept by Blanche Rings.

HAILEY (Harley), ANTHONY, Gallia co

Ref S 41624 Pens Bur corrects spelling as usually listed "Harley" to Hailey. Pvt Va Contl. Servd 5 yrs. Appld for pens in Hammond co Va May 19 1818. In 1820 was pensr in Gallia co. B 1759; several chldr (none ment). Letter of 8-25-1842 says: "Wf died a few days before he did." Rept by State D A R French Colony chpt repts found no deeds; wills; estates; or mar in name Hailey in period fr 1818 to 1842.

HAINES, NATHAN, Mahoning co

Pens appl Circuit ct Warren O. Also N H Men vol 2 pp 256-260-263. B Conn son of Joseph Haines. Power of Atty for the heirs of Joseph Haines from brother Ebenezer in Conn. Rept by Mahoning chpt.

HALL, ASA, Portage co

Servd as carpenter; rank also shown as pvt Capt Willcox's Co Col Jeduthan Baldwin Regt. Artificers Contl Trps Conn. Enl 2-17-1778 for 3 yrs; disch 2-19-1781; b abt 1760 Conn. Mar Elizabeth Hall (same name) Wallingford Conn 1787. Atwater Hall who mar Permelia Haskins is given as an only chld. Ref Pens R 4460 (R means rejected). He d 1814 Portage co O. Son b 1-28-1799 1st chld b Atwater O. There are sworn statements for Rev serv tho appl 1851 by son for arrears was rejected. Rept by Mrs. Finch Regstr of Mississinewa chpt Portland Ind.

HALL, JOHN, Wood co

In deaths of Rev soldiers fr the American Almanac and Repository of useful knowledge reads: "Jan 1840 at Perrysburg O aged 89 John Hall a native of Conn who was a Lieut in Rev Army and served at Bunker Hill, Ticonderoga, and Trenton." Rept by Mary Steinmetz, Reading Pa.

HALL, JOHN, Clinton co

Pvt Va State Trps. Enl May 1 1780 Patrick co Va. In 1811 remvd to Ky; thence to Clinton co O whr Sept 5 1832 appld for pens; b 1751. Ref S 2589 Va. Rept by State D A R.

HALL, MOSES, Ashtabula co

Pvt Mass Contl. Enl June 1780 in Berkshire Mass in 12th Reg Mass Line; b Oct 1762 New Marlborough twp Mass. Servd 6 mo. Livd at Berkshire till 1781; thence to Washington twp Conn. 5 yrs later to Lenox twp Mass; thence in 1811 to Ashtabula co O. Ref Mass S 4326. Rept by State D A R.

HALL, PETER L, Shelby co

Pvt N J Milit. Enl æ 15 as substitute for brother-in-law. Servd 2 yr 9 mo. Was b 10-26-1764 Monmouth co N J whr he livd at enl. Aft war in 9 yrs movd to Phila Pa; thence to Valater whr liv abt 15 yrs; then 8 yrs in Ind; thence to Warren co 2 yr; then to Shelby co O. Appld for pens 5-6-1833 Shelby co; whr liv in 1840 æ 77 in Orange twp. Ref N J S 16856. Rept by State D A R.

HALL, RICHARD, Clermont co

Pvt and Indian spy 1778-82; b Washington co Pa; mar in 1793 to Pheobe Beggle, (b 1770); one dau was Phoebe; d Clermont co. Ref 114, D A R lin p 251. Cop by Mrs Oehlke, Nathan Perry.

HALLADAY, JOHN, Pike co

Pvt N C Contl. Enl Guilford N C in fall of 1775 or 6. Servd 9 mo. Appld for pens in Pike co O 2-7-1819; and in 10-14-1822 stating wf very old and infirm; had two grchldrn Halladay Wiley æ 10 or 11 in 1822 and Milinda Wiley past 9. Ref N C S 41627. Rept by State D A R.

HALLAM, THOMAS, Clinton co

Pvt in Capt Evan Cesna's Co Rangers of Frontier Bedford co Pa Milit 1778 to 1783. Was son of John and Isabel (one repts Elizabeth) Fell Hallam; b 3-10-1748 Hagerstown Md. Was gr-son of emigrant Thomas Hallam who came to Md abt 1701. He mar first: Mary Berkshire (Beshear) in Hagerstown by whom had eight chld 3 died in infancy others were: John; Charles; William; Deborah (Kinkaid); Nancy (Hagan). Mary d in 1798 and Aug 26 1798 he mar again to Sally Vorhees dau of Isaiah Vorhees. She was b 6-1-1773 and d 12-23-1841 Sabina O. By second mar had 8 chld: one d infancy; others: Thomas; Sophia (Morrow); Absalom; Samuel; Sarah Margaret (Stone); David; Isabel (Goodrich). In 1828 Thomas traded their land in Washington co Pa whither they movd after Rev for 1000 acres in Clinton co O. Here he raised blooded horses. He d July 31 1829 at Sabina Clinton co O whr stone is intact. Many ref given by two descendants who proved service and are No. 49895 Mrs. O C Brown Indianola Iowa; and Mrs

Ralph Henderson No. 59242 Sioux City Ia each of whom has rept these facts to Ohio D A R Chairman.

HALLMAN, STEPHEN, ? co

Listed as half-pay pensioner (but pens papers are as a soldr in War 1812). Might have srvd in both wars. J D.

HALTER, JOHN, Highland co

Incorrect spelling of Hatter, John which see.

HAM, THOMAS, Belmont co

Was b 1766 Fredericksburg Md; d 1838 Belmont co; mar 1785 to Jane Hampton (1754-1844). Srvd in Capt Richards Stringers Co Md Line; Pensr 1832; 12 chldr: John d young; Elizabeth unmar; Sarah mar Henry Meek; Richard mar Fannie Meek; Wm mar Susannah Sharp; Rizin mar Mary Myers; Polly mar Jacob Eggy; Rebecca mar Jacob Wilson; Catherine mar Michael Ault; Samuel mar Elizabeth; Charity mar Jacob Myers; Thomas mar Polly (Mary) Hardesty. Rept by Zane's Trace chpt.

HAMBLIN, LEVI, Cuyahoga co

Pvt Conn Contl. Enl Hartford co Conn Feb 14 1778. Servd 3 yrs. B 1765. Appld for pens in Cuyahoga co O Nov 7 1818. Ref Conn S 41617 Pens Bur. Rept by State D A R.

HAMILE, EBENEZER, Preble co

Exec Doc 37 of 1852 refused a pens as servd less than 6 mo. By Wm Pettit.

HAMILTON, CHARLES, Adams co

Corp Delaware Contl in Regt of Col Hazlett for 6 mo. Enl abt May 15 1775. Appld for pens Apr 16 1818 and 1819 residing in Adams co O. Ref Del S 41614;p 330 Adams co Hist. Rept by State D A R.

HAMILTON, JOHN, Hamilton co

Musician Mass Contl. Pensd in Hamilton co O 1827. (No record of pens found at D C — J D). Cop fr Census 1840.

HAMLIN, JOHN, Delaware co

Pvt N J Milit. Enl in fall of 1776. Servd 9 mo. Also servd 2 yr as teamster; b 7-2-1759, Huntington N J. He was a substitute for his father. Aft Rev movd to Washington co Pa and aft 6 yrs went to Washington co Ky and aft 8 yrs to Delaware co O whr appld for pens 11-20-1832. Ref N J S 17465. Rept by State D A R.

HAMMOND, JACOB, Trumbull co

Pvt in 2nd Battl Northampton co Milit Co 6 May 14 1778. Ref Pa Arch V 8 5th S p 114; b in Germany 1750; mar Anna Hottel Apr 12 1774; chldr: John Jacob; Anna Margaret; Mary Magdalene; George; John; Elizabeth; Anna Maria; Anna Charlotte; Christina; Gideon; and Lydia. He d 2-3-1824 N Bristol Trumbull co O; bur at Bristolville on his farm (the Francis Norton) whr is stone with dates and name erected by family. One of first families to settle in Bristol twp. Ref Family Bible rept by Mrs C D Williams Spokane O; Hist Trum-Mahon co V 2 p 234; Biog-Hist E Ohio p 692 by Summers; Will bk 4 p 226 Columbiana co records proba 1821? heirs not named. Rept by Mahoning chpt. Also Rept by Mary Chesney D A R corresponding with other two.

HAMMOND, JOHN, Trumbull co

Ref 27 Rept N S D A R p 128 as bur at Bristolville 1812. Rept by Nathan Perry chpt. (One John Hammon was pensd 1832-34 while living in Ohio; and in Cens 1840 one ment as pensr in New Center O — J D. (Also see John Hamond below).

HAMMOND, THOMAS, Athens co

Pvt Md Contl;b 1763; mar Sarah Boyles 1-28-1793 Montgomery co Ind. Enl Marlborough Prince George co Md Mch 1781; pvt in Capt Williams and Edward Price Co's Col Peter Adams 3rd Md Regt; was at Yorktown; dischgd 1783; pensd in Athens county 1820; liv in Crawford co Ind 1828; in Adams co Ill in 1831. Widow æ 76 liv in Washington co Liberty twp was allowed a pens on appl 12-27-1850. He d Nov 1832 (no place stated referred to "children" but no names). Ref W 4224 Pens Bur and Mrs L A Hart 516 Vermont Pl Col O fr whom this rept accepted by St Chairman. Rept by Jane Dailey.

HAMOND, JOHN, Hamilton co

This name listed as a pensr Act of June 7 1832 on Rolls of 1832-34. In Census of 1840 Some name listed as pensr Fulton twp Hamilton co O æ 87 yrs. (b then in 1753). Rept by Jane Dailey.

HAMPTON, JOHN, Pickaway co

Bur Hillside cem east of Bazetta; cop fr 27th Rept N S D A R by Mrs. Oehlke Nathan Perry chpt.

HAND, EDWARD, Highland co ?

Ref Census 1840 as pensr liv in Salt Crk twp Highland co O. Cop by Jane Dailey. Research failed to corroborate the fact.

HANDLIN, MATHIAS, Butler co and Ind

Pvt N J Milit. Enl abt 1776. Servd 2 yrs; had servd over a yr in Milit previously. Resident of N J. Three yrs aft dischg movd to various places before coming to Butler co O whr had livd abt 10 yrs; mar Anna Head Sept 10 1787; chld named were Burton and Phebe; he d Nov 2 1840 at Pleasant Hill Ind. (widow states). First appld for pens in Butler co O Oct 10 1832. Ref W 4218 New Jersey. Rept by Ohio D A R.

HANKS, THOMAS, Logan co

Exec Doc 37 of 1852. Refused a pens as servd less than 6 mo. Rept by Wm Pettit.

HANNA, HENRY, Jefferson co

Rev service confirmed by a Miss Kinsey of Mt Pleasant who knew descendant of Henry and rept to Mary D Sinclair who located stone data; b 1738; d 1820; bur Old Seceeder cem Mt Pleasant O Jefferson co. Rept by Steubenville chpt.

HANNAH, WILLIAM, Mahoning chpt

Pvt 4th class Cumberland Milit. Ref Pa Arch S 5 Vol 4 p 80. Mar Ester; three chld were: Thomas; Betsey; William. D abt 1814 at Poland O. Ref Will bk 2 p 46 Trnscr records Mahoning co 1814. Rept by Mahoning chpt.

HAPTONSTALL, ABRAHAM, Gallia and Ill

Pvt N Y Milit of Orange co N Y under Capt Thomas Moffett, Seth Marvin and Francis Smith 1775-1777. Twice a substitute for Rhineus Helms. In Battle at Ft Montgomery Oct 6 1777; pensd in 1833. A farmer he left Gallia co in 1835 and d in Knox co Ill. Ref Preston and Va Papers VI pub of Wisc Soc Draper Mss fr Bernice O'Brien this information to St. Ch and French Colony chpt.

HARAKIN, JOHN

Is incorrect spelling for "John Karakin" of Knox co O which see (Jane Dailey).

HARAMAN (Hariman), DAVID, Preble co

Found incorrectly listed as Harman David; a pvt Md Milit 1777 or 1778. Enl Baltimore Md whr he then resided. Servd 6 mo; b 1761. Appld for pens in Preble co 1834; listed in Cens 1840 as liv in Monroe twp Preble co with Chas Van Horn æ 84. Ref S 9560 Md. Cop by State D A R.

HARBERT (or Harbit), WILLIAM, Scioto co

Pvt Va Contl. Servd 3 yrs; b 1750; mar Margaret Traver during his service; four chldr b in Pa before they movd to Ky; Samuel youngest son b in Ky; William Harbit is a grand-son. He appld for pens in Nicholas co Ky 1818; same in Clark co Ky 1820 while liv in Fleming co Ky; pens trnsfr to Scioto co O 1830 whr he d Mar 20 1835. His widow appld for pens same co. Nile twp July 8 1847. An affidavit of a witness names other chldr: Elizabeth; Polly; Susannah; John; Henry; and Samuel. Ref W 7673 Va. Cop by State D A R.

HARBISON, ROBERT, Preble co   27

Enl Washington co Pa; srvd 17 mo in Pa Trps under Gen Hand and Capt James Leach. B in Pa 1758 mar Sallie James; had 8 chldr; recd pens July 1833; d Eaton 1837; bur Mound Hill cem. Rept Commodore Preble chpt.

HARDAN, SAMUEL, Butler co

Exec Doc 37 of 1852. Refused a pens as servd less than 6 mo. Rept by Wm Pettit.

HARDESTY, FRANCIS, Portage co

Pvt Pa Milit. Enl fall 1776; servd 6 mo. B 3-24-1757. Appld for pens Portage co O 3-12-1834. Ref Penn S 8684. Cop by State D A R.

HARDESTY, OBADIAH, Belmont co

Pvt 1st Regt Pa Line. Pensd Act of 1828 in Belmont co. Servd under Capt J Finley Ref S 46362. Cop by State Chairman J D. Mary Steinmetz Reading Pa repts death as 7-29-1830 in Belmont co. Ref Pa Arch list.Zanes Trace chpt Mrs McCommon repts: b 1758 Va; d 1830 Belmont co; mar Polly Paris 1784 a French girl; 9 chldr: Urias b 1785 mar Elizabeth Clark; Solomon mar Catherine Warren; Kaziah mar John Hatcher; Rebecca mar Ralph Hardesty; Lewis mar Sarah Warren; Catherine mar Jesse Campbell; Sarah mar Daniel Warren; John drowned in creek flood 1818 with his wf and five chldr; Polly (Mary) mar Thomas Iiams and d in Morrow co at æ of 102 in 1907.

HARDEY, PARY, Cuyahoga co

Pvt N H Contl. Enl 1775; servd one yr 7 mo and 12 da. B 5-9-1757 Bedford Mass. Went to Onandaga co, Delaware co, and Ontario co N Y and for "past ten mo in Cuyahoga co O." Appl for pens Cuyahoga co 3-14-1833.Ref S 18436 N H. Cop by State D A R.

HARDIN, JAMES, Hamilton co

Pvt Capt John Pearson's Co 9th Pa Regt Contl line. Ref Pa Arch Vol 3 5th Ser p 455; also certified copy of Record fr Hardin Bible; and Biog Miami Valley. B Philadelphia 5-10-1757 son of James and Martha Hardin; mar Eleanor Davis dau of Samuel Davis 11-6-1783; chldr: Samuel (m Mary Cilley); James (m Susan Withrow 1st and 2nd Darino Carter); Rebecca (m Wm Poole); Martha (m David Kennedy); Susan (m Amos White); Mary (m Thomas Hueston); Catherine (m Samuel Potenger); Eleanor (m Jacob Smith). He died 6-26-1837 on his farm Colerain twp whr he is bur in family graveyard (South of Bevis). Servd 4 yrs. Also as a Privateersman buying land with money secured fr the capture of prizes. Bot form 2-26-1800 and his log house used for holding elections the yr Thomas Jefferson elected Pres. His mother's wedding ring is preserved as a treasured relic by descendants who belong to chapt rept this data Cincinnati.

HARDIN, RICHARD, Ross co

Incorrectly listed as "Harding;" a pvt Pa Contl. Enl in Redding twp Pa. Servd 3 yrs. Aft Rev movd to Ross co O whr appld for pens 7-13-1818 stating æ as 65. Some discrepancy in dates as Pa Arch list says he d 10-15-1825 in Ross co O æ 67. Ref Penn S 41604. Cop by State D A R.

HARDY (or Hardey), NATHANIEL, Portage co

Pvt Conn Contl. Enl Ashford Conn and servd till 1780 whr dischgd at Elizabeth-town N J. Servd 3 yrs. Appld for pens 2-9-1820 in Portage co O Stating had a wf æ 64; a gr-son Anson Hardy æ 14; he was æ 60. Ref S 41598 Conn. Cop by State D A R. See p 173 Roster Vol 1 whch gives possible burial place.

HARMAN (or Harmon), CONRAD, Muskingum co

Pvt in Capt John Clark's Co Col Daniel Broadhead's Pa Regt. Enl 1777 dischgd 1783 Sept pensr 1818 æ 70 in Muskingum co whr he d 6-9-1823. Mar Christina ——; she was æ 60 in 1820 and chldr: Esther 24; John 19; Boston 14; Conrad 16. Ref S 41611; Hist Wash Co Pa p 82. Rept by Mary Chesney chpt. Pa Arch list rept by Mary Steinmetz, Reading Pa as d Muskingum co O 6-9-1822 æ 75; and Mississinewa chpt Portland Ind.

HARMAN, GEORGE, Pickaway co

Drummer boy Va Milit. B 3-21-1761 in Va. Parents: George and Mary Foss Harman; mar Mary —— abt 1791 or 2; chldr: George 1793; David 1795; Jacob 1797; Barbara 1799; Eli 18—; Susanna 1805; Othias 1809; John 1812; Amos 1814; Sarah 1816. He d 12-28-1832 and bur in abandoned High st cem Circleville north side nr center end by side of wife; stones carry above data. Marked 1932 by Pickaways Plains chpt bronze marker. Ref Rost Rev Soldiers of Va p 202. R W War 4 p 225. Rept by Pickaway Plains chpt.

HARMAR, JOSEPH, Washington co

Major; associated w settlement of Marietta; descendants likely bur in Washington co. Cop fr Scrapbook list.

HARMON, JOSEPH, Cuyahoga co

Pvt 1776 Lieut Saml Harmon's Co fr Suffield Conn whr he was b. He mar in 1778 Eleanor King (b 1760); one son was named Carlos; d Euclid O. Ref V 117 p 188 D A R Lin No. 116606. Rept by Nathan Perry chpt.

HARNESS (Harnish), JOHN, Mahoning co

Pvt N Y Men in Rev p 182; Chldr: Mary; Elizabeth; David; Susannah; Hannah; John. He d abt 1817 Green twp Mahoning co. Ref Ohio Patriot Apr 12 1817 est John Harnish; Deed bk O p 342 Columbiana trnscrbd Mahoning co John Harnish 1820. Compare p 174 Ohio Roster Vol 1. Rept by Mahoning chpt.

HARN, FREDERICK, Montgomery co

Listed incorrectly various places for Frederick Harp which see Ohio Roster p 174 Vol 1. Sometimes called Herb. Ref 7624 Pa. By Jane Dailey.

HARPER, DANIEL, Meigs co

Pvt N H Contl. Mar Mary — 1-21 1790; chldr named: Sally; Amos; Amy; Lavina; Betty; Ezekiel; Steven; Greaty Temple. He d 8-3-1839. Appld for pens in Athens co 6-20-1818; removd to Orange twp Meigs co whr appld again 7-25-1820. Ref W 4221. Cop by Mrs John Chase Pomeroy.

HARPER, JOHN, Adams co

Buried Winchester Adams co. Rept by Sycamore chpt.

HARPER, JOSEPH, Trumbull co

Ref Trumbull co Probt Court Recds V 1 p 39 says: "Major Joseph Harper late of Richfield d 17th of May 1805 and there was pension due him from the Gov." Cop by Mrs Winnagle Warren O.

HARPER, WILLIAM, Harrison co

Pvt Pa Contl. Enl for 3 yrs. Mar 15 1776 in Pa. Taken prisoner in Long Island New York and escaped abt 8 mo later. In 5th yr of war re-enlisted was taken prisoner by Indians and held for 5 yrs. Appld for pens in Harrison co O 6-15-1825 at æ 76. Ref Penn S 41608. Rept by State D A R.

HARRELL, GEORGE, Meigs co

Pvt Va State Trps. B in Shenandoah co Va May 11 1755 movd to Kanawha co. Thence to Letert twp Meigs co O whr appld for pens 6-7-1832. Cop by Return Jonathan Meigs chpt — Mrs Chase.

HARRIMAN, DAVID, Preble co

Bur Israel twp. Rept Commodore Preble chpt.

HARRINGTON, JOHN, Portage co and Ill

Pvt Mass Contl. Enl June 1781 at Landisfield (?) Mass. Servd 3 yr fr Ontario co N Y whr appld for pens 4-25-1818; appld for trnsfr to Portage co O 7-23-1821; and trnsfr to Hancock co Ill 2-10-1841 (whr prob died). In 1818 states æ as 54; "had 3 chldr and one gr-child (unnamed). Was a shoemaker. Ref Mass S 36014. Cop by State D A R.

HARRINGTON, SETH CAPT, Erie co

Bur Sand Hill cem family monument. Was b in R I 1754 son of Col Johnathan Harrington of Concord Mass. His mother was dau of Bishop Madison of Va. He mar Hulda dau of Gen Smith. They livd in Shirley Mass. 1775, 7 das in Capt Henry Haskells Co Col Jas Prentice Regt. Apr 26 1775 Capt Robert Langleys Co Col Asa Whitcombs Regt Lieut Holds Co Col Julius Regt 6th Middlesex co. Dischgd at Littleton Sept 17 1777. Joined Capt Smiths Co Col Bigelows Regt term 3 yrs. In 1780 went with Justin Elys men to reinforce army for 6 months. Marched July 12 1780. Rept by Marjorie Cherry.

HARRIS, ISAIAH, Columbiana co

Native of N C. Came to O 1805 w wf and 7 chldr: Chalkley; Ann; Carney; Nathan; Sarah; Robert. Carney b 1798 in N C mar Rachel Yates. Entered land in Butler twp 3 mi s of Salem. Was ship carpenter. Ref Columb co Hist McCord p 744. Rept by Wilma Molsberry.

HARRIS, JOHN, Montgomery co

Was b 1766, d 1841. N J Men of the Rev pp 619, 620. Battl 1st Sussex Co and also Conn line. Capt Jacob Teneick. Bur at Rehoboth cem south of Centerville. Rept by Wm Pettit S A R.

HARRIS, LUTHER, Erie co

Capt Harris Easter Battl Morris N J 1775 1777 Naval Service list Capt Harris. Bur Milan cem; family monument. Captain Luther Harris was a brother-in-law of Rev A H Betts. He was old when he settled here; d 1842 æ 86; b 1756; wf Mary. Ref Officers and Men of N J p 393, 871; Firelands Pioneers O S Vol 1 No. 2 p 42; Williams History p 442, 484. Rept by Marjorie Cherry Sandusky.

HARRIS, MOSES, Trumbull co

3rd Battl Gloucester Col Summers St Trps. Ref N J Men in the War of Rev. P 620. Mar Phebe Brooks; chldr: Timothy; Hannah; Elizabeth; and others. Was a resident of Lordstown; came to Trumbull co fr N J with his brothers-in-law. Rept by Mary Chesney chpt.

HARRISON, ALEXANDER SR, Franklin co

Ref p 393 Williams Bros Hist Franklin co O. "Alexander Harrison Sr was a soldier of the Revolutionary war from Winchester Va; to Hamilton twp in 1802; first was at Lancaster." Rept by Blanche Rings Col O; From Pens No. Va B L wt 1884-100 comes this note: "Charles Booth was the heir of Alex Harrison He appt Vespasian Ellis to prosecute his claim to bounty land due Alex Harrison who died just before the Rev war ended." (There is a discrepency in these two reports which note — J D).

HARRISON, STEPHEN, Richland co

Pvt N H Milit; enl Apr 1775 Mass; Servd 2 yrs; b 4-21-1757; mar Mary ——— in Brookfield N Y. Aft Rev worked in diff places in New England but in 1800 settled in Paris Oneida co N Y. In 1860 movd to Scioto co O aft 4 yrs to Wayne co; thence in 1829 to Madison co whr appld for pens 6-7-1821 a resident of Chester twp; thence to Richland co whr appld for pens 9-24-1832. Ref S 18433 Conn Mass; N H and Vt. Rept by State D A R.

HARRISON, THOS, Erie co

Harrison Cem Birmingham quarries; family mon b Apr 17 1753 in Florida Montgomery County N Y. Srvd from 1775 at various times as private and teamster in N Y Milit under Capt Amanniel De Grauf; Gerrit Putnam; Veeder; Colonels Frederick Fisher; Harper and Volkert Veeder. Was in battles of Stillwater; Cherry Valley; Johnstown; was in many scouting parties in pursuit of Tories and Indians. Length of service about 2 years. Pension 1832 S 8646 He d 1838 æ 85. Wf Petty d 1844 æ 81. Ref Peakes History p 919. Rept by Marjorie Cherry.

HARRISON, WILLIAM, Logan co

Servd as Major Lieut-Col of a Regt under McIntosh in the expedition of the latter into Indian country at the bld of Fort McIntosh and Fort Laurens Autumn of 1778 O. Also member Col Wm Crawfords expedition vs British and Indians at Sandusky 1782. Born in Va son of Lawrence Harrison; mar Sarah Crawford dau of Col William Crawford. Chldr: Sally; Nancy; Harriet; Battell; John; Polly. Killed by Indians nr Wapatomica (nr Zanesfield) Logan co O. His body was recognized by John Slover a captive of Indians who later escaped. Was a lawyer-high-minded and educated. Ref Crawford's Campaign vs Sandusky by C W Butterfield — many and various pages; Cleveland Plain Dealer issue Jan 20 1937. Rept by Clara G Mark Jacobus Westervelt D A R.

HARROFF, JOHN, Mahoning co

Pensr. Srvd Pa; b 1750; d before 1840 in Austintown. Bro of Jacob Harroff p 175 O Roster. Ref List late Henry Baldwin S A R; Hist Trumbull and Mahoning co V 2 pp 38, 39, 175. Rept by Mahoning co

HART, JONATHAN, Washington co

In scrapbook list of Marietta settlement. Major; listed here for continued research. List fr Marietta chpt.

HARTHORN, JAMES, Hamilton co

Lieut. Enl Lancaster co Pa in Pa Contl. Servd 12 mos fr 1775; b 1747 same co. Aft war movd to Va; thence to N C; then back to Va; thence to Hamilton co whr appld for pens 8-14-1832. Ref: S 2279 Penn. Cop by State D A R.

HARTWELL, NATHAN, Licking co and Sandusky co

Pvt. Enl 1780 in 4th Regt Mass Line. Servd 3 yrs; mar Sally Ripley 11-7-1789; chldr: Hannah 17; John 14; Henry 10; Rosey 8 (in yr 1820). He pensd 5-25-1820 in Licking co No. 18160; he d 1822 æ 59 in Sandusky co O. Wf pensd in Union co 4-8-1839 and on the Census 1840 list at Paris O that co. Ref W 3803 Mass. Cop by State D A R.

HARVEY, ASA, Hamilton co

Major Conn; b 1739 Conn; mar 2nd 1760 to Esther Stewart Cone (1742-1826). Elizabeth was one dau thro whom is estab. No. 124556 Vol 125 p 168 D A R lin. He d 1826 Hamilton co. Rept by Nathan Perry chpt.

HARVEY, EDWARD, Hamilton co

Enl Alexandria Va 1770. Servd 3 yrs in Contl. B 1752; mar Mary ——. Appld for pens 5-20-1818 Hamilton co O. Ref S 41606 Va. Cop by State D A R.

HARVEY, GEO, Erie co

Huron cem Huron O Government marker. Pvt Penn Continental line Corporal Jacob Bowers Co 6th Penn Reg commanded Lt Col Josiah Harmar Sept 9 1778. Pvt a Patenter 10th district Penn Donation Lands running on Northern boundary line found to lie without the State. Military abstract from the Executive Minutes Oct 26 1791. Ref Penn Arch Ser 5 Vol 2 p 772; S 5 Vol 3 p 134; S 6 Vol 4 pp 26-44.

HARWICK, DAVID, Clinton co

See Hamrick, David p 171 Vol 1 Ohio Roster.

HASKELL, ELNATHAN, Washington co

Capt. Cop fr scrap book list of Marietta Settlers, for research.

HASKILL, MOSES, Washington co

Pvt. Enl Feb 1781 Mass Contl Bolton twp; dischg Nov or Dec 1783; servd 2 yr; b 1759; pens appl 5-4-1818 in Washington co Marietta twp. Ref S 41610 Mass. Cop by State D A R.

HASSINGER, ABRAHAM, Ashland co

Listed p 142 in "History of North Central Ohio" by Wm A Duff as a Rev soldier; bur old cem nr Perrysville. Rept by Nathan Perry chpt.

HATCH, JAMES, Washington co

Appld for pens 8-17-1840 Com Pleas Ct Marietta O. Ref V 8 p 615. An Admstr appt for estate of James Hatch. Rept by Mrs. Helen Sloan Marietta chpt. (cf Elijah Hatch Sr who had a son James p 178 Vol 1 Ohio Roster).

HATTER, JOHN, Highland co

Pvt. Enl Northumberland co Pa Milit. Servd 8 mo. B 1750 Wirtenburg Germany. In 1802 movd to Highland co O whr pens appl 8-29-1833. Ref S 9570 Penn. Cop by State D A R. (Erroneously spelled Halter).

HATTON, WILLIAM, Champaign co and Ind

Pvt Va Line; pensr June 6 1820 Champaign co O; trnsferd to Ind. Listed here to avoid continued research. — Jane Dailey.

HAWBEARD (or Hawsbeard), THOMAS, Muskingum co

Enl July 4 1776. Pvt Pa Contl. Servd 6 yrs. B 1744; appld for pens 5-4-1818 in Muskingum co O. Dischgd at Trenton N J Jan 1782. Ref 41609 Penn. Cop by State D A R.

HAWKINS, PHILIP, Guernsey co

Pvt Capt S Smith Co; enl Baltimore Md Col Smallwood's Regt Contl Inf. Appld for pens 3-23-1832 and May 1820 a resident of Guernsey co. Pensd Apr 18 1832 stating æ 76; had a family of himself; two daus; one æ 23; one 28; wf d abt June 1831; Had disposed of 50 A land in Belmont co O to Saml Tillett May 1827 for $134 and $16 note. Ref S 41612. Cop by Jane Dailey.

HAWKINS, THOMAS, Washington co

Pvt enl 1776 or 7 in Va Milit. Srvd 8 mo. Was b 1758 Charles co Md. Pens appl 10-29-1832 Union twp Washington co. Ref 4310 Va. Rept by State D A R. P 275 Va Milit in Rev states he d 11-8-1832. Cop by Jane Dailey.

HAWLEN, NATHANIEL, Delaware co

Enl 1776 pvt N J Milit. Srvd 6 mo. Was b Sussex co N J 2-5-1757; Movd to Pa; in 1800 to Columbus O; aft 8 yrs to Delaware co O whr appld for pens 11-20-1832. Ref: S 2603 N J. Rept by State D A R.

HAWLEY, CALEB, Columbiana co

Pvt in Capt John Underwood's Co. (comp of East Bradford) 2nd Co of Col John Hannums' Battl Chester co Pa Milit. Pvt in East Bradford Chester co Milit of 1780. Chldr: a son Benjamin was b in Chester co Pa who mar Mary Davis dau of Samuel. Came fr Pa to O in 1802-voted in 1809. Ref Pa Arch 5 V 588 p 851 and county recds. Rept by Wilma Molsberry Youngstown.

HAWLEY, EBENEZER, ? co

Not located. Compare Eben Rice Hawley, Vol 1 Roster of O; Ref Doc No. 31 1-6-1831 whr listed as pvt; but since he srvd in a Co not on Contl Estab was refused a pension. Rept by Blanche Rings Col O.

HAWLEY, OZIAS, Portage co

Enl July 1779, marched fr Simsbury twp. Hartford co Ct to Horse Neck, whr was on duty for one mo dischg. Returned home. re-enlisted June 1780. B 1764 Hartford co Conn. Mar Sarah 12-5-1786; d 6-18-1836. Resided in Simsbury Conn; Otis and Sandysfield Mass; then to Portage co O whr livd in Freedom twp whr wf appld for pens 7-7-1845. Ref W 4484 Conn. Cop by State D A R.

HAYS, JAMES, Fayette co

Pa Frontier Ranger. Bur Bloomingburg cem nr Washington C H. Grave mrkd by Washington C H chpt and descendants. Ref Miss Dora Hays Bloomingburg O.

HAYES, LEVI, Licking co

Fifer Ct St Trp for 9 mos. Was b Apr 1764 Simsbery? Conn. Pens appl Licking co O Nov 1 1832. Ref Conn S 4328. Rept by State D A R. An issue of Oct 15 1847 Ohio State Journal Daily "Hays, Deacon Levi, æ 84 at Granville Licking co a soldr of the Rev and one of the early pioneers of that county." Cop by Blanche Rings.

HAYWARD, HENRY, Washington co

.   B 1733; d 1818. Thought to be a Revolutionary soldier in Washington co but not proven. Rept by Helen Sloan, Marietta.

HAZEL, HENRY, Champaign co

Enl 1777 for 3 yr as matross Co 7; was at Valley Forge and other battles; in Va and Md Regts; mar Sarah Johnson; one child was named Abraham who mar Catherine Taylor. Livd in Washington co Pa; movd to Ky; with wf and chldr (all except William). Movd to Champaign co O in 1805 nr Mechanicksburg whr livd to 93rd yr. Ref Pens cl No. 7579 cop by Jane Dailey. From stone data Urbana D A R repts d June 16 1838; bur Maplegrove Mechanicksburg O. On appl said body removd fr old Hazel burying ground to Jacob Hazel's lot in new cem.

HAZELTINE, JOHN, Butler co

Pvt in Co of Rangers under Capt Timothy Beedle Mass Regt whch went to Fort St John Canada. B 1755; mar Elizabeth Hayne 1785; a dau named Elvina mar Judah Hinckley 1825. D in Butler co 1832. Ref V 105 D A R Lin No. 104655 cop by Jane Dailey.

HAZZARD, ARTHUR, Monroe co

Enl Mar 1777 Del Contl. servd 6 yrs. Appld for pens in Monroe co O June 13 1818. Ref S 41615 Del. Rept by State D A R.

HEADLEY (or Headly), CAREY, Monroe co

Enl June 1776 Pvt N J St Trps. Servd one yr. Was b 1760 Morris co N J; mar Mary Hathaway Nov 1787; had eleven chldr: Isaac; Francis; Sarah; Huldah; Experience; Phebe; Francis; Rachel; Mary; Cary son; Susannah. He d July 13 1839. He had appld for pens in Monroe co O 9-21-1832; his widow appld there 2-15-1850. Ref W 4741 N J. Rept by State D A R.

HEALD (Hale), NATHAN, Columbiana co

Pa Arch S 6 Vol 2 p 208; b Chester co Pa 1735; d 1825; mar Rebecca Hutton abt 1764. S A R ref 50693. By Wm Pettit.

HEART, REUBEN, Portage co

Enl Jan 1779 in Hartford co Conn Contl. Servd 3 yrs. Appld for pens 5-2-1818 Portage co O æ 55; mentions Alpheus and son-in-law Edmond Ferrill. Ref Conn S 41633. Rept by State D A R.

HEATH, ISAAC, Ashtabula co

Ct Contl Regt of Col Elmore; b 1729 d 1816; bur at Kingsville Ashtabula co O; grave located by Mary Stanley chpt. Ref: 18 and 21st rept N S D A R pp 207, 97 respt. Cop by Nathan Perry chpt.

HEATH, RICHARD (or Robert), Erie co

Bur Barber cem Berlin twp family monument. Initials R W on his stone. He is vouched for by Geo Uri Stevenson of Chicago member of the Md Historical Society. Rept by Marjorie Cherry.

HEATON, DAVID, Butler co

Pvt in battles of the Jerseys; b 1742 Morris co N J; d Middletown Butler co O 1839; mar Phebe Johnson. Ref Vol 25 p 116 D A R in bk No. 24327 through a son James. Rept by Nathan Perry chpt Mrs T R Oehlke.

HEBER, JACOB, Montgomery co

Ref 5th Ser Pa Arch V 8 p 231; Was b 1762; d 1835; bur at Ellerton, Montgomery co O. Mrkd by Monument. Rept by Wm M Pettit. State Sec S A R Dayton O.

HECOX, TRUMAN, Meigs co

(Various spellings). Pvt in Capt Matthew Smith's co Col Webb's Regt Conn Trps also N Y Service; b 1765 N Y; mar Sarah Hecox (1766-1838); Jeptha was one chld mentioned; d 1837 in Meigs co O. Ref V 124 No. 123298 D A R Lin. Cop by Jane Dailey.

HEDDLESON, WILLIAM, Adams co

Spelled also Huddleson and Heddelson; pvt first enl Carlisle Pa July 1776 nr whch place he livd Cumberland co. Servd 7 yrs. B Nov 1756 Belfast Ireland; mar Elizabeth Brockman 1-6-1830; d 9-2-1845 in Adams co O. He movd fr Carlisle Pa to Bourbon co Ky in winter 1778; in 1779 movd to Washington Mason co Ky whr livd till Mar 1831; thence to Brown co O and same yr to Winchester twp Adams co O. Here his widow appld for pens Apr 18 1853; and in Oct 9 1857. She was liv in Hillsborough Highland co O. Soldier appld for pens Adams co 10-27-1832. Ref W 5107 B L wt 26015-160-55. Rept by State D A R.

HEDGES, ELIJAH, Fairfield co

Pvt U S Army; enl 1791 not Rev; Va Rangers 1791; Old War Ind File 4342; formal cert issued 11-24-1824 in Brooke co Va; movd fr here to Fairfield co O prior to 1824; appld for trnsfr of pens 11-13-1824; Name listed p 406 Wiseman's Pioneer People of Fairfield co O as Rev. Rept by State D A R.

HEETER, SEBASTIAN, Montgomery co

Pvt. Ref Pa Arch S 5 V 4 p 241. Born 1760 Hopewell twp Bedford co Pa. Srvd in frontier rangers and it is claimed he servd in east and was at Valley Forge. Settld in Perry twp 1815; d 1846; bur in New Providence Lutheran Ch cem Perry twp. Grave markd June 30 1835 with Richard Montgomery chpt S A R conducting impressive ceremonies. Fifty-three descendants present. Name spelled Heater also. Rept by W M Pettit S A R Dayton O.

HELMEN, MARTIN, Columbiana co

Rev soldr b 1764; d 1845; bur Center twp Columbiana co. Mar Magdalena (b 1763 d 8-3-1838 bur Center twp). Ref Columb co cem recds. Rept by Wilma Molsberry.

HELPHENSTON, PETER P, Madison co

Major in Rev War. A native of Va. Came to Ross co Chillicothe O 1805 settld in Madison co 1807. Cop fr 20th rept N S D A R p 69 by Nathan Perry chpt. (Extensive research failed to find more data — J D).

HEMENWAY, JAMES, Mahoning co

Pvt Mass Soldiers and Sailors v 7 p 702 and 797; mar Elizabeth; chldr: James; Isaac; Sarah mar David Park; Martha mar Stacy Cook; Rebecca Mar Audrey Parks; Elizabeth mar Allen Cox; Abigail. He d before 1823 at Goshen. Came to O in 1818; his son James was clk of twp in 1827. Ref Hist Trumbull Mahoning co V 2 pp 193 and 204; Deed bk R p 88 Jas Heminway heirs 1823; Deed bk O p 138 James Heminway, names heirs 1826. Rept by Mahoning chpt.

HENDERSHOT, JOHN, Monroe co

Pvt Pa Milit. Enl June 1780 Bedford co Pa whr b 1754; aft Rev movd to Washington co Pa. Thence to Monroe co O whr he appld for pens March 1824; and in 1834 was pensd there. Ref S 9574 Penn. Rept by State D A R.

HENDERSON, JONATHAN, Brown co

Pvt Mass Contl Capt Child's Co Col Putnam's Regt; servd 2 yr; mar Eleanor 9-3-1790 in Washington co Pa. Chldr: in widow's appl for pens in Brown co 2-23-1839 names ten: Elizabeth 1791; David 1792; Martha 1795; Jonathan 1797; Martha 1799; Linsey

1804; Stephen 1806; Josiah 1809; James 1811; Benj 1815; in 1819 he was pensr in Belmont co; 1838 she appld in Brown co whr he d 5-26-1833. He was a cooper. Ref W 3809. Cop by Jane Dailey.

HENDRICK, CHARLES, Ross co

The Chillicothe Advertiser of Oct 8 1831 carried the following: "A Revolutionary soldier died in Chillicothe the 28th of Sept 1831 at the advanced age of 85 years. He was formerly from Va." Rept by Mrs. Orion King Pickaway Plains chpt.

HENDRICKS, ELIJAH, Wood co

Bur on Theodore Jenson farm 5 mi S E of Bowling Green O on burial plot reserved in deed; b abt 1752. Cop fr 18th rept of N S D A R p 207 by Nathan Perry chpt.

HENDRICKSON, WILLIAM, Richland co

Pvt Md Milit. Enl July 1776 Frederickstown; servd 7 mo 10 da; b 12-23-1757 N J. Aft Rev livd abt 20 yrs at Ft Cumberland Md; thence to Wheeling Crk nr Ohio state; then to O. Appld for pens 9-7-1832 Richland co O. Ref S 2301 Md. Rept by State D A R.

HENDRY, DAVID, Ashtabula co

Pvt 1st Regt N Y Line under Goose Van Schauck; b 1754; at Bridgewater Mass; mar Selina Hotchkiss 1786; d at Harpersfield Ashtabula co O 1827. Cop fr V 106 No. 105604 D A R Lin by Jane Dailey. The following was copied by the State D A R fr Pens Cl N Y; he servd as pvt 7 mo 7 da and as musician 20 da in N Y Line. (Above notes verified by them). He enl 4-24-1776 in Delaware co N Y; was taken prisoner by Indians Aug 1777. His widow pensd 9-8-1840 in Ashtabula co O.

HENNING, CONRAD, Stark co

Enl in Pa as a rifleman; on appl of heirs by Geo B Henning for pens Stark co O 1-16-1855 same was rejected on the ground there was no record on file of Conrad Henning having servd as alleged. Affidavit of heirs stated he mar Mary Magdalene who d 5-4-1837; chldr: Jacob; Catherine Bair (widow); Rebecca Eckhart (wid); Abraham and the affiant George B. Ref R 4887 Penn. Cens 1840 names Conrad as a pensr. He is bur Lutheran cem Paris O Stark co. Cop by State D A R.

HENRY, JOHN, Stark co

Fr Pa Arch list of Pa soldiers who livd in O is name John G Henry as residing in Stark co O 1833 aged 75. Rept by Mary Steinmetz Reading Pa.

HERBERT, THOMAS, Pickaway co

Exec Doc 37 of 1852. Refused a pens as servd less than 6 mo. Rept by Wm Pettit.

HERBERT, THOMAS, Richland co

Pvt N J Milit. Enl 1776 Monmouth co. Servd N J Line one yr. B Monmouth co 1753; appld for pens 10-24-1832 Richland co O. Ref S 18443 N J. Rept by State D A R.

HERRON, JOHN, Licking co

Pvt in Col Samuel Miles Pa Rifle Regt; b in Ireland; mar Nancy Cook; chldr: Katherine; Sherwood and others; soldr d Newark O; Ref No. 13682. Rept by Hetuck chpt.

HERRON, SAMUEL, Preble co

B in S C. Bur Israel twp Hopewell cem. Rept Commodore Preble chpt.

HESS, DAVID, Knox co

Ref Cens 1840 a pensr liv in Berlin twp æ 97; was b 1742. Ae indicates Rev service but none found (J D).

HETHERLY, THOMAS, Brown co

Pvt Va Contl. Enl 12-25-1776. Servd over 3 yrs. Fought at Brandywine, Germantown and Monmouth; resided in Leesburgh Loudon co Va when enl. Dischg at Little York Pa 1780. He appld for pens in Brown co O 6-24-1832 giving æ 77. Ref S 2612 Va. Cop by State D A R. Addit information rept by Taliaferro chpt. He mar Mary Heaton; he d 5-30-1835 æ 85; bur Ash Ridge ceni Jackson twp Brown co. His grave located by Meryl Markley; has stone with data on it. In 1811 he resided in Eagle twp. Will made in 1810 copy probated 4-24-1841; will witnessed by Lydia Heaton and Patience Osborn. Mary Heaton Hetherly's brother Dr James Heaton named Executor.

HEYWOOD, BENJAMIN, Washington co

Listed in news-clipping by L A A found in old scrap bk as Rev soldr taking part in or interested in settlement of Marietta and no doubt bur in Washington co cem. Many had descendants liv there and served in Indian War never recompensed by U S Gov. Listed here for continued research for proof. Rept by Marietta chpt.

HICKOX, DAVID, Trumbull co

Or spelled Hicox, Hicock; pvt Conn Contl. Enl 5-14-1777 dischgd 1-7-1780. Servd 3 yr. B Jan 1757; appld for pens 6-21-1818 while residing Vienna twp Trumbull co O. In appl of 1820 mentions wf æ 56 and adopted boy æ 11. Ref S 41637 Conn. Rept by State D A R. Other data rept by Mary Chesney chpt additional: soldier was in battle of white Marsh, Monmouth, and Stony Point. Dischgd at Morris N J wf name Phebe; chldr: Jesse; Olive; Phebe; Irene; Almira; Eunice; Emily; possibly others. Resided at Fowler whr he died.

HICKCOX, GILES, Medina co

Pvt Mass St Trps. Enl Edgemont Mass 1782. Servd 9 mo; b 1765 at Durham Conn. Aft war livd in Conn and N J thence to Granger Medina co O whr appld for pens Oct 1832. Ref: S 2311 Mass. Rept by State D A R.

HICKEY, EDWARD, Licking co

Listed as Rev soldier in Licking co by Hetuck chpt Newark in 15th rept of N S D A R. Cop by Nathan Perry chpt. Hetuck chpt repts b Cork Ireland; d æ 75 in Mary Ann twp Licking co; wf d in Winchester Va.

HICKS, DURFEE, Hamilton co and N Y.

Marine U S Navy. Enl in spring of 1775 at Little Compton Mass. Was pensr 1818 in Hamilton co O. Made appl for trnsfr 1820 to N Y stating had wf æ 64; a stepson William Chase (?) æ abt 12. Ref Navy R I S 43680. Cop by State D A R.

HICKS, JOHN, Monroe co

Enl Mar 1776 in a Co under Capt Westfall in Va; servd 2 yr. Dischgd at Valley Forge Mar 1778. Appld for pens 6-25-1819 Monroe co O; again 1820 stating had wf Sarah æ 45; chldr: Benjamin æ 24; William æ 16; Nana (?) æ 14; Betsy 12; Nathan 9; Leonard (?) æ 7; and Joseph æ 3. He was æ 66 yrs in 1820. He d 10-28-1837. Ref S 41638 Va. Rept by State D A R.

HIGGINS, DANIEL, Butler co

Enl at Pittsburgh Pa June 1777; Servd 8 mo. Then hired a substitute; enl again serving in all 4 1-2 yrs. Livd at Pittsburg abt 12 yrs aft close of war; thence to Brook co Va for abt 2 yr; thence to Ohio whr lived abt 8 yr one of that in Butler co. He was b 8-25-1759 in Ireland. Appld for pens 8-1-1832 in Butler co O. Ref S 5527 Va. Rept by State D A R.

HIGHT, JOHN, Columbiana co

A pensr. B 1757; was living in St Clair twp in 1840 æ 83. In 1785 lived in Fayette co Pa (Bullskin twp). Ref S A R yr bk 1912-13 Rev pensrs of Columbiana co; Pa Arch S 3 V 22 p 574 and Cens of Pensrs 1840. Rept by Wilma Molsberry Youngstown.

HILDEBRAND, MICHAEL, Stark co

Pvt in Capt James McConnell's Co 5th Battl Lancaster co Pa Milit; b in said co; d Stark co. Cop fr Vol 146 p 217 D A R Lin by Jane Dailey.

HILDERBRAND, GEORGE, Washington co

Servd as pvt in Capt George Reese's Co Lancaster co Pa Mil 1777. Was b 1753 Lancaster co Pa. Mar Mary Elizabeth Kinsley 1776; she d at Marietta O. One dau Mary mar Daniel Vailles 1820. Soldr d at Marietta 1827 and grave marker placed by Marietta chpt 1934. Rept by J D and Marietta. Cop fr V 108 No. 107765 D A R Lin by J D.

HILL, GEORGE, Pickaway co

Enl fall of 1779 Shenandoah co Va. Servd 18 mo. Appld for pens 5-8-1818 in Licking co O and for new one 10-27-1820 giving his æ as 65. Ref S 41642 Va. Cop by State D A R. From Pickaway Plains is rept the following data which we believe refers to same soldier: In 1780 George Hill enl fr Culpeper co Va as pvt Lieut McGuire Col Green's Regt. In 1781 enl as pvt in Capt Parson's Co Col Washington's 3rd Regt of Light Dragoons; was in battle of Camden and Eutaw Springs, whr was wounded. Was b 1754; mar Hannah Hickman Culpepper co Va. She was dau of James Hickman; mar Oct 15 1785; mar bond signed by George and Joseph Hill; she d Apr 1830; He d Apr 25 1838 grave not located. He was pensd 1813 in Hampshire co Va. Later to Ross co; thence to Monroe twp Pickaway co. In 1833 livd in Mechlenburg twp æ 79. Ref Williams co Hist p 335 states he opened 1st grocery store in Darbyville 1827. Ref W 4987 (D C) (See also same name p 186 in Fairfield co O adjoining Pickaway co Ohio Roster Vol 1).

HILL, HENRY, Franklin co

Enl at Courthouse Geauga co Va as pvt; servd 18 mo. Appld for pens in Franklin co O 5-11-1818; also 6-10-1819; also 1820 stating æ 69 yr; a wf æ 54; had no family. Ref S 41639 Va; Order bk 2, 257, Court Recd Col O. Rept by State D A R.

HILL, JAMES, Fairfield co

Pvt in Capt Sears' Co Col Thompson's Regt Md Milit. Servd 7 mo 10 da. Brot to America wh young by Father; settled Cecil co Md. After war livd Chester co Pa 4 yr. Thence to Fairfield co O abt 1807 whr still resides (Nov 13 1834) Pensr 1-26-1835. Ref S 9579 Md. Rept by Jane Dailey.

HILL, JOHN, Mahoning co

Pv.t Ref Ser 3 V 23 and Ser 5 V 4 (p 242) Pa Arch Many ref. Crumrine's Hist Washington co Pa p 81; Will bk 4 p 117 John Hill Trumbull co records — Proba 1825; W Reserve Chron Nov 11 1825 Est John Hill Coitsville; Tax list 1826. D abt 1825 Coitsville. Mar Elizabeth; chldr: John; Rebecca; Jonathan; Isaac; Daniel; Elizabeth; David; Mary mar —— Hazen. Rept by Mahoning chpt.

HILL, JOHN, Washington co

Enl Bucks co Pa 1777 Newton twp whr he resided as pvt Pa St Trps. Servd 7 mo fr 1777; mar Elizabeth 6-2-1783; he appld for pens 7-26-1832 fr Union twp Washington co O. His widow appld there 4-22-1850 Stating he d Nov 1842 Wash co. Union twp. A witness stated they had "5 or 6 chldr when I knew them 45 yr ago". He was b 1760. Ref W 5298 Penn. Rept by State D A R.

HILL, ROBERT, Mahoning co

Ranger. Ser 3 V 23 p 338 Westmoreland co 1776-1783 Pa Arch. Also N Y Men Supp pp 204-219; and Mass Sold and Sailors V 7 p 898 et al. He mar Patience Rogers one chld Rogers Hill was b 1799. Livd at Austintown O. Ref Hist Trumbull and Mahoning co V 2 pp 138 & 175. Rept by Mahoning chpt.

HILL, SIMON, Licking co

Enl in Sept the mo before Cornwallis was taken at Fauq——? C H Va. Servd one yr; Appl for pens 1818 in Licking co O stated æ 57 living with wf Margaret æ 60 and son Jesse "all unhealthly." Ref S 41644 Va. Rept by State D A R.

HILL, SOLOMON, Ashland co

Listed p 104 Hist of N Central Ohio by Wm A Duff as a Revolutionary soldier Ashland co O. Rept by Nathan Perry chpt.

HILL, WILLIAM, Pickaway co

"Died in Wayne twp March 10 1838 Mr William Hill late of Jefferson co Va æ 77 and 2 da. The deceased was a Patriot of the American Revolution; was at the taking of Cornwallis; and served two campaigns under Gen Wayne. He removed with his son to this co about 3 yrs since." Cop fr Old Newspaper by Pickaway Plains chpt.

HILLYER, SETH, Ashtabula co

Enl Granby Conn in Contl line 1776 whr he resided; servd 2 yr; Appld for pens in Ashtabula co O 8-7-1832 stating æ 75; mar Sibil Mar 1783; residing Andover æ 81 in Cens 1840; widow appld pens here 11-29-1844. Ref W 4696 Conn. Rept by State D A R. The Mary Redmond chpt repts he d 6-22-1841 at Andover; grave not located.

HIMROD, ANDREW, Delaware co

Enl 1780-81 in spring; was liv in Northumberland co Pa. He was b 2-4-1763 Somerset co N J. Appld for pens Delaware co 11-19-1832; became insane 1838 or 9. He d 4-18-1842. Ref S 2616 Penn. Rept by State D A R.

HINE, NATHAN, Trumbull co

Made appl for pens fr Trumbull co O. No data found to determine if Rev or 1812 service. Rept by Mary Chesney chpt.

HINKLEY, NATHANIEL, Washington co

Volunteered abt May 1776 Brunswick twp Cumberland co Mass whr livd dur Rev moving to Washington co O Sept 1789. Servd as pvt Q M and Ensign Mass Contl for 22 mo. Was b Cumberland co Pa 8-14-1755; appld for pens 7-27-1832 Roxbury twp Wash co O and Aug 17 1840; d abt 1841. Had wf Sarah. Ref S 4377 Mass. Rept by State D A R.

HINMAN, JOHN, Mahoning co

Pvt. Ref Conn Men in Rev p 466; also Vt Men pp 155-375-343; Hist Trumbull & Mahoning co V 2 p 60-64-69; Deed bks K p 534 and C p 314; mar Mary ——; chldr: Catherine, mar Daniel McConnel; Betsy mar John Webster; Sally mar John Reed; Polly mar James Laughlan; John; Samuel; Jacob minors in 1818; Daniel; James; Jane. D before 1818 Poland O. Rept by Mahoning chpt.

HINSDALE, JACOB JR, Trumbull co

Servd fr Conn in Capt Amos Wilson's Co Col Fisher Gage's Regt. B 4-18-1759 Canaan Conn Parents: Capt Jacob Hinsdale and wf Mary Brace; he mar Sarah Barber 1-16-1782; chldr: Jacob; Abel; Almira; Sally; Betsey; Mary; and others. Came to Braceville abt 1834 to liv with son Joseph; d there 10-26-1839. Ref Pens Cl R 5038 (Meaning no pension allowed). Rept by Mary Chesney chpt.

HISE, JACOB, Columbiana co

Pvt N J Milit. B Titusville N J; mar Phebe ——; he d at Salem O. His musket and hat perforated with bullet holes in possess of family. Ref V 30 No. 29854 D A R Lin. Cop by Nathan Perry chpt.

HITCHOCK, ISAAC, Perry co

Exec Doc 37 of 1852. Refused a pens because his service was as a privateer. Rept by Wm Pettit.

HITES, JOHN, Holmes co

Came to America with Lafayette when aged 18; fought with him at Rachambeau; was at surrender of Cornwallis; had an express job as told in pension claims. Is bur on W O Miller farm north of Millersburg O Holmes co abt 5 mi on high hill called Work's Hill just south of Holmesville O. Grave in an old peach orchard and marked by old stone marker; data fr Pens Claim D C as rept by Mrs Arthur Brogue of Mason City chpt Mason Cy Ia.

HIXSON, ELIJAH, Monroe co

Enl at Leesburgh Loudon co Va 1779 or 80; pvt Va Contl; servd fr 1779 to 1782; b 1760; appld for pens 11-1-1823 Monroe co O names 3 chldr: Rachel æ 17; John æ 17 (Twins); Burnett æ 14. Ref S 41636 Va. Rept by State D A R.

HOADLY, PHILO, Delaware co

Enl in spring 1780 as pvt Conn Milit; servd one yr; b 10-12-1763 Waterbury Conn whr resided during Rev. Father's name was Ebenezer.. Appld for pens Delaware co O 11-21-1832 whither he came in 1807. Ref S 2624 Conn. Rept by State D A R. Delaware chpt repts bur in Berlin twp possibly.

HOAK, HENRY, Erie co

Bur oldest cem Berlin Heights Govt Marker. Corp in Capt John Withers Co of Milit Col John Ferries Battl of Associators in Lancaster co dated Aug 19 1776. Was b 1745 d 1832. He also srvd in Capt Abraham Dehuggs Co Col Samuel J Atlee. He srvd in the Jerseys. Ref Williams Hist p 477; Pa Arch S 5 Vol 2 p 490 and Vol 7 p 972. Rept by Marjorie Cherry.

HOBAUGH, PHILIP, Madison co and Ind.

Enl 1779 Pittsburgh Pa. Pvt Pa line for 4 yrs. Pensr 5-3-1819 in Madison co O. In 1820 appl states æ as 58; wf name Christena mar 7-14-1789; chldr: Molly æ 14; Michael 12; Elizabeth 10; Susan 8; Peter 6. He d 8-6-1836. Ref W 10125 Pa. Rept by State D A R. Was trnsfrd to Ind.

HOBBY, JOHN, Washington co

Capt. Cop fr scrap bk of Marietta settlers. Listed for continued research. Rept by Marietta chpt.

HOBDAY (or Hoddy), RICHARD, Ross co

Sergt in Capt Lipcamps Co 7th Va Regt under Col Alexander McClenachan. Was b Va 1759; mar Jennie; chldr: Robert; Keziah. Soldr d abt 1830. He and his wf bur in Ross co nr Frankfort O. Ref No. 177830 D A R. Rept by Mrs. Paul R Minich.

HODGKINS, SAMUEL, Brown co

Enl in Harford co Md; marched to Baltimore in Capt Bennett Bussey's Md Co; servd abt 4 wks; re-enlisted 1775 and in 1776 serving one term of three mo and another of nine mo. The latter in Capt Bussey's Md Co Flying Camp. In spring of 1777 servd

2 mo and in fall of 1782 for 6 wks; was b 6-6-1757; mar Lydia Wright 3-9-1831. She was b 1789 and d Oct 1-1863. She was allowed bounty land No. 44806-160-55. He d Oct 13 1845 and bur on farm of George Perkins Pleasant twp Brown co O. Stone standing with usual dates. Ref R 5092 Pens cl A proven D A R line. Rept by Taliaferro chpt.

HODGSON, JOSEPH, Hamilton co

Service for Md. Ref Md Arch Vol 18 p 427. The name is found spelled "Hudson" on several deeds. Was b 1760 son of Capt Jonothan Hodgson and Francinda Bassett. Grandparents were Robert Hodgson Jr and Sarah Borden; gr gr parents were Robt Hodgson Sr and Alice Shotten. This Robert was the immigrant who arrived 1657 in America. Soldr d 1840; bur Oxford O twp cem. Rept by Mrs. Jos Baldridge Bellevue Pa. Bur; birth and death dates rept by Oxford Caroline Scott chpt.

HOFF, ISAAC, Butler co

Enl in Hunterdon co N J in Milit. Servd 16 mo. Was b 4-2-1758; livd with father till enl; aft Rev movd to Ky; thence to Butler co O 1803; appld there for pens 8-1-1832. Ref S 4408 N J. Rept by State D A R.

HOFF, JOHN, Delaware co

Enl Jan 1776; was Sergt N J Milit serving 1 yr. Was b 2-18-1760 Huntington co N J; mar Martha Moore 12-24-1781; chldr: James; Catherine; John; Hiram; Bartell; Owen; Ambrose; Almon; and Joanna. He d 3-5-1838; he appld for pens 11-19-1832 Delaware co O. During Rev resided in Sussex co N J; thence to Pa in 1787; thence to O 1815 and in 1817 to Delaware co. Rept by State D A R. See Huff, John, p 195 Ohio Roster Vol 1.

HOFFMIRE, SAMUEL, Knox co

Pvt. 1st Regt Monmouth co Milit under Capts Shepherd Bennett and Polhemus and Lt Hendrickson. Servd monthly tours in 1780; 81 and 82; a res of Monmouth co N J. B there 12-26-1763; mar Sarah Conroy 3-1-1787; she b 4-18-1765 and d 8-19-1833. Chldr: Sarah; Isaac; William; Thomas; Martha; Alice; Catherine; John; and Eliza. He d 7-30-1837; bur on own farm 1 mi fr Batemantown Knox co O. Aft 97 yrs his great-grandson Geo Dick of Mt Vernon O had remains removed and re-interred across the co line in North fork cem Morrow co O. In the grave was found three brass buttons of different sizes one the size of a quarter had the name "Landon" on it. The skeleton of the soldier was found in perfect state of preservation as a kodak view of it lying in the bottom of the grave revealed. He was a pensr 1833; Kokosing chpt marked the grave in 1934. Ref: Adjt Gen office Trenton N J; Pens Cl Wash D C. Rept by Mrs. Emma Ewalt Kokosing chpt.

HOGEBOOM, JOHN, Medina co or N Y

Pension office states there is no record of this soldier ever living in Ohio but believe this is the man who was in Ohio in 1840 as of same age. The Cens of 1840 stated: a pensr æ 83 living in Harrisonville Medina co O with Bartholomeu Hogeboom. Ref S 13427 N Y States enl Greenbush Keneselmer co N Y 1775; app pens Albany co N Y 1832. Rept by State D A R to avoid further research.

HOLAM, SAMUEL, Pickaway co

Pvt Pa Contl. Enl Bethlehem Pa. Servd in Capt Caleb North's Co Col Anthony Wayne's 4th Pa Battl; enl again in 1777 serving in Capt John Christie's Co and Thomas Bonde's (?) Co Col Francis Johnston's 5th Pa Regt. In Batls Brandywine; Monmouth; Germantown; Stony Point. Was b 2-16-1760; pensr 5-12-1819 residing in Ross co; in 1820 liv in Pickaway co. In 1819 one Benj Holam made affidavit in support of soldier's claim for pens. No relation ment in pens papers. Ref: S 41647 Pa (?) Grave not located. Rept by Pickaway Plains chpt.

HOLCOMB (-or-be), ELIJAH, Muskingum co

Pvt. Pa. Contl. Enl Feb 1776; dischgd at end of 9 mo. (tho cert states he servd one yr). Appld for pens 11-27-1820 and also in 1818 in Muskingum co O. Stated he was æ 70 wf was Nancy "One son lives with me" in 1820. Ref S 41654 N J Pa. Rept by State D A R.

HOLCOMB, JAMES, Knox co

Exec Doc 37 of 1852. Refused a pens because he serv less than 6 mo. Rept by Wm Pettit.

HOLCOMB, JOHN G, Muskingum co

Enl at the Highlands in N Y Dec 1780; servd till 1783 was honorably dischgd at West Pt. Pvt Conn Contl Appld pens Hartford co Conn 4-17-1818 æ 58; appld again 11-24-1820 Muskingum co O where he was receiving a pens 1818; a farmer. Ref S 37116 Conn. Rept by State D A R.

HOLDEN, JOHN, Washington co

Capt. Cop fr scrapbook list of Marietta settlement for continued research.

HOLDEN, JOSEPH

Listed in Doc No. 31 Jan 6 1731 as refused a pens because he deserted the service. Rept by Blanche Rings Columbus O.

HOLDREN, LEVI, Washington co

Capt. Cop fr scrap book list of Marietta settlement for continued research.

HOLE, DANIEL, Montgomery co

Settld in Montgomery co O 1795-6; came fr Va with Father and family; mar Hannah Delay; services see Va Lib rept (1912) 1 P D 92; D 152 also Beer's co Hist p 132. Rept by Richard Montgomery chpt S A R Dayton.

HOLE, JACOB, Columbiana co

9th Battl Lancaster co Milit; b Adams co Pa 1760; d 1831; mar Christena Tonlk 1766; S A R ref 42107. By Wm Pettit.

HOLE, ZACHARIAH, Montgomery co

Setld in Montgomery co O 1795-6 on Sec 21 called Hole's Crk. In 1798 erected a blockhouse; mar Phoebe Clark; chldr: William mar Ruth Craine; Daniel mar Hannah Delay; Polly mar David Yenzell; Betsy mar John Craig; Phoebe; Sarah mar ——— Eaton; for service see Va Lib Rept W D; 1 P D 58. Rept by Richard Montgomery S A R Dayton O.

HOLLISTER, APPLETON, Cuyahoga co

Ref Conn Men of Rev p 166; Hist Coll of Rev Soldiers V 8 p 119 see Hollister Geneal also Wadham's p 46. He was b Bolton Conn son of Charles and Charity Wadham Hollister; he mar first Sarah Carver dau of John and Sarah (Talbott) Carver in 10-4 1787; she d 1802; chldr b to this mar: Sarah 1788; Enos 1789; Harvey 1791; Patty 1791; Clarissa 1794; Carolina 1796; Alva 1798; Ann 1799; Lucina 1802. He mar second: Lucina Carver coz of 1st wf: who d 1807; chldr to 2nd wf: Rachel b 1804; he mar third wf: Anna Carver sister of 1st wf and had chldr: Samuel b 1810; William 1812; Deodat 1815. (She mar again d in Pa). He d 12-15-1831 æ 69 & 2 mo; bur Shaker Heights (old Warrenville) Cuyahoga co Lee Rd n of Kinsman Rd. Rept by Lakewood chpt Mrs Louella Wise.

HOLMES, JOHN, Greene co

Rev Pensr bur Old Pioneer cem Bellbrook Greene co.

HOLMES, SETH, Richland· co

Enl Williamstown Mass 1778; servd 9 mo as pvt Mass Contl; was b 1747; in appld for pens 1820 says had a wf æ 66 and one son æ 43; appld for pens Susquehanna Co Pa May 2 1818; and also in Richland co O Sept 1820 whr he was liv in 1833. Ref S 41645 Mass. Rept by State D A R.

HOLT, JOHN, Knox co

Cens of 1840 listed liv in Chester twp Knox co æ 80. Cop by Jane Dailey.

HOLT, THOMAS, Trumbull co

Ref S 4400 Pa as cop by State D A R states: Pvt Pa Trps. Enl 1778 Cumberland co Pa whr he livd till he removd to Guernsey co O. Here he appld for pens Oct 18 1832 a res of Madison twp. He stated b Apr 17 1761 Cumberland co Pa and that he servd one yr. From Mahoning chpt the following data sent: he was pensr in Trumbull co O 4-6-1833; was a Ranger on Frontier ref S 3 V 23 pp 273 and 590 Pa Arch Birth given as 1760; died 9-28-1848 Milton twp; bur Eckis cem. Ref Old pens bk V 3 Trumbull co; also list of H R Baldwin S A R; grave located by S A R 1912-13.

HOLTON, JOHN, Franklin co

Pvt Pa Contl. Pensr July 23 1819 Act of 1818. Cop fr Ohio list Pensrs 1818 by J D. Rept by Columbus chpt Mrs W S Van Fossen that he was b 1743 being æ 76 in 1819; he mar Rachel ——. A son John d Franklin co 1869 bur Greenlawn. Born 4-7-1784. Ref Greenlawn cem Asso Col O.

HOMAN, EBER, Preble co

Enl 1779 Mengham twp Morris co N J. Servd 6 mo in Capt Wards Co Major Hayes N J trps. Dischgd 12-15-1779; enl 1782 Capt Powers Pa Co. Was b 9-9-1764; mar 3 times; had 8 chldr by each wf (so descendants say); at Lebanon Courthouse mar recd of Eber Homan to Anne Marshall 6-14-1818. Chldr located: Eber; Benjamin; Peter; James and Rachel (b 1821 mar Wm Turner Frazee). Bur at old part upper cem Lewisburg Preble co O. Inscr on stone: Eber Homan d March 25 æ 76 yrs 6 mo 18 days. At æ 2 or three came with his father to Morris co N J; thence to Fayette co Pa in 1780; pensd 10-4-1833. Ref Homer Royer Eaton O. Proven line of Mrs. Geo Young Los Serranos D A R Ontario Cal. Rept by May Hart Smith 637 East D St Ontario Cal.

HOOVER, FELIX, Montgomery co

5th Ser Pa Arch II p 652 First Pa Con Line Capt James Ross company 1777. Bur at Baptist Cem Centerville; has monument. B 1752 d 1828 Will. Rept by Wm Pettit.

HOOVER, JACOB, Mahoning co

Pvt 7th class 1782. Ref S 5 V 7 p 497 516 Pa Arch. Also S 5 V 8 pp 318, 328, 356, 366. Chldr: Isaac mar Susannah ——; Jacob mar Elizabeth ——; David; Catherine mar John Stallsmith; Polly mar Jacob Musser; and Israel. He d before 1821 in Springfield twp Mahoning co O. Ref Hist Trumbull and Mahoning co V 2 p 47; Will bk 4 p 461 Columbiana co Recds-Prob 1821; Deed bk P pp 533, 534, Trnscr Mahoning co 1828; Jacob Hoover's heirs Springfield twp. Rept by Mahoning chpt.

HOOVER, JOHN GEORGE, Licking co

Pens July 8th 1834. Pvt in Pa Line at Monmouth and Stony Point. Wounded in neck; lost an eye. Was captured and exchanged. B in Germany in 1752. Mar Barbara Smith in 1783 in Chester co Pa. Chldr "Coonrad;" Charles; Henry; poss Andrew. D Nov 8th

1834 at Newark. Bur in Sixth Street Cem Newark. Widow allowed Pens Oct 26 1838. Rept by Hetuck chpt.

HOPKINS, JAMES, Champaign co

Enl in Va Sept 1775; pvt Contl; srvd 2 yrs. Was b 1747; d 9-27-1823. Appl for pens in Champaign co 4-13-1818 æ 75. Was a pensr in Clark co O 1819. Ref S 41650 Va. Rept by State D A R.

HOPKINS, JOHN, Brown co

Was b 1732; d 1797; bur at Red Oak nr Ripley O Brown co. Grave located by Ripley chpt. Ref 16 Rept N S D A R. Cop by Nathan Perry chpt.

HOPKINSON, JOSIAH, O

Sergt and Major in Md.

HOPWOOD, WILLIAM, Fairfield co

Was drafted abt 2 mo before the capture of Cornwallis; pvt Va Milit. Srvd 7 mo. Movd fr Shenandoah co Va to Fairfield co O abt 1806. Appld there for pens 10-31-1832 æ 68. Ref S 2324 Va. Rept by State D A R. Name listed p 406 Wisemans Pioneer People Fairfield co and p 275 Va Milit in Rev. Cop by J D.

HORN, JOSEPH, Highland co

Compare listed p 192 Vol 1, O Roster Rev bur at Newmarket. He resided in Cumberland co Pa before and aft Rev. Then movd to Mason co Ky; aft 2 yr to Adams co O and aft 18 yr to Highland co whr pensd 1833. A pvt 5 mo and Sergt 2 mo. Pa milit. Was b 1-12-1758 at Chester co Pa; d 5-31-1841; bur Presb cem at Marshall O. Gr mrkd by D A R. Ref S 2620 Pa. Rept by State D A R.

HORN-BAKER (Hornbaker), PHILIP, Portage co

Claim No. S 2363 pens. Enl at Juniata or Carlisle Pa 1775 in Capt Hendrick's Penn rifle co and was annexed to Col Morgan's Regt in Col Arnold's expedition to Quebec whr wounded in battle and taken prisoner held till 1776 and released. As pvt in Capt John Petty's N J Co; was at Battle of Monmouth. Ref Jersey men in Rev p 215 gives name as Hornbaker. Born 1747 Mansfield Sussex co N J nr Germantown; twice mar. Livd in various places in Trumbull and Mahoning cos; later went to Ravenna to live with grand-dau whr he d 2-28-1839. Rept by Grace M Winnagle, Warren O.

HORTON, HENRY, Trumbull co

Found spelled Hoston and now spelled Haughton and as such filed p 178 vol 1 of Roster; but pension papers contain "Horton" on original appl in Trumbull co Recds. Addit data to Vol 1; was pvt Conn Contl. Pens 1818 and 1820 in Trumbull co a resident of Southington twp. B 1766 (other bk says 1764). In 1820 ment wf; dau æ 15; dau æ 9; son æ 7. Ref S 41652 Conn (pens). Rept by State D A R and Mary Chesney chpt.

HOSBROOK, JOHN, Hamilton co

Sergt 1st Regt Contl Line N J Vol. Ref Stryker's Men fr N J. B in Ireland; mar Lydia Kitchell 1781 in Hanover N J (dau of Moses Kitchell); chldr: Daniel mar Eunice Bates; he was b 8-3-1785; d 11-22-1868; mar 9-5-1788; Archibald and Hannah. Soldr abt 1798 Madeira Hamilton co O; bur by rd side on his farm; grave unmarked. A farmer; he came to Columbiana 1798; thence to his farm adjoining present site of Madeira; family still possesses farm. Ref Allegra Frazier Centralia Ill. No. 77474 D A R Lin bk Vol 78 p 182. Rept by Mrs. Whallon Cincinnati chpt.

HOSIER, ABRAHAM, Montgomery co

Chester Co 5th Ser Pa Arch V 795 Milit 7th Com 1780 Capt McClaskey Col Geo

Pierce. Had 13 children when he came to county in 1806-7. Burial place unidentified. Rept by Wm Pettit S A R.

HOSKINS, CORNELIUS, Washington co

Found incorrectly spelled Haskins; a pvt Mass Contl. Enl 1775 or 76 Middleberry Mass. B 1745; mar Elizabeth æ 47 (in 1820); chldr: Mary; and James Dill. Appld for pens Mifflin co Pa Oct 6 1819 and again in 1820; appld for trnsfr to Washington co O Mar 6 1827; and also 10-24-1835 (V 7-226 Wash co courthouse) whr states he left a widow Elizabeth Hoskins. Ref S 41648 Mass. Rept by State D A R and Marietta chpt.

HOSKINSON, ISAIAH, Licking co

Pvt. Va Milit. Enl abt Aug 1777 or 78 Martinsburgh Va. B 12-27-1749 Prince George's co Md. Appld for pens Licking co O 11-3-1832; Had resided in Ohio since 1805 and had livd in Md; Va; and Pa. Ref S 16157 Va. Rept by State D A R. Was J of P in Franklin twp Licking co repts Hetuck chpt.

HOSTETTER, DAVID, Columbiana co

Rev Soldr Rec not yet found. Was b 1760; d 1820 Jan 6 æ 60 yrs. Bur Center twp. Livd Lisbon. Fr York co Pa whr he was listed as single man in 1782. Estate settled 1820 at Lisbon. Ref Col co cem records; Pa Arch 3 XXI p 561; Census 1840; The Ohio Patriot. Rept by Mrs. Wilma M Molsberry.

HOUGH, WILLIAM, ? co

Trnsfrd to O fr Warren co Indiana Mar 4 1834. Notified of death Sept 15 1838. Rept by Ind Hisorical Com.

HOUS (Hout), ——, Champaign co

Another soldr bur Mt Tabor cem Champaign co; inscript illegible. Rept by Urbana chpt.

HOUSER, LUDWICK, Stark co

Or Hauser; pvt Pa Contl; enl Apr 1776; srvd 2 yrs. Appld for pens 4-25-1833 Perry twp Stark co O æ 87. Ref S 2623 Pa. Rept by State D A R.

HOUSER, MARTIN, Stark or Franklin co

Pensr 1840; bur Harrisburg O. Cop fr Census. J D.

HOUSTON, JOHN, Warren co

Pvt of Cavalry N C Milit. Serv in Co of Capt Barnes Col McDowell Regt N C Line two yrs; and one yr in Cavalry; b 1763 Mecklinburgh co N C. Appld for pens in Warren co O Oct 3 1832 resident of Turtle crk twp æ 69. On one scouting exp 1780 made prisoner by scouts of Col Patterson a British officer and conducted to Camden S C; thence to Charleston to a British ship; thence to Brit hospt in Charleston and kept pris till 1781 Mar 1. He and three others escaped. Livd in Meck N C; thence to Madison co Ky; and in 1800 to Williamson co Tenn. 1807 to Miami co O. In 1809 to Warren co O whr livd.

HOVER, HENRY, Trumbull co

As Lieut in 3rd Batl and later as Capt in protecting the frontier and in N J Campaign was attached to Washington's army. Ref N J Men in Rev p 393; was b Apr 4 1740 Walpak Sussex co N J son of Hendrick Hover; wf's name Mary; chldr: Henry; Jane; Manuel; Catherine; Jonathan; Peter; George; Samuel; Judeth; John; Mary; Isaac; Joshua; Susanna. He d at Hubbard; bur Corner Church (Disciple cem) Hubbard O. Name only on stone. Rept by Mary Chesney chpt.

HOWARD, ADAM, Ross co

Pvt Va Milit. Pens 1834 Ross co O. In 1840 liv in Buckskin Twp æ 90 yr. (Cens 1840 ref). Rept by J D. Nathaniel Massie chpt located Will bk EF p 83 case 3082 naming wf Catherine?; chldr: John; Elizabeth; Katherine; Christena; Mary; Christopher (youngest son); Margaret; Phebe; Soldr d 1848 (Will probated April 11).

HOWARD, GORDON, Clinton co

Pvt. Enl Sept 1775 Pa Contl; servd 5 yrs. B 1753; in 1827 Apr 4 appld for pens Clinton co O. In 1831 was receiving pens there. Ref: S 41657 Pa and Va. Rept by State D A R.

HOWARD, JOHN, Lorain co

Enl Sharon Conn early in 1776 as pvt in Capt Benjamin Mill's co Col Bradley's Conn Regt; taken prisoner in Bat of Ft Washington Nov 16 1777; held till March 1777 when paroled. Was allowed pens Apr 22 1818 whl a resident of Peru Clinton co N Y æ 59. In 1820 refrd to wf Rachel æ 54; son John æ 18; and gr-son Abel Irish æ 7; in 1837 liv in Columbia twp Lorain co with chldr not named. Ref Bureau Pens. From Genl Acct Office Wash D C data; he d 12-5-1844 in Columbia twp Lorain co O and left no surviving widow, and only one chld named John. Rept by Nathan Perry chpt. (Listed in Cens 1840 as pens there æ 83 — J D).

HOWARD, JOHN, Montgomery co

5th Ser Pa Arch II p 551 state regt of foot; vol III 125 Sixth Pa Con Line from Reading 1778; 1780, 1781, served 10 months under Col Rawlings received $66.66 depreciated pay. Berks Co. Burial place Worman Cem Clay twp. D 1839 aged 81. Rept by Wm Pettit.

HOWE, EBENEZER, Butler co

Pvt. Enl Boston Mass Spring of 1782; servd a term of 3 yrs. Apr 9 1793 he mar Sarah Sears; Chldr: Alethea (?); Mary Ann; James; Milton. He d July 10 1829 Butler co O whr had appld for pens Sept 1 1826 Ref: Mass W 7766 B L Wt 17870-160-55. Rept by State D A R.

HOWE, JAMES Warren co

Enl March 1781 Richmond co Va; servd 3 mo as substitute for his brother-in-law Wm Jones in Col Nelsons Va Regt. Enl July 1781; servd 3 mo as subst for brother Thomas Howe in Capt Saml Fauntleroy Va Co. In Oct 1781 enl servd 2 mo as pvt in Capt Northem or Kelsick's Va Co. Was at Yorktown siege. Abt 1821 movd to Warren Co O whr was pens 1832-34; he mar Margaret Dean Jan 6 1803 in Frederick co Va. Soldr bur Seceder cem. She was pensd 1853 æ 72 a resident of Clinton co O. No ref made to chldr. Rept by Wm Pettit S A R Dayton data fr D C and by State D A R. Ref W 7765 B L Wt 26608-160-55 Va.

HOWELL, JONATHAN, Belmont co

Pvt Va St Trps in Capt Jos Ratiken Lieut Col Clapham Co. servd 17 mo in various enl. B June 20 1760 (Appl) in Huntingdon co N J. Enl Leesburg Va Loudon co; again in Ohio co Va; Wash co Pa. In 1814 he went as subst for Richcard Hardesty; thence to Belmont co O whr pens 1833. Ref S 2326 Va. Cop by Jane Dailey fr pens recd.

HOWELL, REUBEN, Columbiana co

Sergt Va Line 7 mo. Enl Aug or Sept 1780 Loudon co Va. B 2-26-1762 Trenton N J. "At the æ of 15 mo his father movd to Loudon co Va whr livd till 1810 thence to Columbiana co O whr pensd 3-5-1833 at Salem. Ref S 2327 Va. Pens No. 6543. Rept by State D A R. Mrs Molsberry Youngstown repts name in 1840 list.

HOWEY, THOMAS, Crawford co

D May 25 1835. No certain but this name was found among cemetery records as a Rev Soldr. Rept by Mary C Hise Bucyrus O.

HOYL, JOHN, Mahoning co

Pvt Capt John Ashton's co Ref Pa Arch S 5 V 7 p 248. Wf Catherine; chldr: David; William b 1804; Nicholas; John 1783; Peter 1790; Jacob; Polly mar —— Klineman; Nancy mar —— Courtney; Catherone mar —— Crawford; Lydia mar —— Kinnamen. He d abt 1831 Berlin twp. Ref Hist Col and Mahoning co V 2 p 194- 5; Tax list 1826 Peter and John Hoyl. Rept by Mahoning chpt.

HOYT, NICHOLAS, Morgan co

Pvt 9 mo 22 da N H St Trps. Enl 1781 Deerfield Rockingham (?) co N H. Dischgd Dec 1781; re-enlisted servd 6 mo 22 da. Livd in Deerfield 2 yr aft war; 2 yr in Maine; one yr again in Deerfield; in Conway N H 2 yrs; and 2 yr in Pa. 21 yrs in Waterfield ? O and 17 yr in Morgan co O whr now resides. He appld for pens there July 19 1832. Ref N H and N Y S 2618. Rept by State D A R.

HUBBARD, ASA, Medina co

Pvt. Enl 1776 Hartford Conn Milit. Srvd 6 mo 12 da. Aft Rev livd Enfield and Windsor Conn; Amherst; Springfield; and Long Meadow; Mass; Bristol; N Y and Granger Medina co O whr appl for pens Oct 23 1832 whch was allowed. Was b 1757 Enfield Hartford co Conn. Ref S 2333 Conn. Rept by State D A R.

HUBBARD, JOHN, ? co

"Pvt servd in late war; no evidence of being wounded in line of his duty as soldier" — this given as reason for rejection of pension claim p 81-82; Doc 31; Jan 6 1831 O S Libr. Rept by Blanche Rings Col O.

HUBBELL, JOHN, Warren co

Enl 1777 Elizabethtown N J Line. Was Sergt. B 1752 (being 66 in 1818 whn appld for pens in Warren co O Apr 16. Mar Mary —— Aug 1st Thursday 1778; chldr: John; Daniel; Abijah; Rachel; Anna; David; S d Apr 17 1834. In 1820 he had appld for pens in Fayette co Ind; and Apr 6 1840 widow appld fr Henry co Ind æ 81. Ref W 9484 N J. Name listed here to avoid further research as he d in Ind likely. Rept by State D A R.

HUBBERT, EPHRAIM, Fairfield co

No doubt this is same listed p 196 Vol 1 of Roster as "Ephraim Hulbert" Hancock co with no data. He was pvt N J Milit. Enl abt 1776 under Capt Dickerson. Servd 11 mo 6 da. B 1759 N J; appld for pens in Fairfield co O 5-29-1833. His name is listed in Wiseman's Hist Pioneer People p 406. Ref: S 2643 N J. Rept by State D A R.

HUBER, JOHN, Clermont co

Col Lancaster co Pa Milt 9th Battl b 1751 Pa and fr stone in Williamsburg O only "d Sept 21 18—" can be deciphered. Mar Christina Brinkle (1759-1821). Four have joined D A R on line of his sons Jacob and John. One ref: V 75 p 22 No. 74065 D A R Lin. Rept by Nathan Perry chpt.

HUBLER, MICHAEL, Montgomery co

Ref S 5 V 8 p 220 Pa Arch Northampton co Associator Col W Roup. D 1849; bur Ellerton cem Montgomery co O. Grave mrkd by Richard Montgomery chpt S A R who rept this data thro Wm M Pettit State Sec.

HUDDLESTON, THOMAS, Hamilton co

Pvt in Capt Augustus Willet's Co of Middletown twp Bucks co Pa Milit Aug 21 1775.

B Bucks co Pa son of William Huddleston (1702-1776) who mar Dorothy Walsh Nov 14 1727. Thomas mar Catherine Elizabeth Stinger Aug 1763; chldr: Jacob; Thomas; Susanne (b Apr 8 1789; d May 13 1864); mar Rezin Bryant Newell Mar 22 1806 (he was b 1784 d 1855). Soldier d at Newton Hamilton co O whr bur. Ref Pa Arch 5 Ser V 5 p 307. Data secured fr Lansing Glen Lytle Sayre No. 1518 S A R Los Angeles by Jane Dailey.

HUDDLESON, WILLIAM

See "Heddleson."

HUDNALL, THOMAS, Athens co

Pvt Va Contl Col Harrison's Regt in Artillery; servd 3 yrs. B 1760; d at æ 93; bur Union cem Athens co. Grave mrkd by Gov marker; he livd in Alexander twp. One son was William; family driven fr France in 1685. Ref Dept Interior S 41664 Va Contl. Cop by Jane Dailey; with family dates fr Mrs. Emma Robinson a descendant.

HUFF, PETER, Trumbull co

Drafted in Frederick co Md in 1777. Servd till 1778; drafted again and marched to Carlisle Pa; servd abt 6 mo. B in Germany; came to America with parents when æ 9. Livd in Berkeley co Va nr Potomac riv till abt 1807 came to Hubbard O whr was liv 1837. Ref S 9597 pens cl. Rept by Mary Chesney chpt.

HUGHES, JONATHAN, Gallia co and Va.

Pvt Va Milit. Servd under Capt Cook Col Posten Regt. Appld for pens 1833 in Jefferson co Ind; same in Gallia co O. Mar 9 1834 whr recd pens. Ref S 9591 Va. On July 7 1835 appld for trnsfr to Thurman co Va whr prob bur. He was b Mar 25 1753 Hampshire co Va. Rept by State D A R. Listed p 276 Va Milit in Rev as liv in Gallia co æ 81. Cop by J D.

HULET (Hewlett, Hulett), ASA, Lorain co

Enl abt June 1781 Berkshire co Mass. B 1764 same co and state: mar Polly —— on Mar 8 1812. He d Oct 8 1846, at Russia, Lorain co O. In 1838 Jan 31 appl for pens Livingston co N Y widow appl in Lorain co O. Oct 27 1856; later in Cuyahoga co 1858. Cens of 1840 lists name as pensr liv Brunswock Medina æ 82 with Elisa Mason. Ref R 5362 (meaning rejected) B L Wt 84049-160-55 Mass. Rept by State D A R.

HULET, SYLVANUS, Portage co

Pvt Mass Line servd 9 mo enl July 8 1779 Mass Line. in 1819 June 14 appl for pens Portage co O. and pensr 7-15-1820; stating he was æ 63; had wf Mary; chldr: Charlotte; Sylvester; Francis; and Mary. Ref S 41672 Mass. His appl for a pension was rejected, on grounds he was not in indigent circumstances, under act of May 1 1820. (Ref Doc 31 Jan 6 1831 list Rept by Blanche Rings Col O). Rept by State D A R.

HULL, AARON, Athens co

Inspector of Provisions Mch 13 1780; b 1736; son of Nathaniel Hull and Elizabeth Burr; he mar Abigail Whitlock Oct 8 1770; chldr: Stephen; William; Huldah; Samuel; Sarah; Jabez; Abigail died at Shade Athens co 1825. Ref Conn Men in Rev pp 24-71-419. Rept by Nabby Lee Ames chpt.

HULL, ABNER, Cuyahoga co

Pvt Ct Contl enl June 1776 servd 13 mo 5 da b May 4 1759 New Haven Ct. Appld for pens Cuyahoga co O. Nov 7 1832. Ref S 2335 Conn. Rept by State D A R.

HULL, ANDREW, Mahoning co

Pvt Ct Men in Rev 1775; Pvt Ct Histor Soc V 12; son of Solomon Hull, a Rev soldier; mar Elizabeth; chldr: Manuel (Emanuel) b 1791; Andrew; Eve; Mary b 1795 (mar Wm Hamilton). Soldr d abt 1822, at Boardman, bur Cornersburg (perhaps) Berlin twp Grave not located. Soldr was b Westmoreland co Pa; came to Berlin twp 1809; d at home of son Emanuel. Ref Hist of Trumb and Mahon cos V 2 pp 84-88-115; Hist Mahon co V 2 p 280 by Butler; Will bk prob Oct 1 1822. Deed bk E p 257 From Andrew Hull heirs Boardman 1850. Rept by Mahoning chpt Mabel Askue Chairman.

HULL, GEORGE, Mahoning co

Pvt Pa Ref Pa Arch S 5 V 4 pp 405-713; b Aug 15 1761; mar Abigail (1768-6-12-1840). He d July 23 1833 Boardman twp; bur Cornersburg O. Is prob a son of Solomon Hull p 197 Roster Ohio Rev Sold Vol 1. Ref cem recds of Henry R Baldwin's Rev S. Rept by Mahoning chpt.

HULL, ISAAC, Scioto co

Enl early 1776 resid in Middlesex co N J as pvt Milit. Servd 1 yr 8 mo; b Feb 10 1740 Middlesex co. Movd to Ky, Mason co Fall of 1792; thence to Scioto co 1812. Here he appld for pens Sept 26 1833. Was wagon-maker; ref S 9599 N J; and p 331 Evans and Stivers Hist. Rept by State D A R.

HULL, ISAAC, Mahoning co

Pa Pensr. Ref Pa Arch S 3 V 23 pp 218, 583; N J Men p 373. Was bur probably at Old Market St cem. Settled in Canfield twp. Rept by Mahoning chpt.

HULL, JOHN, Ross co

Placed on pens roll Aug 9 1833. Enl at æ 15; servd under Gens Gates and Green and present at Yorktown. Movd to Chillicothe Aug 20 1833. Bur in old cem. Bones remvd to Grandview cem to lot of John D Madeira whr they now lie (1900). Old stone on his grave. Cop fr 4th rept N S D A R p 300, by Jane Dailey.

HULL, SAMUEL, Licking co

Was b 1735 Hartford co Md. Mar Martha Glover 1764 in Culpepper co Va. Son Levi killed by Indians. Had 14 other chldr. D Gratiot O 1814. Ref Va Rom 32 p 231 also Hull Genealogy. Rept by Hetuck chpt.

HULL, URIAH, ? co

Pvt servd in "late war"; name listed in rejected claim for pens, as having no evidence of his having been disabled while in the service of the U S. Ref Doc 31 Jan 6 1831 p 81-2 O S Libry, Rept by Blanche Rings Col O.

HULLINGER, DANIEL, Champaign co

Pvt and Sergt Pa Contl Pensd 1833 Champaign co. Was son of Christian who was also "called into service 8 mo." He was b Mar 12 1757 Warwick twp Pa d July 22 1839 æ 82 plus. Bur Rector cem Valley Pike and Terra Haute Rd. Was teamster; re-enlisted as pvt and honorably dischgd as Lieut. After war movd to Shenandoah co Va whr mar Ann Shockey (b 12-6-1767 d 8-20-1836) in 1783. Movd to O abt 1788 to Champaign co. Had eleven chldr: Christopher b 1785 Va d 1859 mar Mary Crabb; Daniel Jr b 1788 Va d 1856; Jacob b 1788 Va d 1830 mar Mary Mathena; Nancy b 1790 d 1873 mar Reuben Maggert; Valentine b 1793 d 1855 mar Elizabeth Maggert; John b 1795 d 1836 mar Olive Coe; Elizabeth b 1797 d 1867 mar Geo Arbogast; Rosanna b 1798 mar Daniel McIntire; Catherine b 1799 d 1834; Joseph b 1800 d 1865; Abraham b 1801 d 1873 bur at Tremont. Ref S 2329 Pa as rept by State D A R and rept by Miss Gaumer Urbana chpt.

HULSE, HENRY, Trumbull co

Altho Nathan Perry repts name as Rev Soldr cop fr 27th rept N S D A R Mary Chesney chpt Warren found the following to be facts: "There is no stone for him in Disciple cem, "Corner cem" nr Hubbard, but there are many unmarked graves, and his may be one. Henry Hulse came to Courtland in that twp fr Shelby co Ky in 1802. He was too young to be a Rev soldier, but is soldier of 1812. His father may have come with him and settled in Hubbard as a Henry Hulse (Hulz of Hubbard acknowledged service of subpoena to testify before Com Pleas Ct in 1803)." Data given here to avoid further research and to correct Rev statements found. J D.

HUMPHREY, GEORGE, Jefferson co

Pvt 2nd Trp 1st Regt Light Dragoons Contl Trps 1782 1783 under Capt John Watts. Enl fr Va early yrs of war servd along Va and Pa frontier. B Dec 19 1749 North Ireland son of David Humphrey Sr; mar 1st Jane Wilson Nov 2 1775; 2nd Elizabeth Jolly Jan 15 1788 sister of Henry Jolly; chldr of first wf: Agnes mar Wm McMunn; Alexander unmar; David mar Eliz Ramsey; Elizabeth mar Joseph son of Wm Mc Caughey. Soldr d Mar 26 1834; bur. Old Seceder S E part of town of Mt Pleasant east side of cem Insc: "In memory of George Humphrey who departed this life Mar 26 1834 aged 84 yr 3 mo 7 d." Was a member of 1st Const Convention of Ohio; Representative 1809 & 1812. Ref Va State Libry Richmond War 4:219 War 33:12 et al; No. 265352 D A R. Rept by Clara Mark, Histor. Jacobus Westervelt D A R Westerville O (Photo of stone was attached).

HUMPHREY, JOHN, Jefferson co

Enl Pa Dec 1776; Orderly Sergt in Capt Patrick Jack's Co Col John Allison's Pa Regt. Enl 1777 Capt White's Regt; in 1778-79 Capt John Taylor's Co; Capt in Col James McDowell's Pa Regt et al. Was b 1752 nr London Cross Rds Chester co Pa. Was son of David Humphrey Sr; mar Elizabeth McKee; chldr: James; Robert; John; William; Mary (mar John Trimble); David; Nancy; Elizabeth (mar Thomas McElroy); George (mar Virginia Lewis). Soldr d June 30 1841 Warren twp Jefferson co O; bur at Warrenton O (accd to written statement of son and gr-son). Pensd in 1833; Cens of 1840, was liv in Warren twp. During war livd Cumberland Pa (now Franklin) nr Mechanicksburg. Ref Pens Cl No. S 8744 Pa; Recds Divis No. 25785 Rev War Ohio Agency; co recds Chambersburg Pa and Wheeling W Va Belmont & Jefferson co Hist. Rept by Clara Mark Westerville O.

HUMPHREY, ROSWELL, Cuyahoga co

Volunteered 1781 in Litchfield co Ct St Trps. Pvt. Servd 11 mo 20 da; b 1765; mar Elizabeth Norton, Aug 16 1792; he d Mar 12 1835 Cuyahoga co O. Appld for pens Aug 4 1832 there; Widow appld there July 5 1839. Ref W 4998 Conn. Rept by State D A R.

HUMPHREYS, JACOB Licking co

And sometimes "Jacox," it is thot. Pvt Va Contl Enl Charleston Md Spring 1775. Appld pens 1818 æ 69 liv w wf who was a cripple. Was farmer; Ref Va S 41667. Rept by State D A R.

HUNGERFORD, LEMUEL, Franklin co

Order book 6-133. Made declaration for pens under the act of June 6 1832 and the clerk is directed to issue certf as directed by the War dept. (9-29-32). Ref Court recd Columbus. Rept by Blanche Rings.

HUNT, JAMES, Clark co

Pvt Md Contl. Enl May 1778; b May 1745; ments "wf" no name; appld for pens Oct 1831 Clark co O. Ref 641663 Md. Rept by State D A R.

HUNT, JONATHAN, Knox co

Enl from Somerset co N J (whr he was b) in Capt Philip Phillips Co on May 10 1777 Huntertown N J. Sergt. Dischrgd Sept 20 1777. Re-enl Oct 1 1777 Capt Corles (Corliss) Troop Light-horse at Huntertown N J. Mar Christianna; soldr d Hunts Station 5 miles S of Mt Vernon O; bur Boyles cem; lot not numbered. Inscript on mrkr "Jonathan Hunt d July 5th 1825 æ 83 yr 2 mo 4 das." Grave mrkd by fam monument and Rev mrkr placed by Kokosing chpt D A R in 1937. The B and O R R passed through

Jonathan Hunt's farm and Hunt's Station was named in honor of Jonathan Hunt. Ref Inscript on Monument and Hunt fam hist. Rept by Kokosing chpt Emma Blair Ewalt chr.

HUNT, WILLIAM, Mahoning co

Pvt in 1st Co 2nd Battl Cumberland co Milit. Ref S 5 Vol 6 p 161 & 191 Pa Arch. He mar Elizabeth ——; chldr: Elizabeth; Martha; Seth; John. He d before 1830 in Green twp. Ref Will bk 7 p 88; Columbiana co Recds Probated 1830; Deed bk 0 p 570 Wm and Elizabeth Hunt to Wm Hunt Jr 1827. Rept by Mahoning D A R.

HUNTER, ANDREW JOHN, Mahoning co

Ref N Y Men in Rev p 238; Mr Andrew Hunter Qr p 132; he mar Jane; chldr: Mary (mar R P Justice); Ann (mar Ralston); Pearsey; Robert; Hariett; William; Thomas; George. He d abt 1837 Poland O. Ref Deed bk F 380 John and Jane Hunter to R P Justice 1835; also "F" p 426 John Hunter Heirs 1838; Tax list of 1826 John Hunter Poland. Rept by Mahoning chpt.

HUNTER, BENJAMIN, Pickaway co

Enl Fort Montgomery N Y servd in Capt Titus Co Col Henry B Livingston's 4th N Y. Was at Capture of Burgoyne, Monmouth. In Gen Sullivan's Expedi vs Indians; wintered at Valley Forge; enl at Phila again; servd in Capt Heard's Co of Light Horse; trnsf to Capt Christies (?) Co Col Richard Butler's Pa Regt. Was b in 1752; d Apr 11 1829 æ 77 in Circleville twp accd to old newspaper; grave not found; was pensd Apr 23 1818 æ 66 residing in Ross co O. In 1821 was liv in Pickaway co Ref No. S 41673 N Y. Rept by Pickaway Plains chpt. From Mary Steinmetz Reading Pa comes ref: Pa Arch. Ohio list one "Benjamin Hunter resided in Pickaway co 1832 æ 82" which if same man may be conflicting dates.

HUNTER, JOSEPH, Franklin co

Pvt Capt James Howells' Co 7th Batl Cumberland co Pa Aug 1782, Col James Purdy. B Aug 8 1763 Cumberland co Pa son of Joseph Hunter. He mar Margaret Mc Gaughey Oct 17 1782; chldr: Robert b 1783 mar Ann Riddle; Martha 1785 mar Sam Robinson; Isabella 1787 mar William Shaw; John 1789 mar Miss McGowan; Joseph Jr 1793 mar Eunice Starr; William 1791 mar Margaret McElvain; Nancy 1796 mar David Mitchell; Jane 1801 mar Andrew McElvain. Soldr d June 6 1834 Columbus O whr bur in Greenlawn cem. Insc: Joseph Hunter, Esq born Aug 8 1763 died June 6 1834. Early settler before 1800; one of founders of 1st Presby church at Franklinton O. Ref Pa Arch S 6 Vol 6; Old N W Quarterly; Martins Hist Franklin co. Rept by Columbus chpt and F C McElvain Topeka Kan.

HUNTER, JOSEPH, Fairfield co

Born in Va whr servd as Capt of Trps. Mar Dorotha Berkshire of Md. Chldr: Judge Hocking H Hunter b 1801 d 1872 on his farm at Lancaster O. Joseph d in Fairfield co. He came to Ky at close of War thence to O in 1798 the first settler in Fairfield co. Ref Biograph Cyclopedia of Ohio Vol 1 p 183 pub 1883 Cincinnati O by Western Pub Co. Cop by Mrs. Whallon Cincinnati chpt.

HUNTER, ROBERT, Warren co

Pvt Capt Tutt's Co Col Huger's S C Regt. Enl 1775-6; Servd 15 mo; b Sept 16 1750 supposedly in Ireland; mar Katherine Kyse (Keyse). Chldr: Thomas mar Phoebe Lollar or Lawler; Elizabeth b Va 1790 mar David Fudge; Nellie b Ky mar William Hatfield. Exact no. of chldr not known. He d March 11 1830 Salem twp Warren co O. The "Western Star" of Lebanon states he was bur in Union twp grave not known. Movd from S C to Henderson Ky; thence to Warren co O in 1803; whr settld in Salem twp in 1804. Was farmer. Ref Pens Cl S 41678 S C; pens allowd May 29 1818; and Natl No. 40431 S A R. George Rogers Clark; Rept by Catherine Greene chpt Mrs. Reed. Also rept by State D A R same recd with 1747 as date of birth, cop fr Pens Cl.

HUNTER, ROBERT, Fairfield co

Ensign and 2nd Lieut N Y Contl under Col Wm Malcom. Was b 1761 Carlisle Pa. Mar Elizabeth ——; one son was named Thomas who mar Ann Morrow. He d 1846 Fairfield co O. Ref V 106 and 117 p 278 D A R lin Bk No. 116888. Rept by Nathan Perry chpt.

HUNTINGTON, HEZEKIAH, Portage co

Though found listed in Ohio should be Conn. Ref Vol 46 p 32 D A R Lin. Cop by Jane Dailey.

HUNTLEY, DANIEL, Ashtabula co

Exec Doc 37 of 1852. Refused a pens as servd less than 6 mo. Rept by Wm Pettit.

HUPP, PHILLIP, Monroe co

Pvt Va Line servd during War; he mar Mary —— July 23 1782; he died Nov 9 1831; appld for pens Apr 9 1829 in Monroe co O. His widow appld for pens Jan 21 1837 in Monroe co. Ref W 4239 Va. Rept by State D A R.

HURLEY, CORNELIUS, Ross co

Pvt enl 2-14-1776 Prince Williams co Va. Servd 2 yrs. Was æ 65 in 1821 whn appld for pens in Ross co O. He stated he had 3 sons, four daughters all married; wf was dead. Ref S 41677 Va. Rept by State D A R.

HUSTON, ALEXANDER, Montgomery co

Early settler at Beavertown whr is bur in Presbyterian Cem. Ref Ser 5 Pa Arch. Vol 1 p 50; V 2 p 500 503; Vol 5 p 116; Vol 7 p 570 585 1069; Vol 6 p 189. Rept by Wm Pettit S A R State Sec Dayton.

HUSTON, DANIEL, Columbiana co

Exec Doc 37 of 1852. Refused a pens as servd less than 6 mo. Rept by Wm Pettit.

HUSTON, DAVID, Greene co

Early settlr at time Montgomery and Greene co were a part of Hamilton co. Name in 1790 census fr Franklin co Pa. On tax list 1798; Ref Ser 5 Pa Arch. Vol 7 pp 269, 276, 282, 373, and 176. Livd and d in Greene co whr servd on bench; credited as being a brother of Alex Huston a Montgomery co settlr. Rept by W M Pettit S A R Dayton.

HUSTON, HUGH, Pickaway co

Enl June 1779 in Capt John Jourdon's Co pvt Pa Line æ 69 in 1818 whn appld for pens in Pickaway co. Wf was 70 æ in 1820; chldr: Rebecca æ 24; John 22; and gr-dau. Eliza Read æ 13 in 1820 appl. Ref S 41679 Contl Pa. Rept by State D A R.

HUSTON, WILLIAM, Columbiana co

Pvt Pa Line servd 4 yrs. Pensd 10-9-1820 in Columbiana co O stating his age as 66, and wf's age 57 name Prudence; Ref S 41675 Penn. He enl 2-17-1777. Rept by State D A R. Fr Mrs Wilma Molsberry Youngstown comes data: resided in Columbiana co 1834 æ 72. Ref Pa Arch Vol 23 S 3 p 575; 1833-4 Pens Rec U S. Fr Census of 1840 by St Chairman is data: living in Canaan Wayne co O in 1840 pensr æ 78; (Fr seven sources, we give the above as authentic, tho Cens of 1840 would indicate if same man he might have d in Wayne co).

HUSTON, WILLIAM, Miami co

Conflicting data permits no authentic statement but we give it here to avoid further research:Ref No 70416 D A R Lin states he was fr Lancaster co Pa; he d after 1822 at Piqua Miami co. (Cop by State Chairman). See also No. 70415; No. 55786; cf No. 124416; and p 126 Vol 125 D A R Lin.

HUTCHINGS, GABRIEL, Butler co

Enl N J March 1782; dischgd June 25 1783; pvt servd 15 mo. In July 17 1820 appld for pens in Butler co O stating age 62; wf old and infirm; Shoemaker; Ref S 41668 N J. Rept by State D A R.

HUTCHINGS, WILLIAM, Butler co

Enl 1776 Morris co N J as pvt N J Milit servd one yr and 6 mo. In 1795 removd to Pa and after 6 yrs to Ohio whr resided in Butler co for 15 yr (Appl). Appld for pens 5-31-33; gave age as 75 in 1832; b Essex co N J. Ref S 2334 N J. Rept by State D A R.

HUTCHINS (or Huchins), JACOB, Cuyahoga co

Enl 1775 Mass St Trps servd 2 yr. B 1759 Worcester Mass. After war movd to Plattsburg N Y thence Orangeburg Canada; then to N Y State 11 yrs. to Pittsburg Pa then to O. Pensr 1832 Cuyahoga co. Ref S 4414 Mass. My State D A R.

HUTCHISON, JAMES, Wayne co

Pvt in Capt Hugh Campbell's Co 2nd Batl York Co Col Robert McPherson while at Perth Amboy Sept 17 1776. Listed also in York co Milit May 27 1778 signed by John Travis in War of Rev. Was b 1743 County Antrim Ireland; mar Jane Kelly; chldr: Matthew; Mary; Jane; Nancy; Betsey; an infant; Jinnie; Daniel; William; Jimsey; Isabella. He d 12-17-1817 Fredericksburg Wayne co O whr bur in East cem. Insc James Hutchison d Dec 29 1817 aged 74 yr. Jane his wife d Apr 15 1845 aged 97. Family came to America with Kelly fam abt 1754. In 1815 came to Wayne co fr Westmoreland co Pa. A corrected record of burial place was sent to Wash D A R Sept 1927 with photos. Complete data fr Mrs. Oscar Finch Portland Ind. Regstr Mississinewa chpt. Ref No. 250379 D A R. Secured by Jane Dailey St Ch.

HUTTON (or Hutten), GEORGE, Scioto co

Enl York co Pa 1776; servd 3 yrs as Pvt Pa Contl; b 1752; On Aug 13 1818, appld for pens in Scioto co O. whr liv in 1840, Nile twp æ 86 with son John Hutton, accd to census. Ref S 41676 Contl Pa. Rept by State D A R.

HUXSON, MATTHEW, Warren co

Or "Hicxson". Enl in Hunterdon co N J in 1776 in Amwell twp whr was born 12-12-1756. Pvt under Capt Eli and Col Martin one yr. Appld for pens Oct 3 1832 Warren co O. Ref S 18022 N J. Rept by State D A R.

HYDECKER, JACOB, Richland co

In cem at Bellville O recently was placed a marker, with insc: "Hydecker, Jacob born in France 1759 Came to U S with Genl Lafayette's Army. Fought in Rev war. Placed by gr-grand-son, Sherman Painter." Investigation by Jared Mansfield chpt found this fact was handed down in family, but have no papers to prove it. This same man fought in war 1812 fr O as a substitute for a Mr Stout who had been raised by a Grubb family; which name Hydecker assumed is not known; he mar in Va to —— Meadows; perhaps some one may be helped with this information. (St. Chairman).

IAMS, JAMES, Belmont co

Pvt Capt Walker's Co Col Dorsey Regt of Md Line (not Pa) Appld for pension 10 Mar 1834 residing in Richland twp Belmont co where he had come from Bethlehem twp Washington co Pa where he had lived five yrs. B Amarandall co Md 1754 where he enlisted. Ent on Ohio rolls 26 Mar 1834 papers sent to Wilson Shannon St Clairsville O. Ref S 8751 Md Pens Clms. (This record was discovered when seeking one "Thomas James pvt Pa Milit for whom no data was found at Wash." Cop by Jane Dailey.

IIAMS, THOMAS, Belmont co

Or Imes etc; servd in 2nd Md Regt; dischg 1-1-1780; b 1754 Md; d 1834; mar Catherine Hampton 1791; S A R 52601. Rept by Wm Pettit.

INGALLS, ISRAEL, Hamilton co

Pvt Capt Barne's Co Col Wyman's Regt New Hampshire Milit 6 mo. Enl Dunstoth (?) N H. Remvd to Corinth Orange co Vt; thence to Bath N H; thence to Penobscot River Me; thence to Columbia twp Hamilton co 20 June 1832 æ 77. Born Andover Essex co Mass 25 Dec 1754. Ref S 9740 N H. Cop by Jane Dailey at Wash.

INGERSOLL, GEORGE, ? co

Capt; listed in scrapbook item as interested in Marietta settlement, many been verified. Filed for continued research. List fr Marietta chpt.

INMAN, EDWARD, Ashtabula co

Pvt in Capt John Franklin's Co 5th Regt Connecticut Milit serving at Wyoming Pa in 1782. B 1733; d 4 May 1821 in 88 yr; bur S E Corner Wayne twp Ashtabula co. Grave found 30 Sept 1913. Ref Pa Arch 3-23-461 (Baldwin). Rept by Wilma Molsberry Youngstown.

INMAN, JOHN, Mahoning co

Pvt in Capt John Franklin's Co 5th Regt Connecticut Milit; servd at Wyoming Pa in 1782; bur in Mahoning co. Ref Pa Arch 3-23-461 (Baldwin). Rept by Wilma Molsberry Youngstown.

INMAN, RUFUS, Washington co

Enl 28 Oct 1780 Lutton Mass as pvt. Servd 3 yrs. Appld for pension Aug 1820 in Jefferson co O which states he was b 1762; mar Elizabeth æ 49; had 4 chldr: James æ 18; Aaron 16; Nathan 14; Samuel 10 (date at time 1820). Dischgd 28 Oct 1783 at West Point N Y. Ref Mass S & S V 8 p 642; Pens Clms S 41680 Mass. His name listed as pensioner 1821 in Washington co where we have listed him. Cop by State D A R.

IRELAND, DAVID, Preble co

Enl N Carolina made Capt. B N Carolina 1765. Mar Nancy Mitchell; came to Preble co 1808. Bur in Jefferson twp. Rept by Commodore Preble chpt.

IRVIN, EDWARD, Fairfield co

Pvt. Enl 1777 or 8 in Penn Milit. Servd 6 mo. Pensd 6-22-1833 in Fairfield co O stating was born 7-5-1748. Came to U S with father abt 1757; and movd to Miflin (?) co Pa in 1780 movd to Ky; thence to Fairfield co. Ref Wiseman's Pioneer People Fairfield co p 406; S 5598 Pa (Pens Clm). Cop by State D A R.

IRWIN, FRANCIS, Perry co

Exec Doc 37. Refused a pens as servd less than 6 mo. Somerset O Perry co. Rept by Wm Pettit.

IRWIN, JAMES, Butler co

Pvt Penn Milit. Enl 1777; enl 3 times; was in Capt William Grahams Co. Made two tours vs Indians under Capt David Boal. Pensd 12-27-1833 while liv in Butler co. Mar Agnes (Irwin); one son was Robert; d 1847 æ 89 in Butler co. (This data cop by Jane Dailey from V 10 p 283 D A R Lin No. 9800 also rept by Nathan Perry chpt on No. 7312. Pens Clm S 9743 Pa from which he states born 16 Oct 1758 Cumberland co Pa. Drafted in Autumn of 1777; livd for 37 yrs in Ohio mostly Butlet co. Cop by State D A R. Ref S A R 15548.

IRWIN, JAMES, Champaign co

Corporal Mass Contl. Enl 1777; dischgd 1782 West Point; Servd 5 yrs. Appld for pens 4-22-1818 fr Champaign co recd 1819. B 1741. Ref S 41681 Mass (Pens Clm) (Data that he was bur in Wilmington Clinton co remains to be proven). Cop by State D A R.

IRWIN, JOHN, Clermont co

Exec Doc 37. Refused a pens as servd less than 6 mo. Rept by Wm Pettit.

IRWIN, JOHN, Mahoning co

Pens appl Circuit Court Warren O Bk 6 p 185. One son was John? Soldr d Ellsworth twp. Ref Tax list 1826 John Erwin Elsworth twp; Deek bk H p 55 to John Erwin 1844. Rept by Mahoning chpt.

IRWIN, WILLIAM, Mahoning co

Pens appl Warren O Circuit Court Bk 6 p 183. Mar Mary (Wallace) Scroggs. Soldr d Youngstown O. Tax list 1826 Youngstown O names Thomas Christopher and Jacob Erwin. Res soldr bro of Christopher Egle. Ref Egle Notes p 114 Ohl; Deed bk H p 142 Edwin Wm from Turhand Kirtland 1824. Rept by Mahoning chpt.

ISBEL, (or Isbell) JOEL, Wayne co

Though this soldier d in Mich the data is included here that further research may not be made in Ohio for his grave. Name occurs in Ohio lists as pvt Conn Contl pensd in Wayne co O 11-29-1819. Fr Pension Clm R 5500 Conn. (R meaning rejected) we take the following data: Servd 3 yrs Conn Line. B Mar 1766; parents Lymen Isbel father who made affidavit for Joel 10-12-1819 in Medina co O. Mar Mary Chatfield 1-30-1793; 6 chldr: Herman Swift æ 18; Normy ? æ 15; Albert æ 13; Joel æ 10; Myram 8; Mary 5. D Sept 17 1838 Monroe co Mich accd to affidavit of son James 1839 fr widow's appl for pens in which she states reside Shortbridge Mass at mar moving to Whitestown N Y at once; after 5 yrs to East Bloomfield N Y; aft 5 more to Clarence N Y; aft 12 yrs to Ohio; in 1836 to Mich where he d. Cop by State D A R.

ISHAM, GEORGE, Clark co

Enl 1776 Colchester Conn. Servd 3 yrs as pvt. B 1763 he states in application for pens 3-27-1819, residing in Clark co O. Mentions "wife and four children oldest being 14." Farmer; in October 1819 he is listed as pensd in Hamilton co where he may have removed by that time. No data on burial. Ref S 41682 Conn. Cop by State D A R.

ISRAEL, JOHN, Belmont co

Cadet in Capt Mitchell's Co Col Wood's 12 Va Regt. B 1749 Md. Mar Rachel Clay 1787. D 1822 Belmont co O. Ref S 17510 Va. D A R Lin V 110 p 156 No. 109504. Cop by Jane Dailey.

ISRAEL, JOHN, Butler co

B Albermarle co Va 1765; Enl while a resident of Wilks co N C; livd there till 1811 when came to Butler Co O remaining till 1821; removd to Franklin twp Johnson co Ind where appld for pens 11-12-1832. Rept by Jane Dailey, to avoid further research in O.

JACK, THOMAS, Adams co

Sergt Pa Contl. Enl 3-1-1776. Ren-enl 1777; dischgd Jan 1781; resided in Pa till aft dischg then movd to Adams co O. Widows appl states he was 71 yrs old in 1820. Chldr: Nancy; Betsy; Margaret; and grand-daughter Jane. Farmer; d 8-9-1831 in Adams co O. Ref W 4705 Penn; Pa Arch list of O Soldrs. Rept by Mary Steinmetz Reading Pa. Cop by State D A R. Ref Courier of Liberty 1831; and Evans & Stivers Hist Adams co p 331. Wf name Jane Kincaid. By Meryl Markley.

JACKMAN, WILLIAM, Jefferson co

Grave located by Mrs Sinclair Steubenville stone data: b 1751. d 1818; bur Island Creek Cem Jefferson co O. We submit the following data as ref on same name but have no positive proof it is the same; cop fr V 5 p 222 D A R Lineage bk No 4628 by Jane Dailey: William Jackman in 1777 pvt in Col Stickney's Milit. Regt that marched to Ticonderoga; in 1778-9 servd in R I camp as Sergt; in 1780 drafted fr the Militia for "new levies" in Contl Army.

JACKSON, ALEXANDER, Miami co

Enl 4-4-1777; served in all abt eleven mo as pvt Pa Milit. Resided in Green co Pa till 1809 when movd to Ohio. Appld for pens 9-27-1832 in Miami co stating was b in Lowden co Va 1759. Ref S 4435 Penn. Cop by State D A R.

JACKSON, DANIEL, Morrow co

Bur Franklin twp Yankee St cem Morrow co. Rept by Mt Gilead chpt.

JACKSON, ISAAC, Columbiana co

Pvt and Sergt Pa Line 1777-1783; enl in March 1777 in Chester co Pa (appl) Pensd 1829; Bounty land Wt 549-100 was granted 250 A Ohio Military Land. Pvt Washington co Pa Co Capt John Christie 5th Regt; Sergt Capt Budes Co 3rd Regt Pa Line; Dischgd at Philadelphia 1783. Ref S 46451 Pa; Pa Arch reports of Colum co. Cop by State D A R & rept by Youngstown chpt. Was brother of Joseph Jackson of Licking co

JACKSON, JAMES, Cuyahoga co

Enl Maryland 1-29-1777 pvt Md Contl. Servd 6 yrs. Appld for pens in Cuyahoga co O 4-13-1818; states born 1743; "had no family and never had any;" Butcher by trade; pensd allowed 1819. Ref 41690 S Md. Cop by State D A R.

JACKSON, JOHN, Mahoning co

Pvt. Ref Pa Arch Ser 3 V 23 p 317. Capt Nicholas Shinn's Co. B in Ireland; chldr: Joseph Jr mar Agnes; John; David b 1793; ? Samuel b 1800 Va. Came in 1803 fr Washington co Pa with sons Joseph & John; was trustee. Ref Hist Trumbull & Mahoning co V 2 p 176; Hist Mahoning co p 485 by Sanderson; Name on tax list 1826 John Joseph & David Coitsville. D Coitsville Mahoning co. Rept by Mahoning chpt D A R.

JACKSON, JOSEPH, Mahoning or Licking co

Pensd for service as pvt in Pa while residing in Licking co 8-24-1818. Servd fr Chester co Pa in Capt John Christies Co Col Johnson's Regt 1777. Dischgd Aug 1783 (at Phila Pa). D 1819 Newark O; bur in 6th St cem abandoned in 1877 at which time "Jackson" was only legible word on stone. Rept by Hetuck chpt. Verified by State D A R as S 41687 Penn; and B L Wt 550-100 Pens Dept. Also rept by M S Askue Youngstown adding he recd 100 A land in O before pensd 200 A shown in survey; given $8.00 a mo.

JACKSON, RICHARD, Jefferson co

Enl June 5 1777 Somerset co N J; as Sergt in N J Contl Line. Servd 6 yrs. Appld for pens 9-25-1820 in Washington co Pa at which time was 75 æ; had one mar dau no name stated; on June 23 1828 appld for transfer fr Pa to Jefferson co O. Ref S 41683 New Jersey Pens Dept Cop State D A R.

JACOBS, JOHN, Trumbull co

Enl 3-13-1776 Pa. State Regt under Capt Miles as pvt. Pensd 1-27-1819 residing in Poland twp Trumbull co O. In application of 1818 said æ 64; that he livd with brother-in-law. Ref S 41689 Penn-Pens Dept. Cop by State D A R.

JACOBS, WILLIAM, Morgan co

Enl Apr or May 1776 as pvt Md Milit. To Oct 1780 as Sergt. Was taken prisoner soon aft enl and held till Oct 1780. B June 19 1755 Frederick co Md. Chldr: Elizabeth; William; Van and Catherine. Movd to Frederick co Va; thence to Hampshire Va; thence to Morgan co O where pensd 5-28-1833. D abt June 3 1836. Ref S 2289 Md. Pens Dept. Cop by State D A R.

JAMES, JOHN, ? co

Srvd fr Preston in Lexington Alarm; Con in Rev pp 20, 617. Ancestor of Joseph Benson Foraker. Ref 2475 S A R. By Wm Pettit.

JAMES, THOMAS, Belmont co

No record found. See Thomas Iams, Belmont co

JAMES, WILLIAM CAPT, ? co

Listed in news clipping found in old scrap book no date by L A A "as Rev soldr who participated or interested in settlement of Marietta." Filed here for continued research. Rept by Marietta chpt.

JAMISON, FRANCIS, Ross co

Enl Aug 1775 in Westmoreland co Penn Contl. Servd one yr. In 1820 was æ 64; appl states had ten chldr: seven at home; eldest being æ 16 in 1820; pensd in Pa. appld for trnsfr 10-19-1822 in Ross co O. Cop by State D A R. Ref S 41686 Penn. Pens Dept. Pickaway Plains repts fr history "Francis Jamison a Revolutionary soldier d Mar 27 1823 in Ross co."

JAMISON (Jemison), WILLIAM, Ross co

Servd in Capt John Lowden's Co Pa Riflemen Col Wm Thompson's Battl. Also in Capt Marpole's Co. B 1746 Phila Pa. Parents: Robert Jamison of Ireland & Sarah McKee; both d in Phila 1802. Mar Susannah Lockhart 1771 dau of Jacob Lockhart Moreland twp. Chldr Charles 1772; William; John and Matthew 1785; George; Jacob 1786; Samuel 1795; Merrit 1780; Sarah 1773; Elizabeth 1778; Mary 1777. He d Ross co 1804; bur on farm Ross co but removed to Concord Presb church nr Frankfort O whr stone plainly marked. Came first to Bourbon co Ky; thence to Ross co 1796 with Nathaniel Massie. Ref 33. Rept N S D A R p 111. Rept by Washington C H D A R. Nathaniel Massie D A R. Ross co repts Will p 19 V A B C D Ross co Probate Court 1805; Mentions his Ky plantation; Executors: James Davis, Susannah Jamison & John McClain.

JANUARY, JAMES, Greene co

D A R Magazine Aug 19 29 page 505 and 485 lists him as private under Cols John Todd, Daniel Boone and Stephen Trigg at Battle of Blue Licks Ky. B near Lexington Ky. Spent later life in Greene County. A son Robert mar Mary Wadham. Soldr d 8-21-1824. Rept by Catherine Greene chpt. Further reference in Evans and Stivers Hist Adams County p 92. He owned one of the earliest taverns in the county. Rept by Meryl B. Markley, Vice Chairman.

JAQUA, GAMALIEL, Preble co

Enl 1781 Litchfield co Conn. Servd one yr. B 1-29-1764 in Litchfield co Conn. Mar Eleanor —— 9-23-1785; Eleven chldr: Roxina; Darius; Betsy; Judson; Almira; Jenny; Julia; Rachel; Clarissa; James; & Malinda. He d Apr 20-1835 Preble co O at New Paris Jefferson twp where he is bur in Spring Grove cem. (fr D A R Eaton) In 1785 he remvd to N Y State; thence to Pa Bradford co; thence to Preble co Jefferson twp. There in July 13 1833 he appld for pens. On Feb 22 1839 widow appld fr there; she again appld 9-1-1851 fr Wabash co Ind; on 4-23-1855 again fr Darke co O. She names grand chldr: Reuben Harrington; Gamaliel Jaqua; Mason Allen; & Charles Jaqua. Ref W 7888; B L Wt 26826 Conn. Cop by State D A R.

JAQUA, SIMON, Trumbull co

Sergt with Vermont Trps under Col Ethan Allen at the storming of Quebec and taking of Burgoyne at Saratoga. Mar 12-9-1784 to Ruth Hanchett Salisbury Conn. Chldr: Family incomplete one was Milton; and another son both of whom d in 1811; Charity; Drusilla; Mary; he d in Fallowfield twp Crawford co Pa 6-25-1825. Since he was long a resident of Johnston Trumbull co O and first Justice peace is recorded here. Rept by Mary Chesney chpt.

JEFFREY, JOHN, Wayne co

Ent Rev 1777 Cumberland co Pa; b 5-22-1756 England; came to America before æ 18. Resided Cumberland co for 6 or 7 yrs aft Rev. Then movd to Pittsburg; thence to Moreland co Pa; thence to Franklin co Pa; thence Ohio co Va; thence to Jefferson co O. Thence to Wayne co O; mar Demaries (Demerris) Jeffrey as rept by Wooster-Wayne D A R who says he d in Wayne co 1839; livd nr Orville and Dalton as witnesses & admstr are resident of that section. In Oct 2 1832 widow appld for pens fr Wayne co and in 1839 was resident Sugar Crk twp. Ref W 4708 Pa and S C sea service. Cop by State D A R.

JEMISON, DAVID, Muskingum co

Enl 1776 York co Pa Milit pvt; servd seven mo. Born 1-15-1759 Chester co Pa. Appld for pens Nov 1832 res Hopewell twp Muskingum co O. Ref S 2290 Penn. Cop by State D A R.

JENKS, JACOB, Ashtabula co

Enl 1776 fr Smithfield R I Col Morey's Regt. Pensd 1832; b Smithfield R I 1761; mar Martha Morey (1763-1824) in 1781. One dau was Martha. Soldr d 1842 Saybrooke O whr was a pensr in 1840 living with John Sherman. Ref V 121 No 120408 D A R Lin. Rept by Jane Dailey.

JENNINGS, ESBON, Medina co

Enl Nov 1779 Stratton Conn. Dischgd 1783 Highland N Y. Pvt Conn Contl. Appld for pens Genesee co N Y May 5 1818; again 1820 in Cayuga co N Y Scipio. Also Feb 2 1833 Medina co O & in census 1840 liv in Kinkley name spelled "Isbuel" born 1764; mentions "children" in appl. Ref 41695; B L Wt 2208-100 Conn. Cop by State D A R.

JOHNSON, ALEXANDER, Ross co

Exec Doc 37 yr 1852. Suspended pens. His service not admitted. Rept by Wm Pettit.

JOHNSON, BENJAMIN, Highland co

Located by Wah-wil-a-way D A R Hillsboro. Ref 15th Rept N S D A R p 9165. Rept by Nathan Perry chpt.

JOHNSON, CALEB, Ross co

Enl 1776 Essex co N J. Servd 12 mo Pvt; 5 mo Sergt. B 5-9-1749 Essex co N J; mar 4-12-1772; chldr Mae; Phoebe; Mary; Hannah; Susan; Sally; Haette Rachael;

Nancy; Caleb; & Harriet Baldwin. D 12-31-1836. In Sept 1776 the British entered his hometown Newark now Orange N J and ran him wife and family away from home and burned his furniture. In 1820 he movd to Ross co O where he was pensr in 1833; in 4-22-1835 appld for trnsfr to Madison co Ill. Grave not located. Ref W 4251 N J. Cop by State D A R.

JOHNSON, DAVID, Mahoning co

Pvt. Ref Md Arch V 18 p 429; b 1762; mar Margaret —— who d Jan 5 1835. He d 1852 Poland Mahoning co; bur in Presb Church cem. Ref Henry Baldwin S A R list. Rept by Mahoning D A R.

JOHNSON, JAMES, ? co

Pvt listed in rejected pens appl. Ref Doc 31 Jan 6 1831 as deserted the service. Rept by Blanche Rings.

JOHNSON, JAMES, Clermont co

Enl 1777 York co Pa Militia; Servd 1 yr 2 mo. B 1750; appld for pens Clermont co Aug 1832 resident Franklin twp. Pensd 8-29-1833. Ref S 16165 Penn. Cop by State D A R.

JOHNSON (or Johnston), JAMES, Warren co

Enl Lancaster co Pa 1776; Capt Brown Co Col Hedrick Regt. Servd 6 mo. Appld for pens in Warren co O Oct 3 1832; allowed 4-20-1833 there. Ref S 2666 Penn. Cop by State D A R.

JOHNSON, PHILEMON, Muskingum co

Pvt N H Contl. Enl Aug 1 1778; Dischgd Allentown Vt for 1st term; at Castleton for last term. Servd 21 mo. In 1818 was æ 56; appld for pens Muskingum co O May 5-1818 also 1832 residing in Rich Hill twp. Ref S 2667 Vt. Cop by State D A R.

JOHNSON, SILAS, Muskingum co

Enl Mar 20 1780; dischgd June 14 1783; pvt Va Contl. Servd 3 yrs. In 1829 was æ 59; mar Sarah —— æ 49; chldr: Silas 17; Tunis 14; Henry 11; Peter 6; fr appl 1820 in Muskingum co O. Ref S41705 Va. Cop by State D A R.

JOHNSON, THOMAS, Mahoning co

Pvt Pa. Many ref; Pa Arch. Pensr 1818 Trumbull co O. Old Book 1818; mar Ann ——; chldr: Jonathan; Jacob; Margaret mar —— Hunt; Ann mar —— Ladd; Rodney mar —— Owen; Mary mar —— Borton. D before 1848 Smith twp. Ref Will bk p 109 Columbiana co probated 1848; Deed bk R p 242 Thos & Ann Johnson to Isaac Votaw 1830; Deed bk S p 292 Thos & Ann Johnson to Jona Johnson 1832. Rept by Mahoning D A R.

JOHNSON, THOMAS, ? co

Appl for pens Washington co July 25 1820 in Com Pleas Court Marietta O. Stated property value at $30.00. Ref V 3-420. Rept by Helen Sloane.

JOHNSON, WILLIAM, Cuyahoga co

Enl Worcester co Mass. Servd 3 yrs. B 1758; In appl 1834 states "wife Abigail dead; family scattered; resides with a dau & her husband." A dau Olive Thorp made appl for pens. Her affidavit says he d Spt 2 1851. He appld for pens in Delaware co N Y May 30 1818. Also on June 26 1834 Cuyahoga co. (Here is copied N Y not Ohio. There is a Cayuga co in N Y). S A R lists him in Cuyahoga co O 8-20-1832. Ref S 10295 Contl Mass. Cop by State D A R.

JOHNSON (or Johnston), WILLIAM, Huron co

Enl Apr 1775 in Conn Line residing in Middletown Conn where he was b 1754; servd 17 mo 6 da; appld for pens in Huron co O Fitchville twp 3-24-1838. Ref S 8761 Conn; & 18th Rept N S D A R p 217. Cop by State D A R. See Johnston, William p 204 Vol 1 Roster Rev Soldiers in O and Johnston, William, Richland co (this Vol).

JOHNSON, WILLIAM, Fairfield co

Sergt Md Contl. Servd 3 yr. Enl Fredericktown Md 1778; appld pens Fairfield co O 5-15-1818; farmer; was æ 70 in 1818. Chldr: "had 13; 8 now living; 2 sons live with him æ 19 & 17; and a dau æ 25 who has a child." (appl) Ref S 41704 Md; & p 406 Wiseman's Pioneer People Fairfield co. Name listed. Cop by State D A R.

JOHNSTON, JACOB, Columbiana co

Pvt N Y and N J milit. Servd 8 mo. Enl in Rockland co N Y 1775-6; again in N J Movd to Columbiana co O 1816 or 17; pensr there 1-21-1833. Ref S 2660 N J & N Y; Census 1840. Cop by State D A R; also Rept by Mahoning chpt.

JOHNSTON, JAMES, Mahoning co

Conn Men in Rev. Many refs; d Canfield O 1-28-1820. One of proprietors of Canfield O; a bro of Archibald Johnston who d 1805; Ref Mahoning Despatch 4-9-1897; Hist of Canfield by Truesdale; & S A R List of Henry Baldwin. Rept by Mahoning D A R.

JOHNSTON, JOHN, Mahoning co

Pvt Pa. Ref Ser 3 V 23 Many pps Pa Arch. Mar Jane Caldwell of Beaver Pa. Chldr: Mary mar Elmer Gilmer; John b 1773 mar Caroline ———; Margaret mar Samuel Moore; David mar Mary Ann; Samuel mar Elizabeth; Elizabeth mar Alex Moore; Thomas mar Martha; Francis; William. He d abt 1831 Coitsville twp. Came with chld fr Mercer co Pa. Ref V 2 p 167 Hist Trumbull & Mahoning co; Will Bk 6 p 211 Trumbull co Recds probated 1831; Deed bk K p 538 Transcd Mahoning co Johnston John Heirs 1843; on Tax list 1826 John Johnston. Rept by Mahoning D A R.

JOHNSTON, SAMUEL, Ashtabula co

Pvt and Sergt Mass Contl under Capt White Col Smith Regt for 10 mo 12 da fr Lancaster Mass. Servd various enl. Resided in Geneva twp Ashtabula co Oct 20 1832 æ 79; Pensr there 7-24-1833. Ref S 18475 Mass. Cop by Jane Dailey.

JOHNSTON, SIMON, Ross co

Findley and Putnams Hist p 42 listed as Rev soldr. Rept by O S Librarian Mrs Rathburn.

JOHNSTON, WILLIAM, Richland or Huron co

Enl Penn York co Oct 1776; servd Pa Line 2 yrs. 1752 Lancaster co Pa. Mar Sidney Larrimer Apr 16 1776; chldr: Sidney; Mary; Martha; Margaret; John; Agness; Andrew; and Ester. (Fr Widow's appl). D Apr 27 1838 (stated on widow's appl). Aft Rev he resided in Allegheny co Pa; then Fayette co Pa; then Westmoreland co Pa. "For last yr has resided in Richland co O (appl). On 12-4-1833 appld for pens residing in Plymouth twp Richland co O. On 1-31-1834 pensd there. His widow appld fr Huron co O July 29 1839. (This fact leads the State Chairman to believe this is the William Johnston Huron co p 204 Vol 1 Ohio Roster Rev Soldiers). No place of bur was given by widow. Ref W 4250 Penn. Cop by Ohio D A R. From C M Garber Butler O Sec S A R at Mansfield comes data: "William Johnson bur Terris cem Worthington twp Richland co O; d Sept 20 1849 æ 90 yrs." (There is a difference in dates).

JONES, ASA, Cuyahoga co

Enl 4-1-1777 at Plainfield Conn Sergt Conn Contl. First appld for pens in Cuyahoga co O 5-5-1818 stating was æ 63; wife was dead; mentions son "William" with whom he resided; and two daus names not given. Listed as pensr 6-16-1819 Cuyahoga co. Ref S 13558 Conn. Cop by Ohio D A R. Wm Pettit repts B 1755; d 1834; mar Lucy Park. Ref 34578 S A R.

JONES, CROCKER, Delaware co

Enl in Wyoming Valley Pa winter 1777; pensr 3-24-1819 Plymouth Pa for service of 3 yrs. Was æ 70 in 1818; appld in Luzerne co Pa in 4-22-1818 for pens; & on 5-5-1819 for transfer to Delaware co O. D 12-27-1839; bur Berkshire cem Delaware co. Ref S 41702 Conn. Cop by Ohio D A R.

JONES, GEORGE, Vigo co Ind

Supposed to have d somewhere in O or N Y. The record states he was going to N Y in Dec 1834 and is thot to have d whl passing thro O. Was never seen or heard of again in Ind.

JONES, HENRY, Champaign co

N J Contl Line; b 1734 Wales; d aft 1901; mar Hope Lippincott Wallace 1763; ref 54960 S A R Rept. by Wm Pettit.

JONES, JOHN, Clinton co

Pvt Pa Milit under Capt Pearce; b 1756 N J. mar Lina (or Linna); one son was Samuel; d 183— Clinton co O. Ref 122526 V 123 D A R Lineage. Cop by Jane Dailey.

JONES, RICHARD, Gallia co

Fifer under Capt Watson Col S B Well Conn Line. Servd 3 yr June 1777 to June 1780. B May 15 1767; mar Elizabeth Clark June 29 1806; had five chldr. Soldr d July 23 1852 Floyd co Ind. he appld for pens in Gallia co 3-20-1830; merchant; appld for trnsfr to Floyd co Ind 2-23-1836. Dischrgd at Springfield N J. His widow appld for pens in Floyd co Ind Apr 9 1853. Ref W 765; B L Wt 5439-160-55; Conn Contl. Cop by Ohio D A R.

JONES, RICHARD, ? Cuyahoga co

Servd as pvt under Capt Van Lawrence Gross Col Marimis Willett N Y Levies. B 1755 Poughkeepsie N Y. Mar Hester Van Bibber 1808; a son named Alexander P mar Irene A Gilbert; d 1919 Euclid O. Ref V 106 D A R. Lin No 105 938. Cop by Jane Dailey.

JONES, SAMUEL, Brown co

Enl Winchester Va 1776 as pvt Va Line; servd 4 yrs. Pensd 9-6-1819 in Brown co O. Was 56 in 1818 (July); mar Elizabeth (æ 64 in 1821). Chldr: Catherine 17; Lewis 15; Elizabeth 13; Matilda 11; Westley 9; Stephen 7; (at time of appl). Ref S 41706 Va B L Wt 1848-100. Cop by Ohio D A R.

JONES, SOLOMON, ? co

Ensign: listed in rejected pens appl. Ref Doc No 31 Jan 6 1831 as not being in indigent circumstances accd to Act of May 1830. Rept by Blanche Rings.

JONES, THOMAS, Mahoning co

Pvt Pa. Ref many in Pa Archives; b 1760; Mar Sarah Wilson (1775-1865); 15 chldr: Thomas mar Rachel Webb; Mary mar Asher Squire; Margaret mar James Bruce; James mar Huldah Tanner; Joseph mar Ann ——; John mar 1st Nancy Calhoon; 2nd Desire Phelps; Samuel mar Betsey; Rosanna mar Columbia Lancaster; Elijah mar

Phebe Manchester; Matthew mar Eliza. He d before May 2 1852 Ellsworth twp. Came to Mahoning co 1804; was second family in twp. Ref Hist Trumbull & Mahoning co V 2 pp 99 & 98; Hist Mahoning co p 199 & 999 Sanderson. Also Republican Sentinel 5-2-1852 states d as above noted. Est Bk 1 p 372 Ellsworth twp. Rept by Mahoning D A R.

JONES, THOMAS, Belmont co

Pvt in Capt Nathan Adam's Co Del Regt Contl Trps under Col John Hazlett in barracks at Dover Apr 12 1776. The same being in Capt Manlove's Co part of the Flying Camp under Col Samuel Patterson; enl Oct 1 1776; also pvt Capt Thomas Watson's Co fr Dec 17 to Dec 27 1776. B Wales 1-9-1750; mar Rebecca Smith. Chldr: William b 9-17-1788; Samuel b Feb 7 1791; Thomas b July 1794; James b June 4 1796; Rebecca b Sept 18 1806; Benjamin b Jan 31 1799; Mary or Polly b Apr 7 1802. He d at Barnesville Belmont co O Aug 1854 where he is bur. At early age left an orphan; a few yrs aft mar he and family went to Pa; thence to Ohio. Ref State Achivist Delaware; Mrs J H Smith No 196492 D A R former member of Nathan Perry D A R who rept this data thro Mrs T R Oehlke.

JUDD, ARUMAH, Ashtabula co

Enl in Mass Regt under Capt John Chadwick May 1778. Pensd 12-28-1818 Saratoga co N Y. Later trnsfrd to Ashtabula co O. Servd 9 mo. B 12-16-1747. Mar Sarah ——— 11-24-1773; chldr: Sallah b 1774; Mercy 1776; Asa 1782; Ozias ? 1784; Lois 1786; Arumah 1788; Rebekah 1791; one baby b 1794 the last. Soldr d 7-11-1836. Ref W 4252 Mass. Cop by Ohio D A R.

JUDD, REUBEN, Portage co

Enl 1779 Mass Line; servd 9 mo. Mar 11-27-1791; widow d June 1839 leaving sev small chldr; one dau Sophia æ 14; 1 son Solomon 5; now living with him (appl 1820). He d Oct 1834 Portage co O where his pens had been trnsfrd Sept 4 1832; in 1820 was liv in Hampden co Mass. Ref S 41712 Mass. Cop by Ohio D A R.

JUDY, JOHN, Pickaway co ?

Pvt Pa State Trps. In 1777 was 2 mo in Capt Jacob Shartell Co Col Bolser Gheer's Regt. In 1778 2 mo Capt Menhacker's Co in Col Bolser Gheer's Regt; in 1780 2 mo in Col Michael Kindemuth's Co; in 1781 2 mo Capt Henry Knause Co same Col B Feb 2-1759 Montgomery co Pa; at æ 4 movd to Berks co Pa. One child was called Peter; allowed a pens Sept 18-1832 while living in Pickaway co O nr Tarlton in Salt Creek twp whr had livd 26 yrs. Came 1805 fr Berks co Pa. Ref S 4462 Penn. Rept by Pickaway Plains D A R.

JUDY, JOHN, Union co

Srvd in Rev as soldr in Artillery Corps. Was b Basle Switzerland 1760 coming to America at the æ of 10 w his father's family Martin Judy and settled on South Branch of the Potomac. In 1782 movd to Flemingsburg Ky whr his son John Judy Jr was b in a block house. In 1793 movd to Greene co O and in 1800 to New Harmony twp Clark co O nr Plattsburg. In 1831 movd to Union co O hr he d at æ 81 yrs. He mar Phoebe Lamaster 1783; chldr: Temperance b 1789 mar Michael Wilson; John 1791 mar (1) Lydia Hull 1822 (2) Anna Hull 1826; Benjamin 1793 Elizabeth Osburn 1815; Martin; Elanor mar Valentine Wilson; Nancy mar Nicholas McCally: Jesse mar a Johnson; Frances mar Aquilla Turner; Joshua mar Irvin; Richard mar Truett; Phoebe mar (1) Sargent (2) Peter Smith; Samuel mar Inskip. Ref No 114722 D A R. Rept by Indiana Histor Commission.

JULIAN (Julin), ISAAC, Miami co

Enl 1778 Pvt Pa Milit. Servd 7 mo; enl summer 1779. B 1741 Frederick co Md. Was æ 91 in 1832; livd in Greene co Pa during Rev and to 1812 when remvd to Ohio Miami co Sept 1832. Pensd there. Ref S 46054 Penn. Cop by Ohio D A R.

JULICK, JULIAN, Butler co

Bur at Jacksonburg Wayne twp Butler co. Ref 4th Rept N S D A R p 295. Cop by Nathan Perry chpt.

JUSTICE, ROBERT, Franklin co

Pvt Pa Contl. Pensd 5-13-1819 in Franklin co æ 68. From Ohio State Journal issue 12-11-1835 is taken following: Obituary "Soldier in Revolution aged 86. D in Columbus O Nov 30 1835." Rept by Columbus D A R. (Mrs J J Rings).

KARAKIN, JOHN, Knox co

Name found listed as Harakin, John which is incorrect. Pvt Pa Contl 7 mos. Pens 5-3-1833 Knox co. Ae 74 Feb 1760 Northampton co Pa.

KARMMERER, PHILIP, Fairfield co

Pvt Capt Thos Robinsons co Lancaster Co Pa Milit. B 1759 Lancaster co Pa. Mar Rose Ann Hyle (1761-1818) in 1787; Had son Samuel. Soldr d Fairfield co O 1827. Ref No. 123985 D A R Lin. Rept by Jane Dailey.

KARR, ANDREW, Warren co

B 1744;d 1828. Servd Pa. Came Warren co 1806. Elder Dicks Creek Pres Church frm 1816 to death. Grave mkd by Richard Montgomery chpt S A R of Dayton by Wm M Pettit.

KECK, MICHAEL, Mahoning co.

Pvt 8th Class 7th Co Capt Geo Smiths 6th Bn Northampton. Mar Catherine. Chldr: Daniel; Michael. Soldr d 1808 in Springfield twp to whch he came 1806. Grfather came from Germany 1732. Ref Hist Columbiana co p 793 McCord. Will Bk I p 104 Columbiana co Records. Deed Bk O p 48. Rept by Mahoning chpt.

KEHR, DAVID, Madison co

Enl 1780 Apr as Indian Spy. Svd 2 yrs. B July 25 1763 near Phil Pa; wf d prior to 1839; chldr: Hannah Sutherland; Jane Watson. Will probated 1812 case 3923 Madison Co. Pensd Mad co Oct 8 1833; transfd Pike Co Ill Feb 1839. Ref Pa S 32359. Lvd Northumberland co Pa 10 yrs aft war; thence Bourbon co Ky 5 yrs; then to Ross Co 20 yrs; thence Madison. Rept by State D A R.

KELLOGG, JASON, Ross co

Wounded siege Boston and Harlam Hgts, Re-enl and svd close War. B 1754 Sheffield Mass. Mar Miriam Dewey 1780; soldr d Sept 5 1821 Chillicothe while visiting son. Lvd Hampton N Y. Ref Vol 112 D A R Lin Bk p 101. Cal S A R Bull for 1901 No. 3430 S A R. Cop by Jane Dailey.

KELLY, JOHN, Washington co

Svd wth Col Washington wounded at Cowpens; mar Elizabeth Askins; chldr: John; William mar Jane Brandon. Soldr d Wash co O. Lvd Brandonville Va (now W Va); came to Wash co 1800. Ref D A R Lin Bks. Rept by Mississinewa chpt Portland Ind.

KELLEY, NATHANIEL, Trumbull co

Enl 1779 in Capt Stones Co at New Hampton Stratford Co N H. Re-enl 1781 Capt Smiths Co. B 1765 or 6 in Brentwood N H. D Sept 17 1842 probably in Lordstown. Came to Edinburgh twp Portage co fr New Hampton; Was 75 in 1840 Cens and "head of his family." Appl Pens Portage co Aug 8 1832. Ref N H S 4472. Rept by Jane Dailey and Mary Chesney chpt.

KELLY, WILLIAM, Hamilton co

Enl Franklin Co Pa as pvt Va State Trps. Srvd 1 yr 6 mos; b 1758 Sussex Co N J; appl Pens Hamilton Co Sept 3 1832; Came to Ohio 1800. Ref S 2689. Rept by State D A R.

KELSEY, THOMAS, Miami co

Enl pvt Ulster Co N Y Milit May 1776. Servd 14 mos. B 1754. Appl pens Montgomery co 1832 lvg with son. Resided Miami co 1833. Ref N Y S 2687. Rept by State D A R.

KEMP, JOHN, Licking co

Exec Doc 37 of 1852. Refused a pens as servd less than 6 mo. Rept by Wm Pettit.

KENNARD, JOHN, Perry co

Enl pvt 1775 Ringwood twp N J; svd 6 yrs; dschg in hospital Buckingham Pa. B 1753; mar Sarah. Soldr d July 14 1823. Shoemaker. Appl pens Perry co Apr 25 1818. Ref Pens list 1835-111-0-82; S 41723 N J. Rept by State D A R.

KENNEDY, ANDREW, Knox co

Enl spring 1777 in Huntington twp York Co Pa. Srvd 6 yrs. B 1758. Appl pens Knox Co July 25 1818. Ref Penn S 41713 and Pa Arch. Ser 2 Vol 10 p 633. Rept by Mrs. R Winnagle and State D A R.

KENNEY, STEPHEN, Warren co

Enl Preston Conn Feb 1778; srvd till 1781 under Capts Kurney, Whitney, Latham and Ward. B Mar 6 1762 Stonington Conn; d at sons home July 19 1848. Appl pens frm Clear Creek twp Warren Co Oct 3 1832. Bur near place of death. Rept by Mary Fox Miller.

KENT, APOLLUS, Ashtabula co

Conn Service. D Sept 4 1838 æ 76. Bur Amboy Conneaut twp. Ref Conn Men in Rev p 552. Rept by Mary Redmond chpt.

KENT, ISAAC, Perry co

Enl pvt 1781 in Md Contl; servd 9 mos. Dschgd Annapolis. B 1759; wf d Dec 12 1834. One chld lvg Susannah who res Morgan co. Soldr d Feb 11 1824 Perry co. Appl pens Muskingum co May 1 1818. Ref Pens 1835-111-0-82. S 41725 Md. Rept by State D A R.

KENT, JOHN, Muskingum co

B 1748. Pens Wayne twp Musk Co 1842 at æ 92. Not thot to be same as Vol 1 p 210. Cop by State D A R.

KENT, SAMUEL, Meigs co

Pvt Conn Contl and Milit. B 1757 at Suffield Hardford co Conn; mar Mary Noble in Rupert Va 1783. Chldr: Bershaber; Samuel; Mary; Anna; Amasa; Elisha; Filinda; Harriett; Sina. Went from Suffield to Bennington co N Y; in 1817 to Salem twp Meigs co. Appl pens there; also in Gallia co 1831. Ref Filing Env W 5306 Conn. Rept by State D A R.

KENTON, SIMON, Logan and Champaign cos

Servd as Scout Pvt and Gen in Va Line. B Fauquier Co Va 1755 son of Mark Kenton of Ireland. Mar 1st Martha Dowden May 14 1787; 2nd Elizabeth Jarbo. Chldr:

Matilda; Mary; William; Elizabeth; Ruth Jane. 1st wf had 2 sons and 2 dau; 2nd wf had 1 son 5 dau. Soldr d Apr 29 1836 in Logan co at spot where he had once escaped frm Indians. Body removed to Urbana and monument erected. Scout in Dunmores Army 1774 Ohio Exped. Scout Clarks Exped 1778 and in Miami exped of 1780. Srvd with Wayne after Rev. Pens late in life special act Congress. Ref Randalls and Ryans Hist Ohio. Ohio Arch and Hist Soc; Vol 105 No. 104304 D A R Lin and Vols 13-17-25-27-67-71 D A R Lin. Rept by Nathan Perry chpt Martha P Mills Rensslear Ind Jacobus Westervelt chpt.

KEPHART, MARTIN, Stark co

Enl pvt Frederickstown Md 1775; svd 3 yrs; B 1758; wf b 1758; Had 2 daus. Soldr d July 5 1832. Cooper. Pensd in Stark co June 7 1819. Ref Md S 41727. Rept by State D A R.

KEPNER, BENJAMIN, Pickaway co

Pvt in Capt Daniel McClellans Co 7th Bn Cumberland Co Pa Milit. B Berks co Pa Dec 1765; mar Elizabeth Huebsche in 1790; chldr: Mary Elizabeth b 1790; Jacob; Catherine; Benjamin; Mary; Andrew; Sarah; Barnhart (or Barnhard). Soldr d May 30 1818 Salt Crk twp; bur Tarlton south side nr tree. Inscpt on stone "Kepner b 1765 d 1818 æ 52" Came Salt Crk twp 1802 frm Berks Co Pa. Ref Family Bible. Deed record of Admstr Pa State Lib Williams Hist Franklin and Pickaway cos. Arthur H Hopkins Rensslear Ind. Rept by Pickaway Plains chpt.

KERNER, PHILLIP, Ross co

Rev Pensr 1840 æ 75 Colerain twp. Rept by State D A R.

KERNS, GEORGE, Mahoning co

Frontier Ranger; b Westmoreland co Pa; mar Julia ——; chldr: Julian; Elizabeth; Margaret; George. Soldr d 1805 Springfield twp. Father of soldr from Holland to Westmoreland co. Ref Pa Arc. Ser 3 Vol 23 p 302; Hist Fayette co p 753; Will Bk I p 156; Columbiana co Records; Deed Bk I p 47, Geo Kerns heirs Apr 1 1810. Rept by Mahoning chpt.

KERR, JOHN, ? co

Pvt refused pens as sevd in Regt not on Contl Estab. Doc 31 Ohio St Lib. Cop by Blanche Rings Columbus. Not thot to be same as Vol 1 p 211.

KERR, JOSEPH, Jefferson co

Enl 1776 8th Pa Regt Contl Line; Name on Rolls York Co Milit 1782. Born Edinburgh Scotland Aug 9 1760; mar Jean Chambers, Bingham Aug 26 1790; chldr; John Smyth; Robt Bingham; Nancy Smyth (mar Jos Kennedy); Mary Moore; Leander; David. Soldr d July 14 1848 Kings Creek Va Brook co; bur Toronto cem Toronto O lot No. 10; gr mrkd by Michael Hyers chpt; inscpt on stone "1760-1848." Ref Pa Arc Vol 3 p 316 5th ser. Also Vol 2 6th Ser p 659. Rept by Michael Myers chpt.

KESLING, PETER, Warren co

Lstd pg 278 "Va Milit in Rev" as lvg Warren Co æ 77. Cop by Jane Dailey.

KESLER, JACOB, Preble co

Enl pvt York Co Pa 1775 or 6; Srvd 10 mos; b July 1747 Berks Co Pa; had wf and chld. d 1837 near Lafayette Ind. May be bur Indiana. Appl pens Preble co Harrison twp Sept 21 1822. Dischgd May 17 (yr not stated). Settled on farm s of Lewisburg 1811. Ref Preble co Hist Contact with descndts. Pens S 2688 N C. Rept by Commodore Preble chpt.

KEY (Kee), STEWART, Trumbull co

Enl pvt Apr 1775 Hampshire Co Mass State Trps. At Bunker Hill. Svd 9 mos. B 1753 Hillsborough Conn; mar Sarah Paddock at Ware Mass Mar 30 1775. Chldr: Ebenezer; Ephriam; Sarah wf of John Kakefield; Rhoda wf of John Harrington; Joanna wf of William Alger; Lucinda and Ira. Soldr d May 31 1833 Trumbull co Green twp; bur old cem south of Kenilworth. Wf d 1844. Soldr appl pens Aug 1832. Widow appl pens July 25 1842. Ref Mass 7956. Rept by Mary Chesney chpt.

KEYES, DANIEL, Medina co

Enl Sgt Mass Contl Roxbury Mass Apr 20 1775. Srvd 6 yrs; b 1754. Appl pens Medina co June 16 1818. Resd Richfield twp. Farmer. Ref Mass S 41720. Rept by State D A R.

KIGER (Kyger), GEORGE, Fairfield co

Sold in Pa or Va Line Contr supplies to Rev Army. B Pa 1741; mar Margaret or Catherine Beeler. Soldr d Lancaster O Dec 12 1835. Head family 1790. Cen Shenandoah Co Va. Ref Pa Arc 3 Ser Vol 2 p 234 and Fairfield and Perry Co Hist p 180. Also No. 249 S A R of Cal Vol 7. Copied by Jane Dailey.

KIMBALL, ANDREW, Meigs co

Pvt N H Contl. B 1751. Blacksmith. Pensd Meigs co. Sept 22 1819. Ref S 41728. Rept by State D A R.

KINDER, GEORGE, Warren co

B Pa. Early settler Warren co. Emigrated 1789. Ref Pa Arch. 5th Ser Vol 6 p 184 195. Rept by W M Pettit Dayton S A R.

KING, CHARLES, Muskingum co

Enl Feb 1775 Cambridge Mass. Sgt and Maj Va Contl. Srvd 2 yrs from 1777. Dschgd Phil Pa Dec 13 1779. B 1756; wf Elizabeth. Chldr: Elizabeth; Caleb; Catherine; appl pens Brooke co Va Sept 14 1819. Appl pens Muskingum co O Nov 24 1820. Ref Mass Va S 2700. Rept by State D A R.

KING, GEORGE, Richland co. Enl May 1780 Fauquier co Va. Svd 3 yrs. Dischd Salisbury N C 1783. B 1761; mar Mary 1797. Soldr d Dec 5 1838. Appl pens Richland co Oct 21 1828. Wid appl pens Ashland O Vermillion twp Apr 22 1850. Ref Va W 2736. Will rec Richld Co Court No. 123. Rept by State D A R.

KING, GERARD (Gerrard), Warren co

Enl Pvt Capt Peytons Co Va Milit. Svd 6 mos. B July 1759 Charles co Md. Mar Keziah Thurston 1794 at Martinsburg Va. One chld known, John. Soldr d June 7 1840; bur Friends Cem Waynesville Warren co O. Pens 1832-1834; pens for 20 mos issued 1837; Pensr stated 1836 had been Ohio 40 yrs mostly sycamore twp Hamilton co; thence to Fayette to Warren. Ref W 7984. Wid pens Feb 20 1848. Rept by State D A R.

KING, JOHN G, Fairfield co

Enl Lancaster Pa May 1779 Pa Contl; svd 4 yrs; b 1761; mar Jane McAffee (d 1847). Chldr: David b 1809; Nancy Jane b 1814; Rachel Turner widow and Peter. Soldr d Oct 28 1830. Appl pens Fairfield Co 1818. Ref Wisemans Pioneer People Fairfield co p 406. Pa R 5953. Rept by Jane Dailey and State D A R.

KING, WILLIAM, Montgomery co

5th Ser Pa Arch Vol 3 p 53. Fifth Pa Con Line Nov 20 1779 Col Johnson. 1782 Vol 5 p 663 Capt John Harris Chester co milit. Vol 7 p 105 srvd as member of court martial in Lancaster co. Numerous other services. Early settler of county. Burial place not identified. Rept by Wm Pettit.

KINGSBURY, JOSEPH, Lorain co

Vol Aug 1779 Sandisfield Mass 5 wks pvt Capt Collars Mass Co. Enl May 1780 pvt Capt Noah Allens Co Col Smiths Mass Regt. Dschgd 1781. Guard over Maj Andre when latter executed. Enl 1783 Col Sprouts Mass Regt; dischg Dec 23 1873. B 1760 Endfield Conn.Remvd Brighton Lorain co 1820. Appl pens Aug 1832. Soldr still lvg 1850. Ref Pa and Mass S 2707 and Gen Acct Off Washington D C. Rept by Nathan Perry chpt by Mrs T R Oehlke.

KINGSBURY, LEMUEL, Huron co

B 1759; d Dec 20 1844; bur Wakeman cem. Listed as Rev soldr and pensioner by H G Mains in 1859. His granddau Mrs M V Armstrong livd at Wakeman at that time. Ref Pioneer Women of Western Reserve p 561; Firelands Pioneers O S Vol 2 No. 2p 28. Rept by Marjorie Cherry Sandusky.

KINNAN, EDWARD, Clermont co

Exec Doc of 1852. Refused a pens as servd less than 6 mo. Rept by Wm Pettit.

KINNEY, JOHN, ? co

Pvt lstd rejected pensions appl ref Doc 1 Jan 1 1831 as deserted from service. Not same as Vol 1 p 215. Rept by Blanche Rings.

KINNISON, WILLIAM, Belmont co

B 1757 Cens 1840 lvg Richland twp æ 83. Not found in Rev Pens Claims. Rept by Jane Dailey.

KINNY, JOHN, Knox co.

Enl pvt Greene co Pa 1778. Indian spy and sct. Srvd 3 yrs. B 1755 pensd Oct 21 1833. Ref Pen Roll 1835:0:137; Pens S 16180. Rept by State D A R.

KIRK, JOHN, ? co

Pvt refsd pens as srvd in Regt not on Contl Etabl. Ref Doc 31 Jan 6 1831 Ohio State Lib. Rept by Blanche Rings Columbus O.

KIRKPATRICK, JOHN ROBERT, Knox co. Pvt pens 1789; bur Martinsburg Knox co O. Ref Md pens Rolls of Invalids p 21. Rept by Clara Mark Westerville O and Gertrude Moore.

KIRKWOOD (Kirckwood), **DAVID,** Champaign co

Enl 1776 Hagerstown Md. Resd at Pittsburg Pa at time had gone to Hagstn to get salt when he volunteered. Srvd 2 yrs. B Ireland 1740; mar Margaret (may have been 2nd wf) May 18 1794. Had 11 chldrn John eldest æ 65 in 1851. Soldr d June 25 1847; bur Muddy Run Cem Union twp. Inscpt on stone states d at age 100 yrs. Came to this country frm Ireland 1772. Aftr Rev lvd Pittsburg 20 yrs Ky; 1 yr Whythe Co Va; thence to Champ co. Appl pens Oct 10 1832. Ref Md W 29916½. Rept by Jane Dailey.

KITCHELL, SAMUEL, Hamilton co

Servd sevrl yrs pvt. At battle Brandywine under Lafayette. B 1755 in Pa; descd of Robt Kitchell fr New England. Soldr d 1839 near Columbia on frm; bur Armstrong Chapel Indian Hill. No marker. Bought lot in Hamilton co 1789. In 1792 was a subscriber of Fst Pres Church. Owned farm in Sycamore twp. Ref Compilation of Gen

Samuel Cary in 1898 S A R Yr book. Kitchells name in real estate court records. Rept by Cincinnati chpt by Mrs Whallon.

KITLEY (Kitler), JOHN, Hamilton co

Enl Jan 1780 in Mass. Srvd 3 yrs as musician; b 1763. Appl pens Hamilton co Sept 20 1826. Appl Pike co Ill. June 15 1840 made declaration Rush Co Ind May 1846 for bounty land. Had wf and dau Mary Marsh æ 16 in 1826. Ref S 35510 B L Wt 2410-100. Rept by State D A R.

KLINE, JACOB, Knox co

Enl Sussex Co N J as pvt Apr 1776. Srvd 13 mos. B 1755 N J. Aft Rev lvd N J and Pa; then to Knox co. Pensd 1833 at æ 78 O pens Roll 1835:111:0:137. N J S 4479: Rept by State D A R.

KNAPP, EDWARD, Delaware co

Enl pvt Boston Mass 1781; srvd 2 yrs; b Sept 23 1763. Son of Daniel Knapp; mar Esther Skell Nov 25 1790. Chldr: Hannah b 1792; Betsy b 1795; Daniel b 1797; Edward b 1800; Sythene b 1802; Jerusha; Charles and Tizzy. Soldr d Mar 23 1821 Delaware co. Appl pens Apr 30 1818. Ref Mass W 24979. Rept by State D A R.

KNAPP, JOHN, Pickaway co

Enl Spring 1777 Va Contl Fifer; srvd 6 mos. b 1762; bur Huron O. Grave located Sandusky chpt. Resd Pickaway co Sept 28 1819. Dischgd Pittsburg 1783. Ref Rept 18 N S D A R p 220 Va S 41735. Rept by Nathan Perry chpt.

KNAPP, JOSHUA, Stark co

Enl Dec 1778 or 79 Northumberland co Pa Robinsons Rangers. Srvd 2 yrs. Appl pens 1830 in Columbiana co. Appl Stark Co 1833. Granted July 16 1830. B Oct 15 1756. Brother Samuel Knapp Tompkins co N Y. Ref Penn S 8802. Pa Arc Ser 3 Vol 23 p 195. Dockt Bk 5 p 335 Columbus O. Rept by Mrs Wilma Molsberry Youngstown and State D A R.

KNAPP, OBEDIAH, Delaware co

Ref Old N W Qurtly Vol 9 p 258. Rept by Mrs R Winnagle Warren O.

KNAPP, SAMUEL, Crawford co

Enl June 30 1775 N Y St Trps Rock Island Co N Y; svd 6 mos. B 1759 Orange co N Y. Soldr d July 22 1846 æ 87; bur Sycamore cem. Appl Pens Crawford co 1833; lvg same co 1840. Reared Watertown N Y. Service could not be proven tho numerous aff one frm bro David in Mayfield N Y and other statements but pens denied. Undbtly a Rev Soldr. Ref Col William Crawford chpt Jeanette Knapp Griswold Old Lyme Conn Martha Pitkin chpt.

KNIGHT, ELIJAH, Gallia co

Pvt Md Contl. B 1758; wf and 3 chld lvg 1820. Appl pens Gallia Co 1818. Appl Pickaway co 1818. Pensd 1819. Ref Conn S 41732. Rept by State D A R.

KNIGHT, JACOB, Belmont co

Enl Frederick co Md July 1776 or 77 in Capt Benj Prices co. B 1753. Pensd Belmont co Nov 27 1819. Ref Md S 41733. Rept by State D A R.

KNOTT, IGNATIUS, Clermont co

Enl 1776 Hagerstown Md as pvt Md Contl. Srvd 2 yrs. Appl pens Clermont co 1832. Ref Md S 4481. Rept by State D A R.

KNOWLES, CHARLES, ? co

Listed in old scrap-book as Rev soldr participating in settlement of Marietta. Doubtless bur Washington co Cem. Never paid for Indian war services. Cont research suggested. Rept by Marietta chpt.

KNOWLTON, ROBERT, Meigs co

Pvt Mass Contls. B 1748. Appl pens Athens co June 1811. Movd to Meigs co whr appl July 1820. Appl states soldr has no family to care for him. Reported by Return Jonathan Meigs by B Chase.

KNOX, WILLIAM, Butler co

Lvd Liberty twp with Robert S Knox. Cens 1840 at whch time soldr æ 70. Rept by Jane Dailey.

KOON, PHILIP, Washington co

Exec Doc of 1852. Refused a pens as servd only 3 mos. Rept by Wm Pettit.

KOWNS, CHRISTIAN, Hancock co

9th Va Contl Line. Was b 1759 Rockingham co Va; d 1837; mar Anna Lamp. Ref 50894 S A R. Rept by Wm Pettit.

KRICKBAUM, JOHN WILLIAM, Stark co

In Casper Stoevers Lancaster co Pa Milit. Was b 1754 Berks co Pa; d 1818; mar Catherine Garman 1782. Ref 44948 S A R. Rept by Wm Pettit.

KRONINGER (also Groninger, Croninger), JOSEPH, Stark co

Enl 1776 Northumberland co Pa as pvt. Srvd 2 yrs. b 1755; mar Elizabeth "about time of Treaty of Peace" Chldr: Benjamin; Jacob; Henry; Katherine Minnis. Appl pens Wayne co Oct 18 1821. Soldr d May 15 1841. Stark co O, æ 92. Pensd 1833. Widow appl Stark co Sept 8 1842. Ref Pa R 2499. Rept by State D A R.

KUDER, ELIAS, Pickaway co

Capt 1781 under Col John Keller in Pa Milit fr Bucks co Pa. Rept by Margaret Rider, Tontogany O.

KYLE, THOMAS, Butler co

Pvt and Ranger Pa Line in same Co with bros; Joseph; Robert; Samuel; William. Srvd 3 yrs or more. B Feb 6 1756 in Bart (now Eden) twp Lancaster co Pa. Early taken to Franklin co Pa. Son of Samuel and Jean Bell Kyle. Mar 1785 Elizabeth Chambers dau of Rowland Chambers; mar 2nd Sarah Patterson 1805. Chldr: Jean; Samuel; Anne mar John Kyle 1st cousin; Rowland; William; James; Joseph. Soldr d Aug 6 1828 Kyles Station Liberty twp Butler co; bur Lower Monroe cem at Monroe. Grave has stone with legible inscrptn. Complete data available thru those giving ref: Fayette Co Pa Hist p 714-718; Hist Butler Co Vol 1 has eight refrs. Etta M Kyle Genealogist Kyle Fam. Rept by Etta M Kyle 144 W Rayen Ave Youngstown Ohio.

LABONI, PETER, Lorain co

Listed p 144 in Hist North Central Ohio by Wm A Duff as a Rev soldier. Rept by Nathan Perry chpt.

LACEY, SAMUEL, Licking co

Enl May 1777 at Elizabethtown N J in Contl servd 9 mo. Came to Licking co O in 1834 to liv w wf and son. Was laborer. Pensd 1818 and 20, stating age at 67; wf

Eunice abt 40 ae a cripple; he d 10-16-1839. Ref S 41745 Contl N J. Rept by State D A R.

LACKEY, JOHN, Ross co

P 294, Chapman's Bros Hist of Fayette, Pickaway and Madison cos 1892 is following date "Lackey, John who was a Capt in the War of the Rev came fr Pa to O in 1813; located in Ross co whr he and wf both died. Their chldr: Reason; Thomas; Ira; Hannah (mar Groves); Richard; Sanford; Ann (mar J Henley); Maria (mar John Richey); Susan (mar Kennell)." Rept by Pickaway Plains chpt.

LAKE, ARCHIBALD, Washington co

Commissary Dept. "Scoured the surrounding country procuring provisions and fresh vegetables for sick wounded soldiers in the Genl Army Hospital Camps at Fiskhill and New Windsor N Y. Was b 1720 England; mar Mary Bird (b abt 1728); chldr: Thomas; William; George; James; Andrew; Sally; Margarette. He d 1798 July 1st ae 78. Bur Rainbow cem Washington co. Bronze tablet and Rev marker placed 1930 by Marietta chpt. Worked in Fishing Banks Newfoundland aft the War was shipbuilder N Y. Came to Marietta, 1789. Ref: No. 263167 D A R; Hildreth's History of Wash co p 464. Rept by Helen Sloan, Marietta chpt.

LAKE, JOHN, Warren co

Pvt N J Milit. Enl Monmouth co N J. Servd under Capt Cardart ? Regt of Col Holmes 2 yrs. Was b July 8 1760 Monmouth N J whr resided till 1819; thence to Warren co O whr livd ever since. Appld there for pens Oct 1832. Ref S 4486 N J. Rept by State D A R.

LAKE, MRS. MARY BIRD, Washington co

Matron of Genl Army Hospt at Fiskhill and New Windsor N Y. Often personally commended by Washington for her excellent service and care of sick and wounded soldrs. B 1728 Bristol Eng; mar Archibald Lake; chldr: Thomas (Rev soldr); William George; James; Andrew; Sally; Margarette. She d Apr 27 1796 Rainbow whr bur (7 miles above Marietta). Grave first mrkd with granite shaft by Sunday School Asso of O in 1890 as Mary Bird taught the first S S in 1789 in Campus Martius. In 1930 a bronze tablet was placed by Marietta chpt. Ref Hildreths Pioneer Settlers p 320; No. 263167 D A R; Williams Hist Wash co p 464. Rept by Marietta chpt.

LAKE, THOMAS, Washington co

N J Milit under Capt Cornelius Carharts Co; Col Sylvanus Seely's Regt. Was b 1760 son of Archibald and Mary Bird Lake (both have Rev service); mar Elizabeth Bertine dau of James Bertine N Y Cy; chldr: Peter Bertine (1797-1874); Mary (Mrs Daniel Dunbar); James; Ann (1800-1895) mar David Williams; Martha R mar Richard Morris; Deborah 1808-1856 mar John Payne. He d Aug 29 1854 nr Layman and Bartlett O Wash co whr bur in Union cem Rt No. 50. Insc: "Thomas Lake, a native of N Y d Aug 29 1854 in 94th yr of his age." Ref: Pay abstract Col Seeley's regt N J Milit; Hildreth's and Williams Hist Wash co Court recds and Deeds. Rept by Helen Sloan, Marietta chpt.

LAMA, WILLIAM, Belmont co

Pvt Pa Contl. Regt of Col Wayne. Servd one yr. Was native of Tyron co N Ireland b 1757; d 1821 Apr 8 Belmont co O; was liv in Flushing twp whn appld 1818 for pens. Stated he came to America to Chester co Pa 1773 or 4. Latter part 1775 enl there for various services. In appl of 1820 gives ae 62; residence Belmont co; had a "wf" who is old; chldr: nine: Joseph ae 16; Kitty 16; Sally 14; John 12, lame; James and Nancy twins ae 10; Wiley, helpless, ae 8; Harris 6; Lucinda 4. Ref S 41749 Pa and Pa Arch S 3 Vol 23 p 574. Cop by Jane Dailey.

LAMB, JAMES, Fairfield co

Serv fr Cumberland co Pa (thence to Ky). Servd as Sergt in Capt Grier's Co. Later as Lieut in Capt Hughes Co. Son of Samuel Lamb, "an ardent patriot who sent 5 sons to the army." James mar Ann ——; one child was Margaret mar James Long, in Ky. He d Fairfield co O bur Turkey Run cem Baptist Ch-yd. Insc illegible. Ref: Pa Arch S ? Vol 15 p 406; Vol 10 p 367. Rept by Mrs. W S Van Fossen, Columbus chpt.

LAMBORN, DAVID, Mahoning co

Pvt Ref Pa Arch S 6 V 3 p 310; military roll 1783-1787 Chester co. Was b 1764; d 1855 Smith twp Mahoning co. Ref: cem recds of Henry Baldwin S A R. Rept by Mahoning chpt.

LAMBRECHT, DANIEL, Fairfield co

Pvt Pa Milit. Enl 1779 Bucks co Pa whr he then livd. Servd 10 mo. Appld for pens 1834 Fairfield co O whence he came abt 1812 fr nr Sheppardstown Va; he had movd there fr Frederick co Md aft war. Stated he was ae 84 in 1834; a gunman. Ref Pa S 8815. Rept by State D A R. (Listed p 406 Wiseman's Pioneer People Fairfield co). J D.

LANDON, JAMES, Delaware co

Pvt. Enl March 1778 N J Line; was liv in Sussex co then servd 3 yrs. in 1818 appld for pens Delaware co O; in 1820 gave age as 70 yr. Rept by State D A R, fr Ref S 41738 N J data fr Capt Wm Hendricks chpt addit to above; was pvt in Capt Luce's Co Col Shreve's 2nd N J Regt. Wounded at Monmouth July 28 1778; recuperated returned and servd to end of war. Born in America May 1750; bur Shoup cem 4 mi south of Prospect O. Insc on stone: "James Landon died Sept 13 1838 aged 88 yrs 3 mo 18 days." Bronze mrkr was placed June 4 1932, by Capt Wm Hendricks chpt. Fr Lucerne co Pa he came to O 1818.

LANE, EZEKIEL, Seneca co and N Y

Enl Apr 1777 whl resid in Sandytown Sussex co N J. Pvt Pa and N Y and N J Milit 18 mo; was b 12-13-1755, east side of North riv. Pensd 11-5-1833 in Seneca co. Trnsfrd to Chatauqua co N Y 4-26-1844. Ref: S 23760 N J; Pa; N Y. Came to O 1833. Rept by State D A R.

LANE, HENDRICK, Butler co

Enl fall of 1776 in Somerset co N J. Servd over one yr. Pvt N J Milit. Pensr 1833 Butler co whither he came in 1807. Stated his birth July 20 1760 Somerset co N J. Ref: S 4494 N J. Rept by State D A R.

LANE, JOHN, Trumbull co

Enl at Cheshire Newport co N H in 1776 as volunteer in Capt Samuel Weatherby's Co Col Wyman's Regt. Under General Gates marched to Ticonderoga. Enl again in fall 1777; served as Corp. Was b Killingworth Ct Jan 15 1755. Since lvd in Green and Dutchess co N Y. Came to Newton Trumbull co O 1807. Rept by Mary Chesney chpt. See p 220 Vol 1 Roster of O.

LANE, JOHN, Mahoning co

Pvt. Mar 1st Mary Low; 2nd Mary Woodrow (1786-1868); Chldr: 9 — Henry; John; Albert; Artilissa mar Joseph Drake; Woodrow; William; Mary; Rachel; Effie. He d at Austintown. Ref: Pa Arch S 5 Vol 2, many lists; N Y Men pp 34, 142; N J Men p 230; Conn pp 228, 481; Vt pp 140, 797; Mass Men V 9 p 478. Tax list 1837 and 1826. Deed bk J p 559 to John Lane Austintown 1814. Rept by Mahoning chpt.

LANE, MORDECAI, Clermont co

Pvt Pa Contl. Servd 2 yrs. Enl in 8th Regt in 1777 Pa. Appld for pens in Clermont co O 7-29-1818; in 1820 appld again stating his age 67 and wife Margaret's ae 52. Ref: S 41739 Pa. Rept by State D A R.

LANEBAUGH, JOSEPH, Lawrence co

Enl May 1781. Pvt Va Contl; servd 6 mo and 14 da. B 1763. Appld for pens June 7 1832 Lawrence co O; pensr 1834. Ref: S 8816 Va. Rept by State D A R.

LANED, ABIJAH, Ashtabula co

Another spelling for "Larned" and "Leonard," Abijah; the latter recorded p 225 Vol 1 Ohio Roster Rev soldrs. New data under Larned this vol. (Jane Dailey.)

LANGHAM, ELIAS, Madison co

Enl 2-19 1777 under Lieut Richard C Waters in 1st Regt of Artillery. Servd throughout the war; was Lieut in Va Line; pensd 9-28-1818 Madison co O. In 1821 appl gave his age as 61 and had 6 chldr none liv w him. Ref S 41747 Contl Va; B L Wt 1309-200-Lieut issued 8-10-1789 to Richard Platt assignee. Compare p 221 Col Elias Lanham V 1 Roster of O Rev soldrs. Rept by State D A R.

LANIER, JAMES, Preble co

Capt in Col Wm Washingtons Regt. Distinguished for efficiency during the war. Servd also in Gen Anthony Waynes N W Terr Campaign. B in Va; mar Elizabeth Washington daughter of John; d nr or in Eaton; likely bur in Frame cem. Rept by Commodore Preble chpt.

LANKTON, LEVI, Washington co

Entered as cook in Commissary dept. B 1754 Southington Conn. Mar 1st Elizabeth Crane (1765-91); he d 1843 Marietta O whr bur in Mound St cem. Grave mkd by Marietta chpt. Ref V 124 No. 123722 p 230 D A R Lin. Rept by J D and Marietta chpt. (See p 221 Roster O Soldrs Vol 1).

LANTERMAN, WILLIAM, Mahoning co

Another spelling for "Launterman, William" recorded p 222 Vol 1 O Roster of Rev Soldrs which see. Rpt by Wilma Molsberry Youngstown.

LARNED, ABIJAH, Ashtabula co

Pvt N H St Trps. Appld for pens in Ashtabula co O 9-24-1832; enl in Northumberland co. Grafter (?) twp N H last part of June. Ref W 8016 N H Contl. Rept by State D A R. It is thot by Mary Redmond chpt and St Ch that this is another spelling for Abijah Leonard recorded p 225 O Roster Rev Soldrs Vol 1. Filed here to avoid further research on this spelling.

LASH, PETER, Wayne co

Drafted to serve in Sussex co N J Sept 1776; pvt Pa Contl servd one yr; was b 1764 Sussex co N J; mar Susannah —— on Dec 21 1828; he d Aug 1843 Wayne co O. Was pensr there 7-8-1834; resided in Washington co Pa previous to coming to O. Widow appld for pens in Ashland co O Apr 18 1855. Ref W 12066; B L Wt 28617-160-55 N J. Rept by State D A R. Reasearch in Wayne co found land sold 1839 naming wf Katherina in the deed (which may indicate a second wife). This data by Wooster-Wayne chpt.

LASLEY, ABRAHAM, Gallia co

Pvt in Capt James Craven's Co 5th Batl Washington co Milit June 1782. Ref p 188 Volunteers Pa Arch Ser 6. Was b Oct 11 1753; mar Hester (Ester) Craft (b Aug 28 1755. Chldr: John; Benjamin; Elizabeth (Betsey); David; Caty; Hannan; Abraham;

Jonathan; Lydia. He d 1828 Gallia co O; bur Runnels cem Addison twp; was farmer; brick mason having built the first brick house in Addison. Was elected "fence viewer" in 1802. Rept by French Colony chpt.

LASTER, THOMAS, Knox co

Enl in spring 1777 in barracks at Phila Pa. Pvt Contl. Served 3 yrs. In appl for pens 1818 gave age as 58 yr. Listed in O Pens Roll of 1835 V 3 p 0-71. Ref S 41748 Penn. Rept by State D A R (N B Compare Thomas Lester p 225 O Roster Vol 1).

LATIMER, JAMES, Perry co

Exec Doc of 1852. Refused a pens as servd only 3 mos. Rept by Wm Pettit.

LATTIMER, JOHN, Mercer co

Pvt N J Milit. Enl Maidenhead Hunterdon co N J (whr he resided) in Capt Van Cleve's Co Col Johnson's Regt. Servd 17 mo. On Nov 12 1831 his age was 81; last pens pd July 15 1839; pens arrears appr Nov 12 1860. He d Oct 5 1841 Mercer co O; leaving no widow. One son was William. Pens of 1833 sent to Crane Schenck Dayton O. Mr A L Bulwinkle 9th Dist N C Gastonia N C asked for his record. Ref Vol A p 214; S 4507 N J; Certificate 13010. O Agency Records Division R 18488-J D. Cop by Jane Dailey.

LAUGHAM, ELIAS, Madison co

This is found listed but is incorrect spelling for Elias "Langham" and "Lanham" which see.

LAUGHEAD, BENJAMIN, Clinton co

Pensd Act of 1832-34 as pvt in Capt Jamison Co Col Lacy Regt Pa Militia for 8 mo. Pens date 19 Dec 1834. Was b in Bucks co Pa 1761 whr liv dur war. Son of John Laughead (named in appl); wf "Agness" who was ment in son's letter for pension for his mother who d 1842. One son was Elisha of Masontown Pa (letters dated 12-30-1848); others: James, John; Johnson; Elizabeth; Nancy; and Mary. He d 1837. After war went to Canacocheig now Franklin co Pa; thence to Huntington co Pa till 1813; thence to Fayette co Pa till 1831; thence to Clinton co O whr he then livd 1832. His last pens pd to 4 Sept 1836. Was Elder of Presby Ch before coming to O livd in Union twp ae 73 on 27 June 1834. Ref S 7128 Pa. Copied by Jane Dailey.

LAUGHEAD, DAVID, Greene co

Cop fr 108 No. 107238 D A R Lin by Jane Dailey is data: Pvt 6th Co 6th Bn Lancaster co Pa under Jos Walker Col James Taylor. Was b Lancaster co Pa 1755; mar Elizabeth Mitchell 1786; one chld was named Eliza and mar John Bradfute; Soldr d 1825 Greene co O. Fr Catherine Green and Cedar Cliff chpts comes location of grave in Massie's Creek cem nr Cedarville. Insc on stone: In Memory of David Laughead who d June 29 1824 aged 67 yrs. Came fr Pa to Ky with George R Clarke 1780; to Greene co 1804. Fr Mrs Geo Skinner Oxford No. 259745 comes: he was son of James and Eleanor McKnight Laughead. Ref Pa Arch S 2 Vol (?) p 306; and 5th S Vol 7 p 605 May 27 1782; servd in Exp vs Shawnees at Old Chillicothe Aug 1780.

LAW, BARTON, Clermont co

Enl 1780 in Prince George co Md. Servd in Pa Milit as pvt for 6 mo. Appld for pens Nov 8-1833 residing in Monroe twp Clermont co O aged 62. Pensr there 1834. Ref S 8817 Pa. Rept by State D A R.

LAWRENCE, JACOB, Adams co

Enl as Vol July 1 1781 Pa Milit whl residing Fayette co Pa in Co of Capt Cato Col Laughery for 19 mo. Was pensd 1833 in Fayette co and trnsfd to Adams co O Mar 1846. "Died in Adams co a few yrs ago" affidavit of witness bur Hopewell O Adams co. Ref S 4521 Pa. Rept by State D A R and Sycamore chpt.

LAWRENCE, WILLIAM, Guernsey co and Pa

Enl 1774 Baltimore Md pvt Md Contl. Srvd 3 yr. Was b 1750; mar Rachel Roberts July 29 1828; he d Sept 15 1833 Pittsburg Pa. In 1818 appld for pens in Guernsey co O; was receiving one there in 1821; petition for aid Act of 3-18-1818 on file Nov 1820 Guernsey co C H. Ref W 5309 B L Wt 338-60-55; and B L Wt 6-100-55 Md. He was dischgd Phila Pa 1780. Widow appld for pens May 25 1855 from Muskingum co O. Rept by State D A R.

LAWS, JOHN,   Licking co

Enl Aug 1 1776 in 11th Va Regt. States age ae 60 in 1818 appl; mar Margaret ——; chldr: Sally age 4, in 1820; John 18 mo. He d 2-27-1840. He movd fr Va to Licking co O in 1829 to be w his family. Ref Va S 41754. Rept by State D A R.

LAYNE, SAMUEL, Lawrence co

Enl 1777 Va Fluvania co as pvt Milit. Servd 13 mo. Was b Jan 14 1759 Goochland co Va. Aft Rev livd in Bedford and Patrick co Ky. "Has livd in Lawrence co O 3 yrs 1832. Ref S 4493 Va. Rept by State D A R.

LEACH, JOSHUA, Butler co

Enl in Calvert co Md 1776; pvt and sergt Md Milit. Servd abt 28 mo. Was b 5-10-1756 Md; mar Priscilla Wilkinson Jan 6 1783; he d June 6 1845. Pensd in Butler co 1832-3 to which he came in 1817. Ref Md W 1786. By State D A R.

LEBY, CHRISTIAN, Ross co

Rev service found p 608 Roster Rolls York co Pa 1775-1783 Pa Arch Ser 6 Vol 2. Capt Jacob Biebe?s Co 1776. Was b 1759; mar Anna Musselman; chldr: Christian mar Mary Heath in 1818 who was dau of Samuel and Mary Wood Heath who was b Feb 2 1802 d Oct 11 1872; the son Christian d Aug 27 1823 age 32 yr 11 mo 7 da. He was in War 1812; the Rev soldr d nr Kinnickinnick Ross co O March 4 1830; bur Crouse chapel at rear and to left of church. Inscr: "In memory of Christian Liebe d March 4 1830 age 71 yr 6 da. Anna, wf of Christian Liebe d March 2 1847 in 81 yr of her age." After Rev he came west to take up grant at mouth of Scioto Riv. Learning his wife's bro was in Ross co nr Chillicothe he went up Scioto to locate nr him whr he lvd and died. His grant prob in Ind. Rept by Mt Sterling chpt. (Liebe is German spelling).

LECROY, JOB, Brown co

Drafted April 1779 Salem co N J and continually drafted every other mo until close of war 1783. Pvt N J Contl. Servd 2 yr 3 mo. Pensr Brown co 9-16-1833 age 72. Ref N J S 16449. Rept by State D A R. Research by Taliaferro chpt found wife's name Prudence; and chldr: Job; Mary Latta; Hannah Stilwell; fr will, probat March 21 1833 Vol 1 p 249; Brown co Recds. (But he had appld for pens in Apr and July 1833 there; so there is some discrepancy). J D.

LEE, EZRA, Erie co

Bur Huron cem; govt mrkr. Lieut-Ensign Jan 1 1777; Lieut Jan 1 1778; Regimental Qrtrmstr Nov 16 1778; Brigade Qrtrmstr 1779-80 and 81. Was of Lyme 1st Reg Conn Line Quartermaster Gen Huntington Brigade June 16 1779 record 1781. Quartermaster Nov 16 1778. Was also in War of 1812. Ref Conn Men in Rev p 145, 146, 143; Block-houses and Military Posts of the Firelands p 37-66. Rept by Marjorie Cherry.

LEE, JAMES, Logan co

Enl Stafford co Va 1776 Contl; servd 4 yr. Was b 1749; pens appl 1818-19 Clark co O and in Logan co O in 1820 ment one son residing w him, Enoch ae 14. Ref S 41762 Va. Rept by State D A R.

LEE, LEMUEL, Ashtabula co

Pvt in 4th Co of Capt Summer's 2nd Regt Conn Line. Was b 1760 Lyme Conn; mar Sally Sterling in 1783; she was b 1761-d 1833; he d 1826 Ashtabula co. Ref V 125 p 185 D A R Lin No. 124613. Rept by Nathan Perry chpt.

LEE, SAMUEL, Ashtabula co

Lieut and Capt 1783 Conn Line; b 1749 Salisbury Conn; mar 2nd wf Elizabeth Brown who d 1857. He d 1829 bur at Colebrook O; grave mrked by Luther Reeve chpt. Ref 15th rept N S D A R p 164 and No. 89793 Vol 90 D A R Lin (by J D). Rept by Nathan Perry chpt.

LEE, WILLIAM C, Richland co

Enl Sept 1776; pvt Md Contl; servd one yr. Appld for pens 1-16-1819 in Richland co O mentioned a wf; a dau aged 23 and gr-son ae 10. Pensr in Richland co 6-26-1833. Ref S 41757 Md. Rept by State D A R. Research by Mansfield chpt locates one "William Lee a wheelwright liv at Olivesburg O whose will was filed in Richland co Court house Adm Ruth Lee; final settlement 1841."

LEE, WILLIAM, Columbiana co

Enl 1775 Bedford co Pa. Servd as Sergt Pa Contl during the war. Appl for pens in Columbiana co O 1818; gave age 75; mar Mary B —— who was 50 yr old then; Chldr: Ann ae 19; Rachel ae 17; Dorothy 14; William 12. He d 1-6-1832. Ref S 41755 Penn. Rept by State D A R. From Youngstown chpt (Mrs Molsberry) comes the following data with some addit facts and differences in wife's name, which one should work out; other facts seem to indicate it is the same William Lee. Data: Pens d 1819 Pa Contl Line; Sergt and many services; O S 9852-100 A. Issued Nov 1789 for Rev serv not claimed in 1828; was b Nottinghamshire, Eng 1743; mar Barbara Shoemaker; chldr: Sarah (Smith); Mary (Earick); George (b 1793) Middleton twp O and d 1870); William; Ann (Coulson); Dorothea (Ward); Rachel; Elizabeth; Catherine (Freed); Hannah (Skelton); Soldr d Jan 6 1828 ae 85 Middleton twp Columbiana co O. Came there in 1793; Estate settled 1828; servd 7 yrs in war; sttld on soldiers grant; liv nr East Palestine on Bull Crk. Ref: Pa Arch 2-10-661; Ohio Patriot; Hist Columbiana co; Amer St Papers Vol 5 p 16.

LEEDOM, THOMAS, Muskingum co

Enl Burke Hill Pa Mar 1777; Contl servd Pa Line 2 yrs. Appl for pens Muskingum co Oct 26 1832 liv in Rich Hill twp. Gave ae as 78 yr. Ref S 4578 Penn. Rept by State D A R.

LEEDS, ROBERT, Clermont co

Enl 1777 under Capt Payne; pvt (Va) ? Contl. Srvd one yr. Pens appl in Clermont co O 7-14-1819 and 11-9-1832. Was b Glaston co N J 7-7-1757. Movd fr there to Clermont co O abt 1804. Ref S N J 14489. Rept by State D A R.

LEETON, BENJAMIN, Brown co

Enl Feb 15 1779 Amelia co Va. Servd 18 mo. Pensr in Brown co O 6-19-1819; was 62 yr old 1820. Ref S 41756 Va. Rept by State D A R.

LEGG, JOHN, Champaign co

Enl 1776 in Capt Blackwell co. Pvt Va Contl. Pensr 7-14-1819 Champaign co O. Was ae 63 in 1818. Liv w him a wf ae 56 son ae 20 (in 1820). Ref Va S 41758. Rept by State D A R.

LEGORE, JOHN, Fayette co and Ind

Enl Lancaster Pa Apr 1 1776. Pvt Pa Line six yrs. Pensr 4-2-1819 Washington Fayette co O. Was trnsfrd to Ind 6-27-1828. Was ae 64 in 1819 had wf Esther; a step-dau ae 12 in 1826; He d 7-7-1829 in Ind. Ref S 35521 Pa Contl. Rept by State D A R. (Was on Ohio Pens Roll 1818 — J D.)

LEIGH, DANIEL, Pickaway co

A native of Allentown N J b 1756; came to Madison co Pickaway co in 1823 whr soon d. Was soldr of Rev; had 6 chldr: Zebulon S; Charles; Wateous; Elisha; Sarah (wf of Samuel Savage); who remained in N J; Eliza wf of Capt Buzzengarger and settled in Ind. Ref Williams Bros Hist Madison and Pickaway co. Rept by Mrs. Orion King Pickaway Plains chpt.

LEIM, SAMUEL, Clinton co

This is mis-spelling for Linn, Samuel Clinton co filed p 229 Vol 1 Ohio Roster. Frequent copying through the years often leads to incorrect spelling. Listed here to avoid continued research.

LEMRICK, Patrick, Brown co

Or "Limerick" sometimes spelled; Enl 2-4-1776 Pa. Dischgd 1779 in N J Servd 4 yrs. Pensr Brown co O 5-10-1822; was ae 80 in 1820 and had no family with him. Ref S 41772 Pa. Rept by State D A R.

LEONARD, JAMES, Brown co

Enl in Pa 1776 for 2 yrs. Dischgd at Valley Forge Jan 1-1779. Pens appl in Highland co in Aug 28 1832 giving ae 98; wf was Elizabeth Watson mar 12-22-1780; had "seven chldr," Thomas one made appl for amt due. Ref W 5465 Penn in which the widow states he d Feb 6 1836 Perry twp Brown co O. Rept by State D A R. Taliaferro chpt (Meryl Markley) Brown co corroborates name and place of death adding a daughter's name Lebery a gr-son Joseph Cahil; soldier was among the first 23 to vote in Perry twp in 1815. His will probated Aug 15 1835 Vol 1 p 314 — Probate Crt Brown co O.

LEONARD, JAMES, Warren co

(Compare this record with James Leonard above; tho there is a difference of one year in date of discharge and in the cem whr bur errors often are found; each record comes fr authentic data.) Servd in 13th Regt 10th Co Col Walter Stewart Col Miles Rifle Regt. Dischgd at Valley Forge Jan 1 1778. Was in battles: Long Island, White Plains, Trenton, Brandywine, et al. Pensr resident of Warren co O 1831 age 87. Bur in family cem nr Zoar Hamilton twp. Ref S A R No. 48171. Rept by William Pettit Dayton O.

LEONARD, JOHN, Mahoning co

Pvt. Ref: Ser 3 V 23 p 270 Cumberland co; Ser 5 Vol 2, 4, 8, many services — Pa Arch; mar Nancy ——; chldr: John b 1782 mar Rebecca; George mar Margaret; Nicholas b 1795 mar Isabel; David b 1800 mar Ann; Rachel mar Wm Robinson; Benjamin mar Fanny; Sally mar James Burnett; Peggy mar John Shatto; James mar Sussan. Soldr d 1813 at Ellsworth O. Ref Hist Trumbull & Mahoning co V 2 p 99; Hist Mahoning co by Saunderson p 179; Deed bk C p 464 to John Leonard Heirs 1816. Pens Appl Bk 5 p 76 Circuit Crt Warren Trumbull co O. Rept by Mahoning chpt.

LEONARD, Patrick, Hamilton co

Born 1740 resided Cincinnati 1817. Ref Ohio list Pa Arch. Rept by Mary Steinmetz Reading Pa (Could this be error for Patrick Lemrick of Brown co which see) J D.

LESH, JACOB, Preble co

Pvt in Capt Michael Wolf's Co Berks co Pa Milit. Was b Berks co 1757; mar Anna Moyer in 1782; she b 1763 d 1851; Jacob Jr was one son; soldr d 1820 Preble co O. Cop fr V 107 No. 106819 D A R Lin. by Jane Dailey.

LESSIER, HENRY, Columbiana co

In Army of France. Came w Marquis De Lafayette. Servd to end of war. B 1748 Poland; d Feb 11-1845 Columbiana co Home. Came fr Polk Missouri here a few mo before his death. Had every attention in the county home. Ref Ohio Patriot Feb 1845. Rept by Mahoning chpt (Mabel S Askue).

LEWIS, BENONI, Washington co

In Commissary dept. B Rhode Island Sept 2 1752; mar Mary Walton b Conn Sept 4 1753 d July 13 1845. Had eleven chldr: Nathan b 1776; Waterman b 1798; Frederick b 1793; Lucy b 1781; Mary b 1796; Lydia b 1785; Thomas 1790; these are bur by Benoni and wife, and the 2 wives of Hezekiah Lewis are bur in same plot — prob dau-in law of Benoni. Soldr d at Belpre; bur in cem there on Rt 50. Stone inscr: Benoni Lewis b Sept 2 1752 d Sept 23 1821. "He had been Capt of an ocean ship and was employed dur the Rev in the Commissary dept. In 1802 he emigrated w his fam to Va and in 1807 settld on the Ohio side." Ref Williams Hist Washington co. Rept by Marietta chpt.

LEWIS, CHARLES, Perry co

D in Perry co 2-16-1825 aged 78. Name listed in Pa Arch list of Pa soldrs who came to O. Rept by Mary Steinmetz Reading Pa. Fr Hetuck chpt comes data: Charles Lewis b 1751 died 1-16-1829. Listed in Morgan co

LEWIS, EBENEZER, Marion co

Altho his appl for pens was rejected because he did not furnish proof of service in Contl Estab as required by law listed here to avoid continued research and to preserve his record as he stated b Mar 19 1764 Fairfield co Conn. Pens appl in Marion co Θ 1835 states he enl Aprl 1779; served 23 mo as pvt in Capt Nash's Co Col Dimon and Whiting Ct Regt. Re-enl Mar 24 1781; served 25 mo as pvt in Capt Thomas Nash Co Lieut Col Dimon and Col Whiting's Ct Regt; and that he was in attack of enemy at Fort Ridges 1782. Six yrs aft serv movd w father to Rutland co Vt; 15 yrs later to Onondaga co N Y; and 1823 to Marion co O. No ref to family other than father. Ref R 6311. Rept by Capt William Hendricks Chpt (Mrs S L Leeka). From Col Chapt comes data: Cop fr Ohio State Journal Sept 3 1836 —— "D Ebenezer Lewis aged between 107 and 112 yrs. D Aug 10 1836 at residence of John Y Thorp in Claridan twp Marion co O. A veteran of the Rev; native of an eastern state and came here abt 14 or 15 yrs ago." Could this older Ebenezer have been father to other one who in 1836 would be only 72 yrs old? (J D).

LEWIS, HENRY, Knox co

Enl Cumberland co Pa spring of 1780 as a guard. Servd 8 mo. Pens appl in Knox co O. 5-6-1833 states ae abt 78. Listed 1835 V 3 O 137 pens roll. Ref S 4532 Pa. Rept by State D A R.

LEWIS, ISAAC, ? co

Pvt refused a pens as no satisfactory evidence of service exhibited. Ref Doc 31 Jan 6 1831 O S Libry — Rept by Blanche Rings. Col O.

LEWIS, JACOB, Knox co

Exec Doc of 1852. An Express rider, not pensionable. Rept by Wm Pettit.

LEWIS, JOSEPH, Franklin co

Pvt Pa Contl; pensd 6-12-1820 in Franklin co (Cop by J D). Research on this record by Columbus chpt (Mrs K H Van Fossen) repts he was found to be 77 yrs old June 12 1820 whn pens there. Fr Adm Docket 1-143 Franklin co he d Aug 20 1820; Adm appt Aug 22 1820. Judging fr these two records it is believed the date of death in the following is an error: sent by Mary Steinmetz Reading Pa. ——"Died in Franklin co

8-10-1830 ae 77 Joseph Lewis. Ohio list of Pa soldiers Pa Arch. Later authentic research states 1820 is date of death. Wfs name is Hannah. Ref 2-278 and 2-300 Court Recds Columbus O. Cop by B R.

LEWIS SAMUEL, Perry co

Corp Pa Contl. Pensd 2-1-1819 Perry co O. Servd 5 yrs; b 1746; mar Jane ——; Carpenter. On Ohio Pens Roll 1835 V 3: 0-82 gives death Feb 16 1825 (data also on back of pens cert at Wash). He livd in Westmoreland co Pa abt 40 yrs; livd in Ohio since 1816. Ref S 41763 Penn. Rept by State D A R.

LICHTY, CONRAD, Montgomery co

Ref Berks co Pa S 5 Vol 4 p 263 Pa Arch; bur at Ellerton cem Montgomery co O. Marked by Richard Montgomery chpt S A R of Dayton. Rept by Wm Pettit Dayton S A R.

LIEURANCE (Lorrance or Lowrence), GEORGE, Clinton co

Is filed here to avoid oft reported data as a Rev Soldr. He servd instead in war 1812. Ref W C 30097 B A J Ill.

LIEUZADER, ABRAHAM, Guernsey co

Exec Doc of 1852. Refused a pens. Service of 7 mo and 19 da admitted. Rept by Wm Pettit.

LIGGETT, WILLIAM, Ross co

Pvt in Capt Peter Bryan Bruins Co Col Daniel Morgan's Va Regt. Was b 1750 Londonderry Ireland; mar Mary ——; one son was John. D in Ross co O. Ref V 121 D A R lin p 213 No. 120687. Cop by Jane Dailey.

LIGGINS, WILLIAM, Columbiana co

Enl York co Pa 1777; pvt Contl Line; servd 6 yrs. Pens appl 3-30-1819 in Columbiana co O stating age 59; wf Betsey; Step-dau Jane Patterson ae 14 (in 1820). Ref S 41769 Pa Contl B L Wt 501-100. Rept by State D A R. Fr Youngstown chpt (Wilma Molsberry) comes Ref Baldwins Records Pa Arch S 3 Vol 23 p 575; gives death as June 17, 1824.

LIGHTFOOT, JEPTHA, Clermont co

Rev soldr d 1828; second person to be bur in West Woodville cem Blanchester. Family repts he was captured at N Y and kept on English ship for several yrs. Papers destroyed by family. Rept by Mrs Jesse Garner Blanchester thro Warriors Trail chpt.

LIMING, JOSEPH, Brown co

B near Phil Pa the son of Henry Liming. Rev soldr taking part in many battles. Came to Lexington Ky 1799 and to Clark twp Brown co 1806. His father and his two brothers settled near him. Chldr: Jonathan; Abraham; Samuel; Sarah; Joseph; William; James; Ahira Dellaplane. Samuel fought Indians under Wayne and Abraham, James and Joseph were in war 1812. Soldr said to be buried "under apple tree on his farm." Ref Beers Hist Brown co pp 521-524. Rept by Meryl B Markley Vice Ch.

LINCOLN, RUFUS, CAPT, ? co

Listed in news clipping by "L A A" found in old scrapbook no date as Rev soldr participating or interested in settlement of Marietta; with few exceptions they (who have descendants in this section) are bur in cem in Washington co; many active in Indian war at own expense never reimbursed by U S. Filed here for continued research almost half having been verified. List fr Marietta chpt.

LINDSEY, JAMES, Champaign co

Enl 1775 in eng Regt Va Line Capt Alexander; pensr 9-9-1819 Champaign co abt 60 yrs old; mar Priscilla Stubblefield Jan 1812; he d 2-4-1824. Ref W 25476 B L Wt 44 933-160-55 Va. Widow mar John Thomas 5-10-1826; he d 2-19-1846 and she appld for pens in Champaign co O 1856. (A note found on one James Lindsey bur at Centerville O but no other data found. Town is in Montgomery co O — J D). Rept by State D A R.

LINDSAY, SAMUEL, Meigs co

"Samuel Lindsay first settler at the mouth of East Sandy Creek in Cranberry twp Venango co Penn. Later moved to Meigs co O whr he d. He servd in the Rev" — cop fr Hist Venango co Pa pub 1890 pp 263-265 by Presque Isle chpt D A R Margery Bacon Erie Pa.

LINDSLEY, SIMEON, Delaware co

Or Linsly. Pens 6-22-1833 in Delaware co for service in Col Enos Regt Capt Gillett et al Cos for abt 9 mo. Enl at Litchfield Conn whr was b 21 Sept 1761; mar in Vermont previous to 1794 to Rutilly ——; he d 22 Sept 1844 Delaware co O. Ref S 4553 Conn. Cop by Jane Dailey. Fr Capt Wm Hendricks chpt (Mrs. S L Leeks) repts: bur in Shoup cem 4 mi s of Prospect O. On stone is : "Simeon Linsley d Sept 22 1844 aged 84 yr who spent a part of his youthful life in the service of his country in the Rev War of 1776."

LINE, BENJAMIN, Butler co

Enl Lancaster co Pa Line; b 1754 Lancaster co Pa; mar Rebecca Jewell; one chld was Eunice mar Saml Adam; he d in Butler co O 1816. Cop fr D A R Lin V 109 p 150 by Jane Dailey.

LINE, JOHN, Butler co

Enl 1782 Essex co N J; dischgd Dec 15 1782; served 9 mo as pvt N J Milit; pens appl 1832 states b June 6 1764; was 68 yr old in 1832; resident Butler co O for thirty yrs. Liv there July 27 1832. Ref S 4547 N J. By State D A R.

LINE, JOSEPH, ? co

Pvt. Refused pens as servd in Regt not on Contl estab. Ref Doc 31 Jan 6 1831 O S Libry Col O. Rept by Blanche Rings Col O.

LINGAN, GEN JAMES MACUBBIN, Ross co

Was allowed 300 A bounty land for service as Capt on Contl Estab by Warrant issued 19 March 1792 No. 1294. No papers on file as destroyed in war office fire 1800. A letter fr a Commissioner states he was killed 7-18-1812. Ref Md B L Wt 1294-300-Capt (no papers). Rept by State D A R. Fr Columbus chpt (Mrs. Van Fossen) comes data: "Rev soldier native of Md died at Chillicothe O — cop fr Chillicothe Supporter" date of Aug 22 1812.

LINN, ADAM, Guernsey co

Servd 6 mo in Capt McLean's Co in Flying Camp; later enl Gettysburg Pa in 1776; was 1st Sergt under Lieut McPherson Col Irvin's 7th Pa Regt; was in numerous big battles; present at hanging of Major Andre and servd till 1781. No date or place of birth stated; he livd aft the Rev in Pa, Md and Va, moving to Guernsey co O in 1811. Pens appl Sept 19 1833 ae 83 liv in Guernsey co O. He mar Ann Hefflebower Aug 17 1780 in Hagerstown. She was alld a pens 1841 whl liv in Jefferson twp Guernsey co aged 80; in 1846 she said had livd said twp abt 34 yrs coming fr Augusta co Va. Chldr: John b 11-20-1784; Joseph b 2-18-1787; Gorg ? b 3-2-1790; Samuel b 9-3-1793; Aaren b 12-10-1796; Andrew F 36 yr ae in 1841. This data fr W 5023. Pens Cl office. Accompanying the above recd is data from Mary E Stone of Anna Asbury Stone chpt. George Linn came fr Va to Guernsey co O in 1813; his bro Samuel fr Pa 1807; George later returned to Pa and brot his father and 2 sisters; they took up large farms on adjoining sections. Adam b 1748 d 1834; wf was Ann Hefflebower; will in Guernsey co Crt dated Sept 25 1834. To the chldr she adds: Gordon; William; Mary mar James McMichael; Nancy mar John Sargent; Sarah mar William March; Margaret mar Samuel Dunning; Elizabeth mar David Ralston. Soldr is bur at Winterset Guernsey co O. Ref Pa Arch V 2 p 1091 Pensions Adam Linn Feb 19 1777-1781 et al. (This is not Adam Linn of Butler co p 228 O Roster).

LINN, JAMES, Mahoning co

Sergt. Ref Ser 3 V 23 p 464 Genl Armstrong nr Phila Pa Arch. Wf name Esther; chldr: John; Joseph; William; James b 1785; Annie; Polly; Eliza. He d abt 1828 Coitsville twp Mahoning co; was amg early settlers there. Ref Hist Trumbull and Mahoning co. V 2 p 167; Will bk 5 p 21 Trumbull co Recd. Tax list 1826 Coitsville James Linn. Rept by Mahoning chpt. (Mabel Askue).

LINSCUTT (or Linscott) SAMUEL, Trumbull co

Enl May 1782 Newton Mass. Dischg June 30 1784; b Apr 11 1763; in appl 1820 mentions "wf" son Thomas ae 28; 3 other sons ae 19; 17; 13; and one dau ae 6; 1st appld for pens 8-16-1818 Trumbull co O. Ref S 41775 Mass Contl. Rept by State D A R. Mary Chesney chpt repts one son's name was Ithamer; resided in Farmington twp.

LINTNER, PETER, Butler co

Volunteer 1777 Jan 1 in Farmanough twp Cumberland co Pa. Servd pvt Pa Milit Line for 6 mo. Pensr in Butler co O 3-27-1833 whr had livd past 25 yrs. He was b Mar 27 Hunterton co N J 1760. Ref S 3912 Penn. By State D A R.

LISK, JAMES, ? co

From Marietta chpt comes data: Appld for pens Com Pleas Crt Marietta O Washington co. Ref V 7 3. Addit data: d Feb 5 1831 leaving no widow but one son Nicholas Lisk.

LISKE, JOHN, Monroe co

Enl abt 7-10-1779 in 9th ? Va Regt; servd 10 mo. Pens appl 1818 gives ae 63; 1820 he names wf Elizabeth ae 55; Nicholas ae 19 "works for himself." Ref S 41773 Va. By State D A R. (Compare James Lisk above to whom a son Nicholas is recorded. Each record comes fr authentic sources — J D).

LISLE, JACOB, ? co

Refused a pens as servd in a Regt not on the Contl Estab. Ref Doc No. 31 Jan 6 1831 O S Libry. Rept by Blanche Rings Columbus chpt.

LIST, JOHN, Pickaway co and Ind

Enl Anbany N Y in 1st Regt N Y line; dischgd at Snake Hill N Y 1783. Aft Rev movd fr N Y to Pa; was b Mar 2 1753; had "wife and one dau."; Pens appl fr Washington co O 1-19-1819; fr Pickaway co O 5-20-1818; in 1820 livd with wf and dau ae 12 in Butler co O whl resident Ross twp; was a mason; in 1822 Jan 15 appld for trnsfr to Owen co Ind. Ref S 35523. Rept by State D A R. (Also one same name pensd in Richland co O 1-19-1819 who was trnsfrd to Ind — J D).

LLOYD, DAVID, Miami co

Enl spring 1776 Huntington co Pa. Movd fr there to Miami co O in 1811; servd 10 mo as pvt Sergt and Lieut in Pa Milit. B May 1755 Frederick co Va. Pens appl Sept 27 1832 Miami co. Ref S 4590 Penn. Rept by State D A R.

LOCK, AYRES, Tuscarawas co

Pvt Mass Line; pensr 4-27-1819 Act of 1818. Trnsfr to N Y. Listed here to avoid further research in Ohio. Cop by J D.

LOCK, CAPT JOHN, Preble co

Servd thro the Rev; made Capt; b Md 1755; d 10-4-1818; bur Roselawn cem Lewisburg Preble co O. Rept by Commodore Preble chpt. Fr Wm Pettit Dayton comes data cop fr stone: "Capt John Lock d Oct 4 1818 ae 63 yr 8 mo. Soldr of War of 1776."

LOCK, PHILIP, Franklin co ?

On the back of the original marriage certificate of Ansel Mattoon and Almira Mattoon Apr 17 1845 written in pencil is the following notation: "Eunice Lock widow of Philip Lock a pvt in the Rev war d July 30 1846. The last she drew pension was Sept" The rest of paper was torn so you could not read it. There is nothing to indicate who this Eunice Lock was but listed here for evidence on Philip as a Rev soldr.

LOCK (alias Starr), WILLIAM, Jefferson co

Enl Browns Mill Frederick co Va Dec 1779 U S service. His real name is William Starr but aft secession fr British army changed it to Locke enl by that name in American service. Capt of Cavalry Va Milit; servd 2 yr; was b Mar 1 1754; in letter of June 12 1843 said he was "dead." Pens appl 8-28-1832 allowed 12-30-1833 in Jefferson co Ross twp res. Ref Bur Pensions D C. Rept by State D A R. Listed in "Va Men in Rev" p 280 from Jefferson co O ae 89. (J D).

LOCKWOOD, DANIEL, Belmont co

This is an error found in lists but should be David Lockwood recorded p 230 Vol 1 Roster O. To which we add data fr research. Ref W 5030 Navy N Y. His widow appld for pens Apr 5 1792, in Ohio co Va; resident of Meade twp when in Belmont co O. Rept by State D A R.

LODGE, JONATHAN, Columbiana co

Ranger Robinson Volunteer Northumberland co Pa; b 1762; wf b 1769 d Jan 8 1844; bur by side of husband in Center twp; he d Mch 21 1844. Ref Col co cem records; Pa Arch S 3 V 23 p 196, 278. Rept by Wilma Molsberry Youngstown.

LOGAN, JOHN, Hamilton co

Pensr 1832-34; pvt Col McCoy Regt Pa servd 9 mo. In 1831 removd to Miami co and Sycamore co O; he d 31 Mar 1836 Hamilton co O leaving no widow or minor chldr. Ref S 8855 Special Act of Congress 28 June 1836 for his relief apprvd. Cop by Jane Dailey at D C (Cf p 230 O Roster for John Sr who had a son John).

LOGAN, PATRICK, Butler co and Ind

Enl Dec 1776 or Jan 1777 at Red Stone Pa. Servd 3 yr. Appl for pens as pvt Va Contl in Butler co (not Franklin as sometimes found listed). Giv ae as 68 yr. Appld for trnsfr fr Ohio to Franklin co Indiana 10-3-1820; stated had no family. Was a weaver. Ref S 41778 Va. Rept by State D A R. A ref fr Doc 31 Jan 6 1831 O S Libry lists him as dropped fr pens list under Act of 1820 as not being in indigent circumstances. Rept by Blanche Rings Col O.

LONG, JAMES, Warren co

Corp in Capt Persifor Frazer's Co Col Anthony Wayne's Regt 1776; b Lancaster co Pa; d Warren co O; mar Elizabeth Douglas; Ref Vol 27 p 228 D A R Lin No. 26785 thro son Samuel; No. 69973 thro son Stephen; No. 68862 thro son John. Rept by Nathan Perry chpt Mrs. T R Oehlke.

LONG, MICHAEL, Montgomery co

5th S Pa Arch IV 144. Received depreciated pay. Vol III 45 Fifth Pa Contl line 1778. Vol II 727 First Pa Contl Line 1777; Cumberland co 1782 VI p 650 Capt Wm Lamb. Rept by Wm Pettit S A R.

LOOKER, OTHNIEL, Hamilton co and Ill

Enl Elizabethtown Point N J May 1776; resided there (Morris co) 31 yrs; thence to Vt one yr; thence to N Y for 15 yrs then to Hamilton co O. Servd 10 mo 14 da as pvt Mass St Trps. Pens appl in Hamilton co O Aug 15 1832; pensr 5-6-1833. Rept by State D A R. Ref S 32386 N J. From Cincinnati chpt comes data: Othniel Looker was 4th Gov of Ohio; he mar Pamela Clarke dau of Abraham a signer of Dec of Independence; their dau Rachel mar Judge Joseph Kitchell to whose home in Palestine Ill the soldier went late in life and d there; bur on fam lot of Jos Kitchell. Was St Senator 1814; 3 terms; St Rep 3 terms; Speaker of House; Gov 1814 filling out term of Return J Meigs; came to Harrison Hamilton co 1801 to a land grant; Proven recd of Mrs. Bessie M K Richey Robinson Ill. Mrs. Whallon Cin O repts: a few wks before his death he arrayed himself in his uniform worn in Contl serv and appeared upon the platform in a 4th of July celebration making an impressive speech.

LOOMIS, ASA, Portage co

Enl Apr 1776 residing in Torrington Conn. Pvt State Trps. Servd 8 mo 21 da; b in Conn 1757; came to O abt 1821 to Charleston. Pens appl Portage co O 8-27-1832. Ref Conn S 4568. Rept by State D A R.

LOOMIS, GILES, Ashtabula co

4th Regt 3rd trp Light Horse Conn; d 1812 Windsor O. Grave located by Mary Stanley D A R. Cop by Nathan Perry chpt from 18th Rept. N S D A R p 223; and 21st rept p 1002; Mary Redmond chpt repts he was a Capt; d 7-2-1812 ae 56. Ref Loomis Gen.

LOOMIS, JONATHAN, ? co

Pvt. Refused a pension as servd in a Regt not on the Contl Estab. Ref Doc No. 31 Jan 6 1831 O S Libry. Rept by Blanche Rings Col O.

LOOMIS, URIAH, Clark co

Exec Doc of 1852. Refused a pens as servd less than 3 mo. Rept by Wm Pettit.

LOOP, PETER, JR, Sandusky co

Service Albany and Dutchess co Milit N Y; S A R Ref 51465; b 1766 N Y; d 1855; Woodville O which is in Sandusky co; mar Rebecca Gilbert. Rept by Wm Pettit.

LORD, ABNER, Franklin co

Ref Marvin Gen Desc of Reinold and Matthew p 62. Rept by Mrs. R Winnagle Warren O.

LOTZ, JACOB, Vinton co (various spellings)

Enl 1778 whl resident of Stoverstown Va servd 3 mo as pvt in Capt John Brown's Va Co. Re-enl spring of 1781. Servd 3 mo in Capt Thomas Marshall's Va Co. Fall of 1783 movd to Winchester; aft 3 yr to Berkley co; thence to Greenbrier co; aft 6 yr Bath co; thence to Gallia co O whr pensd 4-25-1833 in Wilkesville twp. He is bur in cem here which is now in Vinton co. He was b 12-21-1761; a visit to grave found tombstone data: Jacob Lotz 1760-1839 "A soldier of the Revolution;" on one side "Sarah Wolf Lotz 1761-1839; Rachel Lotz 1808-1888; Fr J Boyd Davis Col O a descendent comes Ref S 4567 Va and chldr Mary mar Matthew Edmiston; Margaret mar Isaac Hawk; Isaac mar Nancy Knox; Clara mar William Humphreys; Abraham mar Nancy Carpenter; Susan mar Renick Brown; Sarah unmarried; Catherine mar Cornelius Carr Jr; Rachel unmarried.

LOVE, HENRY, Hamilton co

Pvt Va Line. Servd 9 mo 16 da. Pensr 1-9-1834 in Southampton co Va and in 1840 in Colerain twp Hamilton co O ae 85; was "ae 77 in 1832;" enl Southampton co Va Milit. He d 2-27-1840 (agency bk). Ref Va S 8858. By State D A R.

LOVE, MORDECAI, Clermont co

Tho found listed is a mis-spelling for "Lane, Mordecai," which see, this volume. (J D).

LOVE, THOMAS, Meigs co

Pvt Va Milit; b 1755 Ireland; came to U S in 1763; mar Roseanna McClure Feb 1 1787; d 12-22-1834 prob in Letart twp whr he came fr Mason co Va; thence to Meigs co. Livd also in Augusta co Va first. Ref W 8055 Va. Rept by Return Jonathan Meigs chpt. Cop fr "Va Milit in Rev" p 280 by Jane Dailey "at ae 79 liv in Meigs co. Trnsfr fr Ky."

LOVELAND, ELISHA, Portage co

Responded to first call for trps; b 1738 Glastonbury Conn; mar Lucy Sparks; one chld was Abner b 1764 mar Lois Hodge in 1787; he d at Freedom O Portage co. Ref V 107 D A R Lin 106513 p 158. Cop by Jane Dailey.

LOVELESS, GEORGE, Trumbull co

Pvt enl 1777 as subst for his father; Va Milit; servd 8 mo; b Sept 5 1760; son of John Loveless drafted 1777; he appld for pens 10-15-1832 Newton twp Trumbull co. Rept by State D A R and same by Mary Chesney. Ref S 4575 Va adding death Feb 26 1833; and he was prisoner of war Detroit. Named a brother John.

LOWERY, DAVID, Montgomery co

5th Ser Pa Arch Vol 4 p 243. Contl Line. Came to county in 1796. Burial place not found. Rept by Wm Pettit S A R.

LOWTHER, WM, Jefferson co

Ref Vol 58 or 75 pp 145, 154 D A R Lin bk; bur Island Creek cem Jefferson co; b 1762; d 1842. By Mary D Sinclair Steubenville chpt.

LUCAS, JOHN, Butler co

Enl Pa 1776-7 in St Trps. Servd 10-12 mo; b Sept 7 1760 Frederick co Md. Movd fr Pa to Ky and aft 12 yr to Butler co O whr has lived 30 yr (appl). Ref Penn S 4584. Rept by State D A R.

LUCE, BENJAMIN, Montgomery co

Pvt Morris co N J Milit; b 1730 Marthas Vineyard Mass. Mar Elizabeth Hopkins; one chld was Benjamin Jr. Soldr d 1814 Montgomery co O. Ref V 123 No. 122659 D A R Lin. Cop by Nathan Perry chpt.

LUCK, ADAM, Ashland co

Listed p 142 in History of North Central Ohio by Wm Duff as a Rev soldier. Rept R Lin. Cop by Nathan Perry chpt.

LUDLOW, JOHN, Hamilton co

Capt tho military service not found; his obituary stated he was a Capt. He was b Morris co N J son of Cornelius and wf Catherine Ludlow; mar first Catherine dau of Daniel Cooper Jr a Rev soldr; 2nd wf Demun. Chldr: Agnes; Huriss; Daniel C; Mary; John; James; William. He d Cincinnati O; bur Spring Grove cem with usual insc on tombstone; a fam monument. Came to Cin 1789 fr Buffalo N Y. Owned lots in first sale; 1st name contributing to church bld. First sheriff of Ham co; Memb 1st Legis of O; one of founders of city. Ref D A R No. 3967; and 33 rept N S D A R p 111. Rept by Mrs. Whallon of Cincinnati chpt.

LUDWIG, DANIEL, Pickaway co

Pvt livd Berks co Pa dur Rev whr was b June 4 1748 son of Daniel and Mary Ludwig natives of Germany. He mar 1st Appelona dau of Michael and Susannah Miller who d May 14 1787. Had four chldr: John; Christina; Daniel, George. Mar 2nd wf Eve 1788 dau of Casper and Rebecca Grismer; she b 1766 d 1800; 2 chldr Thomas; Joseph. Mar 3rd wf Elizabeth Shupert in 1802; chldr: Catherine; Mary; Jacob; Elizabeth; Rachel; Susannah. Soldr d Pickaway co O June 9 1825; bur on D S Ludwig farm 2 mi s e of Circleville; mrkd 1932 by Pickaway Plains chpt. Came to O 1806. Rept by Pickaway Plains Columbus and Ann Simpson Davis chpts.

LUKE, JOHN, Wayne co

Enl 1776-7 in N J Milit. Resid Middlesex co whr was b Nov 1761; movd to Northumberland co Pa 1796; thence to Wayne co O 1823 whr appld for pens Jan 25. Ref S 4582 N J. Rept by State D A R. Wooster-Wayne chpt found no trace of soldr.

LUNT, DANIEL, CAPT, ? co

Listed in old scrap bk as "Rev soldr who participated or interested in settlement of Marietta. Filed here for continued research. Rept by Marietta chpt.

LUSHER, JOHN, ? co

Pvt. Refused pens as deserted the service. Ref Doc 31 Jan 6 1831. O S Libry. Rept Blanche Rings Col O.

LUSK, SAMUEL, Montgomery co

Enl Rowan co N C 1780 whr living; pvt N C St Trps. Servd 5 mo; 9 1-2 mo in Cavalry; 3 mo Qrtrmastr; was 72 yrs old in 1832 whn appld for pens Sept 11 in Montgomery co O. Ref S 4583 N C. Rept by State D A R.

LYMAN, FRANCIS, Ashtabula co

Pvt Conn Contl. Pensr 8-1-1833 Ashtabula co. Mary Redmond chpt reports (1931) he d 7-17-1840 at W Andover O. There is no tombstone but descendants say he is bur there by his wife whose grave is mrkd.

LYON, ABRAHAM, Muskingum co

Enl Nov 15 1775; servd 1 yr pvt in Capt Meeker's Co Col Wind's N J Regt; also in Capt Squire's Co Col De Hart's N J Regt. Dischgd 1777 at Elizabethtown N J. Pensr 1818 in Muskingum co O ae 69. Ref S 41788 N J; Rept by Mrs. Alena Lyons Martindill Wellston O cf No. 134224 D A R.

LYON, JOHN, Hamilton co or N Y

Artifier N J Contl. Pensd Hamilton co (cop by J D). Report from Pens Claim office gives the following on "John Lyons" stating it is the only recd there but no indication he ever livd in O b 1753 Newark N J. Enl in Fall 1776 at Morristown N J. Movd to Oswegachie N Y in 1799 and now (1832) resides there." Ref N J R 6558. Rept by State D A R.

LYONS, BARNABAS, Trumbull co

Enl 1779 in Capt Westbrooks N J Co as substitute for father who had to support large fam. In 1781 was teamster; later pvt guarding the frontier vs the Indians. B 1762 Morris co N J. Came to Hubbard twp Trumbull co O more than 29 yrs ago (1834). Rept by State D A R and Mary Chesney chpt who add: Soldr bur Old North cem Hubbard O with stone insc: "D Oct 18 1841 in 80th yr." On stone is name Mary ——— only legible data. Ref R 6563 N J.

LYTLE, JUDGE ROBERT, Butler co

Pvt. Servd 2 mo ea yr 1776-8-9; pensd Mch 4 1831; on U S pens roll 1833 Butler co Vol 2 p 107 with $20 annually. Was 1st J P for Milford twp 1806-1809 Butler co. Came to O 1802 passport reading "Permit Robert Lytle Esq wife Margaret and ten children to pass and repass." He was b Cumberland co Pa June 28 1753; mar Margaret Sanderson; chldr: Sarah mar James Blackburn 1784; Margaret mar ——— Blair; Rachel mar Andrew Lintner; Hannah mar Mcbride (co historian); Nancy mar King; Mary mar Bone; Jane mar Robert McCain 1807; Ann mar John Douglass 1813. Soldr d 1838. Rept by Mrs. Whallon Cin chpt.

McADAM (or Macadam), JOHN, Champaign co

Pvt Pa Milit. Pensr 5-27-1833 liv in Champaign co æ 71. Ref Pa Arch Vol 23 S 3 p 584. Cop by Jane Dailey. Randolph McAdams Urbana repts: b Mar 30 1763 Northumberland co Pa; d June 16 1839 Champaign co; bur Kingston cem Salem twp. Mar abt 1797 Lycoming co Pa Katherine Steward (b 1763-d 1839; bur in same cem). Came to this co 1803; both members Baptist Ch; was 1st J of Peace in Salem twp. Srvd as spy in Rev War æ 15 for 1 yr 10 mo 20 das. By Urbana chpt.

McBRIDE, ALEXANDER, Ross co

Pvt Pa Contl. Pensr 7-21-1819. Will dated 19 Aug 1833 Prob 22 Oct 1833. Lived Adelphi; child Alexander Jr; other children not mentioned. Ref Vol A B C D Wills page 342. Rept by State D A R and Nathaniel Massie chpt.

McBRIDE, ROGER, Meigs co

Pvt Del Contl. Pens 4-29-1820. Bur prob in Syracuse twp; Linen weaver. Filing Envelope S 41846 and B L Wt 219-100. Rept by Mrs John Chase, Return Jonathan Meigs chpt.

McBURNEY, JAMES, Franklin co

Pvt N J Contl. Pensr 6-10-1819 Franklin co. Enl in 1777 in 1st Reg N J Line. (appl) Appl for a pension 1820 stated æ 70 yrs. He and wf live alone in Franklin co in 1820. (appl). Ref N J S 41839. Rept by State D A R.

McCALL, JAMES, Brown co

Servd 3 yr in the Privateer Navy (during Rev went to Pa). B Ireland; mar Jane Ramsey 1785; chldr: Margaret; John; Robert; James; Nancy; Samuel. Bur West of Fairview Ch across White Oak Creek Scott twp Brown co; limestone marker; identified through family. Rec by McCall's gr-gr grand-dau. Ref Beers' Hist Brown co pp 625-520. Landowner Scott twp Brown co 1829. Servd on first Board of Trustees Scott twp. Selected on first Jury in Clark twp 1811. Rept by Meryl B Markley Taliaferro chpt.

McCALLA, THOMAS, Columbiana co

Pvt Pa Line Pequea twp Lancaster co Pa. Bur Old Cem East Palestine. Lived Pequea twp Lancasted co Pa before coming to Columbiana co. (cf McCullough, Thomas Mahoning co this vol). Ref S A R 1912 yr Bk; Pa Arch 3 23 817. Rept by Mrs Wilma M Molsberry Youngstown.

McCANDLESS, JAMES, Montgomery co

5th S Pa Arch V 6 p 591 et al. Fr Cumberland co Pa. Capt James Poe; also 8th Battl 3rd Co 1st call 1777 p 540. (Not a pensr D C). Bur Woodland cem Montgomery co O. Rept by W M Pettit Dayton.

McCANN, JAMES, Noble co

Enl on the Juniata R in Pa on Easter Sunday 1776. Serv as pvt and fifer in Capt John Murray's Co Col Miles; Daniel Brodhead's; Bulls and Walter Stewart's Pa Regts; was in battles Long Island and Brandywine. Dischrgd at Valley Forge aft servd one yr and 9 mo. B Ireland 1759; mar Jane Quayle (Quaile) Sept 9 1779 in Sherman's Valley Pa. Chldr: Thomas b May 14 1791; d Dec 26 1838 mar Ann Morris (b 1795; d May 2 1862). (Names of other children not available). Soldr d Mch 4 1839 Center twp Noble co March 1819 was a resident of Green co Pa. Later he came to Ohio. Settled in Noble co; specialized in raising blooded stock. Appl for pension Green co Pa. Ref R 6609 Pa. March 16 1819 age 60 yrs. In 1832 he lived in Guernsey co O with son name not stated. Rept by State D A R also Columbus chpt. Filed by Ethel Millhone Anna Asbury Stone chpt.

McCARROLL, JOHN, Butler co

Pvt Pa Contl. Enl in Phil in April or May 1777 and served 6 yrs. Discharged fall May 14 1778. Appl for pens Jan 5 1818 Butler co O. Ref Pa W 7418 B L Wt 2195-100. Pens was transferred to Smith co Tenn in Aug 15 1820. Trnsfrd back to Butler co 4-15-1822. Rept by State D A R.

McCARTNEY, JAMES, Ross co

Pvt Pa Milit. Enl about 2 yrs aft com of War; served 6 mo and 15 days (cert). B 4-11-1745 Londonderry co Ireland. Mar Sarah ——; came to America 4 or 5 yrs before the Rev. Landed at Phil Pa; moved to Westmoreland co Pa; moved to Bourbon co Ky about 1793 and stayed abt 28 yrs. Later moved to Ross co Ohio. Estate probd 1836 (case 5739). Appl for pension 10-10-1832 in Ross co. Ref Pa S 2772. Rept by State D A R.

McCHUKIN, MATTHEW, Preble co

B 1757 in S C. D 1847 in Israel twp. Bur Hopewell cem. Rept by Commodore Preble chpt.

McCLANE, WILLIAM, Columbiana co

Pvt in Pa Navy Dec 1 1776 on the "Washington" commanded by John McFabich. B 1759; d 1829; bur W Weaver twp. Ref Columbiana co cem Records. Pa Arch 3 S V 23 p 21. Rept by Mrs Wilma Molsberry Youngstown O.

McCLAIN, ABIJAH, Columbiana co

Ranger Westmoreland co Pa Richard Johnston's co. Pensd in Fayette co Pa 7-15-1833. B 9-2-1754 Middlesex co N J. Mar Lydia May Feb 1836; d 7-11-1848 Green co Pa. Came to Columbiana co from Pa. Lived in Monmouth co N J until 20 yrs of age; from thence he and his parents mvd to the Flats of Grane creek O co Va whr he enl in the Pa Fifle Regt in 1776. Mar and moved to Allegheny co Pa whr he lived 10 yrs. Then moved to Green co Pa. Widow appl for pens in Green co Pa 2-18-1854. Ref Pa Arch 3- 23 Volume pp 225- 325; pensd Pa W 7408 B L Wt 17 584-160-55. Rept by State D A R; also by Mrs Wilma M Molsberry Youngstown.

McCLAIN, WILLIAM, Monroe co

Pvt Pa Contl. Srvd 6 yrs. Enl in Md July 1776; dischrgd in Phil Pa end of Rev. Was b 1754; mar Betsey æ 52; chldr: Martha æ 19; Rachel 16; Betsey 14; Hannah 11; Matilda 10; (Martha infant of Rachel's with them). (1820). Pens Monroe co 1820. Pensr 1840 æ 81 liv in O twp. Weaver. Ref S 41838 Contl Md. Rept by State D A R and Mrs E B Acomb Athens O.

McCLEAN, FERGUS, Brown co

Bur nr Ripley O æ 101. Had but one child son John; was living in Union twp as "Fogus McClain." Came from Pa during Whiskey Rebellion. Ref Beers Hist Brown co p 415; 18 Rept N S D A R. Rept by Nathan Perry chpt; Taliaferro chpt.

McCLELAND (McClelland), HUGH, Stark co

Pvt Pa Contl. Enl Mar 1777 Lancaster co Pa. Served 6 yrs. Age 67 in 1820. Wife age 52 (appl 1820). "6 chldr living with me; 4 daus & 2 sons: Sarah; Wm; James; Nancy; Elisa; Lilla." D Sept 9 1825; (recorded on pens. certf). Appl for pens Stark co O Apr 18 1818. Stone Mason. Ref S 41834 B L Wt 1116-100 Contl Pa. Rept by State D A R.

McCLELLAND, JOHN, Mahoning co

Pvt. Ser 3 V 23 p 214 Pa Arch. B 1763; D 1847 Poland O. Mar Jane —— (b 1769; d 12-1-1857). Chldr: Robert; James W; Rebecca; Eliza; Mary; Margaret; William. Bur Pres churchyard; came from Monmouth N J. Ref List of H R Baldwin S A R; Will vol 1 p 38 Mahoning co probated 1847. Tax lists 1826 1837 Poland O. Rept by Mahoning chpt.

McCLELLAND, ROBERT, Fairfield co

Pvt Pa Milit. Enl in 1776 in Lancaster co Pa. Pensr 1-8-1833 Fairfield co. Served 6 mos. Aged abt 80 yrs in 1832. Applied for pens in Fairfield co O 10-3-1832. Ref name listed p 406 Wiseman's Pioneer People Fairfield co Pa S 2765. Rept by Jane Dailey.

McCLOUD (McClurg), SAMUEL, Medina co

Pvt Mass Contl. Enl Feb 1776 in Boston Mass. Pensr 3-28-1829 in Portage co. Servd 1 yr; disc Jan 1777 in Peekskill N Y. Pens 4-28-1820 Ontario co N Y; trnsfrd to Medina co O 9-4-1821; aged 60 yrs in 1821. Mar Hannah —— aged 56 in 1821. Chldr: George aged 19 yrs in 1821. Appl for a trnsfr from N Y to Ohio 2-27-1821 in Medina co O. Ref Continental (N H) S 41820. Rept by State D A R.

McCLUNG, MATTHEW, Preble co

Pvt Pa Milit. Enl Dec 10 1776 Northumberland co Pa. Served 10 mos. B Oct 1757 Cumberland co Pa. Mar —ane —— Nov 29 1785. Chldr: Sarah; James; Mathew; Elizabeth b 1796; Wm Laughlen; Samuel Cassiday; Mary Jane; Margaret; Elizabeth b 1830. (family record). Soldr d June 2 1844 Preble co O. Appl for pens Preble co O Sept 19 1832. Ref W 9984 Pa. Has lived in O about 29 yrs 1832. Wid appld for pension Sept 11 1844. Rept by State D A R.

McCLUNG, THOMAS, Muskingum co

Pvt in Capt Abraham Scott's co 7th Battl. Lancaster co Pa Milit. B Ireland 1753; mar Nancy Graham 1774 (b 1758 d 1847). Margaret was a dau. Soldr d 1832 Pleasant Valley O. Ref Vol 113 p 82 D A R Lin No 112252. Rept by Mrs Oehlke Nathan Perry chpt.

McCLUNIE (McCluney), MICHAEL, Washington co

Pvt Pa Milit. Enl at Mount Rock near Carlisle Pa 5-27-1776. B 1742 age 68 yrs in 1820. "Have no family" (appl). D 7-31-1823. On file in Pens Bureau. Appl for pens Wash co O May 22 1818. Res of Newport twp. Weaver. On July 24 1820 appl in Marietta in Com Pleas Court stating property valued at $5. Ref S 41 845 Pa; Vol 3 p 413. Rept by Helen Sloan; also by State D A R.

McCLURE, HUGH, Fayette co

Exec Doc 37 of yr 1852. Refused a pens as srvd less than 6 mo. Rept by Wm Pettit.

McCLURE, JAMES, Washington co

B 1759; d 1826. Rept by Helen Sloane.

McCLURG, ROBERT, Scioto co

Pvt N H Contl. Pensr 5-31-1820 Medina co. Servd 3 yrs. Enl 1775 Entram Mass. B 1756; mar Hitabel; chldr: Uriah; David; Asa; Abraham; Polly; John; Harriet. Appld for pension Ontario co N Y May 14 1818. Appl for trnsfr of pen to Medina co O Jan 27 1827. Appld for trnsfr of pension to Scioto co O Jan 3 1839. Ref S 41859 Continental Mass N H. Rept by State D A R.

McCOHAN, THOMAS B, Preble co

Pensr 1840 Dixon twp Preble co. (No æ so might be war of 1812). Rept by Jane Dailey.

McCOLLOUGH, ROBERT, Hamilton co

Sergt Conn Contl. Pensd Hamilton co 1818; age 65 yrs in 1818. Enl in March 1776 at Morristown N J. Ref Conn S 41,833. Rept by State D A R.

McCOLLUM, CORNELIUS, Clermont co

Ensign N J Milit. Pensr 6-22-1833 Clermont co. Served 2 yrs. B 1-4-1749 Monmouth co N J. Enl in 1776 in Glouster co N J under Genl Washington Capt Paine. Ref N J S 2767. Moved to Glouster co N J at the age of 17 yrs. Resided for about 29 yrs in Glouster co N J after the war and moved to Clermont co O. Rept by State D A R.

McCOMAS, WILLIAM, Jefferson co

Capt co of Milit Harford co Md. B in Ga; mar Aramanthe ——; dau Rebecca McComas Gillis. Soldr d May 27 1828 aged 89. Bur Pioneer Cem located in S E edge of E Springfield. Family marker. Ref Md Arch 1775-76. Pp·387-538 Harford co Md; Oath of Fidelity Brumbaugh Md Recs V 2-p 247 Mar 24 1778. Rept by Mrs W S Van Fossen Columbus chpt.

McCONNELL (McConnel), FRANCIS, Belmont co

Pvt N J Contl. Pensd 1819 in Belmont co. Enl Nov 1 1775; served in Regt commanded by Col Wind one yr. B Ireland 1754. Mar Mary —— Jan 14 1781. Chldr: Francis McConnell age 16; also an orphan child Austen Henry æ 7. Soldr d Feb 21 1833 appld for pens Belmont co Mar 18 1818 & again Aug 5 1820. Emigrated fr Ireland to N J 1774. Mary McConnell appl for wid pens Belmont co O Mar 20 1846. Ref W 3846 N J. Rept by Jane Dowd Dailey Albany O St Ch.

McCOOK, GEORGE, Columbiana co

Rev soldr rec not yet found. Was b 1752; mar Mary McCormack (b 1763 d 8-3-1833; bur beside husband). Soldr d 1822 July 4; bur Center twp. Ref Col co Cem Recds. Rept by Mrs Wilma Molsberry.

McCORMICK, REV FRANCIS, Hamilton co

Enl age 17 served through two campaigns. Present at surrender of Lord Cornwallis. Recorded on Pension Rolls of Hamilton Co of 1832 Va Line Pvt military record cop from Gen Samuel F Crey; parents George McCormick & wf came fr Scotland 1759; mar Rebecca —— (b 1767 d 1840). Soldr d Anderson twp 7-26-1836. Bur Salem churchyard Hamilton co O. Came to Milford O 1795 to farm; built a cabin here; to Anderson twp in 1807. Was associated with Rev Philip Latch in Meth ch work in Va; two were earliest Meth Preachers in the Northwest Territory; conducted great revival Meetings in early years in Hamilton co following 1 yr like work in Va; preaching in great Camp meetings and revivals. Ref D A R descendant Mrs Bertha (C E) Thuma Jamestown O. Rept by Mrs E P Whallon Cin chpt.

McCORMICK, JOHN, Adams co

Enl Apr 1788 and dischrgd Franklintown 1779. His pension claim rejected because he did not serve 6 mos. Ensign in 6th co Milit Battallion of Pa. (A list of the 8 Milit. Battl of Cumberland co Pa Field officers & rank in battl is on file in pens bureau). B July 9 1756 Cumberland co Pa. Parents came to Va when John was 3 yrs old; mar Hannah ——. Chldr: Crowell Sill; Mary Anderson; Sarah; William; James. Soldr bur Winchester Adams co O Miller operated McCormick Mill for many yrs. Justice of the Peace. Will probated June 16 1837 V 1 p 373. Probate Court Brown co. Ref Beers Hist Brown co Biog Sec page 76; also p 582; R 6652 Pa. He was living in Eagle twp Adams co O Aug 10 1841 (appl). Rept by State D A R; Meryl B Markley Taliaferro chpt; also Sycamore chpt.

McCORMICK, JOHN, Richland co

Exec Doc 37 of yr 1853 refused a pens as srvd less than 6 mo. Rept by Wm Pettit.

McCOY, ALEXANDER, Columbiana co

Ranger Washington co Pa; ranger Westmoreland co Pa; pvt Capt Robt Samuel's Co 8 Battl Cumberland co Milit on a tour of duty in the Kishacanquilles valley in 1782. (In this same co are fellow settlers of Trumbull and Mahoning cos, Moses Dickey, James McGill, Wm Carson). One son was James (b 1806 Center twp); Soldr d 9-24-1826 very old; livd in Center twp. Ref Pa Arch 3 XXIII 201; 213 etc 454. Rept by Mrs Wilma Molsberry.

McCOY, DANIEL, ? co

Capt. From old scrap bk clipping of Rev Soldrs interested in or participating in Marietta settlement descendants of whom are bur in Washington co. Listed here for research by Marietta chpt.

McCULLICK, WILLIAM, Mahoning co

Pvt. "Va Men in Rev" pp 127, 175. Chldr: John b (1781-12-31-1818) mar Eunice dau of Wm Logan Rev Soldr. Rept by Mahoning chpt.

McCULLOCK, ROBERT, ? co

Sergt. Listed in Invalid pensrs of U S belonging to Ohio paid at Chillicothe annually $48. Cop fr p 172 Pensrs 1818 by Jane Dailey (cf p 238 V 1 Ohio Roster).

McCULLOUGH, THOMAS, Mahoning co

Pvt in Co 7 9th Battl Lancaster co Pa Milit 1780. Pa Arch. B 1762 Pa; mar Rose Ann Addison in 1804. One known chld was Mary b 1808 mar Thomas Kirkpatrick (1792-1863). Soldr d 1858 Youngstown O. Ref No 124632 D A R. Rept by Nathan Perry chpt to Mahoning chpt.

McCUMSEY, ROBERT, Mercer co

Pvt Capt Collier's co Gen Whitley Regt Pa for 12 mo; resided in Harrisburg Pa when enlisted. "Was 76 on 7th May last 1832" cop fr pens appl. Nov 2 1832 appl for pens Act June 7 1832. Lived in Franklin co Pa until 1828; came to Ohio where he lived (1832). Crane Schenck Dayton O Nov 8 1818 sent appl papers. Pens Act June 7 1832 bk E Vol 8 p 10. Recd $40 begin Mch 4 1831; iss 5-6-1833. Rept cop Jane Dailey fr old Pens Office D C.

McCURDY, ROBERT, Wayne co

Pvt Pa Contl. Pensr 9-22-1819 Wayne co. Enl Carlisle Pa July 1 1775. Srvd 1 yr. Ae 65 1819. "Wf d" (appl 1821). Chldr: "dau." Appl for pens Harrison co O June 8 1819 res Wayne co. School master. Ref S 41 851 Pa. Appl for pens Wayne co O July 3 1821. No will; no deed; Francis McCurdy Admst of Chattels. D in Wayne co Dec 12th 1824 aged 69. Ref Pa Archives 5th S V 2 Page 729. Rept by Wooster Wayne chpt; State D A R; Mary Steinmetz Reading Pa; Hetuck chpt.

McDANIEL, EDWARD, Brown co

Pensr 1840 Huntington twp Brown co age 95. B in Maryland, parents Watson and Nancy McDaniel; mar Mary Waldron; chldr: Hiram b 1822 in Mason co Ky. Only one found. Bur Evans Cemetery in Huntington twp. Rept by Meryl B Markley Taliaferro chpt.

McDANIEL, PATRICK, Adams co

Pvt Pa Contl. Pensr 7-7-1819. Enl June 1775 in Pa. Dischrgd Dec 1776 in N J. Served 1 yr. Age 76 in 1818. Res Hamilton co O May 1 1818. Res same co Sept 4 1820. Ref S 41 861 Pa; Evans and Stivers History of Adams co p 331. By Meryl B Markley vice chairman and State D A R.

McDANIEL, WILLIAM, Clinton co

Exec Doc 37 of yr 1852. Refused a pens as srvd less than 6 mo. Rept by Wm Pettit.

McDERMOT, MICHAEL, ? co

Pvt. Listed in Invalid pensrs of U S belonging to Ohio pd at Chillicothe $96 annually. Cop fr Pensrs of 1818 p 172. By Mrs O D Dailey Albany O.

McDONALD, JAMES, Mahoning co

Pvt. Pens appl bk 6 p 167 Circuit Ct Warren Trumbull co O. Soldr d Coitsville. Rept by Mahoning chpt.

McDONALD, COL JOHN, Ross co

Mrs Catherine McDonald consort of Col John McDonald a Rev sold of Popular Ridge Ross co O d Mar 22 1850; she was mar Feb 15 1799. Copy fr Scioto Gazette May 15 1850 by H C Pemberton. Rept by Mrs. Orion King Circleville. One McDonald, John b 1760; d 1837. Rept by Helen Sloane in Washington co O.

McDONOUGH, REDMONT, Warren co

Pvt Va Contl Warren co. Pensr 3-9-1819. Enl in Penn Mar 1777 in Perth Valley Northumberland co Pa. At Battle of Brandywine he was taken prisoner and remained prisoner of the Br between 15 & 16 mos; then released (he believes on parole). Served in Regt commanded by Col Hendrick Va Line 3 yrs. After having enl in Penn he was marched to Phil then to Somerset co N J where he was drafted with his co & 2 other cos to fill up the 6th Va Regt & while in this service was taken prisoner as afsd. B 1745; mar "Jane —— æ 60." (appl in 1820). Made appl for pens at Lebanon Warren co O Aug 22 1820. S 41852 Va. Rept by State D A R. Listed in rejected pens appl. Ref Doc No 31 Jan 6 1831 as not being in indigent circumstances accd to Act of May 1830. Rept by Blanche Rings.

McDOUGAL, ALEXANDER, Richland co

Serg 2 yrs N Y Line. Pensd 12-31-1832 in Argyle N Y. Pensr 1840 Madison twp Richland co age 86 liv w Jas A McDougal. Enl Aug 1775 and was dischgd Feb 26 1780. Ae 78 yrs in 1832. Transferred from N Y to Ohio to be with son and back to N Y to be with his other children (appl). Appl for a transfer from N Y 8-12-1839 in Richland co Ohio. (Appl). Ref S 29320 N Y. Rept by State D A R. (Compare w other record, this vol).

McDOUGAL, ALEXANDER, Hardin co Ky or O.

Pvt & Lieut in Co commd by Capt Blissinghom Regt commd by Col Fare in S C for 18 mos and 2 mos lieut. B North part of Ireland May 1 1741. Appl for pens Hardin co Ky Jan 21 1833. Sailed from Ireland 1762 & in Aug of same yr landed in Phil Pa. Remained there 3½ yrs; then moved to Wilmington N C where lived abt 7 yrs; then to S C near Indian line & in 1773 to Union co. Enl 1777 1801 moved to Hardin co Ky. Ref S 30576 S C by State D A R. In deaths of Rev Soldiers fr American Almanac and Repository of Useful Knowledge is "Mar 3 1841 in Hardin co Ohio in his 102nd yr Rev Alexander McDougal a Baptist minister and a soldier of the Rev." Ref S 30576 S C. Rept Mary O Steinmetz Pa. Further research must prove whether in O or Ky. (J D).

McDOUGAL, JOSEPH, Scioto co

Exec Doc 37 of yr 1852. Refused a pens as srvd less than 6 mo. Rept by Wm Pettit.

McDOWELL, JOHN, Jefferson co

Surgeon's mate; recd sword for distinguished service; original member of the Cincinnati; 6th Pa battl. Enl 1776; in 1778 rose to rank of Surgeon. Mar Martha Johnston (e); chldr: two sons were Alexander and John. Soldr b 1750; d Steubenville O 1825 age 77. Ref D A R Lin V 10 p 242; V 5 p 45;V 19 p 236; Pa Arch Vol 1 p 167 No 18570 S A R. Rept by Wm Pettit and Nathan Perry chpt.

McELHANEY, FELIX, Fayette co

Pensioner in 1840; aged 90 residing in Union twp. B 1750. Rept by Washington C H chpt.

McELROY, JOHN, Trumbull co

Fife Major 2nd Pa. Entitled to 200 acres of land for service Pa Arch S 3 V 3 P 696. Chldr: Mary; James; Jane; John; others. Soldr d Warren O Feb 18 1841. Ref In "Adler's (Pa) Journal 16 Mar 1841" deaths of Rev Soldiers is an account and "d in Warren O Feb 18 1841 John McElroy, aged 83 b in Ireland. Was in 16 engagements." Ref Amer Almanac Reposit Information Boston. Rept by Mary Owen Steinmetz Reading Pa; Mary Chesney chpt.

McELROY, JOHN, Jefferson co

Pvt of cavalry N Y Contl. Pensr 3-26-34 in Jefferson co Act 1832. Trnsferred to Ill. Listed here to avoid further research in Ohio. Rept by Jane Dailey.

McELROY, WILLIAM, Jefferson co

"Soldr of Rev." Ref Doyle, Joseph B 20th century "History of Steubenville and Jefferson co O." p 467. Rept by Mrs Rathburn, Librarian Ohio State Libry Columbus.

McELVAIN, SAMUEL, Franklin co

Pvt. Under Capt Gibson & McTeer Col Wilson also Ensign in Capt McAllister's Co Col Purdy's Pa Regt. B 1753 Lancaster co Pa (prob). Parent Moses and Agnes (Miller) McElvain Lancaster & Cumberland cos Pa. Mar Elizabeth dau of Col James Purdy Cumberland co Pa; now Juniata co Pa 1779; b 1761-1840. Chldr: William b Sept 26 1780; Fermanagh twp Cumb co Pa d Upper Sandusky O; Martha (King) b 1782-1846; James b 1784 killed by Blackhawks 1832; Robert b 1786 d young; John (f Henry L Doherty) b 1789-1858 Andrew b Sept 3 1791 Bourbon co Ky (now Harrison) d Lincoln Ill 1861. Mar 1st Patsy Hunter; 2nd Jane Hunter Columbus O; Joseph b 1794-1834 mar Margaret Hunter b 1796-18—; Purdy b 1800 d 1848; Matilda (O'Harra) b 1804-1874. Two d in infancy. Samuel McElvain d Columbus O Feb 8 1806; bur Old Sullivant burying ground on Scioto R Franklintown now Columbus O. Headstone broken and misplaced. With Sullivants party surveyed military lands Franklin co name on tablet in

Memorial Hall. Ref V 123 p 45 D A R Lin No 122143; Old N W Quarterly Mag V 15 1912 p 167-177; Pa Arch 6th S V VI pp 243, 249, 251. Reptd by F C McElvain 1258 Topeka Blvd Topeka Kans; also Columbus chpt D A R and Nathan Perry chpt.

McEVER, JAMES, Athens co

Pvt Mass Contl. Pensr 7-7-1819. Serv 2 yr and 6 mo. Mar Louisa 1779. Seneca ? was one; Soldr d Jan 24 1829. Appl for pens July 5 1820 in Athens co O. Ref Mass S 23936. Enl at Hancock Mass in 1781. Rept by State D A R.

McFARLAND, WALTER, Knox co

Pvt Pa Contl. Pensr 4-30-1819 in Knox co age 78. Served 3 yrs. Age 62 yrs in 1818. Enl in 1778 at Carlisle twp Pa. Appl for pens 8-17-1818 Knox co O. Ref O Pen Roll 1835 111 0-71; Pa S 41835. Rept by State D A R.

McFARLAND, WILLIAM, Greene co

Muster Roll Pa Navy of the Ranger Galley commanded by John Mitchell Dec 1st 1776 to Jan 1 1777. Was drummer boy. Also named as Frontier Ranger 1777-1783. B 1763; d Sept 1st 1816; bur Old Massie Creek Cem near Xenia. Family stone in good condition. Ref Pa Arch 3rd S V 23 p 204. Rept by Cedar Cliff chpt.

McGAFFEY, NEAL, ? co

Lieut. From old scrap bk clipping of Rev soldrs interested in or participating in Marietta settlement descendants of whom are bur in Washington co. Listed here for research by Marietta chpt.

McGEE (or Magee), WILLIAM, Washington co

Pvt N H Contl. Pensr 5-21-1819 Washington co. Served 3 yrs fr 1777. B 1749. Mar Margaret —— age 60. Enl N Y 1777. Servd in N H Line. Disc 1780 Danbury Conn "formerly res of Cambridge co of Charlotte N Y." (certified by one of his former officers). chldr: William liv w son Robert is a widower in 1823. N H S 41840 Appl pens July 24 1820. Ref V 3 p 413 property value $350.27 and May 9 1823. Ref V 4-119. Stating property value at $24.00 in Common Pleas Court Marietta O. Rept by Helen Sloane; also by State D A R.

McGHOGAN (Gougan, McGoogin), ALEXANDER, Belmont co

Pvt Pa Contl. Enl Dec 1775 Lancaster co Pa. In Regt commd by Col St Clair Pa Line 1 yr. Was b 1748; mar Jane —— Westmoreland co Pa 1793. No chldr. (appl 1820). Soldr d Sept 1833 Belmont co; bur Union cem St Clairsville O. Inscript on monument "Soldr of Rev." Was a weaver. Pens appl Belmont co O July 24 1820. Ref W 2681 Pa. Wid appl Warren co O Dec 4 1880. Rept by State D A R.

McGILL, JAMES, Mahoning co

Pvt. Ser 3 Vol 23 pp 222, 240 Pa Arch; Ser 5 Vol 2-4-6. Mar Isabel; son James mar Margaret. Soldr d Poland twp. Settled on Sec 12 Ellsworth; later removed to Poland. A Rev soldr from Washington co Pa. Ref Hist Trumbull and Mahoning cos Vol 2 p 99; Hist Washington co Pa p 83; Deed bk C p 526 James and Isabel McGill to Ellsworth 1818; Tax list 1826 Milton twp son James. Rept by Mahoning chpt.

McGOWAN, CHARLES, ? co

A wagoner listed in rejected pens appl. Doc No 31 Jan 6 1831 as case not provided for by law. Rept by Blanche Rings.

McGINNES (or McGuinnes), JAMES, Stark co

Enl 1776 Cumberland co Pa. Srvd 1 yr. Pens appl June 30 1818 Stark co O. Ref S 41850 Pa. Rept by State D A R.

McGOWN (Goen), JOHN, Franklin co

Rev soldr d Aug 31 1825 æ 75 in Columbus O. Was a refugee from Nova Scotia; joined the standard of U S in their struggle for freedom. Had a masonic funeral. Ref cop fr Col Gazette Sept 1 1825 issue by Blanche Rings.

McGUFFEY, WILLIAM, Mahoning co

Pvt. Ser 5 Vol 6; S 6 p 621 Vol 2 York co Pa Arch. Was b 1742 Scotland; mar Ann McKittrick (1746-Feb 8 1826); one son was Alexander b 1768 (mar Ann Holmes) father of Prof Wm McGuffey compiler of the readers. Soldr d Feb 21 1836 Coitsville twp Deer Creek cem Lawrence co Pa D A R dedicated June 1932. Joined Contl Army 1779 Washington co Pa 1789 and to Coitsville twp O in 1800. Ref Trumbull and Mahoning cos Vol 2 pp 166-196; Sat Evening Post 1926 Youngstown Vindicator June 21 1832. Rept by Mahoning chpt.

McGUIRE, CHARLES, Butler co

Pvt Pa Contl. Pensr 11-25-1819 Butler co O. Enl for 3 yrs in 1777 in Lancaster co Pa. Servd 3 yrs. Discharged in Jan 1781 at Trenton N J. Age 65 in 1819. Chldr: "granddaughter age 8." Res Butler co O Aug 9 1819. Res Madison twp Butler co O Aug 28 1820. Ref S 41,831 Pa. Rept by State D A R.

McHENRY, ROBERT, Muskingum co

Pvt Va Contl. Pens 10-8-1822 Muskingum co O. Servd 3 yrs from first of June 1779. Age 69 in 1820. Appld for pension Nov 27 1820. Ref S 41,849 Pa. Rept by State D A R. Enl Dec 1775 Pa; disc Jan 1777 Phil Pa. Enl again first of June 1779 in Pa and served till disc in Feb 1781.

McILHANY, FELIX, Logan co

Pvt Pa Contl. Pensr 6-2-1819. No data found aft going to three different towns. All said ancestor came f rom Ireland only two generations ago. Rept by Bellefontaine chpt. Pa Contl Pension No 11221. Pvt 7th Pa Regiment 1 yr. Enl in the fall of 1775 in Co commanded by Capt David Greer. Pensd in Harrison co Ky 6-2-1819. Transfrd to Logan co O. Age 63 yrs in 1818. Chldr: Mary aged 52 yrs; Sarah 37 (a cripple); Rebecca 35 yrs in 1829. Lived with dau in Logan O Feb 1831. Ref S 41848 Pa. Rept by State D A R.

McINTIRE, JOHN, Champaign co

Pvt Pa Milit. Pensr 9-21-1833 Champaign co. Enl in Dec 1776 when a res of Warwick twp Bucks co Pa since the war he has resided in Cumberland and Westmoreland cos Pa and moved to Champaign co O in 1813. B Jan 1759 Warwick twp Bucks co Pa. Res of Harrison twp Champaign co O in 1833. (appl). Ref Pa S 2802. Rept by State D A R .

McINTOSH, MAJ DUNCAN, Ashtabula co

2nd Regt Conn Line; bur Cem Windsor O. Ref 18 N S D A R rep p 225. Cop by Nathan Perry chpt.

McINTYRE, THOMAS, Madison co

Pension No 15567 put in the Pa Line 1 yr. Pensd 10-4-1818 in Clark co O. Enl 1-1-1776 6th Pa Regt co commanded by Robert Adams. Age 70 yrs in 1820. Mar Margaret aged 75 yrs in 1820. Ref S 41,854 Pa. Rept by State D A R.

McKAIG, PATRICK, Wayne co

Pvt Capt John Duncan's Co 6th. Batt Lancaster co Pa Milit. Name of child A Patrick McKaig Jr mar Rachel Starr in 1799. Bur Wayne co O no grave found. Ref VIII p 170 No 110537 D A R Lin. Rept by Jane Dailey.

McKEAN (McCane), ROBERT, Mahoning co

Pvt 3rd class Ser 5 V 6 p 450 Pa Archives. Capt Wm Strain. Mar Mary ——; chldr: brot up 8. D abt 1843 Ellsworth. Ref Hist Trumbull & Mahoning co V 2 p 199; Deed Bk H p 180; McCane Robert & Mary to —— Milton 1838. Tax list 1826 McCane Robert. Rept Mahoning chpt.

McKEAN, THOMAS, Mahoning co

Pvt 3rd class. Ser 5 V 6 pp 82, 110 Pa Arch. Capt James Young. D early Ellsworth O. 3 sons & 1 dau. Ref Hist Trumbull & Mahoning co V 2 p 99. Rept by Mahoning chpt.

McKEE, SAMUEL, Franklin co

Pvt in Washington co Pa Milit. B 1744 Pa; mar 1781 Rachel Davidson, b 1756-1841. Eli was one son. Soldr d Ohio July 20 1823 Columbus Psd Apr 26 1819 aged 69. Ref V 125 p 76 D A R Lin No 124249 Franklin co Adm Docket I-187. Estate 0414 adm apptd 8-30-1823. Rept by Nathan Perry chpt; Mrs W S VanFossen Columbus chpt.

McKELVEY, WILLIAM, Huron co

Pension No 14534. Pvt Pa Line. Enl 5-18-1777 in Chester co Pa. Pensd in Greenfield twp Huron co O 9-6-1819. B in 1760 in Ireland. Chldr: Robert T age 19 yrs; Eliza 16; Polly 13; Julian 8 in 1820, with whom he liv in Greenfield twp Huron co O. Ref S 41844 Pa. Rept by State D A R.

McKENSIE, JAMES, Columbiana co

Pvt in Capt Jacob Stark's Co 10th Pa Line May 1780; June to Aug 1780; enl May 3 1777; enl May 5 1777-1778. Was b 1756; mar Eleanor (b 1779 d 9-21-1768). Soldr d 2-20-1855 æ 99 yrs 3 mos in W Beaver twp. Came to Col co in 1807; Capt in war of 1812. Ref Cem records of late Henry Baldwin; Hist Col co; Pa Arch III p 538, 561, 567, 577. (Cens of 1840 lists one James McKenzie Ashland co as pensr Orange twp æ 71. J D). Rept by Wilma Molsberry.

McKINLEY, JOHN, Wyandot co

Officer in 13th Va Regt. Memb Col Crawford's Exped against Indians 1782. Killed & beheaded by Indians June 1782 on banks of Little Lymochtee creek near where Crawford was burned at stake. Ref Randall's & Ryan's Hist of Ohio V11 p 368; Lineage No 71977 Mrs Willis Jones 55 East Longview Ave Col O; also No 162,062 Miss Hilda S McKinley 1374 Neil Ave Col O. Rept by Jacobus Westervelt chpt.

McKINNIE, HENRY, Mahoning co

Pvt Ser 6 p 132 Wash co Pa. Pa Arch. Mar Barbara Stewart (1764-1814); chldr: Alexander b 1786 N Y; James b 1793; Matthew 1795; Alexander 1799 mar Nancy Dickinson; Agnes 1802 mar David Fusselman; Elinor b 1805 mar John Price; Henry 1808; John. Henry McKinnie d abt 1812 Youngstown. Ref Deed Bk C p 79 McKinnie Barbara from John Young 1812. Land contracted for by Henry McKinnie decd. Deed Bk B p 164 Henry McKinnie fr Youngstown ht 1808. Mahoning Free Democrat 1852 decd James C McKinnie. Rept by Mahoning chpt.

McKINNON (McKennon), JOSEPH, Columbiana co

Fought in Rev. Was also paymaster in Indian Wars. B 1734 in England. Mar Margaret Dillon (d Mch 27 1830 age 73 yrs 6 mos). Chldr: Michael b Aug 1 1781 at Raccoon Washington co Pa (He was mar 3 times); George D; Nancy mar Riley d. aged 104 yrs; George mar Ada Babb dau John Babb (1768-1829) the 1st owner of Babb's Island which he bought fr the government. Soldr d June 22 1809 aged 75; had lived with his children. Came to America with father before Rev. Father was Episcopal clergyman with allegiance sworn to King; he returned to England at beginning of Rev. Joseph remained in America and fought. Was School teacher. Came to East Liverpool in 1795 aft losing property in Pa. Stopped in Wellsburg W Va aft Pa. Ref Hist Col Co McCord p 471, 462. No 269373. Rept by Mrs Wilma M Molsberry 143 Broadway Youngstown O. Bethia Southwick a new chpt in 1929 had only time to list the name, Vol 1 Ohio Roster.

McKNIGHT, ELI, Belmont co

Pvt Va Milit. Pensd 1833 Belmont co O. Served in Co Commd by Col West Va Milit 6 mos. B 1760. Father moved to Loudon co Va. Appld for pens Loudon Co Va Nov 16 1832. S 2710 Va. Rept by State D A R. Listed p 281 "Va Milit in Rev" as liv in Belmont co O where he was transferred fr Ky. Cop by Jane Dailey.

McLAIN, JOHN, Mahoning co

Service in Cumberland co Pa Milit. Pa Arch Ser 5 Vol 23 p 634. Was b in Scotland. Ref 17931 S A R. Rept by Wm Pettit.

McLENE, JEREMIAH, Trumbull co

Served in Legislature fr Columbus District; Secy of State for 25 yrs. Rev Soldier. Ref Galbraith's Collection of Ohio History for Asso Press. Rept by Hetuck chpt.

McLEROY, JAMES, ? co

Pvt listed in rejected pens appl. Ref Doc No 31 Jan 6 1831 as no satisfactory evidence of service exhibited. Rept by Blanche Rings.

McLLANAN (McClanan), MORDECAI, Montgomery co

Pvt N J Milit. Pensd 7-27-1833 Montgomery co 3 yrs 6 mo serv. Enl 1776 or 7 into the N J Militia. Was residing in Hunterdon co N J at the time he entered the service. He moved fr there to Montgomery co O 14 yrs aft the war B Oct 6 1762. Ref N J S 18506. Rept State D A R.

McMAHAN, ABNER, Trumbull co

Pvt N J contl. Pensr 9-6-1819 Trumbull co Enl at Hackettstown N J in fall of 1775 and marched to Canada. Pension claim S 41832. Resident of Bazetta twp Trumbull co O. Rept by Mary Chesney chpt.

McMAHON, CORNELIUS, Ross co

Pvt listed in Invalid pensrs of U S belonging to Ohio paid at Chillicothe annually $64. Cop fr p 172 Pensrs 1818 at S of R Libry L A by Jane Dailey.

McMAHON, JOHN, Ross co

D in Ross co 17-4 ? age 94 Pa Arch. Rept by Mary Steinmetz Reading Pa.

McMAHAN (or McMahon), JOSEPH, Adams co

Pvt Va Contl. Pensd. Apr 10 1828 in Adams co O. Served 3 yrs fr 1777. Enl Spring of yr 1777. Geo Rice' Co Col Heath's Va Regt May 1761. Mar Mary Schryhauser (b 1771) mar 1792. Chldr: Abner age 19; Phebe age 15; Gregg age 12; Oliver age abt 18; other children: John; Elizabeth; James; Benjamin; Joseph; Robert; Sarah (cop fr family record submitted by wid). D Apr 1838 Cincinnati O. Res Adams co O. Mar 19 1828. Widow res in Whiteside co Ill on Jan 23 1850. Albany twp age 79. Ref W 23941 Va; B L Wt 385 a 160-55 V 112 No 111294 D A R Lin; Evans & Stivers History Adams co p 331 by Meryl B Markley. Rept by State D A R & Jane Dailey.

McMANNERS, JOHN, Ashtabula co

5th & 8th Reg Conn Line. Pensr 1840 Sheffield twp age 80. Cem Gageville O. Located by Mary Stanley chpt. Rep 18 N S D A R p 226; 21 Rept N S D A R p 103.

McMEEN, JOHN, Warren co

B Cumberland co Pa 1756; d 1828 Service in Cumberland co Milit. 3rd Ser Pa Arch Vol VI pp 214 238. Ruling Elder of the Dick's Creek Pres Ch fr its orig until his death. Bur Dick's Crk Pres chyd. Mkd by Richard Montgomery S A R Dayton.

McMILLEN, DANIEL JAMES, Ross co

Drummer Pa Milit. Served 9 mo. Enl in the Spring 1776 Chester co Pa. B May 1760 Ireland; appl for pens June 4 1833 in Ross co O. Came from Ireland to America in 1774 and went to Chester co Pa. Resided in Del and Md until 1819 when he movd to Ross co O. Ref Pa S 9007. Rept by State D A R.

McMILLEN, JAMES, Muskingum co

Under Col Crawford in Sandusky Campaign 1782. B Dec 1st 1758 in Pa. Parent William and Margaret. Mar Jane Bell. Chldr: Andrew; George; William; James; Isaac; Theodosius; Mary and Diver. D 1821; came fr Washington co Pa to Licking co in 1808; thence to Muskingum co 1812. Rept by Hetuck chpt.

McMINNIS, JAMES, ? co

Pvt refused a pens as srvd in regt not on Contl Estab. Ref Doc No 31 Jan 6 O S Libry. Rept by Blanche Rings.

McMULLEN, JAMES, ? co

Pvt refused a pens as srvd in regt n ot on Contl Estab. Ref Doc No 31 Jan 6 1831 O S Libry. Rept by Blanche Rings.

McMURRAY, WILLIAM, Noble co

1st Reg Pa Line Capt Lowden. Applied for aid Act of 3-18-1818. Was 67 yrs in 1820; farmer in Beaver twp Noble co. Mar Anne. Chldr: Anne; Wm; George; Mary; Betsy; Patty; Hannah; Daramirah. Bur Founder's cem. (family). Owner of McMurray Inn (Old Buckingham place) estate of over 100 A. Ref Record of deed given by Wm McMurray & wife Lucinda McM. (Military twp). Rept by Anna Asbury Stone chpt.

McNEALY, JAMES, Wood co

Rev War Soldr bur Sugar Grove Cemetery old cemetery on the Reason Whitacre farm east of Cygnet Cem opened 1841 Wood co O. I see by Wood co History that a Hannah McNeely mar Edward Whitacre a bro of above Reason Whitacre. This Edward Whitacre d 1846 Wood co. I suppose that is why McNealy was bur there. Rept by Margaret C Rider Tontogany O. Black Swamp chpt.

McNETT, ADAM, Delaware co

Bur Sunbury Cemetery O. D June 25 1848 age 85. A patriot of the Rev. Rept 21 N S D A R. By Nathan Perry chpt.

McNINCH, ARCHIBALD, Franklin co

Order bk 6 133. Appld for pens from Franklin co June 7 1832. Cop by Blanche Rings. Miss Eva McNinch Columbus O gives the following: "Archibald McNinch came in 1816 from Alleghaney co Pa to O and settled nr Portsmouth Scioto co; later came to Franklin co and settled nr Worthington O. Was an Indian fighter. Date and place of his death unknown but thot to be close to Columbus. Was survived by wid; and two sons; Archibald; Andrew Jr. Archibald Jr was never mar; was badly burned when æ 4 and had bad feet; aft his fathers death he livd with his mother until her death; aft her death livd with his bro Andrew J McNinch. Soldr may be bur in Saunders gr-yd Franklin twp. Andrew was b Oct 8 1812 in Pa; d Oct 18 1896 Franklin twp this co; both boys bur Wesley Chapel cem nr Saunders Gr-yd. Rept by Blanche Rings.

McNITT (or McKnight), ADAM, Delaware co

Pvt Mass Line 3 yrs. Pensd 5-24-1820 Chatauqua co 'N Y. Transferred to Licking co O 11-23-1832. Later transferred to Delaware co O. Age 69 in 1832 Wooster Mass. Mar Mercy Sarles ? Nov 1821. Enl Jan 1781 in Shilburn Mass. Came to Licking co in 1832 and moved to Delaware in 1848. Chldr: Ezra age 18 in 1820; Prudence age 14; Molly 12; Harriet 8; Alvira 5. D 5-25-1848 Berkshire O. Ref 21st Rept N S D A R; Mass W 559; B L Wt 26088-160-55. Rept by State D A R & Jane Dailey.

McNUTT, ALEXANDER, Columbiana co

Depreciation Pay Pvt Chester co Militia. Pvt in Capt John Addams Co 4th class 5 Battl Cumberland co Pa Militia Oct 1777. Served as Pvt in various companies of Cumb co Milit thru Aug 1782. Came from Va. Ref Pa Arch 5 S IV V p 297; 5-6 V pp 326, 338, 559, 650. Rept by Mrs Wilma M Molsberry 143 Broadway Youngstown O No 269373.

McNUTT, ALEXANDER, Preble co

    Served thro war; also in War of 1812; was Lieut of Ohio Riflemen. Surveyed Cumberland Trail or Natl Rd thro Preble co O. B Fredericktown Md 1769. Mar Elizabeth Tillman in Tenn. Had a large family. Bur in old cem near Lewisburg. Rept by Commodore Preble chpt.

McNUTT, ALEXANDER, Mahoning co

Pvt 4th class S 3 V 23 P 802 Pa Arch Capt Wm Wilson 8th Battl 1780-81. Also S 5 V 4 559 Cumberland co. Capt —— Col Alex Brown Mar Rachel ——. chldr: Elizabeth; Samuel b 1798; Robert; William; Abraham; Alexander; Nancy; Sarah; Rachel; Barned; David; Hannah. D abt 1827 Springfield twp. Came from Va Henry R Baldwin Deed Bk O p 497 to Alex McNutt 1812; Deed Bk W p 657 Alex McNutt Heirs 1837. Will Bk 5 p 400 Alexander McNutt Probated 1827. Rept by Mahoning chpt.

McNUTT, BENJAMIN, Mahoning co

Pvt Ref S 5 Vol 6 p 250 Pa Arch; Revolutionary list of Henry R Baldwin S A R. Rept by Mahoning chpt.

McPIKE, JOHN, Adams co

Pvt Pa Milit. Pensr 5-24-1833 Adams co. Enl Mar 15 1775 in York co Pa. Completed his term and re-enlisted at Sandy Creek Glades and 5 other re-enl to Nov 1777. Cens of 1840 liv in Liberty twp age 90. 14 months 1st Lt about 3 mo Orderly Serg; was 81 yrs old in 1832. Appl for pens Act 27 1832. Ref Pa S 2810. Rept by State D A R. Ref Evans and Stivers Hist Adams co p 331. By Meryl B Markley V Ch.

McQUEEN, ALEXANDER, Muskingum co

Pvt & ensign Va Milit. Ordered out in Sept 1775 & marched to Bridgetown N C. Discharged last time Nov 6 1781. Served 22 mos. Mar 17 1751 Culpepper co Va whr lived till 1829; moved to O & lived in Muskingum and Perry cos. Appl for pens Muskingum co O Oct 26 1832 res Newton twp. Ref S 5075 Va. Listed p 281 "Va Militia in Rev" as transfer fr Tenn to Ohio. Liv in Muskingum co age 83. Cop by Jane Dailey. Rept by State D A R.

McQUOWN (McGowan, McCune, McQueen & McCown), JOHN, Licking co

Pvt Va Contl. Only one of this name in Rev Rec. Enl Fauquier co Va 1776 Capt John Skelton & John Blackwell's co Cols Mercer, Weedon, Thos Marshall 3rd Va Regt. B Apr 25 1751 (Bible Rec). Mar wife Mary —— b 3-1-1757. Chldr: Elizabeth b 1784; Myra and Lyra b 1788; Robert b 1791; d 1860; John b 1794; d 1829. Soldr d 1828 Mch 1827. Cem not stated. No widow Pensd 1819 in Licking co. In 1820 stated he was 70 yrs old;

named a wife "Mary" aged 64 & a gr child Solomon McQuown age 12. He had twin sisters, Joan & Elinor b 2-24-1754. Ref S 41821; No 225856. Mrs W M Francis Elk City Okla. D A R on this record. Rept by Jane Dailey St Chairman.

McVEY (or McVay), BENJAMIN, Monroe co

Pvt Pa St Trps. Served 1 yr. Enl 1781 in Washington co Pa. Since Rev liv in Washington co Pa; Belmont co O; Wash co O; then Monroe co O. B 1765 Bucks co Pa. Mar Elizabeth ——— Apr 28 1834. Wid made appl for pens May 27 1853. Soldr d Jan 6 1847 Monroe co. Applied for pens Monroe co O Sept 21 1832 res of Wayne twp. Ref W 2405 B L Wt 26191-160-55 Pa. Rept by State D A R.

McWHINNEY, THOMAS, Preble co

Enl Aug 28 1780 Capt Samuel Pattons Co 4th Battl Pa Milit under Col Samuel Culbertson Pa Arch S 5 V 6 pp 278-279. Enl May 2 1782 8th Co 4th Battl Pa Milit under Walter McKinney Pa Arch V 6 p 305. Came to Preble co 1816; d Jackson twp 1826. Rept Commodore Preble chpt.

MACUMBER, JOHN, Astabula co

Pvt Mass St Trps. Enl Dec 1776 Dartmouth Mass. Srvd 13 mos. Was b 1760; mar Philadelphia Harrendeen June 1783. Soldr d 6-5-1844. Pens appl in Ashtabula co O 9-24-1832. Pensd 4-10-1833. Trnsfrd to Cass co Ill 9-4-1837. Ref Mass R 6673. Rept by State D A R.

MADAN, JOHN, Mahoning co

Pvt Lancaster Co Milit Col Wm Irwin. S 5 V 2 p 238 Pa Arch. Enl 1-20-1776. Was b 1760 in Ireland; mar Jane Thompson (1764-1811); chldr: Nancy b 1798 mar Abraham DeHuff; Mary mar John Mikesell; Martha mar Isaac Rush; Betsey mar Fleming Powers; Margaret b 1809 d 1840; Jermiah b 1783 Pa mar Susannah. Soldr d May 13 1840; bur in Old cem. Came with family to Poland co in 1806. Ref Biog E O p 785 Sommers; Memoirs of Pioneer Women of Western Reserve p 974; Mahoning co Reg July 21 1860 d Jeremiah Lee Madan b 1783 Pa. Rept by Mahoning chpt.

MAGAW, WILLIAM, Preble co

Pvt and Capt in S C Trps. B 1750 Ireland; d 1836 Preble co; bur Hopewell cem Israel twp. Rept Commodore Preble chpt.

MAGEE, PETER, Perry co

Lieut N Y Contl. Srvd fr 1776 to 1783. Pens appl Perry co O May 19 1818. Dropt fr roll act 5-1-1820. Occupation was a school teacher. Ref O Pens Roll 1835; III; 0-82; S 41804 B L Wt 1395-200 Lieut issued Mar 8 1794 N Y. Rept by State D A R.

MAGIN, CHARLES, Adams co

Pvt Md Contl. Enl Apr 1776. Was b 1745-6; mar Sarah ae 64 or 65 (1820). Res Adams co O May 12 1818 and Aug 11 1820. Ref S 41812 Md. Rept by State D A R.

MAHANA, JOHN, Morgan co

Pvt Mass Contl. Enl 1781 Holden Mass and srvd 3 yrs. Was b June 25 1760. Soldr d May 1839. Appl for pens May 18 1818 in Washington co O states "chldr all mar." Ref Mass S 41811. Rept by State D A R.

MAHON, NEIL, Franklin co

Cop fr Ohio State Journal, "D in Hamilton twp Sept 4 1827, very suddenly. Was a soldr of Rev ae 66 yrs." Ref Courthouse Franklin co; Estate 1666 Hamilton twp — James Mahan appt adm Sept 13 1827 with John Stombaugh and George Clickinger. Rept by Blanche Rings.

MALLORY, CAPT GILL, ? co

A Rev soldr at Lockport May 2 1849. He was at capture of Ticonderoga and Crown Point, Battle of Bennington and surrender of Burgoyne. Cop fr Ohio Statesman.

MALLOW, ADAM, Ross co

Pvt Va as ranger and scout. Was b 10-6-1751. Native of Pendleton co Va; son of Michael and Mary Mallow; mar Sarah Bush (b 5-16-1753 d 2-4-1850) dau of Lewis Bush and sister of Michael and Leonard. Chldr: Adam Jr (Maj in 1812 mar Phoebe Dice); Eve mar Wm Dice; Henry (Capt in 1812 mar Sarah Popejoy); Margaret mar Jacob Carr. Soldr d 11-27-1841 Concord twp Ross co O; bur Mallow or Hegler cem of W side of N Fork of Paint Cr abt 1 mi N of mouth of Herrod Cr. Inscript on monument "In memory of Adam Mallow, Sr who departed this life Nov 27 1841 ae 90 yr 1 mo 21 das." Wife bur at his side (east end of cem) Grave mkd by family; Kodak of stone filed. As a chld taken by parents to Valley of S Branch of Potomac nr Fort Seybert, Pendleton co W Va (now). In Apr 1758 captured by Indians who brot him to village of old Chillicothe, now Frankfort Ross co O. In 1764 ae 13 returned to his parents. Called John Brown by Indians; in 1806 returned and bought land whr he had livd in captivity. Was in battle Pt Pleasant. Ref Biog Hist Pickaway, Madison and Fayette co; Centen Hist of Ross co; Clara G Mark, Historian of Bush Fam Asso. Rept by Jacobus Westervelt chpt.

MALONE (or Meloney), JOHN, Trumbull co

Musician N Y Contl. Enl New Haven Conn 1779. Srvd 3 yrs. Was b 1762; mar Betsey Brown Aug 21 1808. Soldr d Jan 27 1835 Trumbull co O. Pens appl Addison co Vt Apr 20 1818 and Trumbull co O Oct 3 1820. Wid pens appl Ashtabula co O June 12 1856 and Madison Lake co O June 7 1857. Ref W 6820 B L Wt 19694-160-50 Contl Conn 30th U S Inf (1812). Rept by State D A R.

MALT, MOSES, ? co

Pvt but since he servd in a Regt not on Contl Estab was refused a pension. Ref listed Doc No. 31 1-6-1831. Rept by Blanche Rings, Cols.

MANAL (Memel), WILLIAM, Columbiana co

Pens May 8 1830 N J St Trps. Ae 75 in 1833. Was b 1758. Ref Pens Vol V p 335 (appearance Docket Columbiana co); Census of 1840. Rept by Mrs. Wilma M. Molsberry.

MANELY, JESSE, Franklin co

Order bk 2-257 came into Ct and an appl for pens having subscribed and sworn to the service and the Ct being duly satisfied with the correctness of the schedules thereunto annexed do order they be filed and certified. Rept by Blanche Rings Col O.

MANKER, WILLIAM, Highland co

Pvt Va Milit. Enl Berkley co Va whr he livd for 8 yrs aft close of Rev. Srvd 6 mos. Was b Jan 7 1765 Baltimore Md; mar Sarah Powers July 1 1817. Soldr d Apr 29 1839 Highland co O whr he had appl for pens Oct 28 1833. Soldr mvd to Hampshire co Va for 2 yrs, thence to Belmont co O, Clinton co. before going to Highland co. Ref W 9942 B L Wt 73506-160-55; Ind Wars of 1790. Rept by State D A R.

MANLEY, JOHN, Fairfield co

Enl fr Elktown Md in Lees Legion. Was at White Plains, Valley Forge, Cowpens, Guilford C H. Was b 1759; mar Susannah Cox 1790. One dau was Susannah. Soldr d 1814 Rushville O. Widow was pens on his service as Corp. Ref Vol 113 p 220 No. 112676 and No. 20642. Cop by J D.

MANLOVE, WILLIAM, Montgomery co

Pvt Del Contl. Enl Dec 1775 Kent co Del. Srvd 1 yr. Soldr was b 1748. Pens appl Aug 22 1818 Montgomery co O. Ref Del S 41813. Rept by State D A R.

MANLY, JESSE, Athens co

Exec Doc 37 of 1852. Rejected as he servd less than six mo. Rept by Wm Pettit.

MANLY, JESSE, Fairfield co

Exec Doc 37 of 1852. Rejected as servd only three mos. Rept by Wm Pettit.

MANN, ISAIAH, Trumbull co and Pa

Was at Bunkerhill, Trenton, wintered at Valley Forge, at New Garden meeting house and Battle of Brandywine. Was b 1757; mar Hannah; chldr: Sarah; Jane; Isaiah; Thomas; Eliza H; all alive in 1855. Soldr d June 3 or 30 1836 Uniontown, Fayette co Pa. He came fr Ogletown, New Castle co Del to Weathersfield but d at home of a dau Eliza. Rept by Mary Chesney chpt.

MANNING, WILLIAM, Franklin co

Sergt Pa Contl. Enl at beginning of Rev. Was 80 yrs old May 18 1819. Appl states wf (æ 70 yrs) and he livd alone at the time he ppld in Franklin co O 6-14-1820. Ref Conn S 41814. Rept by State D A R.

MANNON, HENRY, Lawrence co

Pvt Va Milit. Enl June 1780 Henry co Va. Srvd 13 mos. Was b 1759 Buckingham co Va. Letter written 4-9-1839 states soldr was d. Aft Rev mvd to Franklin co Va for abt 10 yrs; then Kenauka? co for 20 yrs; thence to Lawrence co in 1821 whr he appl for pens Mar 11 1833. Ref S 16187 Va. Rept by State D A R.

MANSFIELD, JONATHAN, Trumbull co

Pvt Mass Contl. Was b Oct 29 1752; mar Martha Howard Dec 15 1773 in Douglass Mass. One son was Daniel. Soldr d Apr 18 1833 Southington Trumbull co O. Pensr 7-12-1819 Trumbull co. Ref Pens rec W 18471. Rept by Mary Chesney chpt.

MANTZER, JAPAT, Licking co

Pvt Pa Milit. Enl Sept 1776 in Pa line for 1 yr 2 mo. Was b 1755; mar 1-15-1829; d 9-13-1841 Licking co O whr he had appl for pens Nov 5 1832. Ref Pa W 9541. Rept by State D A R.

MAPES, JOSEPH, Franklin co

Pvt N J Contl. Was b 1761. Issue of Aug 30 1834 Ohio State Journal "Joseph Mapes, Rev pensioner, to Mrs. Eleanor Swardon, each 73." (Aug 28 1834 Franklin co marriage recds). At ae of 79 was liv in Truro twp (Cens 1840) Pensr 4-5-1833 in Franklin co. Rept by Mrs. J J Rings, Columbus chpt.

MARK, JOSEPH, Fayette co

Pvt Capt John Rutherfords Co 3rd class 4th Battl Lancaster co Milit Pa. Was b 1752 Frederick co Md; mar abt 1773 Julia ———?; 2nd wf Catherine Plaugher (also Blocker) 1815: Chldr all by first wf: Peter mar Mary Legore; Mary mar Jacob Protzman; John mar Christina ———; Jacob; Henry; Elizabeth d young; George mar Polly Free; Susan mar George Seaver; Samuel mar Elizabeth Hare; Jonathan mar Susana Plaugher. Soldr d 1820 Fayette co O; bur fam cem on farm of son Peter Mark. Now a twp cem in N of Concord twp. Soldr lvd in Frederick co Md during Rev war but enlisted in Pa. At close of war mvd to Huntingdon co Pa; thence to Buckskin twp Ross co. Thence to Concord twp Fayette co O whr d. Ref Pa Arch 5th Ser V 7 pp 402, 407, 1040; Census of 1790, 1800, and 1820; family and co Rec in Fayette and Ross co by Clara Mark Westerville O. Rept by Jacobus Westervelt chpt.

MARKHAM, DANIEL, Summit co

Exec Doc 37 of 1852. Rejected as servd less than 6 mos. Rept by Wm Pettit.

MARLOTT, THOMAS, Adams co

Pvt and Sgt in Md Milit. Pens June 1833. Ref Evans and Stivers Hist Adams co p 331. Rept by Meryl B Markley. This is another spelling for Malott, Thomas p 246 Vol 1 Ohio Roster listed here to avoid continued research — J D.

MARQUIS, THOMAS, Logan co

Pvt and Lieut Capt Henry Grahams Co John Marshalls Regt Washington co Pa Milit. B Winchester Va 1753; mar Jane Park (1751-1841) in 1776. Chldr: James; William; Thomas; Sarah mar Rev Joseph Stevenson; Susannah mar John St Marquis; Mary mar George Newell, Knox co O; Jane mar Caldwell; Ann mar Joseph Clark. Soldr ·d Sept 27 1827 Bellefontaine whr bur on Stevenson lot, slab stone covers grave on which are dates and Bible verses and "Livd in Cross Creek Pa for 33 yrs." Chpt mrkd grave by having the words "A Rev Soldr" carved on the stone. Was the pastor Pres Ch in Pa for 30 yrs. Ref D A R No. 121645. Rept by Bellefontaine chpt.

MARSH, ABIJAH, Ashland co

Name listed p 142 Hist of North Central Ohio by Wm A Duff as Rev Soldr Sullivan twp. Rept by Nathan Perry chpt.

MARSH, ELEAZER, Medina co

Pvt Vt Milit. Enl Bennington co Vt. Srvd 1 yr. Was b Oct 11, 1755 Dunlap co N Y. After Rev livd in Bennington co Vt abt 33 yrs. Aftwards came to Medina co O whr appl for pens Aug 31 1832 Res Live Foot twp. Ref S 2723 Vt. Rept by State D A R.

MARSHALL, JOHN, Richland co

2nd Lieut 3rd Pa Regt and Capt 1779. Was b 1746 Lancaster Pa; mar 1782 Mary Park (1761-1831). John S was one son. Soldr bur Ontario cem Ontario O Richland co. Inscript on stone "Sacred to the memory of John Marshall who departed this life Sept 27 1821 in the 74th yr of age." Ref V 121 p 289 D A R Lin No. 129932. Rept by Nathan Perry chpt. Jared Mansfield chpt repts "There is a grave marker in Mansfield cem (Old Part) for Mary wf of Col John Marshall. Mary d Sept 22 1821 ae 70 yrs and from appearance of ground there had been a grave beside it, evidently Johns. These graves had been movd fr an old cem."

MARTIN, ABSOLOM, Belmont co

Rev soldr mar to a sister of Ebenezer Zane. A son Ebenezer mar a gr dau of Jonathan Zane for 2nd wf. Soldr d 1801. Bur Zane burying gr, Martins Ferry Belmont co O. Emigrated fr N J 1787 to Va side of O river and later mvd to extensive lands bot on O side. Established a ferry fr which Martins Ferry received name. Ref C H Galbreaths Short Stories of O (Col Dispatch). Cop by Jane Dailey.

MARTIN, BENJAMIN, Champaign co

Ref Pa Arch S 3 Vol 23 p 235; b 1750 Pa; d 1834; mar Mary Vertener; S A R ref 23233. Rept by Wm Pettit.

MARTIN, HENRY, Carroll co

Pvt Pa Milit 15 mos. Enl 1779 Cumberland co Pa. Was b 11-10-1756 York co Pa. In 1785 Mvd to Westmoreland co Pa. Mvd to Carroll co O 1827 whr lvd in 1834. Ref Pens Roll 1835; Pens 1840; Cens in Orange twp Carroll co O ae 83; (cf p 250 Roster O for same) Pa S 8990. Rept by State D A R.

MARTIN, JACOB, Perry co

Pvt Md Milit. Was b Aug 18 1759 Oley Pa. Mvd with fathers fam to Frederick co Md. Mar Loudoun co Va. Vol't June 1 1776 at Fannytown Md. Aft 4 yrs in Va mvd to Bedford co Pa whr he res 18 or 19 yrs; then to part of Muskingum co which is now part of Perry co whr he appl for pens Nov 7 1833. Ref O Pens Rolls 1835; III; O 151; S 8998 Md. Rept by State D A R.

MARTIN, JOHN, Athens co

1st Lieut N J Contl. Enl 1776. Col Martin Regt. Pensr 1-6-1834 Athens co whr trnsfrd fr Tyler co Va abt 1820. Was 81 on Oct 23 1820. Wf d before 1823. Chldr: Ephraim; Susannah with whom he livd in 1820; James and Samuel grandsons. Soldr d May 14 1847. 1776 1st Lieut Wm Bond Co 4th N J Regt comd by Ephraim Martin to serve during war. After 2 yrs dischrgd by Washington on acct illness. 1820 appl for pens living with dau and widow; had other chldr. Ref No. 7190 Va. In 1811 had 80 A land Tyler co Va whr livd. Gave to gr-son John Martin (minor) (Mar 1820). In 1816 sold it and purchased 1-4 sec in Athens co O for gr-son. In 1820 gave 100 A to James Martin; 60 A to Samuel, in trust for his mother Susannah Wilson, James mother. Cop by Jane Dailey.

MARTIN, LEVI, Miami co

Enl 1780 Pa Regt Col Piper and srvd 2 yr 6 mo in Cos under Capts Paxton, Mc-Intyre, and Enslow. Was b Chester co Pa Nov 1764; mar Delilah Corbly Miami co. One son was Andrew Cleveland O. Soldr d Miami co O 3-22-1835. Mvd to O Oct 1788. Returned to Pa 1790. Came back to O 1791. Mvd to Miami co 1800 whr appl for pens Sept 25 1832. Ref Sons of Rev Bulletin of Calif V 3 p 288; Pa S 2731. Rept by State D A R and Jane Dailey.

MARTIN, ROBERT, Pickaway co

Pvt Md Contl. Enl 1776 Col Wm Smallwoods Md Regt. In 1777. Capt Archibald Candersons Co Cal Thomas Price Regt. Srvd 3 yrs. Dischrgd 1-2-1780. Was b Jan 1755. Mar Nancy sister of Reeves Phebus in Prince Ann or Somerset co Md Mar 1780. Chldr: John and 5 others unnamed only ones at home. Six living: Elizabeth; George; Luther; Ann; Dorthy; Cassie V. Soldr d 11-30-36 Pickaway co O; bur Alkire Deer Crk twp Pickaway co. Resided in Princess co Md in 1780. Liv in Bullit co Ky 1810. Pensd 5-18-1818 in Pickaway co O. Widow movd to Ind and appl for pens in Fountain co 4-25-1845.She d there Sept 19 1845 at home of son John P Martin. Ref Md W 9535; Mrs F W Johnson Altadena Cal. Rept by State D A R and Pickaway Plains chpt.

MARTIN, SIMEON, Mahoning co

Pvt Conn Men in Rev p 468 1776; also Pa Arch Ser 3 V 14 pp 545, 822 V 15 p 219. Was b 1735; mar Elizabeth; chldr: George b 1798 mar Susanna Sneath; John; Simeon b 1766 mar Elizabeth; soldr d 1818 Springfield twp. Martin came fr Germany; son Simon came to Mahoning co 1818. Ref Biog E O p 611 Summers; Deed Bk P p 80 Martin Simeon Patent 1814. Rept by Mahoning chpt.

MARTIN, THOMAS, Ashtabula co

Pvt Conn St Tr. Enl May 1775 Colchester Conn. Srvd 13 mos. Was b 11-16-1752 Lebanon Conn. Aft enl mvd to Washington Mass. In 1810 mvd to Harpersfield twp Ashtabula co O whr appl for pens 2-4-1833. Ref Conn S 2730. Rept by State D A R.

MARTIN, WILLIAM, Mahoning co

Pvt. Ser 3 V 23 p 706 Pa Arch; also Mass Men V 10 p 301; N J men Conn Men — Vt men. Pensioner Old bk 1808. Was b 1748; d 1-3-1820 Coitsville. Was Supervisor of Highway. Ref Hist Trumbull and Mahoning co V 2 p 197 Sanderson; Mahoning Reg 1-6-1865; Early Settlers in Coitsville 1811; Deed bk I p 38 to Wm Martin fr John Kinsman 1806 Manning. Rept by Mahoning chpt.

MARTINDALE, JAMES, Gallia co

Pvt. Re-enl as Lieut. Srvd under Col Brandon fr Union co S C. Was in Battle of Kings Mt and siege of 96. Was pens under name of James Martindill 1834. Was b 1754 Bucks co Pa. Son of Wm Martindale. Mar 1st Miss Bishop Union co S Car; 2nd Miss Alexander Greenbrier co Va; 3rd Mary Gillmore, Gallia co O. Chldr of 1st wf: Samuel; Thomas and Mollie. Chldr of 2nd wf: John; Moses; Joseph; Andrew L; James A; Druzella; Tabitha; Mary. Soldr d July 7 1840 Addison twp Gallia co O. Bur Country cem nr Bulaville Addison twp. Emigrated to S C; Res Dist 96 during War; thence to Greenbrier Va (now W Va) thence to Gallia co O abt 1811. Ref W L Martindale, West Milton O Will prob 1840, D p 405. Rept by French Colony chpt.

MARRS, WILLIAM, Columbiana co

Pvt Capt John Nelsons Co 4 Battl Northampton co Pa Milit. Pvt Rangers of Westmoreland co Pa. Was b 1769; d June 17 1847 ae 78 yrs; bur Deer Creek cem. Ref Stone data. Pa Arch 2 XIV 3 XXIII 229. Rept by Mrs Wilma M Molsberry.

MASON, ELIJAH, Portage co

Notes of late Alice Boardman D A R State Librarian lists him as liv in Portage co in 1820 at Hiram O. Gr mrkd at Hiram cem by Old Northwest chpt 1932.

MASON, MARTIN SR, Ashland co

Listed p 142 Hist of North Central O by Wm A Duff as Rev soldr — Nankin. Rept by Nathan Perry chpt.

MASON, MICHAEL, Huron co

Pvt Mass Milit. Drafted 1776 living in New Providence Berkshire co Mass. Enl Jan 1778 Mass. Pens 1833 Huron co O. Ae 72 in 1832. Rept 18 N S D A R p 227 bur at Huron O by Sandusky chpt. "Removd fr Erie co O lately to town of Ft. Ann Washington co N Y" (appl Nov 1 1842). Res Huron co O Vermillion twp July 27 1832. Ref S 28804 Contl Mass. Rept by State D A R.

MASON, THOMAS, Adams co O

Pvt Del Contl. Enl July 16 1778 Del. Srvd Regt commanded by Col Hall Del line 1 yr. Taken prisoner by British at Battle of Gen Gates defeat; soon aft was retaken by Gen Marion and mrchd to Wilmington N C; thence to Hillsborough N C whr he joined the Regt under Gen Gates and afterwards by Gen Greene. He cont in service. Was b 1761. Appl 1823 mentions "wf 10 chldr 4 of whom act for themselves." Others: Jefferson ae 13; Malin Jackson 7; Wilson Campbell 2; Eliza 15; Polly 8; Margaret 5. Made appl for pens in Adams co O Apr 16 1818 Warren co 1819, Adams 1823 and 1837 going to chldr in Montgomery co Ind. Ref S 36691 Del. Rept by State D A R.

MASTEN, PETER, Mahoning co

Pens appl Circuit Ct Warren O 1832; also N Y Men p 244. Mar Elizabeth; chldr: Peter b 1809 mar Charlotte (perhaps); John; Peter; Landon; James; Eleanor. Soldr d abt 1832 Goshen twp. Ref Will bk 7 p 358 Trumbull co Recds Probated 1832; Mahoning Free Democrat 1857; Census Mahoning co 1860. Rept by Mahoning chpt.

MASTERS, STEPHEN, Stark co

Pvt N J Contl. Enl 1775 N J. Srvd 3 yrs. Was b 1753; mar Judith Sept 16 1783; "2 sons living with me John æ 19 and Ira 15" (appl 1820) Other chldr: Lydia; Abram; Stephen; Elizabeth; William; Joseph; Sally; Elias; Caroline. (fr fam recd as evidence for wid) Soldr d Jan 3 1835 Stark co O whr appl for pens July 22 1818; 1820. Wid appl pens Stark co Sept 14 1839 and Sandusky co O June 1 1849. Ref W 5340 B L Wt 185-60-55 N J. Rept by State D A R.

MASTIN, THOMAS, Ashtabula co

D Aug 19 1822 ae 62 "A faithful soldr of the Rev". Given as bur in the 1st gr yd South Ridge Conneaut twp. County recds locate his farm in Salem later given to Monroe twp. His wfs name was Sally. Records mention chldr but no names. Rept by Mary Redmond chpt.

MATHENY, ——, Adams co

Rev Soldr bur Wamsleyville O Adams co. Rept by Sycamore chpt.

MATTHEWS, ABEL, ? co

Capt. From old scrap bk clipping of Rev soldrs interested in Marietta settlement descendants of whom are bur in Washington co. Listed here for research by Marietta chpt.

MATTHEWS, GARRET, Guernsey co

Pvt N J Milit. Enl Sept 1776 Amboy N J. Srvd 1 yr and 3 mos. Was b 1750. Appl for pens Guernsey co O Sept 17 1832 Res of Madison twp. Ref S 17564 N J. Rept by State D A R.

MATTHEWS, THOMAS, Mahoning co

Pvt Conn Men in Rev p 541 "Sailor" and p 597. Was b 1754. Soldr d 7-25-1838 Poland twp bur Old Churchyd. Fr Washington co Pa. Ref List of late H R Baldwin; Tax list 1826. Rept by Mahoning chpt.

MATTSLEY, BENJAMIN

This is incorrect spelling for Benjamin Maltby whose complete data appears on p 246 of the Roster Vol 1. Filed here to avoid further research. Rept by Mary Chesney chpt.

MAXWELL, JOHN, Stark co

Pvt Md Contl. Enl 1777 Church Hill Del. Srvd 16 mos. Ae 79 in 1820. Soldr d Dec 16 1826. Appl for pens Stark co O Aug 8 1820. Ref S 41817 Md Pa. Rept by State D A R.

MAYBEE, JASPER, Trumbull co

Made application for pens in Trumbull co. No data to decide if Rev or 1812. Rept by Mary Chesney chpt.

MAYBERRY, RICHARD, Muskingum co

Research found no Richard, but "William", this roster.

MAYBERRY, WILLIAM, Muskingum co

Enl as fifer Morristown N J in 4th Regt of Pa Artillery. Dischrgd in Phila abt 1782. Ae 56 in 1818. Chldr: Nancy ae 20; Susan ae 5. Appl for pens Gallia co O June 27, 1818 and in Muskingum co, Jefferson twp on Nov 5, 1832. Ref S 41807 Pa Contl. Rept by State D A R.

MAYBERRY, WILLIAM SR, Muskingum co

Pvt Pa Contl. Enl in Phila Pa. Dischrgd abt Christmas 1782, at Phila Pa. Soldr b abt 1738. Appl 1820 states "wf ae 63. Only child a son." Appl for pens Aug 7 1820 Wood co Va and Muskingum co O Sept 24 1824. A refiner of iron. Ref S 41819 Navy Pa. Rept by State D A R.

MEANS, ROBERT, Athens co

Pvt N J Milit. Capt Howell Col Wines Regt for 1 yr 4 mo. Enl fr Morris co N J. Was b Trelick Ireland. Came to America at 12 yr of ae. Was 17 at beginning of Rev. Inscr on Ohio Rolls Aug 9 1833, ae 75 yrs. Livd in Mendham twp Morris co N J at 1st enl; aft War came to Pa then to O whr livd for last 20 yrs. Livd in Athens co, res of Lee twp, ae 75 May 9 1833. Pensr 8-9-1833 Athens co. Soldr d Feb 20, 1838. Cop by Jane Dailey.

MEASON, JOHN, Fayette co

Capt John Meason or Mason srvd in 3rd Battl Westmoreland co Milit formerly associated in Va from Berkeley co. Was made Major John Mason under command of Col Nehemiah Stokelly of same Battl. Was b Feb 22 1753; son of Thomas and Elizabeth Meason; mar Hannah Frost 1770 dau of Wm Hannah Frost. Chldr: Isaac; Elizabeth; Martha; Hannah; John; Nancy; Mary; Thomas; Fannie; George. Soldr d Aug 1805 Fayette co Pa. Supposedly bur on his farm in Bullskin twp Fayette co; location destroyed by coke works. Reared in Frederick co Va whr mar and removd to Berkley co Va aft marriage. Most of his family had already movd to O so his widow and other chldr removd to Lancaster Fairfield co O. Surveyor and interested in iron. Ref Pa Arch p 281 Vol 2 S 6; p 314; Natl No 217620. Rept by Chickasha chpt Chickasha Okla.

MEDLEY, WILLIAM G, Washington co

Appl for pen Marietta O June 23 1834. Was b 1763; d Mar 17 1838 ae 75 yrs; bur Tice cem Ludlow twp. Inscript on mon "Here lies the body of William Medley who d March 17 A D 1838 in the 75th yr of his age." Grave mrkd with old sandstone in poor condition. Ref Wash co Court of Com Pleas Vol 7 p 71 Pen Appl. Rept by Helen Sloan, Marietta.

MEEDS, CATO, Portage co

Pvt Conn Contl. Enl Norwich twp Conn 3-1-1778. Pensr 3-5-1819 Cuyahoga co O. Renewed in Portage co. Ae 57 in 1818. Ref Conn S 41866. Rept by State D A R.

MEEK, SAMUEL, Columbiana co

Ranger, Washington co Pa. Of Irish descent; mar Elizabeth (d 1845). One son was Joseph b 1813. Soldr d 1856; bur Old cem East Palestine. He came to Unity twp early with wf. Ref S A R 1912 Yr bk; Upper Ohio Valley Col Co 1 p 282; Pa Arch 3 XXIII 210. Rept by Mrs. Wilma Molsberry.

MEEKER, A C, Trumbull co

Bur Dugan Fowler twp S of Nutwood. Cop fr Rept 27 N S D A R p 129 by Nathan Perry chpt.

MEEKER, ROBERT, Lorain co

Pensd 1832. Pvt; Indian spy and commanded a Co of Rangers 1779. Was b 1752 Reading Conn. 2nd wf Catherine Vandensen (1763-1844). Surviving the widow were chldr: George; Robert; Betsy Lewis; Lucy Blair. The arrears of pension due Catherine Meeker at d were pd to John Taylor Pittsburgh Pa Sept 16 and 30 1850 as atty for the chldr. Soldr d 1835 Amherst O, Lorain co. Ref V 106 D A R Lin 105018. Rept by Nathan Perry chpt.

MELICK (or Melish), JOHN, Perry co

Several enl. Ref Pension Claim W 4283 fr N J. Was b Dec 1753 New Germantown N J whl a res of Somerset co N J of German ancestry. Mar Mary Oyster May 29 1828 Perry co. Two chldr Alexander and Isaac Melick livd at Mt Perry O. Soldr d Perry co O. Was pens 1832 in Madison twp Perry co O. Came here fr Allegheny co Pa. Ref News clipping July 4 1828 fr Somerset O paper. Rept by Hetuck chpt.

MELLOT, BENJAMIN, Richland co

Pvt Pa Milit. Enl 1776 res in Bethel twp Bedford co Pa. Was b 3-19-1759 Egg Harber N J. Aft the war liv in Washington co Pa Monroe co O and aft 1830 in Richland co O whr appl for pens 11-6-1833 while a resident of Congress twp Richland co O. Ref Pa S 2822. Rept by State D A R.

MELONEY, JOHN, Trumbull co

Musician N Y Contl. Was in battle of Bunker Hill and at Yorktown. Also War 1812. Was b in New Haven Ct; mar Aug 21 1808 at Bristol Vt Betsey Brown (She may have been a 2nd wf). One boy was Melvin, at least four, possibly more. Soldr d Jan 27 1825 in Fowler Trumbull co O. Rept by Mary Chesney chpt.

MELLINGER, JACOB, Mahoning co

Pvt 5th class Lancaster co 1780. Pa Arch Ser 5 V 7 pp 153, 174, 226. Capt David Krause. Mar Mary —— (2nd) mar Jacob Baughan; chldr: Jacob mar Polly; Melchoir b 1805 mar Elizabeth; Leah mar Solomon Harmon; Rachel; Benedict. Soldr d before 1839 Beaver twp. Ref Hist Trumbull and Mahoning co V 2 p 192; Hist Mahoning co p 173 Sanderson; Hist Columbiana co p 523 McCord; Deed bk p 59 1813; Deed bk w 124 1839. Rept by Mahoning chpt.

MENELY, JESSE, Franklin co

Pvt N J Contl. Pensr 10-14-1819 Franklin co. Was 75 in 1819. Soldr d May 8 1825. Hannah Menely app Adm 6-20-1825 Franklin co Adm Dock 1-245. O State Journal one Amos Menely mar Susanna Wynkoop (both of Columbus) 2-1-1827 at Lancaster. Rept by Columbus chpt.

MERCER, AARON, Hamilton co

Soldr d Dec 10 1800 ae 54 yrs. This found on stone, in Baptist cem between Davis Lane and Carroll St adjacent to Pa R R Cin O a note "reputed to be a Rev Soldr" is added. Rept by Cincinnati chpt.

MESSERLY, PETER, Mahoning co

Pvt. Ser 6 V 2 p 589 or Ensign York co Mil Pa Arch. Mar Christaina; chldr: Molly mar Philip Sibe; perhaps Geo b 1775 and others. Soldr d abt 1808 Springfield twp. Came to O 1805. Ref Hist Mahoning co p 597 Sanderson; Will bk 1 p 152 Columbiana co Records prob 1808; Deed bk O p 205 Peter and Christain Messerly 1808. Rept by Mahoning chpt.

METCALF, VACHEL, Ashland co

Listed p 142 in Hist of North Central O by Wm A Duff as Rev soldr Sullivan twp. Rept by Nathan Perry chpt.

METZ, JACOB, Mahoning co

Pvt. Ser 5 V 2 p 463; V 3 p 707 Pa Arch. Chldr: Betsey mar Abraham Augustine; Barbara mar Peter Bernhart; Magdalen mar Abraham Kehter; John mar Elizabeth; Abraham mar Sarah; Hoseph mar Rebekah; David; Susannah; Jacob. Soldr d before 1819 Beaver twp. Was among early settlers. Ref Deed bk O p 369 trnscrbd Mahoning co 1819 Jacob Metz Heirs. Rept by Mahoning chpt.

MEYERS, HENRY, Montgomery co

Early settler who d in 1804 having settled in Miami twp. Ref Ser 5 Pa Arch vol 55 p 335; vol 7 p 151. Burial place not identified. Rept by Wm Pettit, Dayton.

MEYERS (Myers or Moyers), JOHN, Perry co

Pa serv Milit. Vol in Berks co Pa July 1776, whr res till 1806. Was b Apr 4 Berks co Pa; mar abt Dec 1778. Mvd to Union co Pa. Aft 5 yrs in 1811 mvd to Perry co O. Pens appl Sept 19 1833. Ref S 9039 Pa. Rept by State D A R.

MIDDAUGH, ABONJAH, Brown co

Exec Doc 37 of 1852. On suspended list as not in regularly organized corps. Rept by Wm Pettit.

MIDDLESWART, JACOB, Brown co

Pvt Pa Milit. Enl 1779 Washington co Pa. Srvd 1 yr and 6 mos. Was b 1761; mar Jane Feb 22 1787; chldr: James Martin; Mary; Sarah; Elizabeth Martin Middleswart; Hannah. (family records) Soldr d May 1 1837 Brown co O. Res Brown co O Apr 25 1834. Wid appl for pens Brown co O Apr 25 1843 res Jackson twp ae 74. Ref W 4034 Pa Va. Rept by State D A R. Meryl B Markley Taliaferro chpt repts Zilphia a dau mar 1810 Oliver Reynolds son of Stephen. Soldr settled at mouth of Eagle Crk. Later movd to interior of co. Ref Beers Hist of co p 441 and Evans and Stivers p 331.

MIDDLETON, JOHN, Highland co

Pvt Va Milit. Enl 1777 Woodstock Va. Srvd 1 yr. Was b Apr 24 1764 Lancaster co Pa. Pens appl Oct 28 1833 Highland co O. Ref S 2847 Va. Rept by State D A R.

MIDDOCK (Midagh), Moses, Hamilton co

Sergt N J Contl. Enl June 1775 Colonel Thompsons Regt of Pa Line. Was b 3-13-1751. Wf b Aug 22 1752. Family consists of wf and one orphan child ae 13 yrs in Feb 1821. Ref N J S 41870. Rept by State D A R.

MIGHT, JOHN, Columbiana co

S C St Trps. Pvt and Musican N C Line 1 yr. Enl abt 1780 "Snow Island" in North C. Was b 10-15-1757 in Prussia; mar Kerankappock Stilwell May 1781 at Pilsaman Washington co Pa; chldr: Mary b 1788; mar John Stevens; George 1790; Elizabeth 1792 mar William Welker 10-18-1814; John 1794; William 1797; Barbara 1800 mar John Green; Samuel 1802 mar Abbie Farr; Sarah 1804 mar Isaac Welker. Soldr d 1-1-1846 in St Clair twp Columbiana co. Came to this country abt 1778 w German trps as a British soldr but deserted and joined U S army. Aft Rev livd abt 4 yr in Berkley co Va; thence mvd to Washington co Pa. In 1805 mvd to Columbiana co O. Ref S C W 4548. Rept by State D A R.

MIKLE (Mitchell or Mickle), JOHN, Clermont co and Ind

Pvt Pa Line. Srvd 3 yr in Artillery Artificers of Col Flowers Regt. Pens Act of March 1818. Appl Marion Ind under Act 7 June 1832. In pens appl of 1820 names Juda wf ae 65; and chldr: Michael 12; Barbary 15. Soldr d Jan 11 1851 (agency bk). Inscribed on pens roll Madison Ind issued Nov 8 1850 stated he went to Ind to live with chldr in appl of Jan 16 1847 Marion co. Pensr 5-7-1820 Clermont co. Ref S 33114 Pa. Cop by Jane Dailey.

MILBURN, ANDREW, Columbiana co

Pvt Va Milit 1 yr. Enl 1780 Loudon co Va whr he was b 1763 and livd for 8 yrs. Livd with his father until 4 yr aft the war. Mvd to Cammel co Va and 10 yrs later mvd to Columbiana co O. Appl for pens 10-15-1832 Columbiana co O. Ref Va S 2845. Rept by State D A R.

MILES, JOHN, Licking co

Pvt Md Contl. Enl at Elkridge Md whr he livd. Servd 1 yr. Was b 1755 Annarundel co Md. Aft the war went to Pa; then to Licking co O. Pens appl Licking co O 10-29-1832. Ref Md S 2827. Rept by State D A R.

MILKOLLIN, JONATHAN, Clark co

Pvt Va Milit. Enl Jan or Feb 1782. Discharged 1783. Pens appl Clark co O Oct 2 1832. Ref S 16971 Contl Va; p 283 Va Milit in Rev (J D). Rept by State D A R.

MILLER, ABRAHAM, Stark co

Pvt Capt Henry Hardmans Co Md Contl line. Was b 1749 Bavaria Germany. Mar 1st Elizabeth Clapper (d 1796) 2nd Savilla Lower mar 1798. Chldr: Susannah 1784; Catherine 1785; John 1786; Abraham 1787; Elizabeth 1789; Mary 1790; Henry 1792; Lewis 1794 all by first wf; Christine 1801 by 2nd wf. Soldr bur Snyders Church nr Cairo O Stark co. Inscript on Stone "Abraham Miller d 1824 ae 75 yrs. Sevilla E his wf d Oct 1832 æ ——". Grave mrkd by Canton chpt D A R May 28 1933. Srvd in Seven Yrs War in Germany. Landed in Baltimore abt 1776. Located in Funkstown Md whr he enl in Contl army. Ref No. 123975 V 124 and No. 119114 V 120 D A R Line; "Lewis Miller" by Hendrick published by G P Putnams Sons N Y. Rept by Jane Dailey and Canton chpt. Wm Pettit repts mar Elizabeth Clapp 1763. Ref S A R 15545.

MILLER, ABRAHAM, Mahoning co

Ranger Northampton co Pa. Ser 3 V 23 p 801 German Regt Col Ludwig Weltner 1776. Mar Sally Bailey; chldr: William mar Rebecca Pow; Joseph b 1800 mar Jane; Daniel; Magdalene; Elizabeth mar —— Fox; Mary mar —— Fox; Catherine mar Lynn; Sarah; Abram b 1777 mar Magaalena. Soldr d Jan 17 1850 Beaver co. Ref Hist Mahoning co p 619 Sanderson; Will bk I p 179 Mahoning co probated 2-12-1850; Deed bk 1843; Early tax list Beaver twp. Rept by Mahoning chpt.

MILLER, DANIEL, Montgomery co

5th S Pa Arch V 2 1056 Fourth Pa Contl Line 1777 Capt Fishbaum; Vol 7 p 640 Lancaster milit Capt James Brown. Other services. Came to Montgomery co 1802. Bur place unidentified. Drafted from Fourth C L to Pa C L Artillery in 1781. Rept by Wm Pettit.

MILLER, DAVID, Montgomery co

Emigrated to county in 1800. Ref 5th Ser Pa Arch V 2 p 218; V 4 p 219; V 5 p 577; v 6 p 457; V 7 p 65; etc. Burial place not identified. Rept by Wm Pettit, Dayton.

MILLER, FREDERICK, Preble co

Pvt Va Milit. Enl May 1778 Rockingham co Va whr he was b Aug 8 1760. Srvd 13 mos. Mar Elizabeth Sharpe b in Pa 1792; Had 5 chldr. (appl of 1822) Soldr d 1835 south edge of New Lexington Twin twp Preble co. Bur Presb ch-yd on the Nisbet farm. Place not cared for. Srvd through Rev and gave distinguished service in war of 1812; his home was a gathering place for soldrs. He was one of the leading men of the county. He and his wf d the same yr. Ref Hist of Preble co by H Z Williams and Bro 1881. Family records. Rept by Commodore Preble chpt by Grace Runyon and State D A R. Ref S 2831, Va.

MILLER, HENRY, Butler co

Exec Doc 37 of 1852. Refused a pension because under age. Rept by Wm Pettit.

MILLER, HENRY, Franklin co

Resided in Franklin co 1832 ae 69. Pa Arch. Rept by Mary Steinmetz, Reading Pa. Also cop fr Order bk 6-133 dated Sept 29 1832. Made declaration for pension under act of June 7 1832 and the clerk is directed to issue certificates as directed by the War Department. By Blanche Rings.

MILLER, ICHABOD, Butler co

Pvt N J St Trps. Enl Elizabethtown N J July 1776. Srvd 8 mos as pvt, 6 mos as Waggonner and 6 mos as wagon master. Was b Apr 7 1759. Mar Joanna Ross Sept 13

1806; d Mar 2 1836. Appl for pens July 30 1832 in Butler co O. Ref N J W 2646 B L Wt 30927-160-55. Rept by State D A R.

MILLER, JACOB, Montgomery co

Lib Rpt 1912 p 213 says in 12th Va Contl Line. W D 246 1. Beers also says Rev Soldr in county history. Came from Hampshire co Va whr census of 1784 listed his family as having six chldr. Burial place not identified. Rept by Wm Pettit S A R.

MILLER, JAMES, Adams co

Service Capt Clarks Artillery Co. Contl Trps under Col Thomas Lamb Gen Henry Knox. Enl Dec 25 1776. Driver May 1777. Matross June 1777. Last on Roll Jan 3rd 1780. Was b in Ireland 1740. Mar Elizabeth Hemphill in New England. Came to Adams co 1798. Chldr: William; Elizabeth; Hannah. Soldr d Dec 25 1830 ae 90. Refused a pens. Ref Evans and Stivers Hist. P 337. By Meryl B Markley. Vice Chairman.

MILLER, JAMES, Montgomery co

5th Ser Pa Arch Vol 2 p 517 Lancaster co Milit. Col Bull Capt Anderson 1777 Vol 4 p 219 received depreciated pay. Vol 7 p 191 2nd Lieut Col Anderson. Rept by Wm Pettit S A R.

MILLER, JOASH (Joas), Pickaway co

Enl 1776. Pvt Cop Andrew Ream Co of Lancaster co milit. Made Sergt under same Capt. Was b 1754 Pa; son of Michael and Catharine Miller. Mar Nancy Anna Stubsch Nov 2 1777. Chldr: Catherine; Rebecca; Peter; Marg; Joseph; Susannah; Nancy; Elizabeth; Edward. Body of soldr removed to Reber Hill cem Pickaway co Lot 107 Sec 13 fr private cem by gr-son Stephen Miller. Inscript on Stone "Joash Miller d Feb 11 1819 ae 65 yrs. Nancy his wf d Aug 21 1839 ae 81 yrs."Grave mrkd 1932 by D A R. Soldr mvd to Martinsburg W Va aft the d 1785 of his father. Then the family came to O 1804. Settled in Walnut twp Pickaway co. He was a blacksmith. Rept by Pickaway Plains chpt.

MILLER, JOHN, Carroll co

Exec Doc 37 of 1852. Refused a pension as serve only 4 mos. Rept by Wm Pettit.

MILLER, JOHN, Mahoning co

Pvt. Ser 5 Many rec Pa Arch; also Conn Men in Rev many N Y Men pp 24, 54, 166, 268 . Del p 404 N J p 690. Chldr: Elizabeth; Isaac mar Catherine Lynn; Mary mar Robert Crooks; Sara. Soldr d abt 1824 Poland twp. Ref Will bk 3 p 461 Columbiana co rec Prob 1824; Deed bk b p 15 trnscribd Mahoning co 1836; Tax list 1826; Wstern Reserve Chronicle 11-22-1824 Est John Miller Poland. Rept by Mahoning chpt.

MILLER, JOHN, Muskingum co

Srvd 2nd Regt Md 1777; dischrgd 1780; b Md; d 1811; mar Elizabeth Sullivan. S A R ref 50670. Rept by Wm Pettit.

MILLER, JOSIAS, Franklin co

Pensd Franklin co O 1818 ae 77. Joseph Miller Adm app Oct 17 1821 Franklin co O. Ref Franklin co Adm Docket 1-157; Order bk 2-260 Pens appl. Rept by Mrs. W S Van Fossen Columbus chpt.

MILLER, MATHEW, Holmes co

Rev Soldr. Rec not yet found. Was b 1732 Ireland. Mar 1762 Margaret Corrneban. Chldr: Robert William; Isaac (b Greensburgh Westmoreland co Pa Feb 8 1798, mar Jan 26 1819 Sarah Dabney. Movd to Trumbull co first having come to Youngstown 1832; then to Farmington Trumbull co 1850. D Apr 2 1875) Soldr d 1817 æ 85. Bur Millersburgh Holmes co. Came to America 1760; then to Westmoreland co Pa whr he mar and in

1814 came to Holmes co whence his son movd to Johnstone twp Trumbull co in 1854. Rept by Mrs. Wilma Molsberry.

MILLER, NICHOLAS, Columbiana co

Pvt Pa Arch S 5 V 7 p 1121; S 6 many references. Was b 1758; d Mar 23 1844 Hanover twp. Ref The Aurora Mar 1844. Rept by Mabel S Askue Mahoning chpt Youngstown O.

MILLER, PHILIP, Highland co

Pvt Capt Philip Graybells co in German Battl. Contl trps under Col Baron Arendt and later Col Housegger. Enl for 3 yr July 1777 on a list on board a frigate. Was b Bavaria Germany; mar Christena Windomaker. Chldr: George; Mary mar Daniel Hoop; John mar Eleanor Chaney; Jacob; Elizabeth mar —— Windomaker; Barbara mar Geo Broadstone; Fanny mar Stephen Moberly Aug 17 1821 Highland co O; Sophia mar Daniel Roads Jan 7 1830 Highland co O. Soldr d Aug 20 1825. Bur 2 1-2 mi S E of Hillsboro O on Marshall Pike in fam gr-yd. Grave mrkd by gov marker erected by descendants May 1934. Came to U S 1760. His organization was formed accd to Res of Cong May or June 1776 that a Battl of Germans be raised for service of colonies. 4 mo Pa and 4 mo Md. Rec not show in which state he srvd. Ref Adj Gen U S. Rept by Waw-wil-a-way chpt.

MILLER, THOMAS, Ross co

2nd Lieut 1778 4th Va Reg. Lieut 1779 wounded at Eutaw Springs 1781. Enl Mar 3 1777 Va line. Was b 1760. Mar 1784 Ann Ball (d 1840). One son was Samuel Thomas. Soldr d 1821 Chillicothe O. Mvd fr Cicil co Md to Chesterfield co Va. Recd bounty land in O. Appl for pens in Franklin co O May 2 1818. Occupation School master. Ref V 60 p 189 D A R lin; Pens Claims. Rept by State D A R and Nathan Perry chpt. Wid pensr 12-22-1838 Pottsylvania co Va.

MILLER. WILLIAM, Pickaway co

Cop fr Chapman Bros Hist P 385. Also Van Cleaf Hist Pickaway co page 493. William Miller was a native of the old Dominion and a patriot in the Rev war. He came to Pickaway co to visit his son William A Miller fr Shepherdstown Va (Said to be buried near Darbyville whr some of the descendants still live. Rept by Mrs. Orion King, Pickaway Plains chpt.

MILLER, WILLIAM, Wayne co

Pvt N H Contl. Enl 1775 Chester co N Y. Srvd 6 mo. Was b 4-17-1846 Old Chester N H; mar Sarah Perkins; chldr: Sarah; William; Ann (children of Sarah) Margaret Hurford his dau. Soldr d 1844 Wayne co O. No grave found. Later livd Orange co Vt for 20 yrs thence to St Lawrence co N Y thence aft 7 yrs to Wayne co O. Owned land in Fayette co Pa whr will was made Feb 6 1824. South half of Sec 26 twp 17 Range 11 of Wayne co was sold at Canton when youngest child became of age. Ref 2832 N H. Rept by State D A R and Wooster-Wayne chpt.

MILLS, ELIJAH, Montgomery or Butler co

Pvt 11 mos; Ensign 2 mos; lieut 3 mos and Capt 3 mos. Enl 1776 in Frederick co Md. Was b 9-5-1757 Frederick co Md. Movd from Pa to Butler co O whr he res when pensd 12-29-1832. Ref: Md S 2825. Rept by Wm Pettit, Dayton S A R and State D A R.

MILLS, JACOB, Greene co

Srvd as associater in Rev under Capt Stites, being under sixteen, in Va. Was b Va Mar 22 1770; son of Thomas Mills and Martha Phillips Mills; mar Mary Webb dau of John and Rachel Davis Webb. Chldr: Daniel; George; John; Lewis mar Rebecca Fitzpatrick; Huldah mar Nayl Baker; Hannah; Owen; Thomas; Rachel mar —— Wilson; Patsey mar Stephen Conwell; Helen mar —— Scheeley; Letitia mar Henry Garlough; Catharine. Soldr d May 30 1850 Miami twp Greene co O; bur Clifton cem, village of Clifton, Greene co. Inscript of marker "Jacob Mills emigrated to Ohio 1796" and dates as above. Stone very old but in good condition. Fr Va to Mason co Ky; then to O whr he was the first settler n of Lebanon Warren co later one of the first in Greene co. First Justice of Peace Miami twp 1808. Ref Robinsons Hist of Greene co; Dills Hist of Greene co. Rept by Catharine Greene Xenia O. Mrs. Leon Reed.

MILLS, JOHN, Washington co

Pvt Conn Contl. Enl 1777 Sept 24 on Lake George at Sandy Point, N Y. Was b 1745. Appl mentions chldr. Pens appl Washington co O May 5 1818 res of Marietta twp (and 7-25-1820 as rept by Helen Sloan). Occupation was a wheelright. Ref S 40161 Contl N Y. Rept by State D A R.

MILLS, MENAN, Montgomery co

Albermarle Co. Pensioner Va Lib 1912 Rept p 214; Pens 3 Ky 69 s of W 1835. Bur on his farm family cem in Perry twp. Later reinterred elsewhere. Exact place unknown. Rept by Wm Pettit.

MILLS, WILLIAM, ? co

Capt. From old scrap bk clipping of Rev soldrs interested in Marietta settlement descendants of whom are bur in Washington co. Listed here for research by Marietta chpt.

MILNER, BEVERLY, Highland co

Rev Soldr   85 pensr in Fairfield twp Highland co. Ref Cens 1840. Rept by Jane Dailey.

MINARD, JOSHUA, Mahoning co

Pvt Conn Men in Rev pp 120, 124, 580. Was b 1763 Conn; mar Phebe (1774-4-19-1841). Chldr: Nathan b 1791; Phebe 1793; James 1796 mar Rachel; Joshua 1797; Betsey 1798; Polly 1801; Harriett 1808; Harmon 1805 d 1875-6-mar Mary Vosburg in Salisbury Conn Aug 25 1830 (d in O); Daniel; Samantha 1810; Rachel 1814; Henry 1816. Soldr d Sept 21 1844 Berlin twp Mahoning co; bur 1-2 mile east of Berlin center. Ref List of Cem rec V 4 late H R Baldwin S A R; Index of Administrations Trumbull co 1844; Will bk 1 p 44 Berlin Probated 2-1-1848. Rept by Mahoning chpt. Chldr rept by E F J Tafe Libr, sons of Revolution Los Angeles Cal.

MINCHELL, WILLIAM, Madison co

A British soldier. But interesting data filed here to avoid continued research. "I made a trip to a grave today and this is what I find on stone: "William Minchell d Dec 25, 1848. 'A stranger I am but here I must lie. My name you can see but my æ is not known'." He was a British prisoner had one leg. His crutches were bur with him and he would never return to his own country as he said he felt disgraced to have been taken a prisoner. This information was furnished by my husband's people who said he was a traveling cobbler and had stayed at the home of his gr-grandfather many times when he made shoes for the family. A clipping in the paper credited him with being a soldr in war 1812 and said he was a Frenchman. I am inclined to believe rather the information of this relative of my husband, who is abt 80 yr old, a well informed woman with a mind clear as a bell, who stayed a great deal at the home of her grandfather and great-grandfather of my husband. Rept by Mrs. J T Martin Cook O.

MINGUS, JOSEPH, Athens co ?

Pvt N Y. No other data located. (J D).

MINGUS (or Mingos), MOSES, Muskingum co

Pvt N Y Line. Col Malcoms Regt Capt James Black. Pens issued Sept 19 1818 sent to Danl Stillwell Zanesville O. Pens appl Muskingum co June 25 1818 æ 59; also

Nov 24 1820 æ 61 appl serv in 1st Regt Col Goshen Vanskyke, Capt Tybouts Co N Y line. "Resided with his sons." Ref S 41006. Rept by State D A R.

MINOR, THOMAS, Jefferson co

Pvt Va Contl. Enl Oct or Nov 1775 Va. Servd 1 yr. Was b 1761. Mar Ann Jennings of Cameron twp London co Va Mar 14 1781 license issued. (Fr all evidence she was called Ann and Nancy also) Chldr: John æ 21; Margaret 25; Rebecca 30; (appl 1822). Also Elizabeth, Robert, Spencer, Thos Ekridge; Peggy; Ann. (Nancys appl) Other chldr: John; Thos Jefferson; Ann Williams Minor; Marthey Jennings Minor. (Family record) Appl Jefferson co O Oct 21 1822. Nancy appl for pens Jefferson co O Feb 26 1840 res Salem twp æ 78. Ref W 4494 Va. Rept by State D A R.

MINS (or Nims), ASA, Huron co

B Franklin Mass. Ref 4th Rept N S D A R p 299. Rept by Mrs. Winnagle, Warren O. See Nims, Asa this vol. (J D).

MINTER, JOHN, Delaware co

Pvt Pa Milit; Capt 6 mos. Bro-In-Law Col Crawford. Was b 1755 Culpepper co Va. Possibly bur in Radnor twp. Mvd fr Va to Westmoreland co Pa 1770. Aft Rev he mvd to Harrison co Ky. Remained abt 20 yrs. 1808 he mvd to Delaware co O whr appl for pens 11-21-1832. Ref Pa S 9027; Howes History. Rept by State D A R and Delaware chpt.

MINTURN (Mintun), JOHN, Montgomery co

Sergt and Major N J Contl. Was b 1752; mar Rebecca Jan 2 1775; d July 7 1826. Pens appl Aug 18 1818 Montgomery co O. Ref N J W 9203. Rept by State D A R.

MITCHELL, AMASA, Hamilton co

Fifer Mass Contl. Enl 1779 West Point N Y. Was b 1752. Wf was liv in 1839. Chldr: John æ 19; Lucy 17; James 14; Harvey 10; Eliza 6. Movd to Indiana in 1839 to be with his chldr. (appl 1821) Pens appl in Kanawha co Va 3-13-1821; in Hamilton co 6-11-1823; trnsfrd to Madison co Ind 1839. Ref Mass S 36699. Rept by State D A R.

MITCHELL, David, Trumbull co

Pvt N C Milit. Pensr 2-22-1833 in Trumbull co. Report fr Pension Bureau "not found." (Would not be proof he did not serve. J D). Rept by Mary Chesney chpt.

MITCHELL, ELIJAH, Preble co

Pvt. Enl Apr 1779 Mecklenburg co N C. Srvd 9 mos fr 1799. Was b Mar 6 1761 Va. Soldr d Aug 1 1847. Letter written fr Huntingdon co Ind July 9 1845 stated that the soldr Elijah Mitchell had movd fr Preble co O to said co and state and asked for his pens money to be sent there. Ref S 2838 N C. Rept by State D A R.

MITCHELL, JAMES, ? co

Pvt but only srvd 6 mo in Contl Regt so was refused a pens. Ref: Doc No. 31 1-6-1831. Rept by Blanche Rings. Col O.

MITCHELL, JOSEPH, ? co

Because he servd in Regt not on Contl Estab he was refused a pension. Ref Doc No. 31 1-6-1831. Rept by Blanche Rings. Col O.

MITCHELL, NATHANIEL, Washington co

Pvt Pa Line 3 yrs. Enl 8-10-1776 8th Pa Regt of Capt David Kilgore Col Enos McCoy. Was b 1750; mar Nancy 12-27-1782. Chldr were all of æ (youngest æ 22). He had living with him one gr-son æ abt 6 yrs in 1820. Soldr d 5-20-1836. Pensd 12-18-1818 Washington co O. Wid pensd 9-7-1839 Washington co O and renewed 12-20-1843. Ref Pa W 3850. Rept by State D A R.

MITCHELL, ROBERT, Belmont co

Ae 80 in 1820. Pvt pensd act Oct 2 1818; in Capt Bruin co Col Morgan Regt of Va. 2 yr Musician. Pens issued to widow Eve Mitchell Oct 2 1844 sent to Carroll or Pennington St Clairsville O. Appl for trnsfr to O co Va Aug 12 1826. Soldr mar Eve —— July 1773 Winchester Va by Rev Mr Mitchell, a Lutheran. One girl was Mary Bramball æ 55 in 1839. Widow says "Had no record of mar of births of chldr." Soldr d June 1827. He enl in Winchester Va 1774-5. Pens of Eve Mitchell widow inscrib on roll of Wheeling Va. Pens iss June 13 1839 sent to John Eaton Jun. Morristown O Belmont co. She livd in Union twp. (cens 1840) æ 85. Ref W 7459. Rept by State D A R and Jane Dailey.

MITCHELL, SAMUEL, Preble co

Pvt and Sergt Pa Trps. Enl 1776 Pa. Srvd 14 mos as Sergt and 2 mos as pvt. Was b Apr 1751 Derry co Ireland. Came to America 1772 and settled in Cumberland co Pa whr res till 1781 when mar and settled in York co Pa. Movd to Washington co Pa. Aft 5 yrs came to Ohio co Va; aft 20 yrs came to Preble co O in 1814. Had 2 chldr (appl) Pens appl Greene co O Nov 24 1832. Ref S 2837 Pa. Rept by State D A R.

MOE, JACOB, Ashtabula co

Exec Doc of 1852. Refused a pension as servd only 3 mos. Rept by Wm Pettit.

MOLER, GASPAR, Morgan co

Pvt Va St Trps. Enl June 1778 Martinsburgh Va Berkly co whr he then res with his father. Srvd abt 7 mo. Was b 1759 three mi above Harpers Ferry; d Feb 17 1845. Five or six yrs aft war movd to Bedford co Pa whr he lived abt 14 yrs; thence to Washington co Pa. Aft 18 yrs movd to Pittsburgh Pa. Stayed abt 8 yrs and movd to Morgan co O. Ref Va S 2874. Rept by State D A R.

MOLER, JOSEPH, Highland co

Pvt Md Milit. Enl Frederick co Md 1778. Servd 2 yrs. Was b Apr 1749 Lancaster co Pa. Movd to Rutherford co N C Jan 4 1778. Then to Washington co Ga for abt 10 yrs. Then to Highland co O. Pens appl Highland co O Oct 29 1833. Ref S 9033 Ga Md. Rept by State D A R.

MONCRIEF, JOHN, Columbiana co

Rev Soldr rec not yet found. Was b 1764; d 1852; bur W Beaver twp. Ref Col co cem rec. Rept by Mrs Wilma M Molesberry.

MONTIETH, JOHN, Mahoning co

Rev soldr bur Hopewell Pres Ch cem. Rept by Miss Etta Kyle, Youngstown O.

MONTGOMERY, HUGH, Butler co

Pvt Va Line trnsfrd to Ind. Pensr in Butler co O Feb 1 1819. Enl Feb 12 1777 Pittsburg Pa in Regt of Col Russell in Va Line. Dischrgd Apr 19 1780. Was b Feb 25 1754. Appl Oct 1822 mentions wf and 1 boy. Livd with sons Michael and Robert. (appl Dec 1825). Res Butler co O Feb 1 1819. Res Decatur co Ind on Oct 7 1822. Also on Dec 23 1825 whn he appl for pens. Ref S 35525 Va. Rept by State D A R.

MONTGOMERY, JOHN, Columbiana co

Ranger Washington co Pa. Was b 1756; d 1827; bur Madison twp. Ref Col co cem Recs; Pa Arch 3 XXIII 215. Rept by Mrs. Wilma Molsberry.

MONTGOMERY, JOHN, Franklin co

Order bk 9-17. Last will and testament brought into court and proven by Joseph Pegg and Matilda Pegg Sept term 1838. Elizabeth Montgomery. Exc. Order bk 9-75. Joseph Pegg a citizen of Franklin co swore that John Montgomery a Rev pensr d at his res in Franklin co on Sept 12 1838 leaving Elizabeth Montgomery his wid and relict. Rept by Blanche Rings.

MONTGOMERY, JOHN, Fairfield co

Pvt Pa Line 5 yrs. Enl Lancaster Pa 1780. Pensd in Fairfield co O. Was b 1756. Wf æ 36 in Mar 1819. Chldr: Mary æ 16; Elizabeth 12; Jane 10; Elmer 8; Hugh 6; Sarah 4; Thomas 2; Joseph 4 mos in Aug 1820. Ref Contl Pa S 40177. Rept by State D A R.

MONTGOMERY, MITCHELL L K, Guernsey co

Pvt Pa Line. Enl Aug 19 1776 Fayette co Pa. Pensd 7-15-1819 Guernsey co O. Wid pensd 6-30-1857 Guernsey co O. Was b 1-5-1750. Mar Rebecca McNeely Sept 1793. Chldr b Mar 1796; Isaac 1798; James 1800; and five step-ch. One named John Mc-Neely. Soldr d 11-11-1845. Ref Pa W 5142. Rept by State D A R. Anna Asbury Stone chpt located pens appl in clerks office of Guernsey co

MONTGOMERY, ROBERT, Ashtabula co

Service ref Milit land bounty rights. 1st Regt Capt Simon Lefever p 145 Hist Ashtabula co by Williams Bros stated he came fr Ireland; reputed a cousin of the Robert who fell at Quebec. Mar Mary (name on stone beside him). Soldr d 10-15-1822 æ 84 yrs. Bur city cem Conneaut O. Came to Conneaut 1799 and it is told held first church services in his home. Ref N Y Men in Rev p 260 Ulster co. Rept by Mary Redmond chpt.

MOODEY (or Moody), ALEXANDER, Muskingum co

Pvt Pa Contl. Srvd 1 yr. Enl Jan 1 1777. Was 76 in 1820. Had Elizabeth æ 26; 2 grand daus: Mary æ 5 and Rebecca æ 3 (appl 1820) Pens appl Muskingum co O Nov 24 1820. Ref S 41891 Pa. Rept by State D A R.

MOONEY, JOHN, ? co

Pvt but since he servd in Regt not on Contl estab was refused a pens. Ref listed No. Doc 31 1-6-1831. Rept by Blanche Rings Col O.

MOORE, ABRAHAM, Jefferson co

A free man of color. Pvt Pa Milit. Entered Rev 1781 then living with Augustine Moore in Fayette co Pa. Srvd 8 mos and 28 days. Was b Oct 1838. Aft Rev res Washington co Pa till 1796 movd to Jefferson co O whr appl for pens May 17 1833. Ref S 2855 Pa. Rept by State D A R.

MOORE, DANIEL, Clark co

Pvt N J Milit. Srvd 13 mos and abt 15 days. Ae 79 in 1833. Enl 1775 N J. Pens appl Clark co O 7-17-1833. Ref N J S 16208. Rept by State D A R.

MOORE, ELIJAH, Jefferson co

Pvt N J Milit. Enl March 1770 in Deerfield Cumberland co N J and srvd 2 yrs. Ae 70 yrs 1819. Appl mentions a granddau. Pens appl Jefferson co O Sept 22 1818 and recd it. Later movd to Va Brooke co and appl for trnsfr. Listed here to avoid cont reasearch for grave in O. Ref N J S 38244. Rept by State D A R.

MOORE, EPHRIAM, ? co

Name listed No. Doc 31 1-6-1831 as pvt but refused pens because he deserted the service. Rept by Blanche Rings. (cf same name p 261 V 1 Roster of O).

MOORE, FERGUS, Pickaway co

Srvd 5 yrs as pvt Pa milit. Was b Ireland Jan 18 1751. Mar Elizabeth 1785 (d Jan 22 1825 æ 75 yrs) Chldr: Fergus; Elizabeth wf of John Flemming; James. Soldr d Wayne twp Pickaway co O Apr 20 1806; bur Westfall cem 6 mi west of Circleville in central part of cem. Inscript on Monument-Fergus Moore dates above. Grave mrkd by Pickaway Plains chpt Bronze markr May 1932. Emigrated fr Ireland whn a young man; mar in Pa; later movd to Ky. Then 1798 to Chillicothe O. Later 1802 bought a tract of land in Wayne twp Pickaway co O. Rept by Pickaway Plains chpt.

MOORE, GEO, ? co

Pvt servd in Milit draft but refused a pens as case not provided for by law. Ref Doc 31 1-6-1831. Rept by Blanche Rings Col O.

MOORE, JACOB, Scioto co

Ensign Va Contl. Enl in Rev Va 1776. Srvd 5 yrs. Was b 1750 in Huntington co N J. Had movd fr N J to Va before war. Pens appl Scioto co O May 16 1818. Ref S 40167 Va. Rept by State D A R.

MOORE, JAMES, Mahoning co

Pvt. Ser 3 V 23 Ser 5 V 2 & 3 Pa Arch. One boy James mar Jane Calhoun. Soldr d abt 1813 Ellsworth. Ref Trump of Fame Estate Nov 24 1813 James Moore Ellsworth adm Tryall Tanner (Rev Soldr) and Joseph Coit. Rept by Mahoning chpt.

MOORE, JAMES, Preble co

B in N C gave services there came to Preble co 1804. One of founders of Camden. D 1832-33. Bur in Camden cem. Rept Commodore Preble chpt.

MOORE, JOHN, Columbiana co

Ranger Pa Washington or Bedford co. Livd in Center twp in 1802. Ref Hist McCords Col co p 478 Pa Arch 3 XXIII p 230, 232. Rept by Mrs. Wilma M Molsberry.

MOORE, JOHN, Ross co

Exec Doc of 1852. Died before act passed. Rept by Wm Pettit.

MOORE, JONATHAN, Warren co

Pvt N J Contl. Enl 1775 N Y city. Srvd Regt of Col Dayton 7 yrs. Was b 1754; mar Elizabeth Berkley co Va 1790; d Sept 25 1853 Bartholomew Ind. Occupation a tailor. Pens appl O May 14 1818 and Aug 22 1820 Lebanon Warren co. Sept 4 1829 Jonathan Moore made declaration for purpose of having his pens made payable in Ind whr he intends to remain. Made appl for new certif in Warren co O Oct 1 1838. Wid appl Bartholomew co Ind Apr 3 1855. Ref W 4743 B L Wt 8595-100 in 1789 and B L Wt 349-60-55. Contl N J and N Y. Rept by State D A R.

MOORE, JOSEPH, Huron co

Was b 1761 Upper Freehold N J whr he enl as pvt New J trps. Various enls. Movd to Mansfield Burlington co N J. Aft Rev movd to Hanover N J; fr there to Philadelphia Pa; then to Coshocton on Delaware River; thence to great bend of Susquehanna River; thence to Newfield, Tomkins co N Y; thence to Enfield Thomkins co N Y. Pens in Enfield N Y 1832. In 1833 livd in Stark co O and in 1834 in Bronson Huron co O. Soldr d in 1849 in Huron co O. Wf d in Enfield N Y abt June 1833. Her name not given. In 1834 a son and a dau of the soldr were living in State of O their names not given. In 1853 a son Joseph B Moore livd in Middlebury Elkhart co Ind. Anna Ivins was named as another heir of soldr. Relationship not stated. Ref Bureau of Pensions Wash D C. Rept by Nathan Perry chpt Mrs. T R Oehlke.

MOORE, JOSEPH, Logan co

Pvt. Pa Arch V 2 5th S p 369. Was b 1765; mar Lydia Ferguson; chldr: David; James; Eliza Steele; James; Margaret; Marian; Serena; Josiah. Soldr d 1859 West Liberty bur at Bellefontaine O. Rept by Bellefontaine chpt.

MOORE, SAMUEL, Montgomery co

Pvt Capt Jas Clarks co Col Joseph Taylor Regt Pa milit. Was b 1760 Chester co Pa; mar Ann Doane (1764-1845); Sally was a dau (1799-1876); soldr d 1838 Montgomery O. Ref No. 123249 V 124 D A R Lin. Rept by Jane Dailey.

MOORE, THOMAS, Columbiana co

Ranger Westmoreland co Pa. Pvt in a Va Regt six yr. Enl Jan 1777 Pittsburgh Pa. Pensd 3-18-1819 Bracken co Ky. Ae 59 yr in 1820. Wf æ abt 58 yr in 1820. David and Jonathan (twins) æ 15 yrs in 1820. Soldr d 8-18-1825. Came to America in the time of the colonies. Srvd under John Beaver in surveying western Pa; then settled on Little Creek and became a miller there. He was the gr-father of Homer Laughlin the founder of the Homer Laughlin Pottery. Occupation Brickmaker. Ref Pa Arch 3 XXIII p 224, 322. Hist Col co. Pa and Va S 36169. Rept by State D A R.

MOORE, THOMAS, Perry co

Pvt Mass Contl. Vol in Mass 1778 then a res in Worcester co Mass. Srvd 9 mos. Was b Sept 3 1761 Worcester co Mass. In cens 1840 says was living with Israel Moore in Madison twp Perry co whr he appl for pens Nov 9 1832. Ref O Pens Roll 1835: III; 0-151; S 2853 Mass. Rept by Jane Dailey and State D A R.

MOORE, WILLIAM L, Franklin co

Order bk 9-75. R W Cowles a citizen of Franklin co swore that William L Moore a Rev pensr d at his res in Franklin co on Sept 1 1838 leaving Susannah Moore his wid and she gave power of attorney to Cowles the same day. Rept by Blanche Rings.

MOORE, WILLIAM, Trumbull co

Pvt Conn Men in Rev p 58. At Bunker Hill lost his gun. Also Conn Men in Rev p 334 Capt Butts co; Am State Papers V 5 p 30 Md. Chldr: William K; Edward; Jacob. Soldr d 3-21-1813 Liberty. Ref Trump of Fame Mar 1813; American State Pa papers V 5 p 30 Service in Md. Rept by Mabel S Askue.

MORELAND, JOHN, Clark co

Pvt Va Contl. Enl Mar 1776 Regt under Col Meyrs. Was 67 yr 10 mo and 13 das 8-14-1820; mar Catherine æ 65 in 1820. Appl mentions a son-in-law. Pens appl Clark co 5-12-1818. Ref Contl Va S 40170. Rept by State D A R.

MORFORD, DANIEL, Brown co

Pvt N J Milit. First entered service Nov 1 1776. Was living at that time in Middlesex co. Srvd 1 yr and 1 mo. Was b Oct 1740 Woodford co N J. Resided in Bracken co Ky and for abt 40 yrs res abt 30 mi fr his present res in Brown co O whr he livd in Brown co O July 1 1833. Ref S 16209 N J. Rept by State D A R.

MORGAN, EVAN, Montgomery co

5th Ser Pa Arch V 2 p 77 1776 of Capt John Nelsons Co of riflemen Col D Hoos Battl to Canada in Nov 1776. Srvd under Gen Wayne and under Col Johnson in 5th Pa. Rept by Mrs. Lindsey Brien, Dayton O.

MORGAN, GEORGE, Belmont co

Pvt Pa line for yrs. Enl Jersey Huts N J. Was b 1761 Chester co Pa. Mar Jane Dec 11 1793; Chldr: Henry 18; George 12; Elizabeth 8; Mary 5. (appl 1820) Soldr d

Nov 2 1845 Belmont co O. At age 92 living in Somerset twp Belmont co O whr appl for pens Apr 15 1819. Pens appl Guernsey co O July 17 1820. Wid appl for pens Monroe co O Oct 20 1849. Wid also appl Guernsey co O Aug 6 1850. Ref W 1635 B L Wt 153-160-55 Pa. Rept by State D A R. Ref Pa Arch V 2 p 732, 892, 109; Certif pens No. 11946. Act of 3-18-1818 (Guernsey co) Rept by Jane Dailey.

MORGAN, GEORGE, Guernsey co

Pvt 1st Pa Contl line Capt Smith and later Capt Bond. Was æ 75 in 1834; Anna Asbury Stone chpt repts wf named Jane; chldr: Henry; George; Elizabeth; Mary. Pens Cl No. 11946 Act of 3-18-1818. Ref Pa Arch Vol 2 pp 732, 892, 109. Pensr in Guernsey co 6-15-1819.

MORGAN, JESSE, Lorain co

Pvt Conn Contl. Srvd 6 mos and 10 days. Enl Apr 1 1779 Danbury Hartford co. Res there till 1816. Was b 1761 Hartford co Conn. 1816 movd to Oneida co N Y to live with chldr. In 1821 went to La Grange Lorain co O whr appl for pens Aug 2 1832. Appl for trnsfr to Cortland co N Y Feb 5 1847. Ref S 5099 Conn; General Acct Office Washington D C. Rept by State D A R and Nathan Perry chpt.

MORLEY, DANIEL, Washington co

Pvt Conn Contl. Enl 3-6-1781 nr West Point N Y. Pensd 6-30-1818 in Washington co. Srvd 2 yrs. Was b 1765. No family residing with him 1820. Soldr d 8-11-1822. Appl pens Washington co July 25 1820. Was a cooper. Ref S 40180 Conn. Rept by State D A R.

MORLEY, JOHN, Trumbull co

Pvt Conn Contl. Pensr 7-31-1823 in Trumbull co. Record S 40176. Srvd fr 1775 to 1777 was in battle of Long Island. Was b Oct 25 1753. D in Trumbull co May 1827 Probater Vol 4. Rept by Mary Chesney chpt. State D A R reports had wf and one son 25 in 1820. Pens appl Trumbull co June 1 1818 res Bristol twp. Ref S 40176 Contl Conn.

MORRIS, BASIL, Monroe co

Pvt Va Contl. Enl 1778 Va. Srvd 10 mos. Was b 1760 Hampshire co Va. Since Rev livd in O co Va, Belmont co O and Monroe co O. Pensr appl Monroe co Sept 21 1832 and pensd 1840 in Enoch twp with Robert Morris æ 82. Ref S 5103, Va. Rept by State D A R.

MORRIS, BENJAMIN, Miami co

Pvt Va Line. Enl Aug 1780 in Va. Srvd 8 mos and 12 das. Pensr 4-11-1833 in Miami co O. Cens 1840 pensr Cynthiana twp æ 76. Was b 6-4-1763 Spotsylvania co Va. Ref Va S 2863. Rept by State D A R.

MORRIS, CORNELIUS, Clark co

Pvt Md Contl. Enl 1779 or 80 in Capt Lloyd Bells Co. Mar Sarah æ abt 53 yrs in 1821; chldr: Jane 19; Cornelius 16; Harriet 15; Elizabeth 10. Soldr d 8-6-1833. Pens appl in Clark co O 5-13-1818. Ref Act Cong 1818 (Col O) æ 76. Md S 40175. Rept by State D A R.

MORRIS, EZEKIEL, Pickaway co

Pvt Capt James Archers co 2nd class 1st Batl associators and milit in 1781-2 Co of Washington Pa. Was b 1744 in Berks Pa; mar Mary abt 1769; chldr: John b 1770 (wf Elizabeth Wills) Samuel b 1778 (wf Amelia); Henry b 1788; Richard; Elizabeth Cline; Rebecca Sarah Linly; Anna Thomas; Rebecca Bowman; Elinor Shelby; Lydia

Morris. Soldr bur old Morris and Evans cem on H Montelius farm Pickaway twp on south side nr center. Inscript on monument is "Ezekiel Morris b 1744 d Sept 24 1822" Grave mrkd by Pickaway Plains D A R May 8 1934. Came fr Berks co to Washington co Pa. In 1809 Feb 1 received by patent a land grant signed by Thomas Jefferson in Walnut twp and still owned by Marris family. The old Morris Bible reads "Ezekiel Morris Seignior departed this life aft a short illness Sept 24 1822 æ 78." Rept by Pickaway Plains chpt.

MORRIS, JAMES, Montgomery co

5th S Pa Arch III p 985, 3rd Lieut Pa Artillery Con Line Apr 1 1777 Col Thomas Proctor. 1782 Vol IV p 640 1782. Capt Moore Chester Co Militia. Rept by Wm Pettit.

MORRIS, JAMES, Fairfield co

Pvt Va Milit. Enl early. Srvd 6 mos. Was b 1757 Berkley co Va. Res in Berkley co Va at the time of enl. Movd to Fairfield co O abt 1808. Pens appl in Fairfield co O 10-30-1832. Ref Va S 2865. Rept by State D A R. Name listed p 406 Wisemans Pioneer People Fairfield co; and p 283 Va Milit in Rev (by J D).

MORRIS, JOHN, Ashtabula co

Exec Doc of 1852. Reinstatement of pens under act of 1848. Rept by Wm Pettit.

MORRIS, JOSEPH, Mahoning co

Pvt. Ser 3 V 23 p 459 Pa Arch. Was b 1767. Mar Rachel (1774-July 8-1863) Chldr: Abraham; John; Joseph; Caleb. Soldr d Mar 17-1825 Goshen twp; bur Center cem. Ref Will bk 5 p 84 Columbiana co Rec prob 1825; Deed bk 2 p 169 Rachel Morris to 1828 land bequethed from deceased husband to son Joseph Morris. Rept by Mahoning chpt.

MORRIS, REUBEN, Warren co

Pvt Va Contl. Enl 1776 Orange co Va. Srvd in Co under Capt Greene Regt of Col Henery 2 yrs. Was b May 4 1756 Culpepper co Va. Pens appl Oct 3 1832 Warren co O res Union Village. Ref S 9036 Va. Rept by State D A R.

MORRIS, STEPHEN, Madison co

Pvt Capt Smith Co Col Summer Regt N J Milit. Was b April 15 1751 Egg Harbour Shore Gloucester co N J whr he livd till came to O 1831. A son was mentioned in a letter of Mar 1 1837 fr Jas McKill Jefferson O to Pens office. Pens appl Dec 31 1836 London O æ 85 under Act 7 June 1832. Granted. Ref S 9031 N J. Cop by Jane Dailey.

MORRIS, WILLIAM, Muskingum co

Pvt Pa Contl. Enl Pa 1777. In appl of 1820 mentions a wf æ 53; a dau Kittura æ 20; (Britton O ?); Louisa 14; Thomas 12; Jannetta 9. Soldr was deceased before 1-26-1832. Pens appl Loudon co Va Apr 10 1818; also 1820; Muskingum co O June 1823. Ref S 40173 Pa. Rept by State D A R.

MORRIS, WILLIAM, Highland co

Sergt Md Milit. Srvd 2 yrs. Was b Aug 4 1744 Worcester co Md and movd fr there to Highland co O 1816. Pens appl Highland co O Oct 28 1833. Ref S 9040 Md. Rept by State D A R.

MORRIS, WILLIAM, Montgomery co

Sergt Md. Enl Monmouth co N J. Srvd 18 mos. Was b 1761; mar Martha Hillan Oct 5 1831; d Dec 3 1838. Pens appl Montgomery co O Mar 12 1833. Mid appl Montgomery co O Apr 30 1844. Ref W 10520 B L Wt 26384-160-55 N J. Rept by State D A R.

MORRISON, A——, Wood co

From D A R record No. 130488 of Delaware O we copy following but we do not certify it is the same man: "Andrew Morrison srvd in 3rd Va Regt under Capt John Chiltons Co. Had a son Andrew" Was bur Beaver Creek cem Grand Rapids O. Cop by Jane Dailey. Margaret C Rider, Tontogany O repts bur at Perrysburg Maumee O.

MORRISON, JOHN, Cuyahoga co

Exec Doc of 1852. Refused a pension as srvd less than 6 mo. Rept by Wm Pettit.

MORRISON, JOHN, Mahoning co

Pvt Cumberland co Pa Ser 3 V 23 pp 687, 700 Pa Arch. Mar Eleanor Jackson. 7 chldr: James went to Holmes co; John went to Trumbull co; Thomas to Pa; Jane; Nancy; Martha; Mary Ann mar David Johnson and livd in Jackson. Soldr d before 1828 in Jackson twp Mahoning co. Came fr Washington co Pa to Jackson twp in 1805. Ref Hist Trumbull and Mahoning co V 2 p 148; Memoirs of Pioneer Women of Western Reserve p 933. Rept by Mahoning chpt.

MORSE, ELIJAH, Ashtabula co

Pvt Mass Milit. Pensr 4-2-1833 Ashtabula co. Mary Redmond chpt repts (1931) soldr d 8-5-1837 æ 72; bur at Williamsfield O.

MORSE, ISAAC, Washington co

Pens appl July 22 1820 Com Pleas Court Marietta O. Ref V 3 p 410. Rept by Helen Sloan. (see Isaac Morris p 263 Vol 1 Ohio Roster).

MORTON, SOLOMON, Lake co

Pvt Capt Evans Co Col Chapin and Frothingham Mass Line. Was b 1763 livd in Hatfield Mass; mar 1784 Eunice Tower (1764-1850) Richard was one son. Soldr d at Painesville O. Cop fr V 115 No. 114696 D A R Lin by Nathan Perry chpt.

MOSES, ABNER, Trumbull co

In Capt Baldwins Co Col Swifts Regt Conn Line 1781-1783. 1st wf Ruhama Johnson 2nd ——; chldr: Abner; Polly; Azariah Wilcox; John; Nancy; probably others. Soldr d June 1808 Vernon. Of Hartford Conn came to Vernon fr Hartland Conn. Livd in Vernon all his life. Rept by Mary Chesney chpt.

MOSES, EZEKIAL, Champaign co

Pvt Conn Milit. Enl 9-1-1776 res of Simsbury Conn. Was b 2-3-1762 Simsbury Conn; mar Eunice 3-17-1790; chldr: Loice b 1791; Inna 1792; Theda Bob 1794; Phebe 1795; Loice 2nd 1797; William 1799; Ivan 1801; Eliza 1803; Eunice 1806; Truman 1810. Soldr d 11-15-1834. Res of Jackson twp Champaign co 1833 a pensr. Ref Conn W 4551. Rept by State D A R.

MOSEY, JOHN, ? co

Ref S A R No 33355; b R I 1762; d 1816; also srvd in War of 1812. Located Milton O (which one of 3 co's). By Wm Pettit.

MOSIER, DANIEL, Athens co

Pvt Mass Milit. Enl Dartmouth Mass pvt in Col Russells Regt for 9 mos. Was b 1745 Newtown Mass; mar Elizabeth (b July 17 1746) Dec 13 1763 Dartmouth Mass. Trupp, son res of Roxbury twp Washington co O in 1845 stated he was 3rd child b Dartmouth Mass Aug 12 1768. Had an elder bro Daniel. (Sons deposition for mother Eliz in Athens O Feb 7th 1815). Soldr d Feb 7 1840. Pens appl Athens co Oct 13 1832 res of Marion twp of Athens æ 87. Livd in Dartmouth Mass; then Hoosar; then Kennebec Me; thence to O. Wid Eliz appl for pens in Washington co O on May 13 1842. Ref R 7454 Mass. Rept by State D A R.

MOSS, ISAAC, Washington co

Pvt Mass Contl. Pensr 5-21-1819 Washington co. Ref Mass Soldiers and Sailors Vol XI p 165. Rept by Marietta chpt.

MOTT, EZEKIEL, Portage co

Enl June 1777. Pvt N Y Line. Srvd 3 yrs. Pensd 12-4-1819 Portage co Deerfield O. Was b 1737; mar Jane (d 11-16-1838) abt 1775; chldr: Elujah; granddau Eunice Carter. Elijah pens appl Stark co O 4-13-1854. Soldr d abt 1823 Deerfield Portage co O. Ref N Y R 7463. Rept by State D A R.

MOTT, JOSIAH, Clark co

Sergt enl East Hartford Conn 1780. Pensr 12-10-1830 Clark co. Mar Eunice Palmer 9-14-1811; chldr: Josiah b 1812; Eliah 1813; Amey 1816; Andrew Jackson 1818; William 1820; Lewis Davis Mott 1822; Eunice 1824; Rhodah Palmers Mott 1826; Sarah Smith Mott 1828; Mary Ann 1829. Soldr d 10-21-1836 Clark co O. Wid appl for pens Miami co O Feb 15 1872. Ref W O 8154; W C 4878. Rept by State D A R.

MOTT, SAMUEL, Portage co

Pvt N Y Contl. Enl 1778 3rd N Y Regt under Col Gansvont. Was b 1754. Movd to O to reside with his chldr. Pensr 1-19-1819 Orange co N Y. Trnsfrd to O 9-4-1829 Portage co. Ref N Y S 40178. Rept by State D A R.

MOWDY, JOHN, Ashland co

Pensr 1840 Vermilion twp æ 95 Richland co, now Ashland co O. Ref Will filed Richland co Ct House No. 247 Final settlement 1845 in Aug. Rept by Jane Dailey and Jared Mansfield chpt.

MOWREY, REUBEN, Trumbull co

Pvt Mass St Trps. Enl fr Granville with the Mass No. S 2875 trps. Later fr Hartland Conn with the Conn Trps. Was b 1754 Glouster R I; mar Lucy Couch; chldr: Lucy; Lucretia; Zilka; Ezekiel; Stephen; Plinny; Loisa; Isaac; and three others. Soldr d Gustavus 1841. Was liv in Hartford Trumbull co O 1832. Pensr 5-10-1833 Trumbull co. Pens Cl Conn and Mass S 2875. Rept by Mary Chesney and State D A R.

MOYER, JOHN, Mahoning co

Ranger, Ser 3 V 23 pp 252, 296; 1778-1783 Westmoreland co and Northumberland co Pa Arch; mar Barbara; chldr: John; George mar Catharine. Soldr d abt 1813 Springfield twp Mahoning co. Ref Will bk 2 p 33 Columbiana co Records probated 1813. Rept by Mahoning chpt.

MOYER, MICHAEL, Montgomery co

Berks co 2 p 40; 5 p 205. With Capt Nagles Co of riflemen that marched to Cambridge 1775. In milit 1777 Capt Philip Creek (Krick) Co as 2nd Lieut. Was b 1761; d 1828; bur Walkey farm Elberton Montgomery co. Rept by Wm Pettit.

MUMY, CHARLES, Morgan co

Listed in Va Milit in the Rev p 284 as liv in Morgan co O æ 80. (The family name of "Mummey" is found in Morgan co O. See Christopher Mummey p 266 Roster Vol 1) Jane Dailey.

MUNGEE, WILLIAM, Champaign co

Was b 1744. Corp Mass Contl. Enl Apr 1775 Roxbury Mass. Stated he had no family and was resident of Franklin co O 1818; and of Champaign co in 1820 whr was a pensr. Ref Mass S 40189. Rept by State D A R.

MUNN, FRANCIS, Athens co

Enl Providence R I 1777 as pvt in Capt Gilsons Co of Artillery. Enl for 12 mo more under Col Eliot. Pensd 1833. Was b 1759 England. Parents of soldr never left England. Mar Sarah Wickham; chldr: Francis Jr; Sarah; Polly; Bailey; Honor; Alexander; George. Soldr d 2-25-1844 Rome twp Athens co O; bur in cem now a field all traces gone. 1st enl with British army then deserted and joined American forces. Ref P 125 Deeds Athens co Bought land in Rome twp Sept 14 1812. Rept by Nabby Lee Ames chpt Helen Townsend.

MUNROE, LEONARD, Delaware co

Pvt Conn Contl. Enl Mar 14 1777 in Conn. Was b 1757; chldr: Denis æ abt 15 and one child æ 12. Pens appl Madison co O Aug 1 1818. Transfr to Delaware. Occupation was a tailor. Ref Conn Contl S 40188. Rept by State D A R.

MUNSON, CAPT HERMAN, Medina co

In 1781 he was commissioned to secure recruits for the American and was called "Captain" Was b Wallingford Conn Oct 28 1738; son of Caleb Munson and Abigail Brokett; mar Anna Bronson July 27 1769; chldr: Mary; Abigail; and Anna. Soldr d Medina Feb 12 1829 bur Old cem Medina. Relatives have kept his grave and others in good condition. Inscript says "Sacred to the memory of Herman Munson who died Feb 12 1829 æ 91 yrs" Mrkd by a slab of sand stone and a bronze star showing Rev service. Ref No. 39032 D A R; Service in The Munson Family by Myron Munson. Rev War Rec of Waterbury p 28 Vol 7. Rept by Nancy Squires chpt Oberlin.

MURIEL (or Murrel), WILLIAM, Columbiana co

Pvt N J Milit 10 mos. Enl July 1776 Salem co N J. Was b 9-13-1759 Mt Holly N J; chldr: One girl was Elizabeth Maud (not mar) æ 26 in 1818. Soldr d aft 1832. Res at time of enl in Salem co N J fr there he movd to Wallington co Pa. Thence to Green twp Columbiana co O. Pens appl Columbiana co O 4-15-1818 and again 8-16-1832. Occupation was a carpenter. Ref N J S 2884. Rept by State D A R. (NB One Wm Murrell listed in rejected pens list as he servd in Regt not on Contl Estab Doc No. 31 1-6-1831). Rept by State D A R.

MURPHY, JAMES, Warren co

Pvt Pa Contl. Enl in Pa 1779. Was b 1760; mar Elizabeth Turk (2nd wf); chldr: Ross æ 10 in 1820 and Jacob æ 8. Soldr d 11-16-1830 Warren co O. Pens appl in Clermont co O 2-16-1819. Wid appl for pens in Warren co O 9-2-1856. Ref Contl Pa W 25739 B L Wt W 87-60-55. Rept by State D A R.

MURPHY, JOHN, Ross co

Pvt Va Contl. Enl 2-2-1777 12th Va Regt. Srvd 6 yrs. Was b 1750-51; mar Elizabeth abt 1780. Pens appl 7-10-1818 Ross co O. Ref Name listed p 406 Wisemans Pioneer People Fairfield co O Va S 40191 B L Wt 564-100. Rept by State D A R.

MURRAY, NEAL, Ross co

Pvt under Capts Miller, Porter and Clark; Cols Mackey, Wilson, Brodhead and Lamb Pa line. Was b Ireland; mar Elizabeth (d 1825); William was one son. Soldr d 1832 in Ross co O. In 1818 a Neal Murray was pens in Clermont co as pvt Pa Contl; likely the same. Cop fr V 114 No. 113531 D A R Lin. By Nathan Perry chpt.

MUSGROVE, WILLIAM, Belmont co

Pvt Va Contl. Enl Jan 1777 Va. Dischgd Apr 18 1780 Pittsburgh Pa. Was b 1760; mar Abigail; chldr: Sidney; Ephraim. Pens appl Frederick co Va Nov 12 1819; trnsfd to Belmont co O Aug 14 1826. Ref S 40190 Va. Rept by State D A R.

MUSSER, SAMUEL, Mahoning co

Pvt Ser 6 V 2 pp 236, 646, 678; York co Pa Pa Arch; Srvd Armand Legion p 287 Contl Congress York Prowell Pa. Was probably b York co Pa; mar Mary —— (Anna Alavia); chldr: Samuel b 1767; Michael; Jacob; Eve mar Michael Snider; Margaret mar David Woltinger; Mar Magdalena 1-9-1787-d young; John Conrad 1789-d young. Soldr d 1808 Springfield twp. Removd fr York co Pa to Washington co and in 1801 with bro Peter Mussey a Rev Soldr to Springfield. Ref Will bk p 100 prob 1808; Contl Cong at York by Geo B Prowells; Farley, Mercer Fam Rec Belmont Farley in Cong Libry. Rept by Mahoning chpt.

MYER, DAVID, Mahoning co

Pvt Ser 5 V 8 p 113 Pa Arch. Mar Catharine; chldr: Elizabeth mar Daniel Krieder; Ann mar Joseph Kauffman; Catherine; Mary mar Abraham Landis; Benjamin; Susanna; David; John; Magdalena. Soldr d abt 1827 Beaver twp Mahoning co Ref Will bk p 518 Columbiana co records prob 1827; Deed bk W p 579 David Myer Heirs to 1837. Rept by Mahoning chpt.

MYERS (or Moyer), ADAM, Huron co

Pvt Pa Milit. Srvd 7 mos. Was b Mar 15 1755 Fort Town Va on Northfork of Potomac River in Va. His father kept record of chldr æ's in Dutch language in Bible. Mar Mary Wiedman Aug 2 1779. Names of chldr not found. Soldr d Dec 15 1844; bur Huron O grave located by Sandusky chpt ref Rept 18 N S D A R p 232. Pens appl Huron co O June 8 1833. Raised in Pa had res in Ridgefield twp Huron co O for abt 15 yrs. Wid appl for pens Huron co O Sept 30 1845. Ref W 10552 Va. Rept by State D A R. (N B One Adam Myers is listed in rejected pens because he servd in Regt not on Contl Estab. Doc 31 1-6-1831).

MYERS, CHRISTOPHER, Knox co

Pvt Md Milit. 1833 pensr.

MYERS, HENRY, Columbiana co

Pvt Pa Line. Had one son Samuel (b Col co 1806 a physician in O and then Elkhart Ind d 1861). Soldr d Columbiana co O or Ripley co Ind. From Janiata co Pa to Columbiana co O 1786 and livd Ripley co Ind in 1834 æ 87 (July 12). Ref Warners Beaver co p 701; Pa Arch 3 XXIII 600. Rept by Mrs Wilma M Molsberry.

MYERS, HENRY, Crawford co

Pa State Trps. Enl Apr 1776 Yorktown York co Pa. Srvd 15 mos. Was b 3-15-1756 Berkley co Va; mar Susannah (d 2-26-1839) chldr: Mary Thornburgh; Susanna Nichols; Priscilla Start. Soldr d 3-23-1834 Crawford co O. Was liv in York co Pa at the time of enl but livd in Berkley co Va aft the war. Soldr d 3-23-1834 Crawford co O. Ref Pa R 7544. Rept by State D A R.

MYERS, JOHN, Perry co

Pvt Pa Milit Pensr 1-6-1834 in Perry co æ 82. Listed on O Pens Roll. Rept by Jane Dailey.

MYERS, MATTHEW, Jefferson co

Ref Pa Arch S 3 Vol 23 pp 237-239. Was b Pa 1758; d 1840; mar Eve Figley, S A R ref 52605. By Wm Pettit. Mary D Sinclair Steubenville chpt repts: Pvt Capt Hawkins Boone's Co 12th Pa Regt Col Wm Cooks; bur Union cem Steubenville O.

MYERS, MICHAEL, Jefferson co

Was given the rank of Capt of Scouts in the Crawford Expedition. Gave great service to govt in quelling the Indians. Was b Winchester Va 1745. Mar Catherine Strickler; chldr: Mollie; George B; Elizabeth; Jacob; John; William b 1811; Michael. Soldr d Aug 11 1852 Toronto O; bur Toronto cem Toronto O Lot No. 6. Grave mrkd by tall grey granite monument Auver Mike Muers Indian Scout 1745-1852. Mrkd by Michael Myers chpt D A R. A part of his duty was patroling fr Mingo Bottom up the west Bank of Ohio River to the mouth of Yellow Creek. In 1795 he located on section 25 twp 4 range 1. Ref This record was found in the "History of Upper Ohio Valley" published by Brant and Fuller 1890 Madison Wis Vol 2 p 159 also pp 33-157. This mans record is well known by the major population of Toronto. Rept by Michael Myers chpt and Wilma Molsberry.

MYERS, NICHOLAS, Montgomery co

Srvd Northampton Pa in Rev. Ref 5th S Pa Arch V 8 pp 594, 599. Capt Safoos 1781. Was fr Mifflin co Pa. Rept by W M Pettit.

MYGATT, COMFORT, Mahoning co

Fifer in Conn Co. Was b Oct 17 1763 Connecticut son of Eli Mygatt officer in Rev War. Mar 1st Lucy Knapp; Mrs. Eleanor Stiles (1777-18 O) 2nd; chldr: Comfort; Elizabeth mar Zalman Fitch; Lucy mar Asahel Adams; Martha; Amanda mar Wm McFarlane; Eleanor mar Allison Kent; Hannah mar W S Otis; Juliana mar Elisha Whittlesey; Almira mar Lewis Hoyt; George; Eli. Eoldr d Oct 17 1823 Canfield O. Bur at Canfield Center Mahoning co. He once pointed out a bridge in Conn which he said his Co crossed during Rev War and he was a fifer. Ref Hist Trumbull and Mahoning co V 2 p 313; Memoirs of Pioneer Women of Western Reserve p 390; Mahoning dispatch Nov 12 1897; Art No. 42 —— Truesdales Notes on Canfield Pioneers. Rept by Mahoning chpt.

NAGLE, JACOB, Stark co

Pvt and seaman U S Navy; pensd 9-16-1833; b Pa; at æ 79 liv in Canton twp Stark co with John Black. Ref Cens 1840. (by J D). Fr Mrs Owen Steinmetz Reading Pa cop fr Adler's Journal Pa of Mar 16 1841 "D Feb 17 1841 in Stark co O. Jacob Nagel æ 80 yr born in Pa" an account is given in German.

NAGLEY, GEORGE, Clark co

At the residence of Elias Nagley Madison twp Clark co O on Oct 17 1837 aged 77-7-2. He undoubtedly went into the service of his country and served four months in the Rev struggle for liberty. (Ohio State Journal and Political Register Issue Nov 1 1837.) Rept by Blanche Rings.

NAIL, HENRY, Richland co

Service 3rd Ser Pa Arch V 23 p 423. B 1755 Pa; d 1835. Ref 25366 S A R. Rept by Wm Pettit.

NANTZ, FREDERICK, Washington co

Enl Va Line 1776 for 3 yrs under Capt James Foster; servd as Sergt under Capt Thomas Willis; was under Capts Thos Moore and Joseph Knight. B 1761 Lunenburg Va; mar Martha Hughes Watkins; one known chld was Martha Hughes Nantz (No. 32015 D A R) He d Washington co. Ref V 33 p 5 D A R Lin. Rept by Nathan Perry D A R. Marietta chpt repts a Rev marker ordered in 1934 for his grave.

NASSEY, EZEKIEL, ? co

Listed in rejected pens appl. Ref Doc No. 31 Jan 6 1831 as served on a vessel not on the Contl Estab. Mariner. Rept by Blanche Rings.

NAYLOR, RALPH, Clermont co

Pvt 7th Co Cumberland co Pa Milit. B 1762 Harrisburg Pa; mar Nancy Stewart 1791. D 1827 New Richmond O. Ref V 105 p 42 No. 104122 D A R Lin. Cop by Jane Dailey.

NEAL, JOHN, Mahoning co

Pvt. Ref Ser 5 Vol 5 p 585 Pa Arch. Mar Rachel; a son was Thomas; a dau was Jane who mar Alex Harsh. Soldr d abt 1802 Canfield O Mahoning co whr he was on tax list 1801. Ref Hist Trumb and Mahoning co V 1 p 49; V 2 p 16; and Deed bk A p 250 Rachel Neal et al fr (1802); also No. D p 134 Rachel wid John Neal to (1823). Rept by Mahoning chpt.

NEBLET, AARON, ? co

Pvt. Listed in rejected pens appl. Ref Doc No. 31 Jan 6 1831 as srvd in a Co not on a Contl Estab. Rept by Blanche Rings.

NELSON, JOHN, Clermont co

Pvt Pa Milit. Pensr 3-28-1833 Clermont co O. Srvd 6 mo. He movd to Cumberland abt æ one yr whr he livd until he enl in the U S service summer of 1776-7 or 8. Cumberland co was divided and he livd in Mifflin co part. In 1789 mvd to Ky; thence to Dayton O abt 1807; to Cincinnati abt 1816; and to Clermont co abt 1825. Here he appld for pens 11-8-1832 liv in Batavia twp. Was b 3-3-1763 Cecil co Md. Ref Pa and N W Indian War of 1790; S 4601 Pens Dept Wash. Cop by State D A R.

NELSON, MOSES, Starke co

Pvt N C Line; enl 1780 in Rowan co N C where resided. In May 1781 movd to Phila Pa. Aft 9 mo movd to Washington co Md. Aft 3 yrs to Franklin co Pa; then back to Washington co Md and in 1812 to Stark co O. Appld for Pens there Oct 12 1832. Cens 1840 states was living with Charles Hartz Plain twp Stark co a pensr æ 80. Ref S 4616 N C Pens Dept Wash. Cop by State D A R. (N B Research places a Moses Nelson in Clark co O. Pensd 2-27-1833 for N C Service.)

NESBITT, WILLIAM, Summit co

Name appears as pvt on Roll of Lieut Daniel Smith's Co Cumberland Co Milit 1779 in War of Rev. Also as Pvt 6th Class Roll of Capt John Wood's co First Battl Cumberland co Milit 1781 1782 in Rev War. Ref p 693 Vol 23; and pp 104, 138, and 623 V 6 Pa Arch 3rd and 6th Ser respectively. Data by H H Shenk Archivist Pa State Libry. Frederick A Godcharles Director Harrisburg. Information furnished and sworn to by Thomas A Graven M D Major M O R C Post 68 Amer Legion. Bur at Northfield Macedonia cem Summit co. Rept by Cuyahoga Portage chpt.

NESSLE, CONRAD, Huron co

Pvt N Y State Trps. Enl 1778. Servd till 1783. B 5-11-1762; d 1-8-1833; bur Huron O (18 rept N S D A R p 223). Appl names a dau Catherine Curtiss; and gives Norwalk Huron co as residence. Pens 7-20-1833 Huron co. Cop by State D A R.

NESTLER, JOHN, Washington co

Listed in Washington co as pvt N J Contl. Pensr 6-9-1819. He appld for pens July 24 1820 in Common Pleas Court Marietta. Ref V 3 p 414. Rept by Mrs Helen Sloan Marietta.

NETTERFIELD, WILLIAM, Trumbull co

Pvt Flying Camp Pa. Drafted 1776 Pa. Servd 8 mo. B Oct 5 1750 nr Bethlehem

Pa. Mar Mary Aug 13 1835. He d Apr 2 1846. Appld for pens Aug 21 1832 residing in Warren twp Trumbull co and receiving one there 7-6-1833. Ref W 569 Pa. Wid appl for pens Trumbull co May 7 1853. Cop by State D A R. Mary Chesney D A R (Warren) adds: a Mrs Mary James prob a 2nd wife; chldr: Samuel; Betsey; William; Jesse; Sally; possible others (not in order of birth).

NEWBERRY, WILLIAM, Brown co

Pvt and fifer N J Milit. Enl 1777 Monmouth co N J. Servd 7 mo. In 1833 Nov 5 appld pens in Clermont co O. Listed in Brown co as pensr 12-2-1833. Aft Rev war lived abt 30 yrs in Glouster co N J; then movd to Clermont co O and aft 5 yrs to Brown co where resided when appl fr pens. Ref S 4602 N J Pens Dept. Cop by State D A R.

NEWCOMB, ETHAN, Trumbull co

Pvt N J Milit. Pensr 7-24-1833. Ref N J in Rev p 703. B 1-1-1763; d 5-7-1837 Brookfield Trumbull co grave unlocated; mar Amelia Summers; chldr: Sarah; Ethan; Abigail; John Thomas; Elizabeth; Joseph; Ruth; Daniel. Rept by Mary Chesney D A R. Add to this cop by State D A R from Pens Dept Wash. Ref S 18523 N J. He was b in Cumberland co N J. (1762) Servd one yr; abt 1808 removd to Trumbull co O Brookfield twp.

NEWCOMB, JOHN, Trumbull co

Pens appl fr Trumbull co; no other data; rept by Mary Chesney chpt.

NEWELL, ROBERT, Logan co

Pvt; b 1741 Ireland. Landed in Phila Pa 1760; mar Christina Williams; went to Ky; settled on land; afterwards claimed by a Rev officer; then he came to West Liberty O. D 1829 in home of dau Margaret Hubbard in West Liberty O. Bur Muddy Run west of town W L. Rept by Bellefontaine chpt. Nathan Perry chpt repts in 16 rept p 142 N S D A R a Robert Newell was listed by Kokosing D A R Mt Vernon as bur there Knox co.

NEWLIN, WILLIAM, Guernsey co

Exec Doc 37. Refused a pens as servd less than 6 mo. Rept by Wm Pettit.

NEWMAN, JACOB, Fayette co

Service Va Milit; b Halifax co Va 1742; d 1837; mar —— Spencer; ref No 46249 S A R. Rept by Wm Pettit.

NEWMAN, WALTER, Licking co

In Battles Long Isl; Brandywine; Paoli; Germantown; Red Banks; Monmouth; Stony Point; Springfield; Camden; Cowpens; Guilford C H; Yorktown; etc. B 1758; d April 1851 Newark O. Bur 6th St cem. Enl with twin bros at æ of 16 fr his father's home Lancaster co Pa. Had first tavern in Gallipolis O. Rept by Hetuck chpt. Addit research at Pens dept Ref W 2230 Pa by State D A R found: b 9-27-1761 Lancaster co Pa; mar Elizabeth Wheeler 10-15-1840. Enl as a substitute for his father in 1777. In 1832 appld for pens living in Fairfield co and 1833 a pensr there. (Name listed p 406, Wisemans Pioneer People Fairfield co and 1840 census living in Walnut twp æ 79. J D).

NEWTON, HANANIAH, Muskingum co

Pvt Mass Contl. Enl July 10 1778 Middlesex co Mass. Appld for pens in Erie co Pa June 2 1818 at æ 56; later trnsfrd to Morgan co O. Mar Chloe Wood July 18 1785;

chldr: John; Armon; Trumon; Abigail; and Amelia. He d April 14 1826 Zanesville O. Ref Mass Contl S 40198 Pens dept.

NICE, WILLIAM, Ross co

Pvt. Enl 1777 Pa Line Contl. Servd 3 yrs. Pensd 10-21-1818 in Muskingum co; transfrd to Ross co O (no date). Was 72 in 1821. Ref S 40205 Pa. Pens Dept. Cop by State D A R.

NICELY, JACOB, Highland co

Pvt 8th Regt Va Line. Pensr June 19 1829 Highland co. Ref S 46335 Va Pens Dept. Cop by State D A R.

NICHOLAS, JAMES, Portage co ?

Listed by Western Reserve D A R in 13th Rept p 123 N S D A R. Filed by Nathan Perry chpt. (Compare James Nichols p 272 Vol 1 Ohio Roster — J D).

NICHOLAS, JOHN, Montgomery co ?

One served Pa Line. Ref 5th S Pa Arch V 6 p 159; also V 4 p 247; servd in Contl Line. V 7 p 444. Deeds in Montgomery co say he came fr Dauphin co Pa. Early Dayton O papers say he was a Rev soldier. Grave unknown. Filed by Wm Pettit S A R Dayton O.

NICHOLS, JONAS, Lake co

Pvt in Col William Malcom's N Y Levies. B Vt 1758; mar Elizabeth Smith who was b 1758 d 1812. He d at Perry O 1843. Cop fr D A R lin Vol 109 p 182 by Jane Dailey. this is similiar data to Jonas Nicholas p 272 V 1 Roster Ohio Rev Sold but "Nichols" is the proven lineage. (J D).

NICKENS, MOSES, (Colored), Franklin co

Ref Beers W H "Hist of Madison co O" p 629 reads: "Moses Nickens was a soldier in the Continental Army under Washington and also in the War 1812; enlisted fr Jefferson twp Madison co O." Rept by Nathan Perry chpt; also by Edith Rathburn O S Librarian. Ref 20 rept p 74 N S D A R.

NIKS, DAVID, Ashtabula co

Pvt N Y Milit. Pensr 9-17-1833 in Ashtabula co. Prob bur in old Monroe cem. (J D). Compare David Niles Vol 1 Ohio Roster.

NILES, GAIUS, Gallia co

Pvt N H Contl. Pensr in Gallia co 6-9-1819; b England; mar Rebecca ——; who d May 11 1832 æ 64 (on stone). He d 3-10-1840 and bur in Sec 16 Gallia co on Alfred Wilcox farm. Stone data "Gaius Niles d Mch 10 1840 aged 95." Grave and data located by Grace McGrath 184 Westwood Rd Col O. Secured by Jane Dailey.

NIMS, ASA, Huron co

Enl 1776. Pvt in Capt Benj Phillips Co Col Elisha Porter's Hampshire co Mass Regt. B 1760 Shelbourne Mass; mar Mary Worthington; a dau named Climena Nims mar Joseph Sweet 1827; soldr d 1840 Bellevue O. Cop fr V 105 D A R Lin No. 104354 by Jane Dailey. (The 4th rept N S D A R p 299 lists as Mins, Asa, cop by Mrs. Winnagle Warren O.) Ref p 701 Pioneer Women Western Reserve gives sketch. (J D). Marjorie Cherry sends chldr: Samuel mar Mahala Long; Elihu mar Zilpha Long; Worthington mar Betsy Barnard; Mary unmarried.

NISBET, WILLIAM, Preble co

Pvt 6th Class 7th Co comm by Capt John Woods 1st Battl Cumberland co Milit under Col James Johnston Aug 18 1780. B in Pa 1734. Mar Elizabeth Irwin in Pa came to Preble co 1805. Soldr d June 1809. Bur in Presb grave yard on farm. Rept by Commodore Preble chpt.

NIXON, GEORGE, Clinton co

Pensr Act 1832-34 as Pvt and Lieut in Capt Evans Co Col Duffee Regt N J Milit. (Fr Wilmington O). Ref S 8919 Pens dept gives following: Enl at New Castle co Del. Was æ 81 in 1833; at whch time names a dau Seeds Nixon æ 41; and son Francis æ 37. Cop by Jane Dailey.

NIXON, THOMAS, ? co

Colonel. From old scrap bk clipping of Rev soldrs interested in or participating in Marietta settlement descendants of whom are bur in Washington co. Listed here for research by Marietta chpt.

NIXON, WILLIAM, Wayne co

Pvt N J Contl. Enl Mar or April 1776 in Cumberland co N J. Servd one yr. Appld for pens Feb 22 1820 in Wayne co O aged 65; names wife Mary to whom mar Apr 28 1804. Names chld a son William æ 16; a dau Gena æ 13. He d Sept 17 1825 in Wayne co O as stated in widow's appl for pens fr Fulton co O July 5 1853 while a resident of Delta in said co. Ref W 806 N J Pens dept. Cop by State D A R.

NISBET, FRANCIS, Mahoning co

Pvt Pa Arch S 5 V 6 p 133. B 1749; mar Annie ——— (b 1751 d 1-7-1823); three chldr were: Francis Jr (1786); John; and William. He livd in Poland O until a short time before his death in 1852 at Westfield Pa where bur just over the Ohio state line. Ref Henry Baldwin list. Rept by Mahoning chpt.

NOBLE, CALEB, Ashtabula co

Lieut in Col Wessons Regt Mass Trps 1779. B 1741 Westfield Mass. Mar Mercy Kellogg (d 1819); one son was Achsah Noble (1771-1855) and one Caleb; he d 1804 Ashtabula co. Ref V 107 p 25 No. 106086 D A R Lin & No. 115565 V 116.

NOLD, JACOB ("Bishop"), Columbiana co

"Soldr in Rev." Pvt N Y Milit. B Aug 13 1765; mar Susanna (b Nov 14 1765 d Aug 22 1836); a son was named "Deacon" Jacob Nold (b 1798 d 9-30-1864); a gr son Abraham b 1826. Jacob d 3-6-1835; bur Old Cem East Leetonia "Mennonite" Fairfield twp. Ref Baldwin Notes Pa Arch S 5 Vol 4 p 475; and 1912 S A R yr bk. Rept by Mahoning chpt Wilma Molsberry.

NOLF (or Nulff), GEORGE, Columbiana co

Enl March 1776 at Eastown twp Northampton co Pa. Was Sergt; Lieut; and Capt in Pa Milit 8 mo. A native of Germany; mar Susanna Edleman ?; a son John mar Sarah Reedy whose parent in Rev and livd in Armstrong co Pa where their son Matthias was b who came to Fairfield twp Columbiana co; other chld: Catherine Close (b 9-1-1775); Susanna Zeigenfuss (b 6-21-1777); Barbara Brown Miller; Conrad; Elizabeth Greener; Isaac; Sarah Hauler (?); Rachel Jameison; and Jacob. He d Sept 1830 accd to certif and was 120 yrs 2 mo 20 da old; was a man of great physical strength; widow appld for pens in Lehigh co Pa 9-14-1847. Ref Upper Ohio Valley Vol 2 p 433; Pa Arch S 3 V 19 p 369 and Pa W 3188 Pens dept. Rept by State D A R and part by Mahoning chpt (Mrs Molsberry).

NORMAN, BAZABEEL, (Bazael), Washington co

Pvt Md Contl. Enl in Fall of 1777 in Regt of Col John Gunby; livd for a time in Va; servd four yrs. Pensd in Washington co 3-5-1819; and widow pensd there 8-2-1847; he was b 7-12-1760; mar Fortune Stephens Sept 1782 in Frederick co Md. chldr Rebecca Norman Grayson; Aquilla; Bazil; (these three living in 1841); other chldr: James (deceased lving widow Lucinda and son Columbus); Joseph decsd lving widow Sarah Ann and ch Mary Ann and Betsy Ann. He d July 17 1830; bur Roxbury twp Washington co. Ref V 3; V 6 Com Pleas Court; Md Mar recds Frederick co; Md W 5429 Pens Dept. Wife d 2-3-1841. Rept by State D A R and Marietta chpt (Helen Sloan).

NORRIS, ARNOLD, Ross co

Ref 4th rept N S D A R p 300; d in Deerfield twp 1835-6. Bur in graveyard many yrs abandoned on farm of James M Reeves abt ¾ mile s w of Clarksburg. Rept by Mrs Winnagle Mary Chesney chpt.

NORRIS, BETHUEL, Hamilton co

Pvt N J Milit. Enl 1776 at Morristown N J. B 1757 there; movd fr N J in 1795 to Ohio residing (1833) in Sycamore twp Hamilton co where on 5-26-1833 he was pensd. Ref N J S 4619 Pens Bureau. The following data furnished by Albert E Dawson that he is bur in Old Presbyterian cem adjoining his prop abt 2 mi N W of s e corner of Butler co. Grave marked at head and foot by stone slabs. Ref Jones S A R records. Rept by Cincinnati chpt.

NORRIS, RICHARD, ? co

Exec Doc 37. Refused pens as gave only frontier service. Rept by Wm Pettit.

NORTHRUP, JOSEPH, Knox co

Pensr Conn service æ 89 was liv in Pleasant twp Knox co in Cens 1840. Compare sketch of one Joseph Northrup Ref p 840 Pioneer Women Western Reserve. Joseph 1766-1843 b Brookfield Conn and Charity 1769-1857 b Stratford Conn. Removd Feb 1796 to Cornwall Conn; thence to Medina twp 1817. Rept by Jane Dailey.

NORTON, JACOB, Trumbull co

This record is fr fam tradition only. Recommended by Washington for skill in prescribing diet and herbs for afflicted soldr during a plague and caring for the sick. Fam possesses a brass war button reputed to belong to Jacob the soldr. Son of an Englishman; mar Barbara Migner when on a visit to Germany. Chldr: George: William; David; Michael; Sarah; Zaceriah; 11 chldr in all. Soldr d Bloomfield twp Trumbull co; bur on his sons farm known as the Page Place. Came to O abt 1806. Fam and war records burned with the home. Rept by Mrs C D Williams Spokane O to Jane Dailey.

NORTON, THOMAS, Jefferson co

Ref Hist Jefferson and Belmont co p 608 states that Norton tho English so strongly sympathized with the Colonists that he fought under Washington during the entire war. In a cem called Two Ridges was found a stone data: "Thomas H Norton d Aug 6 1823 aged 78" which makes his birth 1745. No proof given for inference of service. Rept by Steubenville chpt. (Mrs Sinclair).

NOTT, THOMAS, Morgan co

Pvt Conn St Trps. Enl 1776 Charlestown N H. Was b June 24 1740 Fairfield Conn. Came to Morgan co O fr N H abt 1800 whr in Oct 24 1822 he appld for pens for 2 yrs service. On 9-2-1833 drawing pens. Ref N H (Green Mt Boys) S 5836 Pens Claims. Cop by State D A R. Addit rept fr Leliabel Birch Col O. Srvd over 3 yrs in Rev; 1½ yrs under Capts Weatherby and White also Col Ethan Allen. Enl from Acworth twp Cheshire co New Hampshire. Was in engagement on Plains of Abraham and in the battle of Stillwater. Soldr d May 15 1834 Bristol twp Morgan co O whr bur.

OAKLEY, MILES, Meigs co

Pvt Conn Milit. Movd fr Fairfield Conn. 1801 mvd to Alfred Allegheny co N Y. In 1806 remvd to Belpre Washington co O. Then in 1811 to Meigs co whr was pensd 7-25-1833. Born Apr 7 1757 Fairfield Conn. A farmer; Ref S 18533 Conn. Cop by Return Jonathan Meigs chpt.

OBLINGER, JOHN, Miami co

Lancaster co Pa Milit 1776 Capt George Fetters Col Elder; servd 3 yrs. Pensr 9-15-1832 Montgomery co. B 6-12-1756; d 12-1-1846; bur in Highland cem nr West Milton Miami co Marked by S A R. First wf thot to be Eleanor ——; 2nd Susannah Carl mar 4-17-1826 in Montgomery co. Three of children were Christian, Joshua, and Gabriel. 2nd wf pensd 1853. Ref: Bur of Pens. W 2235 and B L Wt 26512-160-55 Pa. Rept by State D A R and Wm Pettit.

O'BRIEN, DANIEL, Cuyahoga co

Or 'Brien; 'Brine. Enl 1776 and servd 2 yrs as pvt in Capt John Gists Co Col Gists Md Regt. Wounded in foot in Brandywine battle. Pens appl April 18 1818 whl a res of Williston Chittenden co Ver. Was b 3-17-1752; d Oct 14 1835 in Brecksville O Cuyahoga co. Soldr mar 10-23-1795 Martha Gay a 2nd wf in Bolton Chittenden co Ver. She recd pens 6-1-1849 æ 83 res Brecksville O. In 1858 she livd in Burlington Ver. Ref W 1628 Pens Cl; Cop fr Sons of Revolution Bulletin Vol 13 No. 2 1936 p 4 by Jane Dailey. Compare p 275 Ohio Roster Vol 1.

OFFING, PATRICK, Morgan co

Sergt N H Contl. Enl at Cambridge Mass Apr 24 1775; srvd 3 yrs. Appld for pens in Washington co O July 7 1818 aged 66; in 5-6-1820 was pensr in Morgan co. On 5-17-1821 appld for transfer to Madison co Ill. D Oct 7-1821; chld: Febee; Eros; Lucy; and Nelly. Others not named. Ref S 35542 Contl N H. War 1812; Rejected Bounty Land claim War 1812. Cop by State D A R. Often found spelled O'Flyng.

OGLE, WILLIAM, Adams co

Pvt Cumberland co Pa Milit. Mar Mary Cresap; one child was called Enoch; d Adams co. Ref V 23 p 121 D A R Lin and V 25 p 105. —— filed by Mrs. Oehlke Nathan Perry chpt.

OKEY, LEVIN, ? co

Pvt listed in rejected pens appl. Ref Doc No. 31 Jan 6 1831 as not being in indigent circumstances accd to Act of May 1830. Rept by Blanche Rings.

O'LAUGHLIN (or Laughlin), DENNIS, Clinton co

Pvt Pa Contl. Enl Philadelphia; srvd 7 yrs. Mar Martha Matilda McCloud 6-15-1801; d Sept 13 1826. Pens appl Clinton co O 1818 Aug 4. Widow appl in Warren co Apr 18 1854. She mar Henry Leeman June 2 1827. Soldr is bur in Clinton co. Ref W 8249 B L Wt 12576-160-55 Pa. Cop by State D A R.

OLDS, GILBERT, Washington co

Appld for pens July 25 1820 Washington co see V 3 p 420; personal prop value $59.00. On 6-2-1821 pensr there as pvt Mass Contl. (J D) and Marietta chpt.

OLIVER, ALLEN, Ashland co

Ref History North Central Ohio p 142 by Wm A Duff name appears as a soldier of Revolution Perrysville. Rept by Nathan Perry chpt.

OLIVER, DAVID, ? co

Pvt listed in rejected pens appl. Ref Doc No. 31 Jan 6 1831 as servd in Regt not on the Contl Estab. Rept by Blanche Rings.

OLLINGER, JOHN, Montgomery co

Pensr Pa. In 1833 liv in Montgomery co æ 77. Bur in Bowman cem. (not same as Oblinger). Rept by Wm Pettit.

OLNEY, COGSWELL MAJOR, Washington co

Was b 1743 December 28. Mar Sarah Scott. On the monument of Major Olney is the following data: Washington Olney b Feb 16 1789; d Feb 12 1826; Appia his wf b 7-20-1797; d 10-5-1852; Rev George Washington their son b 11-9-1821; d 12-7-1842. Soldr d July 19 1818; bur Oak Grove Marietta O. Grave mrkd by Marietta D A R 1930 and granite tombstones erected by descendants. Rept by Marietta chpt.

ONG, JACOB, Jefferson co

Ref S A R No 24575; b 1760 in Pa; d 1857; mar Mary McGrew. Rept by Wm Pettit.

ORCHEAD (Orchard), THOMAS, Ross co

Pvt Pa Contl. Enl Chester co Pa; dischgd Trenton N J 1781; servd 4 yrs; b 1760; mar Sarah —— March 29 1785; appld for pens July 13 1818 Ross co. He d Mar 26 1844; Widow appld pens 3-18-1845 in Ross co O. Cop by State D A R. Ref W 5454 Pa.

ORGAN, MATTHEW, Tuscarawas co

Pvt Pa Contl. Enl Bedford co Pa; servd 3 yr-to end of war; b 1758; mentions "wife;" son Resin æ 17; dau Jemima æ 12; 2 gr-chldr: Mathew æ 4; Daniel Duncan æ 3; in his appl for pens 1820 while residing in Washington co Pa. Ref S 40226 Contl Pa but no record of having been in O but Pa Arch lists him in Tuscarawas co O 1824 (Rept by Mary Steinmetz Reading Pa). Cop by State D A R.

OSBORN, ABRAHAM, Mahoning co

Pvt; Lieut.New Jersey Men p 430; b Oct 5 1760; father was Osborn, Nicholas; mar Rachel Potts; d Dec 22 1838; at Canfield O; bur Cornersburg cem. Came with Father and 26 relatives fr Va to Mahoning co in 1804; Ref Pamphlet "Nicholas Osborn and Descendants." Cem record Henry Baldwin S A R. Rept by Mahoning chpt.

OSBORN, HUGH, Morgan co

Various spel. Enl at Boston Mass Dec 1781; Marine on ship Alliance; 16 mo. Pensd 9-10-1819 Zanesville O. Widow pens 6-21-1849; pens no. 13698. Trnsfrd to Maine 1822; Back to O 1837; b 1763; Bridgewater Mass; mar Azuba Wade 1-13-1786. One son æ 19 yr in 1820 (name Ezra ?) Soldr d 5-25-1847 Bristol Morgan co O. Ref Navy Mass W 6889 and (Cop by State D A R) and No. 121644 D A R Lin V 122. Cop by Jane Dailey.

OSBORN, JOHN, Mahoning co

Pvt Mass Soldr and Sailors V 11 p 688; Also pvt "Conn Men in Rev;" also pvt Va Men p 230 — Libr rept Richmond. B Oct 15 1765; mar Mary —— who d 6-11-1821; he d 2-17-1838 Canfield O. Ref Cem records Henry Baldwin S A R —— by Mahoning chpt.

OSBORN, JOSEPH, Warren co

Pvt N J Line. Enl in Amwool ? twp N J 1777; servd 7 yr. Pensd in Warren co O 1819 Widow pensd 6-29-1845 Warren co Pens No 10090. In 1825 stated was 72 æ; mar Rosanna Darch 11-12-1786; chldr: Abraham æ 39; John 37; James 35; Elizabeth 33;

Andrew 30; and Ira 22, accd to pens appl 1825. He d 10-10-1830 Warren co. Ref N J W 5456 B L Wt 81-60-55. Rept by State D A R.

OSTRAND, PETER VAN SR, Ashland co

P 142 "History of North Central Ohio" by Wm Duff listed as a Rev soldier Clear Crk twp. Rept by Nathan Perry chpt.

OTIS, EDWARD, Holmes co

Pvt in Capt Lord's Conn Line; 11 mo. b Lyme Conn 1766; a pensr in Holmes co July 6 1833 resident of Salt Crk twp. Livd in N Y last pens fr Mch 4 to Sept 4 1851 made to Erastus Wright Atty for pensr in Ill. On 9-4-1851 he certified he had lived for 14 yrs in Henry co Ill and had prev resided in Holmes co O. Ref S 32425. (Letter fr Mrs. Maddox Wauseon O states "he movd to Stark co O; then to Putnam co; Myoming Ill; where livd with son Merrill or Edward). Cop at D C by Jane Dailey.

OVERSTREET, JOHN, Lawrence co

Pvt Va Line. Enl Sept 1775 1st Va Regt. Servd 3 yrs. Pensd Lawrence co O 6-9-1819; trnsfrd to Sangamon (?) co Ill 7-19-1827. Was 60 yrs old in 1820 and wife was abt 60 æ. Ref Va S 40231. Rept by State D A R.

OWEN, AMASA, Clermont co

A complete hist in N Enl Hist and Gen Register V 83 p 61. Was b 1753 Salisbury; d 1817 nr Neville Clermont co O. Servd in N Y 2nd Regt Ulster co Milit 1778-9. Came to Clermont co fr Owens Island Pa; bot land 1806. Will names wf Sarah; sons: Elijah; Daniel; Amasa; John; Jacob; and Joseph; daus Delilah Gregg; Sarah Crosiar; Eunice Owen. Name rept by Mrs Winnagle Warren. Data cop by Jane Dailey fr Ref.

OWEN, WILLIAM, Clermont co

Pvt Pa Contl. Pensr 4-1-1818 in Clermont co O. Enl 1776 nr Pittsburg Pa. Ae 95 in 1820. Ref Pa S 40232. Cop by State D A R.

OWENS, STEPHEN, Perry co

Pvt 3rd Regt Md Line. Pensr 9-11-1828 Perry co. Mar Nancy ——— Nov 1 1804; soldr d June 8 1837 Perry co O. Appld for pens Muskingum co Aug 30 1828. Ref W 8281 B L Wt 200-60-55. Wid appld 8-26-1853 in Perry co. Rept by State D A R.

OYSTER, JOHN, Richland co

Exec Doc 37 of yr 1852. Refused a pens as servd less than 6 mo. Rept by Wm Pettit.

OZIAS, JOHN, Preble co

B in N C 1737. Srvd pvt; came Preble co 1804; d 1832; bur Roselawn cem Lewis-burg. Rept Commodore Preble chpt.

PACKARD, JOHN, Mahoning co

Pvt Mass Soldr & Sailors V II p 737. Was b Jan 30 1743. Chldr Mary; Thomas mar Ann Berry; Rachel; Rebecca; Catherine; William; Nancy; Jared 1775. Soldr d 1-7-1827 Austintown twp. Ref Hist Trumbull & Mahoning co V 2; Will bk 4 p 339 Trumbull co Recds Prob 1827; Deed bk C p 624 trnscrbd Mahoning co John Packard 1818. Rept by Mahoning chpt.

PAIN, JOHN, Washington co

Pvt R I Milit. Was b 1762; mar Nabby———; d Waterman O bur Waterman nr Watertown. Stone inscript "In Memory of Mr John Paine d Jan 8-1843 in the 81 yr of his ae. Mrs Nabby Paine, Consort of John Paine, d Sept 18-1824 ae 65 yrs. Soldr came with a party fr R I enroute to a western State — delayed by a flood, decided to remain. Built the Watertown Mill. Pensr 5-3-1833 and Apr 15 1834 in Washington co. Ref Williams Hist of Washington co p 630. Rept by Helen Sloan, Marietta chpt.

PAIN (E), BENJAMIN, Washington co

Pvt R I Contl. Appl pens July 24, 1821 in Com Pleas Court Marietta O V 3 p 509 stating prop value $20.33, cop by Helen Sloan. Pensr 10-30-1831 in Washington co. Also same pensd as Sergt and Corp R I Contl 10-24-1833, cop by Jane Dailey.

PAINE, WILLIAM, Belmont co

Emigrated to Md fr England in 1763. Pvt Md Contl. Enl Oct 1776 servd in Regt of Col Hall Md line 1 yr. Was b in England. In his appl 1820 states had wf ae abt 60 yrs. Pens appl in Belmont co O July 24 1820 also appl same place July 20 1818. Ref S40240 Md. Rept by State D A R.

PAINTER, JACOB SR, Columbiana co

Rev soldr-rec not yet found. Was b 1763 son of John Painter. Soldr d Oct 5 1851. Lvd in Northumberland co Pa 1787. Ref Pa Arch 3XXIII 728 Rept by Mrs. Wilma M Molsberry.

PAINTER, JOHN ADAM, Mahoning co

Pvt 3rd class Ser 6 V I p 497 Pa Arch. Soldr mar Catherine; chldr; Jacob mar Barbara; James; Peter mar Elizabeth; David mar Elizabeth; Adam mar Catherine; Ann mar John Pitts; Elizabeth mar David Rudicill; Margaret mar John Robb; Catrine mar Henry Booge. Sldr d abt 1809 Springfield twp. Ref Will bk 1 p 364 Columbiana co Recds Prob 1809; Deed bk V pp 195-6-7 To John Painter-Heirs. Rept by Mahoning chpt.

PAISLEY, JOHN, ? co

Pvt listed in rejected pens appl Ref Doc No. 31, Jan 6 1831 as srvd in regt not on Contl Estab. Rept by Blanche Rings.

PALM, ADAM, Mahoning co

Pens appl Circuit Ct Warren O bk 6 p 297-9. Soldr d Austintown. Ref Tax list 1826 Austintown Adam & David Palm. Rept by Mahoning chpt.

PALMER, ALVA, Huron co

Bur Fitchville cem (1st bur there) His bros Seeley; Samuel; Linus and 2 sisters Adelia; Hannah came with him in 1818. Alva Palmer Jr was b in Greenwich Conn May 1 1794. Ref Williams Hist p 329-335; Firelands Pioneers Vol 9 O S p 74. Rept by Marjorie Cherry.

PALMER, EPHRAIM, Medina co

Enl Greenville Conn 1777. Srvd 2 yrs as pvt. Was b Dec 17 1760 Greenville Conn; mar in Middlesex co N J aft Rev. Aft Rev settled in Middlesex co N J. Aft 6 or 7 yrs mvd to Saratoga co N Y. Thence to Montgomery co N Y. Mvd to Genesee co N Y before coming to O whr he livd since June of 1832 in Columbia, Lorain and Brunswick in Medina co with his chldr. Pens appl Medina co O Apr 8 1833. Ref S 8940 Conn N. Y. Rept by State D A R.

PALMER, GEORGE M, Tuscarawas co

Pvt 2nd Regt Md Line. Srvd 2 yrs. Mar Mary 1788. 8 chldr 5 survived: Mary; James; John; Charles; George. Soldr d Apr 9 1829. Pens appl Tuscarawas co O Dec 13 1828. Widow appl Tuscarawas co O Nov 18 1840 Res of Lawrence twp. Ref W 4561 B L wt 1775-100 Md. Rept by State D A R.

PALMER, JOHN, Jefferson co

Pvt Va Contl. Pensr 9-27-1819 in Jefferson co. Compare p 279 O Roster Vol 1 cop by J D.

PALMER, JOURA, Ashland co

Listed p 142 in History of North Central Ohio by Wm A Duff as Rev Soldr, Sullivan twp. Rept by Nathan Perry chpt.

PALMER, STEPHEN, Columbiana co

Rev Soldr Rec not yet found. Was b 1777 d 1859 bur Old cem E Palestine Unity twp. Ref S A R Yr bk 1912. Rept by Mrs. Wilma M Molesberry.

PALMER, SYLVANUS, ? co

Pvt listed in rejected pens appl Ref: Dec 31 Jan 6, 1831 as srvd in regt not on Contl Estab. Rept by Blanche Rings Col O.

PALMER, WILLIAM, Mahoning co

Pvt mar Phoebe; chldr Abigail mar Terse Stanley; Joseph mar Ann——; Lucinda mar Seth McDonald. Soldr d abt 1824 Goshen twp. Ref Va men in Rev p 232; Will bk 4 p 540 Columbiana co Wills prob 1824; Deed bk D & W pp 368 618 trnscrbd Mahoning co 1834. Rept by Mahoning chpt.

PANCAKE, Benjamin, Columbiana co

Rev soldr rec not yet found. Chldr; Matilda J. mar 1838 James Davidson & had 8 chldr. Ref Warners Hist Beaver co Pa p 638. Rept by Mrs Wilma M. Molsberry.

PARKE, JOHN, Brown co and Ind.

Pvt Va Milit. Originally fr Conn but settled in Wyoming valley aft massacre went to Va Ky and to O. Enl 1779 Hampshire co Va. Dischgd Ft McIntosh. b 1762. Mar Lettice Moseley dau of widow Helen Moseley. Chldr Enos; Jesse; David; John; Leoli; Sarah; Rachel; Lydia; Pheoba; Elizabeth all by first wf who d Oct 5 1823. Second wf Marg Darrel mar Apr 1 1824 had ch. Names not known. Soldr d at Wea-Wea nr La Fayette Ind whr he went in 1834 with his son Enos. Was prominent in early Clermont co. Pensr 8-9-1833 in Brown co. Descendents are mainly in Clermont co O. Rept by Taliaferro chpt by Meryl B Markley.

PARKER, ASAHEL, Ashtabula co

Exec Doc 37. Refused a pens as did not serve 6 mos. Rept by William Pettit.

PARKER, ASHAEL, Erie co

List of those who received town bounty of 30 lbs for service 1781 1783 fr Waterbury Conn Mar 15 1784. Soldr d 1841 ae 76. 1st wf Phoebe Finch — Second wf Jemime. Soldr bur Parker cem Route 60 S of Birmingham, Family monument. Rept by Marjorie Cherry, Sandusky.

PARKER, JACOB, Preble co

Srvd thro Rev. Was b Morristown N J; twice mar; had large family. Soldr d 1748 bur in cem at East end of West Alexandria for which he gave a part of land. Came to N W Terr. Srvd under Gen Anthony Wayne. Rept by Commodore Preble chpt.

PARKER, JAMES, Mahoning co

Pvt Ser 5 Pa Arch; Conn Men, Va Men and New Hampshire Men. Was b 1750; mar Lucy (b 1779-d 3-29-1872). Soldr d Nov 25 1824 Ellsworth O; bur Center cem.

Ref Cem recds of the late Henry R. Baldwin S A R; Western Reserve Chronicle Nov 1825 Est James Parker. Rept by Mahoning Chpt.

PARKER, JOEL, Ashtabula co

Conn Pension lists p 9 639 pvt. Soldr d 5-29-1814 ae 77 bur Andover O. Rept by Mary Redmond chpt.

PARKER, JOHN, Harrison co

Exec Doc 37. Marriage was aft service. Wid had no claim under this act.

PARKER, JONATHAN, CAPT, Ashtabula co

6th Co 3rd Battl Conn St Trps. Bur Windsor O. Grave located by Mary Stanley chpt. Ref 18th Rept 236; 21st Rept p 105 of N S D A R. Rept by Nathan Perry chpt. Mary Redmond chpt reports (1931) h d 2-26-1824 ae 88 yr. Mary Chesney chpt adds the stone data: "A Capt in Rev and Staff officer under Gen Washington" and dates as above rept.

PARKER, JOSEPH, Ross co

Pvt Pa Milit. Enl Bucks co Pa whr res until aft Rev. Then mvd to Tacoming? co Pa; thence to Ross co O. Srvd 8 mo & 12 das. Was b 11-26-1759 Bucks co Pa. Pensr 12-27-1833 in Ross co. Nathaniel Massie repts he d 1834; No will — Probate case 6049. Ref Pa S 8927. Rept by State D A R. Marietta repts a Jos Parker appl for pens in Com Pleas Ct Washington co O 1832 and 1834.

PARKER, THOMAS, Huron co

Waiter to his uncle, Elisha Parker, an officer under Col Seth Warner. Was b 1767, Providence R. I; mar 1796 Sarah Elliott (b 1769) One son was Seth. Soldr d 1839 Peru O. Ref 120 Vol. No. 119335 D A R Lin. Cop by Jane Dailey.

PARKHURST, JOHN, Mahoning co

Pvt Conn Men in Rev p 70 also N H State Papers V 4 p 293. Mar Hannah——; chldr: Unice; Amos; Phebe; Luther: Soldr d abt 1815 Youngstown. Ref Will bk 2 p 196 Trumbull co Recds prob 1815; Deed bk p 450 John Parkhurst 1828; Tax list 1826 Rept by Mahoning chpt.

PARKS, JOSEPH, Warren co

Was b in Lancaster co Pa 1746 d 1814. Came to Warren co in 1797. Service 5th S Pa Arch Vol VII p 939 Ruling Elder of the Dicks Creek Presbyterian Church fr organization until his death. Bur Dicks Cheek Pres Churchyd. Mkd by Richard Montgomery S A R of Dayton. Rept by W. M. Pettitt.

PARKS, MICHAEL, Huron co

Serg. Srvd 6 yrs and 9 mos. Was in 11 battles among them Bunker Hill and Saratoga. Family was of Flemish origin. D Nov 10 1845; Episcopal cem Norwalk. Ref Firelands Pioneers O S Vol 5 p 2. Rept by Marjorie Cherry.

PARISH, CYPRIAN (misspelled Cypman), Lake co and Mich.

Pvt N. Y Contl for 7 mos 12 das. Enl Apr 1782 N Y. Was b 1766 Frederick co N Y (father kept birth recds in Bible). Had one son John with whom he lvd part of the time. Prob d in Mich. Appl for pens in Tompkins co N Y June 1822. Appl for trnsfr fr N Y to Geauga co O Jan 3 1839. Nov 3 1943 ppl for transfr to Mich whr he was residing with his son. Pensr 1840 ae 74 in Painsville O liv w Lewis Parish. Ref N Y S 29363. Rept by State D A R.

PARMETTER (Parmenter or Parmetar), ABRAHAM, Hamilton co

Pvt Mass Contl Enl 1777 Servd 7 yr Mass line under Capt Fowles. Made appl for pens in Hamilton co O Dec 27 1821. Stated that he lately removed to this co fr Potter co Pa. Was b 1760. Appl 1821 stated wf living ae 59; chldr grown mar and settled. Made appl for pens in Lyeoming? co Pa May 9 1818. Ref S 40235 B L Wt 1071-100 Mass. Rept by State D A R. Ref No. 110030 and No. 32442 D A R Lin and V 125 p 83 is addit data: stated b Sudbury Mass; mar Patience Patterson (b 1762) chldr; a son John mar Mary Hobbs. Sldr d 1842 Cincinnati O. Rept by Jane Dailey.

PARRET (Parrott), SAMUEL, Perry co

Pvt Va Milit Srvd 6 mos fr 1781. Was b Apr 1756 Shenandoah co Va. Livd in Rockingham co Va when ent service Jan 1 1781; mvd to Perry co O 1818 or 1819. Pens appl Perry co O Nov 9 1832. In Cens 1840 says living in Reading twp ae 85. Ref S 17619 Va. Rept by State D A R.

PARSONS, ENOCH, ? co

Mentioned 3rd Rept p 229 N S D A R. Cop by Mrs. Oehlke Nathan Perry chpt.

PARSONS, HARMON, Miami co

Pvt N J Contl Enl June 1779 Easton? Pa. Srvd 4 yrs. Was b 1757. Chldr; James; Elizabeth; John; Amanda; Catharine; Synthia; Rachel; Hiram; and George. Pens appl Oct 6 1819 Miami co O. Soldr was a wheel wright. Ref N. J. S 49234. Rept by State D A R.

PARSONS, REV JUSTIN, Huron co

Was at Ticonderoga, Vt Volunteer. Was b 1759, Northumberland Mass. Mar Electra Frary. One dau was Lucretia. Soldr d 1847 Ridgefield O (Now Monroeville). Ref D A R Lin V 23 p 91 p 239 294. Cop by Nathan Perry chpt.

PARSONS, SOLOMON, Huron co

Pvt Conn St Trps srvd 18 mos. Was b 1766 Windsor co Conn. Bur Huron O by Sandusky chpt. Lvd in Windsor co Conn 29 yrs aft birth; then to N Y; thence to Roxbury twp Delaware co 20 yrs; Movd to Vermillion twp Huron co whr resided in 1833. Ref 18 Rept p 237 N S D A R, S 4646 Conn Rept by State D A R and Nathan Perry chpt.

PARTRIDGE, SHEFFIELD, Ashtabula co

Corp in Capt Wm Jennisons co of minute men at Lexington Alarm. Was b 1752 Holliston, Mass; mar 1794 Hannah Lyman (d 1835) Delcena was a dau. Soldr d 1830 Ashtabula co O Ref V 125 p 85 D A R Lin No. 124280. Cop by Nathan Perry chpt.

PATTERSON, JAMES, Wayne co

Unable to locate. Wooster Wayne rept Bond names James George as admr; filed 1834. Probably died then. No grave found .

PATTERSON, JOHN, Preble co

Pvt S C Milit Enl Aug 1778 as substitute for his father Samuel Patterson in Ninety Six District of South Carolina. In Regt of Col Reed for 15 mos and 15 days. Also srvd in Ga & N C lines. Was b Jan 1763 Ireland son of Samuel Patterson. Aft was res in S C till 1807; thence to Preble co O whr since resided. Was res of Preble co O Sept 13, 1852. Ref S 17626 Ga N C S C Rept by State D A R. Compare same 283 O Roster Vol 1 (J D).

PATTERSON, WILLIAM, Franklin co

Pa pvt. Was b 1761; mar 1st-Jane; 2nd Mary (aft 1856 Mary signs vouchers fr estate as Forsman, having mar Robert Forsman 1856) chldr; minor son Moses and 8 other chldr not named. Settl estate O 1855 names 9 who signed Soldr d 1846, 71 yrs; bur Truro gr yd; inscript on monument: "William Patterson d 1846, 71 yrs" Jane, wf of Wm Patterson d 1821 44 yr. Mary wf d 1834 35 yr. Sarah dau of Wm & Mary d 1828 æ 2 yr. Son Thos chgd $25 for expense to Washington co Pa interest of estate. See Williams Bros Hist p 445. Ref Will bk 251 Col O Ct house made 4-20-1846 his ae abt 68 yr Prob 6-20-1847. Names the above family. One Wm Patterson was appt adm of an estate 9-6-1827. Rept by Columbus chpt and Jane Dailey.

PAULLEY, JAMES, Lt., Mahoning co

Chldr; Elisha; Thomas; John. Soldr d before 1811 Youngstown. Stone in Oak Hill cem probably removed fr Old Market St cem dates not legible only d Apr 18——(H B) Ref Mannings list early settlers 1811 Wid Paulley; List of late H. R. Baldwin S A R; Tax list 1801 Coitsville Rept by Mahoning chpt.

PAWLING, COL ALBERT, Miami co

Cop fr Ohio Statesman Nov 28 1837 Issue the following: d at Troy Nov 16 1837 æ 88 yrs. Was 1st Mayor of Troy. He commanded a Regt in the Rev War and was at the taking of St John's; at assault of Quebec by Gen Montgomery and in battle of Monmouth and White Plains. Cop by Blanche Rings Columbus O.

PAYNTER, NATHANIEL, Erie co

Exec Doc 37. Servd 1 yr as volunteer; 2 yrs as teamster. Rept by Wm Pettit.

PAYNE, ABRAM, SERGT, Fayette co

Listed in news clipping by L A A found in old scrapbook no date "as Rev soldrs participating or interested in the settlement of Marietta. Rept by Marietta chpt. Repts by Jean Howatt as in a list of Soldr of 1776 bur in Washington Court House cem.

PEARCE, BENJAMIN, LIEUT, ? co

Listed in news clipping by L A A found in old scrapbook no date "as Rev soldr participating or interested in the Marietta Settlement. Filed for cont research by Marietta chpt.

PEARCE, MICHAEL, Butler co

Pvt N J Milit. Enl at Essex co N J 1776. Srvd 6 mos at no period for more than three mos at one time. Was b Aug 27 1750 Essex co N J; mar Phebe Squire; had 16 chldr; d June 4 1838 Trenton Butler co. Resided in N J; came to O in 1802 July 10; resided in Butler co for abt 28 yrs. Ref N J S3674. Rept by State D A R and Blanche Rings.

PEARSALL, BENJAMIN, Monroe co

Pvt Pa Contl Enl July or Aug 1778 Pa. Srvd 3 yrs. Was b 1752; mar Catharine; chldr; Nancy 18; John 14 (appl 1818). Appl for pens Monroe co O Aug 22 1818. Ref S 40251 Pa Rept by State D A R.

PEARSON (Pierson), MAHLON, Warren co

Pvt S C Milit Enl Union co S C 1777. Srvd under Capt Avery and Col Branham S C line 1 yr 8 mos. Was b Apr 7 1761 Burks co Pa; mentions fathers plantation. Appl for pens in Warren co O Sept 1832. Removed fr Burks co Pa abt 29 yrs ago fr S C Ref S 3663 S C. Rept by State D A R.

PECK, ISAAC, Cuyahoga co

Exec Doc 37 of 1852. Refused a pens as servd less than 6 mo. Rept by Wm Pettit.

PECK, WILLIAM, Hamilton co

Exec Doc 37 of 1852. Wf refused pens as not wid when act was passed. Rept by Wm Pettit.

PEGAN, ANDREW, Highland co

Marine ship Montgomery. Enl 1776 Phila Pa Srvd 1 yr. Was b 1757. Mentions wf 70 yrs of ae in appl 1821. Appl for trnsfr of pens to Highland co O July 25 1821. Soldr was a weaver by trade. Ref S 40249 Pa Sea Service. Rept by State D A R.

PELHAM, WILLIAM, Muskingum co and Ind

Surgeon Va Contl. Had a son Wm C Pelham. Soldr d Feb 3, 1827 Posey co Ind. Appl for pens Muskingum co O Apr 21 1818. Ref S 3678 Va. Rept by State D A R.

PELTON, JONATHAN, Cuyahoga co

Rev soldr. Was b June 10 1758 son of Joseph and Anna (Penfield) Pelton; mar Elizabeth Doane 12-4-1782 (dau of Seth Doane) b 5-10-1761; soldr d 3-30-1840. Chldr; Deborah mar Samuel Cooper; Jonathan; Elizabeth mar John Wilcox; Parker; Beulah mar Dennis Cooper; Joseph mar 1st Obedience Russell 2 Sally Bedlake; Seth mar Mary Porter; Mary mar Silas Beldon; Sarah mar William Treat. Soldr d Sept 12 1830; bur in Euclid cem trnsfrd fr Pelton Corners at Richmond and Chardon Roads. Mvd to Cleveland O in 1814. Rept by Lakewood chpt.

PEMBER, ELI, Lorain co

Pvt Conn Contl Enl Oct 1775 Lebanon Conn. Srvd 2 yrs fr 1775. Was b Aug 17 1762 Norwich Conn; mar Clarissa Bowen Dec 23 1839 in Carlisle twp O. Soldr d June 22 1841 Lorain co O Since Rev livd in lower Canada and N Y till movd to O Appl Pens Lorain co O Aug 2 1832. Wid appl for pens Lorain co O Feb 14 1853 res of Carlisle twp ae 66. Ref W 2335 B L Wt 11417-160-55 Conn Vt. Rept by State D A R.

PENN, BENJAMIN, Clermont co

Pvt 1776 in Capt Henry Ridgeleys co Col J Carvil Halls Maryville Regt. Was b 1740 Md. Mar Mary Sargent, in 1774 (b 1755-d 1817). One son was Elijah Taylor. Soldr d 1834 Clermont co O. Ref V 113 p 60 D A R Lin No. 112184 also see No. 78224 and 113071. Cop by Nathan Perry chpt.

PENNELL, HUGH, Jefferson co

Service in 6th Battl Lancaster co milit; b 1763 Lancaster co Pa; d 1839; mar Mar ——. Ref S A R 42669. By Wm Pettit.

PENNELL, JOHN, Mahoning co

Pvt Va Men in Rev p 237. Soldr d Mar 22 1818 Milton twp. Ref Deed bk G p 432 1819; List of late Henry R Baldwin S A R. Rept by Mahoning chpt.

PENNISTON, GEORGE, Pike co

"A Rev soldr d Feb 9 1846 at his res in Pike co O. He was under Gen Wayne in the last yr of the Rev. He left a family of 10 chldr." Cop fr Scioto Gazette Feb 19 1846 by Pickaway Plains chpt.

PENSALL, BENJAMIN, Monroe co

Pvt Pa Line enl Aug 1776 8th Pa Reg. Was b 1752. In appl of 1820 mentions wf

Catherine ae 53 yr. Chldr Nancy ae 18; John 14; Ref Pa S 40251. Rept by State D A R.

PEPOON, JOSEPH, Lake co

Sergt in Capt David Tarbox co Col Hosfords 11 Regt Ct Line. Was b 1749 Hebron Ct. Mar Eunice Ayers 1791. A son was Jos Jr. mar Sarah Eunice Starks 1833. Soldr d 1812 Painesville O. Cop fr V 105 D A R Lin 104425 by Nathan Perry chpt.

PERCY, JOSEPH, Trumbull co

Enl 1775 in Capt David Hinmans co Conn Line. Again in 1775 enl under same capt and was dischrgd at Horse Neck Conn. Was b 1755; mar Love —— æ 67 in 1820; Pens Appl was rejected as his regt not on Contl Estab. Ref Doc No 31 Jan 6 1831. Rept by Mary Chesney chpt and Blanche Rings.

PERIL, JOHN, Pike co

Pvt Va Milit Enl Frederick co Md servd 1 yr. Was b Feb 11 1760 Frederick co Va. Mar Elizabeth Price 1787. Chldr Margaret Bennett; Elizabeth McKnight; Rebecca; John; George. Soldr d Aug 5 1837 Pike co O. Appl for pens Highland co O July 17 1833. Ref W 5513 Va Rept by State D A R.

PERKINS, DAVID, Cuyahoga co

Enl Mass Milit Apr 1778 Freetown Mass. Was b 1765 Freetown Mass. Appl for pens Cuyahoga co O 4-23-1833. Ref Mass (Sea Service) S 3656. Rept by State D A R.

PERRY, ABIJAH, Trumbull co

Pvt Conn Contl Enl with Major Jabey Thompson May 1775. Srvd 3 yr. Was b May 1755. Wf was 56 yr old in 1820. Chldr; Eunice; Anna; and others. Res of Johnston, Trumbull co O whr he d Apr 1825. Ref S 40259 Conn. Rept by State D A R and Mary Chesney chpt.

PERRY, THOMAS, ? co

PVT Pa St Trps. Conn Line. Pensr 4-16-1833 in Washington co ae 80 yrs. On roll Feb 28-1781. Was b 1753. Ref State Library & Museum Harrisburg Pa and Pa Arch. Rept by State D A R.

PERRY, JACOB, Pickaway co

Pvt Mass Contl Enl Germantown Pa Pens No. S 40246 Act 1818 at ae 58 appld in Pickaway co O. Last pay 3-12-1827; in 1820 he stated had no family; Rept by Jane Dailey.

PETER, JACOB, Pickaway co

Pvt Mass Contl. Pensr 1819. Rept by J D.

PETERS, PHILIP, Fairfield co

Serv Col Edward Hands Regt 1776 Pa; b Pa; d 1830; mar Mary Ashbrook, S A R ref 34139. By Wm Pettit.

PETERS, TUNIS, Fairfield co

Was b 1759 in Dinwiddie co Va son of Zachariah, also Rev Soldr. Mar Francis Adams Hampshire co Va. Chldr: James mar Nancy Peters; Phillip mar Mary Ashbrook; Samuel mar Amelia Peters; Abigail mar Aaron Ashbrook; Katie mar Eli Ashbrook; Deborah mar Michael Blue; Gershom mar Susan Glaze; Tunis Jr mar Eva Glaze; Mahlon mar Rachel Merridith; Parmelia mar Wm Ashbrook; Jonathan mar 1st Martha Thompson 2nd Rebecca Harmon; John M mar Cynthia Biddle; Absolom mar Tamah Swisher.

Soldr d 1839. Bur Turkey Run abt 4 mi fr Easterlime Pickaway co. Lvd in Hampshire co whr he was high sheriff; was a member of the famous Cockade regt of Petersburg Va in war 1812; came to his son Gersham in O and settled in Fairfield co in 1905. Ref Mr Chas Newton Amanda O. Rept by Pickaway Plains chpt.

PEYDOR, BENJAMIN, Geauga co

Located by Taylor chpt, Chardon O location of cem. Ref 16th Rept N S D A R p 146. Rept by Nathan Perry chpt.

PHEBUS, GEORGE, Pickaway co

Was b 1759; mar Mary (d July 9 1858 ae 83 yr 3 mo). Soldr d Oct 9 1834 ae 75 yr 2 mo; bur Alkire twp Deer Creek. Rept by Pickaway Plains chpt.

PHELPS, CAPT DAVID, ? co

Soldr of Rev ae 84 yrs issue of 5-5-1824 Buckeye Eagle. Rept by Mrs. Blanche Rings.

PHELPS, LAVING, Geauga co and Vt.

Pvt Mass line 1 yr. Enl 3-17-1776. Was b 1758. Mar Lavina 9-21-1785. Had 10 chldr. Soldr d 9-22-1836 Essex co Vt altho Taylor chpt rept he d Sunenburg. Pensd in Lancaster Mass 1-28-1819. Coal miner. Ref Mass W4762. Rept by State D A R.

PHILLIPS, JAMES, Mahoning co and Pa.

Pvt Conn men pp 78, 152, 278. Also New Hampshire Men pp 88, 200, 334. Mar Margaret 1766 July 25 1844. Ref Tax list 1826 James Phillips Mahoning co reg July 7-1864 Poll bk 1813. Cem Recds of H R Baldwin S A R Compare No. 116970 D A R. Rept by Mahoning chpt Research on Ref V 117 p 305 finds he ws of Lebanon co Pa and not O as stated See B L Wt 2025-100 Pa Contl.

PHILLIPS, PETER CAPT, ? co

Listed in News clipping by L A A fd in old scrap bk no dat as Rev soldr participating or interested in Marietta Settlement. Marietta chpt.

PHILLIPS, PHILIP, Medina co

Enl Feb 15 1780 Windsham twp Conn. Was b Windsham Conn 1763; mar Elizabeth Phillips 3-4-1789. Chldr: Augustus with whom he, his wf and son Jewel resided; Benjamin b 9-29-1792; Huldah 4-24-1795; John 1-4-1800; Soldr d 6-15-1838 Medina co O. Pensd 1818 in Medina co O. Appl for transfr fr Conn to Medina co 5-5-1821. Wid appl there 9-16-1839. Ref Conn W 5532. Rept by State D A R.

PHILLIPS, SPENCER, Huron co

Exec Doc 37 of 1852. Wid refused pens as she mar again. By Wm Pettit.

PHILLIPS, WILLIAM, Franklin co

Exec Doc 37 of 1852. Refused pens as servd less than 6 mo. By Wm Pettit.

PHILLIPS, SAMUEL, Mahoning co

Pvt Conn Men in Rev. Mar (2nd) Anna Lane (Aug 6 1790-June 23 1853); chldr: Benjamin 1785; Isaac; John 1793; Samuel; Julia 1-19-1819. Soldr d before 1834 Austintown; cem located Four Mile Run. Ref Warren news letter Oct 23 1834 mar of Mrs. Anna Phillips and Robert Kerr. Rept by Mahoning chpt.

PHIPPS, SAMUEL, Richland co

Pvt in Capt Joe Johnson's Co Goshen Co Chester co Pa 4 Battl. Was b Chester co Pa 1735 son of Nathan Phipps and gr grandson of Joseph Phipps who came fr Bristol Eng with Wm Penn. Mar Mary Marshall. Chldr Sarah mar William Wise; John; Samuel Jr who srvd under Gen Wayne and lost his life on Maumee in campaign with Indians; Rachel; Joseph; Mary mar John Duncan; Robert mar Margaret Halferday; Nathan mar Edith Uptergraff. Soldr d Jan 5 1841 Richland co O bur Mishey Frm Worthington twp back of wagon shed nr Butler O. Monument destroyed and grave plowed under. It was a former family burying gr. Came to Richland co in 1815; is listed on 1840 pension as age 104 living in Washington twp with Jeptha Carlton; on tax recds of Goshen twp Chester fr 1765 to 1785; Pa Arch S 5 Vol 5 pp 612, 633, 662, 674, 644; Hist of Venango co Pa sketch on life of son John Phipps. Rept by Mississinewa chpt Portland Ind to Jared Mansfield chpt.

PICKENS, JOHN, Meigs co

Pvt Pa St Trps. B in Ireland emigrated to Pa the yr before the war thence came to Meigs co O. Pensr 4-28-1834 in Meigs co Ref Pa Arch V 23 Ser 3, p 589. Rept by Mrs. John Chase, Jonathan Meigs chpt.

PIERCE, EBENEZER LIEUT, ? co

Srvd several short enl fr Partridgeville, now Peru Mass. Was b 1745 Woburn Mass; mar Eunich Loomis 1770; Soldr d 1802 Marietta O. Soldr was elected to Leg 1782 whr srvd 18 yr. Cop fr V 44 p 268 D A R Lin. Rept by Jane Dailey.

PIERCE, HUGH, Belmont co

Pvt Md Milit enl Kent co Md was in battles of Brandywine and Germantown. Srvd in Co commd by Capt Henry Regt of Col Henry Md line 9 mos. Soldr b 1756 Kent co Md Pens appl Belmont co O June 7 1832 res of Wheeling twp. Ref S 3690 Md. Rept by State D A R.

PIERCE, JAMES, ? co

Listed in rejected pens appl ref Doc No. 31 Jan 6 1831 on acct of amt of his property. Rept by Blanche Rings.

PIERCE, JAMES, Richland co

Exec Doc 37 of 1852. Refused a pens as servd less than 6 mo. By Wm Pettit.

PIERCE, JOSEPH, Mahoning co

Pvt S 3 V 23 p 318 Ensigg Pa Arch Vt Men pp 38, 286. Mar (1) Ruth Newcomb (2) Mrs. Polly Whetezell 1822. Chldr: Joseph mar Clarissa; Amos. Soldr d Jackson twp. Ref Memoirs of Pioneer Women of Western Reserve V 5 p 135; Tax list 1826 Joseph Pierce Jackson twp. Western Res. Chronicle mar Feb 6 1822, Joseph Pierce Sr and Polly Whetezell. Deed bk D p 279, 1824. Rept by Mahoning chpt.

PIGSLEY, PAUL, Huron co

Pvt Mass Contl enl 1779 Mass srvd 1 yr. Was b 1760. Appl mentions wf; one dau ae 14; one ae 9 one ae 6 and a son ae 3 (1820). Res Huron co O June 13, 1818. Ref 18th Rept N S D A R p 240; S 40263 Mass. Rept by State D A R. Cop fr Pioneer History Clarksfield O by Dr. F. E. Weeks pp 97, 121 Nathan Perry chpt. Paul Pixley, an old Rev Soldr and son Ariel came fr Brighton Monroe co N Y to New London twp in 1817 and settled just south of Barretts Corners. Paul d Rochester O. A dau Delania is mentioned.

PIKE, JONATHAN, Portage co

Pvt Conn Contl. Enl 1775 nr Boston Mass. Srvd 1 yr. Was b 1780; mar Charity ae

63 yr in 1821; one dau was Charlotte æ 15 (1821); Soldr mvd fr Livingston N Y to Portage co O in 1830. Appl for trnsfr of pens fr N Y to O whr liv in Portage co. Ref Conn S 40264. Rept by Jane Dailey.

PIKE, ZEBULON, COL., ? co and Ind.

Contl N J Indian Wars and 1812. Capt in 3rd Regt fr Jan 5 1792 to Mar 1792; Maj fr Mar 20 1800 trnsfrd to 5th regt Apr 5 1802 Lt Col to 1812 in Pa Line. Was b 1751; chldr: James B Pike wf Elizabeth; Maria Gage. Chldr of James & Elizabeth were Wm; George; Montgomery; Catharine; Joseph. Chldr of Marie Gage were Zebulon; Sarah, Clarisa; and an infant 9 mos. Soldr d abt Aug 1834 ae 83 in O. Cop fr Western Reserve Chronicle Sept 4 1834 "Col Zebulon Pike ae 83 d at Zebulon O July 27. He had srvd in many of the Rev battles" by Mary Chesney chpt. Research by State D A R finds him a pensr 1826-28 in Dearborn co Ind. Ref S 36737 Contl N J. Black Swamp chpt reports same death date but he d at Lawrenceburg Ind whr he is bur.

PILES, JEREMIAH, Preble co

Pvt Va Milit. Enl 1780 or 81 Bedford co Va. Srvd 8 mos. Was b Mar 1762 London co Va. Came to Preble co abt 1818. Appl for pens Preble co O Sept 21 1832. Ref S 5155 Va Rept by State D A R.

PIPER, FREDERICK, Wayne co

Pvt Pa Milit. Enl Oct 1 1776 Lancaster co Pa. Srvd 6 mos. Was b 1748. Mvd to Hagerstown Md before war ended. Aft a yr mvd to Shenendoah co Va. Aft 2 yrs mvd to Green co Va. Stayed 3 yrs thence to Wayne co O. Appl for pens Wayne co O Oct 4 1832 Res of Green twp. Ref S 8958 Pa. Rept by State D A R.

PIPER, JAMES, Warren co

Pvt Pa Milit enl Westmoreland co Pa Jan 1779 srvd under Capt Mason 2 yrs. Was b 1762 June 11, Cumberland co Pa whr he mar Elizabeth Anckney Dec 16 1790; chldr: Martha McClandless; Wm; Andrew; Eliz; Enoch; Mary Long; Margaret Bailey all b nr Silver Springs Ch in Pa. Soldr d Oct 15 1837 Warren co O. Made appl Pens Warren co O Oct 3 1832 liv in Turtle Creek twp. Elizabeth Piper made appl for wid pens in Butler co O May 31 1848. Ref W 5547 Pa. Rept by State D A R.

PIPER, WILLIAM, Mahoning co

Pvt Va Men (lib rec) p 241 Pa Arch S 3 V 23 p 278 Ranger. Mar Susan; chldr: Sussana; James; Rachel; Eleanor. Soldr d abt 1805 Springfield twp Mahoning co Ref Will bk 1 Columbiana Recds probated 1805. Rept by Mahoning chpt.

PITKIN, STEPHEN, Portage co

Pvt Conn Contl. Enl Apr 1775 Capt Griswolds Co. Srvd 7 mo 28 das. Was b 9-19-1754 New Hartford Conn. Mvd fr there to Portage co O in 1822. Old Northwest chpt repts soldr bur at Rootstown O old cem. Pens appl 10-19-1832 while liv in Rootstown twp Portage co. Ref Conn S 3675. Rept by State D A R.

PIXLEY (Picksley), ELIJAH, Shelby co

Musician Conn Contl. Enl Dec 1777 into Conn Contl under Capt Smith. Was b 1763; mar Elenor; chldr: Thomas ae 14 in 1821; Plummer 11; Hezekiah 9; Phebe 7; Rachel 5; Mary 3; William 1. Was pens in Adams co but appl for trnsfr to Shelby co 9-5-1821. Ref Conn S 40265. Rept by State D A R.

PLACE, PELEG, Delaware co

Pvt Pa Milit 24 mos. Enl in N Hampton Mass as boy scout 1775 for 24 mos. Was b 1761; mar Ann Bensley 9-1-1784. Soldr d 8-9-1834 Porter twp Delaware co whr he appl for pens 11-1-1832. Ref Pa W 4566. Rept by State D A R.

PLATT, JOSEPH, Mahoning co

Pvt Conn Arch V 13 p 84; Bounty Rolls Contl Army 1780 Chldr: Joseph b 1775 mar Elsy; Eli b 1778. Soldr d abt 1818 Boardman twp Mahoning co, whr he came in 1804 fr Conn. One of founders of St. James Prot Episcopal ch 1809. Ref Cem Rec Boardman twp (Thorne); Will bk p — Trumbull co Recds Prob 1818. Rept by Mahoning chpt.

PLUMER, WILLIAM, Washington co and W. Va.

Pvt and Lieut Pa Milit. Marietta repts soldr d and bur at Buffalo W Va nr Charlestown. Pensr 6-11-1832 Washington co. Appld Marietta 10-26-1832. Rept by Jane Dailey.

POLLY, DANIEL, Gallia co

Pvt Conn Contl. Srvd in regt of Col Butler for 3 yrs. Pens 6-23-1818 and 21. Ref S 40285 Conn Soldr b 1759. Gallia co Probate Ct Will Rec C 650 Apr 18-1831 an appl for administrator was made. Daniel Jr was appointed. Rept by State D A R and French Colony chpt.

POLLOCK. ELIJAH, Huron co

Pvt Va Contl. Enl 1775 Brookfield Worcester co Mass. Was b 1757 Conn. Appl mentions wf; one son ae 23; a dau ae 12 (1820). Soldr bur Huron O located by Sandusky chpt and marked by Gov Marker. Res Huron co O in Oct 1820 whr he appl for pens 1818. Ref 18 Rept N S D A R p 241 by Mary Chenney chapt; S 40286 Conn. Rept by State D A R. Marjorie Cherry Sandusky gives "service under Capt Harwood and Bissell in Conn. Trnsfr to Washingtons Life Guard at Valley Forge." Ref Firelands Pioneers N S V 20 p 2026; and Williams Hist p 471.

POLLACK, WILLIAM, Mahoning co

Pvt N Y Men in Rev pp 137, 147. Was b Feb 19 1757 Down co Ireland. Wf b 1767 (liv 1859). Soldr d Apr 19 1859 Poland O. Came to America 1776. Ref Mahoning co Sentinel Apr 19 1859. Rept by Mahoning chpt.

POMPELLY (Pumpilla), JOHN, Clermont co

Pensr act 1832-34 as pvt Capt Bensons co Col Vase Regt Mass Line 16 mo 4 da. Also Marine, ship Nancy Tarter. Pens issued Mar 21 1835 to Batavia O. Mar Mary (b Taunton, Mass July 17 1771) at Turner, Oxford co Me by Rev Strickland Sept 11 1788. Chldr: Polly; Charlotte; Celia; Betsy; Lemira; John; Hariot; Cyrus; Polly II b 1807. Soldr d Oct 20 1837 Clermont co O. List of 68 citzs testify to truth of Pomellys statements in appl (1833). Ref W 5558 Wid last pensd Jan 30 1844 in Amelia O Act 3 Mar 1843; living in O twp Clermont co Dec 19 1843 ae 72. Cop by Jane Dailey.

POOLE, CHESTER, Clark co

Pvt & Corp Conn Milit Enl in Windham co Conn whr he then resided. Was b 8-12-1761 Windham co Conn. Mar Bridget Kinney 12-6-1785; chldr: William 1786; William 2nd 1788; Sally 1790; Rosewell 1792; Polly 1794; Kinney 1796; Chester 1798; Lois 1800; Warren 1803; Jonathan 1805; Phebe 1808; one not named 1812. Soldr d 6-6-1833. Wid pensd 7-22-1849 Hamilton co O. Ref Conn Vt W 5569 B L Wt 14532-160-55. Rept by State D A R.

POPE, EZRA, Richland co

Pvt Conn Contl. Enl Mar 1778 residing Norwalk twp Fairfield co Conn Soldr b 12-22-1755 Fairfield co Norwalk twp Conn. Mar Mary Shefen 12-16-1789. Chldr: Charles ae 50; Peter 48; John 44; Robt 34; William 79 as stated in wid appl Knox co 10-10-1845. Soldr d 2-15-1840 Richland co O. Abt 4 yrs aft war he had mvd to Otsego co N Y; aft ten yrs mvd to Candad and in 1814 mvd to O finally to Richland co in 1828 whr he and his wife (both very infirm) were liv alone when he was pensd 1-31-1834. Ref Conn R 8329. Rept by State D A R.

PORTER, AARON, Mahoning co

Pvt Conn Milit under Capt Abijah Rowlee Hebron Conn. 12 chldr 3 b in Milton twp; Mary mar John Jones Medina co; Nancy mar Jos McKenzie Huron co; Robin in Ind; Enoch and Joseph liv in 1880. Other chldr: David; William; Bazel; Thomas. Soldr lvd to be 96 yr old; bur Milton twp. Came fr Pa in 1803 with wf and 9 ch. 3 b in Milton twp. All livd to maturity. Located on farm where his sons Enoch and Joseph livd. A strong man of great endurance. Ref Conn Men in Rev p 88; Hist Trumbull & Mahoning co Vol 2 p 179; Deed bks and Tax list 1826; Rept by Mahoning chpt.

PORTER, EBENEZER, Washington co

Rev srv Mass Soldrs & Sailors Vol XII p 586; Was b 1732; d 1826-27 Newbury O whr bur below Belpre O. Grave marked S A R Marker ordered 1934 Marietta chpt. Ref Williams history of Wash co O p 506; Newbury Hist by Laura Curtis Preston. Rept by Marietta chpt, Mrs. C. R. Sloan.

PORTER, ELI, Clermont co

Pvt Va Contl. Enl Contl line Jan 1777. Ervd 3 yrs. Was b 1760; mar Mary 12-6-1817. Soldr d 11-4-1848. Pens appl Stonelick twp Clermont co 10-7-1829. Widow appl for pens White co Ind 8-11-1854. Ref Va R 8349. Rept by State D A R.

PORTER, HUGH, Guernsey co

Pvt Pa Contl enl 1776. Srvd 3 yrs. Was b 1758. Appl mentions wf Jane; dau Margaret; gr-son Hananiah. Soldr d abt 1841 as will prob then; livd Madison twp names Jane Porter wf; Hugh, oldest son; Archibald, youngest son; Hannia Wilkins (gr son); Nancy oldest dau; Margaret Porter Matthews, sec dau;—— Burnworth, youngest dau. Appl for pens Guernsey co O Aug 22 1818. Ref S 40289 Pa. Rept by State D A R.

PORTER, JAMES, Montgomery co

One of the earliest settlers German twp. 5th Ser Pa Arch Vol 7 p 17. Flying corps 1776; Quartermaster fr Lancaster co. Vol 6 p 400 1780 Cumberland co Capt Wm Marchant. Burial place not identified and may have gone to Tennessee as a pensioner of name srvd in First Pa Con Line appears in Vol 2 p 735; Vol 4 p 121 sergt. Rept by Wm Pettit S A R.

PORTER, WILLIAM, Mahoning co

Pvt S 3 V 23 Pa Arch Many ref. William was one son. Soldr d Sept 28 1826 Coitsville Mahoning co; bur Hopewell Pres Ch cem New Bedford Pa. Ref Deed bk C p 247 trnscrbd Mahoning co to Wm Porter 1811. Rept by Mahoning Chpt.

PORTERFIELD, ROBERT, Delaware co

Pvt Mass Contl enl Mar 10 1777 Mass Line. Corp 2 yr. Was b 1757. Mar Agnes——Nov 1791. Chldr :John 17; William 16; Lucinda 14; Robert 11; Lorenzo 8; Mary 5 (appl 1820). Soldr d 9-20-1824 Delaware co O. Appl for pens in Delaware 5-21-1820. Ref Contl W 5568. Rept by State D A R.

PORTERFIELD, WILLIAM, Trumbull co

Pvt Contl Line fr Cumberland co Pa. Pa Arch S 5 V 4 p 637. Was b 10-21-1759. Mar 4-21-1795 Mary Shannon. Chldr: John; Robert; Jane; William; James; Sarah; Mary; Soldr d 9-14-1831 and bur Hubbard Trumbull co O. Rept by Mary Chesney chpt.

POTTER, JOHN, ? co

Enl in Capt Wrights Co 1777-78. Was b 1760 Soughington, Conn. Mar 1783 Lydia Harrison (1766-96). Samuel Young was one son. Soldr d 1832 in O. Cop fr V 124 p 187 D A R Lin No. 123584 by Nathan Perry chpt.

POTTER, JOSEPH I, Butler co

Pvt N J Contl. Enl Elizabethtown N J abt July 1 1776. Srvd 6 yrs in N J Line. Was b 1749. Pens appl in Butler co O June 9 1818. Occupation shoemaker. Ref N J S 40283. Rept by State D A R.

POWELL, DAVID, Wayne co

Pvt Pa Milit. Enl Lancaster co Pa whr livd 1780-81-82. Srvd 10 mos. Was b Jan 1759 Lancaster co Pa. Aft Rev livd in Franklin co and Somerset co Pa, Cecil co Md and thence to Wayne co O whr appl for pens May 29 1834. Ref S 8975 Pa. Rept by State D A R.

POWELL (Powl or Paul or Powel), JOSEPH, Marion co

In the pens cl Rejected File 8400 it appears that he was b Sept 3 1760 in old Lancaster co Pa. He alleged that he enl there in Aug 1776; srvd one yr pvt under Capt Curtis Grubb and Col Green; also that he re-enl servd one yr and 9 mos as Sergt in Capt Isaac Sencingers Co Col Elders regt. He appl for pens 1838 liv in Marion co O but his claim was rejected as he failed to furnish sufficient proof of service as required by the pension laws. He d Sept 1 1844 or 1855. Rept by Capt Wm Hendricks chpt. Rept by State D A R soldr livd in Delaware co O 1813 to 31 then movd to Marion co. The Buckeye Eagle issue of 9-18-1844 carried announcement of soldr death.

POWERS, ABRAM, Mahoning co

Certif of S Gen Dist Land Bounty Rights in Reg Army. Payment made of land because of lack of specie. Also N Y men in Rev p 213. Was b 1743 Pa son of Isaac Powers. chldr: Abraham mar Betsey Woodruf; Isaac b 1777 mar Leah Frazee; Jacob b 1787 mar Nancy Pumphrey; James; John. Soldr d Sept 11 1832 Youngstown likely bur at Daulingtown Pa. Soldr was Scotch Irish. Livd nr border of N Y N J and Pa. Came to O in 1797-8 fr Beaver Pa. Ref Hist Trumbull and Mahoning co V 1 P 362; Biog Hist of Mahoning co p 665 Sanderson; Hist Coll Mahoning Valley p 71; Hist E O p 783 by Summers. Rept by Mahoning chpt.

POWERS, SIMEON, Cuyahoga co

Pvt N H Contl. Enl 5-8-1777 at Charleston twp N H. Soldr b 1745; mar Lydia Dwinnell 1768 Sprinfield Vt. Lvd with a son for a No. of yrs. Chldr: Simeon Jr b 1769 mar Mary Goodyear; William b 1770; Joseph b 1773; Asahel b 1775-6 mar Sarah Seward; Nathaniel; Jonathan d young; a dau mar —— Gould. Ref N H S 40284 B L Wt 489-100 and N H Rev War Rolls pp 594 471; Vol 2 pp 77 270: Powers family p 37 by A H Powers Rept by State D A R and Mrs. Fred Kimmons, Toledo O.

POWERS, WALTER, Madison co

Rev soldr bur in Alder cem nr West Jefferson O. Grave marked Sept 1934 by London chpt D A R who rept this data.

PRATT, ELNATHAN, Ashtabula co

No service established. D 2-15-1840 ae 78 yr bur Williamsfield O. Rept by Mary Redmond chpt.

PRATT, JOEL, MAJOR, ? co

Listed in News clipping by "L A A" found in old scrap bk no date as Rev soldr participating or interested in Marietta settlement. By Marietta chpt.

PRATT, JOHN, Monroe co

Pvt Va Contl. Enl Pillsburg Pa Apr 1779. Srvd 18 mos. Was b 1751. Appl of 1832 mentions of wf and 2 sons living in Monroe co O and 2 dau Nancy and Polly. Pensr 1840 ae 83 liv in Centre twp. Appl for pens Apr 12 1819. Greene co Pa. Appl for pens Monroe co O Oct 8 1832. Ref S 49296 B L Wt 13901-160-55. Pa Rept by State D A R.

PRATT, PHINEAS, Licking co

Artificer Mass Contl, Enl in Granby ? twp Conn. Was b 1744. Mar Hannah, Was a carpenter. Pensr 6-6-1820 Licking co. Ref Conn Contl S 40303. Rept by State D A R.

PRESTON, ABIAH, Hamilton co

Pvt and Boatman on Frontier of Cumberland and Cape May. Was b 1760 N J. Mar Margaret Simpson Warden 1793. Robert Simpson was one son. Soldr d 1813, Hamilton co O. Cop fr V 122 p 123 D A R Lin No. 121381 by Nathan Perry chpt.

PRESTON, DAVID, Portage co

Pvt Conn Line 3 yrs. Enl 2-15-1776 in Litchfield co Conn. Pensd 11-30-1819 in Tallmadge twp Portage co O. Was b 1758. Ref Conn S 40291. Rept by state D A R.

PRESTON, ROBERT, Hamilton co

Pvt Fairfax co Va 3rd Va Regt 1777 Thomas Marball Co. Lt Col Wm Heth Col Alexander Spotswood. Recd bounty land; see p 272 saffell. Was b in Va son of William and Sarah Preston. Mar Rachel ——; Chldr: Lavina mar Simon Whallon in 1826; Sarah mar Abraham Patterson; and Mrs. Abner Rude; Soldr d Springdale bur Springdale Presb cem. Name on Tax list in 1809 in Springfield twp Ham. co; Official board of Presb Ch Springdale; also an officer of the town. Rept by Mrs. Mary Rude Molyneaux to Cincinnati chpt Mrs. E. P. Whallon.

PRESTON, SAMUEL, Fairfield co

"D at the res of his son ae 86 yrs in this city (Columbus) of cholera. In the Rev acted a soldrs part. Was b at Ashford, Conn in 1763 and in 1795 removd to Montpelier Vt whr he res till the fall of 1842 when he removed to this city. He was an honest man and much loved by all who knew him. He was bur yesterday and followed to the grave by numerous friends" (Ohio Statesman, July 19 1849). Soldr was b Dec 12 1763 d July 17 1849 at Col O. Was son of Samuel Preston (Fr Green Lawn cem rec). Had one son Samuel D (who is son above) b Jan 3 1813 Montpelier Vt d Nov 22 1856 at Col. Son of Samuel and Lydia Preston. Rept by Blanche Rings Co. O.

PRESTON, WILLIAM, Hamilton co

Regt Artificer Fowlers Artillery. Enl 1776 in Col Wm Montgomerys Co. See Heitmans. Was b in Va; mar Sarah; chldr: Robert; Joseph; Harp; Abijah. Soldr d Springdale O 1802; bur Presb Ch cem. Came to Springfield O before 1800. One of the founders of Springdale town. Was member of 1st board of Elders in 1800 Springdale, and was a founder of the Presb Cr. by Mrs. Mary Rude Molyneaux. Rept by Cincinnati chpt. Mrs. E P Whallon.

PRICE, JOSEPH, Franklin co

Order bk 11-273 an appl for pens and having subscribed and sworn to service and the Ct being satisfied with the correctness thereunto annexed do order same to be filed and certfied. Dated 1820. Order bk 3-292, Joseph Price, a Rev soldr, this day produced his declaration ad made solemn oath to the correctness of same which is ordered to be certified under the seal of this Ct to the Sec of War dated Apr 12 1822. Cop by Blanche Rings.

PRICE, NATHANIEL, Knox co

Pvt Md Contl. Enl 1780 at Annapolis Md into the Co of John Michell. Pensr in Knox co 5-15-1819. Was b 1751. On O Pens Roll 1835 V 3 O-71. Ref Md S 40298. Rept by State D A R.

PRICE, NATHANIEL, Belmont co

Gunner N Y Contl enl Nov 1775 2nd Reg of N J. Was b 1764. Chldr: Elizabeth ae 29 yrs; two gr chldr Ephraim Burch 7; and Mary Burch ae 3 yrs (1820). Appl for pens 7-24-1820 in Belmont co O. Occupation Weaver. Ref N Y S 40295. Rept by State D A R.

PRICE, SAMPSON, Ross co and Iowa

Pvt Va Milit. Enl Mar 1781 Shenandoah co Va whr he then resided; 14 yr aft war he movd to Ky; later to Ross co O abt 1827. Was b 6-24-1761 Culpeper co Va; livd with father until Rev. Pensr in Ross co O 1834 asked for trnsfr to Iowa in 1850. Ref Va S 18167. Rept by State D A R.

PRICE, SAMUEL, Trumbull co

Capt De Bows Co Eastern Battl Morris co also Capt Jonathan Wards Co; also State Troops and Contl Army. Ref Jersey men in the Rev p 727. Was b Aug 5 1750 in N J. Mar 1st Mary Stenson, 2nd Mrs Mary Hoover. Chldr: James Stinson; Archibald; Sally; David; Betsey; John; Susan; Jacob; Richard. Soldr d Dec 20 1827 in Hubbard and bur in Old North cem. He was a mill wright and came to Hubbard fr N J in 1807. Rept by Mary Chesney chpt.

PRICHARD, NATHANIEL, Lawrence co

Pvt Conn Milit. Enl New Haven co Conn 1776. Srvd 1 yr 4 mos. Was b 1762. Mar Comfort Gillet 1787. Chldr: Mary Churchill, a dau the only surviving heir (her appl Mar 18 1853 Gallia co O) Soldr d Aug 31 1843. Since Rev livd in Conn, N Y & O. Wid d Sept 6 1848. Soldr grave marked by Capt Lawrence D A R 1931. Pens appl Lawrence co O Aug 28 1832 Res of Rome twp. Ref W 5582 Conn. Rept by State D A R.

PRIEST, JOHN, Licking co

Pvt Va Contl Enl Apr 1780 Washington, Culpepper co Va whr he livd. Mvd to O Licking co later. Was b 1750 Prince William co Va. Pens appl Licking co 3-13-1833. Ref Va S 3739. Rept by State D A R.

PRIEST, WILLIAM, Fairfield co

Pvt Va Contl Enl in Culpepper co Va Apr, 2 yr prior to capture of British at Little York. Was b 1765. Ref Name listed p 406 Wisemans Pioneer People Fairfield co; Va S 40292. Rept by State D A R.

PRILLIMAN (Prilliamen), JACOB, Miami co

B 1752 probably Va. Chldr: Elizabeth b 1778 mar Moses Fuller in Montgomery co Va; Anna Prillaman b in Va mar Lewis Winters; William b Dec 1789 mar Margaret ——; and others. Soldr d Miami co shortly aft 1840 and is bur there. Ref His name is on Pens Roll of 1840 as living in Elizabeth twp Miami co O ae 88; Also Jay co (Ind) Hist. (See D A R Mag March 1933) Mary Chesney chpt. Rept by Mississinewa Chpt Portland Ind Registrar, Mrs. Oscar Finch.

PRINTIS, WILLIAM, Brown co

Found listed as pvt N J Contl pensr in Brown co 7-21-1819 is thought to be a misprint for William Printy, Brown co p 297 Vol 1 O Roster. Rept by Meryl Markley, Vice St Ch.

PRITCHARD, COMFORD, Lawrence co

Exec Doc 37 of 1852. Claim good under act of 1848. Rept by Wm Pettit.

PROSSER, DANIEL, Richland co

Pvt Va Contl. Was b 1745; mar Margaret b 1763; chldr: Abraham ae 17 yr; Eliza 19 (appl 1823) Soldr d 8-11-1829. Livd in Plymouth twp Richland co when he appl for pens 10-23-1823. Ref Will filed in Richland co Ct House No. 42. Final Settlement 1841. Va S 40297. Rept by State D A R and Jared Mansfield chpt.

PROUGH, PETER, Ross co

Pvt Pa Contl. Enl at Reading Pa 1775. Srvd 1 yr. Was b 1757. Pens appl in Ross co O 6-16-1823. Ref Pa S 40304. Rept by State D A R.

PROWS (Prowse), THOMAS, Gallia co and W Va

Pvt N H Contl srvd in Col Scammels Regt fr 1776 to 1783 pens 10-12-1820. Also made statement of his service in Hamilton co May 27 1818. Was b 1759. Mar Margaret Jamison Apr 17 1817. One son was Samuel. Soldr d July 12 1828 while visiting at Mason co W Va. Also srvd in War of 1812. Margaret Prowse made appl for pens in Butler co O Aug 17 1855 as widow. Thomas Prows made appl in Gallia co Feb 24 1820 and a declaration made Aug 1 1820. In wfs appl a statement was made by her dau May Jamison Polkamas (by Marg Prows first husband John Jamison) that she was present at the mar of her mother and Thomas Prows on Apr 17 1817. W 6878 N H Ref. Rept by State D A R and French Colony Chpt.

PUGH, JOHN, Harrison co

Servd 5 yrs as teamster in Rev; b Chester co Pa 1747; in 1792 he w Benjamin Johnson crossed Ohio Riv at Wheeling Va and settld in Harrison Co. Mar Rachel Bennett; one son William mar Bashaba (dau of said Benjamin above). One of William's 5 sons was E B Pugh who settled 1851 at McArthur a wagon maker b Harrison co 1819. Ref Heitmans Reg p 337; S A R 49834; p 1258 Hist Hocking Valley. Rept by Hannah Dowd Vanderford chpt.

PURVIANCE, SAMUEL, Hamilton co

Chrman Md Com Safety. Purchasing agt of Cont Cong for Md 1775 & 1776 Memb Md Provincial Cong 1774-76. Was a citz of Baltimore. Was b County Tyrone, Ireland abt 1728. Mar Susanna Schleydorn of Phila. One dau was Susannah. Soldr d nr Cin O 1788. Cop fr App No 14 Calif S of Rev p 109 Vol 1 Feb 1929. By Jane Dailey.

PUTNAM, JETHRO, CAPT, ? co

Listed in news clipping by "L A A" found in old scrap bk, no date, as Rev soldr who participated in or interested in settlement of Marietta. Rept by Marietta chpt for investigation.

QUEEN, JOHN (or Jonah), Columbiana co

Pvt Capt Elgins Co. Was b 1755 Ireland; mar 1785 Catherine Marsh (d 1845); chldr: Samuel (1790-1840) who mar Mary Hesser (1792-1884). Soldr d 1847. Rept by Mrs Wilma Molsberry. Compare No 232075; No 180760; No 181376 D A R.

QUIGLEY, SAMUEL, Columbiana co

Ref Penn S 4746 Bureau of Pensions Washington D C. Pvt Pa Line; servd 8 mo. Appld for pension in Columbiana co O 8-14-1832. A farmer; age 75 in 1832 (born therefore in 1757). Enl Aug 1777 in Shippensburg Pa where he resided. Was pensioner 12-18-1832 in Columbiana co (Certif) and Mch 2 1833 same. Fr Youngstown D A R comes report: Samuel Quigley Sr listed in Census of Pens 1841. Servd Pa Milit. Residing in Columbiana co pens granted 12-18-1832 age 77. (Which is same data as above). Living 1840 in Calcutta twp in his own house and 1841 age 84. Ref Pa Arch S 3 V 23 p 585. (There is confusion between this name and Samuel Quinby which see).

QUINBY, SAMUEL, Columbiana co

"A Revolutionary soldier who livd in Trumbull co. He was given a military funeral and taken to Oakwood cem at Sharon Pa where he was buried." Filed by Mary Chesney chpt Warren O Ref p 445 V 1 Roster of Rev Soldiers Buried in Ohio. (This data is filed here to avoid further research in Ohio for the grave. See "Samuel Quigley" — it is my opinion these are two different men. J D).

RADABACH, NICHOLAS, Fairfield co

Exec Doc 37 of yr 1852. Refused a pens as servd less than 6 mo. Rept by Wm Pettit.

RAGER, LEONARD, Butler co

Pvt Va Contl. Enl Sheperdstown Barclay co Va in fall 1775 for two years. At expiration of term was dischgd at Valley Forge Pa. Res in Lemon twp Butler co O on 8-20-1818; appld for pens there 5-1-1819; and 1820. Stated he was ae 72 in 1818; his wf Catherine d 10-1-1831. She was 70 in 1820; he d 4-20-1833 Tippecanoe co Ind. On 2-29-1856 his son Burket Rager appl for arrears of pens in Jefferson co Ky. Fr family records he gave "Leonard Rager mar Catherine Hays 10-25-1781." Soldr named two gr-chldr: Daniel Boyer ae 11 and Jonathan Potter ae one in his 1820 appl. Was a farmer. Ref Pens Cl Va S 40315. Rept by State D A R.

RAINS, WILLIAM, Brown co

Pvt Va Milit. Pensd 6-6-1833 in Brown co; mar Jane Edwards, dau of James a Rev soldr. Chldr: John b 1796; Elizabeth Stewart; Eleanor Lash; Susan Howard; Jane Anderson; Nancy Richmond; Mary Rains. He was bur 1-2 mi west of Aberdeen Huntington twp. The cem was "plowed under" and now the A and P Highway passes over the spot. He was constable in Cedar Hill then in Adams co in 1798. Collector for same 1798. His will prob 5-2-1837 Vol 1 p 355. Prob Court. Fr pens cl W 4314 B L Wt 34854—160—55 Va was secured the following: (additional) Enl in service of U S on Mar 1781 in Fauquier Co Va. Srvd 6 mos; b Nov 23 1764 in Fauquier co Va; mar Jane Edwards Oct 23 1787; d 1-30-1837; Wid appld for pens Brown co 10-29-1838; he had res in Va until 1784 movd to Ky now Mason co and in 1796 went to Brown co whr he now resided. Rept by State D A R.

RAINSBURG (or Rainsburger), JOHN, Carroll co

Enl Fredericktown Md whr he livd 12 yr aft dischrgd. Pvt in Capt Camps Co Col Johnston Regt Md milit 6 mo. Was b Frederick co Md 1759 Jan. Appld pens Aug 19 1834 fr Orange twp Carroll co. Fr Md livd 3 yr at Redstone settlement Pa thence to O Carroll co. Under Act 1838 unclaimed pens issued Mar 10 1835 sent to Saml Stokely Steubenville O. A letter was filed in Pens Bur fr George Reinsberger, Eldora, Hardin co Iowa Oct 9 1861. Ref S 7351 Md. Cop by Jane Dailey.

RAMEY, JOHN, Muskingum co

Va Contl Line 6th Regt; b 1753 Stafford Conn; d 1834; mar Edith Browning 1778; ref 54316 S A R. Rept by Wm Pettit.

RAMSDELL, JOSEPH, Erie co

Seaman of Brigantine "Freedom." Enl July 10 1776 until June 1 1777 under Capt John Christen 10 mo 21 da. Son of Kymball and Mary. Soldr b 1767 Oct 22; d in Bloomingville 1828 whr he is bur. Ref Firelands Pioneers O S Vol 10 p 97; Stewart and Page Atlas p 1; Blockhouses and Military Posts pp 30, 67. Rept by Marjorie Cherry, Sandusky.

RAMSAY, JAMES, Mahoning co

Pvt S 2 V. 14 p 743 Washington co Pa Arch Substitute for bro in law 5 mo in Army of the north tho 2 yrs in Army of the south; served till end of war. In battles of Brandywine, Cowpens, Eutaw and others. b 1752 Lancaster co Pa. mar Margaret; chldr: Hugh; John; James b 1785 mar Abigail; Mary b 1787 mar Nathaniel Kirk; Margaret mar Elihu Warner; Betsey mar Josiah Wetmore; Martha mar Thomas Maxwell; Sally mar Alex Scott; Rebecca mar Robert Wallace; Anna mar David Wallace. Soldr d Aug 2 1818 Canfield O. Ranger under Capt Samuel Brady and recognized many places at Bradys Lake after he settled at Canfield. Ref Hist Trumbull and Mahoning co V 2 p 431; Mahoning co register 5-19-1859, 8-8-1867; Deed bk J p 16 trnscrb Mahoning co James Ramsey fr 1812; Tax list 1826 James Ramsay heirs. Rept by Mahoning chpt

RAMSEY, WILLIAM, Preble co

B in Ireland 1749 came to Va. Mar Martha Ochletree; came to Preble co 1806; d Israel twp 1737; bur Hopewell cem. Rept Commodore Preble chpt.

RANDALL, CHARLES, Huron co

Soldr of the Rev d Wakeman O in 1846. Mention made of a son Marquis D Randall. Ref Pioneer History of Clarksfield O by Dr. F. E. Weeks p 149. Rept by Nathan Perry chpt.

RANDALL, JOSEPH, Butler co

Pvt N Y Contl. Enl Weschester co N Y where he was b 1742. Ae 90, Pens appl July 30 1832 Butler co O whr had movd fr N Y 16 yr before. Ref S 16234 N Y. Rept by State D A R.

RANDALL, JOSHUA, Erie co

Pvt in Capt Augustus Odles co Col John Abbotts Vt Milit b 1758 Plymouth Mass, mar 1793 Keziah Hawley (b 1767) one son was Zalmon Randall. Soldr d 1828 Erie co O. Cop fr V 121 No. 120212 D A R lin by Jane Dailey.

RANDOLPH, CHRISTIAN, Perry co

Research in Pens Cl dept Washington on this name was returned as Christian Rudolph, data filed this volume (J D).

RANKIN, WILLIAM, Fayette co and Ill.

Rev soldr went to Logan co Ill wh he d and is bur nr Lincoln Rept by Jean Howatt Washington C H chpt.

RANSTEAD, JAMES, Licking co and Ind.

Pvt Mass Contl enl 1780 in Hampshire, Mass; mar Jane McMullen; chldr: Leonard ae 16; John 14; Almira 10; Joel 8; Jane 6; James 4 (appl of 1820). Soldr d 8-20-1836 St Joseph co Ind. Pensd in Switzerland co Ind 4-15-1819. Trnsfrd to O 10-27-1830. Ref Mass W 26352 B L Wt 57784-160-55. Rept by State D A R.

RAPE, JOHN, Preble co

Came as soldr with Gen Lafayette servd thro Rev. Was so infatuated with this country he refused to return to France, deserted, and forced inland. b in France mar Eva Catherine Dickard in London co Va. Soldr d 1831 bur West Alexandria cem Preble co. In 1805 came to O located in Twin twp. Rept by Commodore Preble chpt.

RAPP, JOHN, Mahoning co

Pvt Capt Chas Collins co 61st Battl Berk co Milit Col Joseph Heister 1780. Mar Catherine; chldr: Gottleib mar Susanna; Abraham mar Catherine; Catherine mar Abraham Guise; Mary; John. Soldr d abt 1829 Beaver twp. Ref Will bk 6 p 558 Columbiana co recds probated 1829; Deed bk W p 210 1839; Deed bk O p 589 1820 and Deed bk O p 24 1806. Rept by Mahoning chpt.

RATCLIFFE, JOHN, SR, Mahoning and Trumbull cos

Pvt Md Arch V 18, pp 575, 580, 583; b 1762 mar Mary Vandyke (1762-3-28-1840); chldr: John Jr b 12-17-1799 mar Elizabeth Wilson (1797-1875) of Westmoreland co. Soldr d Mar 6 1842 bur Howland cem on Reeves farm. John and Mary Ratcliffe b Delaware came from Pa in 1811. In 1798 mvd to Westmoreland co Pa then to Beaver co Pa in 1801 thence to Trumbull co O. Ref Western Reserve Chronicle Feb 1842; Tax list 1826; also cem records of late Henry R. Baldwin; Hist Trumbull co V 1 p 498 and V 2 p 213; Pioneer Women of Western Reserve p 712. Rept by Mabel S. Askue Ch Rev Soldiers records Mahoning chpt Youngstown O.

RATHBEN, JONATHAN, Clermont co

Exec Doc 37 of 1852. Refused a pens as service was as privateer. Rept by Wm Pettit.

RATLETON, EDMUND, Cuyahoga co

Cop fr 13 rept N S D A R ;p 122 as marked by Western Reserve   D A R by Nathan Perry chpt.

RATTAN, THOMAS, Brown co

Pvt. Pa Contl enl for 3 yrs in Nov 1776 in Northumberland co Pa. Dischgd Jan 15 1781 in Trenton N J served 3 yrs. Res Brown co O Dec 21 1819 ae 64; appl for pens there July 24 1832. Pens trnsfrd to Putnam co Ind on Nov 14 1835. Ref S 16232 Pa Rept by State D A R.

RAUB, PETER, Mahoning co

Pvt 2nd class 6th Co Northampton co Mil Ser 5 Vol 8 p 334 Pa Arch. Mar Mary; chldr: John;; Mary mar Peter Benedict; Barbara mar Conrad Myers; Peter; George; Catherine; Magdaline; Henry b 1781. Soldr d abt 1827 Springfield twp Mahoning co whr he came in 1818 about same time as brother Henry. Ref Will bk 5 p 493 Columbiana co records probated 1827; Deed bk O pp 24 1806; Deed bk R p 360 Peter and Mary Robb to John Robb 1809. Rept by Mahoning chpt.

RAWLINGS, MOSES, ? co

Va cont line b in England mar Mary Cornwell Loudon co Va 1760; chldr: Ezekiel; Moses; Nathan; David; Asa ("Sale") Michael; Samuel; Jane; Letitia; Ellen. Soldr killed by Indians in Ky 1787. Ref p 569 Sept D A R magz and Mrs. Clara Hitchcock Washington C H O cop by Jane Dailey.

RAY (Rea), JOHN, McRUSH (McCrush), ROBERT, Washington co

Volunteered June 1775 srvd 1 yr Capt Henry Millers co Col Hands Regt. Enl for 2 yrs in same Pa Co and Regt. Srvd last 2 yrs in Morgans Rifle men. Appld for pens at Marietta O May 8 1818; also Nov 9 1821. B June 15, 1736 d Aug 21 1825, bur Wesley twp. Pens appl stated was a weaver; his house burned in 1803. Was living on charity of his sons who had large families to support. Ref S 40, 990-Pa V 3, p 9530. Rept by Marietta Helen Sloan. His last name has been incorrectly found listed as "Roberts" (JD).

RAYMER, PHILIP, Ross co

Pvt Pa Contl. Enl in Berks co Pa 1782 command of Col Hampton 2nd Reft. Pensd 5-21-1819 in Ross co. Served 1 yr. Ae 60 in 1818 (appl) Ref Pa S 40312 Rept by State D A R.

RAYMOND, THADEUS, Huron co

Bur Raymond cem 1 mi E of Hunts Corners S of the main road on a cross road. His wf's name Keziah. Letter of Cyrus Hunt "Thadeus Raymond came to Sandusky 1832. They speak of him as a soldr of the Rev. His family were Simeon; James; William." Rept by Marjorie Cherry.

REAGLE (Rigal), JACOB, Mahoning co

Pvt 2nd class Cumberland co Milit Capt Philip Martin Pa Arch Ser 5 V 6 p 501. Mar Mary; Chldr: Solomon; Benjamin; John; Jacob; Elie; Catherine; Mary mar —— Wansetter; Betsey b 1800 mar John Eckman; Lydia; Sally; Margaret. Soldr d abt 1822 Youngstown twp. Ref Will bk 3 p 248 Trumbull co recds Prob 1822; Tax list 1826 Jacob Rigal Heirs Youngstown. Rept by Mahoning chpt.

REAM (Reem, Reme, Reame), ABRAHAM, Fairfield co

Came fr Lancaster co Pa bur farm cem nr Lancaster Fairfield co. Jacob is one son. Known as the "Miller" Rept by Joseph Spencer chpt.

REAM, ANDREW, Clark co

Pvt Pa Milit and Contl liv in Lancaster co Pa whr enl in 1777. Pens appl in Clark co O 7-28-1832. Ref Pa S 4067. Rept by State D A R.

REAM, JACOB, Fairfield co

Pvt Pa Milit. Enl in Lancaster co Pa in 1777. Pvt 5 mo; in hospital 6 mo; teamster 2 mo. Son of Abraham Ream; bur farm cem nr Lancaster O Appl for pens in Fairfield co O 1832 ae 78. Ref Name listed p 406 Wisemans Pioneer People Fairfield co; Pa S 4765. Rept by State D A R.

REAM, NICHOLAS, Columbiana co

Rev soldr rec not yet found. B 1764; d 1839; bur Hanover twp. Ref Col co cem recs. Rept by Mrs. Wilma M. Molsberry, Youngstown O.

REAMS, WILLIAM, Logan co

Enl Carder co N Carolina in 1782 for 18 mo. Bur Old Friends Church cem Rushcreek twp. Rept by Descendant O K Reams, Zanesfield O to Bellefontaine chpt.

RECORDS, JOSIAH, Ross co

Commissioned capt of a co of soldrs to repel attack of Indians. B 1741 Sussex co Del; mar 1761 Susanna Tulley (b 1743); one son was Spencer. Soldr d 1809 Ross co O. Cop fr V 121 No. 120889 D A R Lin by Jane Dailey.

REDDEN, CHRISTOPHER, Portage co

Living in Portage co at Hiram O 1820 a Rev Soldier. Cop fr notes of late Alice Boardman, State Librarian of D A R by J D.

REDICK, JOHN, Muskingum co

Enl Lancaster co Pa. Mar Susan Mar 30 1830 Muskingum co O. Pensr 1840, Hopewell twp. Muskingum co. Soldr d Dec 30 1851. Widow appl for pens Perry co O Aug 10, 1853 but was rejected on grounds that description of husbands services were too indefinite. R 8642 Pa Rept by State D A R.

REDDICK, WILLIAM, Clermont co

Pvt. Pa Contl. Enl in Philadelphia Pa in a Co Commanded by Lawrence Fain. Srvd 6 yrs. Mar Margaret 1785; chldr: Joshua ae 14; Celia 12; Lucinda 10; Rachel 8. (appl of 1820) Soldr d 10-3-1830 or 31. Pens appl in Clermont co O 8-8-1818 ae 58. Widow appl for pens in Ind 11-22-1838. (appl) Ref Pa W 96620; B L Wt 40674-160-55. Rept by State D A R.

REDDINGTON (Readington), DANIEL, Warren co and Ind.

Pvt Mass contl Enl in Regt of Col Jackson 22 mo 27 days. B 1762; mar Anna Prince, May 5 1786 license issued in Hillsborough co N H Pens in Warren co O 9-21-1819. Appl for pens Dearborn co Ind No 8 1832. Soldr d Aug 17 1834. Widows appl in Decatur co Ind June 17 1845. Ref W 9623 Mass. Rept by State D A R.

REED, AMOS, Belmont co

Pvt N J contl Enl 1776 in N J Trenton. Srvd in Regt under Col Shreve N J line 6 yrs; b 1737; mar Gemima Konnard July 1780. chldr: John; Jane Wilkinson; Gemnina

Pryor; and Rachel Vance. Pens appl July 24, 1820 in Belmont co O. Soldr d Jan 7 1834, Belmont co O Ref R 8657 New Jersey. Rept by State D A R.

REED, BENJAMIN, Huron co

Pvt Mass Contl pensd in Huron co 9-23-1833. He believed he served two yrs as pvt; b 1756; Res in Chittenden co Vt, Susquehanna Pa and left for O abt 1818. Ref 18 Rept N S D A R p 24 by Sandusky O chpt who locates bur in Huron O. S 4055 Mass. Rept by State D A R.

REED, JAMES JR.,Mahoning co

Pvt Ser 6 V. 4 p 301; V 6 p 680; V 7 p 596 Pa Arch. B 1764 son of James Reed Sr; mar Elizabeth Calaway (b 1762-d Jan 22, 1860) chldr: Mary 1791 mar Joshua Bowman; Rosanna; Jemina mar Jacob Rudisill; James Jr 1790 mar Mary Turner; Eleanor mar George Turner; Anne 1806; John C. 1809; Hiram 1811; Joshua 1812; Rachel 1801 mar James Turner Soldr d Apr 11 1813 Canfield. Came to Ellsworth 1804 thence to Canfield 1805 — Set up a distillery to furnish whiskey to soldiers in 1811, that being considered an essential part of their rations. Ref: Hist Trumbull and Mahoning co V 2 pp 14 and 90; Mahoning Despatch Mar 26 1897; Hist Canfield Truesdale; Pioneer Women of the Western Reserve p 394; Will b 2 pp 162 and 212 Trumbull co rec Prob 1815. Rept by Mahoning chpt.

REED, NOAH, Mahoning co

Pvt Mass Soldr and Sailors V 13 p 87. Chldr: William; Leonard mar Nancy; Angelina; Alvelina; Soldr d abt 1815 Goshen twp. Ref Will bk 2 p 303 Columbiana co records probated 1815; Deed bk p 86 Noah Reed from — Trnscbd Rec Mahoning co 1813. Rept by Mahoning chpt.

REED, TALCOTT, Huron co

Exec Doc 37 of yr 1852. Gave team service but refused a pens as not come under Act. Rept by Wm Pettit.

REED, WILLIAM, Delaware co

Pvt 6 mos Pa Milit. Pensd 3-21-1833 Del co O. b 12-12-1751 Tyrone co Ireland. Enl 1777 Cumberland co Pa. Left Ireland 1773 for America. Landed at Newcastle Del and went to Philadelphia. Soon settled in Cumberland co Pa. Aft No. of yrs movd to Del co O about 1812. (appl) Appl for pens in Del co O 11-19-1832 resident of Troy twp. Del chpt rept he prob bur at Norton Marborough twp. Ref Pa S 4951. Rept by State D A R.

REESON, BENJAMIN, Highland co

Bur Overman frm 10 mi E of Hillsboro in Highland co O. Cop fr 4th Rept N S D A R p 298 by Nathan Perry chpt.

REEVES, JOSIAH, Pickaway co

Rev soldr b Charles co Md 1767. He mar Elizabeth Davis (b Mar 2 1764 d June 23 1842); chldr: Pensey mar John Blue; Anna mar twice; Wm mar Ann W Hays; Thomas mar twice; Jane; Owen; Josias; Jared; and James Madison; Soldr d Sept 22 1848 in Pickaway co O; bur cem Browns Chapel Ross co. Lived on James River Culpeper co Va; came to Ohio in 1806 locating just over in Ross co O Ref Bk 3 p 38 Will of Joshiah Reeves Circleville, Pickaway co O; Marriage Rec Bk 3 p 2 p 26 p 146. Rept by Pickaway Plains chpt. (Similar and conflicting data on this and Josias Sr. next below, must be left to investigator as each fr authentic source. J D).

REEVES, JOSIAS SR., Pickaway co

Soldr Rev War B Charles co Md Oct 1760 (old style) d at his res in Pickaway co Sept 22 1841. After the Rev settled in Culpepper co Va whence he emigrated to O in 1824; left an aged widow with whom he lived 60 yr; left many desc. Cop fr Ohio State Journal of Oct 6 1841. Rept by Blanche Rings.

REEVES, NATHAN, Ross co

Rev soldr d around Oec 10 1831. Ref Chillicothe Advertiser of Dec 10 1831 fr H C Pemberton's copy. Rept by Mrs. Orion King.

REEVES, WILLIAM, Brown co

Listed p 287 "Va Milit in Rev". Enl in Prince Wm co Va Oct 1 1780. Then res there dschrgd Mar 1781 (appl); served 7 mo. B Apr 8 1765 Prince William co Va. Moved to Ky 1790 whr lived 22 yrs then to Brown co O thence to Scott twp in Brown co. Pensr of Washington twp Brown co. Ref S 17645 Va Rept by State D A R.

REILY, JAMES, Trumbull co

B 1761 D Feb 5 1834. Ref Pa Arch. Rept by Hetuck Chpt.

REMINGTON, ANTHONY, Portage co

Pens claim lists service fr 1776-1781 as marine and soldr. B 4-4-1758; mar Hannah in Mar 1782 at Westerly R I (she d at Fowler O at home of dau) Chldr: Rhoda, Joseph; Fannie; Charles; Huldah; Hannah; Sally; Morey (Merey); Lyman; Virgilous; Anthony Rice; Lyman 2nd. Soldr d at Freedom Portage co O Nov 30 1833 and is prob bur there. Rept by Mary Chesney chpt.

RENESON, WILLIAM, Belmont co

Pvt Mass Contl. Enl in winter of 1775 as res of Tuscarawas Valley Pa, srvd 6 1-2 mo; b 1757. Since Rev livd in Washington co Pa 8 or 9 yr; thence to Cross Creek for 1 yr then to Ohio and into Belmont Co Appl for pens Belmont co O Nov 19 1832 Ref S 4060 Pa. Rept by State D A R.

REYNOLDS, GEORGE, Muskingum co

Ensign, N J line 1 yr. Enl Oct 1775; pens'd 11-3-1818 Muskingum co O. Trnsfrd to the District of Columbia in 1820; b Oct 1757; mar a widower in 1820; chldr: Catharine Jane ae 13; Rebecca Mary 10; William Morton 8; (1820). Ref New Jersey S 36255 Rept by State D A R.

REYNOLD, JAMES, Muskingum co

Pvt of Marines Contl Navy; enl at Philadelphia 1775; b 1750. A gr son James E Reynolds wrote for infor abt serv of this soldr Jan 6 1849 stating he had been dead many yrs.. Appl for pens Muskingum co O Nov 12 1832 as res Rich Hill twp. Ref S 4078 Pa Sea Service. Rept by State D A R.

REYNOLDS, JOHN, Fairfield co

Pvt Pa Contl pensr in Fairfield co 10-21-1833; b 1754; d 1833. In 1840 Census, "John Runnels" ae 89 was living in Clear Creek twp. Ref p 406 Fairfield co Hist (Wiseman) name appears in list pioneer people. Cop by Jane Dailey. Ref Pa Arch V 10 S 2 p 557 given by Mary Chesney chpt.

REYNOLDS, JOSEPH, Brown co

Pvt Capt Peter Van Vorts Co 13th Regt Albany co N Y Milit; b 1749 Rensselaer co N Y; mar Experience Davis; chldr: Joseph Jr mar Jane Abbott 1804; Lettie mar Samuel Dixon; Hannah mar John Abbott Mar 1 1804; Roxie mar Terry Womacks 1815. Soldr d 1824 Brown co O. Bought 1250 A in Eagle twp 1800 whr had a hand mill, later a horse mill. Ref V 106 No. 105213 D A R Lin; Beers Hist Brown co pp 659, 543, 581 and 275 in Biog sect. Rept by Jane Dailey and Meryl Markley.

REYNOLDS, JUSTUS, Hamilton co

Enl Litchfield co Conn Apr or May 1777 to Jan 1 1781 musician under Capts Mat-lock and Munson Cols Chandler and Meigs Conn; b abt 1761; mar Mary; chldr: Nancy Mary Ann; George W; Thomas I. Pensd 1818 Hamilton co O being 57 yr old. Ref Dept Int E W S 40319 Conn. Rept by Nabby Lee Ames chpt, Helen Townsend.

REYNOLDS, NATHANIEL, Adams co

Pvt in Co commanded by Col Tompkins Va line for 7 mos. Enl 1781 King William co Va; pensd Sept 25 1833 ae 71; Ref Cens 1840 ae 77 liv in Green twp Adams co, S 15615 Va. Rept by State D A R.

RHINER, GEORGE, Gallia co

Exec Doc 37 of 1852. Refused a pens as servd less than 6 mo. Rept by Wm Pettit.

RHOADS, GEORGE, Mahoning co

Pvt 4th class Ser 5 V 8 p 402 June 1782 Pa Arch Capt Richard Shaw. Soldr d abt 1825 Springfield twp; ref Will bk 4 p 681 Rhoads Geo Columbiana co Rec prob 1825 Heirs not named; Deed bk W pp 229 230 trnscrbd Mahoning co. Rept by Mahoning chpt.

RHOADES, SAMUEL, Medina co

Pvt May 1775. 8 mo under Capt Seth Ballard Jan 1776; 12 mo under Samuel Par-sons Sept 1777; 4 mo under Harvey Sept 1777; May 1778 2 mo under David Shay. In battles of Forge Point and Saratoga. B 9-25-1753 at Stoughtingham Mass; Son of Samuel and Abigail (Thorp) Rhoades; mar Mary Morse 11-21-1773 at Walpole Mass; chldr: Jabez; Polly; Ireney; Andrew; Francis; Samuel; Jesse; Elias. Soldr d 2-9-1832 at Guilfard (later called Seville) Medina co O. Bur at Seville O. In 1850 cem replatted. Inscrpt on monument of wife "Mary, wife of Samuel Rhodes, died Nov 21 1837 ae 81 yr 5 mo 7 da." A sunken grave adjoining with a 15 ft pine tree growingwhere stone would be is thot to be grave of Samuel. Ref No. 196473 D A R. Rept by Jonathan Dayton chpt, Dayton O.

RHODES, WILLIAM, Champaign co

Pvt Va line; enl 9-1-1775 2nd Regt Va line 3 yrs. Pensd 7-30-1819 Champaign co Ohio; ae 77 yrs in 1822. Mentions a wife and 3 chldr ae 14, 11, and 17 yrs in 1819. Ref S 1324; B L Wt 1026-100. Rept by State D A R.

RIALL, ISAAC, Lawrence co

Pvt N J Milit enl Aug 1776 Morris co N J. Served 13 mos; b July 9 1760 Morris co N J; when about 24 yrs of ae went to Summerset co N J; 1820 to Washington co Pa; Apr 1832 to Lawrence co O. Appl for pens Lawrence co O Mar 12 1833. Ref S 4770 N J. Rept by State D A R.

RICE, BENJAMIN, ? co

Listed in rejected pens appl ref Doc No. 31 Jan 6 1831 as not being in indigent circumstances accd to Act of May 1830 Rept by Blanche Rings.

RICE, CHARLES, Meigs co

Pvt Mass contl pensr in Meigs co 4-24-1833; b Jan 26 1750 Sudbury Mass. Near close of war movd to New Hampshire; 20 yrs later to Meigs co. Ref S 4091 Mass. Rept by Mrs. John Chase, Jonathan Meigs chpt.

RICE, DANIEL, Wood co

Rev soldr d 1830; bur first at Grand Rapids O; later movd to Beaver Creek cem S E of Grand Rapids. His son Isaac was a pioneer of Crawford co and in this line are Dr Chas Tritch Findlay O and James Gillespie Bowling Green. Rept by Georgia D Kimmons, Bowling Green O.

RICE, JAMES, Brown co

Pvt Va Contl two yrs as pvt. Enl July 1775 in King William Court House Va. Dischrgd Oct 17 1777; b 1755; chldr: Michael; Anetta; Betsey; Corneli; Parthena; a son Phillip resided in O; Appl for pension in Brackin co Ky July 30 1823 then in Mason co Ky Jan 28 1824 and in Franklin Brown co O in Sept 4, 1833. Ref Va S 40332; Beers Brown co Hist, p 293. Rept by State D A R.

RICE, LEWIS, Summit co

A Summit co hist states the "gun he used in Rev is still preserved by the family." B probably Conn; bur Darrowville O. Cop by Mabel Steele Taylor, Akron.

RICHARDS, JACOB, Champaign co

Pvt Va Contl. Pensr in Champaign co 1-25-1831. Enl in Augusta Co Va in May 1778 or 79; b 1761; mar Margaret ae 52 yr; chldr: Dorcas ae 13 yr in 1829. Ref Va S 40334. Rept by State D A R.

RICHARDS, JAMES, Adams co

See Richardson, James for data this vol. Erroneously pensd under this name also. (J D).

RICHARDS, JESSE, Wayne co

Enl 1775 Pa. Res in Redner twp Pa Contl pvt; servd 6 mos; b Feb 10, 1756 Chester co Pa. After Rev in Chester co Pa 14 yrs. Thence to Steubenville O whr livd abt 7 yrs thence to Wayne co O. Pensr in 1840 æ 84 living in East Union, Wayne co with James McFadden appl Oct 1 1832. Ref S 4108 Pa Wooster. Wayne chpt repts his will names Eliza his wife and also gives to James McFadden some of his chattels. Rept by State D A R.

RICHARDS, THOMAS, Portage co

Pvt N H Contl. Enl Penmont N H Mar 1776 in the Co of Capt John Strong. Servd 1 yr; b 1753 mar Cynthia Jan 1779; chldr: Rodolphus and Augustus S; Russell; Cynthia; Bruce; Thomas E; William L; Soldr d 1-14-1826. Appl for transfer fr N Y to Portage co O 10-18-1827 whr he resided with his son. Widow appl for a pens in Holcomb ? co Mich 7-4-1836. Ref N H W 5709. Rept by State D A R.

RICHARDSON, DANIEL, Cuyahoga co

Pvt N H Contl. Srvd 11 mos 14 das. Enl 1779 in Goffstown N H Was b 1764. Pens appl 11-5-1832 Cuyahoga co O. Ref N H S 4110. Rept by State D A R.

RICHARDSON, DAVID, Muskingum co

Corp in Capt Elijah Robinsons co Col Elys Regt. Was b 1757 Stonington, Conn. Mar 1785 to Sarah Hudson (1762-1848). One son Alpheus. Soldr d 1843, Otsego O Ref No. 118185 D A R Lin. Cop by Jane Dailey.

RICHARDSON, GERSHAM, Lorain co

Pvt in Capt Elijah Robinson Col Roger Enos State of Conn; six mo service fr May 1778. Was b Oct 17, 1761 Stafford Conn. Son of Gersham Richardson and Abigail Fuller. Mar Rebacah Pasko Dec 5 1782 (she d 1847 ae 89; bur by his side) A son mar a daughter of Peter Rice. Soldr d January 4 1849 at Amherst O; bu Kendeighs Corner Cem Amherst east of center of cem. Grave mrkd by slab stone w usual dates as above. Also marker. Pens appl Sept 4 1832 in New Haven Oswego co N Y. Trnsfr 1835 to Cuyahoga co O whr in 1840 liv w Jane Crossing. Ref S 16237 Conn; Rec Stafford. Conn through Town Clerk. Rept by Nathan Perry chpt and State D A R.

RICHARDSON, JAMES, Adams co

Pvt Va Contl. Enl May 1776 Va. Dischrgd Mar 1778 in N J. Then reenlisted in May in Va. Srvd till close of war. He was erroneously pensd again under name of James Richards; b 1753; d Jan 16, 1833 (Date verified by Meryl Markley but under name of James Richards Ref p 331 Evans and Stivers Adams co Hist) Res Adams co O June 5 1818; res same place 1820. Ref S 40345 Va. Rept by State D A R.

RICHARDSON, JEREMIAH, Licking co

Pa service under investigation. Fr Bucks co Pa; d 1822 nr Newark O. Rept by Joseph Spencer chpt.

RICHARDSON, JOSHUA, Clermont co

Pvt Mass Contl. Enl 1775 Middlesex co Mass; srvd 1 yr; b 1760. On appl 1820 named wf Betsy ae 60; chldr: Betsy ae 20; Polly 17; a Granddau Issabella Richardson ae 9. Soldr d 1-14-1837. Appl for pens 6-5-1818 in Clermont co O. Ref Mass S 40333. Rept by State D A R.

RICHARDSON, MATTHEW, Butler co

Pvt Kent co Md under command of Wm Henry who marched fr said Co Jan 29 1776 and then stationed in Northampton co Va. Ref Md in Rev p 646; Md Arch Vol 11 pp 298-9; and V 18 pp 646. Was b Kent co Md Sept 8 1757; d Jan 1 1838 Butler co; mar Ann Stockton (dau of Major Richard Witham Stockton, a Tory Major) chldr: Sarah; Maria; Rebecca; Betsey; Matthew Jr; Matthew Richardson made the first land in Milford twp 1802; gave the first church and ground for cem in Milford twp. Soldr bur on his farm but later removed to the cem in Collinsville Milford twp Butler co. Ref Hist of Butler co O. Rept by Mrs. W C Moore, Col O

RICHARDSON, SAMUEL, Warren co

Pvt Md Contl. Pensr in Warren co 6-1-1819. Enl 1779 Hagerstown (he thinks) Md. Regt commanded by Col Parsons 5th Md Regt for term of war. Was at Battle of Guilford C H, Eutaw Springs. Was b 1753. Made appl for pens June 26 1818 Warren co O and again 1820 stating none of his family had resided with him during last 25 yrs. Ref S 40346 Md. Rept by State D A R.

RICHEARD (Richard), PETER, Montgomery co

Pvt Fifth S Pa Arch v 240 Vii 153. Family bur in Worman cem Clay twp. Wf d 1829 ae 76. Rept by Wm Pettit.

RICKABAUGH, ADAM, Gallia co

Pvt Va Milit. Pensr in Gallia co 4-15-1833; fr Shenandoah co. Srvd under Col Brown, 2-1-1777 and 1778 Col McCoy 1781. Was b Jan 3 1761 Shenandoah co Va; son of Adam Rickabaugh Sr. Mar Mary Kuntz May 1 1790; chldr: Elizabeth; Peter, Ann; Mary; Joe; Rachel; Adam; William; Mahala; and unnamed baby d in infancy; Soldr d July 23, 1836, Gallia co O. Bur in family cem on Harry Woods farm nr Rio Grande Gallia co O. Also fought in War 1812 under Capt Isaac Butler and Capt Daniel Womeldorff. Ref Miss Gertude C Allen, 139 West Second St. Chillicothe O No. 221603. Rept by French Colony chpt.

RICKART (not Rickhart), LEONARD, Butler co

Pvt N C Milit. He with his father's wagon and 2 horses were pressed into service of the army at Salisbury N C. Srvd 11 mos. Was b 1765; mar Mary Shafer June 14, 1785; d Aug 22 1839 Greene co Ill. Pens appl Aug 2 1832 Butler co O. Ref W 26,385 N C. Rept by State D A R.

RICKEY (Richey), ROBERT, Butler co

Sergt Va Contl. Enl Aug 10 1776 Stanton Va; dischgd 1778; srvd 2 yr. Was b 1750. Had 4 daughters of whom 2 were idiots. Pens appl Dec 1 1819 in Butler co O. Ref Va S 40342. Rept by State D A R.

RICKETTS, EDMUND, Fairfield co

Pa Arch S 5 Vol 4; b 1758 Washington co Md; d 1833; mar Milicent Green. Ref S A R 52610. By Wm Pettit.

RICKETTS, EDWARD, Fairfield co

Exec Doc 37 of 1852. Was refused a pens as he could not furnish proof of his commission as an officer. Rept by Wm Pettit.

RICKETTS, WILLIAM, Hamilton co

Exec Doc 37 of 1852. Refused a pens as servd less than 6 mo. Rept by Wm Pettit.

RICKEY, CORNELIUS, Stark co

Pvt N J Contl. Enl April 1778 Capt Bellards Co. Was b 4-22-1761 in Bernands twp N J; d 4-11-1834 Stark co O leaving five heirs. Resided in Northumberland co Pa till he movd to Wash co Pa whr he liv 7 or 8 mos and movd to Steubenville O. Later movd to Stark co O and into Pike twp. Pens Stark co O 8-5-1833. Ref New York S 4096 Pa. Rept by State D A R.

RICKEY, JOSEPH, Highland co

Pvt Pa Milit and Md Lines; records corrected 3-21-1804. Was b 6-7-1748 in Tyrone co Ireland. In 1771 he emigrated to Chester co Pa fr which place he movd to Cumberland co and there he enl in 1777. Abt 1822 he movd to Richland co O. Pens appl in Richland co O 9-17-1832. Ref Md Pa S 4100; Will filed in Richland co Ct House No. 181 Dec 1837. Rept by Jared Mansfield chpt.

RIDDEN (Redden), CHRISTOPHER, Portage co

Pvt and corp N J Milit. Enl at Barnett twp Somerset co N J. 4 mos and 15 das as corp and 4 mos as pvt Was b 8-19-1753 Woodbridge twp N J; d 2-9-1841. Resided in N J and then mvd to Washington co Pa; lvd there 10 yrs; thence to Partage co O. Pens appl 10-16-1832 res Hiram twp Portage co O. Ref N J S 4059. Rept by State D A R.

RIDER, ADAM, Ross co

Pvt Va Contl. Enl in Va Line 1775. Servd 4 yr. Was b 1758; had 3 chldr and one grandchild. Soldr d 2-21-1826. (Newspaper item) Pens appl 7-20-1818 Ross co O. Ref Contl Va S 40341. Rept by State D A R.

RIDER, JOHN, Athens co

Lancaster co Pa milit; 5th S Vol 7 p 646; b 1753 Holland; d 1850; mar Margaret Engle. Rept by Wm Pettit.

RIDGEWAY, SAMUEL, Pike co

Pvt S C Milit. Enl July 1 1778 in Craven co S C whr he lvd. Was b 1767 Buckingham co Va; movd to S C with father; Movd to O in 1803 Ross co; thence to Pike co. Pens appl Pike co Ohio 10-3-1833. S C S 4119. Rept by State D A R.

RIDLIN, JOHN, Auglaize co

Pvt Mass Contl. Enl 1781 in Mass; srvd 3 yrs. Was b 1752; mar Sarah; a dau Abigail ae 22 in 1820. Pensd in Licking co O 4-28-1818. Ref Mass S 49331; B L Wt 34855-160-55. Rept by State D A R.

RIENHART (Rinehart), MARTIN, Butler co

Pvt Pa Milit. Drafted May 1779 Buffalo twp Northumberland co Pa. Srvd 1 yr fr 1779. Was b Jan 12 1759 Berks co Pa. Bur Millville Bethel cem Butler co O whr he had appl for pens July 30 1830. Ref S 4114 Pa and 4th Rept N S D A R p 295. Rept by State D A R.

RIGGS, Eleazer, Warren co

Exec Doc 37 of 1852. Refused a pens as service was as privateer. Rept by Wm Pettit.

RIGGS, GIDEON, Clermont co

Pvt Mass Contl. Enl Mar 1776 in N J Artillery Co com by Capt Daniel Neale; servd 1 yr. Was b 1763. In appl mentions wf old and infirm and a step daughter who has 3 chldr, oldest 13 or 14. Pens appl in Clermont co O. Mar 3 1818 and again 4-9-1828. Ref Contl N J S 40330. Rept by State D A R.

RIGGS, JAMES, Washington co

Srvd in Pa Regulars Res during war Bedfar co Pa. Was b 1742 Rock Creek Montgomery co Md; d 1818; bur new cem on hill at Matamoras O. Grave mrkd by Marietta chpt 1934. Ref D A R Mag Oct 1929 p 632. Rept by Marietta chpt.

RIGGS, JOHN, Brown co

7th Md reg Frederick Md. Bur Flaugher cem Huntington twp nr Aberdeen. Rept by Mrs. J K Cecil, 530 Kellog Ave, Palo Alto, Cal. to Meryl B Markley.

RILEA (Riley), RICHARD, Brown co

Pvt Va Contl. Enl for 3 yrs Mar 1779 in Leesburg Va. Dischrgd at end of war in Charlestown S C. Was b Mar 27, 1762. Mar Rhoda, June 19 1793. Chldr: Able ae 15; Lavinia 12; Wm 10; Sarah 7; Joseph 2; John. (appl of 1821). Soldr d Aug 7 1839 Brown co O; bur Mt Carmel cem. Grave mrkd by stone with dates legible. Res Brown co O May 8 1819; liv in Washington twp 1825. Was a carpenter and twp trustee 1826 for 3 terms. Wid appl for pens Brown co O Oct 4, 1839. Ref W 2167 Contl and Va in Rev p 287. Rept by State D A R and Taliaferro chpt.

RILEY, JOSEPH, Medina co

Pvt Conn Milit. Drafted Aug 1776 Hartford co Conn. Srvd 6 mos and 14 days. Was b Sept 15 1752 Hartford co Conn. Pens appl Medina co O July 13 1833 Res of Copley twp. Ref S 4105 Conn. Rept by State D A R.

RINEY, JOHN, Knox co

Cens 1840 liv in Chester twp Knox co ae 80 (b 1760) cop by Jane Dailey.

RINGLAND, JOHN, ? co

Quartermaster. Listed in rejected pens appl. Ref: Doc No. 31 Jan 6 1831 as srvd in a Regt not on contl estab. Rept by Blanche Rings.

RIPLEY, JACOB, Jefferson co

Pvt Sergt Pa St Trps. Enl Bedford co Pa liv Path Valley Pa. Servd 13 mos. Was b 1756 near Carlisle Pa. In appl 1833 states he had 3 daus living in Jefferson co O. D Nov 14 1835 Jefferson co O. Aft Rev livd nr Hagerstown Md. Last 20 yrs in Morgan co Va whr he appl for pens Nov 26 1832 and Jefferson co O Oct 1 1833. Lately removd fr Va. Ref S 4768 Pa. Rept by State D A R.

RISING, BENJAMIN, Lorain co

Pvt and sergt Mass St Trps. Enl soon aft Battle at Lexington in Hartford co Conn. Was b Sept 22 1748 Suffield Hartford co Conn. A gr-son Chauncey Parker b 1812 livd with him in Medina co. Soldr d Mar 19 1846 Lorain co O; survived by two chldr: Oliver ae 65; Polly. After Rev livd in Hampshire co Mass and in 1818 movd to Lorain co O. Pens appl Medina co 1826 and Lorain co Aug 16 1832. Ref S 9086 Conn. Rept by State D A R.

RITTER, JACOB, Mahoning co

Pvt 5th Battl Philidelphia. Ref Pa Arch Ser 5 V 6 p 16. Soldr d abt 1817 Canfield O. He came to O in 1805. Ref Hist Trumbull and Mahoning co V 2 p 42; Deed bk B p 19 trnscrbd Mahoning co to Jacob Ritter 1803; Western Reserve Chronicle Dec 6 1817. Est Jacob Ritter Canfield O; Mahoning Despatch July 2 1897. Rept by Mahoning chpt.

RITTER, TIMOTHY, Ashtabula co

Soldr d 1848; bur Windsor O Ashtabula co. Grave located by Mary Stanley chpt. Ref 18 and 21 Rept N S D A R p 246 and 108. Cop by Nathan Perry chpt.

ROACH, WILLIAM, Washington co

Was b 1731; d March 7 1818; bur Deval cem nr Coal Run. Ref Rev service Mass Soldrs and Sailors V XIII p 362-363. Rept by Marietta chpt.

ROACH, WILLIAM, Jefferson co

Pvt Pa contl. Srvd 3 yrs. Was b 1750. In 1820 appl mentions wf ae 66 and a son ae 18; pensd in Jefferson co 5-1-1819. In 1840 ae 100 pensr liv in Ross twp Jefferson co O with Jeremiah Roach, Ref S 40350 Pa. Rept by State D A R.

ROADS (Reed), JOHN

Pvt listed in rejected pens appl. Ref: Doc No. 31 Jan 6 1831 as servd in a Co not on the Contl estab. Rept by Blanche Rings.

ROAFF, PETER, Montgomery co

Pvt Md Contl enl June 11 1777; servd 1 yr. Was b 1761. Pens appl July 24 1821 in Montgomery co O. Ref Contl Md S 40352. Rept by State D A R.

ROBERTS, JOSEPH, Mahoning co

Pvt Ser 5 V 2 p 841 Pa Arch Capt John Irwin. Mar Elizabeth; chldr: William; Henry; Elizabeth mar —— Woodward; Hannah mar Thorn; Sarah mar —— Fullerton; Caroline mar —— Johnson; Jane mar —— Knox; Mary Ann. Soldr d 1836 Jackson, Mahoning co. Ref Will bk 8 p 281 Trumbull co Records Prob 1836. Rept by Mahoning chpt.

ROBERTS, WM, Ross co

Pvt Va Milit Enl 1 1-2 yrs prior to surrender of Lord Cornwallis. Servd 9 mos. Was b 1765-6 Frederick co Va. Livd in Frederick co Va on the Shenandoah river end of war. Movd to Harrison co Va and aft Indian Wars were over movd to Ross co O. Appl for pens in Ross co O 6-14-1834. Ref Va S 7497. Rept by State D A R.

ROBINS, WILLIAM, Carroll co

Pvt N J Contl Pensr on Ohio Rolls 1-8-1820; serv under Col Ogden Regt 3 yr. Was b Mar 1861. Mar Elizabeth (b May 10 1766) Oct 25 1789 in Bucks co Pa, by Rev Nathaniel Irving of Preb Cr. Chldr: William Robins Jr ae 26 an invalid; Elizabeth b 1804; Ruel b 1806; Rebecca b 1809; Martha b 1811; (named in appl for pens 1820). A son John makes sworn testimony 12-1-1840 fr Lee twp Carroll co O. Soldr d Aug 7 1837 Carroll co O at his home. Soldr & wf came fr East to Uniontown Pa Fayette co thence to O whr resided abt 26 yr in neighborhood. (Nov 30-1840). Ref W 4782 N J. Widow pens Jan 4 1841; in Nov 1840 resid in Lee twp Carroll co. Rept by Jane Dailey.

ROBINSON, DANIEL, Portage co and N Y

Srvd 3 yrs. Pensd 11-29-1819 Boston twp Portage co O Wid pensd 9-7-1853 Albany N Y. Was b 1763; mar Jane Robinson? 11-25-1827; chldr: John ae 14; Susan and

Sarah (who livd in N H with a companion of his); Sylvester b May 1814 resided with soldr (appl of 1821). Soldr d 2-19-1852 Hannibal N Y. Ref Mass W 584 B L Wt 36562-160-55. Rept by State D A R.

ROBINSON, JOHN 2nd, Harrison co

Pvt Md. Enl 5-4-1778 at Piscatawa ? Md. Was b 1751; d 6-11-1819. Appl for a pens in Harrison co O 5-21-1818. Ref Md S 40355. Rept by State D A R.

ROBINSON, JOHN, Mahoning co

Pvt. Ser 6 V 1 pp 642, 653, 656, Pa Arch. Also records N Y, Conn, Mass, Del, Va. Mar Fanny (Frances); chldr: Sara; William; Martha; Mary; Fanegan. Soldr d abt 1824 Springfield twp. Came to Columbiana co (Mahoning now) 1802. Ref Columbiana co; Will bk 4 p 623; Columbiana co Records — Prob 1824; Deed bk O pp 3 4 5 Trnscbd Mahoning co fr John and Frances Robinson 1805. Rept by Mahoning chpt.

ROBINSON, MAXIMILLIAN, Licking co

Enl Fauquier co Va 1776 3 yr under Capt Wm Blackwell and Gabriel Long; Col Morgans 11th Va Regt. Was b 1750 or 1752 in Va. Mar Lucinda Gundy (b 1753). A son was Benjamin mar Phebe Grant. Soldr d 1831 in Brownsville O. Pens appl 5-5-1818 in Licking co O. Ref V 106 D A R Lin 105902 and S 40353 Va. Rept by State D A R.

ROBINSON, PETER, Ross co

Rev soldr pensioner ae 84 yr living in 1840 in Scioto twp Ross co O. Rept by Mrs. Orion King.

ROGERS, EDWARD, Medina co

Seaman U S Navy pensr. Enl New London Conn 1775. Srvd 1 yr. Was b Nov 28 1753 New London Conn whr wf d. After Rev lvd in New London Conn for several yrs. Aft wf d movd to Landisfield Mass. Thence to Medina co O. Appl for pens Medina co O Oct 22, 1832, res of Brunswick twp. Ref S 4795 Conn Sea Service. Rept by State D A R.

ROGERS, JOSEPH, Ashtabula co

Pvt N Y Contl Enl April 1780 Orange co N Y and again in 1782. Was b 1764 in New York; d 1844. Pensr in Tompkins co N Y. Trnsfd to Ashtabula co O 9-25-1833 whr in 1840 liv in Denmark twp ae 87. Ref N Y S 11322. Rept by State D A R.

ROGERS, THORNE, Columbiana co

Rev Soldr. Rec not yet found. Son Thomas mar Hope Russell (b Burlington N J); gr son James (b 1812 Burlington N J). Soldr bur Old cem East Palestine Unity twp. Ref S A R 1912 yr bk Hist Upper Ohio Valley p 188 Vol 2. Rept by Mrs. Wilma M Molsberry.

ROGERS, NATHANIEL, MAJOR, ? co

Listed in news clipping by LAA, found in old scrap bk, as Rev soldr who participated in or interested in settlement of Marietta; with few exceptions they (who have descendants in this section) are bur Washington co cem; many active in Indian war at own expense never reimbursed by U S. filed here for cont investigation, as almost half have been verified. List fr Marietta chpt.

ROGERS, WM, ? co

Name fr scrap bk clipping same as described above for Nathaniel Rogers. Filed here for investigation.

ROGERS, WM, Adams co

Pvt N J Contl. Enl May 1777. Dischrgd May 1780. Srvd 3 yrs. Was b 1754; appl mentions chldr: Darius ae 58; Abigail 14. Soldr d in Spencer O; bur there. Res Adams co O June 12, 1818 and 20. Ref 3rd Rept N S D A R p 229; S 40365 Contl N J. Rept by Nathan Perry chpt and State D A R.

ROLL, ABRAHAM, Hamilton co

Pvt Patriot furnished material aid to Contl army. Was b 1759, N J; mar Patty Vance (1763-1843) chldr: Samuel; John. Soldr d 1827 Hamilton co O; bur Springdale Presbyterian ch cem in oldest part; no stone. Soldr went to O 1800 Springdale Farm before 1809. Name Tax List Springfield twp Ham co O 1809. One of the founders of Christian New Light Church Mt Healthly; to Burlington 1800. Ref No. 121381 D A R Lin V 122. Rept by Mrs. James Roll Glendale O. Cincinnati chpt.

ROLL, JOHN JR., ? co

Pvt Morris co N J Milit. Was b Germany. Son of John Roll. Mar Rachel Van Winkle (d 1768). One son was Abraham. Soldr d in Ohio. Cop fr No. 121831 D A R Lin V 122 by Jane Dailey.

ROLLISON, ROBERT, Brown co

Rev soldr liv in Eagle creek twp Brown co. Ref No data found. Rept by Taliafero chpt.

ROOT, DANIEL, Geauga co

Conn Serv under Col Wollcott, 1776; b 1751 England; d 1820; Mar Anna Pease 12-12-177—; Ref 50688 S A R. Rept by Wm Pettit.

ROOT, ELIJAH, ? co

Pvt listed in rejected pens appl ref: Doc No. 31, Jan 6 1831 as did not serve required nine mo. Rept by Blanche Rings.

ROSE, JACOB, Delaware co

N Y Line. Enl Rochester N Y 1778. Dischrgd 1783 Sneekhill N Y. Was b Apr 21 1761 Leobarrie N Y (fr family record) son of Wm Rose and Elizabeth; mar Liza or Lizza Bowker Aug 5 1784; chldr: William; Jacob; Cynthia; Jerusha; Isaac; Samuel; Silas; Sally; Orsamus B. Soldr d Aug 28 1839 Delaware co O. Appl for pens Tompkins co N Y Nov 27 1818 also in 1828. Pensr 7-27-1833 in Delaware co O whr widow appld for pens 8-15-1843 whl resid Trenton twp. (Compare Jacob Roosa p 313 Vol 1 of Roster) Ref W 4578 N Y. Rept by State D A R.

ROSEBOOM, JOHN, Montgomery co

Resident of Dayton 1832 applied for pens but rejected on gr that further proof of living witnesses required. Rept by State Secy S A R Wm Pettit.

ROSS, EZEKIEL, Butler co

Pvt N J Milit Enl Essex co N J 1776 whr he livd. Srvd 2 yrs. Was b 1756 nr Westfield N J; mar Ruth Maxwell (1756-1819). One son was Amos. Soldr d Butler co Millville O. Pensr 3-24-1834 Butler co Hanover twp O. Ref S 7490 N J; No. 17483 D A R; 4th Rept N S D A R p 295. Rept by State D A R and Mrs. Oehlke, Nathan Perry chpt.

ROSS, JOHN, Warren co

Pvt 6th class 8th Co 7th Battl fr Juniata co Pa 1780 and 1781 under Capt James Harrell and Col Pury. Ref Pa Arch 5th S Vol 5 pp 489 496. Soldr b nr Belfast Ireland

1757. Mar 1778 in Ireland to Jennette Irwin wou of James Irwin (fr will of Jas Irwin probated Nov 2 1803 Mifflin co Pa); chldr: William; James; Ann Ross Macready; Hannah Ross Willoughby; George; John; Samuel; Clendenin; Williamson; Robert Irwin; Joseph who d without issue; (76 grand-children). Soldr d 1820 Warren co O bur Stewart, now Union, Warren co O. Rept by Sycamore chpt. Grave markd by May (Ross) Ludwick, new marker 1934. He and 3 bro came to America in 1778 located in Mifflin-town Pa where he livd until 1812 when they emigrated to Ohio locating at a tavern Station known as Twenty-Mile Stand. Here he d. Never secured pension. Ref No. 283485 D A R. Secured fr Roy H. Ross Urbana O thru Mrs. Kate Mason Hawes, Marietta.

ROSS, MATTHIAS, Hamilton co

Ensign in Capt Elijah Squires co 2 nd reg N J milit. b Springfield N J; mar Mary Halsey (d 1826). One son was Ogden. d 1826 Cincinnati O. Cop fr D A R Lin 123 p 297 No. 122972 by Jane Dailey.

ROSS, ROBERT, Madison co

Exec Doc 37 of 1852. Refused a pens as servd less than 6 mo. Rept by Wm Pettit.

ROUNDS, JAMES, Brown co

Pvt Mass Contl. Enl 12 mos in 1775; honorably dischrgd 8-9 mo later. Enl again 1777 in Jan; dischrgd 1780. Served 3 yrs. Was b 1766. Mar Elizabeth Woodruff Jan 1817. Soldr d Jan 3 1843 Brown co O. Pensr 1840 ae 82 liv Clark twp Brown co. His widow later appl for a pension in Putnam co Ind. Ref Mass W 7149. Rept by State D A R.

ROUNDS, LEMUEL, Brown co

Pvt R I Contl. Pensr Brown co 8-23-1828. Also V 124 p 85 D A R Lin says: pvt 1775-76 under Capt Lane Col Varnum Mass Trps. Was b 1756 Buxton Me. Mar 1781 Mary (or Molly) Whitney (b 1764). Chldr: Patience b 1783 mar Bradbury; Miriam mar Wm Gould in Brown co; Elizabeth Lemaster; Mary File; Susannah Park; Lemuel. Soldr d 1836 Brown co O. Ref V 124 D A R Lin No. 123254; and Dept Int. Will Pro 1836 Brown co Vol 1 p 332. Rept by Jane Dailey; Nathan Perry chpt and Meryl Markley.

ROSS, REUBEN, Hamilton co

Pvt Md Contl Capt Alex Smiths co and Col Rawlings. Was b 1755, Harford co Md. One son was Robert. Soldr d 1855, Hamilton co O. Pensr in Clermont co 6-13-1820. Ref V 121 p 220 D A R Lin No. 120707. Rept by Jane Dailey and Nathan Perry chpt.

ROUSE, JOHN, Washington co

Said to be Rev soldr; b 1741 d 1818. No other data. Rept by Helen Sloane, Marietta.

ROUSE, THOMAS, Jefferson co

Pvt Pa St Trps. Enl 1781 Washington Pa whr then res. Srvd 1 yr. Was b 1762 Queen Ann co Md. Mar Nancy 1798. One dau was Ann. Soldr d Aug 27 1832. Since Rev livd on Buffalo in Pa. Some yrs in O before it was a State on Short Creek. Since has livd Brook co, Va Belmont, Monroe, Guernsey cos O and for his last yr in Jefferson co O. Appl for pens Jefferson co O Oct 22 1832 res Smithfield twp. Wid appl Monroe co O Feb 18 1856. Res Wayne twp and Washington co O Feb 20 1832. Ref W 9629 B L Wt 61067-160-55 Pa. Rept by State D A R.

ROUT (Routt), WILLIAM, Pickaway co

Servd as Pvt and corp in Capt Ball co 5th Va Regt commanded by Col Chas Scott Sept 28 1776 Apr 1 1777. Was b 1749 Stafford co Va; son of Peter Rout; mar Ann Staege (now Stage); chldr: Bushrod Jefferson; Frances or Fanny mar John Anderson; Matilda mar Richard Ward. Soldr d Dec 1831 near Ashville Pickaway co. Bur in old Route cem abt 1 1-2 E of Ashville on Wm Whileheads frm. Soldr came to O frm Va and livd and d in Harrison twp. Ref Will bk 1-2 p 134 5 VR-W D 104-1. Rept by Miss Alice Stene Worthington O, Pickaway Plains chpt.

ROWELL, DANIEL, Athens co and Ill.

Pvt N H Contl. d 1847 Paris Ill whr movd. Inscript on marker (D A R) Courthouse yd Paris Ill. Soldr came to Athens co 1810 fr Parkersburg Va. In 1845 went to Ill to live with dau. Raised his family in Lee twp Athens co O. Pensr in Athens co 6-10-1820. Ref Mrs. W J Warren (a gr gr dau) Fort Morgan Colo V 5 V 6 Deeds Athens co name appears. Rept by Jane Dailey.

ROWLAND, HEZEKIAH, Huron co

Servd in nearly the whole period of the Rev war. Mar Grace Rowland a sister to the wf of Capt Samuel Husted. Nancy Rowland mar Ezra Wood. The families livd in Putman co N Y in 1818 when Hezekiah Rowland came to Clarksfield to work in Capt Husted's grist mill. Soldr d there; bur Clarksfield cem. For several yrs operated the Haysville mill. His chldr were: Aaron; Levi; Esther; Nancy. Ref Firelands Pioneers N S Vol 12 pp 431 432. Rept by Marjorie Cherry.

ROWLAND, LUKE, Huron co

Was b Cannon Conn May 12 1758; mar Elizabeth Knickerbocker. Chldr Olive; Jas; Jos; Wm; Elizabeth; Julia; Esther; David; Emeline. Listed as Rev soldr and of 1812. Ref Firelands Pioneers N S Vol 13 p 773 Vol 17 p 1617. Rept by Marjorie Cherry.

ROWLEY, ABIGAIL, Hamilton co

Pvt Mass Contl. Enl 1775 Colchester Conn. Srvd 3 yrs from 1777. Was b 1758; mar Elizabeth; chldr: Cornelia Hall; gr son, Abijah Dickenson; Lydia Johnson; Maria Lively; son Samuel; Elizabeth Dickenson; Cleo Cole. Soldr d July 23, 1850 Fulton co Ill (fr a record of Court of that co & state). Appl for pens Cattaraugus co N Y Jan 7 1818. Appl for trnsfr to Hamilton co O Nov 3 1827. Ref S 32493 Conn Contl. Rept by State D A R.

ROWLEY, JOSEPH L, Lawrence co

Pvt Sergt Seaman comm Milit. Enl Apr 1776 Middlesex co Conn. Was b Apr 16 1750 Colchester Conn. Aft Rev he lvd New Canaan N Y 8-10 yrs then Hooser N Y abt 4 yrs then Geneas N Y thence to Westmoreland co Pa. Remained there 2 or 3 yrs then moved to Allegheny co Pa for 10 yrs. In 1820 mvd to Lawrence co O. Appl for pens Mar 12 1834 Lawrence co O Res of Fayette twp. Ref S 7408 Conn Sea Service N Y. Rept by State D A R.

RUDISILL, JACOB, Mahoning co

Lieut York co Mil Capt Casper Reineke 1778 Ser 6 V 2 pp 539, 707. Mar Elizabeth chldr: Joseph; Mary Magdalena perhaps others. Soldr d 1805 Springfield twp. Ref Will bk 1 Columbiana co Records Prob 1805. Rept by Mahoning chpt.

RUDOLPH CHRISTIAN, Perry co

Pvt Pa Milit Enl in 1776 in Montgomery co Pa where he res with his father. Srvd 13 mos. Was b 1758 on the Rhine in France. Came with father to U S when abt 8 yrs. Appl for pens Fairfield co O Mar 11 1833 Res of Jackson twp. Ref O Pa Roll 1835; 111 15-1; S 4797 Pa. Rept by State D A R.

RUDOLPH, JOHN CHRISTOPHER, Montgomery co

Pvt N Y Contl. Enl Oct 9 1777 in Funck's Milit for during the war; dischgd June 8 1783. Was b 1758. Res Montgomery co O in 1820. Ref S 40374 N Y. Rept by State D A R.

RUE, BENJAMIN, Warren co

Ensign, Pa Contl. Srvd in regt commanded by Col Debar Pa line 9 mos. Was b Jan 22, 1752. Had a son Benjamin and gr-child 15 mos (appl 1820). Pens appl Nov 19 1818 in Warren co O res in Lebanon. Ref S 40370 Pa. Rept by State D A R.

RUFFNER, EMANUEL, Fairfied co

Name listed p 406 Wiseman's Hist Fairfield co as a teamster in the Rev War and belongs to list of Soldiers of the Rev. Copd by Jane Dailey. Rept 1932 by Elizabeth Sherman Reese chpt as mrkd by them w tablet. Fr Roy McNaghten, Detroit a descend comes def data; Va service; bur Ruffneer cem north of West Rushville, Pleasantville Rd; Movd to O 1807; print of stone enclosed on whch is: In memory of Emanuel Ruffner d June 4th 1848 æ 91-2-21. Nr by are stones of: Magdalene, first wf of Emanuel Ruffner d Nov 20 1822 æ 65 yr 8 da; Elizabeth (his second wf) d Dec 10 1842 æ 63-9-6; Henry (their son) d Feb 15 1806.

RUNYON, JOHN, Preble co

B Nov 1763 in Hunterdon co N J. Enl 1780 in Rowan co N C servd until surrender Cornwallis. Came with fam to Preble co 1819. Pens 1832 D 1833. Bur nr Hope Jackson twp. Rept Commodore Preble chpt.

RUMBARGER, GEORGE, Montgomery co

Pa. Lancaster Co. 5th Ser Pa Arch V 7 p 560 Milita 6th battl 1778-79 Michael Moyer Capt. Bur Jackson twp Presbyterian Church cem Montgomery co. Rept by W M Pettit Dayton.

RUMMELL, PETER, Mahoning co

Pvt 3rd Co Capt Venentine Rummel; Pa Arch Ser 6 V 5 p 341. Mar Margaret (1770-1858). Soldr d before 1833 Berlin twp. Came to Mahoning co early in 1800. Ref Hist Trumbull & Mahoning co V 2. Deed bk 2 p 125 Trnscrbd Mahoning co fr Peter & Marg Rummell; Warren News Letter May 20 1833 Est Peter Rummell Berlin twp. Rept by Mahoning chpt.

RUMP, FREDERICK, Champaign co

In a list of deaths of Rev Soldr fr Adlers (Pa) Journal; Dec 23 1841 says "died in Urbana O Nov 9 1841 Frederick Rump in 107th yr of his age" Rept by Mary Owen Steinmetz, Reading Pa.

RUNYAN, JOHN, Champaign co

Pvt Pa Milit Enl 1776 Essex co N J serving 4 terms. Was b 11-26-1756. Mar Mary 2-19-1778. Chldr Betsy 1-17-1779; Stephen 10-21-1780; Debby? 1-15-1783; Richard 2-2-1785; Jenny 5-25-1787; Sally 8-30-1789; Anne 3-4-1791; John 12-14-1792; Polly 2-9-1795; Rosannah 9-13-1791; Peggy 9-26-1799; Elias 4-25-1802; Lydia 8-7-1804. Soldr d 9-14-1836. Ref New Jersey W 4790. Rept by State D A R.

RUNYAN, JOHN, Preble co

Pvt N C Milit Enl May or June 1780 Rowan co N C. Srvd 9 mos and 10 das fr 1780. Was b 1763 Nov 4 Hunterdon co N J. Pens appl Preble co O Sept 21 1832 res of Dickson twp. Ref S 4799 N C. Rept by State D A R.

RUSSELL, ASHER, Morgan co

Pvt Conn Contl Srvd 7 yrs fr 1776 in Rev War. Was b 1760. One son Ashvell. Entered service on Jan 1 1776. Appl for pens in Hartford co Conn Apr 17 1818. Made appl for pens in Morgan co O on Jan 5 1831. Ref S 40368 B L Wt 1195-100 Conn Contl Rept by State D A R.

RUSSELL, ASHUR, Morgan co

Pensioned for service as pvt under Capt Bissell & Walker Cols Huntington & Webb Ct Line; living in Morgan co in 7-10-1818. Was b 1753 Wethersfield Ct; d 1836 McConnellsville O. Ref p 18 V 105 D A R Line No. 104055. Rept by Jane Dailey (who believes this is same soldier as Asher Russell, recorded above).

RUSSELL, ELIJAH, Fairfield co

Pvt Va Contl. Enl in Nov 1776 Culpepper co Va. Servd 2 yrs. Was b 8-15-1758 Culpepper co Va. Pens appl for 10-1-1833 aft he had mvd to Fairfield co in 1813. Ref Name listed p 406 Wiseman Pioneer People Fairfield co; Va S 4169. Rept by Jane Dailey and State D A R.

RUSSELL, CHARLES, Gallia co

Pvt Va Milit. Was b 1759 mar Elizabeth Nolan May 4 1791, Berkley co Va. Chldr Sarah; James C; Thomas; William; Mahlon; Moses; Samuel B; John; Charles Jr. Soldr d Mar 11 1839 Springfield twp. Bur Glassburn cem Springfield twp Gallia co O. Ref Mrs Artie Roush Bidwell O. Rept by French Colony Chapter.

RUSSELL, JOHN, Mahoning co

Pension Appl Circuit Court bk 6 p 292 Warren O. Also Va Men (Library Rec) p 265. D at Poland O. Ref Tax list 1826 Poland twp Mahoning Reg Jan 7 1864; Poll bk Poland 1813. Rept by Mahoning chpt.

RUTHERFORD, ROBERT, Champaign co

Pvt Va line. Enl Shenendoah co Va Oct 1780. Was b 1761; d Mar 16 1851. Pens appl Champaign co O July 11 1818. Ref S 38341 Va. Rept by State D A R.

RUTLEDGE, MAJOR WILLIAM, Ross co

A soldr of Rev did masonry on State house Chillicothe O p 496 Howe's History. Rept by Jane Dailey.

SACKETT, DAVID, Ashtabula co

Lieut Mass Contl. Enl 5-19-1775 whl residing in Hampshire co Mass. Srvd 1 yr. Was b 8-31-1744 Hampshire co Mass. Appl states he had 2 sons-in-law. Pens appl in Ashtabula co O 3-18-1818 and in June 1820. Ref Contl Mass S 40379. Rept by State D A R.

SACKETT, SALMON, Summit co

Was b May 8 1764 Warren Conn son of Capt Justus Sacket and Lydia Newcomb. Mar Mercy Matilda Curtis May 3 1787. 13 chldr named p 159 Sackett Fam Hist. Soldr d Nov 24 1846; bur Tallmadge Summit co O (not verified). Ref 18th Rept N S D A R p 248; p 109 and 159 Sacketts of America, Los Angeles Libry. Rept by Nathan Perry chpt and Jane Dailey.

SADDLER, CHRISTOPHER, Cuyahoga co

Pvt in Rev. Was b in Germany; mar Sophia 1781-2; chldr: Christopher: William; soldr d 3-23-1839 Cuyahoga co; bur Bay Village Dover O. Inscript on marker "Christopher Saddler War of 1776" (a new marker) Came to America as a British soldr abt 1777. Was taken prisoner and held until 1778 when he enl in an independent corps under command of Count Pulaski. Pens appl Cuyahoga co Oct 1833 but refused; wid appl 10-16-1838 Cuyahoga co. Ref Contl (German) R 9135. Rept by Lakewood chpt. Mrs Luella Wise.

SAFFORD, DR JAMES, Gallia co

Pvt Capt William Dyres Co Vt 10-12-1780 to 11-6-1780. Was b July 23 1763 Hardwich Mass son of Challis Safford and Lydia Warner Safford. Mar Joanna Merrill Aug 1 1784; chldr: James; Merrill; Henry; Fanny; Challis. Soldr d Sept 27 1834 Gallipolis Gallia co whr he is bur in Pine Street cem. Was a physician, associate judge of Rutland co Court Vt 1797-1801; representative of Rutland co Vt 1796. Ref Data furnished by S M Culbertson Denver Colo to Ohio Valley Saffords published and edited by S M Culbertson. Rept by French Colony chpt.

SAGER (Seegar), **DR JOHN GEORGE**, Union co

Two enl; pvt Capt John Millers Co Col Robert McGraws 5th Pa Regt Contl line Jan 3 1776 to Jan 3 1777. Was taken prisoner at the battle of Germantown Nov 16 1776 and sent to Prison camp at N Y city and later paroled. Enl 1779 Capt Samuel Rogers Co 8th Battl 6th class Cumberland co Pa milit. Immigrated to Louden co Va 1779 whr last of his chldr were b. Came to Union co O 1805 with 8 chldr: George; Christian; Frederick; Jacob; Henry; Samuel; Abraham; Barbara. Largest pioneer fam in Union co. Dr Johan George Seager founder of family in America came to Philadelphia Oct 5 1737 on "ye good old ship Townshead" and settled in Lancaster co Pa. Cop fr F W Gardners column Columbus Dispatch by Jane Dailey.

SAILOR, PHILIP, Morgan co

Corp Pa Milit. Enl 5th Pa Regt Aug 1 1776 Chester co Pa. Was b Ap 1 1752 Pikeland Pa; d Apr 2 1845. Res Chester co Pa abt 7 yr aft the war. Thence to Cumberland co Pa and res 13 or 14 yr; thence to Morgan co O whr appl for pens Oct 29 1832. Ref Pa S 3852. Rept by State D A R.

SALMONS, SOLOMAN, Fayette co

Bur Salmon cem Paint twp Fayette co O. Stone record: d July 14 1837 æ 75 yr. Ref Mrs J A Wissler Washington C H. Rozilla wf of Soloman Salmons d July ——— (no date). Rept by Wm Horney chpt.

SALTER, JAMES, Scioto co

Enl Va 1776. Srvd 3 yrs. Was b 1754. Was mar. Pens appl Ohio co Va Aug 10 1826. Trnsfr to Scioto co O Jan 9 1838. Cens 1840 pensr Porter twp æ 84 liv w Robert Kenady. Ref S 41125 Va. Rept by State D A R.

SALTER, SAMUEL, Scioto co

Pvt and Va Contl. Srvd 1 yr. Was b 1753; mar Bridget. Appl mentions chldr but no names. Original pens claim Fayette co Pa Oct 29 1822. Appl Scioto co O Jan 19 1833. Occupation was a baker. Ref S 4126 Va. Rept by State D A R.

SAMPSON, SAMUEL, Athens co and Ind

Pvt Pa Milit and St Trps Capt Johnsons Co 15 mo. Pensr Athens co 8-24-1833. Aft Sept 1841 pensd at Madison Ind. Was b Pa. Was farmer and teacher; came to Homer twp (then Athens co) Nov 7 1832 æ 70. Mvd to Clay co Ind. "wf d in O". Chldr livd in Ind Mar 16 1842. Enl Bedford Pa Mar 1782 Boyds Range Lieut Johnsons Co Ensg Hugh Means. In 1800 movd to Green co Pa then to Ohio co Pa; 1821 Morrow co O; May 1831 Athens co Homer twp. Ref July 3 1837 deed of land for Solomon Cokly V 8 p 553 Athens co decds. Pens appl denied as service not in a Co on contl estab. Athens co deeds show names of Jacob 1821; John 1826; Daniel 1837. Cop fr Dept Int Pa S 32506. Rept by Jane Dailey.

SAME (or Sams), **JONAS**, Brown co

Was b 11-18-1756 Pa. One child was Nehemiah. Bur Sardinia O. Grave located by Ripley chpt. Came fr Pa to Ky then to O in 1803. Was with Col Crawford at his defeat 1782. Was not a U S pensioner. Ref 16th Rept N S D A R p 145. (This no doubt is data on "Sams, Jonas" Brown co p 321 Roster Vol 1 J D) Rept by Nathan Perry chpt and Taliaferro chpt.

SANDS, ALEXANDER, Monroe co

Exec Doc 37 of 1852 required further proof as to length of service, in order to secure a pens. Rept by Wm Pettit.

SAYRES, EPHRAIM, Meigs co

Exec Doc 37 of 1852 Suspended pens as servd in Regt not on contl Estab of regularly org corps. Rept by Wm Pettit.

SANDY, WILLIAM, Pickaway co

Pvt Va Contl. Enl in Leads Town Westmoreland co Va. Wf æ 59 in 1820. Chldr: Henry æ 20; Nancy Brownley 33 (appl 1820) Appl pens 1818 in Va for services as pvt in Va Regt commanded by Cols Marshall and Porterfield 5 yrs. Later in 1820 appl Pickaway co O. Ref S 40386. Rept by State D A R.

SARGENT, JAMES JR, Clermont co

Resd Frederick co Md dur Rev; Memb Com of Observation & Support w his father James Sergent Sr. (Ref Mitchell Thirley's Ency Direct Hist & pp 54-101. Soldr bur Woods cem ¼ mi fr Chilo Clermont co whch prob was his old farm; b 1-25--1747 Montgomery co Md; d 12-13-1826; wf Philena Pigman bur same cem; b 12-23-1748; d 7-20-1822. (Ref Walls fam Bible). A framer of Constitutional Conv of O; Senator four terms; Ref: Md Hist Soc Mag Vol 11 No 2 p 172; Callie King Walls, Cin O who repts this recd and states neither James Sr or Jr were settlers in Pike co; that Snowden third chld of James Sr mar Mary Heitman and lived in Pike co. Compare p 322 Vol 1 O Roster of same name Pike co which evidently is James Sr and possibly is confused. (J D).

SARGEANT, WINTHROP COLONEL, ? co

Listed in old scrap bk by Marietta settlers. Filed for continued research by Marrietta chpt.

SATTERLY, SAMUEL, Darke co

Pvt N J Contl. Enl 6-1-1778 Sussex co N J. Srvd 9 mos. In 1827 stated his wf was d and chldr of age. Pens appl Boone co Ky 1817; Darke co O 7-6-1827. Occupation was a tanner and currier. Ref N J S 40381. Rept by State D A R.

SATTERFIELD, JOHN, Pike co

Exec Doc 37 of 1852 refused a pens as servd less than 6 mo. Rept by Wm Pettit.

SAYERS, JOSIAH, Morrow co

Emigrated fr Pa. Was b abt 1764. Only child known Reul. Soldr d Denmark Caanan twp Morrow co O; bur Worden cem Canaan twp. Inscript on Monument "Josiah Sayers d Feb 2 1857 æ 93 a life long member of Baptist Church and a soldr of Rev." Grave mrkd by family tombstone. Ref Sayers Genealogy History of Morrow co by Perrin and Battle p 739. Rept by Columbus chpt. Mrs. W S VanFossen.

SAYLER (Saylor), JACOB, Pickaway co

First class pvt. Srvd in Capt Davidsons Co Col Smith Battl. Bedford co Associators Mar 22 1776; also Capt Wm McCalls Co 3rd Battl Bedford co Milit pvt. Was b 1737 Berks co Pa. Believes fathers name was Henry. Mar Elizabeth 1770. Chldr: Jacob b 1778; John b 1780; Henry 1782; Micah 1787; David 1788; Elizabeth (Whelzel); Katherine Herring; Mary Lutz; Sarah Lutz. Soldr d Sept 21 1800 Salt Cr twp; bur Boggs Pickaway twp nr west side. Inscript on monument "Jacob Saylor d Sept 21 1800 æ 62" (wf stone also). Came fr Berks co Pa abt 1765-70 to Bedford co Pa. Bought 100 A 4 mi N of Ft Bedford. In 1776 into town Bedford, bot lot 149 on which was a spring which supplied Washingtons Trps. Made guns for the army before enl. Movd to Pickaway co O 1799. Also harness maker, owneil grist and saw mill. Ref Pa State Libry; Family history; Saylor Bible printed 1609; old printed and written letters; Hist of Franklin and Pickaway co; Pa Arch 5 S V 5 pp 51-119. Arthur H Hojkins Rensselaer Ind. Rept by Pickaway Plains chpt.

SAYRE, DAVID, Meigs co

Pvt Capt Richard Tomleys Co fr Elizabethtown twp 1st Regt Essex co N J Miilit. Was b Essex co N J 5-30-1736 son of Daniel Sayre (d 4-17-1760) and Rebecca Bond mar on 4-18-1761 Elizabeth N J. Soldr mar Hannah Frazier in 1758 (b 1-23-1741 d 1-31-1825-6); Soldr d 7-11-1826; bur Letart Falls cem Meigs co O. Grave mrkd by descendants official mrkr 1931. Ref Howells Hist South Hampton N Y. Col Doc 2 pp 144-150; direct descend of Thos Sayre b 1597 Eng one of "Lynn Undertakers" of Lynn Mass. Rept by Mrs Katherine F Rathburn Return Jonathan Meigs chpt.

SAYRE, EZEKIEL, Hamilton co

Lt Monmouth co Milit. See p 431 Strykers Men of N J. Was b 1726 Southampton L I; son of Isaac (d 1730) and Elizabeth White Sayre. Chldr: Pierson (1761-1852); Benjamin Sheriff of Warren co O; Levi (1768-1826); John (1771 ——); Hulda Sayre Wallace; Rachel (McCollough). Soldr d and bur at Reading O. Grave mrkd by family. Was in battl of Stony Hill; went to New Providence N J; thence to O 1790. Was a contributor to 1st Presb Church Cincinnati O. Ref Littles "Passaic Valley and Early Letters" and Sayre "General Outline by Theo Bauta;" Jones "History of Cin" Mrs Rose Joel D A R Crawfordsville Ind. Rept by Cincinnati chpt.

SAYRES (Sayre, Rauel), RUEL, Perry co

Rev soldr N J milit. Was b July 1754 Salem co N J. Vol Salem co N J Aug 3 1776. Livd in N J till 1795. Livd in Pa abt 20 yrs and then in Perry co O abt 18 yrs. Cens 1840 says living in Clayton twp æ 87 with Isaac Bennett. Ref S 3855 N J. Rept by State D A R.

SCAMMEL, LESLIE, Washington ? co

Genl; listed in old scrap bk as filed for cont research by Marietta chpt.

SCHAAK, JACOB, Columbiana co

In list of Deaths of Rev Soldrs Adlers (Pa) Journal May 30 1843 as: "D New Lisbon O May 2 1843 Jacob Schaak æ 83 yrs 5 mo 17 da." Rept by Mary Owen Steinmetz Reading Pa. From W M Pettit S A R Dayton comes this addit data. Pvt and spy in McGrubbs and Cunningham's Pa regiments. Flying Corps. Pensioned Nov 27 1832; S A R No 2390. Mrs Wilma Molsberry repts he enl 5 times for short terms. Was b Nov 15 1758 Lebanon Pa; mar Dorothea (1762 1-13-1813) bur New Lisbon; soldr d May 5 1844 at New Lisbon O æ 85 yr; bur Center twp. Res Center twp New Lisbon. Came in 1804 fr Pa. Ref Ohio Soc S A R year bk 1898; Pension bk No 3; Census 1840.

SCHAMEHORN, ——, Pickaway co

Bur Rains cem nr Derby O. Replying to an inquiry abt a Rev soldr by name of Schamehorn, Dr C J Smith Portland Ore answered "Near whr we livd in my early childhood was an old and abandoned cem known as the Rains cem. My father who was b 1839 in the same neighborhood and livd there all his life used to tell us that he saw when a very small boy an old man bur in the Rains cem by the name of Schamehorn and that this man had been a Rev soldr." Rept by Jane Dailey.

SCHEENAM (Schoenham), WILLIAM, Columbiana co

Pvt Va Milit. Pensr in Columbiana co 12-28-1832 æ 82. Ref Pens Rec of 1833-34. Cop by Jane Dailey. State D A R repts was b 1752 Philadelphia Pa. Pvt Pa Line 18 mos. Enl 1776 Cumberland co Pa. Ref Pa S 3868.

SCHERMERHORN, RICHARD, Ashtabula co

Pvt N Y Milit. Srvd 1 yr and 23 das. Was pvt in a Co of Milit commanded by Capt Jellis J Fonda. Mar Nancy or Annatie Vanvoghten 4-28-1777. Chldr: Mary b 1779; Nalana 1781; Marys son John 1795; Nalanas son Peter. Soldr d 4-25-1814 Ashtabula co O. Widow Annatie (or Nancy) pensd 2-26-1838 Ashtabula co O. Ref Contl N Y W 4331. Rept by State D A R.

SCHOFF, PHILIP, Guernsey co

Pvt Capt Asia Hills Cumberland co Pa Milit. Trained with trps at Standing Stone Fort 1778. Was b Apr 2 1770 in Cumberland co Pa. His father Philip Shoff killed in Rev service. Mar Elizabeth Ramsey Megrew 1794. Chldr: John; Sarah; Hannah; Philip; Fanny; Amelia; Harriett; Matilda; Washington. Soldr d Nov 15 1855 Birds Run Wheeling twp; bur on farm. Srvd in Whiskey Insurrection and in War of 1812. Ref Schoff Family Hist; Pa Arch 3rd. S Vol 23 p 165. Rept by Hetuck chpt.

SCOTT, CAPT ISAAC, Trumbull co

Pvt and Capt. Md St Trps. Pensr Trumbull co 8-8-1833. In battles of Trenton, Princeton, Brandywine, Germantown whr he was twice wounded rendering him unfit for service. Was b June 12 1756 Chester co Pa but enl fr Cecil co Md. Mar Jane. Among their chldr were: Matthew; Moses; Isaac Jr. Soldr d Oct 3 1833 Howland Trumbull co O. Rept by Mary Chesney chpt.

SCOTT, JOHN ? co

Pvt appl for pens rejected as no satisfactory evidence exhibited. Listed Doc No 31 Jan 6 1831. Rept by Blanche Rings.

SCOTT, JOHN, Ashland co

Listed p 142 in "Hist of North Central O" by Wm A Duff as Rev soldr (one listed in Warren co) Perry twp. Rept by Nathan Perry chpt.

SCOTT, NEHEMIAH, Trumbull co

Pvt. Ser 6 Vol 4 pp 336, 444 Pa Arch. Was b 1763; d 1834; bur Old Market St stone rem to Oak Hill cem. Livd in Liberty twp Trumbull co O. Rept by Mahoning chpt.

SCOTT, SAMUEL, Mahoning co

Pvt. Ser 6 Vol 23 p 284 Pa Arch. Was b 1750; d 1842 Coitsville twp; bur Deer Creek Lawrence co Pa. Ref List of late H R Baldwin S A R. Rept by Mahoning chpt.

SCOVILL, AMASA, Trumbull co

Fifer in Rev. Was in N Y at evacuation of British 1783. Pensioner. Was b Dec 22 1758 Waterbury Conn; mar Esther Merrill; chldr: Joel; Asahel; Roswell; Ansel; Sarah; Merrill; Esther-Almira; Rachel-Elvira. Soldr d Mar 30 1844 Vienna O. Estate was in Trumbull co. Came from Middlebury Conn to Vienna in 1810. Rept by Mary Chesney chpt.

SCOVILL, MICHAEL, Trumbull co and Michigan

Pvt Conn Milit. Pensr in Trumbull co 7-3-1834. Was b 9-10-1762 Hartland Conn son of Micah Scovil and Mary ——. Mar Hannah Meeker. Was res of Trumbull co for a no of yrs but 1836 movd to Mich to live with chldr res of Wayne co in that state. Ref Pens Claim S 30691. Filed here to avoid cont research in O. Rept by Mary Chesney chpt. Exec Doc 37 of 1852 repts he d before action on his appl. Rept by Wm Pettit.

SCOVILL (Scoviel), THOMAS, Licking co

Bur Johnstown old cem Licking co O. Ref 15 Rept N S D A R p 163 by Hetuck chpt. Rept by Nathan Perry chpt. (No U S Rev Pens located at Pens Dept J D).

SCULL, JAMES, ? co

As rept 19th Rept N S D A R p 280 is thought to be "Stull James" of p 358 Vol 1 Roster of O. Rept by Jared Mansfield chpt.

SEABRIST, JACOB, Columbiana co

Pvt. Mar Christiana (b July 10 1779 d Aug 8 1827); bur Columbiana cem. Inscript on Monument "Co 7 Battl 9 Pa Milit." Rept by Rebecca Griscom chpt. Rept by Wm Pettit fr No 42107 S A R soldr b Adams co Pa 1760 d 1831; mar Christena Foulk. Spelled Seachrist, Seegrist.

SEARL, AARON, Licking co

Pvt Mass Milit. Enl 1779 South Hampton Mass. Srvd 7 mo 15 das. Was æ 71 in 1832. Had res in N Y, Vt and Mass since Rev. Movd to Licking co O abt 1820. Ref Mass S 3870. Rept by State D A R.

SELL, SAMUEL, Mahoning co

Pvt 2nd class Capt Daniel Clapsaddlers Co 1st Battl Ser 5 Vol 6 Pa Arch. Mar Margaret; chldr: John; Christaina mar Jacob May; Susanna mar Michael Fisher; Elizabeth mar Christain Rummell; Samuel. Soldr d abt 1823 Poland O. Ref Will bk 4 p 291 Trumbull co Records Probated 1823; Deed bk F p 102 trnscrbd Mahoning co Samuel Sell Heirs to 1827; Western Reserve Chronicle Nov 14 1826 Est Samuel Sell Poland 1826. Rept by Mahoning chpt.

SERBOR (Seerber), JACOB, Highland co

Pvt Va Milit. Enl 6 times. Srvd 30 mos and 20 das. Pensr in Highland co 11-8-1833. Was b 1744 Germantown Pa. Ref: Va S 4017. Rept by State D A R. Believe this is another spelling. Serber, Jacob, listed in Va Milit in the Rev p 289 as liv in Hamilton co O æ 90. J D.

SELSER, FREDERICK, Richland co

Pvt Pa Contl. Enl July 1777 North Hampton co Easton twp Pa. Pensr in Richland co 5-20-1834. Was b 1758 Shenandoah co Va. He had a large family to support. Movd from Pa to Richland co O in 1815 whr has since resided. At time of appl he was too old and infirm to leave his bed. Res of Milton twp. Ref Pa S 9476. Rept by State D A R.

SERGEANT (Sargent), ELIJAH, Clermont co

.   Pvt Md Milit 6 mos 15 das. Enl in Frederick town Md at the æ of 18 under Capt Thomas Frazier. Was 74 in 1832. Res of Washington twp Clermont co O 1832. Pensd there 8-29-1833. Pensr Delhi twp Hamilton co 1840 æ 82. Ref Md Va S 16245. Rept by State D A R.

SEVERNS, EDWARD, Miami co

Data from Ref R 9394 N J Pens Cl on this spelling proves to be same data recorded on p 327 Vol 1 Roster of "Sevems, Edward," which see. Filed here to avoid cont research on this spelling. Jane Dailey.

SEWELL, THOMAS, Pike co

Pvt Va Contl. Enl 8-5-1776 in Va. Srvd 2 yrs. Was 68 in 1819. Had no family. Pens appl 8-25-1819 Pike co O. Occupation a schoolteacher. Ref Va S 40394. Rept by State D A R.

SEWARD, JAMES, ? co

Pvt listed in rejected pens appl. Ref Doc No 31 Jan 6 1831 as srvd in Regt not on Contl estab. Rept by Blanche Rings.

SEWARD (Seaward), JOHN, Portage co

Pvt Mass Milit. Enl nr beginning of Rev in Granville Mass. Was b 1-29-1758 Granville Mass. Pens appl 8-28-1832 whl residing in Aurora twp Portage co O. Ref Contl Mass S 4812. Rept by Jane Dailey.

SHACKLEE, PETER, Morgan co

Pvt Pa Contl. Enl 1777 or 78 in Pa. Srvd 2 yr 6 mo. Mar Barbara Ann Nov 15 1788; chldr: Peter; Betsy; Vermili; Hannah. Soldr d Mar 19 1834. First appl for pens Apr 3 1818 in Washington co O. Ref Pa W 4799 and Vol 3 p 559 Marietta (Courts). Rept by State D A R.

SHADLEY, DANIEL, Licking co

Pvt Va Milit. Was res in Frederick co Va at the time he entered the service. Srvd 6 mos and 14 days. Was æ 77 Mar 1832; mar Elenor Blake 12-18-1822; d 10-2-1836 Hanover twp Licking co. Enl Sept 1777 Frederick co Va. Pens appl Licking co O 10-29-1832. Ref Va W 6043 B L Wt 26880-160-55; p 289 "Va Milit in Rev War." Rept by State D A R.

SHAEFER, LAMBERT C, Huron co

Pvt N J Contl. Enl 1775 Covershill N Y. Srvd 2 yrs. Was 80 in 1832 Feb 11 1753 Covershill N Y. Bur abt 2 mi s of Birmingham Florence twp O on bank of Vermilion river. Pens appl Huron co O July 1832 res of Townsend twp. Ref 18 Rept N S D A R p 252; S 6059 N Y. Rept by State D A R.

SHAEFFER, PHILIP, ? co

Wagoner. Refused a pens as his case not provided for by law. Ref Doc 31 Jan 6 1831. Rept by Blanche Rings Col.

SHAFFER, ANDREW, Stark co

Pvt Pa Contl. Enl Dec 1 1780 Pa Regt. Srvd 3 yrs. Was 62 in 1819. Pensd in Stark co 4-28-1820. Livd 7 yrs aft pens was granted. Ref S 40403 Pa. Rept by State D A R.

SHAFFER, JACOB, Muskingum co

Pvt N J Contl. Enl N J line Oct 1775; dischgd 1783. Srvd 7 yrs. Pens appl Muskingum co O June 25 1818. Ref S 40405 N J. Rept by State D A R.

SHAFFER, SAMUEL, Mahoning co

Pvt. Ser 5 V 7 p 995 Pa Arch. Chldr: William; David mar Anna; Edward mar Sally; Marie mar Wm Templeton; Eliza Jane mar John Templeton; Henry; John b 1797 mar Lucy; Daniel b 1789. Soldr d abt 1843 Jackson twp. Samuel Shaffer came from Va with 8 chldr before 1820. Ref Hist Trumbull and Mahoning co V 2 p 159; Will bk 10 p 359 Trumbull co Records probated 1843; Deed bk K 418 trnscrbd Mahoning co from Samuel Shaffer Heirs 1843; Tax list 1826. Rept by Mahoning chpt.

SHARON, FOSTER, Medina co

Listed pp 144. 145 in Hist of North Central Ohio by Wm A Duff as Rev soldr. Rept by Nathan Perry chpt.

SHARP, AMOS, Columbiana co

N J Milit. Enl 1776. Srvd 7 mos. Was b 1775 Burlington co N J. Pension no 13385. Pensd in Columbiana co O 7-6-1833. Ref New Jersey S 18593 and Cens 1840. Rept by State D A R.

SHARP, SPENCER, Washington co

Exec Doc 37 refused a pens as servd 3 mo only. Rept by Wm Pettit.

SHARROCK, JAMES, Guernsey co

3rd Milit fr Westchester co N Y Col Pierre Van Cortlandt and Samuel Drake etc. Ref N Y Soldrs in Rev as colony and state by Jas A Roberts Comptroller 1898. Was b 1750 Liverpool England son of a Prot Father Catholic mother. Mar Jane Everard 1785 of England. One known dau Phoebe mar Cornight McCoy; another Polly b 1797 d 1799; named in will are Timothy; Benjamin; Everard; George; John; Phoebe; and Mary. Soldr d 1826; bur Miller cem Guernsey co O nr Salesville O in lot in rear of church. Inscript on monument "James Sherrick who departed this life March 28 1826 æ 76 yrs." Grave mrkd by deteriorating stone. Soldr was educated for priest; rebelled; taken by a Press gang; sent to fight colonists; escaped; joined Contl army. Timothy and Edward were in war of 1812 (lists). Ref "Our Ancestors" by Homer Eiler No 244,- 245 D A R. Will of March 1826; Williams Fam Geneal. Rept by Homer Eiler and Elizabeth Zane Dew chpt.

SHAVER, NICHOLAS, Licking co

Pvt in Rev War. D Nov 19 1838; bur on James Davis farm 3 mi south of Newark. Was a farmer and tax collector in 1820. Ref Pa Arch 5 Ser Vol 4 p 250 and Vol 5 p 93; also Mrs Sylvia Woodbridge descendant. Rept by Hetuck chpt.

SHAW, JOHN, Delaware co

Pvt Md Contl. Enl in the Md line Jan 1776. Srvd 5 yrs. Also spent some time as recruiting serg. Pens appl in Delaware co O 5-15-1818. Ref Md S 40401. Rept by State D A R.

SHAW, RICHARD, Trumbull co

Was at Danbury, Chestnut Hill, Fort Mifflin, Monmouth and Stony Point. Ae 89 pens in Weathersfield head of his household. (Cens '40). Among his chldr were: William; Richard; Henry; Bridget; Zuriah; Ladusia. Soldr d Mar 4 1847 Weathersfield twp Trumbull co O. Rept by Mary Chesney chpt.

SHAWAN (Shawhan), DARBY, Warren co

Pvt in Lieut Jonathan Harneds Co Wash co on list of Milit Rolls 1782-85; also Ensign David Rubles Co; pvt on Depreciation Pay List and List of soldrs of Rev from Washington co Milit. Lieut Capt David Rubles Co 5th Battl Washington co Milit July 7 1784; pvt on List of Rangers on the Frontiers 1778 1783 from Washington co. Was taxed in Bethlehem twp Washington co on 80 A 3 horses 5 cattle in 1781. Man by name of Derby Shawhen was head of fam in Washington co on Census of 1790. Soldr and wf Priscilla bur Zoar cem 2 mi w of Morrow Warren co O. Inscript on gravestones are: "Darby Shawhen d Jan 21 1824 æ 76 yrs;" wfs "Priscilla wf of Darby Shawhan d Apr 9 1837 æ 73 yrs." Both gravestones are in good condition. Ref Wm G Hills Columbus O. Rept by Jane Dailey.

SHAWKE, JACOB, Columbiana co

Another spelling for Schaak, Jacob, which see this vol.

SHAYER, BARTHOLOMEW, ? co

Lieut. (No more data). Listed in Ohio Pensions list by Wm Holden. Rept by Jane Dailey.

SHEARS (Sheese), PETER, Tuscarawas co

Pvt German Regt. Enl Hagerstown Md Aug 2 1776; dischgd Fredericktown Md May 2 1778. Srvd 1 yr 9 mos. Was b 1749; mar Barbary; 9 chldr: 2 born before husband enl in Rev; others: Mary Ellis; Peter; Sarah; Towney. Soldr d Feb 2 1824 Stark co O. (fr son Peter) Pens appl Huntingdon co Pa 1818; Tuscarawas co O July 11 1821. Wid appl Stark co O July 17 1843 res of Pike twp. Ref W 9286 Contl Md. Rept by State D A R.

SHEEHAN (Sceehan or Shean), CORNELIUS, Columbiana co

Pvt Capt Mathew McCoys Co Cumberland co Milit Dec 1780; also 1781 and 82. Came from Pa. Voted in 1816 in Columbiana co. Pensr Pvt Va Milit granted Dec 28 1832 æ 82. Ref Pa Arch 5 V 360 622. Rept by Mrs Wilma Molsberry.

SHEETS, FREDERICK, Columbiana co

Rev Soldr (rec not yet found). Was b 1757; mar Barbara (b 1765 d 1806 bur Forney cem). Soldr d 1817 Nov 11 æ 60 yrs 6 mo 11 das. Bur Unity East Palestine Forney cem. Was a pioneer of East Palestine. Ref Columbiana co Cem Recs; Warners Beaver co Pa p 719. Rept by Mrs Wilma Molsberry.

SHEETS, GEORGE, Gallia co

Pvt in Capt Arbunkle Co Col Boyes Regt Va Milit for 9½ mo. Was b Bucks co Pa. Appl pens Nov 7 1834 Gallia co æ 75; removd to O when quite young. Pens iss Mar 19. Ref S 7479. Rept by Jane Dailey.

SHEETS, MATHIAS, Ross co

Pvt Va Contl. Enl May in the yr of the taking of Cornwallis at Little York. Enl in Shenandoah co Va. Srvd 18 mos. Mar Margaret æ 77 in 1828; chldr: Susannah æ 25 1828; son æ 38 1828. Appl for pens Ross co O 11-4-1835. Ref Name listed p 406 Wisemans Pioneer People Fairfield co; Va S 40423. Rept by Jane Dailey.

SHEFFER, PHILIP, Ashland co

Teamster and Wagon master Pa Milit. Enl 1777 whl a res of Bethlehem or Northampton co Pa. Was b 9-29-1758 Springfield co Bucks co Pa; had one boy Abraham; soldr d 5-27-1847 Ashland co O. 7 yrs aft war movd to York co Pa. Thence to Westmoreland co Pa; thence to Harrison co O. From there to Richland co. Ref R 9415 Pa. Rept by State D A R.

SHEFFLETON, GEORGE, Trumbull co

Pa Arch S 5 V 6 p 488 7th class 7th Co Cumberland co Milit. Soldr d Oct 27 1823 æ 69 yrs a soldr of the Rev. Had sons John and George, others not known. Rept by Mary Chesney chpt.

SHELDON, JONATHAN, Trumbull co

Pvt in Capt Amasa Sheldons Co Col Elisha Porters Regt. Service in the Northern dept. Mass Soldr and Sailors. Was b Feb 27 1749; mar 1st Oct 6 1771 Mary Durffee; 2nd Feb 16 1762 Priscilla Manchester. Chldr: Perry; Prudence; Joseph; Oliver; Ruth; Jonathan; Mercy; Mary; Daniel; Chloe; Lois; Jonathan 2nd; Lucina; Sarah; Rhoda; Benjamin. Soldr d Aug 8 1835 Fowler O; bur Sheldon pvt cem Fowler O. Rept by Mary Chesney chpt.

SHELEY, JOHN, Greene co

Possibly a Va service. Was b 1723; chldr Michael b 1772 Va mar Lois Strong. Soldr d 1820 Silver Creek twp Greene co; bur Sheley cem on original Sheley farm abt 1 mi s of Jamestown on Jamestown Paintersville Pike. No mrkr except field stone. Cem well kept and in beautiful condition. Ref Dills Hist of Greene co p 807 "John srvd 7 yrs in Rev war and d at the æ of 97 yrs." Rept by Catherine Green chpt by Mrs Leon Reed.

SHELLER, HENRY, Ashland co

Listed p 142 in Hist of North Central O by Wm A Duff as Rev soldr Mifflin twp. Rept by Nathan Perry chpt.

SHEPARD, CHARLES, Athens co

Pvt Md Milit. Pensr in Athens co 12-27-1833. Soldr d in Ill. Ref March 3 1838 recd land fr John Clarke Vol 9 p 34 R 14 Town 8 Sec 1 lot 50 A. Co Court Recds. Rept by Jane Dailey.

SHEPARD, JOSEPH, Portage co

Pvt N J Milit. Pensr Trumbull co 9-23-1833. Was b Freehold twp Monmouth co N J æ 84 yrs in 1832. Mar 3 times; 3rd wf Sarah Dowson March 3 1815 Washington co Pa. Chldr Ezekiel; Eliza by 3rd wf; others. Livd in Freehold N J until abt 1795 then movd to Washington co Pa and abt 1807 to Newton Trumbull co O. His late yrs were spent in Paris twp Portage co whr he d. Pens Rec gives two dates of death namely Dec 1 1839 and Nov 7 1838. Rept by Grace M Winnagle.

SHEPERD, JOHN, Brown co

Srvd in Capt Wm Cherrys Co 4th Va Infantry Apr 1777 to March 1788. Was b abt 1749 son of Thomas Sheperd and Elizabeth Van Metre. Mar Martha Wilson 1775 (b 1750); chldr Isaac; Jacob; John; Abraham; and three others names not available. Soldr d 1812 Red Oak O; bur in Brown co O. Represented Adams co in State Senate for many years. Came to Bratton twp Adams co in 1801. Surveyor; helped build Zane Trace. Ref Historic Shepherd town by Dandridge p 346; Evans Hist of Adams co p 413, 116, 119, 99. Rept by Hetuck chpt and Taliaferro chpt. Gr loc by Lieut Byrd chpt in Red Oak Pres cem Brown co.

SHEPERD, WILLIAM, Butler co

Var spellings. Pvt N J Milit. Enl abt Oct 1 1776 in N J Milit at Sussex co N J Crt House. Srvd 2 yrs and 3 mos from 1776. Was b Mar 1759 Sussex co N Y æ 73 in 1832; mar Eleanor or Ellen Oct 15 1792; chldr: Jonathan; Louis; Abraham; John; David; William; Eleanor; Paul; Elizabeth; Mary; Sarah; Henry. Soldr d June 4 1833. Pens appl Butler co O 1832. Had res in O more than 30 yrs in Butler co 20 yrs. Wid appl for pens Butler co O Apr 22 1857 res of Oxford twp. The heirs appl for pens Union co Ind Sept 16 1850 and stated that she d Aug 29 1849 Butler co O. Ref W 6035 N J. Rept by State D A R.

SHERBURNE, ANDREW, Brown co

Seaman; ranger. Enl Apr 1779 battleship Ranger. Pens No 9468; pensd 4-19-1819 Cincinnati O. Trnsfrd to Oneida co N Y in 1824. Was b Aug 1765. Ref Navy (N H) S 42275. Rept by State D A R.

SHERER, JOHN JACOB, Preble co

Was b 1760 in Pa. Mar Catherine Smith b 1762; had 10 chldr; soldr d 1845 on farm in northwest part of Washington twp; bur Sherer cem Washington twp Preble co. Came from N Carolina to O in 1806 settled in Washington twp. Ref S A R yr bk. Rept by Commodore Preble chpt.

SHERLOCK, EDWARD, Ross co

Pvt Pa Contl. Enl Aug 1776 Pa Line. Srvd 3 yrs. Was 66 in 1823. Wf æ 66 or 67 in 1823. Soldr d Feb 11 1825 (fr co Newspaper) Ref Pa S 41152. Rept by State D A R. Mary Chesney chpt rept Ref Hist Fayette co Pa p 81; Hist Washington co Pa p 84.

SHERMAN, TIMOTHY, Washington co

Enl 1-17-1776 in a Co commanded by Col Paul Dudley. Also Capt Asa Barnes Co Col James Knowlton Regt. Pensd 9-16-1819 Waterford twp Washington co O. Living with wf and 2 sons in Waterford O in 1820. Was æ 58 in 1818; mar Polly æ 64 in 1825. Chldr: Wakeman æ 20 yrs; Uriah 15; Abel and 6 other chldr all mar (appl 1820). Soldr d 1820. Mrkr placed by Marietta chpt 1832 in Mound cem as grave unknown. Ref Contl Mass S 40400. Rept by State D A R.

SHERMAN, WILLIAM, Columbiana co

Rev soldr. Rec not yet found. Was b 1757; d 7-6-1837 æ 80 yrs. Grave mrkd livd Gillford (Guilford). Ref Ohio Patriot. Rept by Mrs Wilma M Molsberry.

SHERWIN, ELNATHAN, Clermont co

Pvt Mass Contl. Enl Chelmsford twp Mass 1781. Srvd the war. Was æ 58 yrs in 1820. Mar Abigail æ 52 yrs in 1820; chldr Nancy æ 16; Elbridge Gerry æ 8 yrs. Ref Mass S 40416. Rept by State D A R.

SHEVERDECKER, MICHAEL, Preble co

Pvt Va Milit. Enl in Frederick co Va. Srvd 6 mos and 12 das. Was b 1762 Frederick co Va. Mar Anna Garret Dec 13 1787. Chldr: Elizabeth Hafner appl for arrears of pens in Preble co O June 12 1854; also Catharine d young; Polly Persinger; Luke; Frances; David. Soldr d Mar 3 1833. Appl for pens Preble co O Sept 21 1832 res of Monroe twp. Ref W 6039 Va. Rept by State D A R.

SHIELDS, DAVID, ? co

V 114 p 225 No 113678 D A R Lin gives data: b July 19 1764 Cumberland co Pa. Pvt Pa Line. Mar Nancy McChord; one son was William McChord. Soldr d 1844 in O. State D A R repts from pens claim: srvd in Co commanded by Capt Shields in Pa trps for 1 yr 5 mos 3 das. Pens appl Armstrong co Pa res Red Bank twp Mar 19 1833.

SHIELDS, TOBIAS, Madison co

Pvt. Enl in Capt Fraziers Co 4th Regt in Pa Line in latter part of 1775. Srvd till end of war. Pensd 9-29-1819 Madison co O. Appl states: "Has been totally blind for 14 yrs." Ae 70 yrs in 1818. "Two sons and one dau upon whom he and his wf are dependent." Ref Pa S 40419. Rept by State D A R.

SHIPMAN, ABRAHAM, Trumbull co

Enl Capt John Petty's Regt Col William Williams Regt Milit in Vt 1777. Srvd various enl until close of war. Vt in Rev p 35. Was b Aug 25 1755 son of Jonathan Shipman and Abigail Fox; married May 5 1777 to Hannah Bixby; children: Abram; Frederick; Billy; William 2nd; Hannah; Julianna; Mary; Royal; Adrial; Anny; Josiah. Soldr d Mar 7 1841 Gustavus O. Rept by Mary Chesney chpt.

SHLIFE (or Schlife), JOHN, Fairfield co

Pvt Md Contl. Enl Baltimore Md 6-20-1776. Srvd 3 yrs. Was b 10-4-1754. Chldr: 2 daus liv with him æ 30 and 23 in 1819. Also six other chldr liv elsewhr. A grandson (helpless cripple) æ abt 17. Pens appl Fairfield co O 5-15-1819. Occupation was a blacksmith. Ref Name listed p 406 Wisemans Pioneer People Fairfield co; Contl (Md) S 40417. Rept by State D A R.

SHOAF, PETER, Mahoning co

Pvt in Cumberland co Pa Milit Capt Campbell's Co 4th class. Mar Elizabeth; soldr prob bur Poland O. Owned a gristmill and sawmill on Spring Run on Pa line at an early date. It was run by his sons for some yrs and then sold. On tax list in Poland in 1803. Ref Pa Arch S 5 Vol 6 p 143. Hist Trumbull and Mahoning co Vol 2 pp 59, 61, 69. Rept by Mahoning chpt.

SHUEY, JOHN MARTIN, Montgomery co

Bur Greencastle cem Dayton; gr markd by S A R 1936. Records in poss Ohio chpt S A R. Rept Jonathan Dayton chpt.

SHORT, JOHN, Clermont co

Exec Doc 37 refused a pens as served less than 6 mo. Rept by Wm Pettit.

SHOUSE, CHRISTIAN, Jefferson co

Pvt Pa Contl. Enl Jan or Feb 1776 Pa. Srvd 1 yr. Ae 65 in 1818 Northampton co Pa. Wf æ 61 (appl 1820). Pens appl Jefferson co O July 3 1818. Res of Knox twp. Occupation a house carpenter. Ref S 40418 Pa. Rept by State D A R.

SHOFF, PHILIP, ? co

When a lad carried whl in service such a heavy musket that the General ordered it taken away and one given him more suitable to his yrs. He d in O 1855 at the æ 85; mar Elizabeth Ramsey. Ref Nat No 9071 D A R through daughter Frances. D A R Nat No 4527 states that Philip Shoff of Pa æ 8 was in Capt Asa Hill's Co. Rept by Nathan Perry chpt.

SHREVE, GODFREY, Meigs co

Pvt Mass. Enl 4-19-1775 Rochester Mass. Pensd 10-13-1818 Washington co O. Trnsfrd to N Y 1826. Was æ 50 yrs in 1818. Mar Ruth æ 54 yrs in 1821. No family but his wf. Ref Contl Mass S 42273. Rept by State D A R.

SHUMAN, TIMOTHY, ? co

Pvt stricken from Pens Rolls of 1818 Act of 1820 as not being in indigent circumstances. Ref Doc No 31 Jan 6 1831 pp 70 71. Cop by Blanche Rings.

SIBLISS, THOMAS, Franklin co

Mass Contl. Was b May 13 1819 æ 98. Soldr d Nov 7 1823; Adm app May 1 1824 Franklin co Adm Dock 1-220. Rept by K H VanFossen (Mrs W S) Columbus O.

SIDLE, PETER, Warren co

Musician Pa Contl. Enl 1776 nr York town Pa. Srvd as musician under Col Mercer 3 yrs. Mar Mary Roans Dec 30 1828; one chld Mary Ann 10 yrs of æ. Soldr d Sept 1838 Warren co. Was in Battl of Monmouth. Mar in Warren co O. Pens appl July 6 1818 Warren co O. Occupation was a cooper. Mary Steele former wid of Peter Sidle appld for wid pens in Warren co O Feb 14 1853. Mar Samuel Steele Jan 11 1839 and he also d in Warren co O winter of 1840 or 41. Ref W 6195 B L Wt 26299-160-55 Pa. Rept by D A R chpt.

SILVER, JOHN, Hamilton co

Pvt Col S R Clark Capt Chas Gaiff ? Co of Rangers; on duty August to Nov 1783. Ms in State Libry Richmond Va in Ill papers. Was b Augusta co Va 1762. Was also in Capt Gabriel Madison's Co of Milit. Mar Eliza 1792 (b 1772 d 1817); chldr: John Jr b 1795 d 1846 mar 1817; his dau was Catherine Eliza mar Henry Markley 1848. Soldr d 1813 Mt Washington Hamilton co O. Was a bro Judge James Silver Cincinnati who was 2nd Lieut in Rev War. Ref Nat No 225816 D A R. Rept by Cincinnati chpt Mrs E P Whallon.

SIMMS, JEREMIAH, Perry co

Pvt Va Milit 6 mos. Enl 1777 Culpeper Court house in Culpeper co Va. Was b 7-7-1760 Culpeper co Va. Mar Catharine Madden 1-3-1839; soldr d 5-17-1846 Perry co O. Mvd fr Va to O 1820 and has livd in Perry and Muskingum cos. Cens 1840 says living in Madison twp Perry co æ 79. Wid appl for pens 6-4-1855 Perry co O. Ref Contl Va W 1500. Rept by Jane Dailey.

SIMMONDS, ROBERT, Butler co

Pvt and Sergt Md Milit. Enl July 1776 Kent co Md whr res. Srvd 8 mos. Was b Dec 1757 Kent co Md; æ 75 in 1833. Removed to Caroline co in 1794. In summer of 1795 was in clerks office in Hagerstown Md. Oct 1775 he left for Ky nr Lexington whr livd 6 yrs; then to Harrison co Ky and frm here to Hamilton co O in 1805 or 6. Aft death of his wf he movd from Hamilton co O to Butler co O to live w dau whr had res past 7 yrs whn appld for pens Mar 14 1833 res of Morgan twp. Ref S 4836 Md. Rept by State D A R.

SIMMONS, WILLIAM, Stark co

Pvt Md Contl. Enl Kent co Md 1780. Was 54 in 1818. Mar Elizabeth abt æ 30; chldr: Joseph 10; James 7; John 2. Pens appl Apr 27 1818 Baltimore Md and Harford co Md 8-28-1820. Nov 10-1826 appld in Starke co O. Ref S 40434 Md. Rept by State D A R.

SIMONS, ADAM, Mahoning co

Bur Pleasant Grove cem. Rev soldr mentioned in address of Compatriot Lynn and rept by W M Pettit S A R.

SIMONS, FREDERICK, Ashtabula co

Pvt in Md Trps Capt Creagers Co Col Johnsons Regt. Enl at Fredericktown Md. Was b 1762; mar Barbara Reed; a son Henry mar Sarah Young. Soldr d 1851 Williams-field O; bur Williamsfield Center, Ashtabula co O. Grave located by Mary Stanley chpt. Cop fr No 101093 S A R p 148 Col Soc S A R Bulletin for 1901 and 21st Rept N S D A R p 109. Rept by State D A R.

SIMONTON, JOHN, Preble co

Lieut in Col Wm Irvin's 6th Pa Battl Cumberland co Pa Milit. Was b Ireland 1754; d Preble co O 1828. Ref D A R Lin bk and Vol 109 p 50. State D A R repts frm Pa Arch O list S 40429 Pa was Pvt Pa Contl. Pensr Athens co 5-17-1820 æ 81 for serv in regt of Col Irwin 10 mo. Appl names wf æ 61 one son John æ 15 (1820). He enl Pa in Moses McLean Co Col Irwin Regt York co 6th Pa line.

SIMONTON, THOMAS, Stark co

Pvt Pa Contl. Enl Cumberland co Pa 1777. Srvd 4 yrs. Was 70 in 1818; mar Mary Dec 18 1787; son æ 18; dau æ 12 (1820) Soldr d June 11 1830. Pens appl Stark co O Dec 14 1818 and 1821; wid appl Carroll co O Oct 2 1838 res of Brown twp and Columbiana co O Apr 7 1843. Ref W 3880 Pa. Rept by State D A R. Fr No 46967 S A R rept by Wm Pettit is service in Col Irvine's Pa Regt; b 1750 in Pa; d 1830; mar Mary Clark 1787.

SIMPSON, JAMES, Butler co

Exec Doc 37 refused a pens as servd less than 6 mo. Rept by Wm Pettit.

SIMPSON, JOHN, Pickaway co

Pvt Va Contl. Enl Winchester Va spring 1776. Pvt Capt Berry's Co Col Abrm Bowman's Regt in battle Brandywine; Germantown; Monmouth; seige of Yorktown and taking of Cornwallis. Was b 1752. Grave not located in Pickaway co. Pensr in Picka-day co 4-28-1819; was allowed pens July 27 1818 æ 66 Ross co. In 1821 was living in Pickaway co. Ref Pens No S 40430. Rept by Pickaway Plains chpt.

SIMPSON, JOSIAH, Butler co

Pens in Butler co for services as Pvt in N J line 1776. Was b 1751 Somerset co N J; mar Jane Van Syckle 1775; one dau Mary mar Thomas Powers 1799. Soldr d 1847 Butler co O. Cop fr D A R Lin 106816 by Jane Dailey.

SIMPSON, ROBERT, Adams co

Pvt N H Contl. Pensr in Adams co 2-12-1833. Was b abt 1763 Deerfield N H. Livd w father until winter of 1777. Res Spriggs twp Adams co O 1832. Ref Contl N H S 3910. Rept by State D A R.

SIMPSON, THOMAS, Muskingum co

Corp Md Contl. Enl Md May 28 1777; dischgd Jan 5 1780. Srvd 3 yrs. Was æ 65 in 1821; mar Mary æ 55 in 1821; had a dau æ 14 (appl 1821). Appl for pens Muskingum co O Nov 5 1819 and 1821. Ref S 40436 Md. Rept by State D A R.

SIMPSON, WILLIAM, Warren co

Pvt Delaware line. Enl for war in Kent co Del. (dep of Rhoda; Oliver) Srvd in Regt of Capt Kirkwood. Was at Battle of defeat of General Gates. Pensd Salem twp Warren co O 11-28-1828. Ref S 46322 Del. Rept by State D A R.

SIMS, FRANCIS, Meigs co

Exec Doc 37 of 1852 suspended pens as service not in any regularly organized corps. Rept by Wm Pettit.

SIMS, JEREMIAH, Muskingum co

Enl Culpepper C H Culpepper co Va. Pvt in Capt Tolls Co Col Darke Regt Va Milit 6 mo. Was b Culpepper co Va July 7 1760; mar 1st Elizabeth Saunders abt 1805; 2nd Catharine Madden (æ 62 in 1855) Jan 3 1838 in Muskingum co O. Wf and fam emigrated to O; wf d leaving 6 chldr. No chldr by Catherine Maddon. Soldr d May 17 1846. Came to O 1821 Perry and Muskingum cos. In 1839 livd in Perry co. Nov 14 1832 app for pens in Muskingum co O Newton twp æ 72. Ref W 1500 B L Wt 31586. Nov 15 1870 wid resid Fultonham Muskingum co O Newson twp. Pensr 29 Nov 1870 Col Agency and Previous acts. Rept by State D A R.

SINCLAIR, GEORGE, Butler co

Pvt N J Contl. Enl 1776 at Philadelphia Pa. Srvd in regt commanded by Col Shreve. Wf æ 66 and 2 dau and 1 son. (Appl 1820) Appl for pens Butler co O June 11 1818. Ref S 40438 Navy New Jersey Pa Sea Service. Rept by State D A R.

SIPRILL, NICHOLAS, Ross co

Pvt Pa Contl. Enl 1779. Srvd 2 yrs. Was 59 in 1818. Pensd Ross co 6-30-1819. Ref Pa S 40433. Rept by State D A R.

SKINNER (Shiner or Shriner), JOHN, Wayne co

Other spellings. Pvt Pa Milit. Srvd 10 mos. Was b 1753 Rockland twp Bucks co Pa; mar Barbary æ 86 in 1853. Was mar whn she was 16. Soldr d abt 1839 Wayne co O. Pens appl Wayne co O May 29 1834. Abt yr 1819 John and Barbary left Pa and mvd to Wayne co O. Wid appl for pens Morrow co O Oct 3 1853 res of Congress twp. Ref R 9632 Md; N J; Pa. Rept by State D A R. Wm Duffs Hist of N Central O p 142 lists John Shriner as Rev soldr. Cop by Mrs Oehlke.

SKINNER, MICAH, Huron co

Pvt N Y Contl. Livd in New Lebanon Albany co N Y in month of Apr 1781 whr enl for 3 yrs. Srvd 2 yrs. Was 66 in 1832. Agent was notified soldr d Dec 6 1844. Res of Huron co O July 27 1832 Ridgefield twp. Pensr in Huron co 3-5-1833. Ref S 3916 N Y. Rept by State D A R.

SKYSARD, JOHN, Cuyahoga co

Grave mrkd by Western Reserve chpt. Ref 13th Rept N S D A R p 123. Cop by Nathan Perry chpt.

SLATER, WILLIAM, Mahoning co

Pvt Pa Contl Line. Pensr in Mahoning co 5-10-1833 æ 82. Ref Pa Arch Vol 23 S 3 p 593. Cop by Jane Dailey.

SLAUGHTER (Slater), WILLIAM, Mahoning co

Pvt Mass State. Pensd July 20 1833; also appl bk 5 p 81 Circuit Court Warren O. Soldr d Milton Mahoning co. Ref Old Pension Bk 1833 Vol 3. Rept by Mahoning chpt.

SLIMER, JOHN, Wayne co

Pvt Pa Milit. Pensr in Wayne co 7-8-1833. Cop fr Pa List by J D. Wooster-Wayne chpt repts no grave found and no records found.

SLOTE, PETER G, Franklin co

Pvt N Y Line 6 yr. Enl 1775 at White Plains N Y. Pensd 6-22-1819 Franklin co O. Trnsfrd to N J 11-28-1820. Was æ 54 yrs in 1818; mar Charity æ 50 yrs in 1820. He and his wf liv alone in Bryen ? co N J in 1820. Ref N Y S 33755. Rept by State D A R.

SLOATE, PHILIP, Hamilton co

Pvt N J Milit. Enl Colonel Dye's Regt Aug 1 1781. Liv with uncle at time of enl in Bergen co N J whr was b 7-7-1765. Mar Sally Stagg Sept 1799. Chldr: Mrs Ann S David; Mrs Sarah M Armstrong æ 43 and 37 repectively; Philip; Elizabeth B; John; George W; and Eliphaz Alonzo. Soldr d 1-21-1837 Cincinnati O. Mvd to N Y City abt 1790. Then in 1816 movd to Cincinnati O. Wid pensd 3-5-1851 in Cincinnati O. She appl for bounty land in Scioto co O 6-20-1855. Ref N J W 6076. B L Wt 31719. Rept by State D A R.

SLUTTS, JOHN SR, Jefferson co

Mariner on Sea. Drafted Baltimore Md abt Apr 1 1777. Was b 1757; mar Catharine June 23 1790; large fam of chldr. Soldr d Oct 10 1833 Jefferson co O. Bur Circlegreen cem Jefferson co O. Inscript on mon "Rev soldr on land and sea. D Oct 10 1833 æ 76 yrs 5 da. He was a Rev soldr and father of 12 sons and three daus." Stone well preservd. Wid appl for pens Jefferson co O July 23 1856; mar Frederick co. Ref R 9667 Md. Rept by Steubenville chpt.

SMILEY, JOHN, Hamilton co

An early settler of Hamilton co. B 1745 Cumberland co Pa; d 1808; may be bur in part of Hamilton later Butler co. Services in 9th Pa C L regt and also associator of milit frm Cumberland co. Fifth S Pa Arch Vol 3 p 460; Vol 4 pp 345; 475; 486; 500 in 7th battl 6th class associators under James Purdy. Rept by State Secy S A R Wm Pettit. Ref 54954 S A R.

SMITH, AARON, Medina co

Pvt Mass Contl. Enl 1778 whl res in Hadley twp Hampshire co Mass. Was dischrgd 7-10-1783. Movd to Medina co O prior to 1822 and to Burlington Wis 1835. Was æ 60 yrs in 1820. Chldr: Moses æ 20; Limuel 9 in 1820. Soldr d 9-23-1838 Burlington Wis. Pensd Madison co N Y 9-9-1819; appl for trnsfr to O 7-17-1822 in Medina co O. Appl for trnsfr from O to Wis in Racine co Wis 1-5-1837. Ref Mass S 38388. Rept by State D A R.

SMITH, ADAM, ? co

Bur Mt Zion cem 2 mi N W of New Berlin O. Grave mrkd by stone Ref 18th Rept N S D A R p 253. Rept by Nathan Perry chpt.

SMITH, ANTHONY, Monroe co

Pvt N J Milit. Drafted 1777 Monmouth co N J. Srvd 2 yrs. Was b 1753 Monmouth co N J; d Aug 11 1836. Pens appl Greene co Pa Sept 10 1832. Heirs appl for pens from Woodsfield O June 15 1839. Made declaration Monroe co O Jan 28 1833. Wid d June 1838. Ref S 4856 N J.

SMITH, DAVID, Delaware co

Pvt N Y Contl. Enl Fredericksburgh N Y 3-1777. Srvd 5 yrs. Was b 3-12-1761; mar Chloe Hughes 10-7-1783; chldr: Sarah æ 35 1820; Nathaniel 18; Aluan 14; Almond 11; Chloe 5. Nehemiah named later in appl 1820. Grand chldr named Taylor: William b 1813; Harriet 1815; John 1816; Sarah Elizabeth 1818; Betsy Ann Russel 1816; and Alford Russell 1818. Soldr d 10-5-1823 Delaware co O. Mvd from Dutchess co N Y to Del co O 1814. Pensd 2-2-1819 Fairfield co. Occupation a tailor. Ref Name listed Wiseman's Pioneer People Fairfield co. Ref N Y W 4272 B L Wt 7761-100-pvt issued 12-15-1790 to Tryon Assignee. Rept by State D A R.

SMITH, DAVID, Washington co

Pvt Conn Contl. Pensr in Washington co 6-22-1819. Enl Apr 1777 and srvd; then enl 2nd abt 1781 in Capt Rice's Co. Srvd 1 yr and 6 mo. 2 yrs 10 mo then furnished a substitute. Pens papers state was "72 yrs in 1818." Ref Pen Cl S 40468; Vol 3 p 414 Com Pleas Court Marietta. Rept by Marietta chpt.

SMITH, EBENEZER, Richland co

Pvt Will Gray's Co York co Pa Milit May 27 1779. Was at Valley Forge winter of 1779. Was b Little York York co Pa Jan 4 1751; came from Scotland in 1740 son of Wm Smith. Mar 1st Martha Bently; 2nd Mary Robinson. Chldr of 1st wf: Benjamin; Jedediah; Jane; Elizabeth. Of 2nd wf; Thomas; Mary; Eleanor; Samuel; William. Soldr d Jan 19 1834; bur Mansfield O. Ref S A R yr bk. D A R Nat No 174574. Rept by Jared Mansfield chpt. The burial ground on Ebenezer's farm has been ploughed up. It is said he may have been bur in old cem whr a school bld now stands but bodies were removd to Mansfield cem Amg them some of Ebenezers fam.

SMITH, EDWARD, Morgan co

Pvt Va St Trps. Enl Apr 1781 in Frederick co Va whr he lvd. Srvd 6 mo. Was b Jan 27 1759 Baltimore co Md. Aft 15 yr and to Allegheny co Pa whr aft 12 yr he mvd to O to Washington co and later to Morgan co. Pens appl Morgan co O Aug 9 1833. Ref Va S 7566. Rept by State D A R.

SMITH, GEORGE, Ashtabula co

Pvt Mass Line 9 mos. Enl 6-1-1777 Rutland twp Worcester co Mass. Was b 1761 Rutland twp Worcester co Mass; mar Molly Bent 2-12-1789; soldr d 6-17-1844 Orwell twp Ashtabula co O; bur Orwell Ashtabula co O. Grave located by Mary Stanley chpt. Appl for trnsfr from Mass to O in Trumbull co 6-6-1837; pensd 1840 Orwell Ashtabula co æ 79. Wid appl Ashtabula co 6-26-1846. Ref 21st Rept N S D A R p 109. Mass W 6119 B L Wt 8457. Rept by State D A R.

SMITH, HAZADIAH, Ashtabula co

Exec Doc 37 refused a pens as servd 2 mo only. Rept by Wm Pettit.

SMITH, HENRY, Licking co

Defender of Fort Henry Wheeling W Va Sept 11-12-1782. Was b 1761; son of James Smith; mar Mary (b 177— d 1866). (One rept says mar Sarah b 1770 Hagerstown Md. She d 1867) Chldr: James 25 in 1792; Harriett Beall; Nancy Clark; Nathaniel; Louis Clark; Willia; Caroline; Carnilian and David. To these are added David; George; Henry; William; Nathaniel. Soldr d July 22 1843; bur Cedar Hill cem Newark. Had 1st grocery in Wheeling W Va. Settled in Licking co O 1804. Farmer and associate judge 1809-1823 Licking co Madison twp. Ref De Haas Border War p 281 1809-1823 Licking co Madison twp. Rept by Hetuck chpt. (Anna Priest)

SMITH, HENRY, Monroe co

Pvt Mass Contl. Enl Apr or May 1775 Mass line. Srvd 6 yrs. Was æ 64 in 1818; mar Catherine Oct 19 1793. Chldr: James; Job; Jacob; Nancy; Henry. Soldr d Jan 30 1825. Pens appl July 7 1818 Monroe co. Ref Mass W 6089. Rept by State D A R.

SMITH, HUGH, Mahoning co

Pvt. Ser 5 Vol 5 p 526 Chester co Mil; Pa Arch; N Y men in Rev p 45; N J men p 757. Mar Mary; chldr: Jeannette mar Caleb Baldwin; John mar Nancy Baldwin; Robert; Mary mar J F Scott; Margaret mar Samuel Leonard; Lorenzo D; Gidwon Miller; Reuben Hugh. Soldr d abt 1821 Ellsworth. Came from Md in 1806 w 5 sons and 3 daus. Ref Hist Trumbull and Mahoning co Vol 2 p 99; Hist Mahoning co p 200 Sanderson; Deed bk D p 299 trnscribd rec Mahoning co to Hugh Smith Heirs 1829. Rept by Mahoning chpt.

SMITH, JAMES, Columbiana co

Pvt Capt David Grier's Pa Co and in Col Hartley's Regt. Was in battles Brandywine and Germantown. Dischrgd Apr 13 1778 length of service 1 yr. Was b 1752; mar Jane; one son d 1824. Soldr d aft 1840 St Clair twp. Family of German descent; ancestor came to Baltimore Md at æ 14 yr. Had 5 sons and 6 dau. One son Peter (d æ 82) mar Sophia Cahill and movd to O. Ref Appear Dock Bk 5 p 335 Columbiana co; S 40453. Was allowed pens Apr 13 1830 æ 74. Res in Columbiana co. Certficate no 20145 issued May 19 1830. Rept by Rebecca Griscom chpt and Wilma Molsberry.

SMITH, JAMES, Mahoning co

Pvt. Ser 5 Pa Arch many. Chldr: William b 1784 mar Mary Wishart. Soldr d Youngstown O. B in Ireland came to Franklin co Pa. Ref Hist Mahoning co Vol 3 p. 112 Butler; Hist Mahoning co p 675 Sanderson; Deed bk B p 431 trnscrbd Mahoning co to James Smith 1806. Rept by Mahoning chpt.

SMITH, JOHN N, Belmont co

Pvt N J Milit. Enl June 1780 in Burgan? co N J whr was b Sept 24 1764 Bergan co N J. Srvd 1 yr and 6 mo. Aft war left for N Y Cy and Little Brittain until 1803; then to Belmont co O whr resided. Pens appl June 9 1832 Morgan co O. At æ 76 liv in Flushing twp Belmont co O. Later movd to Va. Ref N J S 18228. Rept by State D A R.

SMITH, JOHN O C, Pickaway co

Pvt Pa Milit. Whl liv in Mansfield twp Sussex co N J he enl May 1776 in Lieut Benj Warner Co under Major Pratt. Enl again 1779. Was b Dec 1760 Oxford twp Sussex co N J; bur in fam cem on Clate Weber's farm. Aft Rev he movd from N J to Md; then to Va; later to O. Pensd Oct 23 1832 whl liv in Pickaway co. Ref S 3921 Pa. Rept by Pickaway Plains chpt.

SMITH, JOHN, Highland co

Pvt Va Milit. Enl 1-1-1781 Halifax co Va whl livd there. Srvd 6 mos and 14 das. Was b 10-1-1742 Amelia co Va. 1821 movd to Fayette co; appl for pension Highland co 8-25-1832. (Pensr in Cens 1840 in Highland co.) Listed p 289 "Va Milit in Rev" æ 90 in Highland co. J D. Ref Va S 3939; S A R 46249 by State D A R.

SMITH, JOHN, Lorain co

Listed p 144 in "Hist of North Central O" by Wm A Duff as a Rev Soldr. Rept by Nathan Perry chpt.

SMITH, JONATHAN, ? co

Pvt. Stricken fr pens rolls of 1818 Act of 1820 not being considered in indigent circumstances. Ref Doc No 31; Jan 6 1831. Cop by Blanche Rings.

SMITH, JONATHAN, Mahoning co

Lieut Va. Enl Dec 15 1776 8th Regt of the Va line. Pensd 7-13-1819 Youngstown O. From pens appl 1820 soldr was æ 64 yrs; his wf Nancy æ 54; and son William æ 11. Fam liv in Youngstown O in 1828. Ref Va S 40473 B L Wt 2079-200-Lieut. Issued Oct 17 1794. No papers. Rept by State D A R.

SMITH, JOHNSTON, Gallia co

Pvt Va Contl. Pensd 8-9-1819 Gallia co. Mar Nancy ——; chldr: Rachel Dyer; Anna Smith; Betsey Smith. Ref Gallia co Probate Court Civ Jr 1 p 60; the heirs of Johnston Smith and wf Nancy, Anna Smith Rachel Dyer and Betsey Smith, made appl for back pens (for services rendered in Rev War) due to Nancy Smith as wid of Johnston Smith. Rept by French Colony chpt.

SMITH, JOSEPH, Belmont co

Pvt Md Milit. Enl Dec 1776 Cecil co Md. Srvd 9 mos. Was b Feb 14 1753 Cecil co Md. Since Rev livd in Md; then 2 yrs nr Pittsburg; thence to Belmont co. Pens appl Belmont co O Aug 2 1832 res of Wheeling twp. Ref S 4861 Md. Rept by Jane Dailey.

SMITH, LORONTZ, Columbiana co

Exec Doc 37. Rev soldr liv in O 1852 or before refused a pens as servd in French army. Rept by Wm Pettit.

SMITH, NICHOLAS, Washington ? co

Enl Fall of 1776 Newark N J. Pensd 6-9-1819 Salem Washington co O. Was 81 yrs in 1818. Had no fam and resided in Salem O 1820. Ref Contl S 40462. Rept by State D A R.

SMITH, NOAH, Portage co

Exec Doc 37 refused a pension as servd less than 6 mo. Rept by Wm Pettit.

SMITH, OBADIAH, Clermont co

Pvt N Y Contl. Enl Feb 1777 Duchess co N Y. Srvd 5 yrs. Was æ 59 in 1818; mar Peninah; chldr: Caroline æ 10; Harriet æ 2 (1820). Pens appl Clermont co 5-19-1818. Ref N Y S 40458. Rept by State D A R.

SMITH, PETER, Wayne co

Pvt Pa Milit. Enl 1776 Berks co Pa whr livd 22 yrs. Srvd 9 mos. Was b 1756 Berks co Pa. Mar Julian ——. The will named wf and following chldr: Peter; George; David; John; Jacob; Catherine mar David Swartz; Mary; Elizabeth mar Christian Lent; Pekey mar Jones Miller; Susan mar John Elinberger; Rosanna mar Christ Specher. Soldr d 1827 Wayne co; no grave found. Ref S 4850 Pa. Rept by Wooster-Wayne chpt.

SMITH, DR PETE, Clark co

N J Apr 1 1777 J Ten Eycks men at Bound Brook. Pvt May 7 1778 Morris co Milit Capt Carters Co Col Seeleys Eastern Battl; Adj Gen office Trenton N J. Was b Feb 6 1753 in Wales; son of Dr Hezekiah Smith. Mar Catherine Stent Dec 23 1776 dau of Sam'l Stent of Hopewell N J. Chldr: Samuel b 1778 d 1856; Ira b 1780 d 1864; Sarah b 1782 d 1824 mar Henry Jennings: Hezekiah b 1784 d 1870 mar Sally Smith; Elizabeth b 1786 d 1809 mar John Ferris; Abraham 1788; Nancy b 1790 mar John John; Margaret b 1793 mar Hugh Wallace; Catherine b 1793 d æ 15; Jacob S b 1799 d 1879; (? mar Joseph Keifer Sharpburg Md); Rhoda A b 1801 d 1840 mar Dr William Lindsey of N C. Soldr d Dec 31 1816; bur on his farm Donnelsville Clark co O. Dr Pete Smith was one of the first physicians in the west. At Cincinnati 1813. Advocated innoculation for small pox and it is recorded that he innoculated 130 persons in Morris co 1777. Accepting this information Jane Dailey.

SMITH, PHILIP, Wayne co

Srvd in Capt Beeson's Co under Col Wm Crawford in Exped against Indians 1782. Was wounded. Was b Feb 1761 Frederick co Md; mar Agnes; four of his chldr living 1873: John P; Jacob P; N W; Mrs Agnes McFadden. Others: Nathan; Jonathan; Christena mar Jas McIntire; George; Philip; James; Valentine mar Jacob. Soldr d

3-27-1838 East Union twp Wayne co. In 1782 livd nr Beeson town (now Uniontown Pa). One of the pioneer settlers of O; came 1784; built a cabin but driven away by Indians; returned 1799; settled nr Steubenville Jefferson co whr livd till 1812; thence to Wayne co O. Ref Crawford's Campaign vs Sandusky by C W Butterfield pp 73, 143, 210, 212, 284-7. Rept by Jacobus Westervelt chpt.

SMITH, ROBERT, ? co

Pvt listed in invalid pensrs of U S belonging to O pd at Chillicothe $96 annually. Cop fr Pensrs of 1818 by Mrs O D Dailey. Cf p 342 Roster of O.

SMITH, ROBERT, Hocking co

Pvt Capt Christian Myer's Co Pa Contl Trps. Lieut Col Ludwig Weltner. Was b 1752 New Carlisle Westmoreland co Pa whr he enl 1778. First wf name not known; had two dau Jane and Anne. Second wf mar 1791; name Susan (1766-1821) had four sons: Robt Davidson mar Mary Rhinehart; William; Benjamin F; John Adams. Soldr d 1813 Logan O; bur in abandoned fam cem one mi n of town; last payroll dated Dec 1780 came to Hocking co O in 1812. Ref V 121 No 120947 D A R Lin. Rept by Jane Dailey and Governor Worthington chpt.

SMITH, SILAS, Delaware co

Pvt Conn Contl. Enl 1777 (substitute of father) Wyoming Pa. Srvd 2 yrs. Was b 12-6-1761 Colchester Conn; d 7-17-1839. Movd to Wyoming Pa at æ of 13. In 1815 movd to Ontario co N Y and in 1827 to Delaware co O whr appl for pens 11-19-1832. Ref Conn S 18597. Rept by State D A R.

SMITH, THADDEUS, Meigs co

Pvt N J Milit. Pensr in Meigs co 8-24-1833. Was b May 6 1742 Amwell N J; mar Ann 1781 or 82 by Wm Abbot esq; chldr: Nancy; Benjamin; Samuel; John; Eliza; Jonothan; Ely. Soldr d April 12 1839. Movd to Rutland Meigs co O from Mill Creek Va in 1829. Ref W 9658. Rept by Mrs John Chase; Return Jonathan Meigs chpt.

SMITH, TIMOTHY 1ST, Medina co

Pvt Mass Contl. Enl July 1779 Mass. Dischrgd Peekskill N Y 1780. Was b 1758; d Nov 20 1837. Pens appl Genesee co N Y May 20 1818; Medina co O Oct 27 1830. Was a pensr of Medina co 3-25-1819. Ref S 40461 Mass. Rept by State D A R.

SMITH, THOMAS, Franklin co

Md Contl. Pensd Sept 27 1826 æ 74 — (probably abt 67). Rev Census 1840 states livd in 3rd Ward æ 81. Chldr: John; Nancy mar Wm Hughes 1-29-1845; Hughes; Margaret mar A M G Elliott 2-1845; Dorothy Blanchard. Grandsons: Thomas Martin; Thomas Hull. Will probated Jan 7 1845 Franklin co O. Ref Will bk B 195; Order bk 4-264 declaration for pens 8-25-1826; O 1672 Estate shows he owned land certif. Stated 3-27-1829 for 50 A land Entry 1648 lying in westward of Cumberland Allegheny co Md. Rept by Mrs W S Van Fossen Columbus chpt.

SMITH, WILLIAM, Darke co

Pvt Del Contl. Enl Jan 1776 in Del with Contl army. Srvd 6 yrs. Was æ 68 in 1818; mar Nancy æ 67 in 1820. Pens appl in the supreme court of O 5-12-1818; in Darke co 7-7-1820. Ref Del S 40460. Rept by State D A R.

SMITH, WILLIAM, Adams co

Pvt. Enl in Va. Capt John Waggoner 12th Va Regt Col Wood. Srvd 4 yrs under Gen Green. Dischrgd at Santee S C 1782. Was b 1752 Va; mar Hannah 1766 ?; chldr: Jacob b 1796; George 1798; Elizabeth 1801; Quiller 1802; Margaret 1806; Hannah 1808. Soldr livd in Clermont co. Was in battles of Brandywine; Monmouth; Guilford

Courthouse; Eutaw Springs; wounded by bayonet on knees and crippled for life. (limped) Ref S 40463 Va. Rept by M S Askue.

SMITH, WILLIAM, Monroe co

Pvt Va Milit. Enl in Martinsberg Va in the fall of 1779. Srvd 2 yrs. Was b 1761 York co Pa. Res in Mantinsburg Va at time of enl. 5 or 6 yrs aft the war he movd to Berkley co O. Then movd to Washington co Pa and livd abt 16 yrs. Then movd to Monroe co O. Pens appl Monroe co O 9-1-1832. Ref Va S 3920. Rept by State D A R. J D rept listed p 290 "Va Milit in Rev" as liv in Monroe co O æ 73.

SMITH, WILLIAM, Butler co

Exec Doc 37 of 1852 suspended list shows service in two places. R I. but details not identified. Rept by Wm Pettit.

SMITH, WILLIAM, Ross co

Pvt Pa Milit. Enl 7-20-1776 York co Pa. Srvd 9 mos. Was b 12-3-1760 York co Pa. Resided with father until beginning of Rev. Movd to Washington co Pa 1783; 1802 movd to Ross co O whr appl for pens 10-15-1833. Ref Pa S 7535. Rept by State D A R. Nathaniel Massie chpt repts he d 1804; no will.

SMITH, WILLIAM 2ND, Mahoning co

Pensr Mass; pensd 1818 Trumbull co; Old pens bk V 3 1833. Was b 1742; d Youngstown. Ref Old Pens bk 1808 Act of 1818 O gives his service as in Delaware. Rept by Mahoning chpt.

SMITH, WILLIAM, Huron co

Soldr d Huron co O. Ref 4th Rept N S D A R p 299. Cop by Mary Chesney chpt. (Suggest "Pioneer Women Western Reserve" p 159 and 184 for research on same name. J D).

SNEAD, SAMUEL, Mahoning co ?

Pvt and Sergt Mass St Trps. Pensr Trumbull co 7-20-1833. Cop fr Ohio list by Jane Dailey.

SNELL, DAVID, Richland co

Pvt Mass Milit. Enl 1776; srvd in Regt commanded by Col Jacobs of Mass Line. Was b Aug 1761 Bridgewater Mass. Mar Mary Baker ? 7-17-1783; d 11-4-1845 Richland co O. Was abt 16 yrs of æ at the time of enl and livd in Bridgewater Mass. He res there for a number of yrs aft the war; later movd to province of Maine and livd abt 20 yrs there. Thence to Muskingum co O and then to Richland co O. Pensr Richland co 7-6-1833. Pensr in Congress twp 1840 æ 79. Wid pensd 12-5- 1846 Richland co O. Ref Will filed in Richland co Ct House No 767; Mass W 6137. Rept by State D A R.

SNIDER, JOHN, Shelby co

Exec Doc 37 refused pens as servd less than 6 mo. Rept by Wm Pettit.

SNOOK, JOHN, Columbiana co

Rev Soldr. Rec not yet found. Was b 1753; mar Catherine (b 1761; d 3-20-1826 æ 64 yrs 5 mo 21 da). Chldr: John mar Mary Rupert dau of Adam Rupert Cumberland co Pa. Grson John b 1832. Soldr d Sept 23 1833 80 yr 8 mo 3 da. Bur Unity twp Forney cem East Palestine. Came to Unity twp from Md in 1807. Ref Columbiana co Cem Recs; Hist Upper O valley Vol 2 p 232. Rept by Wilma M Molsberry.

SNOW, LEMUEL, Hamilton co

Pvt Mass Contl. Enl Mass Line 1781. Dischrgd 1783. Pensr Hamilton co 6-15-1820. Was æ 59 yrs in 1818. Livd in Franklin co Ind in Aug 1818. Appl for trnsfr from O. Ref Mass S 40476. **Rept by State D A R.**

SNYDER, ——, Ashland co

Listed p 142 in "Hist of North Central Ohio" by Wm A Duff as Rev soldr bur McFall cem. **Rept by Nathan Perry chpt.**

SNYDER, GEORGE, Ashland co

Listed p 142 in "Hist of North Central Ohio" by Wm A Duff as Rev soldr. Rept by Nathan Perry chpt.

SNYDER, GEORGE, Mahoning co

Ranger. Ser 3 Vol 23 pp 264, 344 Northumberland co Pa Arch. Mar Mary (1765-1859); one son was George. Soldr d abt 1847 Greene twp. Came to Milton in 1805; movd to Greene. Ref Hist Trumbull and Mahoning co Vol 2 p 180; Deed bk G p 117 trnscribd Mahoning co George and Mary Snyder to 1820; Administration bk 1 p 52 Est Geo Snyder Greene 1847. Rept by Mahoning chpt.

SNYDER, PETER, Richland co

Pvt Md Milit. Pensr in Richland co 5-9-1833. Mar Druscilla Metcalf (Scotch); chldr: Vatchel; Peter; Daniel; Rachel; Catherine; Thomas; John C. Soldr d 1860; bur Emmanuel gr-yd Mifflin twp off Mt Zion Rd 4 mi from Mansfield. German kind hospitable and generous. Came to Richland co in 1815 from Washington co Pa. Ref Bought N E Corner Sec 6 Mifflin twp on which he sttled with his family. Rept by Jared Mansfield chpt.

SOCKMAN, JOHN, Muskingum co

Enl 1-1-1776 in the Regt under Gen Butler Pa line. Was æ 65 in 1818. Mar Catherine Ichner 2-2-1819; one son was John Isaac æ 80 in 1905. Soldr d Nov or Dec 1827 Wheeling Va. Pensd 2-11-1819 Muskingum co O. Wid pensd 5-8-1855 Wheeling Va. Pens No 5188. He trnsfrd to O co Va 1820. Son John Isaac appl for bounty land in Westmoreland co Pa 11-27-1905. Ref Pa W 11513 B L Wt 26893. Rept by State D A R.

SOMERSET, THOMAS, Ross co

Pvt Pa Contl. Enl summer 1779 Charlottesville Va. Srvd 3 yrs. Was 71 in 1825; mar 12-5-1787; chldr: Sarah æ 27 in 1824; Ann 25; William 23; Polly 20; Rebecca 18; Susan b 1788; Harry 1790; John 1792; Elizabeth 1794; Mary 1803; Catharine 1808. Soldr d 3-5-1834 Ross co O. Pens appl 3-31-1825 Ross co O. Ref Contl (Va) W 4826 B L Wt 1171-100. Rept by State D A R.

SOUTHARD, ABRAHAM JR, Licking co

Pvt in Capt Peter Dickersons Co Col Elias Daytons Battl trps. Enl 2-26-1776. Rec as Pvt in War dept Adj Gen rept Washington D C. Rec as pvt State of N J Trenton Office of Adj Gen. Was b Aug 25 1758; presumably in Barnards Town N J. Son of Abraham Southard who rem fr Hempstead L I to Somerset co N J 1751 with 8 chldr; will 1777 mentions son Abraham. Mar 1805 at the æ of 26 Eliza Hull dau of Francis and Catherine Hull of Washington co Pa. She d 12-15-1844 æ 76 6 mo. Chldr: Francis b Washington co Pa Mar 31 1793; Elizabeth 1794; Noah 1795; Abraham 1799; Isaiah 1801; Margret 1802; William 1804; then in Licking co O Rebecca 1806; Hannah 1806; Catherine 1809; Thomas 1811; Joseph 1814; Julian 1815. Soldr d May 20 1855 æ 96 yr 7 mo at Hanover Licking co. Fr N J went to Washington co Pa; thence to Licking co O with his family in 1805. He was a bro of Henry Southard also a Rev soldr. Sheriff in Washington co Pa whr he endorsed so heavily for those in distress that he came to O a poor man. Ref D A R 267793. Secured from Noble Everet Warham Mass and G H Southard Col O by Jane Dailey.

SPACHT, ANTHONY, Washington co

Was in battle of Pt Pleasant 1774. Mar Catharine; soldr d 1803; bur abandoned cem in field at Newbury O. Inscript on monument "Pioneers of O Anthony Spacht and wf Catharine; Hannah wf of Joseph Gutherie; Stratton; Leavens; Bliss; Dunham; one woman and 2 chldr killed by Indians d and were bur on this spot between 1790 and 1810. Erected by descendants 1871. Rept by Marietta chpt.

SPAULDING, SAMPSON, ? co

Sergt in Capt John Trull's Co Col Ebenezer Bridges Regt at Lexington alarm. Was b 1745 Tewksbury Mass. Mar Experience Merrill; one dau was Nancy. Soldr d in O. Ref V 57 p 178 D A R Lin No 56517 and No 29966. Rept by Nathan Perry chpt.

SPEAR, EDWARD, Mercer co

Lieut in Pa Line and Lieut of Artillery when killed 1791 at Fort Recovery O. Mar Jane Holliday; William was one son. Soldr d Fort Recovery O Ref V 125 p 234 D A R Lin No 124771. Rept by Nathan Perry chpt.

SPELMAN, TIMOTHY, ? co

Pvt listed in rejected pens appl. Ref Doc No 31 Jan 6 1831 as did not serve required nine mo. Rept by Blanche Rings.

SPENCE, DAVID, Columbiana co

Rev Soldr. Rec not yet found. Was b 1751; d 1821; bur Madison twp. Ref Col Co cem recs. Rept by Mrs Wilma M Molsberry.

SPENCER, AMOS, Miami co

Va pvt Capt Davis Co Col Wood Regt Va Line 3 yr. Was b 1759; appld pens Miami co June 17 1823 æ 64. Only one of this name on files; erroneously listed Mercer co. See pens files. Ref S 40484 Vol 3 p 483. Rept by State D A R. Agency Ohio 19129 $8 beginning June 17 1823; iss Dec 10 1823; Act Mch 18 1818; May 1 1820; Mch 1 1823. Cop by Jane Dailey.

SPENCER, BEVERLY, Champaign co

Pvt Va Contl. Enl 1775 in the 1st Regt of the Va Line. Pensr Champaign co 9-27-1819. Was æ 70 in 1818 Kent co Va. Res of Champaign co O in 1818. Ref Va S 40491. Rept by State D A R.

SPENCER, JOHN, Portage co

Sergt Capt Benjamin Pollard's Co of Artificers Conn Contl Trps Col Jeduthan Baldwin Engineer. Enl 1777 for war; promoted to 2nd Lieut 1779; name on record last time 1781. Ref Conn Men in Rev p 611. Soldr bur larger Aurora cem Portage co. Rept by Moses Cleaveland chpt.

SPENCER, WILLIAM, Clinton co

Pvt Va Contl. Enl 1776 Hampshire co Va. Srvd 3 yrs. Was b 1743. Appl mentions wf. Pens appl July 27 1818 Clinton co O. Ref S 40487 Va and Indian Wars. (One same name rejected U S pensr as case not provided for by law;Ref Exec Doc 31 of 1831. B R).

SPERRY, ELIJAH, Lake co

Lieut in Capt Osborne's Co of Artificers Col Baldwin's Conn Regt. Also sergt for 10 mo 8 das. Enl 1777 in New Milford? Conn whr he then res. Mar Polly Apr 19 1779; soldr d Sept 4 1818 Warren co N Y. Grave located by New Conn chpt. Movd from Vt to N Y in 1802. Later his wid movd to O. He appl for pens in N Y but never received it. His wid appl for pens Nov 4 1839 Geauga co O. Ref 5th Rept N S D A R p 386 Conn Contl W 3885. Rept by Nathan Perry chpt.

SPERRY, PETER, Ross co

Enl 1778 Capt Craven's Co ? Trps. Was b Frederick co Va 1760. Mar Mary Hammock; one dau mar Elisha Thompson 1781; soldr d 1838 Frankfort O. Ref Vol 106 D A R Lin 105927. Rept by Jane Dailey.

SPOKEN, PHILIP, Perry co

Is a misspelling for Philip Spohn which see this vol. J D.

SPOHN, PHILIP, Perry co

Not "Spoken." Lieut Pa St Trps. Enl June 1776 Burks co Pa whr was b 1755. Srvd 8 mos. Mar Catherine Nov 30 1777; chldr: John; Daniel; Mary Stump (formerly Spohn); Jacob; Sarah Auspack (nee Spohn); Samuel. Also George; Adam; Henry Aussack Heirs of Elizabeth. Movd from Berks co Pa to Washington co Md; then to O in Perry co 1804. Pens appl Perry co O Nov 9 1832. Wid d Aug 28 1838 (affiidavit of heirs.) Ref R 100004 Pa. Rept by State D A R.

SPRAGUE, JONATHAN, Erie co

Bur Huron cem; has govt mrkr. Serg pay roll of a detachment under Capt Stephen Calkins for services assisting Major Whitcomb Nov 6 to 13 1778; Sergt pay roll Stephen Calkins Co in alarm Mar 1780 Col Ebenezer Allen 6 das; Sergt Capt Steven Calking Co Ira Allen Regt Oct 13 to 18 1780. Lieut pay roll Capt Ebenezer Wilsons Co Col Ira Allen Reg service at Castleton Oct 1781. Wf Elizabeth. Ref Vt Rolls pp 92, 163, 197, 372, 373, 462; Pioneer Women of the Western Reserve p 571; Firelands Pioneers O S Vol 3 p 29; Vol 4 pp 12; 69; Vol 7 p 54; Williams Hist p 466. Rept by Marjorie Cherry.

SPRAGUE, JOSEPH, ? co

Pvt Conn. No pens Cl at D C. No other data located. Rept by Jane Dailey.

SPRAGUE, SIMEON (Simon), Mahoning co

Pvt. Mass Soldr and Sailors. Capt Phineas Sterrns Co. On an undated muster roll. Mar Elizabeth dau John Everett R S (1753-4-22-1823). Chldr: William; Ira; John; Augustine mar Sarah; Lona mar Samuel M Hayden; Lodimia mar Ezra Hunt; Belinda mar Azariah Wetmore; Jerusha mar James Gunn; Almira mar Charles A Bonnell; Sarah mar Jared Mill. Soldr d June 12-1823 Canfield O. He came to Canfield in 1802. Ref Deed bk F p 71 trnscrbd Mahoning co to Simeon Sprague 1803; Mahoning Dispatch Mar 12 1897 Hist Canfield Truesdale. Rept by Mahoning chpt.

SPRAGUE, TIMOTHY, Clermont co

Exec Doc 37 of 1852 refused a pens as servd less than 6 mo. Rept by Wm Pettit.

SPRAGUE, WILLIAM, Washington co

Was b 1756; d Sept 17 1826; bur Devol cem nr Coal Run O. Ref Rev Ser Mass Soldr and Sailors Vol XIV p 764 and 765.

SPRINGER, E——, Columbiana co

Rev soldr. Rec not yet found. Was b May 7 1735; mar Anny (b 1751; d 9-15-1820); Soldr d March 1814; bur Center twp. Ref Col co Cem recds. Rept by Mrs Wilma M Molsberry O.

SPRINGER, JACOB, Washington co

Pvt N J Contl. Enl 1781; dischrgd June 3-5-1783. Srvd in Capt Piatt's Co Jersey line. Was b 1763. Wf name not given. Chldr: Susanna æ 17; Jacob 15; Humphrey 13 in 1820. Soldr d Aug 9 1830. Pensr in Washington co 12-18-1818. Ref Pen papers S 40488; Pen certificate No 4927; First appl for pens Marietta May 2 1818 (court recds); Ref for death date Pen recd Col O; Vol 3 p 412 Com Pleas Ct Marietta. Rept by Marietta chpt.

SPRINGUM, JOHN, Morgan co

Pvt Va Contl. Enl 1778 in Va. Pensr in Brook co Va for service of 1 yr. Trnsfrd to Morgan co; was a pensr there 2-1-1819. Was æ 65 in 1820. Soldr d Aug 10 1834. Ref Va S 39850. Rept by State D A R.

SPROAT, EARL, ? co

Major. List in news clipping by L A A found in old scrap bk as "Rev soldrs participating or interested in Marietta Settlement." Filed here for continued research by Marietta chpt.

SPROUSE, DAVID, Gallia co

Pvt Va Milit. Srvd in Regt commanded by Col Harrison for 18 mos. Pens appl Gallia co Sept 27 1832. Pens 4-6-1833. Was b Apr 11 1760 Louisa co Va. Ref S 3958 Va; on back of pens certificate in pens dept is written "Dead letter to Hon C Morris Jan 17 1838;" Va in Rev p 291. Rept by State D A R.

SPYERS, BENJAMIN, Brown co

Md Contl. Bur Liberty Chapel nr Decatur O. Grave located by Ripley chpt. Ref 16th Rept N S D A R p 146. Rept by Nathan Perry chpt.

SPYERS, RICHARD, Brown co

Pvt Md Contl. Enl July 10 1781 Md. Srvd 3 yrs. Was æ 65 in 1818. Mar Rebecca Feb 1787; chldr: John æ 17; Dorcas 15; Henry 13; Jane 10. (Fr appl 1821) Other chldr: Wm and Elizabeth Butt (formerly Spyers) (aff of a witness). Soldr d Mar 19 1838 Brown co O. Pens appl May 1 1818 Brown co O; Apr 5 1821 Brown co; Wid appl Brown co Oct 1840. Ref. Cens 1840 liv at Ripley twp æ 78; W 6145; B L Wt 1672-100 Md. Rept by State D A R. Same as Richard Spires Vol 1 p 346 — Meryl B Markley.

SQUIERS, ASA, Cuyahoga co

Pvt Conn service under Capt Edgar's Co Inf Col Sheldon's Regt. Was b 1764 Conn; mar Eunice —— (1766-1851). Morris was one son (1799-1879) Soldr d 1852 Strongsville O. Appld for pens 1818. Ref No 123059 Vol 124 D A R Lin. Rept by Jane Dailey

SQUIER, BENJAMIN, Mahoning co

Pvt. Mass Soldrs and Sailors Vol 14 p 786. Was b 1750; chldr: Solomon; Jehiel; Abigail; Abiram mar Phebe; Mary Ann; Patience; Meriam. Soldr d Jan 8 1824 Canfield O. Ref Will bk 6 p 72 Trumbull co Rec Probated 1824; Cem Recds late Henry R Baldwin S A R; Records St James Prot Episcopal Ch Boardman O. Rept by Mahoning chpt.

SQUIER, JOHN, Mahoning co

Accd to address of Compatriot Lynn is a Rev soldr bur in cem at Canfield. Rept by Wm Pettit S A R.

STACKHOUSE, AMOS, Guernsey co

Pvt N J Contl. Enl July 1776 N J. Servd 6 yrs. Was b 1758; appl mentions "wf".

Pens appl Choshocton co O May 9 1818; pensr Guernsey co 2-11-1819. Ref S 40528 B L Wt 509-100 N J. Rept by State D A R.

STACKHOUSE, ISAAC, Monroe co

Pvt Va St Trps. Enl 1781 spring in Cheat River Va. Srvd 1 yr. Was b 1751 Hampshire co Va. Soldr d 5-1-1838. Pens appl Monroe co O 9-21-1832. Res in Cheat River when he enl. Later livd in Harrison co Va and Moorefield co Va. Then movd to Monroe co Va. Ref Va S 11473. Rept by State D A R.

STANBURY (Stansbury), SAMUEL, Starke co

Pvt N J Milit and State Trps. Was b Morristown N J 1754; d Canton (Starke co) O 1823. Ref No 130910 D A R. Cop by Jane Dailey. Fr Wm Pettit comes Ref 42657 S A R giving mar to Mary Baxter Andrews 1806.

STANFORD, WILLIAM, Wayne co

Rebecca Stanford his wf d Feb 25 1864 æ 52. Soldr bur Cannan Bend cem Wayne co. Inscript on mrkr "D Mar 25 1843. Soldr war 1776." (See p 684 Cuyahoga co Pioneer Women Western Reserve. In spring 1811 a settlement made in N E part of Brecksville twp and Stanfords one of the family. J D). Rept by Wooster-Wayne chpt.

STANLEY, JAMES C, Mahoning co

Pvt. Conn Men in Rev pp 13, 25, 63. Mar Mary; chldr: Garland; James; Elizabeth; Nathaniel C 1768-1848; Littlebury; Lemuel; Jonathan; Mary. Soldr d abt 1823 Smith twp. Came with wf and 8 chldr from Va 1805. Ref Hist Trumbull and Mahoning co Vol 2 p 200; Hist Mahoning co p 225 Sanderson; Hist Coll p 308 Hist Columbiana co p 300; Will bk P Columbiana co Records probated 1823. Rept by Mahoning chpt.

STANLEY, THOMAS, Mahoning co

Pvt. Va Men in Rev (Library Rec) p 286. Also Conn Men pp 251, 331, 539. Mar Priscilla; chldr: James; John; Elijah; Edmond; Millie; Frances mar Isaac Votaw. Bur Smith twp. Ref Hist Trumbull and Mahoning co Vol 2 p 200; Hist Mahoning co p 225 Sanderson; Deed bk P p 203 trnscrbd Mahoning Thomas and Priscilla Stanley 1815. Rept by Mahoning chpt.

STANNAGE, THOMAS, Logan co

Pvt Va. Enl 5-12-1779 Rockbridge co Va. Pensd 11-26-1818 Clark co O (pension no 13094) and again 5-10-1833 Logan co O. Was b 5-12-1759. Date of death not known. Ref Va S 4905. Rept by State D A R.

STARK, CALEB, Tuscarawas co

Lieut N H Line. Pensr in Tuscarawas co 8-6-1822. Cop fr Ohio lists. Mar Sarah 1788 (she d 9-11-1839). Chldr: Henry; Caleb; Harriet; Charlott and Elizabeth Newell. (aff of Henry) Soldr d Aug 28 1838. Son Henry Stark appl for pens N Y city Jan 25 1844. Wid Sarah Stark made last will in Merrimac co N H Sept 24 1840. Ref W 15391; B L Wt 1351-200 N H. Rept by State D A R.

STARKEY, ISAAC, Wayne co

Pvt Va Contl. Hired as substitute 1780 in Va. Dischrgd in Salisbury N C. Srvd 18 mos. Was æ 61 in 1822. Appl 1822 states Wf æ 42; 7 chldr living with me: John Starkey æ 23; Elizabeth and Effie (twins) æ 21; George æ 16; Levi æ 14; Benjamin æ 8; Deborah æ 5. Pens appl Shenandoah co Va Nov 13 1822; Wayne co Mar 31 1824. Ref S 4053 Va. Rept by State D A R.

STARKEY, JOSEPH, Belmont co

Pvt Va Contl. Was in battle of Eutaw Springs and of Guilford C H; taken prisoner at Camden and retaken by Gen Marion on Santee River. (dep of Joseph Starkey Shenandoah co Va 1822) Srvd under Col Campbell 10 mos from 1780. Was b 1764. He was pensd in Va Nov 13 1822 and pens certif was trnsfrd to O (co in O not given) Sept 26 1825. (from copy of certif for pens on file in Vet Adm Wash) Made appl for pens in Frederick co Va Sept 22 1825. Ref S 40525 Va. Rept by State D A R.

STARKS, PARDON T, Butler co

Pvt Mass Contl. Enl Jan 10 1781 Mass and srvd until Jan 23 1783. Was æ 56 in 1820. Chldr: Hiram; Sally Zachariah. Movd from Mass aft the war to Monroe co O whr appl pens 6-22-1820. Movd to Butler co O. Ref Mass S 40527. Rept by State D A R.

STARNFORD, OLIVER, Mahoning co

Pens Appl Circuit Court Warren O. Also Soldrs and Sailors Col Theophilus Cotton. Chldr: ? Horace b 1785; James. Soldr d Poland twp. Ref Tax list 1826 Poland; Tax list 1837 Horace Stanford Boardman. Rept by Mahoning chpt.

STARR, JOSIAH, Portage co

Conn Trps. Pensr 1835. Was b 1751 Middletown Conn; mar 1773 Patience Goodrich (1732-1807). Josiah Jr was one son. Soldr d 1837 Charlestown O; bur Charleston cem Portage co. Inscript on mrkr "Josiah Starr d Apr 12 1837 in 87th yr of his life" Wf bur in Conn. Ref V 112 p 15 D A R Lin No 111039; No 225 Hist Starr Fam by Burgis Pratt Starr. Rept by Jane Dailey from Mrs W T Taylor Cuyahoga Falls.

STARR, WILLIAM, Jefferson co

Used an alias "William Locke" aft enl U S army for the British. See record this vol under Locke (J D).

STAUFFER, Jacob, Mahoning co

Pvt. Ser 5 Vol 7 pp 688, 701, 757 Pa Arch. Mar Susan (1774-Mar 31 1854) Soldr d Oct 24 1859 Beaver twp; bur Old cem at N Lima. Early resident. Ref Hist Trumbull and Mahoning co Vol 2 pp 197, 208. Rept by Mahoning chpt.

STAUFFER, JOHN, Mahoning co

Pvt. Ser 5 Vol 7 pp 700, 756, 784; and Ser 6 Vol 2 p 531 Pa Arch York co Mil 1782 Capt Andrew Paulley. Mar Elizabeth; chldr: John; Abraham; David; soldr d abt 1822 Beaver twp. Among early settlers. Ref Hist Trumbull and Mahoning co Vol 2 p 198; Lin bk Vol 77 p 203 D A R; Will bk 4 p 452 Columbiana co Records probated 1822; Deeds bk P p 404 and 621 from John Stauffer 1818 to 1822. Rept by Mahoning chpt.

STAUR (or Staur, might be Stow), ABIJAH, ? co

STAYNER (Stainer), WILLIAM, Marion co

Pvt July 1777 Philadelphia City Milit Capt Isaac Austin's Co Col Timothy Mattock. Feb 1781 4th Battl 6th Co Capt James Hood Phila Milit Col McKean. 1783 Capt Curtis Lownes's Co Lieut Col Richard Willing 4th Battl Chester Co Milit. Was b May 4 1759 Boston Mass Son of Roger Stayner and Elizabeth Condy. Mar Mary Renelds Apr 18 1782; chldr: Elizabeth; William Benjamin; Joanna; Jacob; William; Roger; Mary; John. Soldr d Apr 5 1840 Marion co O; bur Deal cem Salt Rock twp Marion co O near center of cem. Inscript on mrkr "William Stayner" (remainder of inscript broken off). Grave mrkd by Capt William Hendricks chpt with bronze D A R mrkr on June 4 1932. Ref Pa Arch 5th Series Vol 5 p 678; 6th S Vol 1 p 280, 320. Rept by Capt William Hendricks chpt.

ST. CLAIR (or Sinclear or Sinclair), JAMES, Hamilton co

Sergt N H Line. Enl 1776 Col Silby's Regt N H Line. Pensr Hamilton co 9-6-1819. Trnsfd to N Y 9-16-1818. Was 62 yrs in 1820. Chldr: James; Levi; Mirriam Mc-Kinstrey; Rachel Culver; Nancy Brown; Betsey; Sherman and Sally Randall. Soldr d 1-27-1836 Orleans co N Y. Res in Genesee co N Y with his son James St Clair in 1820. Ref N H S 42397. Rept by State D A R. Listed here to avoid continued research for grave.

STEELE, ADAM, Summit co

Died 1811 æ 67; bur in Hudson. By Cuyahoga Portage chpt.

STEEL, JAMES, Hocking co

Pvt Pa Milit. Pensd June 22 1833 æ 81 in Hock co. Ref p 587 V 23 S 3 Pa Arch. Cop by Jane Dailey.

STEPHENS, MOSES, Washington co

Exec Doc 37 of 1852 refused a pens as servd less than 6 mo. Rept by Wm Pettit.

STEPHENS, NICHOLAS, Hamilton co

Enl Mar 1777 Monmouth Court House in New Jersey. In appl 1820 states æ 59 yrs; wf aged and infirm; had nine chldr all of age and had livd for several yrs with his chldr." Ref Contl (N J) S 40532. Rept by State D A R.

STEPHENS, PETER, Licking co

Lancaster co Pa Milit July 6 1781. Pa Arch S 5 Vol 7 p 129; S 3 Vol 2 pp 234, 330. Once listed in Dept Int as pensr in Licking co far service in N H line 1st regt. Justice was one child. Soldr owned land in Lurerne co Pa. Was tavernkeeper Johnstown O. In 1820 held 1st Methodist meeting at his tavern. Came to Licking co 1812 with sons family. Rept by Hetuck chpt.

STEPHENS, ROBERT, Mahoning co

Pvt. N J Men in Rev p 290. Mar Hannah; Robert was one son. Soldr d abt 1826 Coitsville twp. Ref Deed bk J p 658 Trumbull co trnscribd Mahoning co Robt and Hannah Stephens to ——— 1812; Western Reserve Chronicle Feb 2 1826 Est Robert Stephens Coitsville O. Rept by Mahoning chpt.

STEPHENSON, GEORGE, Knox co

Lieut. In 1776 in Cumberland co Pa he volunteered and srvd as pvt in Capt Culbertson's Co Pa. Winter of 1776-7 was appointed Lieut and srvd 5 mos in Capt Mc-Cammon Pa Co. In the summer of 1777 he enl and srvd seven mos as pvt in Capt McCammon Pa Co. In 1778 was appointed as 1st Lieut and srvd under that rank for three mos in Capt Culbertson's Co of Pa. He was in battles of Trenton; Princeton; Germantown. Was b 1752. Mar Catharine McCombs Cumberland co Pa 1783; soldr d Sept 18 1838 Martinsburg Knox co whr he is bur in Presbyterian cem Lots 246-247. Inscript on mrker: "George Stephenson. Departed this life Sept 18 1838 æ 86 yrs. So Job d being old and full of days. Job 52 chpt and 17 verse." Grave mrkd by Kokosing chpt D A R govt mrkr 1934. Soldr allowed pens of $18 per annum issued March 14 1833 æ abt 76 yrs and living in Knox co O. His wid Catharine pensd May 12 1847 of $80 per yr. Ref Washington D C Pens Office; Hist Washington co Pa p 934 (Rept by Mary Chesney chpt) Old Church Records of Presbyterian Church at Martinsburg Knox co O. Rept by Kokosing chpt Mrs Ewalt Ch.

STEPHENSON, PETER, Washington co

Name submitted by Helen Sloan Marietta O as thot to be Rev soldr.

STEPHENSON, ROBERT, Mahoning co

Pvt Cumberland co Pa. Pa Arch Capt McConnell. Mar Mary Teeters dau Elisha. Soldr d abt 1844 Green twp; bur New Albany O. Member Ohio legislature. Ref Will prob 1844; Hist Washington co Pa p 934 Crumrine. Rept by Mahoning chpt.

STERRETT, JOSEPH, Greene co

B 1756; d 1809; bur Old Massies Creek cem Xenia O. In Westmoreland co Pa Rangers on the frontiers 1778-1783. Ref Pa Arch S 3 V 23 pp 227, 320; 330; S 5 V 5 p 757. Soldr acknowledged receipt of several sums for services in the milit of Westmoreland co yr 1782. Ref Pa Arch S 6 V 2 p 354. Cedar chpt mrkd by govt tombstone in 1935 replacing the old one of sandstone. Rept by Julia H McElroy to Jane Dailey.

STETLER, CHRISTIAN, Montgomery co

Lancaster co Pa Capt Casper Stiver S 5 Pa Arch V 7 p 171 in 1782. Soldr d Beaverton O; bur Stetler Lutheran ch yd. Rept by W M Pettit Dayton.

STETLER, GEORGE, Montgomery co

Limerick twp Phila co 1780-82. Bur Stetler Lutheran Ch yd Montgomery co O. Ref Rec A 97 Pd supply tax 1782. Rept by W M Pettit Dayton.

STETLER, HENRY, Montgomery co

Lancaster co Pa Capt Casper Stiver S 5 Pa Arch Vol 7 p 171 in 1782. Bur Stetler Lutheran Church Montgomery co O. Rept by W M Pettit S A R.

STEVENS, JOHN, Mahoning co

Ranger Ser 3 V 23 p 234 Bedford co Pa Arch. Mar Letta; chldr: Temperance mar Wm Patterson; Mary mar —— Osborne; dau mar Ashamum; dau mar John Brown. Soldr d abt 1836 Berlin twp. Ref Will bk P Columbiana co Records probated 1836; Western Reserve Chronicle; Est John Stevens 1836. Rept by Mahoning chpt.

STEVENS, JOSEPH, Adams co

Exec Doc 37 refused a pens as servd less than 6 mo. Rept by Wm Pettit.

STEVENS, PAUL, Ashtabula co

Pvt Mass Milit. Enl Berkshire co Mass 7-1-1776. Srvd 18 mos. Was 72 yrs in 1832. Mar Esther 5-4-1785; soldr d 2-26-1835. Pens appl Ashtabula co 9-24-1832. Wid appl Ashtabula co 10-10-1839. Ref Mass W 4821. Rept by State D A R.

STEVENS, WILLIAM, ? co

Not of Ohio. Srvd and d in N Y Harpersfield twp 2-17-1780. His Widow Hannah who mar Nathaniel Skinner 4-27-1783 was a pensr 1840 æ 87 in Harpersfield Ashtabula co O. Her 2nd husband had d 9-11-1795 which made her eligible to pens. Listed here to avoid continued research. Ref W 9294 N Y. Rept by State D A R.

STEVENSON, DANIEL II, Fairfield co

Enl Frederick co Md with Washington at Valley Forge. Wagoner; furn own teams. B Frederick co Md 9-2-1737. Mar Ruth —— (b 1-2-1743 d 6-12-1831). One dau was Mary who mar —— Peters. Soldr d Richland twp Fairfield co 6-3-1827; bur Stevenson cem nr Rushville. Grave mrkd Elizabeth Sherman Reese chpt. Rept by Mary Hedges Sears to Meryl B. Markley V Ch.

STEWART, JAMES, Mahoning co

Pvt. Ser 5 Vol 1 and 2 Pa Arch Many ref. Chldr: John; Margaret mar John Arrel; Kezia b 1779 mar Robert Smith a Rev soldr in Ohio Roster; David and James are gr chldr. Soldr d abt 1820 Poland O. Ref Will bk 3 p 121 Trumbull co Records probated 1820; Hist Mahoning co p 482 Sanderson; Western Reserve Chronicle Dec 12 1820 Est James Stewart Poland O. Rept by Mahoning chpt.

STEWARD, JOHN, Portage co

Research for this record as pvt Mass Contl; pensr Portage co 5-4-1832 as is often found listed brought data fr Pens Cl Office in Wash for "Seward, John" or "Seaward" which see this vol. J D.

STEWARD, WILLIAM, Morrow co

Conn Trps. Was b Jan 16 1752 Westerly R I; mar Desire Crary; soldr d 9-16-1844; bur Fargo cem formerly Mortons corners Morrow co. Whn young his parents movd to Stonington; aft 10 yr to Voluntown Conn. Here he volunteered and marched to Roxbury under Capt Joseph Palmer; enl 1775; srvd 7 mos followed by various enl until paroled 1-5-1777. Movd to Vt 1778; aft 24 yrs to Petersburg N Y; aft 4 yr to Perue Clinton co N Y and in 1812 brot his fam to O whr pensd 9-10-1832 Bloomfield twp Knox co O. Ref S 4890. Rept by Mrs C B Baker Findlay O.

STEWART, JOHN, Pike co

Pvt Pa Milit. Enl nr the commencement of the Rev War. Srvd 2 yrs. Was b 1756 Lancaster co Pa. Res in Northumberland co Pa until 1802 and movd to Ross co O. In 1815 he movd to Pike co O. Pens appl Pike co O 7-25-1829. Ref Pa S 7622. Rept by State D A R.

STEWART, JOHN, Clermont co

Pvt and Sergt Pa Milit. Enl 12-26-1776 Hagerstown Md. Srvd 3 mo Sergt and 6 mo pvt. Was b 2-1-1755 Lancaster co Pa. Movd from Pa to Fayette co Ky aft the war and from there to Clermont co O. Movd back to Ky sometime in 1833. Pens appl Clermont co 8-8-1832. Livd with nephew William Boyde. Ref Md Pa S 14585. Rept by State D A R.

STEWART, JOHN, Trumbull co

In Capt MacLays 1st Battl Cumberland co Milit 1781. Ref Pa Arch S 5 Vol 6 p 149; D A R No 78861. Was b 1725 in Lancaster co Pa; mar 1757 Cumberland co Pa Mary wid of Alex Culberson. Chldr: 1 only by this marriage; Charles who was also a Rev soldr. Father and son came to Hubbard abt 1810 and the father (John) d the same yr (1810 and is bur in Old North cem Hubbard O.) Rept by Mary Chesney chpt.

STEWART, JOHN, Franklin co

Pvt Capt Peter Ford's Co York co Milit from payroll dated July 8 to Sept 8 1781. Pa Arch S VI Vol 2 p 629 (spelled Stuart). Was b York co Pa Sept 28 1752 the son of John Stewart of York co Pa; mar Ann ——; Soldr d Aug 12 1809 Columbus O; removd to Greenlawn Col O from Franklin gr-yd 1859. Secured fr Mrs C E Shirk 809 N 17 Harrisburg Pa by Jane Dailey.

STEWART, WILLIAM, Knox co

Pvt and sergt Conn Milit. Enl Apr or May 1775 in Windham co Conn. Srvd as pvt 11 mo and sergt 9 mos. Was æ 80 in 1832 Westerly R I. Res with parents until the Rev. Movd to Vt 1778; aft 24 yrs went to Pittsburgh N Y; thence to Pa and in 1812 movd to O. Pensr Knox co 9-21-1833 æ 82. Ref O Pens Roll 1835 Vol 3 O 137; Conn S 4890. Rept by Jane Dailey.

STINE, MARTIN, Butler co

Pvt N J Milit. Enl Morris co N J abt close of yr 1775. Srvd 2 yrs frm 1775. Was æ 78 1832; b Mar 1754 Morris co N J. Res Butler co O July 1832. Pensd there 12-29-1832. Ref S 4010 N J. Rept by State D A R.

STIVER (Stoever), CASPER 3RD, ? co

A Capt. Bur Lutheran ch-yd Germantown. Came early to Montgomery co O with family; father and gr-father were famous Lutheran ministers. Rept by Wm Pettit S A R.

ST JOHN, JOHN, Hamilton co

Enl Col Thaddeus Crane's Regt N Y Line. Was b 1750 Westchester co N Y; mar 1770 Anna Lockwood (d 1830). One son was James. Soldr d 1819 Hamilton co O. Cop fr V 120 No 119531 D A R Lin by Mrs Oehlke.

STOCK (Steck), MICHAEL, Columbiana co

Depreciation Pay pvt Northumberland co Pa Milit. Pvt in Jacob Spee's Co on the Frontiers Northumberland co Pa in May and June. Service 28 das. Was b Germany 1750; mar Barbara Ritz; one son was Henry (b in Hanover Pa mar Minerva Stalleup). Soldr d 12-19-1827 Columbiana co. Came from Pa in 1805; had been a soldr in the German army but deserted. Ref Pa Arch 5 S Vol 4 p 695; VIII p 680; Ohio Patriot. Rept by Mrs Wilma Molsberry.

STODDARD, ELIAKIM, Mahoning co

Pvt Dec 1781 Co Capt Jacob Hines. Vt Men in Rev. Mar Sally; Soldr d abt 1816 Boardman twp. Came to O 1805. Ref Deed bk G p 211 trnscrbd Mahoning co 1815; Deed bk G p 476 trnscrbd Mahoning co 1815; Trump of Fame May 3 1816 Est Eliakim Stoddard. Rept by Mahoning chpt.

STOGEL, JAMES, Brown co

Exec Doc 37 refused a pens as servd less than 6 mo. Rept by Wm Pettit.

STONER, CASPER, Starke co

Pvt Pa Contl. Enl 4th Pa Regt abt May 1776. Srvd the war and was wounded at Germantown; exchanged 1-1-1781. Was æ abt 60 in 1819; d 1820 æ 61 in Starke co O. Pens appl Stark co O 11-22-1819. Res Bucks Creek Pa in 1810. Ref Pa S 40524 Rept by Hetuck chpt and State D A R.

STONER, PHILIP, Clermont co

B 8-16-1763 Frederick co Md; aft one yr parents movd to Bedford co Pa whr he volunteered and marched to Shoupe's Fort whr stationed from May to Oct of each yr fr 1779 to 1781 under Capt Joshua Davis Col John Piper of Pa Trps. In 1791 livd York co Pa for 6 yr abt 1802 movd to Clermont co O aft 1½ yr to Warren co; aft 4 yr to Montgomery co; to Clermont co; to Hamilton co; and settled in Clermont Stonelick twp on farm. Pensd 11-9-1832; d 9-14-1837; mar 8-11-1791 to Sarah or Sara Ringer in Dover twp York co Pa; she was b 4-18-1766 Pa and pensd 12-29-1838 Clermont co; she d 1852. Only name of chld given is Joseph the 2nd one. Ref W 6804 S of R Bulletin Apr May June 1936. Rept by Ella Tafe Librarian Sons of Rev, Los Angeles .

STOOPS, PHILIP, Highland co

Pvt Del Milit. Enl New Castle co Del whr livd. Srvd one yr. Was b 8-20-1754 New Castle co Del. Sometime aft war he movd to Rockingham co Va whr he res abt 29 yrs and then movd to Highland co O. Pens 8-25-1832 in Highland co O. Ref Del S 4894. Rept by State D A R.

STORY, ANDREW CAPT, ? co

Listed in news clipping by L A A found in old scrap bk as Rev soldr who participated in settlement of Marietta. Filed here for continued research. Listed by Marietta chpt.

STORY, WILLIAM COLONEL, ? co

Listed in news clipping by L A A found in old scrap bk as Rev soldr who participated in settlement of Marietta. Filed here for continued research. Listed by Marrietta chpt.

STOTHARD, THOMAS, Pickaway co

Pvt Va Contl. Enl Frederick co Va 1776. Pvt Capt Chas Porterfields Co Col Morgans II Va Regt in battles of Brandywine; Germantown. Dischrgd Jan 1779. Was b 1758; grave not yet found. Ref allowed pens May 13 1818 æ 60 yrs res in Pickaway co. Pens No S 40533. Rept by Pickaway Plains chpt.

STOUT, ELISHA, Butler co

Enl June 1776 Monmouth N J. Pens No 15286. Pensd 10-11-1819 Butler co O. Wid pensd 5-16-1857 Cincinnati O pens No 11985. Soldr was æ 64 yrs in 1820. Mar Hulda Robbins 11-14-1788; chldr: Charles R; Elisha; Sarah; Johnston; Priscilla Lee (appl of Charles). Others: John æ 13; and Jesse æ 8 in 1820. Soldr d 5-20-1838 Butler co O. Ref N J W 4080 B L Wt 8707-100 no Papers; D A R No 107707. Rept by State D A R.

STOUT, OBADIAH, Adams co

Native N J. 1st settler Green twp Adams co 1796. Srvd thru Rev war. Had 10 chldr. Two youngest scalped by Indians whl fam livd Graham's Station Ky p 432 Adams co Hist. Rept by Meryl B Markley St Vice Ch.

STOW, SAMUEL, Trumbull co

In 1776 he became a teamster for the Rev Forces. Was b 1733; mar Lucretia Rockwell; chldr: Comfort; Henry; Chester and others. Soldr d May 9 1814 Braceville twp Trumbull co. He was a res of Middletown Conn moving from there to Litchfield from which place he came to Trumbull co. Rept by Mary Chesney chpt.

STRADEN, GEORGE, ? co

Pvt appl for pens. Rejected as deserted the service. Ref Doc 31 Jan 6 1831. Rept by Blanche Rings Col O.

STRAIGHT, HENRY, Ashtabula co

Conn Milit Col Canfield's Regt 1840 æ 80 liv in Rome twp. Was b 1760. Soldr d 1-10-1858 æ 97 yr 6 mo; bur Gageville O Sheffield twp. "A soldr under Washington. For Liberty he fought and won. But as a Christian gained the prize of brighter glory in the skies;" inscript on mrkr. Grave located by Mary Stanley and Mary Redmond chpts. Ref 18 Rept N S D A R p 260; and 21 Rept N S D A R p 110; California S of R Bulletin 14; 14-1937, stating b in Warwick R I. Rept by Nathan Perry and Mary Redmond chpts.

STRAIN, DAVID, ? co

Grave located by Wah-wil-a-way chpt Hillsboro O. Ref 15th Rept N S D A R p 165. Rept by Nathan Perry chpt.

STRAIN, HUGH, Mahoning co

Pens appl. Circuit ct bk 6 p 249 Warren O. Soldr d Coitsville twp. Ref Tax list 1826 Hugh and David Strain Coitsville O. Rept by Mahoning chpt.

STRAIN, ROBERT, Montgomery co

Pvt Pa Milit. Enl Aug 1776 Minute men Lancaster co Pa. Srvd 9 mo and 12 das. Was b May 1756 Lancaster co Pa. Soldr d July 15 1840; bur Woodland Montgomery co. Operated a Traveler's Inn at Dayton O abt 1814. (by S A R Dayton) Pens appl

June 22 1833 in Montgomery co O. Was a teamster. Ref Pa S 3989. Rept by State D A R.

STRAIT, JOHN, ? co

Pvt refused a pens because did not serve 9 mo in Contl Army. Ref Doc 31 Jan 6 1831. Rept by Blanche Rings Columbus O.

STRANGE, JOHN, Highland co

Pvt Va Milit. Enl abt the 19 yr of his æ under Shelby in Va Milit. Srvd 6 mo as pvt of inf; 3 mo as pvt of cavalry. Was b 9-3-1759. Pens appl Highland co O 8-22-1832. Ref Va S 3995. (Listed p 291 "Va milit in Rev" as liv in Highland co O æ 75. J D). Rept by State D A R.

STREETER, NAPTHALI, Trumbull co

Pvt R I Trps 1777 to 1778. Land from 1779 to 1782 with the New Hampshire trps. Was b 1763 in Glouster R I. Mar 1st ——; 2nd Feb 15 or 17 1798 Elizabeth Reynolds. Chldr by 1st wf 3 one of whom was John. By 2nd wf: Napthalia; Aaron; William; Terressa. Soldr d Sept 15 1839 Gustavus Trumbull co O. Rept by Mary Chesney chpt.

STRICKLAND, JOSEPH, Richland co

Pvt N J Milit. Enl 11-1-1776 whl res in Hunterdon co N J. Movd from N J to Jefferson co O; thence to Richland co Vermillion twp. Was b 3-8-1760 Bucks co Pa. Chldr: William S; Mahlon; Joseph b 1-4-1804 in N J; Amos; Sarah Case; Lucinda Mitchell; and Rachel Tiuett ? sp (appl of William). Soldr d Richland co O. Pens appl Richland co O 1-2-1834. Ref N J S 7636. Rept by State D A R. Jared Mansfield chpt repts he d in Seneca co æ 86 yr in 1850 as stated in Knapps Hist Ashland co O.

STRICKLING (or Strickland), ALEXANDER, Adams co

Pvt Va Contl. Enl Mar 1776 Va. Srvd 5 yrs. Was b 1752; mar Jane Bowman Oct 17 1788. 11 chldr; 6 living at time of appl; youngest son Jacob; Elizabeth; Sarah; Jane; Nancy; Matilda. Soldr d Feb 19 1842 Adams co O. Pens appl Highland co O Apr 7 1824. Livd in Frederick co Va till they had 4 chldr; then movd to South Branch of Potomac River whr livd 2 yrs; then to Washington co Pa whr livd 7 yrs; then to O. Wid appl for pens Oct 19 1842. Ref W 6174 Va. Rept by State D A R.

STROCK, JOSEPH, Mahoning co

Pvt. Marker placed by descendants destroyed within last 6 yrs. Was b 1748 Wurtemburg Germany; mar Mrs Elizabeth Bessinger Wid Hessian soldr. Chldr: Maria mar Philip Ludwig; Samuel mar Polly Brunstetter; Jchn mar Catherine Rice; Henry; George mar Elizabeth Lottman; Joseph; William; Samuel; Hannah mar Fred Stittle; Betsy mar —— Clinger. Soldr d 1822 Canfield twp; bur Dutch cem. Came with widowed mother to America 1757. Was at Valley Forge. Came to Mahoning co 1813. Ref Hist Trumbull, Ashtabula and Mahoning co p 319; Will bk 6 p 441 Trumbull co recd probated 1832; West Res. Chr 10-27-1822; Tax list 1826 Joseph; Samuel and Wm Strock. Rept by Mahoning chpt.

STRONG, HORATIO, Meigs co

Pvt many enl. Mass Soldr and Sailors Vol 15 p 191. Was b 5-16-1758. Lenox Mass; son of Oziah Strong d 1807 at Homer or S Courtland N Y. Mar Patience Stevens (b 1755). A dau Lydia b 1790 mar on 3-1-1810 William White sheriff of Jackson co; Jared bur in Bunn cem S E of Jackson O; Ozias; Daniel. Soldr d July 14 1831 Salem O. Farmer and tavern keeper at Great Bend Pa 1787-97 and Athens O 1797. Movd to Scioto Salt Works Jackson co (then Ross) and established works of own; 1803. Exchanged same for 640 A in Gallia co at Salem O (now Meigs). A justice of peace in Ross and Gallia co. Ref Strong genealogy Vol 1; No 245325 on this record; Vol 123 p 9 D A R Lin 122029; No 60087 also 52331; 53455. Recd secured for Mrs J L Short 716 2nd Ave Upland Calif by Jane Dailey.

STROUP, JOHN, Madison co

One of the four who fought in Rev; W B L Wt 40923-160-55 is for "Widow of invalid pensr wounded at Brandywine; mar Hannah Wintworth (?) 7-2-1801; soldier d 1831 in Phila Pa ?" Was a native of Pa. Mar Mary Steel (d 11-4-1835); soldr d 2-4-1832; bur rear of Maxey schoolhouse Madison co O. Inscript cop 1924: "——roup, —eb 4 1832 ——y." By side is stone "In memory of Mary wf of John Stroup d Nov 4 1835 æ 68 yrs. Came to Chillicothe O 1799; movd to Madison co O 1805; mentioned in Clarke co Hist. Rept by Capt Wm Hendricks chpt; Mrs Fred Hoch.

STUMP, CONRAD, Pickaway co

Fr Chapman Bros Hist Fayette Pickaway and Madison cos 1892 p 567 "Miss Mary King of Madison twp Pickaway co was b in Berks co Pa a dau of Henry and Barbara Stump King natives of Berks co Pa. Her gt grandfather Conrad Stump is said to have been in the Rev under Washingtons command." Conrad Stumps Will p 67 Will bk 1-2 made 9-17-1824 mentions wf Juliana; sons: William; Henry; George; daus: Maria wf of Abraham Markel; Catharine wf of Joel Stump; Barbara wf of Henry Koeing (King). Exec sons William, Henry and George. Witnesses S Lutz and Chas Dodson. Probated Jan 1 1825. Grave stones inscript: "Conrad Stump d Sept 24 1824 æ 69½ yrs wf Julian d July 20 1829 æ 70-5-2." Cem Stump twp Salt Creek. Rept by Pickaway Plains chpt; Mrs Orion King.

STUMP, JACOB, Montgomery co

Pvt Va Contl. Enl in Co of Capt John Long Frederick co Va and srvd 4 yrs and 9 mos. Enl abt mo of Mar 1777. Recd honorable dischrge at Little York. Was abt 68 in 1818. Res Montgomery co O July 3 1821. Was taken at an early æ from N J the place of his birth to Va. Ref 41193 Va. Va Lib Rept 1912 Suppl O 292. Rept by State D A R.

STUMP, LEWIS, Licking co

Pvt Va Contl. Enl abt Mar 1777 as a common soldr in command of Capt Porterfield. Srvd 3 yrs. Was æ 63 in 1820; Mar Margaret 3-15-1827; soldr d 9-7-1833 Licking co O. Ref Va W 7201. Rept by State D A R.

STURGEON, PETER, Fairfield co

Pvt Pa Milit. Res in Lancaster co Pa at the time of enl. Afterwards movd to Miffin co and abt 1801 movd to Fairfield co O. Srvd 7 mo. Was b 12-13-1756 Lancaster co Pa. Enl 1776 Lancaster co Pa. Pens appl Fairfield co O 11-3-1832. Ref Name listed p 406 Wisemans Pioneer People Fairfield co. Pa S 4903. Rept by Jane Dailey, and State D A R.

STURGES, LEWIS, Licking co

Pvt and Corp Conn St Trps Srvd 2 yrs. Was æ 76 in 1832. Mar Mary who d 2-28-1831; soldr d 1-6-1838; bur Old Granville cem. Inscript on monument gave dates as above. Enl May 1775 Bridgeport Conn. Pens appl Licking co 6-7-1832. Ref Conn S 17704. Rept by State D A R and Hetuck chpt.

SUDDUTH, WILLIAM, Pickaway co

Pvt Va Contl; 3 yr under Capt Wm Blackwell; selected by Col Daniel Morgan as one of Rifle Regt under Capt Grabie Long. Dischrgd 1780. Was b Fairfax co Va; son of Benjamin and Sil——? Mar 1781 to Sarah Roush (d Dec 16 1827 æ 67 yr); Elizabeth mar Levi Lee; Mary mar Wm Millar; Nancy; Lucinda mar Jonathan Renick; Susannah mar —— Brown; Frances; Jermina W mar John Barnes; Peter; William. Soldr d Apr 13 1830 Jackson twp. Movd from old Renick cem to Forest Circleville twp. Grave mrkd by Pickaway Plains chpt 5-11-1832. Came fr Hardy co Va to Pickaway co abt 1816. Ref Bible and Estate settld in Courthouse; Mrs Orion King, Circleville. Rept by Pickaway Plains chpt.

SULLINGER, JOHN, Trumbull co

Cop fr Hist of Venango co Pa pub 1890 pp 263-265, 1120. Came from Westmoreland co Pa. Mar Lovina Judge of Westmoreland co; came in 1805 to Venango co. Brought his family in 1813. He was a soldr of the Rev; weaver; d at Warren O in 1845 æ 91 yrs. Wf d earlier. Purchased land in Rockland twp Venango co Pa in 1805 and settled there in 1813. Had 12 chldr: John; Alexander; Peter; Samuel; James P; Jacob; Andrew; Daniel; Annie mar Capt William Karns; Mary mar James McDonald; Catharine mar James Hoffman. All of them were dead in 1890 except Jacob who livd in Elizabeth

SUMMERS, WILLIAM A, Canada

Exec Doc 37 of 1852 suspended list of pensr as servd less than 6 mo. Rept by Wm Pettit.

SUMNER, SAMUEL, Hamilton co

Pvt Mass. Pensd 6-23-1818 in Hamilton co O. Trnsfrd to Mass 1822. Was æ 62 in 1820. Appl mentions a wf and chld. Living with son Cincinnati O in 1820. Appld for trnsfr to Boston Mass 11-18-1822. Ref Contl S 33763 Mass. B L Wt 13795 Drummer Iss July 9 1789. Rept by State D A R.

SUTLIFF, DAVID, Trumbull co

Received land grant nr Genoa N Y co N Y for Rev service. Was b 6-16-1760. Allegheny co Pa. Rept by Presque Isle chpt; Margery Bacon Erie Pa.
Mar 1st Jemima Williams; 2nd Sylvia Case Tuller June 26 1799. Chldr: Orpha; Nathan; Alice; Jemima; David; Beulah M; Lucina; Lola; Marilla; Parintha; Uriah C; Watson L; Samuel C; Susan; Henry P; Curtis. Soldr d May 1843. Rept by Mary Chesney chpt.

SUTLIFF, SAMUEL JR, Trumbull co

Recd land grant prob in Herkimer co N Y for Rev Ser. Bapt 4-11-1765; son of Samuel Sutliff (also Rev soldr) and Eunice Curtiss. Mar Ruth Granger. Chldr: Allen Curtis; Samuel Harvey; Levi; Milton; Calvin; Granger; Flavel. Soldr d 2-7-1840 Vernon O; bur Old cem at Vernon O. Rept by Mary Chesney chpt.

SUTTON, PHILIP, Huron co

Pvt N J St Trps. Enl Bridge Water N J in 1778 whr livd. Pvt volunteer in Lafayette co West of the Allegory Mts. Was æ 77 in 1832 July 27. Son of Moses ? Sutton and Susanne Sutton. Bur Huron O. Res Norwalk Huron co O 1832. Pens appl July 2 1832. Ref 18th aRep N S D A R p 261. S 7658 N J. Rept by State D A R.

SUTTON, ZEBULON, Licking co

Pvt Mass Milit. Res Somerset co N J at time of enl 1777. Srvd until 1780. Was b 1752 in Somerset co N J. Pens appl Knox co O 8-3-1832. Ref N J S 16265. Rept by State D A R chpt.

SWARTSWELDER, CHRISTIAN, Columbiana co

Pvt in Capt Martin Bowman's Co 10 Battl Lancaster Co Pa Milit 1777. Tho rept fr Columbiana co O d in Cumberland co Pa 1833. Ref R 10347 Pens Cl. Listed here as a correction to filed record. Chldr: John; Samuel; Benjamin; Jacob; Samuel; Lydia; Philip; Peter; and Margaret. Rept by State D A R.

SWARTSWELDER, JACOB, Columbiana co

Ensign in Capt Martin Bowmans Co 10th Battl Lancaster Co Pa Milit 1777. Ref Pa Arch 5 VII p 978. Rept by State D A R.

SWARTZ, PHINEAS, Huron co

Pvt Pa St Milit. Enl in Rev in yr of Brandywine Battle. Then livd in Lamberton twp Chester co Pa. Srvd 21 mos. Was æ 74 in 1832. Was b Chester co Pa. Wf d 1829. Soldr bur Huron O. Was a res of Huron co May 21 1833 Ridgefield twp. Had also livd in Adams twp Senecca co O. Ref 18th Rept N S D A R p 261 S 15668 Pa. Rept by State D A R.

SWEENEY, HUGH, Perry co

Died 1821. Ref Pa Arch. Submitted by A M Priest Hetuck chpt.

SWEET, PHELEG, Ashtabula co

Enl 1775 Alarm service Capt Boardman's Co Capt Morris Co 5th Conn Regt July 19 to Dec 15 1780; also Capt Sedgwick's Co Col Hinman's Regt. Was b 1758; mar Mary Wilkinson 1777; a dau was Mary mar to Pelatiah Shepard; soldr d 1825 Ashtabula O. Grave located by Mary Stanley chpt (See 21st Rept N S D A R p 110). Inscript on mrkr gives it "Pelig Sweet Sr." Ref p 9 S of R Bulletin (Elmer Shepart) Sept 1830 of Los Angeles Calif proven recd. Rept by Jane Dailey.

SWEIGERT, JACOB, Stark co

Pvt Capt Martin Bowman's 5th Battl Lancaster co Pa Milit. Was b 1761 Lancaster co Pa. Mar 2nd wf Margaret (1768-1854). One dau was named Hannah. Soldr d 1850 Stark co O. Ref V 113 p 84 D A R Lin No 112262 also No 102814. Rept by Nathan Perry chpt.

SWINEHART, ADAM, Carroll co

Son of Peter Swinehart. B June 30 1760; d Apr 8 1852 æ 91 yrs. Bur fam cem on Homestead nr Bowerstown O Orange twp. Fam mrkr with above records. Mar Margaret Leslie (Lesle) in Washington co Pa abt 1785. She was b 1764; d 1851 æ 87. Srvd in Capt Geo Mears 8th class 5th Battl of Washington co Pa. Chldr: Peter; Susan; Hester; Margaret; Katy; Gabriel; Eve; Adam and Elizabeth. Ref Will bk 2 p 32 Washington co Pa or Pa General Records. Also Pa Arch S 6th Vol 2 p 168 and 184. Rept by Canton chpt.

SWISHER, ABRAHAM, Pickaway co

Pvt and Sergt in 1st Regt Sussex co N J Milit; also srvd as Capt in 8th Co 1st Regt Sussex co Milit Nov 6 1780. He received certficate no 780. Was b 1741 N J; mar Hannah Christine; chldr: John mar Mary Peterson; Philip; Abraham mar Sarah; Isaac; and dau who mar John Winterstein. Soldr d Nov 12 1828 æ 87 yrs from old newspaper in Circleville Libry. Likely bur in Harrison twp cem. Settled nr Kingston nr Ross co line; d at home of son in Harrison twp. Ref Helen E Swisher 702 Malvern ave Columbus O. Rept by Pickaway Plains chpt.

SWITZER, PHILIP, Gallia co

Va Milit (pensd under Act of Congress 12-5-1832). Enl 2-27-1778; trnsfrd June 1778 to Major's Co; dischrgd Feb 16 1779. Was b May 5 1756 Lewisburg Va; mar Nancy Bridgeman July 1785; chldr: William; Valentine; John; Mary Lasley; Nancy Blake; Rebecca Blake; Elizabeth Hinkle; Sarah Guthrie. Soldr d July 3 1835 Addison O; bur Bethel cem Addison O. Inscript of mrkr "Phillip Switzer b May 5 1756 d July 3 1835." Ref Ella L Rothgeb Cheshire O. Rept by French Colony chpt.

SYMMONS, THOMAS, Butler co

Spelling for "Simmons, Thomas" Butler co O p 334 Vol 1 Ohio Roster. Rept by Oxford Caroline Scott chpt.

TAFT, MATTHEW, Ashtabula co

Enl pvt at æ 17 Shelborn twp Franklin co Mass June 25 1779 in Joshua L Woodbridge's Co Col Nathan Tyler's Regt. Dischd Dec 25 1779. Served 6 mos 8 days at R I. Newport R I payroll for Dec 1779 allowed him service pay and travel expenses for 141 miles. B Pelham Mass Mar 16 1762 son of James and Martha Gray Taft; mar Mary

Crocker. Chldr: Amasa mar Hannah; Anna mar Joshua Page; BeBtsy mar Silas Davis; Huldah mar Stephen Gage; Nathaniel mar Margaret; Matthew mar Susan Stevens; Mary mar Richard Peck; Almira mar R Peck aft death of Mary. Movd Freetown Cortland co N Y in 1814 and to Kingsville O in 1827. D Kingsville 1838. Ref Pens Rolls Mass S 3754. Appl pens 1832 while liv Kingsville. Rev Soldiers Mass Vol 2; Soldrs and Sailors Rev Vol 15 and Mrs Adelphus Keith Spokane Wash. Rept by Mary Redmond chpt and Mrs. K Leach.

TALLMAN, BENJAMIN, Pickaway co

Enl pvt from Va in Amanda Corps Mar 27 1782. B in Berks Co Pa 1745 son of William Tallman of R I and Anna Lincoln. Berks Co Pa mar Dinah Boon (b 1749 d 1824) Nov 9 1764. Chldr: Patience; Sarah; James; Samuel; Thomas; Annah; Nancy; Susannah; Benjamin; John and two dying in infancy. D in Walnut twp; bur on Mrs. Chester Peters farm 200 yds from house which was home of soldrs son Benj. Grave mrkd 1919 by Mrs Roe Zanesville. Soldr owned 175 A land in Pa and kept tavern Berks co. Movd to Harrisonburg co Va 1776 and on to Ohio 1810. Ref Boon Family Hist H T Sparker; Hist Lincoln Family Waldo Lincoln; Hist Rockingham co Va Steichler; Pa Archives Ser 5 Vol 3 p 877 and Olive Dowdy Circleville. Rept by Pickaway Plains chpt.

TALLMAN, PETER, Belmont co

Enl Loudon Co Va 1778-79. Svd Capt Colemans Va Line 7 mos. B 1755 Winchester Va. Appl pens Belmont Co Nov 16 1832 æ 77. Ref Va Pens S 4679 and Va Mil in Rev p 292. Still liv Belmont Co at æ 80. Rept State D A R.

TANNEHILL, MELZAR, Ashland co

Listed p 142 in Hist North Central States by Wm A Duff as Rev Soldr in Green twp. Reported by Nathan Perry chpt.

TALCOTT, JOSEPH, Trumbull co

On mus rall Capt Clarks Co Col Obediah Johnsons Regt Conn Milit in Service in Providence. D Bristol Trumbull co. Ref Conn Men in Rev p 525. Rept by Mary Chesney chpt.

TAYLOR, EDWARD, Wayne co

Pvt N J Milit. Drafted Hunterdon co N J 1777. Svd 11 mos 2 wks. B 1762 Hunterdon co N J. Mar Anna. Appl pens July 8 1834 in Wayne co. Resided Allegheny Pa; thence to Columbiana Co and to Wayne Co. Ref S 7679 N J pens. Rept State D A R.

TAYLOR, HENRY, Trumbull co

Enl pvt N J State Trps 1777 under Lieuts Kirk and Benoni; again in 1780 under Capt Geo Rible at Newton Sussex co N J. B at Bucks co Pa 1757; son Henry Jr. Soldr d Apr 5 1855 Brookfield O where he came 1817. Pensd in Trumbull co July 20 1833. Rept by Mary Chesney chpt.

TAYLOR, ISAAC, Miami co

Enl pvt N J Milit May 1776 Hunterdon co N J. B Feb 1 1756. Went to Fayette co Pa. Aft war liv there 6 yrs; thence to Ohio co Va liv there 12 yrs; to Lancaster O; to Champaign; to Miami co whr he lvd whn appl pens Apr 11 1854. Ref N J Sea Service S 7678. Rept by State D A R.

TAYLOR, JOHN, Huron co

Enl 1776 Sussex co N J. Svd as Orderly 5 mos in Capt Abraham Chambers Co Col Ephriam Montius N J Regt in Flying Camp. At battles Long Island; White Plains; and Ft Washington. Reenlisted Nov 1776; svd as Sergt 6 mos under Capt Macks N J co. At battles Trenton Princeton. Re-enlisted July 1778 for 4 mos as pvt in Capt Manuel Hoovers N J co and in Spring 1779 in Capt Timothy James co. B Aug 24 1751. Mar

1780; lvd on Pa side of Del River across fr Sussex co N J. D Aug 2 1841; bur Butternut Ridge Laporte near Elyria. Pens appl July 27 1832 while res in Huron co. Ref Pens Dept S 16270 N J and 18th Rept N S D A R p 262. Rept by State D A R.

TAYLOR, JOHN, Trumbull co

Service in Repts of 5th Bn Northampton co 1781 4th Co Class I. Mar Jane. Both bur Seceders Cem Liberty twp. Stone inscpt not legible except "died æ 77". Taught first school in Churchill when he was æ 60. Ref Pa Arch S series Vol 8 p 414. Rept by Mary Chesney chpt.

TAYLOR, RICHARD, Preble co

Enl 1775. Servd pvt and Corp 6 mos Cecil co Md Milit. B Oct 1756; mar Ann Wallace (d Nov 19 1843 Preble co). Only chld James. Soldr d Aug 29 1838 in Preble co. Appl pens July 13 1833 and on Sept 1 1832. Widow appld Sept 12 1840. Ref Pens Dept W 4598 Md. Rept by State D A R.

TAYLOR, WILLIAM, Trumbull co.

Enl 1779 in Capt John Craigs Co Pa Line Dragoons 4th Regt Col Stephen Moyland. Servd 3 yrs. Mar Mary; had one chld. Soldr d July 8 1834 and widow mar William Fellers. Farmer by occupation. Appl pens June 10 1820 æ 70 in Crawford Co Pa. Later appl Trumbull co June 25 1723. Again Crawford co Pa Feb 1824 and trnsfrd to Ohio Rolls. Ref Pens Dept S 40558 Pa. Rept by State D A R.

TEERMAN, JOHN, ? co

Reputed Rev Soldr. Came with Hessians; was taken prsnr by Washington at Trenton. Joined patriot cause and srvd to end of war. Bur Warner cem R 40. Soldr marker at grave.

TEEGARDEN, AARON, Pickaway co

Service S 5 Pa Arch. Vol 4 p 458; b Pa 1754; d 1823; mar Margaret Dibel. Ref No. 29159 S A R. Rept by Wm Pettit Secy.

TERNEY (Turney), JAMES, Ross co

Enl Feb 1776 Pvt Pa Contl. Srvd 20 mos. B 1756 d 1820. Appl pens Ross co July 13 1818. Ref Pens Dept S 40506. Rept by State D A R.

TERRILL (Terrell), JOEL, Lorain co

Enl 1775 Capt Pecks Co Conn. Svd 8 mos Siege St. John and Princeton. Reenlisted 1777; srvd 4 mos as Corp in Capt Theopholus Munsons Co Cols Dunker and Meigs in Conn Trps. At Germantown; Monmouth; and Stony Point. B July 23 1757 at Waterbury Conn; mar Emma Hodge Dec 30 1778 (also called Eunice Hodge). Chldr: Wyllys b 1780; Polly b 1785. Soldr d Mar 22 1825 at Ridgeville Lorain co. Was brother of Elihu Terrel Vol 1 p 365. Ref Pens Bureau and Pioneer Women of Western Reserve p 27. Rept by Nathan Perry chpt.

TERRELL, ICHABOD, Lorain co

Bur Ridgeville Ohio. Ref 3rd Rpt N S D A R p 229. Rept by Nathan Perry chpt.

TERRELL, NATHAN, Knox co.

Enl 1775 in Conn Contls New Milford twp Lichtfield Co Conn. Srvd 20 mos. B 4-12-1755 New Milford twp. Mar Dorothy Phillips Feb 16 1778. Chldr: Elijah b 1791: Joana b 1779. Soldr d Jan 24 1834 in Knox Co Ohio. Appl pens Knox Co 1832. Widow appl June 26 1837. Ref Pens dept W 4083 Conn. Came to Knox Co 1817 frm Conn. Rept by State D A R.

TEST, ZACHARIAS, Columbiana co

Rev soldr record not yet found. B N J Chldr: Isaac B; Samuel; Benjamin; Came to Butternut twp Columbiana co 1803 with 3 grown sons each taking 160 A land. Ref McCords Hist Columbiana co p 825. Rept by Mrs. Wilma Molsberry Youngstown O.

TETER, SAMUEL, ? co

Not on Pens files. Commanded Doddridges Fort 1782. B Pa 1737; mar Mary Dodd-ridge in 1770. Had son Samuel who mar Rebecca Ford. Soldr d Ohio 1832. Located first in Ky in 1799. Ref Vol 107 D A R Lin 106924 and Vol 115 p 94 No. 114304. Rept by Jane Dailey.

THAYER, BARTHOLOMEW, Coshocton co

Reputed Rev Soldr. Bur Geo W Norman farm Keen twp. Cop by Jane Dailey.

THAYER, ELIAS ? co

Pvt refused pens because srvd in Regt not on Contl Estab. Rept by Blanche Rings Col O.

THAYER, JOSEPH, Ashtabula co

Enl Pvt Conn Contls May 9 1775. Mar Abigail Sackett May 8 1776. Chldr: Reuben aged 40 in 1823; and Anna a dwarf. Soldr d May 17 1838. Farmer but not able to work. Pensd Erie Co Pa Oct 16 1823. Widow pensd Chautauqua co N Y 1839. Ref Conn Contls W 18133. Rept by State D A R.

THOMAS, CALEB, Ashtabula co

Srvd Conn Milit 6th Co 5th Bn. Bur Windsor Corners Ashtabula co. Grave located by Mary Stanley Chapter. Pensd Ashtabula co Oct 16 1833. In 1840 lvd with Oliver Loomis Jr and was æ 77. Ref No. 18 and No. 21 Rpts N S D A R pp 263 and 111. Rept by Nathan Perry chpt and Jane Dailey.

THOMAS, JEREMIAH, Washington co

B 1756 d 1849 at Marietta. Bur Mound cem. Ref Mass Soldr and Sailors Vol 25 p 579. Rept by Marietta chpt.

THOMAS, JONATHAN, Clermont co

Listed in "Va Militia in Rev" p 292 as living in Clermont co and æ 76. Cop by Jane Dailey.

THOMAS, JONATHAN, Washington co

Enl Jan 1782 as pvt in Sandburn N H. Servd in 1st N H Regt to end of war. Dschgd New Windsor Hgts N Y. B 1763; mar Elizabeth. Chldr Betsy; Harriett (living in New-port Wash co in 1820) Soldr d Newport 1825; bur Newport twp cem. Grave mrkd 1933 Marietta Chpt. Pensd May 21 1819. Ref Cert No. 10953. Pens papers 40574 Wash co Common Pleas Court. Pens Rolls N H S 40574. Rept by Marietta chpt.

THOMAS, JOSIAH, Muskingum co

B 1757; pensd Harrison twp Muskingum co 1840 æ 83 and lvg with William Thomas. Rept by Jane Dailey.

THOMAS, OWEN, Columbiana co

Enl pvt in Philadelphia co Pa Milit July 31 1775. Reenlstd July 30 1781 in Loudon Co Va. B 1754 in Chester co Pa. D Oct 10 1827. Lvd Montgomery twp Phil co Pa when he enl. Lvd Loudon Co Va 10 yrs; Bartley co Va 16 yrs. To Ohio later. Appl pens Feb 9 1833. Ref Pa and Va Pens Rec S 3785. Also Pa Arch 3-23-585. U S pens rec 1833-34. Rept by Mrs Wilma Molsberry Youngstown O.

THOMPKINS, PHINEAS, Franklin co

Enl Florida twp Orange co N Y Milit 1775-76. Previously lvd Newark N J to age 16. B July 28 1753. Appl pens Jan 20 1834 in Franklin co O Lexington twp. Came to Richland co 1827. Ref Pens N Y S 7743. Rept by State D A R.

THOMPSON, ABRAHAM, Ross co

Enl pvt Dec 1775 near Trenton N J in N J Contls. Srvd 1 yr. B 1752; d Aug 30 1832 at Chillicothe. Appl pens in Ross co June 13 1819. Shoemaker by trade. Ref Pens Dept N J S 40576 and Scioto Gazette issue Aug 22 1832. Rept by Mrs. King Circleville and State D A R.

THOMPSON, JAMES, Scioto co

Enl Apr 1777 Pa Contls. B 1757 N Y city. Farmer by trade. Appl pens Scioto co Apr 24 1818 from Vernon twp. Ref Pens Dept S 40563 Pa. Indian War 1794 and War 1812. Rept by State D A R.

THOMPSON, JAMES, Wayne co

Servd in Col Spencer's 2nd Regt; d 1841. Ref No. 2342 S A R. Rept by Wm Pettit S A R Secy.

THOMPSON, JAMES, Richland co

Exec Doc 37 Rev Soldrs res in O refused a pens as service not in Reg Corps. Rept by Wm Pettit.

THOMPSON, JOHN, Mahoning co

Pvt Conn Line; b 1758; d 1813; bur at Smith. Early settler in above co. Ref "Conn Men in Rev" and Hist Trumbull and Mahoning cos. Vol 2 p 200. Rept by Mahoning chpt.

THOMPSON, JOHN, Adams co

Pvt Pa Milit: bur Old Seceder cem Liberty (Cherry Fork). Grave Located Sycamore chapter. Ref 16th Rept N S D A R p 146. Rept by State D A R.

THOMPSON, JOHN, Athens co

Exec Doc 37 Rev Soldrs res in O 1852 or before refused a pens as servd less than 6 mo. Rept by Wm Pettit S A R Secy.

THOMPSON, JOHN, Franklin co

Enl York co Pa 1777 and marched to Boston. Lieut Co Foot. Promoted to Col of Rangers and Volunteers raised by Pa. Also paymaster Pa Trps 2 yrs. B 1758; d at Columbus Ohio Apr 17 1834. Left only nieces and nephews. Appl pens Mar 25 1818 and trsfd to Ohio, Atty at Law. Ref Pens Rec Pa Contls S 7715. Old newspaper at Col libry. Issue of Apr 19 1834. Rept by Blanche Rings Gives full service written by soldr 20 yr before he d. In Crt House recds are mar of one Sarah Thompson to Robert Armstrong 12-21-1818 by Hoge; will of Mrs. Ruhama Thompson 01163 to dau Sarah Armstrong and to dau Mary Lacey Shepherd — Probat March 1837. Mary Chesney chpt and State D A R.

THOMPSON, JOHN, Butler co

Enl July 1775 in N Y Contls and srvd duration war. B 1751. Pensd Jan 1 1819 in Butler co Ohio. Ref Pens Dept N Y S 40562. Rept by State D A R.

THOMPSON, JOHN, Trumbull co

Colonel in Pa Contl. Pensd Trumbull co Mar 30 1819. No further data. Rept by State D A R.

THOMPSON, JOHN, Brown co

Not same as Vol 1 p 367. Pvt Va Contls and pensd Brown co June 9 1819. Ref Va S 40575. Rept by State D A R.

THOMPSON, JOSEPH, Belmont co

Enl Pvt Mass Contl 1776 at Roxbury Mass. Srvd Mass Line 4 yrs. B Nov 3 1761; mar Thankful (b 1772). Chldr: Joseph; Thankful; Marietta; Ruth; Mary. Appl pens Belmont co May 21 1818. Ref S 40572 Mass. Rept by State D A R.

THOMPSON, RUFUS, Ashtabula co

Enl 1781 in Tolland Conn. Milit as pvt and srvd 6 mos. B 1765 Munsonville Conn; mar Sally Burly Nov 24 1785. Soldr d Jan 6 1841. Pensd Ashtabula co July 6 1833. Widow pensd Mar 3 1847 in Erie co Pa. Ref Conn W 3621. Rept by State D A R.

THOMPSON, SAMUEL,

Pensd 1832. Nothing found to add proof. (J D).

THOMPSON, SETH, Ashtabula co

Enl Sept 1775 N H Contls and srvd 2 yrs 8 mos. B 1760. Chldr: George; Hannah. Mar Mary. Soldr d Nov 25 1828 æ 68. Bur Farnham Conneaut twp. Pensd May 12 1819 in Ashtabula co Salem twp. Widow pens same loc June 12 1843. Ref Mass Contl and N H W 6271. Rept by Mary Redmond chpt.

THOMPSON, THOMAS, Mahoning co

Pvt Pa and Conn Lines. B 1764 d Oct 15 1848 in Coitsville twp; bur Hopewell Pres cem Lawrence co Pa. Ref Cem Records of Henry Baldwin S A R and Mahoning co Register 1865 Coitsville. Early Settlers 1811. Rept by Mahoning chpt.

THORLA, THOMAS, Noble co

Srvd thru War. B in N E 1748 at Newburyport Mass; d Olive Dec 1835; bur Olive cem Caldwell Ohio. He followed three sons to Ohio in 1828 bringing aged wife. Ref Watkins Hist Noble Co p 432. This record was incorrectly filed reversed in Vol 1 p 368. Correction rept by Anna Asbury Stone chpt.

THORNHILL, REUBEN, Knox co

Enl Pvt Va Contls 1778. Servd 2 yrs under Col Francis Taylor and Lt Col William Fountain. B Dec 25 1757. Appl pens Knox Co Sept 24 1830. Pensioner Knox co 1833 æ 76. Ref Va S 3794. Rept by State D A R.

THORNTON, JOHN, Mahoning co

Pvt Berkeley Co Pa Milit under Capt Robt Patterson. Chldr: John; Martha mar Wm Reed; Joseph; Agnes mar Houston; Mary mar Graham; Rebecca mar Robinson; Jean mar Simpson. Soldr d 1815 Coitsville. Ref Hist Trumbull and Mahoning co Vol 1 p 48; Vol 2 p 86; Hist Mahoning co P 1011; Trumbull co Will Book 2 p 332. Also Coitsville Early Settlers. Rept by Mahoning chpt.

THORP, AUGUSTUS, Erie co

Was b 1769 son of Mary Miles Stanley and Joel Thorp; d 1810; bur Deyo-Bolls cem Groton twp. Grave mrkd by gov mrkr. Rolls of the 6th Conn Brigade lost. Not certain whr he first enl but his bro a yr younger was in this 6th Brigade. Find Augustus trnsfrd from the 4th Brigade to serve under Gen Siliman May 1 1778. Ref Firelands Pioneers O S Vol 10 pp 3, 4; N S Vol 5 p 45 and Vol 21 p 2481. Rept by Marjorie Cherry.

TIBBALS, SAMUEL, Montgomery co

Enl Mar 20 1777 at Norfolk Conn. Conductor of teams Conn Lines 16 mos. Mar Miriam Couch March 19 1823. Chldr: Sarah Langdon; Mary Wilcox; Lois A Stedham and Aaron Couch. Soldr d Apr 13 1829 Albany N Y. Movd from Conn to Ohio 1804 then to Mass in 1807. Widow d 1854. Settler Mont twp. Ref Conn and Pa W 6285. Rept by Wm Pettit S A R and State D A R.

TICE, SOLOMON, SR, Washington co

B 1750 probably N Y. Son of Martin and Mary Tice. Mar Ann Collier. Chldr: James 1775-1851; John 1780; Soloman Jr 1783-1864; Jacob; David; Martin; Mary; Sarah b 1798 mar Jacob Newlin a soldr of 1812. She was first white child b in Ludlow twp. Soldr d Nov 14 1838. Bur Tice cem Ludlow twp near Muskingum Valley. Inscpt on Marker "In memory of Soloman Tice who departed this life Nov 14 1838 aged 88." Ref Williams Hist Wash co P 700-701. Wash co Court Rec Vol 4 pp 30-124-305. Rept by Marietta chpt by Helen Sloan.

TIDD, WILLIAM, Trumbull co

Servd with N J Trps as pvt frm Hunterdon co N J. Wife Ann; bur Union cem Niles Ohio. Relationship if any to Martin Tidd Vol 1 p 369 not known. A son John lvd Niles. Ref Jersey men in Rev p 785. Rept by Mary Chesney chpt.

TIGNOR, THOMAS, Union co

Exec Doc 37 Rev Soldrs res in O. 1852 or before refused pens as servd less than 6 mo. Rept by Wm Pettit, S A R Secy.

TILFORD, ALEXANDER, Miami co

Cop fr 5th rept N S D A R p 252 by Mrs R Winnagle Warren O.

TILLMAN, TOBIAS, Preble co

Pvt in Co of Horse 1776 under Capt W O'Neal Col Butlers Regt N C Trps. B Orange Co N C 1751; mar Catherine Sharp 1783. She was b 1753 d 1840. One dau Phebe; son John. Soldr d Lewisburg Preble co. Pens appl Mar 22 1833. Ref No. 120254 D A R Lin Vol 121 and Pens Rec S 6247. Rept by Jane Dailey.

TIMMONS, ROBERT, Ross co

Pvt Del Contl. Pensr in Ross co 9-6-1819. Rept by Jane Dailey.

TINGLEY, EBENEZER, Miami co

Enl June 1776 Morris co N J in N J Milit. Srvd 13 mos; b July 27 1759 Morris Cc N J. Appl pens Monroe co O Sept 27 1832. Aft War movd Essex Co N J 1 yr; thence Fayette co Pa 10 yrs; thence Warren co O 10 yrs; to Belmont Co 6 yrs; to Monroe co. Ref N J pens S 3815. Rept by State D A R.

TINKER, SILAS, Ashtabula co

Pvt and Corp und Capts Jewett and Jones Cols Troop and Latimer Conn Line. B 1748 Lyme Conn; mar Lois Wade (b 1749); son Chauncey. Soldr d 1840 Kingville O. Ref Vol 113 p 118 D A R Lin. Rept by Nathan Perry chpt. Refused a pens as servd less than 6 mo. See exec Doc 37 rept by Wm Pettit.

TIPTON, SYLVESTER, Franklin co

Listed in "West Va Rev Ancestors" by Anne Waller Reddy; was b in Va (now Hampshire co W Va) around 1753; mar 1st Mary Stark (said to be a niece of Gen Stark) and 2nd a wid Poulson abt 1835. Chldr by 1st wf: Elizabeth mar a Corder; Hannah mar a Green; Thomas mar Elizabeth Tomlinson in Ross co O; Sarah mar Richard Heath; Jonathan mar Lucinda Dennison; Margaret mar Dr House; Catherine mar 1st Benjamin Gray; John mar Eliza Tomlinson; Hiram mar Tabitha Southward. Soldr d abt 1843 æ abt 90 yrs nr Reynoldsburg Pleasant twp Franklin co as he was on the tax list of 1844; was a school teacher; teaching in Va; Md and in 1798 in Muhlenberg twp Ross co O. Was in Franklin co by 1815 by Ct Rec. Grave not found but prob bur in Pisgah cem which was loc on the farm of his son Thomas in Pleasant twp. Desc Blanche Tipton Rings.

TISON, MATHAIS, ? co

Enl Goshen N Y 1776 Capt John Littles Co. Reenlstd aft 9 mos sick lve in Md Line; svd 4 yrs to end of war. B 1747; had a son John. Appl pens Wash co Court Sept 10 1818. Rept by Marietta chpt by Helen Sloan.

TOBIN (Tobey), ISAAC, Guernsey co

Pvt in Capt Joshua Corshon Co Col Chambers N J Regt. B 1750 Hunterdon co N J. Mar Phebe Thompson 1775. Had son Isaac Jr. Soldr d 1836 Guernsey co. Ref Vol 120 D A R Lin. Rept by Jane Dailey.

TOLAND, JOHN, Adams co

Enl Mar 1780 while lvg New Castle Co Del in Capt John Rudolphs Co Col Henry Lee's Regt Horse. Battle of Guilford to close of war. B July 10 1762. Wf d before 1833. Soldr d aft 1841 Adams co. Allowed pens 1832 whl lvg Pickaway co. In 1841 lvd with widowed dau Adams co. Her name Mrs. Sarah Trask. Pens N 18628. Cen 1840 states lvg Greene twp Adams co æ 76. Rept by Pickaway Plains chpt.

TOLMAN, ROBERT, Hamilton co

Bur Pioneer cem Cincinnati O. Insc on stone "Robert Tolman Rev Soldier 1794. Ref 20 Rpts N S D A R p 80. Rept by Nathan Perry chpt.

TOMBLESON (Tomlinson), MICHAEL, Ashtabula co

Bur Windsor Corners. Grave located Luther Reeve chpt. Ref 15 repts N S D A R p 164. Rept by Nathan Perry chpt.

TONEY (mis-spelled Tobey), CAREY, Preble co

Enl May 1781 Bedford co Va in Va Milit. Servd 6 mos; b Oct 10 1763 Buckingham co Va; mar Elizabeth 1787 or 88. Chldr: Harmon who made aff for mother 1859 stated he had 7 bros and 1 sister. Soldr d Sept 6 1859 Preble co. Appl pens Preble co Mar 23 1833. Resd Dickson twp. Wid appl pens Nov 16 1859. Aft War sold lvd Kanawah co Va; thence to Preble co. Ref Pens W 14029 B L Wt 53744-160-55. Rept by State D A R and Commodore Preble chpt.

TORRENCE, THOMAS, Fairfield co

Enl pvt 3 yrs Mass Regt. B 1745. Chldr: one known dau. Appl pens Apr 18 1818 Fairfield co. Farmer. Ref Wisemans Pioneer People Fairfield co p 406 pens Mass S 40582. Rept by Jane Dailey.

TOWNSEND, JOHN, Mahoning co

Pvt several services. B 1758; son John F. Soldr d 1813 Youngstown; bur Rider Farm. Ref cem rec Henry Baldwin decd. S A R; Conn Men of Rev Ser 3 vol 23 pp 80-103 Pa Arch. Mass Men Vol 10 p 92. Rept by Mahoning chpt.

TIPTON, LUKE, Holmes co

Enl 1779 Apr Pa Rang pvt Bedford Co. B May 14 1760 Baltimore Co Md. Had son with whom lvd (appl). D Oct 8 1855. Appl pens Holmes co May 1832. Trans appl Henry co Tenn May 4 1846. Cen 1840 pensr Mill Creek twp Coshocton co O æ 85 and liv with Adam Bible. Issued Bounty land Certif May 19 1856. Lvd in Md and Va after War Appl increase pens Weakley co Tenn Oct 3 1853. Ref S 3812 B L Wt 26150-160-55. Rept by Jane Dailey.

TOWNSEND, JOSEPH, Mahoning co

Pvt 4th Class Berks co Pa Milit. Chld: John b 1783. Soldr d before 1826 Youngstown O. Blt first tnnery in Youngstown. Ref Pa Arch Ser 5 vol 5 p 384. Hist Trumbull and Mahoning cos p 164. Rept by Mahoning chpt.

TOWSLEY (Tousley), MATTHEW, Medina co

Enl Mar 1780 Bennington Vt. B 1765. Appl pens Addison co Vt July 24 1832. Appl pens Medina co O Jan 21 1834. Appl pens Orleans co N Y Sept 1839 then residing Geneser co N Y. Ref Pens S 14712. Rept by State D A R.

TRACY, JOHN, Fayette co

Pvt Cumberland co Pa Milit Capt John Jacks Co Second Bn. Chldr: William; Warnel; Soloman. Bur Tracy land now owned by Cockerill family. Grave location gvn 1927 by Mrs Sarah Cockerill æ 90 just prior to her death. Ref Pa Arch Ser 3 p 647. Came to Ohio 1805. Rept by Washington C H chpt.

TREBY (Tribby) JOHN, Trumbull co

Son of John Treby Sr (also a Rev soldr) and his wf Sarah Richardson. B Newport R I Sept 24 1758; d Brookfield O May 1819. Mar in 1780 to Abigail Hazard (a dau of Jeremiah and Phebe Tillinghast Hazard) She was b Feb 14 1764 in Exeter R I; d May 1842 Brookfield O. Chldr: Phebe mar Rice; Anna d young; George mar Martha Witherspoon; John Jr mar Fanny Patton; Abigail mar David Roy. Srvd as sailor on Frigate "Confederacy" launched 1778. Oct 1779 she sailed from Philadelphia having on board French Minister Gerard and the newly appointed ambassador to Spain John Jay. Encountered storm and forced to land Martinique Dec 18. Refitted and put to sea but in March 1781 captured off Va Capes by a British "74" and taken to Charleston S C then in enemy possession. Ref of Maratime Conn by Lewis Middlebrook Vol 1 pp 50, 51. Rept by Mary Chesney chpt.

TRESCOTT, JONATHAN, Trumbull co

Pvt Capt Enoch Nobles Co Col Ezra Woods Mass Regt. B Sheffield Berkshire co Mass. Soldr d May 27 1848 æ 83; bur Mt Pleasant cem St Johnsburg Va. Ref Trumbull co May 9 1833. Rept by Mary Chesney chpt.

TRIBLE, JOSEPH FULCHER, Washington co

Enl Caroline co Va joining Army at Williamsburg last day Feb 1777 for 2 yrs in 2nd Regt Va Line. Re-enl 18 mos 2nd Regt Va Line. Taken prisnr Charleston; escaped after 10 mos. Servd under LaFayette till Cornwallis' surrender. Shot in groin at Savannah. B 1760; mar Elizabeth (b 1783). Chldr: (given pens appl 1820) Roxanna 15 yrs; William 13 yrs; John 10 yrs; Nancy 8 yrs; Elizabeth 5 yrs; Samuel 4 yrs; Andrew 6 mos; soldr d Aug 3 1836. Ref Pens Rec Va S 40588 and Wash co Common Pleas Court (death record). Rept by Marietta chpt by Helen Sloan.

TROTTER, CHRISTOPHER, Adams co

Enl 1781 Martinsburg Berkley Co Va. B Oct 1758. Soldr d 1828. Appl pens Apr 20 1818 lvg Adams co. Ref Contl Va Pension Rolls S 40593. Rept by State D A R.

TROTTER, JOHN, Adams co

Enl June 1774. Winchester Va. Srvd 4 yrs. B 1757. Chldr: Lewis; William; Amy; Betsy and four others all over 21 yrs of æ in 1820. Appl pens Lincoln co Ky Aug 18 1820. Appl trans to Adams co Ohio Mar 21 1825. Ref Va S 42046. Rept by State D A R.

TROXELL, ABRAHAM JR, Montgomery co

Enl July 17 1776 Frederick co Md. Capt Henry Hardmans co. Bur Troxell cem Miami twp. Ref Md Arch Vol 18 p 51. Rept by William Pettit Dayton S A R.

TROXELL, ABRAHAM, Montgomery co

Enl John Kershners Co Frederick Co Md Milit June 27 1778. Guarded prisoners at Frederick. Ref Md Arch vol 18 p 328. Rept by William Pettit Dayton S A R.

TRUSLER, JONATHAN, Franklin co

Lstd Va Milit in Rev. P 293 as lvg Franklin co æ 76. See also Franklin co Order bk 9-75 for John Trusler pensr of U S d at his res in Union co Aug 16 1838 leaving Elizabeth Trusler his wid who granted Isaac Watts power of attorney the same day. Rept by Jane Dailey and Blanche Rings.

TRY, JACOB, Pickaway co

Servd 3 yrs as pvt guarded ammunition at Brandywine. B Feb 6 1757 abt 30 miles fr Philadelphia. Mar Justina Bernhard Aug 1 1793. Chldr: Jacob; Elizabeth; Marie; Catherine; George; Daniel; Sarah; Johann. Soldr d July 31 1833 Circleville. Body movd frm Lutheran cem to High St Cem. Last marker in row of graves. Mar Berks Co Pa. Came to Pickaway Co 1807. Landlord hotel in Jefferson 1st town in co. Ref Pens W 7320. Rept by Pickaway Plains chpt.

TUPPER, REUBEN, Mahoning co

Lstd in Compatriot Lynn's Address as Rev soldr lvg Mahoning co. Bur Canfield cem. Rept by William Pettit Dayton S A R.

TUCKER, ISAAC, Madison co

Enl May 1775 for 3 yrs Faunton twp Bristol co Mass in Mass Line. B 1742. Pensd Fearington Washington co Ohio. No family lvd with friends. Ref 9978 Mass S 40596. Rept by State D A R.

TUCKER, JOHN, Darke co

Enl pvt Feb 13 1776 at fathers house Emily Co Va. Svd 2 yrs. Soldr b 1750. Mar Sarah (b 1780); had son Randolph. Soldr d Aug 28 1829. Appl pens Darke co Dec 12 1819. Farmer. Dischd Valley Forge. Ref Va S 40598. Rept by State D A R.

TUCKER, WILLIAM, Washington co

Svd Col Ebenezer Sproats Regt. D Marietta; bur Mound cem. Stump of stone remains. Inscn on wf's marker "Mary wife of William Tucker d 1822 æ 66." Ref "Mass Solds and Sailors in Rev" vol 116 p 123. Rept by Marietta chpt.

TUCKER, WILLIAM, Hamilton co

Pvt Pa Line. Srvd 3 yrs. B 1757. Wf b 1780. Appl pens Campbell co Ky Feb 27 1826 at which time named wf and 4 daus; oldest 16. Brick-layer occupation. Trans Hamilton co May 3 1832. Ref Pa S 40600. Rept by State D A R.

TUFFS, WILLIAM, Portage co

Enl pvt Mass Milit Apr 1775 near Boston, svd 15 mos. B July 11 1750. Appl pens

Portage co Apr 12 1834. Appl transfer to Allen co Indiana Apr 12 1836. Ref Mass S 32026. Rept by State D A R.

TULLEY, JOHN P, Trumbull co

Srvd Col William Irvines 6th Pa Regt. Taken prisnr Quebec. B Ireland. Had 7 chldr two being James and John. Soldr d 1830 Liberty twp. Bur Seceders cem. Came to Va frm Ireland; to Washington co Pa; to Liberty twp Trumbull co. Rept by Mary Chesney chpt.

TULLIS, MICHAEL, Hamilton co

Enl pvt Berkeley co Va 1775. B Feb 1756 N J; mar Elizabeth Jones 1791. Chldr: Moses b 1792; Thomas b 1794; Leonard b 1796; Jonathan b 1798; David b 1800; Isaac b 1802; Aaron b 1804; Mary b 1807. Soldr d May 3 1832 Franklin co Ind. Appl pens there Sept 19 1827. Widow trans pens to Hamilton co 1832. Wid pens Franklin co Indiana Dec 1852. Trans to D C. Ref Va W 26558. Rept by State D A R.

TUMAN, PETER, ? co

Wf Sally bur Pilgurruh cem Bedford twp. Her husband may be there too. Grave not located. Sally d Aug 26 æ 66. Rept by Luella Wise Lakewood chpt.

TURNER, GEORGE, Hamilton co

Svd Capt 1st Regt S C Line. Pensr Hamilton co 1828. Chldr: Mary (residing Hamilton co and Ky) in 1825. Soldr d in Philadelphia Pa Mar 16 1843. Ref S C S 6283 B L Wt 2228-300. Rept by State D A R.

TURNER, JAMES, Champaign co

Servd in Del. Contl Line; b Ireland 1752 d 1839; mar Ann Ford. Ref No. 34136 S A R rept by Wm Pettit, St Sec.

TURNER, JAMES, Allen co

Enl Hagerstown Md pvt Capt Cresap Co Col Wards Regt Md. Svd 30 mos. B near Baltimore Md 1755; d Jan 31 1839. Appl pens Allen co Aug 8 1832. Pens trans to "Child" Mar 20 1840. Ref S 3841-19892 Allen co Clerks Records Bk E vol 8 p 26. Rept by State D A R.

TURNER, JOHN, Monroe co

Enl pvt Sussex co Del Mar or Apr 1778. Svd 5 yrs. B May 31 1763. Appl pens Washington co O June 6 1818. Appl Monroe co May 5 1828. Ref Del S 40594. Rept by State D A R.

TURNER, JOHN, Guernsey co

Petitioned for aid Oct 3 1818 Guernsey co Clerks records and in Sept 1822. Rept by Anna Asbury Stone chpt.

TURNEY, JOHN, Franklin co

Pvt 8th Class 2nd Co 2nd Bn Northampton Co Pa under Capt Geo Knapingberger. Mar Magdalena (d 1825 æ 78). Soldr d Mar 6 1823; bur Riverside cem Sunbury Road Franklin co O. Inscpt on stone "John Turney d Mar 6 1823 æ 74". Ref Pa Arch 5th Ser Vol 8 p 107. Ohio State Journal June 6 1829. Anna Salzman Mt Pleasant Iowa. Estate Settlement 0406. Compare No. 32321 S A R on James Turney, same wf. Rept by Mrs. W C Moore and Mrs W S Van Fossen Columbus O.

TWAY, JOHN, Fayette co

Enl pvt Flemington Co N J date not given. Servd 3 yrs. B 1757; wf named Sally. Soldr lvd with son appl pens May 9 1821 Fayette co Farmer. Bur Paint twp possibly Salmon cem. Grave not known. Ref Dills Hist and Pens N J S 42045. Rept by William Horney chpt.

TYLER, EBENEZER, Ashtabula co

Servd Conn Milit under Col Johnson. B 1747; d 1824; bur Saybrook Ohio Ashtabula co. Grave loc by Mary Stanley chapt. Ref N S D A R repts p 226 No. 18 and No. 21 p 112. Rept by Nathan Perry chpt.

ULRICH, JACOB, Richland co

Reported a Rev Soldr bur at Mansfield O.

UNDERWOOD, ISAAC, Wayne co

Pvt Masss Cont'l. Pensr in Wayne co 5-23-1820. Enl 1781 Mass Dischgd at Phila 1783. Servd 2 yrs b 1755; mentions wife, son Alanson and 7 chldr with him, in appl of 1820. On Oct 13 1819 appld for pens in Geauga co; and again July 8 1818; on Feb 21 1834 appld for new certif for pens in Wayne co alleging that his son Alanson lost his certif which he was keeping for him. He had appld for pens in Stark co in 1820 and on Jan 17 1822. Cens 1840 lists him in Chippewa Wayne co as pensr æ 74. Ref S 40609 Mass. Pens Claims D C. Cop by State D A R & J D. Wooster-Wayne D A R reports: Sale of land in 1842 Wayne co names wf Zilpha d 1848. No grave found.

UPSON, JOSEPH, Cuyahoga co

Pvt Mass Milit and State Trps. Also Conn. Enl June 1776 at Springfield Mass. B 5-5-1750 Plymouth Ct. D 12-21-1835. Was pensr in Cuyahoga co 5-7-1833. Ref Conn & Mass S 9493. Cop by State D A R.

USMAN, CHARLES, Adams co

Private Va Militia. Pensioned Feb 12th 1833. Ref Evans and Stivers History Adams County page 331. Rept by Meryl B Markley Vice Chairman.

VAIL, SOLOMON, Coshocton co

Enl Winchester twp Frederick co Va in 1775-76; pvt Va Contl; servd 7 yrs. Pensr in Coshocton co 12-8-1818; in 1820 was æ 75. A blacksmith. Ref Va S 40611. Cop by State D A R.

VALENTINE, GEORGE, Fairfield co

Pens Cl S 17171 Md and Pa. Enl 1775 or 6 Lancaster co Pa. Servd 10 mo as pvt; 20 mo as teamster; in Pa and Md Milit. b 1-2-1752 in Lancaster co Pa. Movd to O abt 1811; Appld for pens 11-1-1832 Fairfield co O. Listed p 406 Wisemans Pioneer People that co. State D A R.

VANAKEN, GIDEON, Trumbull co

Pvt N Y St Trps; pensr Trumbull co 9-17-1833; was 77 in 1832 (then b 1755); d Johnston Trumbull co Lieut Abraham Van Aken was his brother. Ref Pens Cl S 16277. Filed by Mary Chesney D A R.

VANAKER, GEORGE H, Logan co

Exec Doc 37 refused a pens as servd less than 6 mo. Rept by Wm Pettit.

VANAUSDALL, CORNELIUS, possibly Knox co

Enl 1776 under Cornelius Lot (?) Capt while residing in Somerset co N J where he was b 12-3-1758. He servd over 10 mo in Va and N J troops. Abt 1777 movd to Augusta co and enl as substitute for Hugh Botkin in 1780. Pensr in Greenbrier co Va 9-26-1833. He was trnsfd fr Va to O 9-4-1839. Ref S 15691 N J and Va Pensl Cl. O pens roll 1835 V 3 137 and p 293 "Va Milit in Rev War" where it states he was living in Knox co O aged 75 (J D). Cop by State D A R. One of similar spelling liv in Mason twp Lawrence co æ 81; cop fr cens 1840 by J D.

VANAUSDALLEN (or Vanarsdlen et al), GARRET, Butler co

Pvt N J and Pa S 7783 ens Cl Enl abt 7-1-1776 Summerset co N J. Servd 6 mo. B Mar 1753 Summerset N J. Appld for pens Butler co O 10-15-1832 whr he livd 22 yrs. Cop by State D A R & J D.

VAN BUSKIRK, JOHN, Licking co

Spy and scout under Major Samuel McCullough Henry Sewitz' Co of Northampton co Pa Milit. On Ohio frontier till 1800 when settled in Licking co. B 1755 N J; mar Elizabeth Hendricks dau of James Hendricks (she d 1840 æ 74; bur Lot 100 grv 140 by him lot 101 6th St cem Newark O). He d Dec 13 1840 æ 83. Chldr: Arilla a dau d 1818 bur lot 100 grv 139; another chld grv 138; a Lewis Van Buskirk lot 99 grv 137 d 1828 æ 31. Stones were laid on the grave and covered by Act of Council-Settled Brooks co W Va with his father 1780; came to Licking co 1800; was mar in Brooks co W Va. Built a mill 1804 on E Church St; also a house same date on E Locust both still standing. First pers in Union twp to own the land on which he settled; taking up 3100 A. Ref Hist Licking co 249-538-546-599-607; county deeds; & Pa Arch 5th S V 8 p 433. Filed by Hetuck D A R.

VANCE, DAVID, Jefferson co

Ranger Westmoreland co Pa for frontier defense. Mar Margaret Colville (b 1746). Aft Rev came to O and held civil office in Jefferson co. Ref Vol 28 p 250 D A R Lin No. 27684 thro son Daniel. Filed by Nathan Perry D A R.

VAN CLIEF, PETER, Washington co

In abandoned cemetery nr Waterford in old apple orchard Righteous Ridge is this insc on stone: "In Memory of Peter Van Clief a soldier of the Rev War who d March 5 A D 1816 in the 53rd year of his age." Marker placed by Marietta D A R 1930. Near by are stones with following data: Mary Ann consort of Peter Van Clief d Sept 1832 æ 87 yr 6 mo 12 da; also "Jane Van Clief d Feb 12 1816 in 20th yr of her age." (Also Mary Grub consort of Peter Grub d Aug 7 1815 æ 44 yrs). Filed by Helen Sloan Marietta D A R.

VANDAMAN, FREDERICK, Adams co

Enl as pvt aged 17 Va Contl Line under Capt Andrew Waggoner serving 18 mo. B Fayette co Pa where he d. In 1789 mar Susannah Hillicost. She was pensd in Adams co O in 1843; therefore listed here for ref D A R lin vol 24 p 131 No. 2337 thro dau Nancy. Reported by Nathan Perry D A R Mrs Oehlke.

VANDERVERT, CHARLES, Ross co

Scioto Gazette of Nov 5 1828 item: "Chas Vandervort a Revolutionary soldier d in Chillicothe on Wednesday last age 75 years." Filed by Pickaway Plains D A R fr H C Pemberton's list.

VAN DE VENDER, BARNABAS, Preble co

Pvt Va Milit. Listed as Pensr in Preble co 3-5-1833 æ 73 in book "Va Militia in Rev War" (who lived in Ohio) p 293. Cop by Jane Dailey.

VAN DUYN, JOHN, Meigs co

Strykers "Officers and Men of New Jersey in Rev War p 797; also Van Dine, John "Capt Strykers Troop Lighthorse" Somerset p 798; also Van Dyne, John, Somerset. B 1745; livd in or at Bound Brook N J; d 4-30-1825 nr Middleport O whr bur in lower cem. Mar 1st Christina Staats 2-10-1765 who was b 1-5-1742; d 4-10-1791. To this union were chldr: James 1768-1771; Hannah b 1770; Henry 1772-1777; James b 1774; John 1776; Henry (again) b 1781; 2nd wf was Jane (Boudinot) White 2-3-1796 (mar) she the dau of Dr John and Rachel (Van Nordon) Boudinot; she b 2-16-1764; d 5-14-1832. Chldr were: Rachel Bradford 1798-1839 mar 1st Col Robert Carver Barton; 2nd John N Smith; Adrienna b 1801-1831 mar Andrew Donnally; William Bradford b 1804-1874 mar 1st Elizabeth Smith; 2nd Abra Ann Crowell. Data filed by Elmer Jacobs Athens O but service not verified by State Ch Jane Dailey.

VAN GORDER, ABRAHAM, Trumbull co

Enl in Northampton co Pa in Capt Van Ettens 1st Co 5th Battl 1780. Was b abt 1760; wf's name Elizabeth. Chldr: Elizabeth; Isaac; and others. He d in Warren O Feb 6 1835. Ref Pa Arch S 5 p 377. Filed by Mary Chesney chpt.

VAN GORDEN (or Gorder), JAMES, Trumbull co

Pvt Ulster Co Rangers; mar Elizabeth b 1767 d 10-18-1840; tax list 1826 N Y Men p 203; West Reserve Chron Oct 1840. Rept by Mabel Askue Mahoning chpt.

VAN GUNDY, CHRISTIAN, Ross co

Sergt 1779 in Northumberland co Milit Col John Kelly. Ref Linn's Annals of Buffalo Valley 1755-1855 pp 171-78. B Lancaster co Pa abt 1742; mar Ann; chldr: Christian Jr b 2-3-1766; mar Mary Magdalena Follmer; Ann Mary mar John Wolfe; Jacob b 4-20-1770 mar Catherine ——; John b 1767 mar Margaret; Barbara mar George May. Soldr came to Ross co abt 1804 as on Oct 29 he entered Sec 21 twp 9 R 21 599 acres there. (court recds). He d here nr Chillicothe 1812. During Rev livd in Buffalo twp Northumberland co Pa (now Lewisburg Pa). Service was estab on testimony of a son and a gr son. Ref Hist Sesq and Juanita Valleys V 2 p 1235 by Everts Peck and Richards Phila 1886 and No. 216706; 234920; 252430 D A R. Rept by Skikelimo chpt D A R Lewisburg Pa thro Mrs Frances Backus.

VAN LILBURG, HENRY, Jefferson co

Was b 1744; d 1826; bur Sugar Grove cem. It is said his wf was shot to death by a Hessian soldr. Her baby was in her arms. Rept by Mary D Sinclair Steubenville chpt.

VAN NESS, GEORGE, Madison co

Srvd thro war; with Washington at Valley Forge. He d 3-22-1832; he movd to Madison co O in 1813. Listed in 20th Rept p 80 N S D A R. Cop by Jane Dailey.

VAN NORMAN, ISAAC, Morrow co

Bur Franklin twp North Fork cem Morrow co O. Rept by Mt Gilead chpt.

VANNOSTRAN, GEORGE, Butler co

Pvt N J Contl. Volunteer at Brunswick and dischrgd at Elizabethtown N J. Srvd 3 yrs. Appld for pens 9-20-1818 Butler co O æ 67. Ref Pens Cl S 40615 N J. Cop by State D A R.

VANTILBURG, HENRY, Jefferson co

Exec Doc 37 refused a pens as servd less than 6 mo. Rept by Wm Petit.

VANTRESSE, JOSEPH, Knox co

Pvt in Capt Tar's Co Col James Johnston's Md Regt. B Aug 11 1750 Delaware. Mar Ann —— 1788; Lucy Ann was one child. He d 1838 in O; appld for pens in Knox co Aug 3 1832. Servd 6 mo. Ref Pens Cl S 4700 Md; and No. 122154 Vol 123 D A R Lin. Cop by Jane Dailey.

VATTER, CHARLES, Hamilton co

Pa Service; b 1760 France; d 1841; mar Pamilia Ann Loring; ref S A R 25355. Rept by Wm Pettit. One Charles Vathier is found cens 1840 pensr Delhi twp Hamilton co æ 78. (J D).

VENARD, THOMAS, Warren co

Pvt Pa Milit. B Loudon co Va 1756 whr livd till æ 20 and movd to Washington co Pa; here enl in 1776. Servd under Capt Goddis Pa Line 11 mo. Then movd to Scott co Ky and after 2 yrs in 1796 to Warren co O where "he has resided ever since" as stated in appl of May 20 1833 residing in Clear crk twp. Ref Pens Cl S 16282 Pa. Rept by State D A R.

VIAH, GIDEON, Gallia co

Pvt Va Milit. Name listed in "Va Militia in Rev War" p 293 as liv in Gallia co æ 79. (by J D) Ref Pens Cl 6311 Va gives service in Col Dickerson Regt 1 yr 8 mo 20 da. B Nov 25 1755. In 1818 moved fr Va to Gallia co Addison twp whr appld for pens 8-11-1832. Cop by State D A R.

VIERS, BENJAMIN, Gallia co

Ref Va S 6313. Bur Pensions (D C). Pvt Va Contl. Servd under Col Blueford Va Line two yrs. Appld for pens in Gallia co O Apr 24 1833. Pensd 5-28-1833 in Gallia co. B 9-3-1752 Charlotte co Va; mar Betsey Long Amherst co Va 1822. Rept by O State D A R.

VOORHEES, MINUE, Hamilton co

Capt and Quartermaster; also Asst in Genl Hospt C A 1777. Born Somerset N J (see Van Voorhees); his father was Abraham Voorhees who dropped "Van" after the War see same p 379 Roster O Rev soldiers. Minue d Reading O where was bur in cem. A maternal ancester was Jennetje Minues who named one son Minue Johannes for whom this Minue Voorhees was named no doubt. Came to Columbia Hamilton co 1792; thence to Reading 1794 joining father and brothers. He was the third son. Entered Sec 32 of land. Ref Stryker "Men of N J in Rev" p 837; pp 808-877 Gen Dept; Nelsons Hist Hamilton co for Voorhees family. Rept by Mrs Whallon Cin D A R.

VOORHEES, STEPHEN, Butler co

Pvt L I N Y. His name is on the Memorial tablet in Hamilton Butler co O Memorial Bld in list of Rev soldiers of Butler co. He was b Long Island N Y Possibly history found in Warren co O. Rept by Cincinnati chpt.

VORYS (or Vories or Vorhees), ISAIAH, Franklin co

Pvt N J. His obituary states he was a native of N Y. Came to Columbus O before the first settlement. Mar Charlotte. About him Ohio State Journal of Mch 22 1834 says in obituary headed "Another Revolutionary soldier gone." Under date of 4-7-1835 Journal has: "Mrs Charlotte Voris mar Elijah Backus." in Probate recds is also found "Charlotte Voris-Ebenezer" name. His will probated 4-3-1833 d 3-16-1834 æ 85. Chldr: Abraham; William; John; Ann Hilson; Sarah Hilson; Polly Rodgers; Hannah Blair. Rept by Columbus D A R.

WADE, JAMES, Ashtabula co

Sergt Capt Isaac Hall's Co at Prospect Hill 1775. Was b Medford Mass 1750; mar Mary Upham; one child was Benjamin Franklin; soldr d Andover O 1826 May 9 æ

75 yr. Grave located by Mary Stanley D A R. Ref V 30 D A R Lin No 29980; also Vs 18 and 21 Hist Ashtabula co O 67 and 84 rept by Mary Redmond chpt. Rept by Nathan Perry chpt.

WAGGONER, JACOB, Clark co

Pvt Germon Regt. Enl 5-4-1777 Pa Line. Was b Feb 1755. Chldr: George W; Mary Ann Eyre; Hannah Eyre Altemus a gr dau; other childr: Barbara æ 19; Polly 17 in 1821. Appl for pens in Clark co O 5-21-1818. Ref Act Cong 1818 Col O æ 68; Contl (Md) S 40628. Rept by State D A R.

WAITE, JONATHAN, Adams co

Pvt Mass Line. Enl at Danvers Mass 1777. Mar Naomi Collins 1-26-1797; soldr d 7-27-1840 Adams co O. Wid appl for pens in Adams co 8-22-1857 but was rejected. Ref Mass R 1105 Rejected B L 297559-55. Rept by State D A R.

WAITE, JONATHAN, Portage co

Was b Northampton Mass Jan 24 1753; d Aurora Portage co Ohio 1838. Rept by Moses Cleaveland chpt.

WAITE, PETER, Medina co

Soldr d Wadsworth O. Ref 3rd Rept N S D A R p 229. Rept by Martha Pitkin chpt.

WAITES, JAMES, Brown co

Pvt Pa Milit Regt of Col Crawford. Enl May 1777 Washington co Pa. Srvd 1 yr 4 mos and 12 das. Was b Mar 1762 Bartley co Va; Mar Margaret Livengood abt 1791; soldr d Mar 2 1855 Brown co O; bur Sterling twp Taylors Chapel. Rept by "James Waites d Mar 21 1855 æ 95 yr." Came fr Redstone Pa to Ky; to O 1794 and 1802 to Sterling twp whr owned 118 A on Four Mile Crk. James Waite res in Brown co Apr 29 1833 and appl for pens there. Livd Brown co for 28 yrs; previously res in Ky. Wid res Brown co O Sept 28 1855; wid res Clermont co O Mar 24 1855. Ref W 25898; B L Wt 27573-16055 Pa; Beer's Hist p 685; Rockey and Bancroft's Clermont co p 685. Rept by State D A R and Meryl B Markley Vice Ch.

WAKLE, THOMAS, Clinton co

Pvt Conn Contl. Enl Apr 1 1780 in Conn. Srvd 1 yr. Was b 1760; pens appl Clinton co O Aug 7 1822. Ref S 40633 Conn. Rept by Jane Dailey.

WALCOTT, JOHN, Pike co

Pvt Pa Contl. Enl latter part of summer 1777 1st Pa Regt. Chldr: Kitty æ 16; Hannah 14; Reuben 12; Hetty 10; Christe 8; Fanny 6; Lucinda 4; (appl 1820). Pens appl in U S court of Ky Oct 2 1818 whl residing in Bourbon co Ky. Trnfrd to O. Ref Pa S 40634. Rept by State D A R.

WALE, THOMAS, Madison co

Listed in "Va Milit of Rev" p 294 as Va soldr living in Madison co O æ 71. Trnsfrd from Tenn. Cop by Jane Dailey.

WALKER, ASHER, Tuscarawas co

Enl 1775 as a substitute for his father. Aft having srvd out this term he volunteered to serve another term. Was b 1757 Monmouth co N J. Pens appl Fayette co Pa Oct 22 1832; and Tuscarawas co O Mar 4 1834. Ref S 3451 N J. Rept by State D A R.

WALKER, BENJAMIN, Muskingum co

Pvt N J Milit. Enl N J 1779; srvd 1 yr and 3 mos. Was æ 72 or 73 in 1833. "He thinks he was b 1761 Rahway ? N J." (Appl). Livd in Rahway N J when called into service. Aftward res Wilkesbarre Pa and now at Muskingum co O whr appl for pens Nov 26 1833 res of Licking twp. Ref S 7801 N J. Rept by State D A R.

WALKER, JAMES, Adams co

Pvt N C Milit. Enl Feb 1 1776 Orange co N C (since Coswell co). Re-enl in 1776 Jan 9. Was æ 77 in 1832. Pens appl Oct 6 1832. Ref N C S 3450. Rept by State D A R. Compare same name fr p 331 Evans and Stivers Hist. Pensr Oct 8 1833 for Pa Milit service. Rept by Meryl Markley and State D A R.

WALKER, JOHN SR, Butler co

Cop fr Cens 1840 æ 74 liv in Fairfield twp Butler co. Rept by Jane Dailey.

WALKER, JONATHAN, Portage co

Listed in "Va Milit in Rev" p 294 as liv in Portage co O æ 69. Cop by Jane Dailey. Compare John Walker, Summit co p 383 O Roster Vol 1.

WALKER, MESHEC, Muskingum co

Pvt N J Contl. Enl into 1st Regt 8-10-1776. Srvd 6 yrs and 10 mos. Was æ 75 in 1826. Wf æ 70 yrs in 1826. Pens appl Muskingum co O 5-26-1818. Ref N J S 40621 B L Wt 362-100. Rept by State D A R.

WALKER, PETER, Adams co

Pvt Pa Contl. Enl May 1777. Dischrgd Jan 1781 Trenton N J. Srvd 3 yrs from 1777 to 1780. Was æ 68 in 1827. Mar Elizabeth Sept 5 1785; chldr: Joseph; Elizabeth Thompson; late Elizabeth Walker) and Rosan Miller (late Rosan Walker). Soldr d Apr 26 1826. Was res Adams co O Aug 11 1820 and Mar 23 1827. Pensd Adams co 1820. Son res Scioto co on Mar 29 1852. Ref W 5161 Pa. Rept by State D A R.

WALKER, SAMUEL, Muskingum co

Pvt N Y Contl. Enl 1779 N Y. Dischrgd Snake Hill N Y June 1783. Was æ 60 in 1820. Pens appl Muskingum co O Aug 9 1819; appl also 1820. Ref S 40635 N Y. Rept by State D A R.

WALKER, WILLIAM JR, Perry co

Srvd as 2nd Lieut in Washington co Md Milit. D Somerset O; mar 1775 Marie Siegfried. Ref Vol 25 p 214 D A R Lin bk; Nat No 24600 through son Josiah. Rept by Nathan Perry chpt.

WALKER, WILLIAM, Darke co

Pvt Va Milit. Enl Sept 1778 Va Whl res Botetourt co. Srvd 8 mos. Was b 1759 Bedford co Va. Aft war movd to N C; aft 11 yrs movd to Knox co Tenn; aft 18 yrs movd to Preble co O; aft 5 yrs movd to Darke co O. Pens appl Darke co O 11-19-1833. Ref Va S 7800. Rept by State D A R. Listed in Va Milit in Rev p 294 as liv in Darke co O æ 75 (J D).

WALKER, WILLIAM, Mahoning co

Pvt. Ser 3 V 23 pp 169; 170, 247, 350 Pa Arch. Soldr d before 1837 Smith twp. Ref Deed bk R p 108 trnscrbd Mahoning co p 1823; Deed bk I 275 trnscrbd Wm Walker by Adm to 1837. Rept by Mahoning chpt.

WALLACE, ISAAC H, Lorain co

Exec Doc 37 refused a pens as servd less than 6 mo. Rept by Wm Pettit.

WALLACE, ——, Morrow co

Bur Cardington twp Greenlawn cem Morrow co O. Rept as Rev soldr by Mt Gilead chpt.

WALLEN, DANIEL, Clark co

Pvt N Y Milit. Enl 1776 or 77 whl a res of N Y. Aft the war livd in New Hartford Conn; Luzerne co Pa; Lake co N Y; Indiana; and Ohio. Was b 3-4-1749 or 50 New Hartford twp Conn. Res of Bethel twp Clark co O in 1832. Ref Pa S 6337. Rept by State D A R.

WALSH (or Walch), JAMES, Adams co

Pvt Va Contl. Enl Culpepper co Va 1776. Srvd 2 yrs. Was æ 68 in 1818. Had a dau Serepta æ 23. Res Adams co O May 18 1818 whr appld for pens 1820. Was a schoolteacher. Ref S 40622 Va. Rept by State D A R.

WALLACE, JOSEPH, Portage co

Pvt R I Contl. Enl in Apr 1777 in Capt Elisha Bluckman's Co. Dischrgd Apr 1780 Morristown N J. Was æ 60 yrs in 1818. Chldr: Betsey æ 14; Frona 10; Sabrina 8; Joseph 6; and Laura 2 in 1820. Appl for trnsfr of pens from N Y to Portage co 8-8-1820. Ref Conn Contl S 40630. Rept by State D A R.

WALLER, ASHBEL, Butler co

Pvt Conn Contl. Enl 1778. Srvd 7½ mo. Was b Oct 12 1759 Litchfield Conn; mar Jane Turner June 7 1832; soldr d Sept 20 1848 Butler co O. Res in Butler co for abt 27 yrs. His wid movd to Jefferson co Ky whr she later appld for arrears of her husbands pens Aug 21 1856. Pens appl July 20 1832 in Butler co O. Ref Conn W 25861; B L Wt 47744-160-55. Rept by State D A R.

WALLER, WILLIAM, Guernsey co

Pvt Va Contl. Enl 1776 as Corp Md and Va Riflemen under Capt Wm Brady Cols Hugh Stephenson and Moses Rawlings. Mar Sarah —— 1779; (b 1759; d 1848). One son was William. Soldr d Guernsey co O. Ref V 115 p 159 D A R Lin No 114514. Rept by Martha Pitkin chpt.

WALTEMYER, GEORGE, Muskingum co

3rd Co 5th Battl York co Pa Milit. Capt Wiley's Co pvt Oct 7 1780. York co Milit Capt Bausley's Co 1776. Was b Germany 1741 Son of Ludwig (Lewis) Waltemyer; mother d at sea; father mar again in America. They came to America 11-2-1752 on ship Phoenix fr Rotterdam. Had 5 sons: Frederick; Charles; David; Philip; Michael mar Margaret Musser in Pa and had 7 chldr. These were all b in York co Pa. At least 2 dau: Katie the youngest mar Frederick Stouvener; other dau mar —— Orwick. Soldr d before 1812 Musingum co O probably bur nr Roseville. Sec wf went to York co Pa and d in two weeks. Ref Pa Arch S 6 Vol 2 pp 526, 606, 689, 695, 699; Rupps 30000 names; Will bk F p 77 York co Pa. Rept by K H VanFossen Columbus chpt.

WALTER, MATTHIAS, Columbiana co

Rev Soldr. Rec not yet found. Was b 1767; d 1854; bur Elk Run. Ref Col co cem Recs. Rept by Mrs Wilma M Molsberry.

WALTERS, JOHN, Monroe co

Pvt 6 mo and 10 days. Enl June 1781 in Pa. Was b 1763 nr Hagerstown Pa. Res Laps Creek Fayette co Pa at time of enl. Movd to Belmont co O aft the war; aft 25 yrs movd to Monroe co. Pens appl Monroe co O 6-3-1833. Ref Pa S 17753. Rept by State D A R.

WALTERS, PETER, Morgan co

Pvt Va Trps. Enl Oct or Nov 1777 in Va. Srvd 1 yr. Was b Apr 1760. 2nd wf was Isabella mar July 6 1797; 2 chldr by first wf; Joseph; and Mary b 1795; 11 chldr by second: Mary æ 25; Ruth æ 21; Jonah 21; Andrew 17; George 16; Ann 17; Solomon 11; Rachel 9; Elizabeth 3; Sarogh ? 1. (appl 1820). Soldr d Feb 15 1834 Manchester twp Morgan co O. Soldr appl for pens Morgan co O on July 18 1832 res Manchester twp. That Peter Walters was formerly mar to a wf who d before his intermarriage with Isabella was stated in letter of Commissioner of pensions. Was res Belmont co O on July 13 1818 and 1820. Wid appl for pens Morgan co O Apr 3 1849 Res of Manchester twp whl res with her son-in-law Wm Archibald. Wid appl for increase of pens Noble co O Feb 4 1854. Ref W 2029 Va. Rept by State D A R.

WARD, JOSIAH, Lorain co

Pvt Mass. Many varied and long enlistments. Enl fall 1777 Dorchester Mass. Srvd 10 mo. Was b Weymouth Mass May 1763; father killed at Bunker Hill battle; bros Nehemiah and Joshua both srvd in Rev; mar Eleanor —— 1795; 1st wf was sister of Samuel Sherman. Soldr d 1843 Jan 18; bur probably Huron O. Res 7 yr in N H aft Rev and movd to northern part of Vt and some time later came to O. His wf appl for pens in Lorain co O Nov 26 1845. He appl for pens Oct 8 1832 in New Huron co O; 1840 liv in Brighton twp Lorain co æ 78. Ref 18 Rept N S D A R p 268; Mass S 7813 Privateer. Rept by State D A R and Nathan Perry chpt. Cop fr News issue of 2-18-1843 by Blanche Rings "He was one of that brave band who assisted in the destruction of the tea in Boston Harbor. During the whole of the Rev he srvd his country with fidelity and whn the strife was over he devoted his time to peaceful pursuit of agriculture."

WARD, OBEDIAH, Ashtabula co

Pvt Mass Milit. Enl Apr 1775 Hampshire co Mass. Srvd 10 mos. Aged 79 in 1832. Pens appl Ashtabula co 9-24-1832; pensd 1833 Ashtabula co and 1840 liv w Elijah Ward at Kingsville æ 87. Ref Mass S 4716. Rept by State D A R.

WARDELL (Wardwell), WILLIAM, Butler co

Pensd 11-26-1819 Butler co O. Wid pensd 7-8-1853 Ind pens no 881. Enl Stanford Conn 1777. Was æ 60 in 1820. Mar Catharine Ray 12-18-1824. Chldr: Harriet 10; Betsy 9 in 1824; Frances Rebecca 3 in 1820. Soldr d 2-12-1848 Oxford Butler co O. Ref Conn W 2030; 4th Rept N S D A R p 295. Rept by State D A R.

WARD, WILLIAM JR, Champaign co

Col Br Greenbrier Co Va in 1784. Son of Wm Ward Sr and Rebecca Anderson Ward. Lived in Kentucky; later a resident of Urbana where he died Oct 10-1841. Bur Oak Dale Cem Urbana. MI "In memory of Col Wm Ward who died Oct 10-1841 in the 57th year of his age. Tho' now laid here, I'll rise to meet my Jesus in the skies." Fur infor Miss Alice Gaumer Urbana.

WARDS, EDWARD, Perry co

Pvt Md Milit; Enl 1776 res of Frederick co Md. Was b 1757 Charles co Md. Movd with his father to Frederick co Md. Mar Lucy Wilson 8-6-1779; chldr: William; John; James; Jermiah; Anna Ward Burgess. Soldr d 3-25-1840 Perry co. Movd to Perry in 1811 whr pensd 1834. Cens 1840 says living Madison twp Perry co æ 86. Ref Md R 11115. Rept by State D A R.

WARE, ROBERT, Belmont co

Exec Doc 37 refused a pens as srvd less than 6 mo. Rept by Wm Pettit.

WARNER, HENRY, Montgomery co

A soldr of Rev is bur at Old Warner cem west of Union. Fifth Pa Arch Vol 2 p 281, 267, 275, 272, 270; Vol 4 p 615 same series in Contl Line. Was b in Pa; d 1816 Randolph twp. Ref 54677 & 54681 S A R. Vol 6 p 620. 1780 in Cumberland milit. The vol 2 p 261 says in Col Miles Regt of riflemen which took part in Battle of Long Island. Another soldr of same name was in Col Broadhead's regt in Battle of Long Island also at Kings Bridge. The vol II ref 375 says "missing aft Aug 27." Rept by W M Pettit Dayton.

WARREN, PETER, Ross co

Pvt Va Line. Enl May 1778 in Cumberland co Maine. Pensd Muskingum co Tanesville twp 1819. Trnsfrd to Maine 1828. Ref Mass S 35702. Rept by State D A R.

WARTHMAN, MATTHIAS, Hocking co

Pa Arch S 6 Vol 1 p 784 Philadelphia co Milit 1777 (Matthias Wartman); same p 773 1780 Matthias Warthaman. Came to America in ship Crawford fr Rotterdam Holland (S 2 Vol 17 Pa Arch); qualified Oct 16 1772. Wf's name Mary Bresler; bought land in Athens co (Court recds); went to Hocking co whr is bur at Enterprise O. One child was Matthias Jr who mar Sally Funk. Rept by Lawyer E E Jacobs Ewings chpt S A R Athens co.

WARTMAN, PETER, ? co

Pvt refused a pens because he servd in regt not on contl estab. Ref Doc 31 Jan 6 1831. Rept by Blanche Rings.

WASHBURN, Anson, Erie co

Ref 3rd Rept N S D A R p 229; bur in Maple Grove cem Vermilion O Erie co. Rept by Mrs Winnagle.

WASSON, WILLIAM, Gallia co

Pvt Pa Milit. Pens 1833 Galia co æ 82. Was b 1752 Antrim co Ireland. Ref Pa Arch p 586 Vol 23 S 3; S 18670. Rept by State D A R.

WATERHOUSE, WILLIAM, Guernsey co

Pvt R I Line. Enl 1775 Cambridge Mass. Mar Lavinia Sept 16 1799. Soldr d Mar 12 1835. Pens appl Guernsey co O Sept 28 1831. Wid appl Guernsey co Aug 31 1849 æ 90. Ref W 6433 R I. Rept by State D A R.

WATERMAN, IGNATIUS, Washington co

Pvt Conn Contl. Enl Norwich Conn fall of 1775. Was b 1759; Mar Eleanor —— æ 61 yrs in 1820. Stated he had no fam except his wf. Soldr d 1848 Salem twp. Grave unknown. Mrkr placed in Mound cem by Marietta chpt. Ref Conn S 40644 Contl; Vol 3 p 411 Com Pleas Ct Marietta. Rept by Marietta chpt and State D A R.

WATERMAN, JOHN, Washington co

Was b 1767 Conn; d Sept 1 1834. Bur Waterman between Watertown and Waterford. Inscript on mrkr "A native of Conn and one of the early settlers of O who departed this life Sept 1 1834 æ 67." Grave mrkd by Marietta chpt. Ref Mass Soldrs and Sailors Vol XVI p 685. Rept by Marietta chpt.

WATERS, ALLEN, Sandusky co

Pvt for nine mos. Enl June 1780 in Conn. Was b 1758 Lime Conn. Pens appl July 27 1832 Huron co O. Livd in Lime Conn when he enl in the milit. Later movd to

New Haven O and later to Ridgefield O in Huron co. Pensr 1840 Cens liv in Green Creek twp Sandusky co æ 81 w William Waters. Ref Conn S 4715. (Compare Allen Watrous p 389 Vol 1 Ohio Roster who is thought to be a different man). Rept by State D A R.

WATERS, JACOB, Licking co

Pvt Pa Milit and St Trps. Service Chester co Pa 1776-77-78. Was b Upper Marion twp Montgomery co Pa. Mar Ann b Apr 1765; d 1849. Chldr: Nathan; Sarah; Jacob; Nancy; Joseph; Rachel; Liddy; Elizabeth; Mary; James; and Jane. Soldr d 1-1-1840 in Hanover twp. Pensr 1833 Licking co. Rept by Hetuck chpt. Exec Doc 37 his wid pens suspended as not a wid at date of act of Congress. Rept by Wm Pettit.

WATSON, WILLIAM, Stark co

Pvt Va Milit. Enl 1780 whl res in Loudon co Va. Srvd 10 mos. Was æ 73 in 1833. Was b Feb 22 1760 Loudon co Va. Aftward res in Frederick co Va for 7 yrs. Movd from Va 17 ago to Jefferson co O for abt 13 yrs and in 1829 to Stark co the part that forms part of Carroll co O. Pens appl Carroll co O Apr 18 1833. Ref S 171780 Va. Rept by State D A R.

WATT, MICHAEL, Medina co

Listed pp 144 and 145 in "Hist of North Central Ohio" by Wm A Duff as Rev soldr, Sharon, Medina co. Rept by Nathan Perry chpt.

WAYNE, WILLIAM, Mahoning co

Pvt Ser 6 Vol 1 p 212 Vol 2 p 599 Pa Arch. Was b 1759; d 1859 Beaver. Rept by Mahoning chpt.

WEATHERHOLT, JOHN, Franklin co

John Wetherhold signed a deed in 1835 for property in Blendon twp to Valentine and wf Mary Bridwiser. Wetherhold prob a widower at this time as no one else signed with him. Rept by Blanche Rings.

WEAVER, JOHN, Clermont co

Pvt in Berkely co Va Milit in Capt Bedinger's Co. B in Holland 1749; mar Catherine who was b 1754; chldr: Susannah; Sarah; Rebecca; James; John; Christina; Simeon; Elizabeth. D in Batavia twp March 1831. Bur in Weaver fam cem two mi southwest of Batavia O. A govt mrkr was set at his grave by descendants June 1936. His wf d 1829. Ref Everts Hist Clermont co pp 246-247. Rept by Achsa Hulick, Beech Forest chpt.

WEAVER, JOHN, Madison co

Pvt Va Line. Pens 1828 Tuscarawas co. No record located at Pens Off D C. We found the following on same name: b Germania Va; a pvt in Capt Heth's Independ Va Inf; mar Keziah Grennam; one son was Wm mar Nancy Ford. Soldr d 1837 in Madison co but did not give the state. Now there is a Madison co in O to which it may refer. Cop fr Ref No 91822 or 69132 by J D.

WEBB, BARRUCK, Clark co

Pvt Md. 3 yrs. Enl June or July 1780 under command of Col Joshua Bell of Md milit. Pensd 10-4-1819 Clark co O. In appl of 1820 states he was æ 60 yrs. His wf Mary æ 45 yrs. Chldr: Harriet æ 12; Noah 9; Asaph ? Z; Marie 6; Thomas 4; Carl Manapah 3 and is deaf and dumb. Ref Md S 40654; the Vet Adm advises Ind History Comm July 1937 this name erroneously listed in Wayne co Ind in 1835 lists. Rept by State D A R.

WEBB, JOHN, Mahoning co

Pvt. Ser 5 Vol 5 pp 819 and 838 Pa Arch. Conn Men; N Y Men; and Md Arch. Soldr d abt 1826 Goshen twp. Ref Will bk 5 p 25 Columbiana co Records Probated 1826; Deed bk Q p 17 trnscrbd Mahoning co 1817. Rept by Mahoning chpt.

WEBB, JOSIAH, Trumbull co

Pvt N Y Milit. Enl Nine Partners N Y in Capt Andrew Harmonts Col Grahams Regt. Pens 1833 Trumbull co. Was b Feb 9 1751 Stamford Fairfield co Conn. Mar 1st —— 2nd at Warren Conn to Rhoda Page. Chldr: (by 2nd wf) Sherman; Harriet; Phebe; Laura. Others not found. Soldr d Jan 23 1842 Gustavus O. Mar at Nine Partners N Y æ abt 24 and enl from there. At æ 28 movd to Litchfield co Conn; aft 47 yrs movd to Gustavus Trumbull co O 1826. Ref Pension record and a grandson. Rept by Mary Chesney chpt.

WEBER, JACOB, Montgomery co

Drummer 8th co 8th Battl Northampton co Pa Milit. Col Balliet Adam Stahler's Co. Was b 1762; d 1835; bur Ellerton Montgomery co Grave mrkd by S A R Richard Montgomery chpt in 1933. Rept by Wm Pettit.

WEBER, PHILIP, Montgomery co

Sergt of the Cavalry in Va Line. Pensr 2 p 128 S of W 1833 Va Libr Rept 1911-12. Wids pens No 11144; pensd 7-14-1857 Ky. Mar Mary 1792. Chldr: Philip; Carolina Ward; Polly Shuck; Fayette; Locky L Graves. Hammit and Spotswood were dead at time of appl. Soldr d Galatin co Ky. Emigrat to Montgomery co 1804-5. Ref Va W 616. Rept by State D A R.

WEBSTER, ANDREW, Washington co

Pvt Mass Contl. Enl for 18 mos June 1782 Dudley Mass. Srvd 1 yr. Dischrgd at cantonments in N Y June 13 1783. Was b 1759; mar Sally Coburn dau of Major Asa Coburn Rev soldr. Had a dau Mrs Charles McCluer. Had a grdau Mary Webster æ 6 yr in 1831. Soldr d 1836; bur Waterford. Grave mrkd by Marietta chpt 1934. Pens 1833 Washington co. Ref Mass Soldrs and Sailors Vol XVI p 770, 771; Pens Papers S 3520; Vol 6 p 241; 214; 251; 314 Marietta crt recds. Vol 7 p 360. Rept by Jane Dailey and Helen Sloan Marietta chpt.

WEBSTER, JOHN B, Guernsey co

Capt Lieut in Pa Line 2 yrs. Enl Oct 1775 Pa Regt. Pensd 7-17-1819 Somerset co Pa. Petition for Aid Act in Guernsey co O March 1829 as Cadet in Co of Capt Joseph Brice 4th Regt artillery Col Thomas Proctor Pa Line. Was æ 66 in 1819. Chldr: Agnes 19; Harriet 17; Lucretia 15; George 13. (1823 appl). Ref Contl Pa S 40663; B L Wt 2391-200 Capt and Lieut Issued Sept 12 1789. No papers. Rept by Anna Asbury Stone chpt and State D A R.

WEBSTER, JOSEPH B, ? co

Listed in rejected pens appl. Ref Doc No 31 Jan 6 1831 as no satisfactory evidence of service given in the Contl Army. Rept by Blanche Rings.

WEBSTER, MICHAEL, Ashtabula co

Pvt Conn Milit. Pens 1833 Ashtabula co. Was b Hartford Conn; mar 1774 to Elizabeth Clard (b 1755). Thro a dau Polly. See 21684 D A R; a son Clark. Inscript on a broken stone "A soldr of the Revolution d 2-15-1850 æ 101 yr 9 mo." Bur old cem Kinsville O. Elizabeth his wf d 10-15-1842 æ 87 yr 6 mo. Ref Pioneer Wom Western Reserve P 535. Rept by Mary Redmond and Nathan Perry chpts.

WEBSTER, SAMUEL, Clermont co

Pvt and Sergt N H Contl. Pvt 8 mos and Sergt 12 mos. Enl Apr or May 1775 Rockingham co N H. Was æ 83 yrs in 1832. Pens appl 8-7-1832 Clermont co O. Since the Rev he has resided in N H and Maine. Livd in Clermont co O abt 15 yrs 1832. Ref N H S 3519. Rept by State D A R.

WEIDNER, DAVID, Montgomery co

Berks co 5th Ser Pa Arch Vol 5 p 194, 197. Captain May 10 1780 1st Co associates. Burial place Trissel's. Was b 1763; d 1844. Rept by Wm Pettit.

WEIGHTMAN, GEORGE, Franklin co

Pvt. 9 mo in Capt Levi Stockwells Co Peter Yates N Y Regt; again in Capt John Chapmans Co Col Seth Warners Contl Regt; prisoner at Fort George 1780; pensr 1818. Ohio St Journal; "George Wightman d here a soldr of the Rev; æ 84 on the 27th and d Nov 27 1844. Resided here over 30 yrs." Was b 1760. Mar Ruth who d 1834 æ 63. In estate "Sarah" wid of Geo Wightman recd several yrs maintenance Apr 9 1845; in 1825 referred to his wf Elizabeth as æ 55. Grave mrkd by Columbus chpt 1935. Ref Bareis "Madison twp p 436; Funeral notice Bell Nov 28 1844 (Germans); Estate 01699-1845 et al court recds. Rept by Blanche Rings.

WEIMER, GEORGE, Montgomery co

Ref 5th S Pa Arch Vol 5 pp 427, 492. Bur Ellerton Montgomery co O. Grave mrkd by Richard Montgomery S A R 1933. Rept by W M Pettit.

WEISELLAKE, GEORGE, Union co

Service in N Y; b N Y; ref 29942 S A R. Rept by Wm Pettit.

WELCH, EBENEZER, Delaware co

Fifer Conn Contl. Enl 6-30-1777. One son was Isaac æ 18 in 1820. Soldr d 1823 bur Liberty twp possibly. Pens appl Delaware co O 5-8-1818. Ref Conn S 40665. Rept by State D A R.

WELCH, JAMES, Mahoning co

Pvt. New Jersey Men. Cummins Regt. Am State Papers Vol 5 p 21. Ref Mahoning Reg Jan 6 1865; Manning's list of Early Settlers in Coitsville 1811; Am State Papers Vol 5 p 21 soldrs entitled to "Bounty Land" not recd in 1828. Rept by Mabel S Askue of Mahoning chpt.

WELLINGTON (Willington), JONATHAN, Columbiana co

Pvt Va Milit 18 mo. Enl abt the mo of July 1781 in Frederick co Va whr he livd. Ae 95 in 1832; mar Rachel abt 1779; chldr: John; William; Jane; Thomas; Nancy; Rachel McKee. Soldr d 2-26-1834 New Lisbon Columbiana co O. Pensd 1-3-1833 Columbiana co. Ref Va R 11305; Va Milit in Rev p 295. Rept by State D A R.

WELLS, ISRAEL, Licking co

Pvt Conn Contl. Enl in Conn 1776 in Jan. Srvd 1 yr. Mar Chloe. Cop fr tombstone: "B 1758; d Apr 3 1831;" bur old cem Granville Licking co (Hetuck chpt). Ref Conn S 40664. Rept by State D A R.

WELLS, SAMUEL, Montgomery co

No pens fcd found at D C as did not know state. Was b 1755; bur Vandalia cem Montgomery co O. Grave not located. Rept by Wm Pettit S A R.

WELLS, WILLIAM, ? co

Capt listed in invalid pensrs of U S belonging to Ohio pd at Chillicothe $240 annually. Cop fr 1 172 pensrs of 1818 by Jane Dailey.

WELSH, DAVID, Knox co

N H Contl. Enl Rutland Fort in Vt in Feb 1777. Srvd 2 yrs as pvt. Was b 1760 Duchess co N Y. Res in Vt for sometime aft the war and movd to Mass; aft 8 yrs movd back to Vt; came to O in 1816 and res in Knox co. Livd there in Middleburg twp with Peter Welsh (in Cens 1840) æ 85. Ref O Pens Roll 1835; III; O-137; Vt S 3504. Rept by State D A R.

WENTWORTH, JOHN, Ross co

Com of a Co 1776 at Ft Edward; srvd Coast Guards and in 1778 guarded Captive prisoners of Burgoyne. Was b 1736 Kittery Me. 2nd wf was Sarah Bartlett (1740-1827). One child was named Foster and mar Catherine Jordon. Soldr d 1781 Chillicothe O. Ref 107591 Vol 108 D A R Lin. Rept by Nathan Perry chpt.

WEST, CLEMENT, Wayne co

Pvt N Y Milit abt 6 mo. Enl in 1778 in Dutches co N Y whr was b 5-20-1760. Aft war movd to Pa and res sev yrs before moving to Wayne co O. Pens appl 10-1-1832 in Wayne co O res of Chester twp. Claim was rejected as srvd less than 6 mo (Exec Doc 37 of yr 1852). Ref N Y R 11337. Rept by state D A R.

WEST, GEORGE, Pickaway co

Major in Va Milit ref: McAllister Va Milit in Rev p 269 Loudon co Va. Chldr: Daniel; Peter; Fredrick; John; George; Elizabeth; Blue; Mary Magdalen Bright; Sarah Barley; Barbara Hall; Margaret Metsler; Catherine mar Philip Trullinger. Inscript on mrkr, George West d 1824 almost illegible. Will probated 12-30-1824; bur John Fry farm Jackson twp. Came to Loudon co Va; thence to Pickaway co 1804 settld on 900 A of Butler survey in s e corner of Scioto twp and n corner of Jackson twp. Ref Will bk 1-2 p 72 Pickaway co. Rept by Pickaway Plains chpt.

WEST, JOHN, ? co

Pvt refused a pens because he srvd in Regt not on Contl Estab. Ref Doc 31 Jan 6 1831. Rept by Blanche Rings. Col O.

WEST, ROBERT, Carroll co

Pensr 1840 Cens æ 86 Carroll co O Orange twp. Cop by Jane Dailey.

WESTBROOK, LEONARD, Trumbull co

Enl in 6th Battl Northampton co Milit 1778. Saw service at Wyoming. Ref Pa Arch S 5 Vol 8 p 427. Was a res of Newton twp Trumbull co O in 1821. Rept by Mary Chesney chpt.

WETHERILL, DAVID, Geauga co

Exec Doc 37 in yr 1852 refused a pens as servd less than 6 mo. Rept by Wm Pettit.

WEYMAN, Andrew, Ashland co

Listed p 142 in "History of North Central Ohio" by Wm A Duff as Rev Soldr Loudonville Ashland co O. Rept by Nathan Perry chpt.

WHALEY, EDWARD, Franklin co

Order bk 2-273. Appl for pens and having subscribed and sworn to the service and the Court being duly satisfied do order same to be filed and certified. Dated June 17 1820. Wm Pettit repts Exec Doc 37 of yr 1852 suspended list account of d before Act of 1842. Order bk 1-278 Sept 25 1839. The most satisfactory evidence produced by oath of Charles Whaley then Edward Whaley a Rev pensr of U S d at his res in Franklin co and left as his wid and relict Elizabeth Whaley who appointed Charles Whaley as her atty. Rept by Blanche Rings.

WHALEY, NATHAN, (Nathan Goforth), Franklin co

Because of sympathy with colonies fled from Eng with 6 other men. All joined Washington's Army 1776. Five of them d at Valley Forge. Nathan Whaley fought throughout war under name of "Go-forth." Was b England; mar 2nd Barbara Freitche (Md); chldr by 1st wf: Barbara; Mahala; chldr by 2nd wf: Sarah; Aner; America; Nutter; Thomas; William; Rebecca. Soldr d Nov 1825 nr Canal Winchester O; bur Kramer cem (S W Corner no mrkr) 1¼ mi south of Canal Winchester in Franklin co. Ref Court records in Fairfield co; a grandson Nathan Whaley of Canal Winchester and a grdau Mrs Mary Kramer of Bowling Green both deceased. Rept by Columbus chpt.

WHEATON, JONATHAN, Holmes co

Pvt Conn Contl. Enl Aug 15 1777; dischrgd Aug 4 1780. Was b 6-26-1755 in Bradford Conn. Mar Penelope Lacy (b 8-25-1756; d 9-23-1828); soldr d 4-23-1838 Millersburg Holmes co O; bur Millersburg cem. Pens appl N Y 1818; Coshocton co 10-14-1820. Rept by State D A R and Wooster-Wayne chpt.

WHEELER, AMOS, Marion co

Pvt Mass Contl. Enl Mass 1776. Srvd 3 yrs. Was b 1762 Middlesex co Mass whr enl in Rev. Movd with father to O. Mar Elizabeth Snow Oct 1788. One son was Horatio N Wheeler. Soldr d Mar 4 1827. Pens appl Scioto co July 17 1818; Delaware co Apr 21 1824; trnsfr to Marion co Apr 28 1825. Ref W 4531 Contl Mass. Rept by State D A R.

WHEELER, ISAAC, Scioto co

Pvt N Y Contl. Enl 1778 Montgomery co N Y. Srvd 5 yrs. Was b 1766. Pens appl Bradford Pa June 11 1819; appl for trnsfr to Scioto co O Apr 8 1825. Ref S 40681 N Y. Rept by State D A R.

WHEELER, NATHAN, Scioto co

Ensign Mass Contl. Enl Apr 1775. Was b 1751. Chldr: Levi; Almira Chaplin; Luther (made appl for pens Scioto co O July 28 1857). Soldr d Mar 14 1823. Pens appl Grafton co N H Aug 18 1819. Appl for trnsfr to Scioto co Jan 17 1822. Ref S 40686 Contl Mass. Rept by State D A R.

WHEELER, SAMUEL, Huron co

Exec Doc 37 suspended list of pensrs as one tour of service 1780 of doubtful duration. Rept by Wm Pettit.

WHEELER, SAMUEL, Licking co

Pvt Va St Trps. Was b Fairfield Conn Jan 1761; d Oct 27 1819. Enl 1778 srvd 6 mo as pvt under Lt John O'dell; enl 1781; srvd 12 mo under Lt Wm Hall; enl 1782 and other times. Ref 48109 Conn. Cop by Jane Dailey.

WHEELER, SIMEON, Trumbull co

Pvt Conn Milit. Was b Jan 10 1761 Cheshire Conn son of William Wheeler and Abigail Fox; mar Anna Sanford 1782; chldr: David; Alma; Jane; Miles; Alfred;

Candace. Soldr d abt 1840 in Ind. Pensr 1833 Trumbull co. Ref Nat no N S D A R 131515. Rept by Mary Chesney chpt.

WHEELER, WALTER, ? co

Pvt efused a pens because he srvd in Regt not on Contl Estab. Ref Doc 31 Jan 6 1831. Rept by Blanche Rings Col O.

WHERRY, DAVID, Guernsey co

Pvt in Capt Joseph Gardner's Co fr East Nottingham twp Chester co Pa 2nd Battl Pa under Col Evan Evans Apr 24 1778. Ref Pa Arch Ser 5 Vol 5 p 522. Was b Chester co Pa Dec 24 1756; d Fairview Guernsey co O May 16 1834; bur in old gr-yd at Fairview. Tombstone placed by descendants still legible. Mar Ann Hall Chester co Pa Dec 20 1778 (b June 24 1764; d Oct 27 1848) settled in Fairview 1801-03. Chldr: Joseph b Jan 1 1779 Chester co Pa mar Elizabeth Van Atta (Vanatta); James 1790-1877 Washington co Pa mar (1) Harriett Pack (2) Cath&rine Wait; Ann 1795 mar John McBurney; Sarah mar Alexander Patterson; John; David mar Mary Ann ——; Mary mar Matthew Stanley Maitland. Ref Family data; Guernsey co Hist (1882) p 503; Records co Probate Court; Pa Arch Ser 3 Vol 12 p 566. Rept by Anna Asbury Stone chpt fr Mrs L M Cox Morgantown W Va (D A R through David line).

WHICKER, WILLIAM, ? co (Warren ?)

Pvt refused a pens because he did not serve 9 mo in Contl Army. Ref Doc 31 Jan 6 1831. Rept by Blanche Rings. Col O.

WHIDDEN (or Whiten), SOLOMON, Clermont co

Pvt Mass line. Pensd 1820 Clermont co. Trnsfrd to Maine. Rept by Jane Dailey.

WHIPPLE, ELIJAH, Trumbull co

Enl from Poquatonnoc (part of Preston) Conn May 1775 with Lieut Ebenezer Brewster in Lieut Col John Tyler's Regt. Was b June 16 1753. Livd in Mesopotania Trumbull co O aft 1835 having come to live with his chldr. Ref Pens cl S 3552 give a lengthy detailed account of his service. Rept by Mary Chesney chpt.

WHITACRE, EDWARD, Columbiana co

Rev soldr. Rec not yet found. Was b Apr 26 1761 in Loudoun co Va son of John Jr and Rachel Whitacre (John b May 14 1794 member Bucks co Pa Falls monthly mtg). Movd to N J 1757; movd to Fairfax Va mthly meeting 1761. Soldr mar Martha Brown (b Dec 1766); one son was Thomas (b Aug 18 1785). Soldr bur Plains gr-yd on Old McKinley Farm. Movd to Ohio in 1806. D nr Minerva O 1840. Ref McCord's Hist of Columbiana co p 838. Rept by Mrs Wilma Molsberry.

WHITAKER, JONATHAN 3RD, Butler co

Enl June 1776 Somerset co N J. Srvd 7 mo and hired a substitute to finish his term. Was dischrgd in 1780. Srvd 13 mo as Sergt. Was b Sept 1758 Somerset co N J; son of Jonathan Whitaker II and Mary Miller. Mar Mary Mitchell Sept 16 1779 Morristown N J. Chldr: Nathaniel mar Agnes Hayden; Abigail d young; Jonathan mar (1) Jane Irvin; (2) Anna McIntyre; (3) Mary Miller; William mar Sarah Skinner; Sara mar David Reeder; Abigail mar Daniel Skinner; Benjamin mar (1) Catherine Telter (2) Hannah Miller; Stephen mar Huldah Skinner; James mar Mary Abbott; Mary unmarried. Soldr d July 13 1840 Butler co O. Movd to Ohio in 1800; Justice of Peace Warren co 21 yrs. Pensd 11-27-1832 Butler co O; pens no 1141. Mary Whitaker's pens No 3839. Ref Whitaker Family Chart; Miss Douglass Hilts 1009 N 12th Boise Idaho; D A R No 155766; N J W 9002. Rept by State D A R.

WHITE, DAVID, Washington co

Pvt Vt Milit. Pens 1833 Washington co. Was b 1765 Hardwick Mass; d 1840 Waterford; whr bur unknown. Marietta chpt D A R mrkr on unknown plot Mound cem. Rept by Martha chpt. Helen Sloane repts appl pens in C Pleas Court Marietta O Oct 25 1832; ref Vol 6 p 351.

WHITE, EBENEZER, Stark co

Pvt Mass Contl. Enl July 1775. Srvd 1 yr. Was æ 61 in 1818. Mar Abigail Nye Mar 30 1797; chldr: Albert æ 17; David æ 15; James æ 11. Soldr d Apr 27 1824. Pens appl Plymouth co Mass May 7 1818; Stark co Aug 8 1820; wid appl Portage co Feb 1 1849. Ref W 1964 Contl Mass. Rept by State D A R.

WHITE, GEORGE, ? co

Listed in rejected pens appl. Ref Doc No 31 Jan 6 1831 on account of the amount of his property. Rept by Blanche Rings.

WHITE, JACOB, Hamilton co

Pvt and Capt Pa Milit. Enl abt the latter part of May 1777 in a Co of Volunteer Rangers. Was b 5-2-1759 Somerset co N J. Liv with father at time of enl in Washington co Pa. Mar Nancy Dews? 3-30-1836. Soldr d 7-20-1849 Gallatin co Ky. Pens 1833 Hamilton co; trnsfrd to Ky in 1843. Wid pensd Owen co Ky 9-20-1853. Ref Pa W 833; B L Wt 98058-160-55. Rept by State D A R.

WHITE, JAMES, Mahoning co

Ranger Cumberland co Pa. Ser 3 Vol 23 pp 249, 338 Pa Arch; also N Y Men; N J Men and Vt Men. Chldr: John; James b 1791; William. Soldr d before 1841 Coitsville. Ref Hist Trumbull and Mahoning co p 168 Vol 2; Will bk 11 Trumbull co records probated 1841; Tax lists 1801 and 1826 Coitsville twp James White. Rept by Mahoning chpt.

WHITE, JOHN, Franklin co

Pvt Pa. Ohio State Journal states: "D on Apr 8 1828 in his 96 yr of æ. Was with Montgomery at Quebec and aftwards took an active part in the Rev War." Had a son Alexander. Another John White d in 1857; left wid Ruth as guardian to 6 minor chldr Sarah B; George; Margaret; under 15 yrs of æ. Last Dr bill was July 1856. Rept by Blanche Rings. Compare 0942, John M White d Nov 1833 left widow Rachel.

WHITE, JOHN MAJOR, ? co

Listed in news clipping by L A A as found in old scrap bk. Listed here for continued research by Marietta chpt.

WHITE, JOSEPH, Muskingum co

Pvt in Capt Mathias Slaymaker's Co Pa Trps. Was b 1741 Franklin co Pa. Mar Mary Hamilton (1754-1853). One son was James. Soldr d 1828 New Concord O. Ref V 108 107080 D A R Line. Rept by Jane Dailey.

WHITE, SAMUEL, Guernsey co

Pvt N H St Trps. Enl 1776 N H. Srvd 11 mos and 7 das. Was b Apr 25 1760 N H. Since Rev livd in Vt; N Y; Pa. Movd from Pa to Guernsey co O. Pens appl Guernsey co O Sept 17 1832 res of Richland twp. Ref S 3540 N C. Rept by State D A R.

WHITE, THOMAS, Butler co

Pvt N J Contl. Enl July 6 1776 Middlesex co N J. Was æ 76 in 1832; b 1756 Middlesex co N J. Mar Mary; soldr d Aug 16 1838. Aft Rev livd in Md until 1823 whn he came to O whr appl for pens Butler co Aug 2 1832; Franklin co Ind Mar 8 1836 appl again. Stated he had recently movd there. Ref S 16291 N J. Rept by State D A R.

WHITE, THOMAS, Belmont co

Exec Doc 37 of yr 1852 suspended list of pensr as widow d before Act of 1848. Rept by Wm Pettit.

WHITE, THOMAS, Belmont co

Exec Doc 37 suspended list of pensr as widow d before Act of 1848. Rept by Wm Pettit.

WHITE, THOMAS, Licking co

Pvt Va Contl. Enl in Fauquier co Va in the fall of 1776. Srvd 3 yrs. Was æ 66 in 1820. Chldr: Nathan; Sally; Susanna Prichard. Soldr d abt 1847. Pens appl Licking co 5-5-1818. Ref Va S 40685. Rept by State D A R.

WHITE, THOMAS, Carroll co

Capt and Ensign 1st Va Milit. Marched from Loudon co Va aft enl 1777 under Capt Thomas and Col Holmes. Was b Mar 17 1754 Newcastle Del son of John and Isabella. Mar Sarah Keyes at Keyes Ferry (she b 1764; d 1845; dau of Humphrey and Sarah Hall Keyes). (Pens cl gives date of mar Oct 1778 whl Mrs Dale gives 1783). Chldr: Elizabeth b 1785 d young; Sarah mar Thos Smith; John mar Elizabeth Loper; Lucretia mar Jonas Walraven; Elizabeth II mar Eli Nichols; Catharine mar Philip Coons; Humphrey mar Elizabeth Stedman; Thomas mar Eliza Norris; James Albert mar —— Loper; Ruth Pemberton mar John McCoy. Soldr d Sept 10 1839 Carroll co whr he is bur in Leesville. Livd in Loudon co Va whn enl; abt 1816 movd from that place to Belmont co O and remained till 1830; thence to Tuscarawas co O. Appl pens Belmont co in Nov 1832. Wid appl Oct 20 1841 same co; she again appld Carroll co Apr 4 1843 res of Orange twp. Ref R 1142 Va; Mrs John W Dale Cin O. Rept by State D A R.

WHITE, WILLIAM, Brown co

Pvt and Lieut Va Contl. Enl 1775 Pittsburg Pa in regt commanded by Col Campbell. Srvd 2 yrs; 15 mos as Lieut and 9 mos as pvt. Dischrgd at Pittsburg in 1778. Was æ 68 in 1821. Mar Hannah Nov 20 1794; chldr: John æ 19; Delila æ 14; Asa æ 10; (appl 1821); also David; Rachel; Joseph; Margaret; Elsey; (wid appl). Soldr d Jan 6 1840. Was res Brown co May 6 1818. whr they came from Pa in 1809. Meryl B Markley repts Commissioner 1818; asso judge 1823-31. Was a cooper. Wid app for pens Brown co June 15 1840. Ref W 10275 Va. Rept by State D A R. Wm Pettit repts: Exec Doc 37 widow refused a pens as she was not a widow at date of Act of 1838.

WHITE, WILLIAM, Portage co

Pvt Conn Contl. Was æ 62 yrs in 1823. Mar Juliana æ 55 in 1820. Chldr: Juliana; Fanny; Philena; William. Pens 6-30-1818 Killingsworth Conn; trnsfrd to Portage co 5-16-1823. Cccupation was a goldsmith. Ref Conn S 40684. Rept by State D A R.

WHITINGTON, EDWARD, Ashland co

Listed p 142 in "Hist of North Central Ohio" by Wm A Duff as Rev soldr Reashaw. Rept by Nathan Perry chpt.

WHITNEY, BENJAMIN, Cuyahoga co

Mass Contl. Enl Apr 1775 Mass Line. Was æ 65 in 1818; mar Delana 5-23-1783; soldr d 3-28-1832. Pens appl Washington co N Y 4-30-1818; trnsfrd to Cuyahoga co O 12-15-1824. Ref Contl Mass W 4858. Rept by State D A R.

WHITNEY, WILLIAM, Ashtabula co

Pvt Mass St Trps. Enl as substitute for his father 1777 whl a·resident of Worcester co Mass Templeton twp. Was b 3-7-1763. Templeton twp Mass; son of Moses Whitney. Resd with son-in-law Alvin Armstrong. Movd from Mass to N Y in 1784 and to Ashtabula co O 1829. Pens appl for trnsfr from Ashtabula co to Rensslaer ? co N Y 11-6-1835. Ref Mass S 15247. Rept by State D A R.

WHITTENBERGER, ADAM, Mahoning co

Pvt. Ser 5 Vol 5 p 285. Capt Richmus' Co 1st Regt Berks Co Mil Lt Col Samuel Ely 1781. Mar Nannah; chldr: John; Solomon; Daniel; William; Michael; Elisha; Murray. Soldr d before 1842 Springfield twp. Ref Will bk 10 p 186 Columbiana co Records prob 1842; Deed bk R p 318 Whittenberger Adam and Hannah to 1830. Rept by Mahoning chpt.

WICK, LEMUEL, Trumbull co

Srvd with the N Y trps from Southampton Long Island. Was b Apr 16 1743 Southampton N Y the 9th of 11 chldr b to Job Wick and his wf Ann Cook. Mar Deborah Lupton; chldr: Rev William; Henry; Phebe; Mary; (list incomplete). Soldr d Liberty twp Trumbull co Mar 20 1813. Rept by Mary Chesney chpt.

WICKERHAM, PETER, Adams co

Was b Germany. Chldr: John; Jacob; Jeter Jr. Soldr bur Locust Grove O in Adams co. Grave located by Sycamore chpt. Was pioneer in Meigs and Franklin twps of Adams co whr he came on a flatboat in 1797 and opened a tavern at Palestine. Built 1st brick house in the locality in 1805. In 1806 the Meigs twp elections were held at his house. Ref 16 Rept N S D A R p 146; cf p 397 Vol 1 Ohio Roster "Wickersham Peter;" Evans Hist Adams co pp 103, 125, 131, 901, 902. Rept by Martha Pitkin chpt and Meryl B Markley Taliaferro chpt.

WICKHAM, JOHN SR, Morgan co

Pvt Pa Milit. Enl springtime of 1775 New Britain Albany co N Y. Srvd 2 yrs. Also srvd in war with France. Was æ 100 in 1834 Rhode Island. Soldr d Feb 19 1835. Res in Albany co during the war. Since he has resided in Pa and Morgan co O. Ref N Y S 7955. Rept by State D A R.

WIDDESS (Widdous), ROBERT, Mahoning co

Pvt. "Va Men in Rev" p 323; Rept of Librarian Richmond Va. Was b 1753; d 1827 Boardman twp; bur cem nr Boardman Center. Ref Cem Rec of late Henry Baldwin; Widdens or Widdous Robert "Va Men" p 230. Rept by Mahoning chpt.

WIGNER, DANIEL, Gallia co

Pvt Pa Milit. Srvd in Co commanded by Capt Valentine Regt of Col McCollister. Appl for pens in Gallia co Aug 11 1832. Pensd 1832 at æ of 99 yrs. Ref S 3695 Pa. Was b July 31 1755 Philadelphia co Pa. When abt 44 yrs of age movd from Philadelphia co Pa to Harrison co Va whr resided until movd to Gallia co O. Ref Pa Arch p 586 Ohio list Vol 23 S 3. Rept by State D A R.

WILCOX, JOEL, Madison co

Pvt Conn Milit for more than 9 mos. Enl in March 1780 2nd Conn Regt. Pensd 6-25-1819 Madison co O. Was æ 57 yrs in 1820. Had eight chldr all of æ except two. Soldr d 9-16-1821. Ref Conn S 40695. Rept by State D A R.

WILCOX, DR ROBERT, Fairfield co

Ref p 406 Wiseman's Hist Fairfield co O. "There are other names believed to belong to list of soldr of Rev." The name of Dr Robert Wilcox surgeon in Rev is in this list. Cop by Jane Dailey.

WILDER, REUBEN, Ashtabula co

Pvt Mass Contl. Enl July 1779 10th Regt Mass Line. Srvd 9 mos. Was æ 62 in 1819; mar Eunice; chldr: Polly æ 16 in 1820. Soldr d 9-25-40. Pens appl Ashtabula co

O 5-2-1818. Wid appl for pens in Ashtabula co O 3-7-1844. Pensd in same co 7-8-1846. Ref Mass W 6545. Rept by State D A R.

WILES, CHRISTIAN SR, Brown co

Soldr b 1760; d Feb 18 1837; mar 1787 to Catherine Meroe (b 1769; d Apr 18 1846). Service: Sergt in Capt Philip Duke's Co 3rd Battl Lancaster co Pa. Christian Wiles is bur on the Fitch farm Ripley Union twp Brown co. Ref Family Bible; proven record. Rept by Meryl B Markley Taliaferro chpt.

WILEY, SAMUEL, Coshocton co

Pvt Mass Contl. Enl N Y Jan 1777. Srvd 6 yrs. Was æ 61 in 1819. One girl was Carolina Ceciley æ 7 yrs in 1820; bur at Keene. He movd from O to N Y in 1826 and from N Y back to Coshocton co O in 1830. Pensd in Coshocton co O and trnsfrd to Oneida co N Y 7-1- 1826. Cens 1840 liv at Keene æ 83. Ref Mass S 40689; B L Wt 646-100. Rept by State D A R.

WILEY, THOMAS, Meigs co

Pvt Pa Milit. Enl in Donegal twp Lancaster co Pa July 1776 whr was b July 1755. Srvd 6 mos and 10 das. Was æ 77 in 1832. Mar Rebecca May 3 1780. Chldr: Mrs Anne Richards dau made appl for pens Jan 30 1855. "Only surviving child." Soldr d Mar 14 1833. In 1780 he movd to Cumberland co Pa to Farmemeck twp (now Mifflin co). In 1805 came to Union twp Belmont co O. In 1817 to Morgan co whr appl for pens Dec 26 1832 res Olive twp. Wid appl for pens Feb 16 1837 Morgan co O res of Olive twp æ 73. Ref R 11534 Pa Contl. Rept by State D A R.

WILKERSON, JAMES, Warren co

Pvt and artificer Va Cont. Enl 1781 Loudon co Va. Srvd in Co of Capt Seldon Regt Col Greene 18 mos. Was b Nov 29 1758. Pens appl Warren co O Oct 3 1832 res of Washington twp. Ref S 4727 Va. Rept by State D A R.

WILKINS, GABRIEL, ? co

Pvt refused a pens because he srvd in a Regt not on Contl Estab. Ref Doc No 31 Jan 6 1831. Rept by Blanche Rings Col O.

WILKINSON, ICHABOD, Butler co

Pvt Conn Contl. Enl 1777 Litchfield co Conn. Was b Nov 4 1743; mar Anna Taylor Apr 13 1775. Pens appl Butler co May 27 1819; Wid appl Erie co Pa Feb 8 1847 res Greenfield twp. Ref W 3202 Conn. Rept by State D A R.

WILKINSON, JOHN, Butler co

Pvt Pa Line. Enl 1777 at Franklin co Pa. Srvd 6 mos. Was b 9-11-1760 York co Pa. Mar Margaret Matthews 1790; chldr: John b 1791; Margaret 1792; Mabela ? 1794; Elijah 1797; Agnes; 1799 d 1802; Abner 1802; George 1803; Mariah 1807; James 1810; Ellanor 1811; Sarah Jane 1813. Soldr d 8-29-1841 Fairfield twp Butler co O. Aft the war returned to Franklin co Pa; thence to Greenburgh twp Pa; thence to Hamilton co O. Aft 26 yrs movd to Butler co O whr resd whn appl for pens in Hamilton co O 2-21-1834. Ref Pa W 9890; B L Wt 33554-160-55. Rept by State D A R.

WILKISON, AMOS, Columbiana co

2nd Lieut Pa Battl from Jan 5 1776; promoted to 1st Lieut May 4 1776; Capt of 4th Contl Artillery Mar 14 1777. Enl as Lieut on ship "Hyderally" (name changed to "General Washington" packet ship) Was in battles of Three Rivers; Brandywine; Germantown. Had a dau Mercy mar John Thompson. Soldr d Oct 2 1833. Soldr went to Washington twp Col Co. Ref McCord's Col co Hist p 525. Rept by Mrs Wilma Molsberry.

WILLARD, JAMES, Union co

Pvt Mass Cont. Enl 2-12-1777 in a Co or Regt commanded by Col Bradley. Was æ 59 in 1820. Mar Elizabeth Wingfield 10-16-1840. No family liv with him but his wf. Soldr d 2-7-1842 Union co O. Was a chairmaker. Ref Hannah Emerson Dustin D A R repts one listed in Union co Hist 1841 at Milford Union co; Mass W 46045; B L Wt 33555-160-55. Rept by State D A R.

WILLIAMS, BENJAMIN, Gallia co

Pvt N C Milit. Was b 1761. Pens in Gallia co O 1834. Appl for pens 10-19-1833. Ref S 7890 N C. Rept by State D A R.

WILLIAMS, DANIEL, Trumbull co

Pvt Conn Milit. Was b Watertown Conn 4-27-1759. Mar 1st Nov 1782 Patience Weed; 2nd Jan 1788 in Watertown Conn Hannah Munson (1766). Chldr: Hector mar Mary Mervin; Roxcenia; Betsey; Sally; Susan. Soldr d Brookfield O 1835 Aug 12. Pens 1833 in Trumbull co. Ref No 111067 p 23 Vol 112 D A R Lineage. Rept by Mary Chesney chpt.

WILLIAMS, DAVID, Belmont co

Pvt Pa State Trps. Enl at Ft Pitt (now Pittsburgh) Pa. Srvd under Capt Croughton and Col Fleming 2 yrs. Was in battles of White Plains; Trenton; Princeton and Brandywine. Was b 1747; d Mercer co Ky. Pens appl Belmont co O Nov 6 1832 then res of Richland twp. Rept by State D A R.

WILLIAMS, DAVID, ? co

Pvt listed in rejected pens appl. Ref Doc No 31 Jan 6 1831 as no satisfactory evidence of service given. Rept by Blanche Rings.

WILLIAMS, JAMES, Pickaway co

Pvt Md Contl. Enl whl residing in Talbot co Ind 1781 in Capt Claggetts Co 5th Ind Regt under Col Sayers. Srvd to close of war. Was b 1756. Wf was 60 yrs in 1823. Chldr: Esther æ 22; Mary 20; Charles 16; John 13; Apr 1823. Grave not found. Was allowed pens May 15 1818 æ 62. Rept by Pickaway Plains chpt.

WILLIAMS, JAMES II, Coshocton co

Pvt Pa Contl enl 1776 Pa Line. Srvd 6 yrs. Was æ 76 in 1821. Mar Peggy æ 64 in 1821. Soldr d Coshocton co O 11-9-1824 æ 79. (Pa Arch Ser 5 O list.) Appl for continuance of pens in Coshocton co O 1-23-1821. Ref Pa S 40690. Rept by State D A R.

WILLIAMS, JOHN, Belmont co

Pvt 1st Regt Md Line. Pensd 1833 Belmont co O. Ref Certf 1085 $80 pre annum. No papers in Vet Admn. Adjudicated in Treas dept. Rept by Jane Dailey.

WILLIAMS, JOHN, Trumbull co

Pvt Pa Milit. Enl 1776 from Exeter twp Berks co Pa. Was in battle of Long Island and several skirmishes. Was b 1758 nr Reading Pa. Soldr d Apr 2 1835 Warren O. Aft the Rev he livd 25 yrs in Va and 26 yrs in Trumbull co. Rept by Mary Chesney chpt.

WILLIAMS, JOSEPH, Jefferson co

Rept he was Rev soldr; bur Mooretown cem; b 1761; d 1849. Rept by Mary D Sinclair.

WILLIAMS, LEWIS, Muskingum co

Pvt Pa Contl. Enl Mar 15 1778 Pa; dischrgd 1782. Srvd 4 yrs. Was æ 77 in 1818. Wm Pettit repts Pa D A R has confirmed his service; was b Pa; d abt 1833. (Rept by Mary Chesney chpt) Ref "Hist of Washington co Pa" p 84; and of Fayette co Pa p 81. Resided in Muskingum co O in 1834 æ 92.) Pens appl Muskingum co O May 4 1818. Appl also 1820. Ref S 40696 Pa. Rept by State D A R.

WILLIAMS, RICHARD, Licking co

Srvd in Col Brodhead's 1st Regt. D at Coshocton. Ref Pa Arch Ser 5. Rept by Hetuck chpt.

WILLIAMS, ROBERT, ? co

Pvt listed in Invalid pensrs of U S belonging to Ohio pd at Chillicothe $96 annually. Cop fr Pensrs of 1818 by Mrs O D Dailey.

WILLIAMS, THOMAS, Lorain co

Pvt Conn St Trps. Enl May 25 1779 Waterbury Conn whr was b Apr 21 1763 and srvd as pvt in Capt Samuel Brunson's Co until July 9 1779; enl Apr 1 1780 and srvd in Capt James Warners Co until Oct 1 1780; Enl Feb 20 1781 and srvd in Capt Crouch's Co Col ạn ield'; Regt until May 9 178 . Pen d ạorain co O Au { 1, 33 res of Colu n-bia twp. After Rev movd from Waterbury Conn to Whitesborough N Y. Removd 1818 to Lorain co O. Last payment of pens to Thomas Williams covering the period from Sept 4 1843 to March 4 1844 made to T J Laughlin at Pittsburgh Pa on July 10 1844 as attorney for the pensr. On Apr 22 the pensr certified that he had resided in Columbia Lorain co O for a period of 15 yrs. Ref General Accounting Office Washington D C; S 6421 Conn. Rept by Nathan Perry chpt and State D A R.

WILLIAMS, WILLIAM, ? co

Pvt refused a pens because he srvd in a Regt not on Contl Estab. Ref Doc 31 Jan 6 1831. Rept by Blanche Rings.

WILLIAMS, WILLIAM, Coshocton co

Pvt in Md Milit. Srvd 21 mos. Was b Anne Arundell co Md whr he enl in the fall of 1775. Bur Plainfield cem in Coshocton co. (Hence must be same soldr p 400 Roster of O Vol 1.) Pens appl Pickaway co O 2-19-1833. Res in Anne Arundell co Md until abt 3 yrs aft war and then movd to Frederick co Md; resd abt 10 yrs there; movd to Leesburg twp Va and resided abt 10 or 11 yrs. Movd to Ross co O; aft 9 yrs movd to Williamsport twp Pickaway co O. Ref Md S 3587. Rept by State D A R.

WILLIAMS, WILLIAMS, Pickaway co

Was pvt in Capt Thom Mullicans Co Col Wm Hydes Md Regt 1775. Enl 1776 in Same Co; also in Capt Disney's Co Col Hall Md Regt. Was in battle of White Plains and surrender of Fort Washington. Srvd 9 mos in Capt Harry Ridgelly's ? Co and Capt John Goodman's Co Col Dorsey's and Ewings Md Regt. Substituted for a bro in Col Ownes Regt. Was b Nov 20 1749 in Anne Arundel co Md. Mother mar a man named Howard. Grave not located. In 1782 or 3 movd from Anne Arundel co Md to Frederick co Ind and 9 yrs later to Loudoun co Va and 11 yrs later to Paint Creek Ross co; 2 yrs later to Crooked Creek Pike co and 9 yrs later to Pickaway co. Had half sisters Mrs. Elizabeth Furley æ 69 in Sept 1833; Mrs Mary Howard æ 66 in Mar 1833 wf of Cornelius Howard of Pike co æ 64 in Jan 1833. Pens No S 3587. Rept by Pickaway Plains chpt.

WILLIAMSON, HENRY, Scioto co

Pvt N J Contl. Enl Sept or Oct 1775 1st Jersey Regt. Was b 1-6-1749 (birth certf); appl states b 1754. Mar Anna 1777; chldr: Mar b 1778; Isaac 1781; William 1782; James 1785; Elizabeth 1788; Joseph 1790; John Wfcoff 1793; Cornelus 1795; Anne 1798. Soldr d 5-4-1832 Henry co Ill. Pens appl Scioto co O Sept 11 1819; Wid appl Mar 19 1842 Jasper co Ill. Ref W 22670 N J. Rept by State D A R.

WILLIAMSON, JOSEPH, Hamilton co

Sergt 1776; 1777 Lieut in Capt Joseph Jenkin's Co Pa Trps. Was b 1755 Lancaster Pa. Mar 2nd wf Mary Benn. One son was Joseph Jr. Soldr d 1840 Cincinnati O. Ref V 125 p 82 D A R Lin. Rept by Nathan Perry chpt.

WILLIAMSON, PETER, Columbiana co

Srvd under Washington. Rec not yet found. Son Gilbert mar Elizabeth Rounce-ville. (Gilbert was b Somerset co N J June 18 1813. Came to O 1819 aft brief stay over line in Pa. Came to Elk Run twp Columbiana co. 1812 soldr under Capt Ditmas. Recd land warrent for 120 A in Morgan co Mo. Had son Lambert b N J Somerset co June 18 1812 who mar Elizabeth Walter dau of Henry (soldr 1812) and Salome Bowman Walter. Henry was from Adams co; Salome from York co Pa). Soldr d Fairfield twp Columbiana co. Ref "Upper Ohio Valley Columbiana co," Vol 2 p 442. Rept by Mrs Wilma Molsberry.

WILLIS, NATHANIEL, ? co

Was b 1755 in Boston son of Abigail Belknap and Charles Willis (who was one of the Sons of Liberty and a member of the Boston Tea Party). During the Rev Nathaniel was editor and proprietor of "The Independent Chronicle" the leading paper of Boston published in Benjamin Franklin's office on Congress St. Mar Lucy Douglass; d 1831 in Ohio. Ref Vol 26 p 273 D A R Lin Bk Nat No 25744 through son Nathaniel (1780-1870); Vol 15 p 242 D A R Lin bk Nat No 14648 through son Nathaniel; Vol 6 p 220 Nat No 5651. Rept by Nathan Perry chpt.

WILLS, BENJAMIN, Brown co

Enl in Philadelphia in 1778 or 9. Srvd 6 mo as marine. Was æ 77 Apr 25 1832. Livd with his parents whn he enl. Mar Mary Altz or Alce Aug 2 1805; soldr d Brown co O Feb 12 1842. Pens appl Brown co Franklin twp July 1832. Pensr 1840 Franklin twp Brown co æ 87 liv w Sarah Rice fam. Ref Pvt of Pa Md ref W 6436; B L Wt 31766-160-55. Rept by State D A R.

WILSON, DAVID Capt, ? co

Listed in news clipping by L A A found in old scrap bk. Probably bur in Washington co cem. Filed here for continued research by Marietta chpt.

WILSON, DAVID, Mahoning co

Pvt Bucks co Pa. Ser 3 Vol 23 men ref. Ser 5 Vol 5 pp40 and 446 Pa Arch. Also "N Y Men in Rev" "Conn Men" and "Vt Men in Rev." Had 5 chldr. Soldr d before 1843 Coitsville O. Came in 1804 from Washington co Pa with 3 sons and 2 daus. Built house in 1815. Ref Hist Mahoning co p 166 Sanderson; Western Reserve Chronicle May 18 1842 Est David Wilson Coitsville; Tax list 1826 David and Wm Wilson Coitsville. Rept by Mahoning chpt.

WILSON, JAMES, Miami co

Srvd in Gen John Stark's Brigade milit; b Windham N H 1759; d 1821; mar Mary Eaton 1785. Ref 52217 S A R. Rept by Wm Pettit.

WILSON, JAMES, Muskingum co

5th Va Regt. Soldr d Muskingum co 8-8-1839. Ref D A R No 70413. Cop by Jane Dailey.

WILSON, JAMES, Warren co

Was b in Ireland 1747; emigrated to America 1770; res Northumberland co Pa. Came to Warren co in 1800 and the log house he built is still used. Was a delegate of the Province 1776 and ensign in milit. Bur Dicks Crk Pres Ch-yd. Grave mrkd by Richard Montgomery S A R of Dayton. Ref Pa Arch S 5th Vol VIII pp 531, 641. Rept by

WILSON, JAMES, Mahoning co

Pvt Pa Arch many ref. Also Conn Men; N Y Men in Rev. Del line and Md. Mar Martha. Chldr: William; Joseph; James; Robert; John; Jane; Agnes mar ——

Templin; Sarah; Margaret; Martha. Soldr d abt 1838 Green twp. Came to Green with sons Wm; John; James and 2 daus. Ref Hist Mahoning co p 303 Sanderson; Will bk 10 p 102 Columbiana co Recds probated 1838; Deed bk I p 363 trnscrbd Mahoning co James Wilson heirs 1841; Deed bk F p 414 trnscrbd Mahoning co James Wilson heirs 1841. Rept by Mahoning chpt.

WILSON, JOHN, Butler co

Pvt Va Cont. Enl Wheeling Va 1776. Srvd 3 yrs. Was æ 85 in 1818. Pens appl Butler co O Aug 8 1818 res Wayne twp. Ref S 40714 Va. Rept by State D A R.

WILSON, JONATHAN, ? co

Appl pens June 23 1834 in Com Pleas Court Marietta O. Ref Vol 7 p 68. Rept by Helen Sloane.

WILSON, MATTHEW, Highland co

Pvt Md Milit. Enl Montgomery co Md Jan 1777. Srvd 6 mos. Was æ 6-23--1834. Ref Md S 7902. Rept by State D A R.

WILSON, MATTHEW, Morgan co

Pvt Pa Contl. Enl May 10 1776. Was sergt 18 mo and a few das; pvt for more than 6 mo. Was æ 65 in 1820 Chester co Pa. Chldr: William; Wilson; James; Ann. Soldr d Nov 2 1844 Morgan co O. Pens appl Jan 9 1819 in Morgan co O. Ref Contl Pa S 16294. Rept by State D A R.

WILSON, MONROE, Coshocton co

Said to be Rev soldr in Coshocton co. Cop by Jane Dailey.

WILSON, MONROE, Butler co

Bur Butler co O. Rept by Jane Dailey.

WILSON, OBADIAH, Licking co

Pvt under Col Crawford in Pa Contl. Enl Pittsburgh Pa 1776. Srvd 3 yrs and 10 mos. Was b 1746. Appl states æ 62 in 1820. Appl for pens Licking co 5-6-1818; pensd Jan 9 1822. Came to O in 1818. Ref Pa S 40708. Rept by Hetuck chpt and State D A R.

WILSON, PETER, Mercer co

Bur Jackson twp Mercer co O. Ref 18th Rept N S D A R. Rept by Martha Pitkin chpt.

WILSON, ROBERT SR, Belmont co

Pvt N J Milit. Enl in the Jersey milit abt the beginning of the Rev. Srvd 2 yrs. Was æ 73 in 1832. Res in Huntington co N J at time of enl. Pens appl 9-22-1832 Monroe co O. Appl for trnsfr to Belmont co 8-28-1838. Was a shoemaker. Ref N J S 177860. Rept by State D A R.

WILSON, SAMUEL, Clermont co

Pvt Pa Milit. Enl in York co Pa abt 177. Srvd 6 mos and 20 das. Was b 2-26-1755 in Lancaster co Pa. Movd to Clermont co O in 1812. Ref Pa S 2844. Rept by State D A R.

WILSON, WILLIAM, Hamilton co

Enl early 1776. Srvd to end. Pvt Pa Trps. Service verified by General Samuel J Cary in S A R yr bk in 1898. Was b Gettysburg Pa 1757. Mar Anna —— in 1815; she d at 49 yrs. 2nd wf Sarah; they had no chldr. Chldr: Martha mar William Baxter; Anna mar Crosley; Polly mar Crosley; Margaret mar Allen Cullum; Catherine mar Bailey; Abraham; David; William; John; Joseph; James; Samuel. Soldr d 1838 Montgomery Hamilton co; bur Pleasant Ridge Ch-yd by side of wf. Grave mrkd by old slab stone by family. Soldr was a leader in the town of Pleasant Ridge. Came early to Hamilton co. Longview Asylum in now on his farm. He removed to Montgomery in 1826 whr he d. Was a founder of the Pleasant Ridge Church and was on Board of Elders. Ref Miss Sylvia Todd of Montgomery O. Rept by Cincinnati chpt.

WILSON, WILLIAM, Clark co

Pvt Capt John Wood's Co 1st Battl Cumberland co Milit. Was b 1735 Londonderry co Ireland. Mar 1771 to Elizabeth Bruce (1750-93); two chldr: Margaret; William. Soldr d 1814 Clark co O. Ref V 114 p 70 No 113205 D A R Lin also No 114, 771. Rept by Jane Dailey.

WILSON, WILLIAM, Mahoning co

Pvt. Ser 3 Vol 23 Pa Arch. Also N Y Men; N J Men; Conn Men and Vt Men. Pensr 1818 Ohio Trumbull co Old bk 1808 act 1818 Trumbull co. Was b 1741; mar Agnes; chldr: James; William; Jane; soldr d June 6 1823. Ref Hist Trumbull and Mahoning co Vol 1 p 482; List of late Henry R Baldwin S A R. Rept by Mahoning chpt.

WILSON, WILLIAM, Trumbull co

Enl in Carlisle Pa abt Feb 1 1777 in 6th Pa Regt. Was æ 76 yrs in 1818. Mar June or Jane 1-20-1778; soldr d 3-27-1824 Bristol twp Trumbull co. Pensd 12-4-1818 Trumbull co Bristol twp. Pens No 16208. Wids pens No 5191 pensd 3-24-1840 Medina co O. Ref Pa W 4296. Rept by State D A R. (One Jane Wilson pensd in Guilford Medina co O æ 82 (Cens of 1840) liv w James Hoffman by J D).

WILYARD (or Williard), PHILIP, Columbiana co

Rev soldr. Rec not yet found. Was b 1767 Md. Had son John b Md (mar Elizabeth Lindesmith). Three other chldr. Soldr d 1853; bur Hanover cem. From Md to Franklin twp Columbiana co. Entered 600 A govt land. Ref Col co cem Recs; McCord's Columbiana co p 422. Rept by Mrs Wilma M Molsberry.

WINDOM (Winham),GEORGE, Belmont co

Various spellings. Pvt in Capt Smith's Co of Md Milit at Flying Camp Sept 25 1777 to Dec 1 1776 (whn Flying Camp disbanded). Pvt in Capt William Wilmot's Co (first in Col Mordecai Gist's Regt and in Col John Eager Howard's Regt) of the Md Continental Line from Spring of 1777 to April 1781. Fought in battles of Germantown; Monmouth; Paulus Hook; Camden; Rugley Mills; Cowpens; and Guilford Court House. Was b in 1760; was living at æ of 16 in Montgomery co Md. Probably b there; may have come from N C. At time of census taken in 1776 he was liv with Elizabeth Windham (æ 52) probably his mother. Father apparently dead. Mar Mary Card (or Cord) December 11 1783 in St Mary's co Md. Chldr Thomas C; William; Harriot; Mary and George twins; Ann; Elizabeth; Meriah and Hezekiah twins; Sarah; Benson. Soldr d Aug 2 1831 Belmont co probably nr present town of Lloydsville in Richland twp. His 1st enl appears under name of George Windom. His 2nd enl under George Windham. His mar license says George Windham. But all his chldr go by Windom. His early life was spent in Md. Aft mar movd to Loudoun co Va whr chldr were b. Movd to Belmont co O early i the 1800's. Ref Edward Patterson 77 Adelaide St Detroit Mich. Rept by Jane Dailey.

WINGARD, JAMES C, ? co

Sergt. Listed as Invalid pensr of U S belonging to Ohio pd at Chillicothe $24 annually. Cop tr p 172 Pensr 1818 of S of R Libry. Cop by Jane Dailey.

WINEGARDNER, JOSEPH, Darke co

Exec Doc 37. Refused a pens as servd less than 6 mo. Rept by Wm Pettit.

WINNER (Wimmer), JOHN, Perry co

Pvt Pa Contl. Enl in the 12th Regt of the Pa line in 1777. Was æ 67 yrs in 1820. Had no family in 1820. Liv with son-in-law John Wright in Pike twp Perry co in 1820. Ref O Pens Rolls 1835; III; 0-82; Pa 3 40717. Rept by State D A R.

WINNER (or Wiswell), ISRAEL, Perry co

Pvt Mass Contl. Enl in 1777 or '78 in the Mass Line. Was æ 67 in 1819. Wf æ 60 yrs in 1820. Chldr all of æ. He and his wf sometimes livd with one son and sometimes with another. Soldr d Sept 29 1822. Livd in Reeding (or Reading) twp Perry co O in 1820. Was a house painter. Ref O Pens Roll 1835; 0-82; Mass S 40713. Rept by State D A R.

WINSLOW, KENELIN, Huron co

Pvt Mass Contl. Enl June 1778 in Mass line for 9 mos. Dischrgd at West Point N Y. Pvt in regt commanded by Col Marshall. Was b Oct 1759. Soldr bur Huron O; rept by Sandusky chpt. Res Bridgewater Windsor co Vt June 10 1819 res Huron co O Aug 1 1828. Ref 18 Rept N S D A R p 274 S 40716 Mass. Rept by State D A R.

WINTERS, JONATHAN, Starke co

Pvt Conn Milit. Pensr 8-9-1833 æ 69 in Starke co O. Rept by Mrs W C Moore Col O. Canton chpt repts he is bur in Quaker cem at Massillon O. State D A R repts he enl May 1780 Canterbury Windham co Conn. Was b Sept 15 1764. Pens appl Stark co O Aug 6 1832 res of Kendall twp. Ref S 17202 Conn. Rept by State D A R.

WISE, PETER, Starke co

Pvt Lancaster co Pa Milit 1782 under Capt Nicholas Lutz. Was b 1758; mar Magdale (Mary) Miller; one son Peter Miller Wise mar Katharine Farmer 1819. Ref D A R No 106798 and No 115492. Rept by Jane Dailey and Mrs Oehlke.

WITTERECHT (Wetrecht), PETER, Mahoning co

Pvt. York co Milit Ser 6 Vol 2 p 61 Pa Arch. Capt Simon Kupenhafer. Was b 1753; chldr: Peter mar Elizabeth; Susannah mar Philip Echoltz; Esther; dau mar Frederick Clitz; dau mar John Myers. Soldr d 1813 Springfield twp; bur Petersburg Springfield twp. Ref Deed bk O p 292 Trnscrbd Mahoning to Peter Wettorecht 1811; Deed bk P p 139 trnscrbd from Peter Wettorecht heirs 1814. Rept by Mahoning chpt.

WITTY, JAMES, Champaign co

Enl 1777 at Guilford N C. Srvd 3 yrs Capt Thos McCrary Regt Col Thos Clark N C Line. Was at Monmouth Charleston; a prisoner 14 mos. Soldr was b Nov 1761 as æ 71 in 1833; b Guilford N C. Soldr d Champaign co O Sept 13 1842 leaving his son Jacob Witty Exec. Oct 3 1832 liv in Jefferson twp Fayette co O whr appl for pens. Movd to Highland co O in 1802; thence to Fayette co. Ref 18662 S Dept Int; Certf bk E Vol 8 p 28 (pens office). Rept by Jane Dailey.

WOLCOTT, BENAJAH, Ottawa co

Ref 4th Rept N S D A R p 299. Pvt in Conn Contl. Grave on the peninsula some distance south of old stone house where he used to live. Head stone has name, æ, and date of death plainly mrkd (1900). Rept by Mrs R Winnagle Warren O. Martha Pitkin chpt repts he was b 1765 Danbury Conn; mar Elizabeth Bradley (see 115351 Vol 116 D A R Lin). One son was William. Soldr d 1832 Danbury twp Ottawa co O. Ref 18th Rept N S D A R p 274 and 4th p 299; and No 115500 D A R. Rept by State D A R.

WOLF, GEORGE, ? co

Pvt Rev Army. Pens 1832 Washington co. Rept by Jane Dailey.

WOLF, JOHN, Harrison co

Supposed to be bur in Harrison co O. Rept by Mrs Mary Piatt Butte Mont.

WOLF, MICHAEL, Clinton co

Pvt Va Contl. Enl Va. Srvd 3 yrs. Was b 1751; chldr all grown Pens appl 1818 Pickaway co O. Appl again 1820. Ref S 40726 Contl Md Va. Rept by State D A R.

WOLFCALE, JOHN, Mahoning co

Not found. Said to have a pension when living with dau-in-law in old æ. Was b in 1752 in Germany. Mar Agnes Conard (1748-1828). Chldr: Abraham b 1785 mar Elizabeth Brouk; John 1774; Jonathan; Sally b 1780 mar Potts; Margaret mar Joseph Osborne; Polly mar —— Nutt; Betsey mar Matthew; Jane mar Russell; Rachel mar Myers. Soldr d July 1 1839 in Austinburg twp; bur Cornersburg cem. Came from Crauel Germany in 1760 bound to a Mr Yates nr Philadelphia; removed to Loudoun co Va 1776; came to O and settled in Austintown. Ref Cem Record of late Henry R Baldwin. Rept by Mahoning chpt.

WOLFE, GEORGE SR, Greene co

Was b 1758; mar Mary Catherine; soldr d Dec 6 1813; bur Union Ch-yr Trebein Road nr Byron in Bath twp Green co. Inscript on monument "George Wolfe Sr b 1758 d Dec 6 1813." Stone old and very much worn. Small metal soldr mrkr. Ref Robinson's Hist of Greene co p 401 and from a newspaper clipping: "Dickey Miller custodian of the cem points out the oldest grave in the cem that of George Wolfe (data as above) a soldr of the Rev." He said that tradition had it that the grave was made in the spot when it was an uncleared wood and that at first heavy logs were put over it to keep wild animals from digging out the remains. Rept by Mrs L O Reed Catherine Greene chpt.

WOLFLEY, JOHN, Pickaway co

Pvt. Pa Arch 5th Ser Vol VII pp 1011-1010-1044-1045 Lancaster co milit. Was b 1755 Middletown Pa 4th son of Johann Conrad Wolfley and Anna Catherine Shockey Wolfley. Mar Elizabeth Heintzleman-McCarthey 2nd wf. Chldr: Lewis; Elizabeth Lutz; Jerome; Phoebe McColloch. Soldr d Circleville O abt 1823. Fam recds say he visited Circleville and d there. Came to visit his chldr and d in Circleville. Grave not found. Srvd in Rev War with his father Johann Conrad Woelfle and his bro Jacob. Both John and Jacob sons were of æ at this time. Recds say he furnished wheat and forage for horses and army. Ref Mrs Eleanor Wolfly Bisell Circleville O. Rept by Pickaway Plains chpt.

WONDER, ANDREW, Wayne co

Pvt Pa Milit. Drafted York co Pa 1782. Srvd 8 mos. Was b 1762 York co Pa. His father kept a record of his æ. Mar Catharine ——. Pens appl Wayne co June 4 1834. Ref S 11880 Pa; Sale of land in 1843 names Catharine as wf. Rept by State D A R.

WOODS, JAMES, Brown co

B in Ireland 1736. Mar Catherine Allen in Ireland 1760. She was b 1736 and d 1823 in Brown co. Enl Washington co Pa in Col Crawford's Sandusky Campaign vs Wyandot towns 1782. Was paid for losses sustained. Chldr: Sarah b Ireland mar William Donaldson; Allen b 1767 mar Hannah Galbreath; Samuel b 1775 mar Alice Richey; Nathaniel b 1777 mar Jane Stewart; Anna mar James Hamilton. Soldr d 1825. Bur in family cem on his farm Route 68 Pleasant twp Brown co. Ref Comp American Gen V 5 p 565; Washington co Pa Crumrine Vol 2 p 130; Hist Brown and Clermont co p

193 Hist Brown co (Beers) and Pa Arch S 6 V 2 p 403 Natl number 295578. Rept by Meryl B Markley Vice Ch.

WOOD, JAMES, Darke co

Pvt Va Contl. Enl at Leesburgh Va Mar 1779. Srvd 3 yrs and 4 mos. Was æ 59 in 1820. Mar Jeremiah Philips 1-15-1793 (b Del 1-26-1774 dau of John Philips) in Botetourt co Va. Chldr: Benjamin æ 16; Nancy 14; Washington 11; Mary 8; Sarah 5; Rachel 1. (appl 1820). Soldr d 1-3-1839; bur New Madison Darke co O. Was pensd 1819 Preble co. Movd from there to Darke co prior to 1839. Ref Contl W 4717; Ellen Wood Mississinewa chpt Portland Ind. Rept by State D A R.

WOOD, JEREMIAH, Muskingum co

Pvt Capt Jos Badcock's Co Col Philip's N J Regt. Enl 1776 July in N J whl res 5 mis from Princeton N J. Was b Feb 2 1755 Woodbridge N J; mar 1778 Sarah Updike (d 1838); chldr: Samuel; Jeremiah (Wood or Wooden) states in appl that he was the only surviving child of above soldr. (Made Oct 6 1854). Soldr d 1853 Rock Island Miss. In 1789 he movd to Washington co on Monongahela River in Pa and resd one and one half yrs; then to Ten Mile Creek; 12 miles from Washington in said co and livd 6 yrs. Then to Ohio co Va 12 miles below Wheeling for 20 yrs; thence to Newton twp Muskingum co O whr appl for pens Nov 13 1834; pensr 1840 æ 86. Ref R 11788 N J; Vol 125 p 299 D A R Lin. (Rept by Nathan Perry chpt) and State D A R.

WOOD, JONATHAN, Stark co

Pvt Vt Milit. Enl 1777 Vt. Srvd 3 yrs. Regt commanded by Col Seth Warren. Was æ 58 yrs in 1818. Pens No 7245; pensd 3-5-1819 Stark co. Livd in Tuscarawas twp Stark co in 1819. In 1840 at æ of 82 was liv w Alvah Woods in Tuscarawas twp. Ref S 3614 Vt. Rept by State D A R.

WOOD, JOSEPH GENERAL, ? co

Listed in news clipping by L A A found in old scrap bk. Probably bur in Washington co cem. Filed here for cont research. Rept by Marietta chpt.

WOOD, THOMAS, Brown co

Resided in Brown co 11-20-1833 æ 75. (Pa Arch). Rept by Mary Steinmetz Reading Pa.

WOODBERRY, NATHAN, Athens co

Pvt Mass Milit in Co of Capt Pool Regt of Col Woods 20 mos. Enl at Beverly Mass. Aft serving a term of 9 mos in May 1778 he was a seaman under Capt Ingerson et al; often a prisoner. Res in Dover twp æ 72 in 1832. Mentions daus: Polly Straight V 4 p 479 Deeds; Betsey Vol 4 p 480. On June 19 1821 deed land of Ohio co Purchase to: John B Woodberry Vol 4 p 476 R 11 twp 2 Sec 17 A 100 and other deeds to Nathan P Woodberry; Wm Woodberry; Betsey; Nancy Woodberry; and Polly Straight. Ref S 3618. Rept by Jane Dailey.

WOODBRIDGE, DUDLEY, Washington co

Was b 1747; d 1823 Marietta; bur Mound cem. Ref Mass Soldrs and Sailors Vol XVIII p 800. Rept by Marietta chpt.

WOODRING, PETER, Fairfield co

Pvt Pa Milit. Pensd 1833 Fairfield co. Name listed p 406 Wiseman's Pioneer People Fairfield co; Census 1840 lists "Peter Wotring æ 83 living in Clear Creek twp." Rept by Jane Dailey.

WOODRUFF, CORNELIUS, Union co

Exec Doc 37 of yr 1852 refused a pens as srvd less than 8 mos. Rept by Wm Pettit.

WOODRUFF, PHILO, Knox co

Pvt more than 10 mos in the cavalry. Sergt 4 mos in Conn St Trps. Enl June 1775 Litchfield co Conn. Entered as subs for bro Samuel. Enl 4 times. Was b 1756 in New Haven co Conn. Bur Mt Vernon O. Grave rept by Kokosing chpt. Movd from Conn to Broome co N Y abt 1822; movd to Knox co O 3-4-1837. Ref 16 Rept N S D A R p 142; Conn S 15720. Rept by State D A R.

WOODS, JOHN, Brown co

Col in the Rev. Possibly Byrd twp Brown co. Filed here for investigation. Ref Brown co Hist. Rept by Meryl B Markley.

WOODS, WILLIAM, Champaign co

Rev soldr. Srvd in Amelia co Va. D A R No 219974. Was b May 5 1748 in Va; son William Woods who came to America from England with bro Richard and settled in Va. Soldr mar 1768 Sarah Stark (b June 12 1752 Md; d Feb 20 1835). 48 yrs a minister of Calvinistic Baptist church. Soldr d July 11 1819; bur nr Urbana O. Chldr: Elizabeth b 1769 mar Dr Goforth Cin O; Christopher b 1772; Phebe b 1774 mar Dr Shannon; Sarah b 1776 mar Wm Coleman of Cynthiana Ky; Jesse b 1779 mar Katurah Thorp; Ann b 1781; Benjamin 1783; Rhoda 1786; Polly 1789; John G 1791; Hester 1793; William 1796. Ref Fam recds Mrs John M Macrea Ontario Calif. Rept by Mae Hart Smith Pasadenda Calif.

WOODWORTH, EZRA, Ashtabula co

Enl Lebanon Conn under Washington June 1780. Srvd 6 mos at abt 17 yrs of æ. Also srvd under Capt Fitch Col John Durkee pvt 4th Conn Regt from July 13 1780 to Dec 1780. Was b 1763 Lebanon Conn; mar Anna Woodworth (1753-1832); chldr: Diodate (1790-1886) mar Juliana P; Cyril; Albigences; Horatio; Luther; Lucinda; Orpha; Hopestill. Soldr d 1834 W Williamsfield O Ashtabula co; bur there. Grave located by Mary Stanley chpt (Vol 114 Lin). Inscript on mrkr gives war record but no dates. Ref 110552 V 111 D A R Lin. Rept by Mary Chesney chpt.

WOOLARD, JOHN, Clinton co

Pvt Va Milit. Srvd 9 mos. Was b 1744 Loudon co Va. Pens appl Sept 5 1832 Clinton co. Ref S 4732 Va. Rept by State D A R. (Listed p 296 "Va milit in Rev." J D).

WOOLEY, STEPHEN, Champaign co

Pvt N J Milit. Srvd under Capt Stadman; Wetherby; Bates and Major Payne Genl Mercer. Was b 1757 Pleasant Mills N J; mar Priscilla Stiles 1781; soldr d Mechanicsburg 1848. Ref Vol 110 D A R Lin p 214 No 109685. Rept by Jane Dailey.

WOOLEY, WILLIAM, Champaign co

Pvt N J Milit. Enl Sept 1776 in N J. Was æ 75 in 1844. Mar Sophia 9-16-1796; chldr: John æ 51 yrs; William 47; Stephen 40; Phebe; Sophia; Grace ?; Margaret. Soldr d 7-18-1844 Champaign co O. Ref N J W 2505; B L Wt 26516-160-55. Rept by State D A R.

WOOLVERTON, THOMAS, Preble co

Srvd thro entire period of war. Rose from pvt to Col. Soldr d on his farm and bur in Frame cem. In 1804 with his family came to O from Pa. Came to Washington twp in 1807. Was very large man and a noted jovial character. Rept by Commodore Preble chpt.

WORTHINGTON, WILLIAM, Hamilton co

Pvt Pa Contl. Enl 1776 in 8th Regt commanded by Col Butler in Pa line. Was æ 82 yrs in 1832. Mar Ann Brown 12-1-1833; soldr d 6-6-1846 Hamilton co O. Ref Pa W 1346; B L Wt 9193-160-55. Rept by State D A R.

WORRAL, BENJAMIN, Morgan co

Pvt Pa Contl. Enl in the Spring of 1777 Lancaster Pa whr he then resd. Srvd more than 3 yrs. Was b March 22 1744. Pens appl Morgan co O Oct 17 1832. Ref Pa S 3478. Rept by State D A R.

WRIGHT, DAVID, Fairfield co

Pvt Pa Contl. Pvt abt 13 mos and 1 wk; scout abt 3 wks. Enl 6-29-1775 Bedford co Pa. Was b 3-26-1757 York co Pa. Pens appl 10-29-1832 Fairfield co O. Ref Name listed p 406 Wiseman's Pioneer People Fairfield co; Pa S 49261. Rept by State D A R.

WRIGHT, ELEPHAS, Licking co

Srvd as sergt in Co of minute men 1775 and in Canadian Expedition 1776. (on Memorial tablet Col O). Was b 1749 Northampton Mass; mar Anna Mosley (1751-85) in 1779. One son was Spencer (1780-1860) who mar Abby Cooley 1804. Soldr d 1813 at Granville O. (15th Rept N S D A R p 160. Rept by Mrs Oehlke). Cop fr D A R No 70164 by Jane Dailey.

WRIGHT, JOSEPH, Mahoning co

Pvt. 3rd Class; Ser 5 Vol 7 p 983 Pa Arch. Mar Rebecca; chldr: Joseph Fr mar Sally; John. Soldr d Smith twp. Ref Hist Mahoning co p 225 Sanderson; Deed bk R p 459 trnscrbd Mahoning co p 1825. Rept by Mahoning chpt.

WRIGHT, ROBERT, Brown co

Pvt Col Gardner's Regt Capt Gardner et al 1 yr 4 mo 12 da. Enl Cambridge Mass. Ohio Rolls pens iss May 19 1835 Brown co O. Was b Cambridge Mass spring of 1759. Soldr d Brown co ?. Oct 30 1833 appl for pens in Brown co æ 74; livd at Cambridge; Bordentown; Philadelphia. 2 yrs aft war movd to Westmoreland Pa whr livd till 1792; then to Mason co Ky for 6-7 yrs; then to Brown co O. Ref S 7975. Abt 1830 found a lost pocketbk in corncrib with money and discharge in it. Rept by Jane Dailey.

WRIGHT, ROBERT, Hamilton co

Cumberland co Pa pvt Capt Brewster's co Coy McKean Regt. Was b Antrim co Ireland 1755. Isaac H was one son (M D Reading O 1840). Came to Phila with father and 3 bro in Aug 1769. In Jan bound to Peter Weaver to learn "breeches making." In 1776 volunteered in Capt Brewster's Co 4th Battl Phila Milit Col Thos McKean. Aft Rev res in Lancaster co Pa; thence to Carlisle abt 1802. Aug 13 1832 appl pens in Cumberland co Carlisle Pa æ 77. In Apr 26 1840 appl for trnsfr to Cincinnati Agency to live with son. Ref S 3620. On Oct 23 1843 res in Clinton co Ind w son Isaac H (since 1841) whr removd fr Reading Hamilton co. Rept by Jane Dailey.

WRIGHT, SOLOMAN, Hebron co

Sergt in Rev War. Was b Lebanon Conn Oct 28 1747; d Salem Conneaut O sometime aft 1818. Co records show he bought 7-7-1814 207 A Lot 52; 251 A in lot 66 twp 13. Soldr supposed to be bur South Ridge graveyd. Mar 1st 1776 Eunice Dewey (b 1745) chldr: Preserved and Lydia; mar 2nd Ruth (Williams) McCall chldr: Diocleitan; Ralph; Sherman; Betsy; George; Maricia; Solomon mar Hepsibah Russell and remained in Wilhaham Mass. The others with exception of Preserved came here with their father 1811. Ref Mrs Daisy Wright Hickok of Owasco chpt Auburn N Y and Mrs W B Wilcox (?). Rept by Mary Redmon chpt.

WROTEN, SHREDRICK, Ross co

Enl fr Delaware co 1806 soldr of Rev. Srvd 5 yr and 6 mo. Was sergt of his Co. D æ 89 6 mo. His son Laban srvd as Capt of milit in his twp. Ref Findley and Putnam "Hist of Ross co O" p 42. Cop by Jane Dailey.

WULLEM, SAMUEL, Clermont co

Pvt Va St Trps. Enl Dec 1779 in the Western Battl commanded by Col Joseph Crockett and was dischrgd at falls of O 12-18-1781. Srvd 2 yrs. Mar Hannah 9-4-1782. Soldr d 9-1-1834 Clermont co O. Was residing at Martinsburgh Barkley co Va at time of enl. Wid appld for pens Clermont co 7-4-1836. Ref Va W 4841. Rept by State D A R.

WYMAN, JOHN JR, Vinton co

Enl whn 16 yrs of æ whl res Charlton Worcester co Mass as pvt Capt Benjamin Allton's Co Col John Rand's Regt serving fr Feb to Oct 10 1780; was 3 mos and 11 das at West Point N Y. Allowed 180 miles for travel home. Was detached to serve 1½ mos as a guard in Col Jamieson's Light Horse and in skirmish at White Plains. His pens claim S 7980 was iss Dec 27 1833; pens began Mar 4 1831 rate $30 per annum. Was b Nov 27 1763 Oxford Worcester co Mass son of John Wyman Sr and his 2nd wf Anna Blood wid of Samuel Town; a gr-gr-grand son of Francis Wyman Jr fr Westmill co of Herst Enl abt 1640 to Charleston Village later named Woburn; now known as Burlington Mass whose home (1666) is owned by the Francis Wyman Assoc Inc. Soldr mar Hannah ——. Chldr: Demarquis Sr mar Permelia Johnson; Lydia mar Lot Warford; Arthur (a part of his fam settld in Knox co Ill); John 3rd mar 3 times: 1st Nancy ——; 2nd Sarah Shry; 3rd unknown; Daniel mar Isabel Crawford (this fam accompanied by his nephew DeMarquis Jr went to Vermilion co Ill in 1852. A caravan of 12 fam journed in covered wagons. With the Wymans were Crawford; Goodwin; Lane; Spencer families being mostly fr Hocking and Vinton cos); Sylvia mar White; a dau mar John Ward; Minerva mar James Robbins; Levi mar Tabitha Cox. Soldr came to Charlton Mass with parents in 1776; in 1783 returned to Oxford. 1789 went to N Y living part of time in Steuben co whr chldr were b. In 1814 he and fam came to O entering by way of Marietta and settled in Elk twp Athens co (now Vinton co). Soldr d in McArthur and bur in old cem there. Inscript on stone legible w dates: "D March 26 1839 æ 75 yr 3 mo 29 das." Wf's "In memory of Hannah Williams Dec 9 1840." Will on file in Athens O. Ref Mass Soldrs and Sailors in the Rev Vol 17 p 983; S A R No 50993. Rept by Hannah Dowd Vanderford chpt and Charles A Goodwin-Perkins Piankeshaw Place Hoopeston Ill fam geneal.

WYRICK, PETER, Guernsey co

Pvt Pa Contl. Enl Aug 9 1776 Pittsburg Pa. Srvd 3 yrs. Was b 1744; mar Sarah Sept 1818; one son William (appl for pens pay aft father's death). Soldr d Sept 18 1823 Guernsey co. Pens appl Guernsey co O July 22 1818. Ref W 11899 Pa. Rept by State D A R.

YOUNG, CHARLES, Richland co

Contemporary of George Washington. Pensr in Monroe twp Richland co O æ 80 liv with Solomon Gladden 1840. B 1767 Va; mar Hester Ford Brook co Va 1791. Chldr: Henry; Isabella; David; Rachel; Salley; George; Charles; Hannah; James; Alpheus; Hiram; John. Came fr Cadiz (Harrison co) O to Richland co. Entered land in Mifflin twp where Yarman's Mill now stands of English origin. Bur Koogles cem by Koogle School (Sec 16); Rt 30 E Mansfield O. Wife bur by his side. On stone:" Charles Young d Sept 21 1840 age 80 yr." This data from a family history which gives his death date 1845 which would give a different birth date. Rept by Jared Mansfield chpt.

YOUNG, CHRISTOPHER, Fairfield co

Ref Va S 40735 Bureau Pensions Washington D C. Pvt Va Contl. Servd 2 yrs. Pensd 1819 in Fairfield co O. B March 1753; "lived with children" (appl). Enl Jan 1776 Waterstock twp Va. Appld for pension in Fairfield co O 5-14-1818; was a mason. Rept by State D A R. Name listed in Wiseman's Pioneer People of Fairfield co p 406. (J D).

YOUNG, CHRISTOPHER, Ross co

"A Revolutionary soldier living in Huntington twp Ross co O with Jacob Miller." Rept by Mrs Orion King Circleville as cop fr H C Pemberton's news clippings. (This might be same man as in Fairfield co above the co adjoin) J D.

YOUNG, CHRISTIAN, Delaware co

Ref New York S 4740. Bur Pensions Washington D C. Enl 1776 Orange co N Y. Pensd 1833 as Pvt N Y Milit. Served 2 yrs. B Oct 1753 Orange co N Y. D 5-22-1828; bur Berkshire twp. In 11-19-1832 appld for pens in Delaware co O. Rept by State D A R.

YOUNG, H H, Knox co

Cens 1840 listed Morris twp Knox co æ 82. Listed for investigation on acct of æ for Rev service.

YOUNG, JACOB, Knox co

Committee on Rev graves of Kokosing D A R Mt Vernon, Mrs Ewalt reports that the "Jacob Young bur at Mt Vernon O. Ref 16 report N S D A R p 142" is the same Jacob Young bur at Washington C H Fayette co p 413 V 1 Ohio Roster which see. St Ch Jane Dailey.

YOUNG, MATHIAS, Ashland co

Ref Penn R 11870 (meaning rejected for pens but not that he did not serve). Enl Apr 9 1777 Pa Line; servd 3 yrs. Was Pensr 1840 in Mifflen twp Richland co O æ 82 liv w Michael Young. B 1759 N J; mar Mary Strayer 1781 or 82; she d 1840 Mifflen Ohio. Chldr: David; Mary McNabb; Michael; Matty Horner (widow); John; Catherine Coon; Jacob (fr appl of chldr). D 4-4-1848 Mifflin twp O. Servd in the Canadian Old Regt under Col Moses Hazen. Livd in Union co Pa until 1815; movd to Potter Chester co Pa 1825 he movd to Franklin twp Pa and in 1835 to Mifflin twp Ashland co O. Rept by Ohio State D A R.

YOUNG, WILLIAM, Lorain co

Listed p 144 in "History of North Central Ohio" by Wm A Duff as a Revolutionary soldier. Bur Huntington cemetery. Rept by Nathan Perry D A R.

ZANE, JONATHAN, Belmont co

Fr Va. Bur in Zane cem Martins Ferry Belmont co O. Cop fr D A R rept Vol 5 p 506 by Grace Winnagle Warren O.

ZEIGENFUSS, JACOB, Stark co

Bur at Waynesburg O. Is a Rev soldr relative of Sicafoose family Starke co Waynesburg O. Located by Mrs L Conrad Canton O.

ZIGLER (Ziegler), JACOB, Pickaway co

War Dept record shows he servd as Ensign in Capt Jonathan Jones Co 1st Pa Battl under Col John Bull; was commissioned Oct 27 1775 his name last in Roll Dec 12 1775 at Barracks at Philadelphia. Servd 1st Lieut in 2nd Pa Regt Jan 1 1777. Born Jan 14 1740 Pa; mar Judith widow of J Sauer or Saures. Chldr: Phillip Jacob b 1767; mar Mary Easter: Catherine b 1768 mar Col Valentine Kieffer; Barbara b 1772 mar Geo Zimmer; Judith b 1774 mar Samuel Watt; Jacob b 1776 mar Susanna Easter; Frederick b 1784; Margaret b 1787 mar John Valentine. Jacob the soldier d Circleville O 2-25-1826 aged 86-1-9; bur Forest cem Circleville twp; middle of west side in Valentine lot. Inscrpt on monument: "Jacob Ziegler d Feb 25 1826 aged 86-1-9." Inscrpt on stone of wife "Judith b 1743; d Mar 14 1819." He came to Pickaway co. Settled on land now occupied by Circleville O in 1805 fr nr Berlin Pa. Mar Judith (as above) of Brownsville Pa abt 1766 and had eight chldr. Gave land on which the city of Circleville is located. One of Founders of Evangelical Lutheran Church in 1811. Ref Williams Bros Hist of Pickaway & Franklin cos 1880 p 228; War Dept Recrds; Will p 76 Bk 1-2 Pickaway co Courthouse. Rept by Pickaway Plains chpt.

ZWEIER, THOMAS, Fairfield co

In list of deaths of Revolutionary soldiers in Adler's (Pa) Journal 19 Sept 1843 it states: "D in Fairfield county O 3 Sept 1843 Thomas Zwier formerly from Berks co Pa aged 90 years." Rept by Mary Owen Steinmetz Reading Pa.

ADDENDA

ADDITIONAL VITAL INFORMATION TO VOLUME ONE; ERRATA; AND INCOMPLETE RECORDS OPEN FOR RESEARCH

ADAMS, ASAHEL, Trumbull co, p 1

B Old Norwich Conn; mar twice: 1st to Olive Avery to whom all 11 chldr belong; 2nd to Olive Mansfield. Ref p 220 Conn Men in Rev. Rept by Etta M Kyle, gr-gr-gr dau, Youngstown O.

ADAMS, GEORGE, Darke co, p 12

Grave mrkd 1930.

ALFORD, ELIJAH, Portage co, p 14

Pvt Mass Contl Line. Was b Becket Mass; d Windham O; mar Olive Adams Higley. One son was levi. Ref V 115 p 92 D A R Lin No 114298. By Mrs Oehlke.

ALLEN, ELIHU, Ashtabula co, p 14

On stone by his side is that of "Triphena, his wf b 7-2-1760; d —— (illegible)". Cop fr cem records of Ashtabula co by J D.

ALLEN, JACOB, Hamilton co, p 14

In cem recds of M E cem adjoining the Pa R R west of Davis Lane Cincinnati O Hamilton co is a stone with this data: "Jacob Allen d Feb 27 1847 ae 82-3-3" (maybe this Jacob). Nr by is a stone: Phebe Allen d Feb 6 1850 ae 80-6-0. Another stone nr: Jacob Allen Jr b Jan 15 1809; d Mar 11 1876. (Cop fr cem recds of Hamilton co by Jane Dailey.)

ALLERTON, JOHN, Mahoning co, p 15

D 1851 Smith twp; bur just over the line in Partage co; was pensr fr Columbiana co 1-3-1833. Ref Allerton Gen. Rept by Mahoning chpt.

ALLIS, MOSES, Lorain co, p 15

Pensd May 2 1818 res of Coventry Chenango co N Y. In 1820 soldr referred to his wf ae 62 yrs and one dau ae 22. One son was Leonard. By Mrs Oehlke.

ALSPAUGH, JOHN, Fairfield co, p 15

Service pvt Pa St Trps. Pensd 5-10-1833 Fairfield co O. (J D).

ALSPAUGH, MICHAEL, Fairfield co, p 15

Srvd as Lieut Pa Milit; pensd 5-27-1833 Fairfield co O. (J D).

AMES, STEPHEN, Lake co, p 16

Pensr Geauga co Jan 20 1820 N H Contl. (J D).

ANDERSON, AUGUSTINE, Morgan co, p 16

Or Augustus is bur Deerfield cem Deerfield twp Morgan co. Amilicent a dau bur there also; d 5-20-1863 ae 81-4-23. By Mrs Robt Henderson, Ashland O.

ANDERSON, ISAAC, Butler co, p 16

Pvt in Morgan's Rifle Regt Pa; later a Lieut. Enl Pa Westmoreland co Aug 1776. Was ae 74 in 1832. Mar Euphemia 11-14-1788; chldr: Robert 1789; Jean 1791; Susanna 1793; Peggy 1795; Fergus ? 1797; Isaac 1799; Euphemia 1802; Joe 1804; William 1808. Bur Vincent cem; was a res in Ross twp Butler co O 1832. Pensr Butler co 5-3-1833; wid appl Butler co Mar 3 1840. Ref Pa W 4628 and 28225 D A R. Rept by State D A R.

ANDERSON, JAMES R, Greene co*

Bur on farm nr Spring Valley. Ref Robinson's History Green co p 898.

ANDERSON, LEWIS, Warren co, p 17

Grave mrkd by Richard Montgomery S A R Dayton July 19 1931, in Tapscott cem Warren co.

ANDREW, JOHN, Jefferson co, p 17

Of Jefferson co; Pa Contl; pensd 1833. Grave mrkd by Steubenville chapter.

ANDREW, JOHN, Hamilton co, p 17

Of Hamilton co. N J Milit 1776 and throughout war. Mar Elizabeth McConnell for 2nd wf; many D A R members thro a son Jesse (26486); dau Mary (24608); son James (6763) in whch is found wf name of Rachel Cunningham. No 46581 gives death as 1811. By Mrs T R Oehlke.

ANTHONY, GEORGE, Jackson co, p 18

Srvd in Pa Contl as trumpeter. Ref p 577 Vol 23 S 3 Pa Arch. In 1828 a pensr in Ross co. (J D).

APPLEGATE, JAMES, Trumbull co, p 18

(1765-1820); bur Liberty Trumbull co accd to recent research. By Mahoning chpt.

ARMSTRONG, ABEL, Jefferson or Logan co, p 19

Is bur Mt Tabor cem Champaign co. Insc on stone: "Abel Armstrong b 1758; d 1837. Data also confirmed by Mrs W N Halsey 750 E 103rd Place Chicago Ill who gave Aug 26 1837 as death date. Rept by B H Johnson West Liberty O to Urbana chpt.

ARMSTRONG, WILLIAM, Columbiana co, p 19

Corp in Capt John Nice's Co Lieut Col Josiah Harmer's Pa Regt; Rangers on the Frontiers 1778-1783 Northumberland co Pa and Robinson's Rangers. Was b Ireland; mar Elizabeth (appl states Mary); chldr: Andrew b Northumberland co Pa 1783 mar Hannah (Shaw) Armstrong. He came to Columbiana co with parents. Andrew (son of Andrew and gr-son of William) b Jan 25 1818; a dau Sarah is named. Soldr d Clermont co abt 1833 (fr appl for pens arrears by son Andrew in Clermont co 5-15-1855). To America whn young; to Northumberland co Pa; to Georgeton Beaver Co for 1 yr; to Middletown twp Columbiana co O in 1799. Squatted; cleared 10 A Section 26. Entered quarter section Elk Run twp whr Clarkson now stands. Built house; survey showed it belonged to another. Ref Upper Ohio Valley (Col co) Vol II p 373; Pa Arch 3 XXIII p 195-7; Pa R 261; No 104093 D A R. Rept by State D A R and Wilma Molsberry.

ARNOLD, THOMAS, Athens co, p 20

Srvd in R I Milit. A pensr Apr 28 1834 Athens co. (J D).

ARTHUR, JAMES, Clermont co, p 20

Pensr 1833 in Butler co O for service in Va milit. (J D).

ARTHUR, JOEL, p 20

Was b 1768; pensr Sept 17 1833 Jackson co for service as pvt Va Milit. Ref p 262 Va Milit in Rev. Copd by J D.

ASHLEY, WILLIAM, Darke co, p 20

Of Darke co and Morrow co appear to be same soldr as following indicates: Pvt Corp and Sergt in Vt Milit. Was b Rochester Mass 1758; d Darke co 1828; mar Phebe Howe; one dau Philinda mar Hiram Burtch 1795. Ref Vol 105 D A R Lin No 104316. Cop by Jane Dailey.

ATWATER, CALEB, Mahoning co, p 21

B 1740; d 1831. Recent research shows he returned to Conn before he died. Rept by Mahoning chpt.

---

* *Open for Research*

ATWOOD, ICHABOD, Mahoning co, p 21

Of Canfield; removd; no place stated. Rept by Mabel Askue.

AYERS, ——, Clermont co, p 22

Is possibly "John" a pensr in Butler co 1832 for service in N J St Trps.

BABCOCK, NATHANIEL, Franklin co (this vol)

Franklin co. Grave mrkd by Columbus chpt 1935. Rept by Meryl Markley.

BACKUS, SAMUEL, Trumbull co, p 22

Bur Portage co Nelson twp; located by Old Northwest chpt. Ref No 36058 D A R thro a dau Assenath. By Mrs T R Oehlke.

BACON, GEORGE, Lorain co

Ref Pens Cl S 1636 Navy (Mass). Res in Huron co 9-18-1822. By State D A R.

BADGER, REV JOSEPH, Wood co, p 22

Is bur at Perrysburg O Fort Meigs cem as rept by Mrs. Robert Newbegin of Ursula Wolcott chpt. The following vital statistics are fr Black Swamp chpt (Margaret C Rider): Was b Wilbraham Mass Feb 28 1757; enl 1775 and 1777 in Capt Nathan Watkin's Co Col John Patterson's Regt Sta at Fort No 3. Mar Oct 1784 Miss Lois Noble; chldr: Henry b 1786 Waterbury Conn; Other chldr all b at Blandford Mass Juliana; Lucius; Sarah d ae 3 yr 7 mo; Lucia; Sarah; Joseph. Also srvd in war of 1812.

BAKER, ABNER, Huron co, p 24

B 1754; d 1845. Pvt Capt John Kirklands Co; Col Ruggles Woodbridge Regt 3 mos 22 das to reinforce northern army; Capt Edward Hammonds Co Col Theophilus Cotton's Regt; Capt Isaac Wards Co; Col Thos Capets Plymouth Co; Lieutenant Abner Baker in John Doty Second Co Col Ebenezer Sprout's Regt. Also to Dartmouth. Rept by Marjorie Cherry.

BALDWIN, ELEAZER, Hamilton co, p 25

Was pvt under his father. Pensr Hamilton co O 1832; b 1764 Killingworth Conn; mar 1785 Jane Redfield (1759-1827) son of Caleb Baldwin (1737-1823) a Rev soldr and Jerusha Parmelee (b 1741) mar 1761. D A R No 25751 through son Wooster; No 61977 through dau Barbara. By Helen M Fox. Nathan Perry chpt.

BALDWIN, SAMUEL, Portage co, p 25

Bur in Aurora Portage co O. "Lieut Samuel Baldwin officer in a Conn Regt. Honorable mention in Rev Records." By Miss Mabelle Olin Kent Ohio.

BALDWIN, SETH C, Cuyahoga co, p 25

Pensd 1820 in Cuyahoga co as pvt Conn Contl. (J D).

BALL, SAMUEL, Licking co, p 25

Was b 1755 (correction of typographical error); was pensr for N J Contl service 1818 in Licking co. (J D).

BALLENTINE, EBENEZER, Marion co, p 25

Proven service No 104691 Vol 105 D A R Lin. Rept by Mrs Oehlke.

BARBER, URIAH, Scioto co, p 26

No 42495 D A R thro a son William E names Rachel Baird as 2nd wf. By Nathan Perry chapt.

BARR, ADAM, Muskingum co, p 20

Mrkd Nov 1931 by D A R and relatives of the soldr.

BARR, CHRISTIAN, Brown co, p 28

Was b in Germany; came to N C; d aft 1811 nr Higginsport O. Located by Ripley chpt Ripley. Ref 16th Rept of N S D A R p 145. Copd by Nathan Perry chpt.

BARTHOLOMEW, JOSEPH, Portage co not Medina ?, p 29

Enl Amity Conn. Srvd as pvt under Lieut Barnabas Baldwin and Col Thompson in Conn trps; enl following winter and srvd 3 mos in Capt Samuel Osborn's Conn Co; 2 mos service the next yr; and in following yr again two mos service under Lieut Aaron Benedict. Was b Mar 28 1758 Wolcott Conn; mar prob 2nd wf Feb 6 1828 at Norton Summit co O; Miss Sina Bronson. Had a large family. Soldr d Oct 31 1854 Suffield Portage co O. Res in Waterbury Conn; Lordstown Trumbull co; O Wadsworth Medina co O; Springfield Summit co O; Suffield Portage co O. by Grace Winnagle.

BASKERVILLE, SAMUEL, Madison co, p 30

Enl 1776 Cumberland co Va. Ref Va S 45238; B L Wt 272-200 Issue of 4-9-1800. By State D A R.

BASSETT, NATHAN, Lorain co, p 30

Mrkd by Elyria chpt D A R 1929 July 21. (J D).

BAUGHMAN, GEORGE, Franklin co, p 31

Grave mrkd by Columbus chpt 1935, rept by Meryl B Markley. St V Ch.

BAY, ROBERT, Guernsey co, p 31

Enl 1777 as Indian Spy. Was b 1760; d 1844. Pens appl 1832 in O and was allowed for 18 mos service as pvt of Pa milit. B in Va; mar Ann Gibson. Ref D A R No 30145 thro son Joseph. Rept by Mrs T R Oehlke.

BEACH, ELIHU, Trumbull co, p 32

A pensr 1821 Trumbull co as pvt in Conn St Trps.

BEACH, OBIL, Madison co, p 32

D A R ref naming chldr: Uri (77337); Lorenzo (122505); Dr Lorenzo (80294). Copd by Nathan Perry chpt. Mrkd by Plain Cy chapt. He was one of nine bro who came to O 1817.

BEAMAN, MOSES, Harrison co, p 36

Beaman is correct; typographical error as Benham, Moses, Harrison co. Record follows fr Pens Cl S 2970 Pa cop by State D A R; (various spellings) was b Aug 8 1757 Cumberland co Pa; wid mar again aft Moses died; chldr: William made appl Feb 20 1856 to obtain due heirs of dec'd father; George; Samuel; Moses; Thomas, Mary; Margaret Heveling. Soldr d Dec 13 1842 Brown twp Knox co O. Made appl for pens in Stock twp Harrison co O Oct 22 1833. Ref S 2970; B L Wt 455-100 Pa. Rept by State D A R. Pvt in Co of Capt Rose in Pa line 2 yrs from May 1781 when he enl. Inscribed on roll of Ohio Mar 4 1831.

BEASLEY, BENJAMIN, Brown co, p 33

Was b in Va; d 1851; bur Beasley cem nr Aberdeen O; located by Ripley chpt. Ref 16th Rept of N S D A R p 145. Copd by Nathan Perry chpt. Pensr 1849.

BECKETT, JOHN C, Butler co, p 34

A pensr 1833 in Butler co O for service as pvt Pa Milit.

BEEBE, DAVID, Lorain co, p 34
Enl in Waterbury Conn 1777; srvd one yr as pvt under Capt John Lewis Col Jonathan Baldwin Conn and as Quartermaster Sergt; D A R No 22541 through son David (1781-1857) states that soldr mar 1768 Lydia Terrill and d in Elyria O. Pens appl 1833 Lorain co whr was living at Ridgeville with Garry Ross. Copd by Nathan Perry chpt.

BEEBE, HOPSON, Athens co, p 35
Marked 1930 by Nabby Lee Ames chpt. Athens O.

BEEM, MICHAEL, Licking co, p 35

Originally Boehm and Boehme. Bur in Universalist Church cem Jersey twp Licking co O located four miles east of New Albany. The grave is nr the s w corner; has large modern monument to Michael Beem and his wf erected by descendants. Inscript reads: "Michael Beem Sen. A descendant of Jacob Beem the philosopher who was b in Saxony Germany A D 1575; d 1624. Michael Sen was b Germany Feb 7 1755; came to America with his parents in 1768; settled in Allegheny co Md; came to O abt 1812; mar Elizabeth Green 1775; to this union was b 8 sons and 3 daus; Richard; John; Andrew; Benjamin; Anna; William; Michael; Daniel; Phebe; Elizabeth; and Jacob. Was a soldr in Rev Army. D Dec 12 1850 ae 95 yr 10 mo 5 da. Elizabeth his wf d Oct 11 1835 ae 80 yr." By Clara Marks Jacobus Westervelt chpt.

BEER, JAMES, Columbiana co, p 35

Pensr in Morgan co O in 1833 for serv in Pa State Trps. Rept by J D.

BELLOWS (Bellesfelt), PETER, Trumbull co, p 36

Pvt in Capt Timothy Jaynes Co of Rangers of Westmoreland co Pa. (Pa Arch Vol 23 S 3 p 327). Was b 7-3-1743 New Jersey; mar Jane Van Horn; chldr: Andrew; Peter; Rachel; Mary; Catharine who mar Eli Young. Soldr d Dec 1844 Farmington twp Trumbull co O; bur on Eli Young farm Section 27. Livd with Eli Young in Cens 1840 ae 83 in Farmington. By Mary Chesney chpt.

BENJAMIN, ASA, Ashtabula co, p 36

One of this name was pensd in Ashtabula co 1820 for service in Mass Contl. Ref D A R Magz Mar 1927 p 228. Cop by Jane Dailey.

BENT, SILAS, Washington co, p 37

Was b Sudbury Mass 1744; d Belpre O 1818; mar Mary Carter. Ref D A R No 29215 thro son Abner; No 44933 through son Silas. Pioneer Women of the Western Reserve p 131 mentions a dau Mary who came to Orwell (Ashtabula co) in 1836. Copd by Nathan Perry chpt.

BICKEL, CHRISTIAN, Hamilton co, p 38

Stone located on Cedar Hills Dairy Farm at Ancor nr Newton O Hamilton co with following: Soldr d Nov 19 1831 ae 78. By side on stone says: "Mary Bickel wf of —— Bickel d May 11 1832 ae 54" and "Catharine Bickel d Aug 1826 ae 19 yrs." Cop fr cem recds of Cincinnati chpt by J D.

BINGHAM, ALVAN, Athens co, p 39

Marked 1930 by Nabby Lee Ames chpt Athens O.

BIGGER, JOHN, (Contgomery co) now Greene co, p 39

Research finds bur in old Pioneer cem Bellbrook, Greene co. Lin bks No 170855 and No 67327. By Catharine Green chpt.

BISHOP, DANIEL, Huron co, p 40

Alonzo was a son; bur also in M E cem. Rept by Marjorie Cherry.

BISHOP, JOEL, Huron co, p 40

Pvt Capt Samuel Barker's Co; enl Feb 17 1777 for 3 yrs. Prisoner Oct 31 1777; returned July 22 1778 disc Feb 17 1780 "Sixth Regt Conn Line 1777-1781. Was son of Reuben Bishop and Ann Wright (mar 1757); mar Phoebe Avery Aug 24 1784; chldr: Chauncy; Joel Jr; Elijah; Reuben; Anna; Clara; Sally; Phoebe; Rachel; Roxy; Martha; Lucinda; Harriet. Soldr d Apr 17 1839 Huron co O; bur Norwich cem 2½ miles s of Havana. Livd in Charleston Montgomery co N Y; thence to Rose Neighborhood N Y; 1836 movd to Havana Huron co O. Ref Conn Men in Rev p 208; Rose Neighborhood Sketches Wayne co N Y by Alfred S Roe p 118; records of No 140194 D A R; No 23139. Copd by Nathan Perry chpt.

BISSELL, JOSEPH, Mahoning co, p 40

Ref No 50385 D A R Lin. Also same No for John Partridge Bissell p 40. Fr cem recds: Joseph P Bissell; Hannah his wf 7-19-1830; 1817; dau John and Ann Fitch Partridge.

BLACK, ISAAC, Delaware co, p 41

Was b 1745 at Tyringham Mass. Soldr d 1826. Ref No 104061 D A R. Cop by Jane Dailey.

BLACKBURN, JAMES, Butler co, p 41

Butler co. Srvd as pvt Pa St Trps; pensr 1832.

BLACKMAN, ELIJAH, Portage co, p 41

Pensd 1818 for service as Capt Conn Line. Was b 1740 Chester Mass; mar Elizabeth Hall; one son was John mar Abigail Rogers; Polly was a dau (No 37011 D A R). Soldr d 1832 Aurora O. Ref Vol 107 D A R Lin 106330. Copd by J D and Mrs Oehlke.

BLAIN, ADAM, Franklin co or Delaware, p 42

Was a pensr in Franklin co 1819. Is this same as "Alam" Blain p 42 O Roster J D.

BLAKE, NICHOLAS, Adams co, p 42

Cop fr notes of late Alice Boardman (D A R Librarian): "Died Sept 8 1831 nr West Union (Adams co) Nicholas Bla—e (4th letter not legible). A soldr of Rev attached to Waynes Brigade." Item fr Courier of Liberty 1831. Cop by J D.

BLAKELY, JAMES, Vinton co, p 42

Srvd as pvt Conn Milit. Pensr 1833. (J D).

BOGGS, JOHN, Pickaway co, p 44

Grave mrkd 1932 Pickaway Plains chpt. On old stone "John Boggs d Mch 31 1838" and nr by "Wf Mary b Sept 1748; d Feb 3 1828 Boggs twp Pickaway co." Rept by Pickaway Plains chpt.

BONNELL, PAUL, Butler co, p 45

"D Butler co 8-26-1820 ae 59 yrs." Pa Arch. Rept by Mary Steinmetz Reading Pa.

BOSS, ADAM, Hamilton co, p 45

Srvd as pvt Md Milit. Pensr 1833.

BOSTWICK, EBENEZER, Portage co, p 46

Enl 1777 fr New Milford Conn as pvt; 1778 made Corp; 1780 Sergt; mar Mercy Ruggles. Cop fr No 12929 D A R thro son Heman. Ref No 11130 D A R states he d in Ohio 1840 ae 87. D A R No 7947 names a dau Lucy; No 28291 D A R thro a son Adriah Hervey (b 1778) staces b New Milford Conn; d Rootstown; wfs name Rebecca Northup (d 1803) mar 1777; names of parents Edmund Bostwick (1732-1826) and Mercy Ruggles (who has been previously named as his wf). Old Northwest chpt has placed a mrkr furnished by co commissioners; grave located by descendants. (Mahoning chpt repts on same name; one came to Canfield Mahoning co w wf and chldr 1805; a second wf Jemima b 1768 d 1842 Canfield). Fr co Histories and Old pens bks 1808 J D repts data of one Eliza Bostwick as pensr ae 83 in 1840 in Portage co.

BOSWORTH, JOHN, Cuyahoga not Portage co, p 46

Of Cuyahoga co; the body was removed fr Baptist cem to Strongsville (same co) whr it was mrkd by a descendant of Miss Bosworth of Western Reserve chpt. (J D).

BOWER, LEWIS, Shelby co, p 47

(Lewis Boyer); Perhaps some vital statistics may be secured fr: Adler's Journal of Nov 7 1843 whch stated "d in Piqua Miami co O Sept 23 1843 Ludwig Boyer in 87th yr" in an acct given. Rept by Mary Steinmetz, Reading Pa.

BOWERS, HENRY, Clinton co or Scioto, p 47

Research finds this Henry was a Lieut 7 yr service; fr Bontetort co Va; mar Dorothy Esterline who d 1-14-1834 in Clinton co O. Rept by Luella Caldwell St Marys O who further states the soldr d 1805 in Scioto co. Rept killed whl at a mill raising or by Indians whl returning home. Member of 1st M E Church blt in Scioto co.

BOWMAN, PHILIP CASPER, Mahoning co, p 47

Pensr 1832; ref No 107245 and 120420 D A R Lin. (J D).

BRADFORD, JOSHUA, Trumbull co, p 48

Ref 27th Rept N S D A R p 128 names John Bradford b 1751; d 1841; bur Braceville. Compare these two. Copd by Nathan Perry chpt.

BRADLEY, ARIEL, Lucas co, p 48

Nathan Perry chpt repts there was a son Herman Allen, ref D A R 21293; and dau Phoebe Marilla ref 39304 D A R.

BRAINERD, ANSEL, Medina co, p 49

No 53397 thro a dau Lucy states parents of soldr are Othniel Brainerd (a Rev soldr) and Mrs Jerusha Shaler Kilborn (1729-1867) mar 1764; No 74313 D A R names Ansel Jr as a son. Rept by Nathan Perry chpt.

BRAINARD, HENRY, Mahoning co*

1754-1824; fr Conn; d at Boardman Mahoning co; have tax, family record but no military data. Lack some dates for authentic statement. Said to have been a sailor.

BRODRICK, WILLIAM, Darke co, p 52

Rev S 2396 Pens Cl: b 2-25 or 6 1760 in Orange co N Y; enl whr livd at Hardyston twp Sussex co N J 1776; servd 2 mos as pvt; and var enl to battle of Monmouth whr wounded by bayonet stab, compelled to return home 1778. Pens appl 5-17-1833 allowed whl liv in Harrison twp Darke co O; d 2-11-1835. Signed his name Brodrick. Came w parents Thomas and Berthenia Brodrick fr Ireland. Father a sea Capt d on water. Chldr of soldr: Isaac; Paul; Sally; pos others.

BROKAW, GEORGE SR, Belmont co, p 52

Fr Pens Bur comes statement he mar Jane Custard; chldr: John; Benjamin; Judith; George (surviving chld of parents) livd around New Athens, Harrison co. Pens arrears pd to wf 1855 in Harrison co whr soldr made pens appl May 1833. Death and birth dates same as Brokaw, George of Belmont co. Cop by Jane Dailey at D C.

BROOKS, JAMES, Lorain co, p 53

Pioneer Women of the Western Reserve p 799 gives chldr of Mr and Mrs James Brooks as: Hannah mar Riley Smith; Fanny mar Stephen Hull; Sally; Calvin mar Amanda Webster; Herman mar Jane Vanderburg; Elisha mar Emily Wilkinson; Samuel mar Sophia Johnson; Hezekiah mar Hannah Johnson. Copd by Nathan Perry chpt.

BROOKS, JOHN, Erie co, p 53

Erie co. Birth date should be 1755; at ae 17 movd to Mississinque N Y. Srvd to close of war; pensr 1834; Pioneer Women West Reserve p 589 gives Rachel Blizzard first wf as mother of John Jr (mar Adaline Squiers); Joseph mar Rachel Barnum; George mar —— Clark; Oliver. Second wf's name was Asenath —— (as rept by Marjorie Cherry); 3rd wf Widow Barnes; 4th wf widow Orvilla Hocum Hancock. Bur Florence twp. Rept by Nathan Perry chpt. 18 rept. N S D A R p 71 states he had 7 wives.

BROWN, SAMUEL, Athens co, p 55

(Athens co). Ref No 22183 thro son John; et al name Rebekah Baldwin as other wf of soldr's father John. By Nathan Perry chpt.

* *Open for Research*

BROWN, SAMUEL, Belmont co, p 56

D A R No 26473 thro a son Richard Montgomery names Elizabeth Fletcher as a first wf; No 23795 is No of Real dau (of 2nd wf) Elizabeth F Lennon; No 63397 is thro a son Henry Cordis stating Mary Newkird as 2nd wf; 43808 thro a son Samuel Washington. Cpd by Nathan Perry chpt.

BROWN, WILLIAM, Hancock co, p 56

Pa Rev soldr. Pensr resid in Walnut twp Pickaway co 1833; ae 75; went to Hancock co whr d ae 90. Ref p 275 Williams Bros Hist; Pens Cl S 2397 Pa. By Pickaway Plains chpt.

BUCHANAN, GILBERT, Mahoning co, p 57

Recent research shows he was b 1761 d before 1826 Poland; bur Edinburg Pa. By Mahoning chpt.

BUCHANAN, JOHN, ? co*

Ref Ohio Valley Genealogy p 13 No Statement as to whether he livd or d in O but a native of Londonberry Ireland; settled in Carlisle Pa before 1776. Srvd in Rev War; thence to Wash co Pa; mar Mary Ross; chldr: John Daniel; Ross; Jane; Samuel; Jonathan; Margaret; Mary; Thomas; Joseph; George; chldr livd Harrison co Mt Pleasant O; Jefferson co O.

BUCK, EBENEZER, Vol 2

Of Ashtabula co filed this vol 2; cop fr cem recd of said co is stone record of his wf "Adah d Apr 19 1857" along with these dates "d 11-2-1837 ae 73." J D.

BUCK, ——, Morrow co, p 57

The Christian name of this Rev soldr is Edmund. Bur in Buck family cem Lincoln twp Morrow co O. Rept by Mt Gilead chpt.

BUCK, WILLIAM JR, Mahoning co, p 57

B in Ireland. Srvd from Pa not Conn. Rept by Miss Kyle. Youngstown.

BUFFINGTON, DAVID, Fairfield co, p 58

Pensr 1833 as pvt Va Contl.

BUNTON, RAYMOTH, Clermont co, p 59

Is probably another name for Bunting Ramoth (this vol) pensd 1-3-1833 Clermont co as pvt N J State Trps. Enl Hunterdon co N J 1775. Srvd 1 yr. Was b 1749; wf named Sally ae 62 in 1820. Ref S 42637. Rept by State D A R.

BURGESS, JOHN, Champaign co, p 59

Pvt N Y Contl. Enl May 1782. Was b 1756; appl of 1820 names wf 62 yrs of ae; one son was Hampton ae 20. Pens appl Champaign co O May 2 1818; also 1820. Ref S 42639 Contl N Y. By State D A R.

BURT, AARON, Lorain co, p 60

Was b Nov 21 1759 Springfield Mass; son of Daniel Burt b Sept 19 1731 and wf Margaret Cooley b Dec 5 1727. Whl a res of No 7 (later Hawley) Mass he en. 1776 as pvt in Capt Aguippa Well's Co Col Woodbridge's Regt Mass Trps; win oth.r enls. Came 1822 to Grafton twp Lorain co O whr pensd Aug 8 1833; d March 17 1843 Grafton O. Soldr mar Dec 3 1790 in Hawley Franklin co Mass Hannah Bass b Aug 12 1759 and who was pensd June 30 1845 whl a res of Grafton O whr she d before 1854. Chldr: Samuel 1791; Ithiel 1792; Caleb Cooley 1793 d Sept 9 1796; Fanny 1795; Violet 1797 mar Ingersol and was the only surviving child in 1854 liv in Lorain co O. Ref Bureau of Pensions. Rept by Nathan Perry chpt.

* Open for Research

BUSH, LEONARD, Fayette co, p 61

Pvt in Capt John Harnes' Rangers Va. B Mar 5 1755 in Hampshire co Va (part that is now Pendleton co W Va). Son of Lewis Bush. Mar 1775 Catharine Stingley (b Feb 2 1755; d July 26 1848). Chldr: Sarah mar Leonard Hire; Leonard Jr mar Catharine Power dau of Martin Power Rev soldr of Hardy co Va; Abraham mar Phebe Peterson; Mary mar Jacob Shobe; Elizabeth mar Edward Feagins son of Capt Daniel Feagins; Catharine mar George Mallow; Jacob mar Sarah Baughan; Susannah mar Robert Burnett son of Robert Burnett Sr and bro of Thomas and Henry; Rachel mar Thomas Burnett; Daniel mar Susannah Baughan; Magdalene mar Henry Burnett; Jemime mar Jesse Peterson; Naomi (also called Amy, mar Joseph Mark Jr); Rebecca mar Elijah Arnold; son of John Arnold. Four sons srvd in War of 1812. Soldr came from Pendleton co Va to Fayette co O in 1810. Wf bur beside him also ten chldr bur in cem; located w of Washington C H. Mrkd w D A R mrkr. Rept by Clara Mark Historian of Bush family Asso. Westerville O.

BUSH, MICHAEL, Ross co, p 61

Son of Lewis Bush. Cildren: John married 1st Mary Wise daughter of Henry Wise a Rev soldr of Hardy co Va; 2nd Kezia Scofield; 3rd Elizabeth Ross; Elizabeth mar Abraham Power son of Martin Power a Rev soldr of Hardy co Va; Michael Jr mar Susannah dau of Martin Power; Eve mar Abraham Stookey. In 1798 migrated with fam to Ross co O Austin Concord twp whr he built the first mill. Ref War 4 116a M S Vol in the Va State Libry Richmond. Rept by Clara G Mark Historian of Bush family Asso.

BUTLER, EBENEZER JR, Franklin co

Ohio State Journal: Ebenezer Butler d at his residence west of this town Sept 12 1828. Judge Ebenezer Butler a soldr of the Rev ae 68 one of the early settlers of western N Y. Cam to Ohio abt 17 yrs. Cop by Blanche Rings Col O.

BUSHNELL, JASON, p 61

In 1780 enl Capt Charles Niel's Co Gen David Waterbury's brigade of milit ordered to defend the coast from Horse Neck to New Have. Mar Hannah Kirkland. Was a pensr. Ref Vol 5 p 315 D A R Lin Bk D A R No 4891; No 9541 D A R through son Daniel or dau Harriet Bushnell. Soldr d at ae of 84.

CAHALL, JAMES, Brown co, p 63

Descendants placed Government marker at grave 1936. Reported by Meryl B Markley St V Ch.

CALHOUN, SAMUEL, p 64

Of Jackson co, tho he livd most of his life in Jackson co is bur nr Vinton Gallia co; relatives report a stone at his grave. By Capt John James chpt rept by Lily Long.

CALKINS, JOHN PRENTISS, p 64

Grave mrkd with bronze mrkr by Elyria chpt D A R 1931 in Avon cem. Addit ref Pioneer Women West Reserve p 48.

CAMPBELL, ALEXANDER REV, Mahoning co, p 65

Founder of Disciples of Christ, who livd awhile in Mahoning, Trumbull and Geauga cos whl organizing the Disciple Churches here was a 1st cousin of my gr-grandfather, Joshua Kyle Sr. Alexander Campbell w b in Antrim Ireland June 1786 and d and bur in Bethamy W Va Mar 4 1866. Filed by Miss Etta Kyle Youngstown.

CAMPBELL, ENOS, Butler co, p 65

One pensd Preble co 1819 for N J Contl service. J D.

CAMPBELL, JOHN, Warren co p 65

A bronze tablet was placed by Wichita chpt of the D A R at Mt Holly cem nr Greene co line with following inscript: "Rev soldr S C Milit; with Col Thomas Brandon 1775-1783." Rept by Catharine Greene chpt.

CAMPBELL, McDONALD, Marion co, p 66

Fr papers of Isabelle Lyphers Goss research finds he d 1845 Marion co O.

CAMPBELL, McDONALD, Morrow co, p 66

In 1930 the Mt Gilead chpt located his grave in Mt Tabor cem Morrow co
O. No 25496 D A R names a dau Margaret as copd by Nathan Perry chpt.

CAMPBELL, WILLIAM, MAHONING Co, p 66

Srvd from Cumberland co Pa and aft 1780 as a ranger from Washington co
Pa received depreciation pay Vol 4 Pa Arch S 5; also S 3 pp 199, 674, 703. Was
b in Ireland; mar Ann Johnson; chldr: John; Allen; William; James; Johnston;
Mary (Campbell) Riddle; Elizabeth (Campbell) McClurg. Pensr 1808. Soldr d Sept
11 1827 at Poland Mahoning co O; bur in Presbyterian Church cem Poland O.
Corrections furnished by Miss Etta Kyle Youngstown O.

CAMPBELL, WILLIAM, Wayne co, this vol 2

Has been located as bur in Dalton cem "Barris Pa Milit — Rev War";
complete recd filed this vol 2. Rept by Edith G Merkel Wooster-Wayne chpt.

CARLTON, CALEB, Portage co, p 68

Mar Margaret Day accd to No 24844 D A R rept by Nathan Perry chpt.

CARLTON, DARIUS, Portage co, p 68

Was bur in Carlton fam cem at McDonald O now the cinder dump of U S
Steel co there. Bodies were never removed. Miss Etta Kyle Youngstown.

CARNAGHEY, WILLIAM, Columbiana co, p 68

Is rept to be bur just across the river fr Columbiana co at Georgetown Pa.
Rept by Rebecca Griscom chpt.

CARPENTER, BENJAMIN, Delaware co, p 68

Enl in 10th Pa regt; was commissoned ensign 1776; 2nd lieut and lieut 1777;
present at surrender of Cornwallis. Mar Mary Ferrier 1773; soldr d 1827. Ref
D A R No 123492 thro son Charles Wesley and 123807 thro son James. Copd by
Nathan Perry chpt.

CARPENTER, DANIEL, Huron co, p 68

B Conn 1755; d Ripley twp 1840. S A R 54306 rept by Wm Pettit. Bur Houfstatter cem Ripley or N Haven pensr 1820 as rept by Marjorie Cherry.

CARROL, WILLIAM, Hancock co, p 70

Pvt Md St Trps. Pensr 1832 Gallia co O. (J D). State D A R repts srvd 7 mos
and 17 das in "Flying Camp" of Md. Was b 1756. Appld for pens in Adams co
O Nov 9 1822; pensr Gallia co 1832; ref S 2197 Md No 26621 names wf Elizabeth
Fees by State D A R and a dau of Elizabeth. Cop by Nathan Perry chpt.

CARTER, JAMES, Clermont co, p 71

Srvd Va Milit. Ref p 266 "Va Milit in Rev." Was in Madison co Va 3-4-1833.
Cop by J D.

CARY, CHRISTOPHER, Hamilton co, p 67

Or Carey; enl from Lyme N H 1778 under Capt Charles Nelson; taken prisoner
1781 carried to Canada and confined in irons; he appl for a pension 1824 allowed
by special act of Congress; was b Windham Conn; had livd N H; 1802 removd
to O; d Hamilton co at Clover Nook, a place made famous by writings of his
gr-dau Alice and Phebe Cary. His parents were Dr Samuel Cary and Deliverance Grant. Mar first 1784 Elsie Ferrel. Ref D A R No 34334 thro son Robert (b
1787).

CARY, EZRA, Shelby co*

Bro of Calvin; mar Lydia Thompson. Reputed Rev service.

CAULKINS, ROSWELL, Delaware co, p 73

Enl at 16 and srvd three yrs with the Connecticut trps. He and his widow pensd. Was b in 1761 Walpole N H; d in Delaware co O 1823. Mar 1782 Eunice Hine. Ref D A R No 28496 thro dau Elizabeth (b 1801); D A R No 4137 thro dau Julia; Vol 12 p 94 D A R Lin Bk Nat no 11241; Vol 12 Nat Nos 11242; 11686. Copd by Nathan Perry chpt. Ohio St Journal 11-15-1823 gives acct. — B R.

CHAPMAN, NATHANIEL, Washington co, p 74

Marietta chpt repts one as d in Salem twp Washington co O 1806. (Could these places be confused?)

CHASE, BEVERLY, Morrow co, p 75

Mt Gilead chpt repts burial in S Bloomfield twp Chase fam cem Morrow co O.

CHERRY, HENRY, ERIE Co, p 75

Capt Pearson 5th N J Contl Col Spencers Regt; Col Wynd 1 yr; dischrgd Ticonderoga; 3 mo under Capt Britten; was b 4-20-1758; d 3-5-1820. Wid Abigail pens 1839 (Marjorie Cherry rept her death 11-30-1844); chldr: five livd in Milan: William; James; Hannah; Tupper; John (went to Canada). Soldr bur in Milan O Erie co whr H School now stands but removd to Cherry lot new cem and mrkr placed 1933 by Martha Pitkin chpt of Sandusky whch rept this data.

CHERRY, JOHN, Mahoning co, p 76

Fr Mahoning chpt later rept it appears he is the John Cherry bur at Niles, Trumbull co.

CHESEBRO, ELIJAH, ? co*

1759-1808. Srvd as matross in the artillery. His widow recd a pens for his service. He was born in Stonington Conn; d in Albany co O (No Albany co in O — one in N Y)

CHURCH, JONATHAN, Erie co, p 77

Gov mrkr at grave in Huron cem; Enl Kingstown Pa Capt Benson Col Zebulon Butler; dischrgd 1780 w broken ankle; mar 12-11-1810; trnsfr to Conn serv. Ref W 1143-39493. Pens Cl. By Marjorie Cherry.

CLARK, ANTHONY, ? co*

Srvd as pvt and sergt in Capt Marshall's Co Col Lucas' Md regt; also pvt in Capt Jarriot's Co Col Darke's Va regt. Was b 1759 in Ireland; d 1833 in Latimer co O. (No Latimer co in O; a town "Latimer" is in Franklin co). He mar 1787 Katie Prutsinger; dau Jinny. Ref Vol 115 p 54 D A R Lin Nat No 114172.

CLARK, EPHRAIM, Trumbull co, p 78

Enl 1775 as pvt Conn trps; was b 1748 Southington Conn; mar Druzilla Balkeslee; soldr d 1828 Mesopotamia Trumbull co. Ref Vol 108 D A R Lin No 107006. Cop by Jane Dailey.

CLARK, ISRIAL, Marion co, p 78

Ref May Calif Sons of Rev Bulletin of 1919, p 9. A proven record on Israel Clark states same b and d and service; but gives in addit mar Mary Kendall; had one child Almira who mar Saml Scribner. Soldr d in Delaware co. Rept by Jane Dailey.

CLARK, ZELOTUS, Summit co, p 79

Was b 1750. See p 30 Vol 105 D A R Lin bk.

COFFINBERRY, GEORGE LEWIS, Richland co, p 81

Ref D A R No 13478 through son Wright Lewis; No 124558 thro dau Mary gives date of marriage as 1786 to Elizabeth Little. No 48897 thro son Salathiel Curtis. Rept by Nathan Perry comm.

Open for Research

COLEMON (Colman), JOHN, Fairfield co, p 82

No pens or rec; b Germany. One son was John b Rockbridge co Va Apr 3 1797. Soldr d nr Canal Winchester (dates unknown); bur in Kramer cem 1¼ mi so of Canal Winchester in Franklin co; tombstone destroyed and inscript obliterated. Ref Old Data furnished by Mr Ed Coleman and L L Moore Americanism officer Leach Benson Post 220 American Legion Canal Winchester. Rept by Mrs W S Van Fossen Columbus chpt. Filed to open up location of service record. Note: This part of Fairfield co since 1859 has been Franklin co.

COLSON, CHRISTOPHER, Lake co, p 83

1st wf named Hannah Robinson mar 10-2-1788; had 7 chldr not named. Dvorced from 1st wf Hannah in 1804; 2nd wf Patty Brown mar 11-23-1806; chldr: Lisa 1807; —— 1809; Emily 1811; Christopher 1814; Patty 1818. Soldr d 8-23-1823 Willoughby Lake co. Ref Pens Cl Mass 25437 B L Wt 1904-160-55. Data by State D A R. Mrs T R Oehlke repts a dau Lovina No 1898 Vol 2 D A R Lin (may be the missing one above).

COMES (Combs), EBENEZER NEWELL, Trumbull co*

Butler's Hist of Youngstown Vol 3 p 603 states he was an ensign of 1st Regt of Milit in 1804 and was probably a Rev soldr. D Aug 1812 in Brookfield leaving wf Mary Ann and chldr: Seth; Mary Ann. Rept by Hetuck chpt.

CONDON, REDMAN, Ross co, p 84

Name is also found listed as Coldon, Redman pvt Pa Contl. Pensr 1818 Ross co.

CONLEY, MICHAEL, Brown co, p 85

Pvt Md Contl; pensr of Brown co O; mar Rebecca; chldr: Joshua; John; Rhese; Michael. Soldr d 1842; livd in School Dist No 1 in Washington twp in 1825. Ref Will bk Vol 2 p 86-87 Probate Court Brown co O. Rept by Meryl B Markley Taliaferro chpt.

CONNER, BENJAMIN, ? co*

3rd Lieut. Rev or 1812? "Servd in late war." Rejected pens as no evidence of having been disabled whl in service. Ref Doc 31 Jan 6 1831. Rept by Blanche Rings.

CONNIE, JEREMIAH, Ashland co, p 85

Name spelled "Connie" Jeremiah listed in Va Contl 1825 in Richland co. Rept by J D.

COOK, CHAUNCEY, Erie co, p 86

Was b 1752. On pension list July 7 1832 as living in Groton twp. We find mention of the home of Chauncey Cook in Wallingford Conn. Rept by Marjorie Cherry, Sandusky.

COOK, JOSEPH, Butler co, p 86

Ref 5th Rept of N S D A R p 369; Under heading of "Ancestors of Knickerbocker chpt N Y. Mar Sarah Langdon. Ref Davis' Wallingford Conn; Ferneau's N Y I pp 271, 347, 348.

COOK, ROSWELL, Delaware co

Drummer Conn Contl Pensr 1819. Bur Oak Grove cem. (J D). Issue of "Delaware Patron," "Died Dec 19 1826 Roswell Cook ae 61 yrs formerly of Farmington Conn. Was under Lafayette." Cop by Blanche Rings Col O who repts refused a pens as not in indigent circumstances. Ref Exec Doc 31 of Jan 6 1831.

COOPER, EZEKIEL, Belmont co, p 87

One of the sixteen Rev soldr settled at Marietta Apr 7 1788. (J D).

COOPER, JOHN, Brown co, p 87

Pvt; Ensign; Sergt Pa Contl; Pensd 1832. J D.

* *Open for Research*

COTTON, BENJAMIN, Medina co p 88

Is the same as one found listed in Cens 1840 pensr Milton twp Wayne co ae 86 as he livd just across the line in Wayne co.

COTTON, JOHN, Mahoning co, p 89

Ensign, Lt and Paymaster Gen. Wrong data and service. Was b in Plymouth Mass. Son of Lt Col Theophilus Cotton. See Mass Rolls for his service. The services given Vol 1 are for a John Cotton b in Ireland and bur in Lawrence co Pa. Lt John Cotton was a descendant of Rev John Cotton of London Eng who was brought to New England as an instructor and afterwards President of Harvard College. Had 5 sons; 2 bur in private cem. Ref Mass Soldr and Sailors of the Rev Vol 4 pp 10, 11. Rept by Etta Kyle, Youngstown.

COUTS, CHRISTIAN, Crawford co, p 89

Grave mrkd by Hannah Crawford chpt 1935.

COVELL, JONATHAN W, Ashtabula co*

Rev soldr. Jane West was the 1st or 2nd wf. Son Alanson James mar Mary Hancock; son Alpheus David mar Lucietia Lyon (whose chldr were: Alphonso A; Merrit Fitzland; Orlensia; Josephine; Mark; John.) Soldr d Sylvania nr Saybrook O. Livd Washington co N Y; then Onondaga co. This was a query in Boston Transcript Feb 2 193?. Rept by Nathan Perry chpt.

COWDEN, JOHN, Knox co, p 90

Grave mrkd by headstone 1935 Kokosing chpt. Mrs C Ewalt chairman.

COWEN, WILLIAM, Clermont co, p 90

Grave in McCollum cem nr Edenton was mrkd 1930 by Warriors Trail chpt.

COX, BENJAMIN, Montgomery co,* p 90

Jas E Passwaters, Dayton wishes to add the name of Isaac to the list of chldr; and states Rachael was the second wf; ref Family recds w addit data open for investigation. (J D).

CRAIG, JOHN, Clark co, p 92

Pvt enl Concord N H. Bro of James Craig of Clark co O. Ref S 42661. Rept by M S Askue Ch of Rev Soldrs Mahoning chpt.

CRAIG, JAMES, Mahoning co, p 91

Pens 1808. Rept by Mahoning chpt.

CRANSTON, JOHN, Champaign co, p 93

Movd w 5 sons and 1 dau to this co in 1815. D on farm nr Woodstock Aug 29 1825; bought a large tract of land N of Woodstock; gave a plot of land to the twp for a cem and is there bur. This cem is on the John R Wilson farm n of Woodstock O. Rept by Urbana chpt which mrkd the grave 1935. Nathan Perry comm submits names of three of his chldr: Stephen (No 25550 D A R); Ephraim (No 37460); Christopher (52608).

CRARY, CHRISTOPHER, Union co, p 93

Grave mrkd 1932 at Curl cem by Bellefontaine chpt with bronze tablet on a stone; dates of service on same. Name of David Culver also on stone, which is nr road side. (Near Logan co line). (J D).

CRAWFORD, JAMES, Franklin co, p 93

Research at Pens Cl Dept by State D A R finds only one record filed for "Crawford" in Franklin co and the name filed is for service of "Samuel" Crawford. The record is exact duplicate of service p 93 for James Crawford. Writing in original appl was interpreted as "Samuel Crawford was mar to Martha Riley (Dicey) July 4 1776"; (another copyist used "either Riley or Dicey" as writing not legible); still another rept fr D A R No 1999 and 2180 thro dau Jane gives wf's name as Martha DeLay! (Cop by Nathan Perry com). Blanche Rings Col

Open for Research

O repts Order bk 9-75 Martha Crawford widow of "James" Crawford is given power of Atty Sept 1838 and Ref Col Gazette Apr 25 1819 appl of "James" Crawford was rejected. (Many not in indigent circumstances but were later restored. Jane Dailey) F A Livingston a descendant Col O repts (perhaps the last word on the discrepany in names) data fr stones in Old Seceder cem for James Crawford b 7-10-1751; d 6-14-1838; Martha Crawford consort of James d July 10 1840 ae 88 plus. However Mrs P B Rumer a descendant of one "Samuel Crawford" sends addit data bur of a Samuel Crawford is in Warren co. (No data given nor has any been filed fr there). This may be a new record.

CRIST, CHRISTIAN, Hamilton co, p 94

Grave mrkd by Cincinnati chpt 1937. Rept by Meryl B Markley, Vice Chr of State.

CRITCHFIELD, JOSHUA, Fairfield co, p 94

Pvt and Artificer Md Contl. Pensr 1833. Elizabeth Sherman Reese chpt. (J D).

CRITCHFIELD, NATHANIEL, Knox co, p 94

Pvt. Enl fr Bedford co pa Apr 1778. Srvd 7 mos as pvt in Capt James Brenton's Co Col Evans' Va Regt. Re-enl 1780 srvd 7 mo as pvt in Capt John Moore's Co Col Pipers' Pa Regt. Re-enl 1781 srvd 2 mos as pvt in Capt Buzzard's Pa Co. Was allowd pens Sept 29 1832. Was b Nov 1761 Shippestown Pa; son of Nathaniel Critchfield Sr. Mar Christiana Welker (d Aug 19 1840). Chldr: William; Isaac; Joseph; Jesse: Benjamin; Mary mar Meshac Casteel; Lucinda mar Jacob Lybarger; Phoebe mar Peres Sprague. Soldr d March 6 1843 on his farm; bur Shrimplin abt two miles s w of Howard. Grave nr center; cem abandoned; inscript on monument "Nathaniel Critchfield d March 6 1843 in the (83rd) eighth-third year of his age." Following Rev War he came to Howard twp Knox co O. Assisted in construction of Fort Laurens O whr his Co was on an expedition against the Indians in northern O. The monument of soldier and wf were restored and reset in 1929 by gr gr grandson Chas V Critchfield who furnished the above information. Ref S 2473 Pa. Rept by Kokosing chpt Mt Vernon O Emma Blair Ewalt chairman of com Rev Soldiers graves.

CRITCHFIELD, WILLIAM, Knox co, p 95

Pvt Pa Line abt 10 mos. Enl Aug 1780 Washington co Pa. Srvd under Capt Joseph Ogle Col Broadhead and Capt Sam Davis. Was ae 68 in 1832. Since the Rev he has livd in Washington co Pa; in Charleston Pa; Coshocton and Knox cos in O. Pens appl Knox co O 9-29-1832. Cens 1840 Rochester Coshocton co ae 77. Rept by State D A R.

CROCKER, JEDEDIAH, Cuyahoga co, p 95

Pvt Capt Ezra Whittlesey's Co Col John Brown detachment of Berkshire co milit; enl Sept 7 1777; dischrgd Sept 26 1777; service 20 days at the Northward; also descriptive list of men raised in Berkshire co for service in the Contl Army. Agreeable to resolve of June 9 1779 returned as recd of Justin Ely commissioner by Capt Christopher Marshall at Springfield July 16 1779 Capt Bradley's Co Col Rossiters regt; ae 18 yrs stature 5 ft 10 in; complexion dark; engaged to the town of Lee. Other enl up to dischrge 1781. Mar Sarah Gifford 1780; chldr: Noah; Jediah Davis; Sarah; Samuel; Elizabeth; Mary; Philena; Aurellia; Alanson; Sylvanus. Soldr d June 1841 Dover Cuyahoga co O; bur Evergreen cem Dover. Grave mrkd by bronze mrkr. Ref Mass Soldrs and Sailors Vol 4 p 120; Records in possession of a descend No 140199 member of Nathan Perry chpt which repts this data.

CROW, WILLIAM, Jackson co, p 96

Pvt Va Milit Pensr 1833 in Jackson co O ae 77. Enl 1779 Rockingham co Va whr he was b; liv there until he movd to Jackson co O. Movd to Ill in 1835 to liv with son James. Soldr d 1-25-1854 (agency bk). Ref Va S 32196. Va Milit in Rev p 268. Rept by State D A R.

CROWL, GEORGE SR. Columbiana co, p 96

Pvt N Y co Milit; bur Catholic cem in Dungannon Hanover twp; came from Pa in 1802; ref Hist of Columbiana co by McCord p 679. S A R 1912; Columbiana co Burials and Pa Arch Ser 5 Vol 4 p 465. Rept by Wilma M Molsberry.

CULVER, DAVID, Logan co, p 97

Name with service inscribed on bronze tablet w Crary Christopher in Curl cem nr Union co. Mrkd by Bellefontaine chpt.

CURTIS, ISAAC, Huron co, p 99

B 1754; d 1843. Enl 1777 Minute Men; servd Danbury, Fairfield, and New Haven whn plundered by British. Capt Lewis Co Col Lewis 8 mos. Capt Wheelers Co Gen Jas Wadsworth taken sick and dischrgd. Pensd Mar 4 1831. Certficate issued at Norwalk O 1833. Also guard under Gen Silliman Col Dennig and Capt Burton. His dau Elizabeth mar Isaac Hill. Ref Firelands Pioneers O S Vol 2 No 2 p 28; Pioneer Women of the Western Reserve p 561; Letters of Rev Zenephon Betts. Rept by Marjorie Cherry.

CUSBOTT, ROBERT, Shelby co, p 100

Robinson's Hist of Greene co states that this soldr left Greene co in 1840 and went to Sidney Shelby co. Rept by Catharine Green chpt.

DANA, DANIEL, Trumbull co, p 101

Removd to Oakwood cem from Old cem Warren O by Gr-sons Charles Dana editor and publisher of the N Y Sun and Julius Dana who wrote a family history. Had a wonderful Rev record; son of Anderson Dana Sr who lost his life in the Wyoming co Pa massacre by the Indians at Wilkesbarre July 3 1776. Rept by Miss Kyle.

DAVIS, DANIEL, Washington co, p 104

One of the 16 Rev Soldrs who landed at Marietta 1788.

DAVIS, JOSHUA, Hamilton co, p 105

Ref Vol 44 p 51 No 43131.

DAVIS, MARMADUKE S, (or Davies ?), Belmont co, p 105

Pvt Capt —— Col Snell Regt Regt Va Milit 8½ mo. Was b Mar 15 1760 Warrenton twp York co Pa. Mar Eleanor Wilson 2nd wf 1816 Jan 30. Soldr d Mar 13 1855 St Clairsville O; bur M E cem. Census 1840 he ae 80 was living in St Clairsville twp Belmont co O. Living at Baltimore but was at Elk ridge landing when ent service. Was a journeyman tailor. Aft mar livd 5 yr Uniontown Fayette co Pa. Aft 1809 livd in Belmont co. Ref W 6967; B L Wt 26188 160 A 1855. Rept by Jane Dailey.

DAVIS, NEHEMIAH, Athens co, p 105

Mrs. Robert Jones 211 Palmetto St New Smyrna Beach Florida regrets (as we do) the omission of her ancestral line thro Mary Stone Davis dau of 2nd wf Phoebe, and sends following data accd to her knowledge but does not state whr proof may be found. Chldr by 1st wf Betty (Merston) mar 1777: Elisha b 1777; Benjamin 1780; Anna 1783; Sarah 1785; Nehemiah 1787. Chldr of 2nd wf Phoebe (Dorr) mar 1793: James Dorr b 1795; Rufus Putnam 1798; Isaiah 1801; Hannah 1803; Judith P 1805; Phoebe 1809; Mary Stone 1811. However we have investigated the mar records of Athens co and find mar of those named by her including a Susan and Reuben (omitted by her but filed Vol 1). Especially found mar of Mary S Davis her line, to Harry Gardner 8-5-1832. Addit ref No 212567 D A R. Rept by Jane Dailey.

DAVIS, WILLIAM, Muskingum co, p 106

Pa Contl; pensr 1824; d 1834; ae 82. Ref Pa Arch V 23 Ser 3. Cop by J D.

DEAN, SAMUEL, Cuyahoga co, p 108

In 1931 the remains were removd to Lakewood Park cem Detroit Rd Rocky Riv. Sec 1 Lot 606 Grave 5. Markd by family with marker flush with ground — uniform size (only kind permitted) with name-birth 8-4-1755; d 4-2-1840. Rept by Lakewood chpt Luella Wise chr.

DECAMP, MOSES, this Vol 2

Grave mrkd by Oxford Caroline Scott chpt rept 1932.

DENISON, JOHN, Trumbull co, p 110

Rev Services. Ref Pa Arch Vol 23 p 283 S 3; S 5 Vol 3 p 247; Vol 4 p 740; Ser Vol 21 pp 605, 737; Vol 22 pp 338, 395, 432; Vol 23 pp 283, 315. Was b 1748 in County Down Ireland; mar Mary McCullough dau of James McCullough who was b in County Derry Ireland. Chldr: Samuel; James; Henry; John; David; Margaret. Rept by Miss Kyle.

DETRICK, JOHN B, Muskingum co, p 109

Grave mrkd by relatives and Muskingum D A R Nov 1931 in Stoverton cem.

DEVOL, JONATHAN, Washington co, p 111

Was one of the 16 Rev soldrs who settled in Marietta Apr 7 1788 which is being celebrated this yr. Copd by Jane Dailey.

DEWOLF, BENJAMIN, Licking co, p 112

Consult D A R No 120401 as to date of birth and wife's name. J D.

DEWOLF, JOSEPH, Trumbull co, p 112

Consult No 120401 D A R; mar Jerusha Carter. J D.

DICKEY, MOSES, Columbiana co, p 113

Pvt Rangers Cumberland co Pa; Pvt Capt Robt Mean's Co 8th Battl Cumberland co Pa Milit 1780 and 1783. Was b 1765; d 1835; bur Bowman cem Elk Run twp. Came to Col co before 1789; srvd in Rev in various capacities. Ref S A R 1912 Col co cem recds; Pa Arch 3 XXIII pp 272, 451, 5 VI 556. Rept by Mrs Wilma Molsberry.

DITTO, FRANCIS, Senecca co, p 114

Rev Exec Doc 37. Henry co his widow pens suspended as not a widow at time of act. Rept by Wm Pettit. Grave mrkd by Dolly Todd Madison chpt June 14 1936.

DIXON, ANDREW, Belmont co, p 115

One son omitted — was James; Rept by Mrs Eliz Jones of Contl Memorial Hall.

DIXSON (Dickson), JOSHUA (Josua), Columbiana co, p 115

Rev soldr. Pvt Chester co Pa milit. Warrantee 183¾ A in Washington co Pa. Surveyed Sept 28 1784. 1781 Followfield twp Washington co Pa owned 330 A. Ref Hist Col co O McCord p 536; No 85334 D A R; Pa Arch 3, XXVI p 550; XXII 731. Rept by Mrs Wilma Molsberry.

DORHAM, ARNOLD HENRY, Jefferson co, p 116

Was agent at Lisbon in Rev and cared for seaman captured by British cruisers. He mar Rachel Banks. Ref No 24368 D A R thro a son Francis Arnold. Rept by Nathan Perry chpt.

DORR, MATTHEW, Athens co, p 116

Ref for other chldr named: Judge Mathew (No 24165 D A R); Russell (No 28641); Joseph (No 38230); Phebe (No 21682); Helen T (No 9781). Rept by Nathan Perry chpt Mrs Oehlke.

DOWD, CONNER, Vinton co, p 118

Grave mrkd at Family reunion 1930 in cem Zaleski O. Father of Hannah Dowd Real Dau for whom McArthur chpt is named. Rept by gr granddaughter Jane Dowd Dailey.

DRAPER, NATHAN, Trumbull co, p 119

Rev Services. Conn Men in Rev p 186. Under —— Brown. Enl Apr 23 1777; dischrgd Jan 1 1778 8 mos service. Mar Hannah Cartwright in 1792; chldr: John; Benjamin; Elihu; Sally; Katie; Polly; Milly Ann. Bur in Union cem Niles O. Ref Hist Trumbull and Mahoning co (John M Edwards 1882) Vol 2 p 224. Farmer and operated a grist and saw mill.

DUNHAM, JACOB, this Vol 2

Kokosing chpt marked grave 1937. Chldr located are Margaret; Frederick; J or I.

DUNLAP, ROBERT, Lucas co, p 120

Grave has been located in private burying ground on east bank of Maumee river of Perrysburg on Rhinefrank farm. Rept by Ursula Wolcott chpt.

DUNLAP, WILLIAM, Trumbull co, p 121

Bur in Trumbull co not Mahoning. Pvt and Sergt from Colorain Lancaster co Pa. Ref Pa Arch Ser 5 Vol 7 pp 599, 621, 1129; S 3 Vol 23 pp 225; 334; S 5 Vol 4 p 435. Aug 1776 and 1777 two mos each under Sgt James Ross Lieut Robert Miller. In 1778 2 mos under Lieut Robert Miller and Col Greenswalt Pa trps. Battles in: Brandywine and Germantown. Res at enl in Colorain twp Lancaster co Pa. Was b June 22 1753 in Chester co Pa; d June 1836 res of his gr-son Peter Carlton in Trumbull co O; bur either Weathersfield twp or Old Carlton family cem Liberty twp Trumbull co O. Mar Margaret Bronn abt 1779 (she d Weathersfield twp Trumbull co O Nov 28 1830). Chldr: John b Bucks co Pa 1780; James b Bucks co Pa 1781; William Jr Washington co Pa 1783; Andrew same co 1785; Margaret same co 1787 mar Joseph Brown; Josiah same place 1789; Elizabeth 1791, mar John Carlton; Mary 1793 mar Peter Carlton; Samuel d whn quite young; Hannah 1779 mar Alexander Marshall. Aft his marriage in 1779 or aft removd to Washington co Pa; thence to Poland O. Bought 200 A; built a house. Aft two yrs exchanged his 200 A of land in Poland for 700 A in Weathersfield Trumbull co O whr he remained.

DUNLEVY, FRANCIS, Warren co, p 121

Pvt Oct 1 1776 to Dec 20 1776 under Lt David Steele Capt Isaac Cox and srvd at Holliday's Cove and Decker's Fort on the Ohio River. July 1777 servd 14 das in Milit at Fort Pitt Capts Scott, Bell, Steele in the fort. Mar 1 1778 went for 1 mos service but was dismissed in 8 das to put in crops. Various other enl to 1782. Was b Dec 31 1761 nr Winchester Va; eldest son of Anthony and Hannah (White) Dunlevy. Mar Mary Craig Carpenter (ref 22356 D A R) and had at least one son Anthony Howard Dunlevy. Abt 1772 Anthony Dunlevy movd his fam across the mts and settled nr Catfish (now Washington) Washington co Pa. Abt 1790 movd w his father's fam nr Washington Ky. 1792 came to Columbia nr Cincinnati whr he and John Reily opened a classical school. Later removd to Lebanon Warren co whr he d Nov 6 1839. Was twice a member of legislature of the N W Territory; member of 1st Constitutional Convention of O in 1802 and member of 1st State legislature 1803. 14 yrs presiding judge of the Court of Common Pleas on 1st Circuit. Pens declaration Oct 3 1832 at Lebanon is said to be one of the most complete on file. Rept by Clara G Mark Historian of Jacobus Westervelt chpt.

DUNN, REUBEN, Greene co, p 121

Bur at Fairfield O instead of Franklin. Rept by Catharine Green chpt.

DURAND, ANDREW, Geauga co, p 444

Pvt Conn Milit. Enl 1777 Cheshire Conn. Srvd 1 yr and 8 mos. Was ae 74 in 1832. Childs Taylor chpt rept for Vol 1 p 444 b Cheshire Conn 1758; son of Andrew Durand and Eunice Hotckiss; carried pkg of letters to Coggswell fr Fishkill N Y to Bemington Vt. Came to Burton O 1806 fr Cheshire Conn; later removd to Ind. Ref Pioneer Hist of Geauga co p 451. Pens appl Geauga co O 8-10-1832 whl res in Burton twp Geauga co whr had res past 23 yrs. Rept by State D A R.

DURHAM, JOHN, Pickaway co, p 121

Musician of the 10th Regt N C Trps. Enl June 28 1777 in Capt Stephenson Co Col Abram Shepards 10th N C Regt. Enl 1778 Capt John Craddock's co Col John Pattous 2nd N C Regt. Taken prisoner at Charleston and held until peace was proclaimed. Was b Aug 13 1761 in N C. Mar Mary Ann (b 1760); soldr d June 3 1853 Perry twp nr New Holland cem Cedar Grove 3 miles s of New Holland. Inscript on monument "John Durham d June 13 1853 ae 92 yrs and 2 mo." Grave mrkd by Mt Sterling chpt in 1911 w Bronze mrkr. In 1840 was a pensr of New Holland. Came to O fr Va in 1816; allowed a pens May 18 1818 whl liv in Pickaway co; in 1820 gave his ae as 65. Res then in Wayne twp Fayette co. Referred to wf as ae abt 60 and one dau ae 12. Ref N C S 42677. Rept by Pickaway Plains chpt.

DYE, ANDREW SR, Miami co, p 122

See D A R Magz p 739 Dec 1929. (Jane Dailey).

DYE, EZEKIEL, Noble co, p 122

Ref Watkins Hist Noble co; second wf was Sarah Paul; had 12 chldr. Jane Dailey.

DYE, JOHN, Brown co, p 122

Grave mrkd by descendants using Govt mrkr. Dedication services were held on one hundredth anniversary of his death Apr 1936. Rept by Meryl B Markley. The State D A R rept addit data fr Pa W 7064 Pens Cl. Pvt Pa Line 3 yrs. Enl Allegania co Pa 1776. Pensd 7-22-1819 Brown co O. Wid pensd 4-5-1839 Brown co

O. Pens no 2344. Was ae 63 or 64 in 1818. Mar Ruth; chldr: Rachel ae 25 in 1838; had five others. Soldr d 4-23-1836 Brown co O. Movd fr Pa five or 6 yrs aft Rev to Mason co Ky. Movd to Illinois abt 8 yrs later and resided 6 or 8 yrs. Then movd back to Ky and resided 4 or 5 yrs and movd to Brown co O.

EATON, JOSEPH, Guernsey co, p 123

Place of birth is stated as Cumberland co Pa. Ref p 15 Bulletin Calif Sons of Rev May 1919. Cop by Jane Dailey.

EBY, DAVID DAVIS, Stark co*

Ref Cop fr D A R Magz Vol 63 No 1 p 60 as follows: "He was a son of ——— and Maggie Davis; movd fr Lancaster co Pa to Va and there servd in Rev. Later removd to Canton O w two sons and d. Information wanted."

EDWARDS, JAMES, Brown co, p 124

According to authentic papers from Brown co court records presented by Mrs Ora Ellis Leeka Marion the town of Aberdeen was laid out by Nathaniel Ellis and not by James Edwards as stated p 124. Edwards sold the land to Ellis (deed recorded at West Union Adams co).

ELDRIDGE, JAMES, Stark co*

No pens service found. Was b before 1745 poss in R I. Mar Sarah Ashcroft dau of Jedediah and Saranna (Rhow) Ashcroft Feb 26 1765 Pomfret Conn. Chldr: Nathan b 17—; William 1766; Stephen (d nr Findlay O); Abigail mar Jonathan Wood; Thomas; Polly mar Viall; Sarah Austin. Soldr d 1815 between Mar 5-12 in his wagon; bur 4 mi s of Massillon in family cem. Initials "J E" on mrkr. Grave mrkd by rough stone. Soldr prob came to O in 1815; bought 160 A in Stark co. Will dated 3-5-1815 Canton O; Rept by Descendant.

ELLENWOOD, BENJAMIN TUCK, Washington co, p 125

Enl May 1775 Capt Archelaus (Areulus) Towne's N H Co Col James Reed stationed at Cambridge Mass. Srvd 8 mos. Re-enl and srvd 12 mos in Capt Jones' Co Col James Reed's N H Regt. Enl in Aug (July) servd 2 mos in Capt Peter lark's Co Col Stickney's Regt (Gen Stark's Brigade). Was b Nov 20 1748 Amherst N H; son of Joseph Ellenwood and wf Abagail; mar Abagail Lamson; chldr: Samuel; Benjamin; Daniel; Jeremiah; Abagail; Betsy; Matilda; Sally; and Polly. Soldr d Mar 17 1827; bur corner of Belpreville cem 2 mils n of O river on e side of R 76 1 mi n of Porterfield. (Not the "Belpre cem"). Inscript "In memory of Benjamin Ellenwood who d March 17 1827 ae 80 yrs." (Days and months obliterated). Soldr came to O abt 1811 with three sons Daniel; Samuel and Benjamin. Ref Secomb's Amherst p 577; Hist of Lyndeborough N H pp 184, 161; State Papers of N H Vol XV; Hist of Wash co O by Williams 1881 p 519, 649; family records; Rev War; Pension cl S-4700; Submitted by W W Ellenwood Wellston O.

ELLIOTT, ROBERT, Hamilton co, p 126

Not Franklin co. This correction and following data is filed by C F Fendrick Mercerburg Pa (1931). "In memory of Col Robert Elliott, slain by a party of Indians nr this point whl in the service of his country. Placed by son Commodore Jesse D' Elliott U S Navy 1835." This is on mrkr in Spring Grove cem Cincinnati. Robert was son of John Elliott who came fr Chester co Pa to Path Valley Fannett twp Franklin co Pa abt 1755; it is assumed his wf d and he mar 2nd Frances (Knot), widow of Richard Childerstone who accomp him fr Pa. Will of John Elliott 1781 names wf Frances and chldr: Margaret; James; John; William; June; Barbara; Benjamin; Robert; Hannah; Robert (mercht of Phila) the soldr mar Jean Wilson 6-6-1773 at now Mercerburg Pa; they each sign deed of land Mch 30 1780 in Bedford co Pa. A mar recd 1st Baptist Ch Phila Mch 16 1781 of Robert Elliott (mercht of Phila) to Ann Duncan of Shippensburg Cumberland co Pa by Rev Wm Roger. V D M. Robert livd at Hagerstown Md; owned land whch chldr sold aft his death; Court recd shows he left widow Ann who mar Daniel Hughes. She d 1825 Hagerstown Md. Chldr: Robert; Patience; Wilson; William; Daniel; Harriet mar Stephen Duncan; John; Jesse; St Clair; Williams (a minor). It is assumed (says Mrs C F Frederick) that the first 4 chldr belong to wf Jean; and last 6 to Ann. (Based on known associations for the names). The Est of a Daniel Duncan Cumberland co Pa shows a dau Ann Elliott who later mar Daniel Hughes.

ELLIS, NATHAN, Brown co, p 127

Hetty is named as a dau instead of Nelly. Inscript on mon in cem overlooking Aberdeen "Capt Nathan Ellis 1749-1819; Soldier in Rev and War of 1812. Founded Aberdeen." Ref "A Tour in the Western Country" by Dr F Cumming 1816; Evans and Stivers Hist Adams co 15 ref found. Established first ferry Maysville to Aberdeen which was called Ellis Ferry to 1816 when he laid out site and called it Aberdeen. Authentic papers from Georgtown court house prove the claim. Mrs. Ora Ellis Leeka Marion O.

ELLIS, SAMUEL, Brown co, p 127

B Oct 22 1752. Correction by Mrs Ora Ellis Leeka Marion.

EMERSON, JONATHAN, Butler co, p 128

Ref p 695 Chapman Bros Hist states: Jon Emerson b in Mass May 7 1756; wf Elizabeth Baley; Saley (Sally) dau of Jon and Eliz mar Richridge son of Samuel of Amesbury Mass son of John who came from England. Rept by Pickaway Plains chpt.

EMMIS, JOSHUA, Lake co, p 128

Another spelling is Emms.

ENEMS, JOHN, Hamilton co, p 129

Is found as "Emmons" D A R No 26785 naming a son Jonathan; No 74022 a son James. Rept by Nathan Perry Com.

ERWIN, CHRISTOPHER, Mahoning co, p 129

Should be Erwin not Ervin. Had 7 chldr instead of five as given. Omitted: Jacob Erwin mar Elizabeth Osborn; Thomas Edwin mar Kate Matrose.

ESPY, JOSIAH, Greene co, p 130

Descendants of this soldr state that he is bur in Lexington Ky. Rept by Meryl Markley.

EVANS, EVAN, Highland co, p 130

1750-1847. See No 21853 D A R.

EVARTS, AMBROSE, Washington co, p 132

Vol 25 p 351 D A R Lin Bk Nat No 24982 names son Timothy; No 38731 names son Gustavus Adolphus (1797-1884); No 20463 names son Silvanus. Rept by Nathan Perry chpt Com.

EVERETT, JOHN, Mahoning co, p 131

Incorrect. Came from Conn. Rev services. Name appears in Co of minute men and Vol 1776 from town of Sharon Conn. Conn Men in Rev p 611. Rev service as given belongs to his cousin John Everett who d in then Northampton co Pa. Fr Miss Etta M Kyle.

EWALT, JOHN JR, Knox co, p 132

Kokosing chpt repts to change the lot of burial to No 66 block 5 Grave 1½ Mound View cem Mt Vernon O. Whn his remains were trnsfrd fr his farm it was found he had been bur in a black walnut log coffin which aft 50 yrs was found in a perfect state of preservation. Mrs. C Ewalt chr.

EWING, THOMAS, Hamilton co, p 132

Grave mrkd by Cincinnati chpt 1936. Rept by Meryl B Markley.

EYMAN, HENRY, Fairfield co, p 133

Mrkd by Elizabeth Sherman Reese chpt 1932.

FALKNER, JOHN, Perry co, p 133

Enl 1776 Capt John Reese's Co Col Arthur St Clair's Pa regt. Placed on pens roll of Perry co O 1818. Mar Elizabeth Hanna. Ref Vol 26 p 233 D A R Lin thro dau Jane gives b 1755; d 1835 whl 14608 gives b 1739 spelled Falkner. Rept by Nathan Perry com.

FANCHER, ISAAC, Fayette co, p 133

1760-1837. Ref D A R Lin Vol III gives service as Va Trps; pensd Fayette co whr he died. Was b Berkley co Va 1760; mar Hannah McCollum; a dau Rebecca mar Jos Parrett in 1811. Ref 110548 V III. Cop by Jane Dailey.

FARRAND, JARAD, Cuyahoga co, p 134

Pvt and sergt Capt Joe Saffords Vt Co; enl 1777 Remington Vt whr then res. Was b Nov 18 1764 Norwich Conn; soldr d 1862 Middleburgh O Cuyahoga co; pens appl Cuyahoga co Oct 21 1824; Chittenden co Vt Aug 17 1832. Ref S 15423; B L Wt 26127-160-55; Contl Va. Rept by State D A R.

FARNAM, ELISHA, Portage co, p 133

Enl in 1776 at West Springfield Mass. Pvt Mass Milit. B 1756 Lyme Conn. Liv Deerfield twp Portage co O whr appl for pens 8-28-1832. Ref Mass S 18297. Rept by State D A R. Mrs Wilma Molsberry repts he mar Thankful Day (1757-1822) who is bur beside him in old cem Deerfield O. Soldr d 1835.

FAUST (Foust), PHILLIP, Mahoning co, p 134

Too young as Miss Etta Kyle repts tombstone recd in Twin Church cem Springfield twp reads: D 2-3-1862 ae 86 yr 4 mo (which makes b 1776). She states data in Vol 1 applies to his father who never came to Ohio.

FEAGIN, DANIEL, Brown co, p 134

Various spellings: fr complete recd filed by Clara G Mark, Westerville we select: mar 2-3-1763 Loudon co Va to Violet (Letty) Combs, dau of Joseph Combs. Chldr: Heathy mar Absalom Craig; Fielding; Daniel (in war of 1812); Elizabeth; Jane; Susannah mar Edward Thompson; Frances mar —— Polk; Nancy; Edward (War of 1812) mar Elizabeth Bush dau of Leonard Bush; Violet mar Levi Arnold son of John Arnold; Willis; 8 others said to have d young. Widow went to Fayette co whr d 2-14-1842 abt 100 yr old. Ref Pens Cl R 3473; Bible recds; co Hists.

FENT, PHILIP, Fayette co, p 135

Clara G Mark Histor Jacobus Westervelt chpt files: he mar Mary Parrett dau of Frederick and Barbara Parrett in Va; thence to Green co Tenn whr a son and a dau mar and remained whn parents came to Fayette co 1814 along w Isaac Fancher, John Parrett (Smokin' Johnnie), Tennessee Joe Parrett and their families. Chldr who came to O: George; William mar Delilah Bodkin; James mar Anna Rose; Rachel mar Jacob Koontz; Mary Nancy mar Isaac Jeffries.

FERREL, JOHN, Licking co, p 137

Servd in Capt James Riggott's Co. (Typographical error).

FERRALL, WILLIAM SR, Columbiana co, p 134

Son of Dominick Ferrall; soldr mar 3 times in Va; first to Judith Goode; 2nd (?); 3rd Mary Baughman of Pa (1772-1845 cem recd). Chldr of first wf: James (d 1861 Carroll co O ae abt 80); of 2nd wf: William Jr (d ae 60); Nancy (Jones) d Williams co O ae 85; of 3rd wf: John (d Iowa ae 88); Elizabeth (Snyder) d East Fairfield ae 92; Jonathan (b 1797 d over 91 yrs old); Edmond d at ae 84 yr; Martha (Booth) d ae 70 yr; Lucy (Kimble) d ae 70; Judith (was liv 1891 very old); Benjamin youngest son liv 1891 in the 90th yr. Dominick progenitor of fam in America came fr Ireland to Charleston S C 1720-30; mar a Quaker here (had above named son William); father and son went to Mill Crk Campbell co Va 1770 or 80; William Sr came to Columbiana co O w 3rd wf and fam abt 1802; built first mill. His sister mar John James who came to O 1802. Ref Upper Ohio Valley Columbiana co Vol 2 pp 114-12-13. Rept by Wilma Molsberry.

FERRIS, JOHN, Lorain co, p 138

Typographical error. Date of death should be 1841; No 48405 thro dau Margaret states he d in Illinois; chldr: Henry (No 42214); Ruth (No 3300 D A R). Rept by Nathan Perry com.

FINK, HENRY, Mahoning co, p 139

Ref Ser 3 Vol 23 p 296 (Pa Arch?). (Data too indefinite for a statement and no opportunity to investigate the ref.) Compare Henry Fike p 138 Vol 1 Roster.

FINNEY, JOHN, Guernsey co

Not Harrison co p 139 accd to following d Jan 30 1839 and bur Peoples cem Centinary Church not far from Cambridge and Newcomerstown Rd. Specific directions are given. Was b Lancaster co Pa Dec 18 1760; bapt by Rev Culbertson; mar Jefferson co O Oct 23 1808 Mary dau of Thos Taylor; son of James Finney and Martha Mays Finney. (James was also a Rev soldr fr Lancaster co Pa; movd to Westmoreland co Elizabeth twp (now Allegheny co) whr he d in 1802 and is bur.) John servd in Westmoreland co milit. Pa Arch S 5 Vol 4 pp 74, 436. Also Westmoreland Contl Line; Rangers on the Frontier 1778-1783. Enl as pvt 1779; under Capt Nehemiah Stokely Col Mayard. Was in an engagement with Indians and British at a fort between Pittsburgh and Fort Wallace. Dischrgd Oct 8 1779. Pens 1833. Rept by Mrs John V Ray Charleston W Va to Anna Asbury Stone chpt.

FISH, EBENEZER SR, Cuyahoga co, p 140

Bur in Denison cem N of Denison on W 23rd nr 25th and Denison Cleveland O Lot No 61; inscript "Fish Ebenezer Sr D Sept 4 1827 ae 70 yrs. Lydia wf of Ebenezer Sr d Oct 15 1848 in her 88th yr. Ebenezer Fish Jr b June 11 1787 in Groton Conn d Mar 26 1880; Joanna wf of Jr d Sept 8 1849; Mary H wf of Jr b Sept 19 1798 d May 3 1884." B in Groten Conn son of Capt John and Lucretia Packer Fish; mar Lydia Fish (his 2nd cousin) b Mar 20 1761; chldr: Abigail mar Ebenezer Foster; Susann mar Clark Reynolds; Lydia mar Alex Ingrahm; Ebenezer Jr; Moses b Oct 25 1789; Daniel mar Matilda Chester; Eunice b Oct 25 1794 mar John Boyden; Jemina b Apr 28 1797 d May 22 1849 mar July 21 1817 Capt Elihu Spicer; Evelina mar Simion Chester; Matilda mar Joseph Williams. He and sons were fishermen. Grave mrkd by family. Rept by Lakewood chpt D A R Luella G Wise.

FISHER, ADAM, Stark co, p 140

Pvt in Capt Krauss' Co 3rd Battl Berks co Pa Milit. Was b 1763 Berks co Pa; d in Stark co O. Cop fr p 217 Vol 146 D A R Lin No 145691 by Jane Dailey. Grave mrkd by Canton chpt.

FISHER, HENRY, Columbiana co, p 140

Pvt Capt Christs Co Col Samuel Miles Regt Pa Trps. Enl 1776. Was b 1760 Berks co Pa or (1757?); mar Mary Keister 4-22-1779; a dau mar John Smith; one Peggy ae 26 and Affy ae 18. (appl 1820). Soldr d 5-1-1826 Columbiana co Fairfield twp; bur Calcuta; pensr 1833; ref D A R Lin No 106849; W 3792 Pa. Rept by State D A R.

FISHER, JOHN, Hancock co, p 141

Was b Berks co Pa 1746 son of John Jacob Fisher and Mary Elizabeth dau of John Frederick. Mar Dec 9 1743. Had bros John A and Christian also soldrs. John mar Magdalene by whom he had two chldr: Magdalene; John Jacob. Had two by 2nd wf: John; Margaret Elizabeth. Came to O 1801; his gr-father servd with English in Queen Anne's War in 1711. Rept by Hetuck chpt. Information fr Chas A Fisher.

FISHER, PAUL, Columbiana co, p 141

In cem 2 mi east of East Liverpool Columbiana co the grave of Paul Fisher is found. Rept by Rebecca Griscom chpt

FITCH, JAMES, Mahoning co, p 141

Name to be withdrawn as Rev soldr as records show he was b 12-25-1787 and too young to have servd. Rept by Mahoning chpt Mabel Askue Ch; Etta Kyle.

FLAHARTY, AMASA, Knox co, p 142

Bur on farm 3 mi northwest of Jelloway Knox co. Located by Kokosing chpt. Ref 16 Rept of N S D A R p 142. Rept by Mrs T R Oehlke. Evidently is same as Fleehorty Amassa filed in Richland co p 142.

FLOYD, WILLIAM, Adams co, p 142

Ref pens Cl S 42728 "Flood or Flud." State D A R.

FOOT, DAVID, Cuyahoga co, p 143

D A R No 22376 names a son Thomas; No 55283 a dau Temperence who gives father of David Foote as Jonathan Foote a Rev soldr (1715-1803). "Pioneer Women of the Western Reserve" p 273 states that Laura Foote wf of J D Taylor b in Berkshire co Mass 1807 came w her father's fam David Foote to Dover in 1815; mar 1824; livd at Rockport. Rept by Nathan Perry chpt.

FOOS, JOHN, Franklin co, p 143

Is spelled Foss, John (1767-1803) in 15 Rept of N S D A R fr Columbus chpt. Cop by Mrs Oehlke.

FOULKNER, WILLIAM, Adams co, p 134

Was liv in Adams co 1834 ae 79 Pa Arch. Rept by Mary Steinmetz Reading Pa.

FRAZEE, JONATHAN, Mahoning co, p 147

Said to have been b in Chester co Pa; his father was also a Rev soldr. Wf's name was Mary Bradford dau of James. Also servd as a Ranger. Ref Pa Arch 3rd Ser Vol 23. Rept by Etta M Kyle.

FREDERICK, THOMAS, Columbiana co, p 148

Ref Pa Arch S 2 Vol 13 p 320; was b 1751 son of Noah Frederick who was killed by Indians; mar Ann Margaret Tibbeus; had 13 chldr. Soldr d 1808; bur Frederick gr-yd N E Corner Sec 12 Center twp. Was captured by Indians. Ref Mrs. Arthur H Kiburz 48 E 53rd St Kansas City Mo a member on this man's service. Family reunions at Lisbon Columbiana co O since 1876. Rept by Nathaniel Massie chpt.

FREEMAN, RUFUS, Medina co, p 148

Pvt N H Milit. Pensr 2-25-34 in Wayne co Act of June 7 1832. Wooster-Wayne chpt repts living in Canaan Wayne co O in 1840 pensr ae 78. No grave found. Sale of land gives name Ruth as wf.

FRENCH, JONATHAN, Licking co, record filed this vol 2

Grave mrkd by Col chpt 1935. Rept by Meryl B Markley Vice Ch.

FRENCH, SEBA, Lake co, p 148

Mary French who in the cens 1840 ae 78 pensr liv in Painesville with Warren French is no doubt wf "Mary Ide" of Seba French Lake co O which see p 148 O Roster. J D. He serv 14 mo in the Mass line and was pensd Geauga co O. Ref Pens Cl Bureau. Rept by State D A R.

FRENCH, WILLIAM, Geauga co, p 148

Is found in Mahoning co as pensr 1833 ae 90 yrs. Rept by Mahoning chpt.

FRISHBY, LUTHER, Trumbull co, p 149

One "Luther Frishby" was pensr under Act of 1818 but taken fr rolls, under Act of 1820 as not considered in indigent circumstances accd to that act. Ref Doc 31 Jan 6 1831 O S Libry. Rept by Blanche Rings. From Mary Chesney chpt: Frisby, Luther ae 80 pens in Gustavus twp (cens 1840). Servd 5 yrs and 8 mo. Was at batteries at Yorktown; dischrgd June 9 1783; b Branford Conn July 1760; mar 1st Mercy Tracy; 2nd Mrs Elizur Talcott. Note correction here fr Roster. Rachel F whose stone stands next to his in cem at Mesopotamia Center he speaks of in his pens recd as his sister. Chldr: Lucius; Sophia; Asher Tracy; Clarissa; Lois Merina; Nathaniel Tracy. Soldr d Nov 19 1842 ae 82 yrs (gr recd); bur Mesopotamia Center cem.

FRYBACK, GEORGE, Pickaway co, p 149

Mrkr placed by Pickaway Plains D A R chpt May 8 1934. We file mar names of those rept by that chpt: Mary Loufburrow; Sarah Anderson; Katharine Emerson; Ann Jackson; Elizabeth Barr; Susannah Robinson. Ref Court Recds.

FULLER, BENJAMIN JR (1760-1848), Clinton co, p 149

Enl in Capt Adial Sherwood's Co Col Morris Graham's N Y Regt; captured 1780 at Fort Ann; exchanged aft two yrs. D in Wilmington O. Mar Polly York. Ref D A R No 35553 names son Gideon Moody; No 6613 thro son William; No 25390 thro son Daniel who gives name of wf as Lovisa Palmer; No 2132 thro dau Betsey gives name of wf as Rebecca Wilder and states that he took with him his son Ephraim only fourteen yrs old. Rept by Mrs Oehlke.

FUSON, WILLIAM, Champaign co, p 150

Fr Bureau of Pens: Enl June 1780 Henry co Va for 3 mo as pvt under Capt George Walter in Va. Sept 1781 for 3 mo under ——— Ruble; In battles of Camden and Yorktown; pens appl Oct 16 1832. Came to O fr Patrick co Va in 1815. Rept by Alice Gaumer Urbana chpt.

GADDIS, THOMAS, Clinton co, p 150

Va milit; appointed Capt 1776; lieutenant-Col 1777 and col 1778 by Gov Patrick Henry. Removd to Monongahela co; built Fort Liberty; took possession of Forts Pickett, Scott, Jackson, and Lindley; servd in Westmoreland co Pa milit in Sandusky exped. Was placed on pens roll for service as Col in 1832. B Frederick co Va; d Clinton co O. Mar Hannah Rice b 1749; known chldr: Priscilla; Leah; Hannah; William. Rept by Mrs Oehlke.

GAGE, REUBEN, Hamilton co, p 151

Listed in "Va Milit in Rev" p 272 liv in Hamilton co ae 68. Cop by Jane Dailey.

GALL, GEORGE, JR, Highland co, p 151

Enl fr Rockbridge co Va 1781 and was present at surrender of Yorktown. Was b Berks co Pa; d Highland co O. Mar 2 nd wf who was Catharine Roads (ref 37025 D A R no of a Real Dau Julia Ann Gall Williams). Rept by Mrs Oehlke.

GALLOWAY, JOSEPH, Greene co, p 151

Correction to Vol 1. Not bur in O but bur Noble co Ind nr Wolf Lake. Grave mrkd by Frances Dingman chpt of Kendallville Ind June 14 1936. Rept by Catharine Green chpt and Indiana Histor Com.

GARD, BENJAMIN, Brown co, p 152

Is misprint for "Gardner Benjamin" which is filed in this Vol 2 of Roster under name Gardner Benjamin. Jane Dailey.

GARD, GERSHOM, Hamilton co, p 152

D A R No 25197 thro dau Ruth Huntington gives b 1738; d 1818; he mar Phebe Huntington (1738-1811). Rept by Nathan Perry chpt com.

GARDNER, JONATHAN, Geauga co, (this Vol 2)

Pvt and sergt N J St Trps. Enl 1-1-1777 Hanover N J at Hanover twp Morris co N J. Srvd 7 mo and 20 das. Was b Mar 1747 Newark N J. 1796 movd to N J; thence to Huntsburg twp Geauga co O abt 1832. Appl for trnsfr to Coles co Ill Feb 24 1838; ref N J S 31051. Rept by State D A R.

GAYLORD, LEVI, Ashtabula co, p 154

Mar Lydia Smith; Lois Barnes was his mother. Proven records of D A R name Mary Potter; David L and Abigail as 3 of chldr. Rept by Nathan Perry chpt comm.

GEORGE, JESSE, Noble co, p 155

B Va 1756; d Feb 4 1845; pvt in Capt Redican's Co Col David Sheppard's Regt of Va line. No 3574 S A R Cal Soc for 1901 p 61. Cop by Jane Dailey.

GIFFIN, STEPHEN, Knox co, p 156

"Giffin" is correct spelling; wf's name Mary Donaldson or Donelson. Rept by Kokosing chpt Emma Blair Ewalt chr.

GILBERT, SEWELL, Licking co, p 156

Is bur in Beech Grove cem Muncie Ind. Broken stone at grave by Ind Histor Research Com.

GILBERY, SEWALL, Licking co, p 156

B 1765; bur Lima twp Licking co. Ref 15th Rept of N S D A R p 163 by Hetuck chpt Newark. (Is evidently same man given as Sewell Gilbert).

GOODALE, NATHAN MAJOR, Washington co, p 160

Commandant of Belpre; capt and carried away by Indians. The mrkr which had been placed in "unknown burial plot" for him was sent (1931) to Col George Croghan chpt Fremont O since they had found his grave at Lower Sandusky. Proven D A R lines are on Elizabeth; Cynthia; Theodocia as daus. Rept by Marietta chpt.

GOODMAN, JOHN, Ross co*

Said to have servd fr Berks co Pa; came to O 1799; d 1830; bur Crouse's chapel nr Kingston O Ross co.

GORDON, GEORGE, Butler co p 161

This soldr bur Springboro cem Warren co; mrkd by monument with dates ae 71; d 1826; b 1755. Rept by Wm Pettit.

GORDON, NATHAN, Geauga co, p 152

Bur Newbury Geauga co; located by New Conn D A R. Ref 15th Rept N S D A R p 387. Mrs Oehlke. Research at Fens Cl brought "no record" bur suggestion to compare Nathan Gawson which is filed p 152 as "Ganson." J D.

GRAY, JOHN, Noble co, p 162

D nr Hiramsburg Noble co O Feb 29 1868 at home of dau; ae 104. Was b 1764. Had not been on pens roll until last yr or two not possessing prescribed proof of military service. "It having come to the knowledge of the congressman of the district that Mr Gray was in needy circumstances and that there was no doubt of his having servd in the closings yrs of the Rev an annuity of $500 per annum was settled upon him." Fr Fireland Pioneers Vol 9 p 46. Rept by Librarian of State O Mrs Rathburn.

GRAY, WILLIAM, Washington co, p 163

One of the 16 Rev Soldrs who came by wagons to Marietta 1788.

GREEN, JOHN, Ottawa co, p 164

Grave markd by De Lery Portage chpt 1932.

GREENE, JOSEPH, Lake co, p 164

Ashtabula co O Mary Stanley chpt in 21st rept of N S D A R p 94 repts one bur in Harpers Field.

GREGORY, NEHEMIAH, Fayette co, p 164

Is incorrect; service given for Jehiel Gregory; Nehemiah his son was in 1812 war. Correct record on Jehiel filed this vol 2. For discrepancies on the birth place of Jehiel Grant Gregory Boston (geneal on Jehiel line) repts prob Bedford Westchester co N Y whr his father Nehemiah livd before Rev; Nehemiah's gr-father et al perhaps came fr Norwalk Conn whr there is a Gregory Pt. No 135756 D A R states Jehiel Sr was b in Gregory Pt Conn. Rept by W P Hay Bradentown Fla (too late to add to record). J D. Other D A R lines are thro chldr: Ann Barnum; Andrew; Odley and Annis.

GRIFFIS, DAVID, Butler co, p 165

Name of David Griffith is given as pensr 1832 Butler co O as pvt Mass Contl. (J D).

GROVE, WENDELL, Mahoning co, p 166

Rept fr pens cl W 4210 Pa gives complete data and correct service; fr which we copy correct data as filed by Miss Etta Kyle Youngstown who has family connections: b Reading Pa 1755 (tombstone data); d Springfield twp Mahoning co; bur Twin ch cem; mar first Miss —— May (5 chldr correctly state Vol 1; 2nd wf Jane Coon mar 1798 at home in Milford twp Mifflin co Pa. Her chldr correct in Vol 1 except Orlando who was her gr-son a son of John. Jane pensd 1855 ae 80 liv w son John Mahoning co and d 3-27-1857.

GUSEMAN, JOHN SR, Fairfield co, p 167

Mrkd by Elizabeth Sherman Reese D A R 1932.

GUTHRIE, WILLIAM, Mahoning co, p 167

B 1766; d 9-14-1848 ae 82-2-25; Margaret (wf of Wm) 1775; 3-17-1849 ae 74-3-7 Poland twp Mahoning co.

* *Open for Research*

HALE, WILLIAM, Montgomery co, p 168

Typographical error for "Hall" as recd shows. Addit ref No 42670 S A R. Rept by Wm Pettit.

HALLIDAY, ELI, Erie co, p 169

Bur Scott cem Huron twp; fam monument; b May 25 1763 in Vt son of Daniel and Anna Halladay; he d at Huron O 1849 May 31; wf Catharine d Feb 3 1842 ae 79; servd with "Green Mt Boys." Pensd Sept 24 1833. Various spellings. Rept by Marjorie Cherry.

HALSEY, LUTHER, Hamilton co, p 169

Mar Sarah Foster; D A R lines name a son John Taylor and daus Abigail Foster and Sarah No 192; No 39903 give wf as Abigail Foster. Rept by Mrs T R Oehlke.

HALSTEAD, EDWARD, Lake co, p 170

D A R No 22958 thro a dau Martha names Martha Ferguson as wf; place b Rickland co N Y. Rept 21 N S D A R of Western Reserve chpt gives bur at Mayfield; (which I find is listed in Cuyahoga co J D). Rept by Nathan Perry chpt.

HALSTEAD, JACOB, Trumbull co, p 170

Was pvt in N Y St Trps; servd continuously fr 1775 to 1781; b 1758 in "Nahaac" N Y. Chldr: David; Jeremiah; Daniel; Isaac; Gideon; Judson; William; Rebecca; possibly others. Rept by Mary Chesney chpt.

HAMILTON, THOMAS, Butler co*

Unable to prove serv as many of this name and State whr servd unknown. Settld Hardy co Va nr Morefield aft war; mar Sarah Seymore. Had 14 chldr. In early 1800 movd to Warren and Butler co O whr livd till d 1827 and wf 1830. Bur Unity ch gr-yd nr Mason, Butler co. Mrkd. Thomas had 4 sons in 1812 war. Data by Adda Hamilton Davis Columbus O.

HAMMOND, ISAAC, Butler co, p 171

B Apr 4 1763 Frederick co Md; Vol fr Augusta co Va Feb 1 1781 pvt Capt Geo Hugstons or Huston's Co Col Morgans Va Regt; at battle Williamsburg and Yorkton. Disch Oct 25 1781; pens 1832 res Butler co O (fr 10 yrs); 1827 res Franklin co Ind; had 5 chldr. Ref Pens Dept Wash No 4327 Va; by Mrs L A Hart Col O; also rept by Ind Histor Research com.

HAMMOND, JACOB, ? co*

Came to O 1815; d 1832-3; was soldr of 1812; fr Westmoreland co Pa. Had son Peter (1804); gr-son George (b 1844).
HAMRICK, DAVID, Clinton co, p 171
Has been found incorrectly listed as "Harwick" David; ref to soldr: W 5292 Va Contl. Rept by State D A R.

HANCHET, JONAH, Lorain co, p 171

Pens Cl states Squire Hanchet b 4-4-1784 claimed to be one of his surviving chldr. Rept by Nathan Perry com.

HAND, EDWARD, not Ohio

Research on name listed Cens 1840 as pensr in Salt Crk twp (? co) found no Rev service. Fr letters recd it is thot that he (soldr) was not in O. One ref found: "Brig Genl Edward Hand d 1802 Lancaster Pa" may be of service. (J D).

HANKINS, RICHARD, Hamilton co, p 171

Pvt Gen Marion's Regt entire period of war. (Verified by Saml F Carey in S A R Yr bk of 1898; also in Hist College Hill by Carey. Was b in N C 1752; son of William Hankins of N J and Mary Evelman of N J. Mar Rochel Letts of N J. Chldr: William; Sarah; Rachel; Elizabeth; Jane mar Nathan Compton (son of Jacob Rev soldr of Hopewell N J); Jane was b 1787 d 1834; Nancy 1811-1890 mar Abraham Tunney of N J 1808-1880. Settld on Forfeit of Sec 36 in 1797; blt log house whch was 1st house in College Hill — still standing tho weather-boarded; located nr Jct of Oak Ave and N Bend Road. Will dated 3-29-1824 gave farm to wf Rachel and a sum of money to a Wm Van Dyke for tuition to school tho he was not related as far as known. Ref: Mrs Corinne Miller Simons 1987 Baltimore Ave Cin O. Soldr d 1823 College Hill. Rept by Cincinnati chpt.

HANNA, JAMES, Montgomery co, p 171

D Oct 1827 instead of 1805. Ref Tombstone in Woodland cem Dayton and Will record in Miami co filed Dec 1827. Rept by Wm Pettit State S A R.

HARBISON, ROBERT, Greene co, p 172

Catharine Greene chpt (Mrs Read Ch) files name as spelled "Harbison" and suggests Preble co for research.

HARDING, GEORGE, AND JOHN, Mahoning co, p 173

Changed their names fr Hardinger aft coming to O. Service (of which man not stated) belongs to a son of Gen John Hardin bur in Ky. Rept by Miss Etta Kyle. Cem data fr German cem Canfield twp Mahoning co give Magdalena 1763-1839. (J D).

HARDENBROOK, LODWICK, Morrow co, p 172

Was b 1755 (a misprint in record).

HARNEST, JOHN, Champaign co, p 174

Pvt Va Milit. Enl May 1777 whn res Shenandoah co Va. Was b 1759 Shenandoah co Va; mar Margaret Feb 25 1784; d June 11 1835. Pens appl Apr 20 1833 Champaign co res of Mad River twp. Ref W 7682 Va. Rept by State D A R. Urbana chpt repts: Myrtle Tree cem E of St Paris Champaign co. Said to be 1st person bur there. Inscript "Jno Harnest — U S Soldr Rev War" — Data fr Lowell Jones St Paris O.

HARP, FREDERICK, Montgomery co, p 174

Ref W 7624 Pa Pens Cl gives mar Catherine Ekolf Oct 1798 (may be difficult to decipher writing); d 2 wks aft came to Montgomery co on 11-21-1833; wid appld 6-12-1834. (Same as "Herb"). Rept by State D A R.

HARPER, JOHN SR, Clark co, p 174

Bur Bloxsam cem in Clark co a short distance fr Greene co line nr Selma. Correction by Mrs I C Davis Cedar Cliff chpt.

HARRIS, JONATHAN, ? co*

Was b N J Sept 22 1763; d Ohio Mar 23 1837; bur "Old Garton gr-yd" Eastern Madison or Franklin co. Bur by his wf. Settld in Canaan twp. Said to be a Major, fifer in Rev and same engraved on stone. Rept by Mrs C F Dickson Iowa.

HARRIS, WILLIAM, Clermont co, p 176

N J Line; enl once for 2 yr and again for 3 yrs. Ref N J Milit p 620; Jerseymen in Rev; in Contl line N J milit p 208. Was a millwright. A proven D A R line. Rept by Matella Doughman Warriors Trail chpt.

HAROFF (Harrouf — 'auf — owf), JACOB, Trumbull co, now Mahoning, p 175

Pvt Pa St Trps. Servd 7 mos. Enl Mar 15 1777 Lancaster co Pa; Dischrgd 1778 Philadelphia Pa. Pens appl Trumbull co July 11 1821 res of Austin Tower twp. Ref S 8647 Pa by State D A R. Miss Etta Kyle repts was mar twice; (1) unknown; (2) Catherine (Kitty) Lynn. Chldr by 1st wf: John and Elizabeth (Betsy); by 2nd wf: Mary (Polly); Susan; Jacob; Andrew; William; Lewis; Leah; Rachel.

HARRIS, WILLIAM, Seneca co, p 176
Grave mrkd by Dolly Todd Madison chpt 1937.

HASKELL, PRINCE, Huron co, p 178
Mar Leah Wilder; 2 dau were Harriet; Adeline. Rept by Marjorie Cherry.

HATFIELD, THOMAS, p 178, Brown co

Data fr stone: b 1761; d 5-18-1845 ae 84; bur West Evans cem Byrd twp Brown co; Martha bur by him d ae 76 4-15-1856; dau of Thos and May Anderson. This may be dates for the one recorded Vol 1. Rec by Meryl Markley Vice Ch.

HAUN, JOHN, Harrison co, p 179

See John Hough V 44 p 332 D A R Lin No 43886.

HAWKS, JACOB, Columbiana co, p 179

Is no doubt incorrect name for Jacob Shawke bur New Lisbon O; (which record see this Vol 2). Rept by Wm Pettit S A R.

HAYWARD, SOLOMON, Gallia co, p 180

His mother was 2nd wf of Edward Hayward (his father) of Bridgewater Mass; her name was Keziah White widow of Edward White; her maiden name was Hall of Taunton Mass. No 101961 D A R. Rept by French Colony D A R.

HEADLEY, JOSEPH, Trumbull co, p 180

Servd w Sussex co N J Trps; never pensd; d at Mecca at home of dau Eunice who mar Benjamin Rowley; wf Abigail bur w him in Casterline cem at Cortland. Chldr: Joseph; Thomas; Samuel; Morris; Amos; Nancy; Phebe; Hannah; Eunice. Rept by Mary Chesney chpt.

HEAGAN, PATRICK, Montgomery co, p 180

Is found listed as "Hagan" 19 Rept N S D A R p 268. By Nathan Perry chpt.

HECK, PETER, Columbiana co, p 181

Is co whr bur not Mahoning; Forney Ch-yd Unity twp. Came fr Windsor twp York co Pa. Rept by Mrs Molsberry.

HENRY, FRANCIS SR, Mahoning co, p 183

Miss Etta Kyle Youngstown authentic genealogist repts her belief this man is not the one who servd in Pa accd to Pens Cl "39679; "Henery, Francis or "Henry" enl 1777 Pa pvt in Capt Wm Bratton's Co Col Hays Regt; wounded at Paoli four times by bayonet; at Brandywine and Germantown; dischrgd 1781. Pens appl 1-26-1819 res Washington co Pa stating ae 66 yr (b then 1753 which is so stated in Roster same recd so far). But "in 1820 liv in Borough of Washington co Pa ae 77 (making b 1743 which is date b of the Francis following); and referred to wf Eleanor ae 55; he d Dec 23 1824" (which is date of death of Francis following filed by Miss Kyle: Henry Francis (1743-1824) mar Agnes Garrison (also Garson ? see No 119208 D A R rept by Jane Dailey); chldr: William mar Polly Buck; Nancy mar James Buck; Francis Jr mar Jane Sherer; John mar 1-10-1822 Jane Kyle (related to Miss Kyle); Elizabeth mar 3rd husband Stephen Reed. Ref Trumbull and Mahoning co Hist p 148; Will bk 3 Warren co O. (From these ref correct solution may be worked out by those interested. J D).

HICKCOCK, DORLIN, Ashtabula co, p 184

Denied a pens as was not in indigent circumstances accd to Act May 1820. Ref Doc 31 Jan 6 1831. Rept by Blanche Rings.

HILDEBRAND, MICHAEL, Stark co, p 185

B Berks co (a misprint in bk); also name Dr A K Zartman is correct spelling. J D.

HILDRETH, DR SAMUEL, Washington co p 185

Bur at Belpre; was later removd to Mound cem Marietta O; mrkd 1930 Marietta D A R who made this rept.

HILL, JOHN, Fairfield co*

Listed p 406 Wiseman's Hist Fairfield co as believed to be a Rev Soldr. D' Walnut twp.

* *Open for Research*

HISEL, FREDERICK, Meigs co, p 187

Return Jonathan Meigs mrkd grave 1932.

HOBART, WILLIAM, Portage co, p 188

Ref No 121270 D A R states b 1743 Compton N H; mar Heziah (?) Brown 1768; Abel was one son; bur Windham O. By Nathan Perry chpt.

HOLLAND, WILLIAM, Mahoning co, p 189

Rept by Etta Kyle Youngstown that research failed to prove the record stated in Vol 1; finds no William or John William Holland a Rev soldr bur in Mahoning co. Court recds and land titles show that William Holland was not in the co of Hollands which came fr Montgomery co Md in 1806. (Suggest research on same name in Fulton co p 189 J D).

HOLMES, JEDEDIAH, Seneco co, p 190

1763-1840; pvt 3rd Regt N Y St line; b Amenia N Y; d Melmore O; mar 2nd 1787 Hannah Brown (1764-1860); Cop by Jane Dailey fr No 110979 V III.

HOLLISTER, NATHAN, Monroe co, p 190

Enl 3-1-1766 Mass; pvt Mass line; srvd 10 mo. B 11-21-1759 Litchfield co Conn whr res at time of war and for several yrs aft; movd to Green co N Y; thence to Ohio co Va; thence to Belmont co. In 1819 was pensd in Monroe co O; in 1820 gave wf's name as Abigail ae 59; chldr: John ae 21; Anne 17; and wf's father Abner Goodrich ae 85. Ref S 4406 Conn Contl. Rept by State D A R.

HOOD, GEORGE, Trumbull co, p 190

Pvt 1st Class in Capt Robt McKee's Co 7th Battl of Lancaster Milit 1782; Pa Arch (? Ser) Vol 7 p 767. Was b Jan 13 1763 Lancaster co Pa (it is believed); mar Elizabeth Goist (Geist) in Bart twp Lancaster co Pa on Apr 15 1791; chldr: Elizabeth; Simon; David; Infant; Amos; Jesse; Leah; George; Levi; Rebecca. Soldr d June 23 1846 Liberty twp Trumbull co O; bur Liberty Union cem Girard O. Adopted by a German fam and sent to Germany to be educated as a Catholic Priest. Returned on a visit and mar and left Catholic church. Aft his marriage livd in Lebanon co Pa; Va; and Washington co Pa; before coming to O 1809. Was a well educated man. Not to be confused w two others of same name who servd fr Pa but in Class 3 and 4 1777. Rept by Etta M Kyle, Youngstown O.

HOPKINS, ARCHIBALD, Brown co, p 191

Son of John and Jean (Gordon) Hopkins; b Rockingham Va 1760; mar 1st abt 1785 Elizabeth Poage; 2nd Elizabeth Shanklin. He d at Red Oak Brown co O Jan 25 1848 ae 88; gr-stone still standing. He removd from Va to Ky; thence to Red Oak (abt 1805). Record secured personally fr Timothy Hopkins San Francisco by Jane Dailey fr his own bk John Hopkins Fam in America; rept by Archibald Hopkins of Granville Ill (1905).

HORTON, HENRY, Trumbull co, 178

Record may be found p 178 Vol 1 Rev soldrs as spelled "Houghton."

HOSKINSON, JOSIAH, Scioto co, p 192

(Not Haskinson); Md Contl enl 1778; srvd 1 yr. Appl pens 1820 Scioto co O: had wf Margaret; dau Polly ae abt 30; 4 small chldr: 2 boys; two girls ae 15, 13, 9, 7; John H oldest son; soldr d Feb 12 1836 Scioto co accd to affidavit of Geo Calvert husband of Emma 1852. Was teacher. Appl 1818 names other chldr: Granville 2nd oldest son; daus: Julia; Ophela; Emma (1818). Ref S 41649 Md Contl. Rept by State D A R. Wid d 1-1-1847 Clinton co O; Heirs made appl 1852.

HOUSTON, WILLIAM, ? co, p 193

Is rept to be bur in Pa not O as stated. A clue points to one fr Lawrence co O; or is it Lawrence co Pa? J D.

HOUSER, MARTIN, Montgomery co, p 193

May be same as Stark co; ref Pa Arch S 5 p 375, Vol 7 Lancaster milit Col Robt Elder Capt Rutherford 1778; same ref p 1036 lists Michael Houser Sr and Jr in Capt Robson Co. Rept by Wm Pettit.

HOVER, EMANUEL, Trumbull co, p 193

Nathan Perry chpt com copd twelve D A R numbers thro chldr: Nancy; Ezekiel; Sarah and Caty. See lineage bks.

HOWARD, PETER, p 193

Bur Greenlawn cem in W Mansfield; grave mrkd by stone as "Rev soldr." Mar Sarah Matten Oct 13 1829; d nr St Mansfield. Rept by Bellefontaine chpt.

HOWARD, SOLOMON, Hamilton co, p 193

Pensr 1832; mar Anna Cary; ref Vol 25 p 315 D A R Lin Bk nat No 24880 thro a son Cyrus. Copd by Nathan Perry chpt com.

HUFF, JOHN, Delaware co, p 195

Bur Sunbury in Berkshire twp instead of Trenton twp. Rept by Delaware chpt.

HUFFMAN, PETER, Butler co*

Will probated Butler co O 1810; one of same name recd land for Rev serv in Ky. Mrs E B L Pueblo Colo.

HUGHES, ELIAS, Licking co, p 196

Mar abt 1780 or 81 Jane Sleeth who d Licking co; bur at Johnstown; gr not mrkd. Chldr: Margaret Jones; Mary Foster; Susanna Leach; Sudna Marlin; Jane Hight; Sarah Davis; Kate; Thomas; Henry; Job; Elias; David; John; and Jonathan (youngest). 2 others d quite young. Came 1797 to Muskingum co; 1798 to Licking co. Said to have been last survivor of Battle of Point Pleasant. Was often called "Ellis" Hughes. Comprehensive acct of his life is given by L V McWhorter "Border Settlers of N W Va." Rept by Clara G Mark, Historian of Jacobus Westervelt chpt.

HULET, JOHN, Medina co, p 196

Mar 1st Sallie Howe (No 68338) D A R; 2nd Hannah Walker (Ref No 13695) of Mrs Betsey (Hulet) Foster a Real Dau (b 1811 Mass). Other D A R lines proven thro chldr: Sally Curtis; Achsah. Ref p 483 Pioneer Women West Reserve mentions a dau Jane Therena mar Aaron Porter; Sally mar Joel Curtis; Betsey Ann mar Nathan Foster; their eldest bro in 1812 war; commending Mrs Hannah Walker Hulet for her care of four step-chldr. Rept by Nathan Perry chpt.

HUTT, JOHN, Ross co, p 199

Va; same bir and death dates found for Hull John, ref 4th Rept N S D A R p 300 indicates error in spelling of name Hull since Hutt is proven record. Data cop by Nathan Perry chpt. Came to Ross co 1801; removd fr old cem to Grand View cem on John D Madeira lot.

HULL, SOLOMON, Mahoning co, p 197

(Holl). Pa Arch S 5 Vol 4 pp 241, 606, Vol 5 p 118; 3rd S Vol 23 p 235. B 1733-40 in Holland and brought to America at an early age. It is believed wf's name was —— Logan. Chldr: George; Andrew; Isaac; Jacob; Henry and probably Logan. Came to O with him abt 1801. D aft 1819 as he witnessed a deed abt that date for his bro-in-law Abner Leach who came to O 1819. Bur Boardman twp Mahoning co O. Rept by Miss Etta Kyle.

HUSTED, SHADREN, Huron co, p 198

Bur on his farm ½ mi n of Hunts Corners; death caused by fish bone in throat. His son Alonzo then livd on the farm. Ref letter to Mrs I F Mack 1901 fr Cyrus Hunt printed in Sandusky Register. Rept by Marjorie Cherry.

HUTCHINS, HOLLIS, Noble co, p 199

B 1744; d Olive twp Morgan (now Noble co) O Aug 5th 1822; Mar Dec 31 1767 Elizabeth Boynton b Jan —— 1745; d Olive twp Morgan co. She pensd Oct 15 1836. Natives of Pownalborough Maine; had sons: John; Joseph; Hollis; David; Daniel. Service is found pens cl W 4243. Enl 1777; dischrgd 1779; pensd 1818. Both are bur R No 21 nr "Hunkidore" school house between Caldwell and Dudley O nr Pine Lake Inn. Rept by Anna Asbury Stone chpt.

* *Open for Research*

INGHAM, ALEXANDER 2ND, Cuyahoga co

Confusion between data on Alexander Sr who was killed in action Aug 27 1776; and Alexander Jr 1764-1858 for whom no evidence of proof of service altho one d Brooklyn Center O Dec 13 (no yr on copy) ae 95 stating a Rev Soldr. (New Eng Histor Geneol Regs p 183 Vol 13); and Alexander 3rd stone inscript d 10-7-1870 ae 82 (Denison and W 25th) whr is also another Alex illegible data; makes it unwise for authentic statement; filed for cont research. Data fr Lakewood chpt.

IRVIN, ANDREW, Clinton co, p 200

Pvt Capt Campbells Co Col Henry's Va Regt. B 1745 Ireland; Mar Elizabeth Mitchell (b 1749) in 1774; a dau was named Elizabeth mar Sam'l Rogers 1830 Clinton co. Ref D A R Lin V 109 p 134; No 108447; rept by Jane Dowd Dailey.

ISRAEL, BASIL, Coshocton co, p 200

Coshocton chpt with ten Anna Asbury Stone members of Cambridge conducted impressive ceremony at the grave of Basil Israel New Guilford cem Perry twp Coshocton twp whn Cordelia O Hopkins of Fort Industry chpt presented a mrkr in memory of her mother Julia S Allison Hopkins (d 1907). Miss Hopkins is gr-gr-grand-dau of the soldr.

JACKSON, BENJAMIN, Knox co, p 201

Grave mrkd 1935 by headstone placed by Kokosing D A R chpt. Rept by Ch Mrs Ewalt.

JACKSON, DANIEL, Knox co, p 201

Grave mrkd by headstone placed by Kokosing chpt 1935. Rept by Ch Mrs Ewalt.

JACKSON, ROBERT, Greene co, p 201

Cedar Cliff chpt reptd plans for mrking 1930.

JAMIESON, WILLIAM, Columbiana co*

And 6 bros rept to be Rev Soldr. By Mrs Molsberry

JOHNSON, RICHARD, Jefferson co, p 203

Was companion of Myers and had been at age of 15; Capt in Braddock's Army; Rifleman in Rev War serving in The Body Guard. One child was Derrick (Capt in War of 1812); soldr d ae nr 100. Settld on what is now known at Bustard farm Steubenville twp 1799; was 7 ft tall. Ref Baldwin Pa Arch; rept by Mrs Molsberry.

JOHNSTON, WILLIAM, Knox co, p 204

D A R lin gives wf's name as Sarah Providence Davis Douglas. Rept by Mrs Oehlke. Mrs Roy Ericson (No 103908 D A R) Stromsburg Neb joins Jared Mansfield chpt and Kokosing in research; In addit to roster they add; mar Sarah Douglas 7-11-1782; chldr: Peter; Samuel; Daniel; James; Insley; Phebe; Sarah; Rachel; Mary; Rosannah. W'd livd Knox co w son-in-law Bartlett Norton; their 3 or 4 sons in 1812 War and William a Capt. In the research Jared Mansfield located following on a William Johnston Richland co; d 9-20-1844 bur Tarries cem Worthington twp ½ mi fr Zion cem (on border line Knox co). See Graham's Hist Richland co. Listed here for research.

JOLLY, DAVID, Ross co, p 204

Addit to: mar 1759 Elizabeth Kelly (d June 8 1791 killed by war party of Shawnee Indians nr Wheeling Va). Chldr: John (killed by Indians June 8 1791); David Jr mar Mary Calvin; James; William mar Elizabeth Catings; Elizabeth mar Hugh McConnell; Mary Ann mar Wm Warnich; another dau killed by Indians June 8 1791. David; James; and William servd in War of 1812 in O. 1785 David livd western Pa; thence to Wheeling region whr during his absence his home was attacked by Indians; wf and 2 chldr killed and son Wm carried away captive. 1796 came to Ross co O nr Chillicothe whr he d "nr mouth of Paint Creek" 1799. 1805 sons went to Highland co. Site of grave unknown; thot to be s of city. Ref D A R Lin Vol XC; Nat No 89722; Hist Ross and Highland cos; Hists; written records made by son Wm and preservd by descendants. Rept by Jacobus Westervelt chpt fr data sent in by Mrs W R McCray Iowa.

* *Open for Research*

JOLLY, HENRY, Licking co, p 204

Wm Jolly a nephew of Henry is recorded as a preacher of moderate ability which raises doubt as to correctness of statement "Henry was a preacher, etc." By mutual understanding Henry Jolly and Michael Beem Sr were bur side by side in Universalist Ch yd cem Jersey twp Licking co O. Rept by F E Harrison Col O. Addit notes fr Clara G Mark Westerville as follows: Mar Rachel (also called Polly) Ghreist b 1766; d 1806; bur Tyler co W Va. Chldr: Kenzie mar Elizabeth Dickerson dau of Thomas; Albert; William; Sidney dau m Vachel Dickerson son of Thomas; 4th son name unknown. Fr Catfish (now Washington) Pa 1774 to Wheeling Va; thence 1799 to Grandview Washington co O. In 1815 in Ohio legislature. In old age went to Licking co O whr d. Wrote his early experiences and observations. Ref D A R 104075; Hist of Panhandle of W Va; W H Hunter's "Pathfinders of Jefferson co"; Co records in Washington Pa; Ohio co; W Va; Washington co O.

JONES, CATLETT, Columbiana co, p 204

Pensr; servd under Boone in Ky. Prob b N C not Orange co Va; mar (1) Ann Barksdale (d in Va); (2) Sarah Crew; chldr Benjamin; Catlett, Joshua; Caleb; gr-son Joshua b 1810 (son of Catlett Jr) and mar Rebecca Miller (d 1890); gr-grson — son of Josua — Byron b 1855. Soldr d ae 80 1829. Came to Butler twp Columbiana co 1798 fr Ky with Col Daniel Boone. Joined Friends here. Ref Hist Col co by McCord. Rept by Mrs Wilma Molsberry.

JONES, JOSEPH, Ashland co, p 205

B 1755; wf d before 1820; mentions grson Joseph Jones ae 14; grdau Betsey Jones ae 17 in appl 1820. Ref S 41703 Contl R I and Mass. Rept by State D A R

JORDAN, JACOB, Noble co

Ref Watkins Hist Noble co pp 422, 549 gives: Went to Jackson twp 1818; his son Peter b 1797 in Green co Pa mar Rachel Albin dau of James Albin a Rev soldr. Nine sons and 2 daus. Rept by Anna Asbury Stone chpt. Also on a Jacob, fr Blanche Finsterwald Athens who believes he is her ancestor bur Canaanville (same name twp) Athens co; b 1760; d 2-22-1849. A second visit to grave found a stone (one in good condition) missing. Reputed Rev service handed down in family but research delayed.

JORDEN, JOHN, Mahoning co, p 206

Misspelled. B in Ireland 1749; pvt; ensign and Capt; later a Ranger. Wonderful service. Came here from Fayette and Washington cos Pa not Chester co as given. Wf Sarah was dau of Major Scott of Red Stone Valley Fayette co Pa who disinherited her for marrying him. Had 10 chldr. Rept by Etta M Kyle.

JOSLEN, DARIUS, Mahoning co, p 206

Accd to newspaper item: "he b 1760; d in Conn 1812; wf d there several yrs later. A dau mar and came to Canfield O." Why then is there a stone in Canfield cem for her Sybil (wf of Darius); d 6-9-1847 ae 87; cop fr Mahoning co cem recds by J D). Questioned by Mabel S Askue chr Mahoning co.

KACKLEY (Cockley), JOHN, Noble co, p 207

Bur in Noble co not Guernsey co on Larrick farm nr Mt Zion ch; Grave mrkd by Anna Asbury Stone chpt 1930 Sept 28 in presence of over a hundred descendants many memb of chpt which sends following addit: Mar Elizabeth Whiteman in Frederic co Va; chldr: Rachel b 1770 mar Michael Yost; Elizabeth b 1771 mar John Millhone; Isaac 1772 mar Katey Millhone; Sarah mar John Drake; Samuel mar Betsy Kackley; Jacob; Margaret b 1784 mar Abraham Buhrer; Hannah 1785 mar George Reed Johnston.

KEETON, GEORGE, Vinton co

Bur Keeton grave-yd at Hope in Brown twp R D Zaleski. Rept by Mart Keeton Zaleski O who knows whr grave is. (This may be same one recorded fr Jackson O).

KELLOGG, JOSIAH, Cuyahoga co, p 268

Fifer Col Seth Warners Regt 1781 and in Capt Morrisons Co Col Swifts Regt; also in War 1812. B Aug 7 1771 Hatfield Mass son of William and Bathsheba Karley Kellogg. Soldr d Apr 1 1847 Middleburg Cuyahoga co O; mar (1) Clarissa Alford; (2) Sarah Fox. 1st mar in Vt 1789; chldr: Sally; Catherine b 1796 mar Isaac Brydia; Hiram b 1798 mar Mrs Sally Marks; John Fox b 1800 mar (1) Elizabeth Killips; (2) Pere Pemberton; Abel T b 1802 mar Sarah Cobb; Wealthy A mar John Himes; Clarissa and Edward d in infancy. Soldr bur Fairview cem Lorain st Fairview twp. Rept by Lakewood chpt.

KEMP, JOHN W, Seneca co, p 209

Is same man as Kent John Seneca co p 210. Rept by Dolly Todd Madison chpt.

KEMBALL (or Kimball), LIEUT MOSES, Jefferson co, p 213

Grave in Warrentown cem mrkd by Steubenville chpt.

KEMPER, PETER CAPT, ? co, p 209

B 1753; d 1829; bur Spring Grove cem Cincinnati Hamilton co. Ref 4th Rept of N S D A R p 298. Cop by Mrs Oehlke.

KIDD, ROBERT, Mahoning co, p 212

D 10-30-1840; Jane wf 1757; 6-6-1841; bur Poland twp Pres Ch cem Mahoning co. Cop fr stone data.

KOHL, GEORGE, Mahoning co, p 217

Wf Maria Kohl (1753-1843) bur Twin Ch cem. By Miss Kyle.

KRIGGER, JACOB, Muskingum co, p 218

Of Cens 1840 is another spelling of Jacob Kreager p 218 Vol 1 O Roster; is found spelled 'Crigger" in Cens 1840. J D.

KUR, ROBERT, Mahoning co, p 218

Should be Kerr as he was of Scotch-Irish lineage not German. Am not sure that Robt Kerr the Rev soldr came to O as cannot locate grave but those dates for his birth and death are correct. Two sons mar into my family and part of that data in the Roster applies to his son Robt Kerr Jr. Rept by Ella Kyle.

KYLE, JOSEPH SR, Greene co, p 218

Grave mrkd by relatives in Cedar Cliff chpt; bur Massie's Creek cem. Rept by Cedar Cliff chpt. 3rd S Vol 23 pp 205, 702, 705. Was b 1749 Bart (now Eden) twp Lancaster co Pa; taken by parents in 1758 to Peters twp; Cumberland (Montgomery now) twp Franklin co Pa. Son of Samuel and Jean (Bell) Kyle. Mar Catherine Chambers dau of Rowland Chambers b 1751; chldr: Samuel; Anna; William bapt Feb 1782; Joseph; and three daus b in Ky. Rept by Etta M Kyle genealogist Youngstown. Mrs Va S Fendrick Historian sends data fr same ref and adds fr Pres Ch Recds Samuel Kyle and wf Jean had chldr: James; Sarah; Isabel; Samuel; Joseph; Robert; William and Thomas. Joseph had a bro who mar Elizabeth Chambers (proven by Rowland Chambers' will).

LAFLER, JOHN, Hamilton co, p 218

Enl Sept 1775 Tappan N Y; servd 12 mos as pvt; 11 mo as ensign; pensd 6-5-1819 Hamilton co; wid pensd 2-10-1840 in Butler co. Appl of 1820 states ae 70 yrs; mar Jemima 12-10-1793; chldr: George ae 15; Joseph 13; James 11; Elizabeth 9; Rachel 7; Ann 3. He d 10-30-1832 in Hamilton co as stated in ref W 5122 N Y Contl; Green Mt Boys. Rept by State D A R.

LANGDON, LEWIS, Lorain co, p 221

B June 25 1749; d June 9 1828; enl Mass May 1778; servd nine mos as pvt under Capt Charles Cotton Col Greaton Mass. Res of Cobleskill Schoharie co N Y. In Palmer Mass 3-2-1775 mar Submit Cooley; she was b 6-4-1750; d 5-4-1842. Pensd 1828 whl liv in LaGrange O.

LANHAM, ELIAS COL, Madison co, p 221

Spelled Langhorn. Major in Rev; b 1755; d Apr 5 1830 at res of Judge Baskerville on whose farm he is bur. Movd to O 1798; settled in Madison co 1807. Ref Rept 20 N S D A R p 72. Rept by Nathan Perry chpt.

LANTERMANN, WILLIAM, Mahoning co, p 222

B 1762 N J; wf Nancy d Oct 20 1856 ae 85; she b Pa; soldr d 1832 not bur in Lantermans cem on farm which settled as said cem was laid out by his younger bro Peter on his own farm several yrs aft Wm Lantermanns death. Had large family: Letitia mar McGrew; Porter; James Reed; Joanna mar William Erwin; John bur in Lantermann cem. Peter Lantermann given as his son was his younger bro a very wealthy man whereas Wm Lantermann did not accumulate a large estate. He was a pensr; record can be secured fr Vteran's Bureau Washington D C. Pensd 1819 whn they gave pens to those not having an estate over $1000. Rept by Etta M Kyle.

LARABEE, JOHN, Licking co, p 221

Chldr: Mary ae abt 15; Elizabeth 13; Daniel 11; Joana 9; William 7; Sylvester 5; Lucinda 3; Lydia 1. Ref Mass Contl S 41743. Rept by State D A R.

LANE (Layne), ROBERT, Clark co

Enl 1779 as pvt Capt Massie's Co Col Lindsey Regt in 1780-81 servd in Capt Wm Grissom's Co Col Geo Matthews Regt. Was b 1758; mar Elizabeth; soldr d 1845. Pens 1832 Clark co O; will probat there 1845; one dau was Susannah. Ref D A R 56981 et al; V 60 p 250 D A R Lin. Rept by Nathan Perry chpt.

LEACH, ABNER, Trumbull co, p 22

Miss Etta Kyle submits complete data fr Pens S 8844. Was b May 4 1750 Mencham Morris co N J whr he enl 1776 and 7; see ref for service; abt 1819 movd w his fam to O. Pensd Feb 11-1834; res Austin twp Trumbull co O; soldr d Feb 9 1846. A son Abraham; dau Nancy and son-in-law Robert Pollack of Youngstown O where liv in 1834. Fr other sources: Mar 1770 Mary Hull b in Holland; d in Champion Trumbull co O July 25 1844 ae 97; chldr Abraham; Hannah mar Alexander Truesdale (son of John soldr who servd fr Pa not N J); John Hull mar Sallie Parthurst; Benjamin mar (1) Dinah Brown; (2) Hannah Raynor; Nancy mar Robert Pollock; Mary. Soldr wf and fam are bur in Champion Center cem; grave mrkd by granite stone with inscript "Abner Leach Dickerson N J Contl Line Rev War." This mrkr has evidently replaced another.

LEACH, ABRAHAM, Trumbull co, p 222

Son of Abner Leach; srvd 1812 war not Rev. Inscript on monument "Abraham Leach Rayon O mil War 1812." By Miss Kyle.

LEMMON, ALEX, Morrow co, p 225

Grave mrkd Sept 14 1929 by Jacobus Westervelt chpt with impressive ceremony. Many relatives present.

LEONARD, NICHOLAS, Mahoning co*

Repts it is reasonably certain he is of right ae; srvd; and bur in Mahoning co. No proof is given.

LEONARD, SILAS, Columbiana co, p 225

Pvt in Lt Col Jas Chamber's Co Col Wm Thompson's Pa Battl of Riflemen (enl fr that part of Cumberland co now Franklin). Pvt Washington co Milit. Recevd depreciation pay; pvt Wash co milit. Was b 1758; d 96th yr; tombstone says Nov 1854; bur old cem East Palestine O; came fr Somerset twp Washington co Pa. Ref Pa Arch II 18; 5 IV 408; 716; Baldwins Records. Rept by Wilma Molsberry.

LETTS, NEHEMIAH, Knox co, p 226

Bur Owl Creek cem nr Utica Knox co O; Inscript on monument "Nehemiah Letts d Sept 3rd 1822 ae 58 yrs and 11 mos; grave mrkd 1934 by Kokosing chpt D A R. Ref No 102243 Vol 103 p 197 D A R Lin bk; rept by Kokosing chpt.

LEWIS, WILLIAM, Morgan co*

Pensr. Living in Morgan co in 1831. A ref found: Hist Fayette co Pa p 81. No proof of Rev service given. Ref Pa Arch.

LINDSEY, JOHN, Marion co, p 227

Soldr d 1837 Feb 28 Marion; bur Deal cem Salt Rock twp Marion co O; inscript on mrkr "John Lindsey d Feb 28 1837 ae 67 yr 4 mo 23 das"; grave mrkd by Capt William Hendricks chpt with bronze D A R mrkr on June 4 1932. Rept by Capt William Hendricks chpt.

LINDESMITH, JOSEPH, Columbiana co

Inscript on mrkr "Joseph Lindesmith d 1817 ae 66 yrs. He was soldr of Rev Bugler and Fifer; srvd during the entire war and was present at the surrender of Cornwallis." Mar in Guilford twp Franklin co Pa May 1772 Anna (or Nancy) Bowman (d Nov 24 1835 ae 82); bur by her husband. Chldr: Elizabeth; Daniel; Jacob (b 1-21-1779; d Dec 19 1849 mar Susanna b 1785-d Aug 1869); John b 1781 d June 1830; Peter mar Susan Ehrhart fr Berlin Pa. Daniel John and

Peter were soldrs of 1812. Came 1769 from Pfaltz Canton Berne Switzerland to Hagerstown Md with his guardian. In 1772 fr Md to Guilford twp Franklin co Pa 1774; Berlin Somerset co Pa; in Sept 1807 to Col co. Rept by Wilma Molsberry.

LINK, ADAM, Crawford co, p 228

Hannah Crawford chpt mrkd grave 1931.

LINN, SAMUEL, Clinton co p 229

A very early rept of George Clinton chpt in 5th Rept of N S D A R p 162 spells name Leim. Rept by Nathan Perry chpt.

LLOYD, GEORGE E, Licking co, p 229

Had a son named George E Lloyd Jr; soldr d Jan 19 1853 Etna O; bur Shaff School House. Inscript on broken monument "Was at Yorktown whr Cornwallis surrendered"; grave mrkd 1931 with new headstone petitioned for by Rev George Weir of U B Church Etna O; G A Shank gr-gr son living nr cem. Rept by Hetuck chpt.

LOCKE, AYRES, Portage co

See same name this vol 2; later rept gives ref S A R 29152 b Mass 1763; d 1839; wf name Mary ——; Pa major. Rept by Wm Pettit.

LOCKWOOD, DANIEL, Belmont co, p 230

Is sometimes found listed; but it refers to "David" filed p 230 Vol 1.

LONGFELLOW, SAMUEL, Washington co*

Wf Lydia Huntoon. Came to Aurelius twp Washington co 1819 fr Portland Me. First cousin to Henry W Longfellow poet. Samuel bur Macksburg O Atkinson cem and thot to be Rev soldr. Ref Mrs W B Burns Kent O.

LOVE, THOMAS, Mahoning co, p 231
B 1767; d 11-6-1847. Cop fr cem recds Mahoning co by J D.

LOVELAND, ABNER, Lorain co, p 231

Pvt 1779-82 different commands. Conn Trps. Was b 1764 Glastonburg Conn; mar Lois Hodge 1787; a son L H Loveland livd Brighton in 1850; soldr d 1847 Brighton O. Pensr 1832 Lorain co. Pioneer Women West Reserve p 462 states in 1821 Mrs Lois Hodge Loveland w husband Abner and 5 grown dau besides a son and his wf came fr Otis Mass. Her son Abner had preceded them in 1820 and built a shelter with such timbers as he could carry on his back. Ref Vol 198 No 107094 D A R Lin; pens claim. Rept by Nathan Perry chpt.

LOVELAND, AMOS, Mahoning co, p 232

Was son of Elizur Loveland; also a Rev soldr and Ruth Sparks; in 1784 went to Vt; bought a farm and there in 1785 mar Jemina Dickerson his distant cousin. Chldr: —— b in Chalsea Vt: Elizur; Milly; Betsey (Elizabeth) mar William McFarlin; Lucinda; Amos; Candace; Cynthia; David mar Lydia Pheil (Pyle) dau of Henry Pheil (Pyle). Bur on his farm Coitsville twp but supposed to have been removd to Riverside cem at Poland O. Rept by Miss Kyle.

LOWRY, ROBERT, Mahoning co, p 232

Not a Rev soldr as contd research on the records finds fr descendants he did not come to America aft the Rev war. What Robt Lowrey does the service refer to? Rept by Mabel Askue.

LUSK, AMOS, Portage co*

Ref "Trump of Fame" for June 2 1813 says: "Capt Amos Lusk d at Hudson Portage co O a native of Conn." Altho he may have had Rev service he was a Capt in War of 1812; Ref p 142 Roster of Ohio Soldiers in 1812.

LYONS, SAMUEL, Columbiana co

Pensr Pa Milit; res of Col co O; pens granted Jan 17 1834 ae 73 yrs; pvt Capt Mathew McCray's Co 1780 Cumberland co milit; pvt same Co 1781-82

Open for Research

Cumberland co milit. Was b 1761-2. Ref Census of pensr 1841. Rept by Miss Mols-berry.

McCAUGHEY, WILLIAM, Jefferson co, p 235

Chldr: Joseph mar Elizabeth Humphrey dau of George; James mar Elizabeth McCune dau of Col Thomas McCune; Janet mar Joseph McCaughey son of Robt; Jean mar Wm McCaughey son of Robt; Margaret mar Isaac Taggart; Elizabeth mar Robt Pollock 2nd James Hogue. Soldr bur Mount Pleasant Jefferson co Old Seceder cem. Monument inscribed "In memory of Wm McCaughey who departed this life Oct 1st 1827 ae 82 yrs 4 mo 2 das. Wf b Mar 1 1746; d Jan 1 1839; bur St Clairsville Belmont co O. Ref Recd of W Ross Cooper; co records. Rept by Jacobus Westervelt chpt.

McCLASKEY (McCaskey — McCloskey), WILLIAM, Columbiana co, p 235

Pvt Capt John Ludwig's Co 6 Battl Col Joseph Hiester Berks Co Pa Milit Aug 10 to Sept 9 1780. Mar 1st Kesia (b 1779 d 1812 in 24 yr; bur Forney cem Unity twp); mar 2nd Ann (b 1787 d 7-29-1847 ae 59); bur Old cem East Palestine; soldr d Feb 4 1845 ae 83 yrs 7 mo 21 da Unity twp Columbiana co; bur Old cem E Palestine O; livd Unity twp; came from Berks co Pa. Ref tombstones; Bald-wins records; Pa Arch 5-5-239. Rept by Mrs Molsberry.

McCLEAN, MOSES, Ross co, pp 235 and 243

A Capt Jan 9 1776; for service see Ref Pa Arch 5th S Vol 2 pp 198, 203, 213; 6th S Vol 2 pp 265, 469; Vol 11 pp 424, 440. Chldr: John mar Margaret McFarland; Elizabeth mar Alexander Speer; Rachel mar Samuel Witherow; Rebecca mar Wm McArthur; Joseph d Young. Mar 2nd Sarah Woods. Chldr: Wm mar Sarah McGinley; Moses mar Margaret Hamilton; Archibald; Alexander; Sarah mar George Nashee; Hester unmar; Tacy unmar; Margaret mar —— Walker. A surveyor in 1766-1767 he and 3 of his bros Archibald, Samuel and Alexander assisted Mason and Dixon in running the celebrated line between Pa and Md and Va. Bur Presbyterian Burial Ground. Ref Monongahela of Old by James Veech p 132: McCollough Genealogy p 95-97 pub 1812 ? by John McCollough III whose wf was a descendant of Moses McClean. Data fr Mrs Va Fendrick Histor-ian of Franklin co Pa chpt D A R. Rept by Clara G Mark.

McCLERMAN, JAMES, Columbiana co*

Ae 75 yr in 1833. Pensd Va Milit. Mrs Molsberry.

McCOMBS, JOHN, Mahoning co, p 236

Enl Pa milit; receivd depreciation pay to 1781; b Ireland; d Poland O; mar Elizabeth Marshall. Ref No 59018 thro son John; Nat no 74443 thro son Robt. Rept by Mrs T R Oehlke.

McCOY, ALEXANDER, Brown co, p 237

Nathan Perry chpt gives Ref 16th Rept of N S D A R p 145 and states b 1760 Pa; d 1837; gr located by Ripley chpt Ripley whr he is bur. Other data fr St Libry of Harrisburg Pa, Gertrude McKinney; Pensd Brown co 1834; b 1764; mar 1787 Catherine Sutherland (1758-1848). Their son George mar Jane Bumpson. Ref Service Pa Arch S 6 V 2 p 122 2nd class Capt Andrew Swearingen's Co.

McCULLUM, JOHN, Mahoning co, p 238

Misspelled. Should be McCollum. Ref Trumbull and Mahoning co (Edwards, 1882) V 2 pp 127, 130. One John McCollum b N J 12-25-1770 mar Mrs Jane (Ayers) Hamson 6-10-1798, b 9-27-1767. The John recorded in Roster erected cabin 1798 and brot fam 1800. Rept by Etta M Kyle who has fam connection w John's son Ira who mar Hannah Kyle. (It appears from above birth date this John is too young to have servd? Jane Dailey).

McDANIEL, VALENTINE, Brown co*

B south bank Potomac Jan 11 1760 mar Sarah Jones 1798. D Jan 13 1846. Bur Huntington twp Brown co. Gr not located. Name among signers asking Gov St Clair for a J P in Adams co 1799. Meryl B Markley and Lieut Byrd chpt.

McDILL, DAVID, Preble co, p 230

Pensd as pvt 1781 Capt Adam's Co Col Lacey's Regt S C Line. B 1763 Ireland; mar Isabella McQuiston 1788; chldr: one son named Thomas mar Janet Caldwell. Soldr d 1843 Morning Sun O. Ref V 106 D A R Lin 105657. Rept by State D A R.

* *Open for Research*

MacDONALD, ARCHIBALD, Champaign co, p 239

Not Logan co. Mar Margaret (1770-1840); parents were Wm McDonald (1727-1822) and Elizabeth Douglas (1730-1814) mar 1751. Ref Nat No 31810 thro son James McDonald and gives Given McDonald his wf. Other lines are thro sons Colin and Duncan, No 71319 who states soldr d in Urbana O. Rept by Nathan Perry chpt.

McILIATH, ANDREW, Cuyahoga co, p 241

Enl 1775 as pvt in Capt Daniel Cook's Co Morris co N J milit and 1776-79 servd sev enls under different commands. Was b in Menden N J 1758; d Euclid O 1820; mar Abigail Cozad; son Samuel. Ref D A R No 57896. (Compare with one filed J D).

McKENZIE, JOHN SR, Mahoning co, p 242

Cop fr cem recds fr Mahoning co are dates b 1765; d 9-19-1852; which are believed to be correct ones. J D.

McKINLEY (or McKinsley), DAVID, Columbiana co, p 242

Pvt Pa line 21 mos; pensd 12-20-1832 Columbiana co. Enl York co Pa 1776; b 5-16-1755 York co Pa; d 9-4-1839. Was res in York co Pa at time of enl; aft Rev he movd to Westmoreland co Pa. In 1814 he movd fr Pa to Columbiana co. Was liv in Center twp (Mrs. Molsberry). Ref Pa S 2812. Rept by State D A R.

McKINLEY, DAVID, Crawford co

Hannah Crawford chpt rept the marking for spring of 1931.

McKNIGHT, JOHN, Clermont co, p 243

Pvt Md Contl. Pensd 1-7-1819 Warren co whl res Clermont co. Enl 1778 servd end of war. Mar Rachel ae 37 1820. Tailor. Ref S 41860 Md. Rept by State D A R.

McMANNERS, JOHN, Lorain co, p 244

Only soldr this name under any spelling (Pens Cl) mar Lucy Colkins (b 1793). She pensd 1853 Marshall co Ill. Chldr: David b 1811 (in Marshall co Ill 1853); Hannah and Clarissa b Clarenden N Y a Real Dau No 96519. Rept by Nathan Perry chpt.

McMILLEN, ROBERT, Knox co, p 244

B 1758 Nottingham twp Chester co Pa; mar Nellie Gilcrist; chldr: Ephraim; Robt; Nellie; soldr d Aug 7 1839 Danville Knox co O; bur Workman cem Danville O old part of cem. Grave mrkd by Kokosing chpt D A R with Rev mrkr and Govt headstone 1937. Pensd July 27 1833. Rept by Mrs Ewalt Kokosing chpt.

McWILLIAMS, WILLIAM, Knox co, p 245

Kokosing chpt D A R placed a headstone at grave 1935. Rept by Mrs Ewalt chr.

MALOY, HUGH, Clermont co*

Pensd 1840 at which time he was liv in Monroe twp. Ref Rockey and Bancroft Hist Clermont co p 198. By Meryl B Markley.

MANNING, WILLIAM, Columbiana co*
"Jail keeper"; d 8-28-1830 at advanced ae. By Mrs Molsberry.

MANSON, DAVID, Miami co, p 248

Pvt Pa Milit. Enl July 1776 York co Pa; Ref Pa S 2755. Was b Oct 1753 Ireland not 1733. Res in York co Pa 1804 then mvd to Cumberland co Pa. Lvd there till 1806 and movd to Warren co O whr he res until 1807 whn he movd to Miami co O whr he appl for pens Sept 25 1832. Rept by State D A R.

MARSH, JOHN, Montgomery co, p 248

(Sergt in Capt Andrew McMayers (Mires) Comm 1st Regt N J Trps under Lord Stirling. Stryker N J Men in Rev p 119. Was b Elizabeth N J 1730; movd to O 1797; mar Nancy Searing). Nine chldr. Sons: John; Jonathan; Searing; David; Timothy. Timothy settld in Preble co d 1845. Soldr d Carlisle 1799 Montgomery co. Rept by Mrs Bernis Brien Dayton Soldr Home.

MARSHALL, JAMES, Mahoning co, p 249

Srvd fr Pa; had long record. Rept Etta M Kyle.

MARTIN, THOMAS, Ashtabula co*

D 3-8-1848 ae 94 yrs; bur Harpersfield O Ashtabula co. Rept by Mary Redmond chpt.

MARTIN, WILLIAM, Columbiana co*

Pvt in Pa Line. Pensd. Rept by Mrs Molsberry.

MASTEN, PETER, Mahoning co*

Reasonably certain is of right age; srvd; and is bur in Mahoning co. No proof given.

MATTHEWS, WILLIAM, Mahoning co*

Rept is reasonably certain he is of right age; srvd; and is bur in Mahoning co.

MATHEWS, JAMES, Columbiana co, p 252

Pvt Capt Mathew Gregg's Co 2nd Battl Cumberland co Pa milit. Was b 1750 Tyrone co Ireland; mar Prudence Garden; chldr: Alexander was one son mar Hannah Krietzer 1804; soldr d 1845 Columbiana co. Ref V 113 No 112031 D A R Lin. (Likely same as one filed as cos adjoin. Rept by Mrs Oehlke.

MAY, JOHN GEORGE, Mahoning co, p 253

This is likely data on John George May p 253 Vol 1 as no George May of same dates in Mahoning co. Rept by Mahoning chpt.

MEAD, MICHAEL, Huron co, p 253

Bought land in Clarksfield lot 31 sec 3. Later his son Luther came and settled there 1830 but whether he brought his father with him or not is not proven. Rept by Marjorie Cherry.

MEEKER, JOHN, Hamilton co, p 253

Research locates bur at Hopewell cem Montgomery O; inscript on monument "John Meeker d Sept 7 1835 ae 75 yrs." Nrby stone: "Elizabeth wf of John Meeker b May 10 1768; d Aug 26 1837 ae 69-3-16." Cop fr cem data submitted fr Hamilton co J D.

MELOTT (or Mallott), THEODORE, Clermont co, p 246

B Nov 7 1755; the Melott fam came fr France to Md; thence to Clermont co. Some settled nr what was later the Brown co section. One son was Prather; one Theodore. Soldr d Mar 10 1845. Bur Union Plains O cem. Inscript on mrkr "Theodore Malott b Nov 7 1755; d Mar 10 1845 ae 89 yrs 4 mos and 3 das. A Rev Soldr." Ref Rockey's "Hist of Clermont co p 307"; Pens Cl Md 2737 gives "Dory" or "Theodore". Rept by State D A R. Rept by Meryl Markley Taliaferro chpt.

MELVIN, ISAAC, Washington co, p 254

Enl fr Concord Mass fr R I duty; mar Abigail Dearborn. Mrs Eliza A M Shrader No 23382 is a Real Dau; d. Rept by Helen Cox Nathan Perry chpt.

MESSERLY, PETER, Mahoning co*

Reasonably certain he is right age; servd; and is bur in Mahoning co. No proof.

MILLER, ABRAHAM, Stark co, (this Vol 2)

Bronze mrkr placed from Co Cimmissioners at grave in Cairo cem nr Canton by Canton D A R.

MILLER, DANIEL, Hamilton co, p 256

Pvt Second N C Battl. Enl Aug 1778 for three yrs. Fam hist states he was prisoner of war on British vessel. B Salem N C Jan 2 1759; d Nov 22 1841 Hamilton con; bur Ebenezer cem out fr Cheviot toward Cleves. Had land grant in N C fr Thomas Jefferson whch was lost by fire. Grave mrkd with govt mrkr placed by fam and formally dedicated by Cincinnati chpt Nov 11 1935. Rept by Cincinnati chpt and data fr Jessie M Markland Santa Barbara Cal to St Ch. J D.

MILLER, JACOB, Butler co, p 257

Teamster and forage master Capt Shipman's Brigade. Was b Westfield N J; mar Lucretia Marsh; d Butler co O; ref V 120 No 119949. Rept by Jane Dailey.

MILLER, JOHN, Muskingum co*

Mar Anne Sullivan Fletcher a wid. Had one dau Elizabeth. Soldr d 1811; wf d 1822.

MILLER, MICHAEL, Miami co, p 257

Because he servd in French army and not provided for by law was refused a pens. Ref Doc 31-1-6-1831. Rept by Blanche Rings.

MITCHELL, DAVID, Greene co, p 259

Grave mrkd by Cedar Cliff chpt 1935. Rept by Meryl Markley.

MITCHEL, PHILIP, Hamilton co, p 259

D Dec 13 1832 Ancor O; bur pvt cem Cedar Hills Dairy Farm Ancor Hamilton co; inscript "Philip Mitchel d Dec 13 1832 ae 115 yrs. A Rev soldr fought at battle of Princeton." Grave mrkd by ordinary tombstone. Rept by Mariemont chpt.

MONROE, LEONARD, Delaware co*

Given as Rev soldr; no proof. Bur Cole cem in Liberty twp. County Hist states he also servd in War of 1812.

MONTEITH, DANIEL, Mahoning co, p 260

Not bur Mahoning co but just over the St line in Hopewell Presb Ch cem New Bedford Lawrence co Pa whr he was deacon and elder for over thirty-five yrs. His bro John also a Rev soldr is bur there also.

MONTGOMERY, M L K, Guernsey co, p 260

Pvt Pa Contl. Pensr 7-15-1819 Guernsey co. Rept by Wm Pettit.

MOODY, JAMES, Mahoning co, p 261

B 1771; liv 1860 at Boardman (census 1860). Dates found later indicate too young for Rev service. Another James may be found for these dates. Rept by Mahoning chpt.

MOOR (Moon), LESTER, Trumbull co*

Made appl for pens from Trumbull co; no data to decide if Rev or 1812.

MOORE, JOSEPH, Lorain co, p 261

Servd 3 yrs Mass St Contl Mass Mar 18 1781 to Dec 17 1783. B abt 1764 Southwick Hamshire co Mass; mar Hannah Miller 1785; chldr: Theron; Hannah; Abigail; Joseph; Norman; Terza; Sophia; Ransom; Seth; Levi; Messina. Soldr d 1846; grave mrkd w bronze mrkr. Pensd Apr 6 1818 Wellsboro Essex co N Y. Ref Mrs C F Jarvis gr-dau No 140636. Rept by Nathan Perry chpt.

MOORE, ROBERT, Highland co, p 262

Pvt Pa Milit. Pensr 6-25-1833 in Highland co. (S A R list) Compare unknown soldr p 262 in Trumbull co; or this may be new name. Jane Dailey.

MORRIS, JAMES, Mahoning co*

Reasonably certain he is of right age; servd; and is bur in Mahoning co. No proof given.

MORSE, SETH, Lorain co, p 264

Elyria chpt placed Rev mrkr on grave of Seth Morse Lorain co Aug 21 1929. Ref Ohio D A R News Vol 1 No 6.

MOWEN, BALZER, Mahoning co, p 265

Was b 4-5-1759; d 8-27-1845 ae 86-4-5; Kathalina (wf) 1766; 12-20-1838; bur Beaver twp Old cem North Lima. Cem recd of Mahoning co changes first name of wf.

MOSES, ROBERT, Montgomery co, p 265

Mrkd by Montgomery co S A R as deeds and wills show he was resident of this co and not Warren. Rept by Wm Pettit.

MOTT, JOHN (Elder), Knox co, p 265

Mrkr placed by Kokosing chpt D A R at Brandon Knox co. Rept by Chr Emma Blair Ewalt. D A R lines are thro chldr: Freeman Hopkins; Mary; Lydia; state N H Contl line for service; and b Richmond. Rept by Nathan Perry com.

MUNRO, JOSIAH, Washington co, p 266

Was at Lexington and battle was fought in front of his father's door on the common. Servd in Burgoyne campaign; was on Lafayette's staff; at surrender of Cornwallis. Was one of the 48 officers who accepted for services Western land and one of the first 16 Rev settlers. D A R lines proven thro dau Sarah; Susanna; son Joseph Fitch. Rept by Nathan Perry com.

MURRAY, JOHN, Cuyahoga co, p 267

From Cleveland Herald of June 15 1827: "June 8 1827 in Euclid Cuy co John Murray S A R pensd in 74th yr. Has been a man of misfortune but of unshaken fortitude and left behind him the enviable character of a patriot and an honest man." Bur Euclid at Nela Ave Cleveland O 1st Presb Ch; has stone w dates; on stone by his "Tryphena Webb consort of John Murray d 1816 ae 60; b 1756." Rept by Lakewood chpt.

NEAL, ROBERT, Ross co*

100 yr old whn he d 1863. Rept by Mrs Peter Blosser.

NELSON, ARCHIBALD, Mahoning co*

Have same dates, but not definite for Rev service.

NELSON, DAVID, Franklin co, p 270

Mar Margaret Logan. Proven D A R lines thro chldr: Nancy; David; and Robert; but thro dau Martha (3 members) all state wf's name as Margaret Jameson. Rept by Nathan Perry chpt.

NELVILLE, GENERAL, Noble co*

Bur Noble co nr Renrock O. Rept by Mrs H Sam'l Wooster Del O. Listed for investigation.

NEVES, WILLIAM, Hamilton co, p 271

In cem nr Blue Ash Hamilton co P on Madisonville Rd is following data on stone: "William Neves d July 11 1838 ae 82 yr" (then b 1756). Cop fr cem recds of Hamilton co by J D.

* *Open for Research*

NEWELL, JOHN, Mahoning co, p 271

Was b N J. P 271 Hist Trumbull and Mahoning cos. Pa Arch S 3 Vol 23 p 216, 254, 703, 738. Bur in Four Mile Run Christian Ch-yd Mahoning co Austintown twp O; was pensr and had wonderful record. Rept by Miss Kyle.

NEWLIN, JOHN, Fayette co, p 271

Pensr in 1840 ae 97 yrs in Concord twp nr Staunton.

NEWTON, ELIJAH, Clermont co, p 271

Bur I O O F cem Edenton Clermont co. (cop fr 4th Rept p 298 N S D A R by Nathan Perry chpt). "Western Reserve Chronicle" Warren O of Aug 20 1873 carries this item: "Elijah Newton resides in Clermont co and is 110 yrs old. P 271 V 1 O Roster no first name says came to O abt 1800. Rept by Grace Winnagle.

NICHOLAS, FRANCIS, Hamilton co, p 271

In cem at Plainfield and Cooper Rds nr Plainfield schl nr Blue Ash Hamilton co was found stone "Francis Nicholas a native of N Hampshire d Sept 30 1808 ae 43-3-13. Cop fr co cem recds by J D. Cincinnati chpt repts (1936) the placing of mrkr at the grave.

NICHOLS, DAVID, Medina co, p 271

Soldr of Rev came to Sharon in 1831 fr N Y. 1st wf was Anna King; had 12 chldr: John and Richard servd in war of 1812. Mar 2nd Mrs Abigail Brown; had one dau Betsey. Ref Pioneer Women of Western Reserve p 961. Rept by Nathan Perry chpt.

NILES, DAVID, Monroe co, p 272

Pvt Vt St Trps 19 mos. Pensd 9-17-1833 Ashtabula co for service in Clarenden Vt. Was native of R I ae 72 in 1832. Ref Vt S 16213. Rept by State D A R.

NOBLE, SETH, Franklin co, p 272

Minister Nova Scotia who took refuge in Mass; servd in milit. Recd 320 acres of land in "Regugee Tract" set apart in O by Govt for sympathizers from Canada and Nova Scotia. Was b Westfield Mass; mar Hannah Barker (Baker) as stated in D A R Lin Bk Vol 25 p 348 thro dau Hannah. Rept by Nathan Perry chpt.

NORRIS, JOHN, Ashtabula co, p 273

Similarity of "Athens" co to Ashtabula may acct for one being listed also as pensr in Athens co 9-16-1833 whr one John Norris of Orange twp (now Meigs co) deeded land to Jacob Spoonele whch was fr Ohio co purchase Dec 25 1845 and bought public land at Marietta. (Of course not one filed Vol 1 who d 1840; but note he was "Jr") Pens appl No 7705 (Rejected) gives same serv as Vol 1 stating; wid d 1846; chldr: one son was Ira; One John Jr who mar Ruth Ladd (both of Tolland) on 3-12-1789; reported that soldr d at Windsor 5-20-1840. Could the Jr have d in 1840 and father John come to Athens co or vice versa ? Rept by Jane Dailey.

OHL, HENRY SR, Mahoning co

Pvt Capt George Shmetters 7th Co 6th Battl Northampton Co Milit command of Major Frederick Sagter and Col Henry Geiger; called out 5-25-1782; returned 7-27-1782. Was b 3-21-1762 or 3 Heidelburg twp Northampton co Pa; son of Michael Ohl (also Rev soldr) and Eliz Barbara Gucker Ohl; mar Abalona Lark (prob 1783); 13 chldr; 9 livd to maturity and came w him to O 1805: Michael b 1784 mar Eva Meyer; David d Lynn twp Lehigh co Pa 1826 mar Magdalena Harding (er); Jacob b 1793 mar Catherine Dustman; John b 1795 mar Maria Katherine Krumrine; Eva b 1798 mar Amos Hood; Maria b abt 1800 mar (1) Andrew Waggoner; (2) —— Kaifer; Henry Jr; Abraham b 1803 mar (1) Catherine Harding (er) (2) Lydia Stroup; Polly (Mary Magdalena) b 1809 mar John Shatto. Soldr d 9-7-1849 Canfield twp; bur Zion cem. Ref Military Pa Arch S 5 Vol 8 p 514; family; Anniversary Hist Lehigh co Pa Vol 3 p 971; Trumbull and Mahoning co Vol 2 pp 142, 177, 179. Corrected by Sarah Ohl Baker 148 Willis Ave; Etta M Kyle 144 W Rayon; Mabel S Askue Chr all of Youngstown Mahoning chpt.

OHLE, HENRY, of Pa

Confused with Ohio soldr. Was Lieut of Marborough twp Phila. Co Pa; b 12-9-1753; d 3-20-1840 Hemlock twp Columbia co Pa; son of Andreas and Eva (Gucker) Ohl. He was a double cousin of Ohio Henry Ohle which led to confusion of data. Filed here as explanation.

OKEY, LEVIS, Monroe co

A letter of this man at Woodsfield Monroe co O date 8-7-1819 (see Adam Crum this vol addt data) indicates he was a res of Monroe co. Jane Dailey.

OLIVER, THOMAS, Jackson co, p 276

Second wf was Eleanor Spriggs mar 12-3-1827 at Gallipolis O. She pensd 1853 liv Jackson co. One Hiram Oliver a res of Pike co in 1860 mentioned but no relationship shown. Ref Pens Cl W 26593 Va. Cop by Jane Dailey.

OSBORNE, NICHOLAS, Mahoning co, p 277

Correction: b 1727 Chester co Pa. Addit to mar of other chldr: John mar Mary Fix (not Fig); Anthony mar Margaret Dieflinger; Aaron mar Hannah McSorley; Mary Mar Wm Nier. Data fr Dr J J Erwin a gr-gr son; rept by Etta M Kyle.

OSWALD, JACOB, Mahoning co, p 277

Service does not belong to Jacob Oswald of Mahoning co who was b 1783-1836; perhaps an older Jacob may be located in his line. Correction by Mahoning chpt.

OWEN, NOAH DR, Licking co, p 278

D 8-2-1821 nr Newark O; reinterred Dec 1875 in Cedar Hill Newark O Lot 623 Grave 1 west side. Lot in name of Eliza Weddell; stone in fine condition has dates and word "Dr" on it. Rept by Hetuck chpt.

PAINE, EDWARD, Lake co, p 279

New Conn Chpt D A R Painesville O reset mrkr of General Paine a Rev soldr N Y Milit in permanent base. Rept by A W Colby. Ref "Pioneer Women Western Reserve" p 42: "Edward Paine came fr Aurora N Y 1799; in 1800 brought wf Rebecca White Paine and 8 chldr; aft 2 yr Eliza was b; she was 1st white child b in Painesville." D A R lines name Sally; Maria; Joel; Charles Henry; a dau who mar —— Parish; and Lydia who names Elizabeth King as first wf mar 1769. Cop by Com of Nathan Perry chpt.

PANGBURN, JOSEPH, Mahoning co, p 280

Does not belong to Mahoning co but Portage co; b 1765; d 1831 Palmyra Portage co. Rept by Mahoning chpt.

PARKER, JAS—, Brown co

Bur Huntington twp. No Rev evidence stated. Mrs. Campbell Georgetown. Since the above data was filed some years ago, the Rev record of James Parker has been established and belongs in the main body of this Volume, but records are often misplaced covering long periods of time and we regret the finding of the record too late to insert earlier. Mrs Preston T Kelsey of Montclair N J is a descendant and furnished the data. Parker. James was born in Pa 1760. Mar Rachel Douglas in Greencastle co Pa in 1795. Srvd in battles Trenton, Brandywine and Princeton. A prisoner in Philadelphia. Chldr: William: (mar 1st Esther Gibson; 2nd Sarah Ruggles; 3rd Maria McAllister)) Ruth mar Joshua Beerbower. Ref Meryl B Markley Vice Ch State.

PARRETT, JOSEPH, Fayette co, p 282

B in Va 1760; one of 7 sons of Frederick and Barbara Parrett. Enl 1776 as pvt Capt Jonathan Clark's Co Col Peter Muhlenberg's 8th Va Regt. Made Lieut and Purchasing Commissare of clothing and provisions for Army at Valley Forge. In battles of Brandywine; Germantown; at surrender of Cornwallis. Dischrgd Nov 1781 Woodstock Va. Pensd with 200 acres Bounty Land in O. Came to Fayette co in 1812. D Aug 28 1847 Wilmington. Grave located in what is now an alley. Mrkr placed in soldrs lot Sugar Grove cem in Wilmington. Was refused bur in Quaker cem because a salute was fired over his grave so he was laid away in Morris Woods just outside cem wall. Ref Miss Dora Hays Bloomingburg O. Jacobus Westervelt chpt Clara G Mark gives mar to Sarah Wendel to which union 7 chldr b. He later mar Anna Hartman of Clinton co. Ref Parrett Fam Hist by Jessie T Mains Greenfield O. (Complete Data).

PARROTT, DAVID, Licking co*

Rept to be a Rev soldr; was b in England; son of Richard Parrott. Soldr d at home of his dau Hannah wf of Peter Headley (a Rev soldr) in Jersey twp Licking co O. Cop fr notes of Eben Condit by F E Harrison Columbus O.

PARSONS, JOHN, Greene co, p 282

Grave mrkd by Catherine Greene chpt 1936.

PATTERSON, JAMES, Mahoning co, p 283

He and wf removd to Wayne co 1823 whr they are likely bur. Rept by Mabel Askue.

PAXTON, THOMAS, Clermont co, p 283

Proven D A R lines give 1739 as date of birth thro 3 of his chldr: Maria Jane; Sarah; Margary. Rept by Helen M Fox Nathan Perry chpt.

PENNY, HENRY, Miami co, p 286

Mrs Clarke Sullivan Dayton wishes to correct the wf's name of Hannah "Thompson" to Hannah "Brown." (d 8-3-1829). (Altho her original paper for Vol 1 rept "Thompson" J D). Confusion arose because Esther Thompson was wf of John Penny Sr.

PETERSON, MATSON, Sececa co, p 287

Grave mrkd by Dolly Todd Madison chpt 1937.

PHIPPS, SAMUEL SR, Richland co

Addit to new record filed this vol two is grave mrkd by Constitution chpt S A R. Ref No 5603 S A R. Rept by Wm Pettit.

PIERCE (Pearce), MICHAEL, Butler co, p 289

Servd as Pvt N J Milit. Pensr 10-30-1832 in Butler co.

PIERSON (or Pearson), JONATHAN, Darke co, p 290

Servd pvt N C Milit. Pensr 5-6-1833 Darke co.

PIERSON, MATHIAS, Montgomery co, p 290

Not Hamilton co. N J Men of Rev p 263 Saus 2nd Regt Conn Line. Bur Rehobeth cem s of Centerville. Rept by Wm Pettit.

PIERSON (Pearson), SAMUEL, Hamilton co, p 290

Enl 1777 in 5th Regt of the Jersey line pvt. Was b 1761. Pensr liv in Sycamore twp Hamilton co O in 1828. Ref Contl N J S 40266. Rept by State D A R.

POE, ADAM, Stark co, p 292

Pvt Pa Line. Pensd 1832 Medina co; was b 1747 Frederick co Md. Mar Elizabeth Cochran; one son was "Andrew." Soldr d 1834 in Tuscarawas co (p 292 O Roster says in Stark co). Ref V 113 p 285 D A R Lin No 112876; also No 86846. Cop by Nathan Perry chpt.

POPE —— GEORGE, (father of), Mahoning co*

Reasonably certain he is right age; servd; and bur in Mahoning co. (No proof given).

PORTER, JAMES, Greene co*

D in 1814; bur Old Pioneer cem at Bellbrook. This information furnished by old resident but no further data as yet available.

POWELL, ABRAHAM P, Champaign co, p 295

B Oct 20 1754; 1780, mar Anna Smith (b Sept 12 1762; d Sept 19 1845); both natives of Va. Member of Patriot army during the Rev. At close of 18th century movd to Ky being thus among the very first settlers of that then western

* Open for Research

county of Va. In 1812 came to this co with his fam entering a tract of land from the govt in Urbana twp one mile west of the present city of Urbana. Was one of the earliest settlers of this co. Rept by Urbana chpt.

PRATT, NATHAN, Warren co, p 295

We list Pratt, Elnathan, pensr 1840 Williamsfield ae 83 liv w Ranseller S Pratt in Ashtabula co for comparison with this Nathan, J D.

PRENTISS, CAPT STANTON, Washington co, p 295

Ohio State Journal issue of 1826 (July ?) carries account of death of Capt Prentiss and gives date of death as 1826 not 1836. Rept by Blanche Rings Col O.

PRICKETT, JOSIAH, Clermont co, p 296

Grave located for marking 1930 on Roudebush farm, Prickett graveyard by Warrior's Trail chpt.

PRINTY, WILLIAM, Brown co, p 297

Found erroneously listed as "Printis" William. Ref S 40301 N J. Rept by State D A R. Govt mrkr was placed at his grave by descendants 1936. Rept by Meryl Markley.

PRYOR, SILAS, Ross co*

B Chester co Pa Mar 16 1745; movd to Va 1770; to Ohio 1807; d Ross co Sept 21 1837; wf d June 1 1845 ae 93 yr 5 mo 7 das. Rept by Mrs Peter Blosser.

RANKIN, DANIEL, Adams co, p 300

Pvt Md Contl. Pensr in Adams co.

RANKIN, JAMES, Harrison co, p 300

Son of William and Anna (Davidson) Rankin; mar Mary Hamilton b Oct 21 1754 mar 1772; chldr: Elizabeth; Ann; Catherine; Rachel; Mary; William Scott; John; Nancy; Samuel; James; Margaret. James Rankin b in Ireland or Scotland came to America with his parents and settled in Fayette co Pa nr Brownsville; he had iron furnaces on Kings Creek. He mar his own cousin. Above data secured when making research on line sent fr Roster; by Mrs Susie M Passmore Butte Mont.

RANSOM, JOSEPH, Erie co, p 300

Pensd Roll of Huron co O 1832 for three yrs service as pvt Conn State Trps. B Nova Scotia; shipwrecked on Lake Erie w cousin John; had left home of son in Berlin Huron co for a visit to his old home in Conn. Mar Lois Mitchell. Ref No 62587 thro son Russell. Rept by Nathan Perry chpt; Marjorie Cherry repts wf named Azuba d 1848 ae 77.

RANSOM, ROBERT, Erie co, p 300

Prob bur in Berlin twp. Chldr of R M Ransom bur there. Servd from Conn. On pens list from town of Colchester who are "some of them hired by two men and part of them we suppose are entitled to $5 per month from the town but have not as yet received any." Rept by Marjorie Cherry.

RATHBONE, EDMUND, Cuyahoga co

Pvt R I Milit. Pensd 12-5-1835 Cuyahoga co. One of this name (no "senior") liv in Newburgh Cuyahoga co ae 83. Cens 1840.

REDMAN, JAMES, (father of), Ross co*

Fr Chapman Bros Hist Fayette, Pickaway and Madison cos 1892 p 327 "James Redman came from Winchester Va to Ross co 1802. His father came from Ireland and servd thruout the Rev war." (It doesn't give the fathers name or whr he d.)

* *Open for Research*

REED, DAVID JR, Meigs co, p 302

Son of David Reed (a Rev soldr) and Diantha Anne Rogers. Mrs Lucretia Helen Regnier No 26016 was a Real Daughter. Cop by Nathan Perry com.

REILY, JAMES, Butler co, p 305

Ref should read: Mrs William Winkler (Adda Stroub).

REMINGTON, JOSEPH, Erie co, p 305

Groton twp; grave not located. Servd fr R I; enl Jan 3 1781 Warwick co of Providence R I under Capt Wm Humphrey Col Orney Regt; servd to Jan 3 1784. Dischcrgd at Saratoga N Y; was in action at taking of Cornwallis; b 1753. Ref Pens records S 40320 R I; Peekes Hist p 334; rept by Marjorie Cherry.

REUBEN, JO (lin or hn or hu), ? co*

Ref 28th Rept of N S D A R p 174 to one Reuben Jo— is open for research.

RICE, JASON, Athens co, p 306

Son of Jonas Rice and Deborah Force; ref D A R Lin bk no 23529 is thro dau Deborah not named in Vol 1. No 44446 states he was b Brimfield Mass. Cop by Nathan Perry chpt.

RIDDLE, JOHN, Hamilton co, p 308

Enl 1778 N J Milit Capt Wm Logans Co; servd 4 yrs. Was b Somerset co N J; mar 1801 Nancy Nutt (1784-1810); was son of John Riddle and Rachel Stockton. D A R members on chldr: Joseph Ross; Adam Nutt (1806-1770); rept by com of Nathan Perry chpt.

RIDDLE, SAMUEL, Mahoning co, p 308

Chldr: David mar Betsey Van Emmons; James mar Jane Bell; Andrew mar Matilda Taylor; Dr John mar Rhoda Winters; Samuel mar Mary Campbell; Catherine mar John McCready; and Ann mar Nicholas Van Emmon. Ref Pa Arch S 3 Vol 23 pp 446, 672, 729; Hist Trumbull and Mahoning cos Vol 2 p 148. Rept by Etta Kyle genealogist.

RIPPITH, WILLIAM, Carroll co, p 310

Grave has been located at Leesville O Carroll co.

ROBINSON, LEWIS, Highland co, p 311

Living ae 78 in Highland co.

ROBERTS, EDWARD, Clinton co, p 311

Grave mrkd Jan 15 1930; Miss Luella Caldwell St Marys. Servd in Md Trps. A Gr dau was Syntha Ann Roberts who mar Henry Sturgis No ——(appears to be "Noble").

ROGERS, BIXBE, Delaware co, p 312

Pensd 1819 as pvt Conn Contl; bur in Burnside cem 2 mi s of Galena the stone data: "d Sept 10 1831 ae 72." Rept in Bonair cem by Jacobus Westervelt chpt.

ROGERS, JOSIAH, Geauga co, p 313

Investigation recommended on data fr 19th rept N S D A R p 279; the date of death 1852 is given to one Josiah Rogers bur Chagrin Falls (Cuyahoga co) O who is already filed p 312 as "Rodgers" Josiah as bur Chagrin Falls. Cop by Nathan Perry chpt.

ROHRER, MARTIN

Listed to avoid continued research for Rev service; was in war of 1812. J D.

* *Open for Research*

ROLL, MATHIAS, Butler co, p 313

Enl 1779 N J Trps Capts Forman and Ogden Cols Ephraim Martin and M Osgood. Pens 1819. B 1762 Elizabethtown N J; d 1831 Hamilton co O; mar 1785 Mary Rutan; a son Isaac mar Hannah Hawkins in 1821. No 11915 V 112; cop by Jane Dailey.

ROOSA, JACOB, Hamilton co, p 313

Cop fr Hamilton co cem records; bur in Hopewell cem. Inscript on mrkr "Jacob Roosa d Dec 24 1831 ae 82-1-26." Also stone "Catherine consort of Jacob Roosa d Aug 7 1823 ae 53-9-0. Ref A number of stones with same family name. J D.

ROSE (not Rase), JOHN, Hamilton co, p 314

Pvt N J Milit; pensr Hamilton co 12-13-1832 res of Anderson twp. Enl Morris co N Y 1774. Since war has resided in Pa and Hamilton co O. Was b 1760 Morris co N J; d 1837. Ref N J S 4787. Rept by State D A R.

ROSS, BENJAMIN, Mahoning co, p 315

Service not from N Y State but from Washington co Pa. See Pa Arch S 3 Vol 23 p 216; Vol 22 p 705; S 5 Vol 4 pp 419, 726 (or Vol 9); Was b abt 1760 York or Chester co Pa; d 1822; bur Ross pvt cem on farm owned by Thos McDonald at corner Bear's Den and Canfield Rds Youngstown O. Mar Elizabeth ———; chldr: Mary b 1787 mar James Fitch 1809; Benjamin mar Mary Palm; Samuel; John mar Phiney ———; Sarah mar Henry Burnett; a son of Henry and Eunice Burnet; Phebe mar ——— Ohl; Ann mar Logan Hull. Rept by Etta Kyle Youngstown.

ROSS, JAMES, Mahoning co, p 315

The service references given belong to James Ross of Pa (aftwards a Senator) who bought land and plotted Steubenville and named it for his officer Baron Steubens. Other data refers to one James who is too young for Rev service as b aft 1800. Rept by Etta Kyle.

ROUNDS, JAMES, Brown co, addit to vol 2

Record filed this vol 2; grave mrkd by descendants using Govt mrkr. Rept by Meryl Markley.

ROWLER, BELZAR, Mahoning co, p 317

Also spelled "Baltzer"; ref for him and bros John and Michael Pa Arch Ser 3 Vol 23 pp 232, 237; Trumbull and Mahoning cos Hist Vol 2 p 198. Rept by Etta Kyle.

RUDISILLY, HENRY, Logan co, p 318

When the record w this name was returned fr Pens Bureau it was spelled "Rudeailly" Henry; same spelling as had been found a pensr Clark co. Ref Pa S 4174 Pens Cl. Cop by State D A R as follows: Pvt; enl 7-4-1776 York co Pa; sergt 2 mos in Pa line. Pensd 4-6-1833 in Clark co. Was b 12-11-1755 Manchester twp York co Pa. Movd from Pa to Trumbull co O thence to Clark co O. Mrs Wissler of Bellefontaine chpt repts: bur nr St Mansfield called Green lawn. Inscript on monument "Soldr of Rev" ae given was 91 yrs; almost obliterated.

RUPERT, ADAM, Columbiana co, p 318

Pvt Pa Contl. B 1754; mar Margaret; chldr: Margaret; Adam; Martin; Elizabeth. Soldr d 1841; bur Brick Church cem on State Route 14 nr Unity O; inscript on mrkr "Rev Soldr." Rept by Rebecca Griscom chpt.

RUPERT, GEORGE, Fayette co, p 318

Mrs Flora Blaine Wood of Nashua Iowa a descendant of George Rupert repts a copy of his pens appl; it names wf Elizabeth; mention a son George mar Catharine Miller and one or two daus are not given. He was of German ancestery; name also spelled Ruperd and Rupard. The 1820 census for Fayette co shows that George Rupert was living Union twp. Son George servd War 1812. Nr his monument one to his wf inscribed "Elizabeth Rupert d Jan 5 1857 ae abt 100 yrs." Rept by Clara G Mark Historian of Jacobus Westervelt chpt.

RUSH, CAPT JOHN, Mahoning co, p 319

Also service ref: S 5; Vol 4; pp 419, 727. Nine chldr: John 1794; Abner; Daniel; Rebecca mar Stephen Baldwin; Susanna; Hannah; Eli; Isaac; Polly. Bur Youngstown twp Williamson pvt cem. Cem data gives d 7-20-1852 ae 75; Amy (1763) d 5-8-1845 ae 82 dau of Senator Abner. Cop by Jane Dailey.

RUSK, JAMES, Perry co, p 319

Grave located by Muskingum chpt. Soldr bur Unity Presb cem Clayton twp Perry co. Rept by Meryl B Markley. Soldr servd as pvt Pa Contl; pensd Perry co 1-25-1819 ae 73; investigate same name bur in Montgomery co. Rept by Jane Dailey.

RUSSELL, CAPT JAS, Washington co, p 319

(1746-1821); grave mrkd at Belpre O Old cem by Marietta D A R 1930. Rept by Marietta D A R.

RUSSELL, WILLIAM, Warren co, p 320

B 1756; d 1832 at Lebanon; is in Warren co not Geauga. See p 24 V 105 D A R Lin bk. Cop by Jane Dailey.

SADLER, WILLIAM, Cuyahoga co, p 321

Lakewood chpt repts William Sadler was in War 1812 and not Rev. (See record of Christopher Sadler this vol 2 who servd in Rev and had a son William).

SEAGE, MARLEIGH (or Harl High), Pickaway co, p 321

Rept fr Manhattan chpt N Y City in addit; son of Benjamin Sage (1725-1813 a Rev soldr) and Abagail Bl—— (illegible copy); Lucinda Stage Pratt was 2nd wf mar in 1811; chldr of first wf not known; chldr: Henry 1793; Susan; Betsey Williamson; Emily Thompson; Harleigh. Gives 1758 as date of birth; bur Forest cem Pickaway co whr are stones w data for him and his wf. D A R Pickaway Plains chpt placed bronze mrkr 1932. Came to co 1811; was post master at S Bloomfield in 1824. Filed by Pickaway Plains chpt.

SAWTLE, BENJAMIN, Cuyahoga co, p 322

Pvt Mass Line 20 mos. Pensr Brooklyn twp Cuyahoga co ae 77 (Cens 1840) liv w Benj Sawtle. Mar Sybel 7-13-1780; chldr: Benjamin ae 15; Nancy ae 13. Soldr d 12-28-1831 Cuyahoga co. Pens N Y 9-25-1818 for trnsfr to Cuyahoga co 7-15-1825; wid appl pens 2-1-1839 Cuyahoga co O. Rept by State D A R.

SCHAEFER, LAMBERT, Erie co, p 323

Grave mrkd by Martha Pitkin chpt 1934 with Govt mrkr in cem on Blair farm S of Birmingham. Was b Feb 17 1753 Coverskill N Y; enl 1775 Capt Christian Browns Co Col Peter Forman's Regt; at Ft Edwards on Lake Champlain 1776 to 1783; honorable dischrg aft 9 mos. Rept by Marjorie Cherry.

SCHLOSSER, TOBIAS, Fairfield co*

Listed p 407 Wiseman's Hist Fairfield co O as believed to be a Rev soldr. Bur in old Reform cem.

SCOTT, MATTHEW, Knox co (Marion co), p 324

12th Va Regt of Foot under Col James Wood; b 1758 Cooper Fife Shire Scotland son of Henry and Sarah Scott. Chldr: John; Henry; Job; Betsy; Nancy; Thomas; Sarah; Martin N. Soldr d 1848 Knox co whr Kokosing chpt honored his memory by mrkr 1931 or 2; whereas p 324 Roster O Vol 1 states remains were removd to Marion co. Rept by Kokosing chpt.

SCOTT, OLIVER, Gallia co, p 324

Pvt enl Mar 1782; dischrgd 1783. Pens cl S 41143 Conn. Mar (1) Permelia ——; (2) Rosanna Hanna 10-13-1822. Chldr: William; Mary; Minerva; George; Oliver; Henry Hudson; Siphrona; Ahira Polley. Bur Vinton Huntington twp Gallia co. Bur Kuntz cem nr Vinton. Inscript on mrkr "Oliver Scott who was a soldr in armies of U S in Rev War and was b in State of Conn in Dec 1762 and d Mar 19 1845 in 83rd yr of his age." Pensd 1821 Gallia co. Rept by French Colony chpt. 8 D A R members rept by Nathan Perry Com through dau Minerva and the number filed in Vol 1 through dau Pamela (not named above). They name Ruth Kingsbury as his wf.

SEVEMS, EDWARD, Miami co, p 327

Should be "Severns" accd to Pens Bur data.

SEXTON, STEPHEN, Mahoning co, p 327

Death notice in Probate Court office states "Stephen Saxton b in N J d 5-2-1857 ae 94 yr." Parents were Lenard and Nancy Sexton. Had 4 sons and 3 dau." Trumbull and Mahoning co Hist p 21 Vol 2; Joseph (4-7-1796); Nancy mar Justice 1812. Rept by Mahoning chpt.

SHAFFER, ANDREW, Highland co, p 328

B Hagerstown Md 1760; d Highland co 1853; 1780 mar Mary Stroup. Ref 110871 D A R cop by Jane Dailey.

SHANNON, GEORGE, Belmont co, p 328

Sept 1929 D A R Magz p 543 contains sketch and marking by descendants Anna Asbury Stone chpt participating. Clara G Mark Westerville repts from Judge Tanneyhill's Article and J A Caldwell's Hist of Belmont and Jefferson cos the following data: He was our first native Ohioan to serve as Governor of the state. George Shannan was brought by father from Ireland abt 1760; orphaned; and reared by Episcopal Clergyman of Wilmington Del. Soon aft his marriage he settled nr Claysville Washington co Pa; 1796 movd to O co Va; 1800 to what is now Warren twp Belmont co O. Mar 1793 Bedford co Pa Jane Milligan. Chldr: George (pvt secretary to Lewis & Clark on their expedition across the continent); Thomas mar Cassandra Anderson; John mar ——— ———; Nancy mar Morgan Gilliland; James mar ——— Shelby; David; Lavina mar Humphrey Anderson; Arthur d young; Wilson mar Elizabeth Ellis (2) Sarah Osborn. Soldr froze to death in a blizzard whl on a hunting trip in 1803 and bur in the "Twp Burial Ground" at the southwest corner of section ten. His fam was considered one of the most prominent in eastern O.

SHEPARD, CHARLES, addit to vol 2.

Pens bur repts error in their rept of 1835, he was in Va Milit not Md. B Dec 25 1763 Baltimore Md and livd in Pa before Rev. Res Winchester Va whn he enl 1780; servd 3 mos in Va Trps. Enl Sept 1781 servd 5 mos Captain James Dunbar's Va Co. Movd to Redstone Pa; then to O. Pensd Nov 15 1833 whl liv in Alexander twp Athens co O. 1841 res Adams co Ill whr he had movd to w Benjamin Ramsey. Ref S 32516 Pens Cl. Rept by Jane Dowd Dailey.

SHERRARD, JOHN, Jefferson co, p 333

Ref Crawford's Campaign against Sandusky by C W Butterfield p 228-229 give excellent acct of the soldr. Filed by Clara G Mark, Westerville.

SHOEMAKER, WILLIAM, Fairfield co, p 334

Pvt Pa Milit. Enl Sussex co N J spring 1776. Pensr Fairfield co 1-9-1834; srvd 2 yrs. Was b 1743 whl coming to U S. Raised Sussex co N J whr his father settled aft coming from Germany. Ref N J S 7508. Rept by State D A R.

SHOTTS, DAVID, Ross co, p 333

Nathaniel Massie chpt has located grave on the farm owned by the fam for over 100 yrs; is now owned by Wm Aikens; 1½ mi n of Denver in Huntington twp Ross co. Stone data has name and 1760-1825. Rept by Mrs P J Blosser Chr.

SHUEY, JOHN MARTIN, Montgomery co, p 333

Grave mrkd by Greencastle cem Dayton S A R. Rept by Jonathan Dayton chpt.

SIMMONS, THOMAS, Butler co, p 334

Oxford Caroline Scott chpt of Oxford mrkd grave at Collinsville O 1932 rept.

SIMON, JACOB, Mahoning co, p 335

Cop fr cem recds of Mahoning co: b 1750; d 9-29-1818; son Andreas and Elizabeth Simon b Md (fr Washington co). Elizabeth wf of Jacob b 10-1-1781; d 7-20-1846 dau of Martin and Elizabeth Degen; (again) Elizabeth wf of Jacob b 1790; d 9-14-1879. Rept by Jane Dailey.

SINCLAIR, JOSHUA, ? co, p 336

Typographical error noted in name which should correctly be mar Abigail Pattee. Ref Feb 1919 Bulletin of Sons of Rev of Calif. Cop by Jane Dailey. (Maumee City mentioned in Lucas co.)

SISK, JAMES, Ross co*

D Aug 27 1836 ae 75 yr 4 mo 18 da; Mary his wf d Feb 2 1801 ae 39 yr 3 mo. Said to be Rev soldr (by descendant). Bur Boudle cem Ross co. Rept by Nathaniel Massie chpt.

SLANTER, EPHRAIM, Lorain co, p 337

Ref Gen Acct Off Washington D C: these names of chldr are given: Hiram Slanter; Jared Slanter; Hannah Jackson; Vastia Spencer; Anna Smith. D A R No 31834 thro son Sylvanus (not named above) gives name of wf as Lydia.

SMALL, ANDREW, Miami co, p 338

Pens Cl No S 3945 Pa states b 2-17-1756 York co Pa; pensr 1833 at Dayton; letter gives same dates of death but no place. Rept by State D A R.

SMITH, JAMES, Columbiana co, p 340

Pvt Pa Contl. Pensr Columbiana co 5-19-1830 whr was yet liv in 1834 ae 78. (J D).

SMITH, JOHN, Butler co, p 340

Oxford Caroline Scott chpt of Oxford mrkd the grave at Riley O 1932. (Addit ref S 4860 N J rept by State D A R).

SMITH, STEPHEN CAPT, Franklin co*

D in 87th yr abt 1823; came fr Scituate R I. (O S Journal issue Nov 24 1823.) Rept by Blanche Rings.

SNOW, OLIVER, Geauga co, p 343

Lakewood chpt repts plans for placing a mrkr at his grave.

SONNER, ANTHONY T, Highland co, p 344

Pensr as pvt Va Milit ae 73 in Hamilton co. Ref 15 Rept N S D A R p 165. Rept by J D and Mrs Oehlke.

SPALDING, ABEL, Delaware co, p 345

The following data probably refers to soldr listed in Delaware co: b 1764; d 1844; pensr 1832 as pvt 1781 Capt Charles Nelson's Co Col Benjamin Wright's Vt Regt of Inf. D in O. Mar Hannah: dau Martha. Ref D A R Nat No 80304 thro dau Martha. Rept by Nathan Perry chpt.

SPRAGUE, JONATHAN, Mahoning co, p 347

In 1935 the remains were removed to Summit co. Rept by Mahoning co.

SPERRY, PETER, Ross co, p 346

Enl 1778 Capt Craven's Co O Trps. Was b Frederick co Va 1760; mar Mary Hammock; a dau Elizabeth mar Elisha Thompson 1781. Soldr d 1838 Frankfort O. Ref V 106 D A R Lin 105927. Rept Jane Dailey.

SQUIER, EZRA, Lorain co, p 348

Addit from Pens Cl Data: Soldr d May 17 1836; mar Mar 4 1788 Betsey or Betsa Pangman (b Aug 1 1769); pensd 1839. 15 chldr: (in 24 yrs): Hannah b 1788; Abner 1790; Anson 1792; Lois 1794 (No 89648); Betsy 1796; Truman 1798; Eunice 1799; Claracy 1802; Amasa 1804; Royal Pember 1805; ——jde 1806; Ezra 1808; Henry Chase 18—(illegible); Champlain 1811; Polly Drake 1812. Ref Bureau of pensions. Rept by Nathan Perry chpt.

STAMBACH, PHILLIP, Mahoning co, p 349

B Northampton co Pa; son of Johann Phillip Stambach and Maria Christina Kuntz; mar Anna Catharine Fusselmann (1766-1821); had 12 chldr; 11 b in Toboyne twp Perry co Pa before he came to Boardman twp Mahoning co O in 1811. Son John was mar before 1811. Full names and ages and marriages are given in

German on their headstones in Lake Park cem Youngstown O. Henry Lenig of Willa (Perry co) Pa is writing a fam hist. Jacob (b 1761) a bro of Phillip d in Perry co Pa. Rept by Miss Kyle.

SHERRARD, JOHN, Jefferson co, p 332

This information may belong with above soldr. Grave located in Quaker gr-yd neglected cem Smithfield Jefferson co. Was b 1750 Ireland; d 1809. Grave located 1930. Rept by Steubenville chpt.

STEARNS, JOHN, Medina co, p 350

Parents were Jonathan Stearns and Beulah Chadwick; was b in Mendon Mass 1751; pensr when he d at Brunswick O. Mar Lucy Merrell 1779. Three D A R lines proven thro Daniel; Mary; and John Jr. Rept by Nathan Perry chpt.

STEELE, ISAAC, Summit co, p 350

Rept by Cuyahoga Falls chpt the parents were Adam Steele and Polly Baker; chldr of soldr: Anna; Elizabeth mar Henry Shuman; Margaret mar Thos Hammontree (went to Ind); Mary mar Freah Horstman (went to Mich); John mar Ann Blendon (Ind); Isaac Jr mar Margaret Steele. Data from Mabel Steele Taylor.

STEPHENS, EPHRAIM, Warren co, p 351

Mrs Thomas R Jones Denver Colo in working out their line on this soldr finds he was b in New Ipswich New Hampshire. His father Joseph Stevens was b at Billerica but removd to New Ipswich before birth of Ephraim. Ref Veterans Adm; Hist of Winthrop (Stackpole) p 609.

STEVENS, JOHN, Champaign co (not Lucas co), p 351

Research Committee of Ursula Wolcott Chapt attempted to verify statement taken fr D A R Lineage bk and have proof fr descendants and Bible recds that he is bur nr Westville, Champaign co and not Lucas co.

STEWART, ALEXANDER, Adams co Pa*

Bur in Seceder's Corners U P Church cem on Logan Road Ext is Adams co Pa not Westmoreland as H R Baldwin gives in his references which latter belongs to Alexander Stewart bur Round Hill Pres Ch cem nr Elizabeth Allegheny co Pa. Rept by Miss Etta Kyle.

STEWART, Hugh, Ross co, p 353

B Dec 19 1757 Philadelphia; mar Sept 16 1780 Margaret Boxburgh Smith (b Phila Aug 25 1763; d May 22 1842). Chldr: George mar Ann P Carr; Elizabeth mar Thomas Fullerton; Martha mar Joseph P Gillespie; James mar Jane Carson Robinson; William died; Robert mar Esther Gillespie (2) Margaret Patton; Margaret mar Lewis Nye (2) Matthew Gillespie; Archibald mar Sarah Linton; Sarah mar James Bogle; twins d young; Jane d young; Mary mar William Arnold Ustick; Hugh C mar Sarah Alibone. In 1809 came to O; settled nr Frankfort Ross co. His "Mansion house" stood between Frankfort and Roxabell across the North Fork of Paint Creek. Was a farmer and distiller. Soldr d May 1 1824; bur on hill in family burying ground; wf d Bloomingburg Fayette co May 22 1842 whr is bur. Information by Miss Emma B Jackson of Washington C H and Hugh S Fullerton Columbus. Rept by Clara G Mark.

STOW, COMFORT, Trumbull co, p 356

Has been found erroneously spelled "Storr."

SUTTON, BENJAMIN, Brown co, p 359

Srvd as pvt Pa Trps; regt of Col Morgan; pensd Sept 6 1833 Brown co O. Servd 16 mos. Enl 1777 Green co Pa. Movd to Va abt 1772 thence to Green co Pa in Mar 1777; thence to Monongahela co Va; thence to Mason co Ky 1788; thence to Brown co abt 1802. Pensr 1840 Decatur ae 87 Res Brown co Apr 29 1833. Ref No 106813 and No 12081; S 16266 Pa. Rept by State D A R.

SWICKHART, MARTIN, Jefferson co, p 361

Mary D Sinclair Chr Steubenville chpt repts he is bur in Mt Tabor ch cem (S W of Osage) stone data reading b 1746; d 1841. C R Swickard Columbus states he arrived Philadelphia w parents on ship Betsy Sept 19 1765. Listed when qualified as Martin "Becker." German name prob "Zwickard."

Open for Research

TANNER, TYRAL, Mahoning co, p 362

B Cornwall Conn 1751; d 11-22-1833 ae 72. Huldah (wf) 1755; 12-29-1803 ae 48; Mary (2nd wf) 1756; 7-13-1845 ae 87. Bur Canfield twp Canfield cem Mahoning co. Stone dates cop fr cem recds of Mahoning co differ from Roster as to which was his first wf. Open for evidence. Name been found incorrectly listed as "Sanner."

TAPSCOTT, JAMES, Warren co, p 362

Mrkd July 19 1931 in Tapscott cem Carlisle Warren co by Richard Montgomery chpt S A R. Address by Hon Mason Douglass Judge Com Pleas Dayton O. Soldr org the church which bears his name.

TAULMAN, HERMANUS, Hamilton co, p 362

In M E cem adjoining the Pa R R just west of Davis Lane Cin O is stone w Rev he suffered (at N Y) under British tyranny for declaring himself a friend to the rights of many. (Imprisoned 11 mo at N Y)." This located his grave. Cop fr Cem recds of Hamilton co. J D.
this data: "Hermanus Taulman d Jan 22 1794 ae 64 yr 9 mo 2 da. In the American

TAYLOR, FREEGIFT, Wayne co, p 362

Pvt N J Milit 8 mos and 14 das. Enl Hunterdon co N J Feb 1777; b 1760 Hunterdon co; had dau Rebecca (mar Sory). Pens appl Wayne co June 4 1834; went to Allegheny co Pa; thence to Columbiana co O and later to Wayne co. Ref Pens Cl S 16267 N J; Rept by State D A R. (No mention of Medina co.)

TAYLOR, JAMES, Columbiana co, p 363

Mar Martha (1752-1831); chldr: Mary mar James Douglass; Jane b 1788 d 1828 mar John McGill; Jane S; Reuben b Pa 1786 mar Rachel who was b Pa in 1808; Enoch; Eligh; Jemina; David dec'd; John. Soldr d 1831; will prob 1831. (Roster must be in error). Bur old cem Springfield twp. Rept by Mrs Wilma Molsberry. Ref Mrs Wm Francis No 225856 D A R Elk City Okla. Jane Dailey.

TAYLOR, JASHER, Cuyahoga co, p 363

Capt Cleveland's Co Col Michael Jackson's Regt. Was b 1753 Ashfield Mass; mar Dolly Carr; soldr d Dover O Aug 6 1827. Ref Cleveland Herald Aug 17 1827: "Jasher Taylor ae 75 yrs at Battle of Bunker Hill Berkshire Mann and Franklin co Mass. Papers please publish." Rept by Lakewood chpt Mrs Luella Wise.

TEMPLETON, WILLIAM, Trumbull co, p 365

S A R descendants claim bur in Trumbull co not Mahoning; was b in Scotland. Rept by Mahoning co.

TERREL, ELIHU, Lorain co, p 365

B 1758 Waterbury Conn; whl living there he enl Apr 1776; pvt Capt John Lewis' Co Col Douglass Conn Regt; dischrgd Dec 25 1776. Drafted Aug 1778; servd one mo in Capt Norton's Co Col Worthington's Conn Regt. Pensd Aug 8 1833 whl living in Ridgeville Lorain co O. Rept by Nathan Perry chpt.

TERRELL, OLIVER, Lorain co, p 365

B Milford Conn; mar 1st Lidda Lewis; ref D A R Lin bk No 51493 thro son Ichabod (b 1763). Rept by Nathan Perry chpt.

THATCHER, AMOS, Preble co, p 366

Servd several enlistments as pvt in N J and Pa lines fr 1775-1781; b 1755 Hunterdon co N J mar Jermima Corwin (1765) in 1783; had a son James. Soldr d Preble co 1834; grave not found. Ref D A R lin No 124554. Ref Mary S Field Washington St Frankfort Ind; Mrs J D Runyon Eaton O. Rept by Nathan Perry chpt.

THOMPSON, ROBERT, Belmont co, p 367

Enl Apr 1777 York co Pa; Sergt in Regt commanded by Col Davis Pa Milit for 12 mos. B Sept 3 1760 nr Lancaster Pa. Lvd Richland twp 1840 ae 81. Pensd O 1833. 1801 lvd Cumberland co Pa; came to O soon aft and livd Belmont co. Ref Pens Cl S 3800 Pa. Rept by Jane Dowd Dailey.

THOMPSON, PRICE, Hamilton co, p 367

In cem at Plainfield and Cooper Roads nr Blue Ash Hamilton co O was found this data on stone: "Price Thompson d Mar 1 1842 ae 85-11-9 a native of East N J; in 1776 he enl for 6 yrs 7 mo as Rev soldr." Nr by is stone: "Molly Thompson consort of Price Thompson d Nov 12 1823 ae 60-9-0. Ref Hamilton co cem Records. Rept by Mariemont chpt D A R who mrkd grave June 1932.

THORLA, THOMAS, Noble co, p 368

Thorla is the surname. Ref p 432 Hist Noble co by L H Watkins and Co Chicago 1887. 3 sons having come to O he followed in 1828 w aged wf." Was b in Newburyport Mass. Rept by Anna Asbury Stone chpt. A pens 3-2-1833 in Morgan co as pvt and Corp Mass. J D.

THRIFT, WILLIAM, SR, Knox co, p 368

Grave mrkd 1935 by Kokosing chpt D A R. Mrs C Ewalt chr.

TIPTON, THOMAS, Champaign co, p 370

Sould have this record: Bur in Johnson cem nr Heathtown (Concord twp) Champaign co. On stone is: d Oct 7 1841 ae 111 yrs. Fr Pens Dept is rept: b nr Baltimore Md; enl Fairfax co Va. Servd various places. Resided in Va all thru Rev. Rept by Urbana chpt.

TODD, JOHN, Columbiana co*

Drummer in Conn milit. (listed for mare data). Rept by Mrs Molsberry.

TOWNSLEY, THOMAS, Greene co, p 371

Enl Cumberland co Pa 1776; Capt Thomas Clark's Co for service in the Jerseys. Drafted as wagoner 1778 and 1781. Under Capt John Nelson. Pensd Green co O 1832; mar Sarah Patterson. Ref D A R No 35519 thro dau Martha. Rept by Nathan Perry chpt.

TRAVIS, JOHN CAPT, Columbiana co, p 371

One pensd 1833 living in Hamilton co for serv as pvt N Y State Trps. J D. Mrs Molsberry states livd in Elk Run twp. He came from N Y State 1808. Was of Welsh descent and Capt in Rev War. Ref Hist Col co 1891 Vol p 176. Rept by Mrs Molsberry.

TRUMAN (Turman or Tuman), PETER, Medina ? (or Cuyahoga) co, p 373

Pvt N Y Contl. Pensr Cuyahoga co 1819. B 1763; d 9-14-1845. Ref 16th and 18th Rept N S D A R. Cop by Nathan Perry chpt. Lakewood chpt repts: In the Pilgurruh cem Bedford twp is inscript on stone: "Sally Tuman wf of Peter Tuman d Aug 6 1826 in her 66th yr."

TUCKER, JAMES, Trumbull co, p 373

Enl Va Dec 25 1776; wf b 1762; soldr b June 15 1761. Pens appl 1820 at which time had 2 gr dau. Ref Va S 40597. Rept by State D A R.

TULLES (Tullis), AARON, Miami co, p 373

Srvd as pvt Capt Hugh Stinsons Co Va Line. B 1753 N J; mar Sarah Thompson (b 1760); soldr d Miami co. Ref No 197354 D A R.

TUTTLE, CLEMENT, Ashtabula co, p 375

Date of birth should be 1756. Ref V 105 p 30 D A R Lin. Rept by J D.

TURNEY, JOHN, Franklin co, Vol 2 new record

Grave mrkd by Columbus chpt 1935. Rept by Meryl B Markley.

* Open for Research

UNDERHILL, DAVID, Huron co, p 376

Commisioned Major in 1793. Son of Capt Abraham Underhill also a Rev soldr. Chldr: Sarah Louise mar A B Beaverstock; Harriet mar Nathan Strong; Thirza mar Morse; Marrian mar Dr Junia A Jennings; Aurelia mar A W Hulett; Isaac mar Amanda Patterson (2) Lydia Gregory; David Jr mar Caroline Wilbur. Soldr was also at Ft Avery in War of 1812.

VALENTINE, GEORGE, Seneca co, p 376

Was a pvt Pa milit. Pensr in Fairfield co 8-8-1833. Name listed p 406 Wiseman's Pioneer People Fairfield co. J D.

VAN BENSCHOTEN, AARON, Erie co, p 377

Govt mrkr. Was baptized Aarlie which led to the mistake in all our histories that there was another Rev soldr named "Orlie Benschooter." Rept by Marjorie Cherry. Fr ref Hist Huron and Erie cos p 487 and 479 a sketch: He and wf came fr Neversink N Y 1816 w family Wm and Danl and a dau who mar Oliver Peak; he was middle age when he came. William purch Lot 27 R 4 when he and wf d 1833. (Their dau Esther mar Joel Fox). Mrs Benschooter d 1877. Cop by Jane Dailey.

VANDEMAN, JOHN, Ross co, p 377

Pvt in Pa Milit and Va. Res at time of enl nr Beasontown (now Uniontown) Fayette co Pa. Mar May 4 1786 Beasontown Pa to Mary Magdaline Hester (b Jan 1763; d Dec 17 1854); chldr: Joseph; Charles; Elias; Mathias mar Margaret LeGore dau of John LeGore a Rev soldr of Washington co Md and Fayette co O; Conrad; Rev Henry; Elizabeth mar —— Perrin; Nancy mar John McLean; John. In 1812 war were sons Mathias, Joseph; John; and Henry. Conrad d in that war. Rept by Clara G Mark Historian of Jacobus Westervelt chpt.

VAN FOSSEN, JACOB, Columbiana co, p 378

Was b Germany; came to Col co 1805-6. Tax collector 1780 Worcester twp Phila co. Ref Pa Arch 3 XV p 570, 572; XVI p 58, 212, 719. Rept by Mrs Molsberry.

VAN GUNDY, CHRISTIAN, Vol 2

William Horney chpt has located his grave.

VAN SWEARINGEN, JOHN, Butler co, p 379

In Rev and War of 1812. B June 4 1764 Frederick co Md nr Middletown; d June 22 1852 nr Mauds O Butler co. Son of Van Swearingen (b 1725 d 1784); mar Margaret Stull. Soldr was mar May 19 1800 to Amelia Dailey (Daly) in Md. She was b Apr 28 1783 dau of Cornelius Daly and Charity Chaney. Chldr: Drusilla; Thomas Van; Margaret; Isaac Stull; Naomi; Elizabeth; Rebecca; John D b 8-20-1819 mar Julia Ann Crane; William; Mary Ann; Washington. Ref Hist and Biog Ency of Butler co pp 590-591; Fam register Garret Van Swearingen. Rept by Mrs C H Wise of Akron to Mrs F J Dayton Akron chpt.

VIOLET, JOHN, Pike co, p 380

Pvt Capt Robt Bell's Co Col John Gibson's Va Regt. Was b Va; mar (1) 1795 Mary Taylor; one son was Samuel; soldr d Adams co. Ref No 115686. Rept by Nathan Perry chpt.

VON ETTEN, JOHN, Mahoning co, p 380

B 1773; d Feb 12 1850 ae 77 yrs War of 1812. Capt. Not the Rev soldr of that name but his nephew who was too young to serve in the Rev. Data given by Miss Eva A Scott a descendant and member of Mahoning chpt D A R who repts this correction.

VOORHEES, JACOB, Jefferson co, p 380

Steubenville chpt mrkd the grave at Center Chapel cem Jefferson co O Mar 30 1932. Rept by Mrs H E McFadden Regent.

WAGGONER, JOHN, Sandusky co, p 381

Servd in Md Dragoons; b 1758 Wassel Alsace Lorraine. Cop fr No 104064 D A R.

WALDRON, JOSEPH, Huron co, p 383

B Feb 7 1753; movd to Bristol Ontario co N Y 1801; came to O 1821; was first burial in Hartland Ridge cem. 3 sons were Sylvester; Stephen; Joseph Jr. All servd in War of 1812.

WALTERS (Watters), JOHN, Guernsey co, p 385

Pvt Pa Contl; pensr 1819 Guernsey co. In Feb 1823 appld for pens Guernsey co. Servd Pa line 1782 Capt Seely Col Wm Butler; later 3rd Regt Col Richard Butler. Mar Katherine ——; chldr: Betsey Rodney; Barbara Jones; Polly; George; John. Was shoemaker and weaver. Ref Pa Arch III pp 314, 717, 1834. Cop by Jane Dailey.

WARD, JARED (or Gerard), Erie co*

Quaker cem Milan twp. Family mrkr. In all our histories he is spoken of as a Rev soldr. Not yet found his record. B 1767; d 1857. Rept by Marjorie Cherry.

WARD, WILLIAM SR, Champaign co, p 387

Under direction of Alice Gaumer chpt chr Urbana chpt convinced that Wm Ward's burial place as history related was in error began a search. The discovery by Otho Robinson as he was plowing along the edge of a wild plum thicket when his tractor plumped into a hole. In the hole Robinson found several human bones. Further investigation uncovered the stone mrkr 2 ft underground on which was engraved the names of Col Ward his wf and two sons. The Sultzbaugh farm was old homestead of the Col Ward family and here the search began and ended. Col Ward laid out the city of Urbana in 1805 on a 160 acre tract. This discovery is claimed to be one of the most important in local historical investigation and plans are now being made to restore the grave and headstne and place a suitable mrkr on the site.

WARREN, EDWARD, Green co, p 387

Pvt Contl and Pa. Pens 1819 11-3 in Green co. Servd 16 mos. Was ae 68 in 1819; mar Susanna who d Jan 1822"; chldr: Samuel 16 and Lydia 9 in 1822. Pens discontinued 11-29-1822. Ref Contl Pens S 10264. Rept by State D A R.

WARREN, JOHN, Pike co*

John and bro Solomon said to have been Rev soldrs; d in Jackson twp Pike co O in 1817 and 20 (respct); originally fr Md; John livd in N C aft war; movd to Pike co abt 1811.

WARRINGTON, WILLIAM, Delaware co, p 388

Mar Nancy Holland (1771-1850) his third wf. Ref Vol 24 p 288 D A R No 23824 thro a Real dau Mrs Julia Ann Weaver. Rept by Nathan Perry chpt.

WARTH, GEORGE, ? co, p 388

Whr in O did he die (1812) or is bur? Hannah Berry his wf; three D A R proven lines on sons George Harrison; and John. (J D).

WATERS, BENJAMIN J, Ashtabula co, p 388

Name found listed as Watrous, Benjamin; pvt Conn St Trps pens 1833 Ashtabula co. J D.

WEAVER, CHRISTOPHER, Champaign co, p 370

B 1761; native of Bucks co Pa; settled in Ky in 1792; came to O 1802. Rept by Urbana chpt.

WEAVER, JOHN, ? co*

Pvt in Capt Heath's Independent Co Va Inf 1777. Was b Germania Va; d 1837 Madison co (no state given — was it Ohio ?); mar Kiziah Grenman; a son Wm mar Nancy Ford.

* Open for Research

WEAVER, WILLIAM, Champaign co, p 390

B 1760 Bucks co Pa; fought in Rev in Ky in 1792; came to O in 1802; located in Champaign co 1807; mar Mary Kiger of Md abt 1783; had 15 chldr. Rept by Urbana chpt. Ref "Va Milit in Rev" p 294 is listed as Rev soldr liv in Champaign co O ae 74. Cop by Jane Dailey.

WEBB, DAVID, Trumbull co, p 390

Pensr 1828 as sergt in 3rd Regt Conn Line. J D.

WEBB, JOHN, Columbiana co*

Came fr Harford co Md in 1805; with 12 chldr. Had son James who mar Kezie dau of Philip Bowman. By Mrs Molsberry.

WEESE, GEORGE, Jackson co, p 391

On Aug 4 1904 an order was issued to correct serv of George Weese of Pa to Va. Appl pens in Jackson co Apr 22 1834 resd at Jackson co ae 70 as he thinks for pens of Act Cong June 7 1832. Ent ser 1781; leaving Hampshire co on tours of 6 mo; under Capt Jos Berry, etc et al service. Hon dischg at Winchester Va. Cop by Jane Dailey.

WEISS, JACOB, Mahoning co, p 391

Name may be found as Rev soldr but he was too young for service. Rept by Miss Kyle, Youngstown. Filed here to avoid future listing. See Jacob Weist p 391 Vol 1.

WELCH, FELIX, Wyandot co, p 391

Upper Sandusky news paper carries complete sketch of this soldr whose grave was mrkd in Mexico cem by Col William Crawford chpt on Decoration Day 1935. Mrs Russell Frantz regent of Dolly Todd Madison gave the sketch of the soldr and his fam of 6 sons and 4 daus; and Mrs R W Main reviewed soldr's life. Rept by Mrs H H Sears Regent.

WELDON, JESSE, Champaign co, p 391

The grave on lot of Joel Reed in Oak Dale cem Urbana. Rept by Alice Gaumer Urbana chpt.

WELLMAN, ABRAHAM, Lorain co, p 392

B in Lyndesborough N H in 1762; enl Apr 10 1777. On acct of leg wounds trnsfrd to Invalid Corps as Corp; sergt in 1781. Pensd Apr 27 1818. D Oct 31 1829 res Russia Lorain co O. Mar in Medford Mass May 17 1781 Rebecca Pearson. She was pensd June 2 1838 Henrietta Lorain co O ae 75. Soldr referred to his chldr: (1820) Elizabeth ae 17; Fanny 15; Ruth 13; gr-child Dolly Clark ae 8. Ref Pens Cl. Cop by Nathan Perry chpt. S A R mrkr placed on grave prob by Western Reserve chpt.

WELLS, ROBERT, Erie co, p 392

Bur Maple Grove cem S of Vermilion; family mrkr. Located 1933 by Martha Pitkin chpt.

WESTON, JOHN, Summit co, p 394

No 24272 thro a son Francis gives b 1755 d 1857. Cop by Nathan Perry com. (Roster date of 1839 prob copd fr stone which could be easily misread. J D).

WHEELER, ASA SR, Huron co, p 394

Drafted as teamster. Came to Trumbull co; thence to Clarksfield 1818 whr he d. Chldr: Lemuel and Anson movd to Kansas; Asa Jr mar Olive Minor; Asa Sr mar mother of Olive Minor (2nd wf of soldr ?); other chldr: William; Bethia; Lovina; Lucretia; Mary Ann; Lucy; and Betsy. Ref Firelands Pioneers O S Vol 9 p 52; Williams Hist p 277. Rept by Marjorie Cherry.

* *Open for Research*

WHEELER, SAMUEL, Hamilton co (not Lucas), p 395*

Research Com of Ursula Wolcott chpt in attempting to verify statement of D A R Lin bk have proof fr descendants and Bible recds that he is bur nr Williams Ferry O (nr Cincinnati) and not Lucas co.

WHIPPLE, ELIJAH, Trumbull co, p 395

(Correct spelling). Was pensr in Gustavus twp ae 89. J D.

WHITMER, PETER, Perry co, p 397

Frequently mentioned in "Linns" annals of Buffalo Valley. (A misprint in bk). Jane Dailey.

WHITRIDGE, JOSIAH, Washington co (?)

Was one of the 16 Rev Soldr of the 48 Pioneers who landed at Marietta 1788. A pvt Mass service. Copd by J D.

WICKERSHAM, PETER, Washington co, p 397

B Washington co Pa 1756; d Adams co 1841; accd to D A R No 27063 thro dau Mary; and No 22326 thro dau Nancy. Cop by Nathan Perry chpt.

WILL, GEORGE, Vinton co, p 399

Remains (few) removd fr Ross co to new cem McArthur Vinton co whr a marble mrkr w bronze tablet was erected by the descendants and dedicated by impressive ceremony 1931. Rept by Jane Dowd Dailey.

WILCOX, ELNATHAN, Geauga co*

D Huntsburg Geauga co; grave located by New Conn D A R. Ref 5th Rept N S D A R p 388. Cop by Nathan Perry chpt. No authentic service yet found.

WILEY, SAMUEL, Coshocton co, p 398

Servd Mass Contl; burial rept at Keene O, Coshocton co. J D.

WILLIAMS, JOHN, p 400

Servd Pa line; when mustered out 1781 recd depreciation pay. D Ohio 1814; mar Margaret Taylor. Ref No 8215 thro son Thomas; filed for research on any "John" found in O. (Delaware co is suggested). Rept by com of Nathan Perry chpt.

WILLIAMS, THOMAS, Hamilton co, p 400

D 1-25-1826 ae 81 (Pa Arch). Rept by Mary Steinmetz. Compare also with No 104107 D A R. J D.

WILLIAMSON, JOHN, Montgomery co, p 401

B N J May 1764; d and bur Phillipsburg O Feb 19 1854. Servd Samuel Meeker's Light Horse Co Elizabethtown N J. Chldr: Joseph; Henry; Jeremiah; John W; William; Betsy; Hannah; Sara. Rept by Mrs W K Sterline. Org Regt Capt Jas Riley Celina. Grave mrkd by Lewis Boyer chpt D A R of Sidney O 1935.

WILSON, WILLIAM, Trumbull co, p 404

Resided in Trumbull co 1840 ae 68. Pensr 1819 for serv in Pa Contl. Ref Pa Arch list of Ohio. J D.

WISE (Weise), JACOB, Mahoning co, p 406

Is bur in Christian Ch cem Four Mile Run and is not Rev soldr whose record is here given. Jacob Wise was b in Lehigh co Pa Jan 2 1786; came to Trumbull, now Mahoning co in 1810. Was son of Johannes Weiss a Rev soldr and early settler of Lehigh co Pa. Rept by Miss Etta Kyle Youngstown fr fam records.

WITMER, PETER, Perry co, p 397

No doubt a misspelling for Whitmer, Peter. Said by C A Fisher to have been a Rev soldr who pioneered in Snyder co Pa. Ref given to him by Anna M Priest. Rept by Hetuck chpt. Witmer Peter found as pioneer Snyder co Pa is no doubt Whitmer p 397.

* *Open for Research*

WOOD, JOHN, Pickaway co, p 408

Grave mrkd 1932 by Pickaway Plains chpt.

WYETH, JOSEPH, ? co*

Pvt Mass. Found listed in Ohio. Research located no def dates.

YEAGER (Yager or Zager), HENRY, Mahoning co, p 412

Correction: not the Henry Yeager who servd from Berks co Pa; but the son of John or Johannes Yeager who servd from Lancaster co Pa and d in Pa Dec 1 1846 ae 69 yrs and wf Susanna d Apr 24 1855 ae 80 yrs. Could not have servd in Rev. Rept by Mahoning chpt.

YAGER (or Yeager), JOHN (or Jonathan), Mahoning co*

Since service p 412 Vol 1 does not belong to Henry Yeager (accd to recent research b 1846) it may belong to this John.

YOUNG, GEORGE, Wyandot co, p 413

Grave mrkd by Col William Crawford chpt May 1933 in Enoch Thomas cem Marseilles.

YOUNG, GEORGE AND JAMES, Portage co*

In 1811 Elizabeth and George Young, and Hannah wf of James Young, and families came from Conn to Portage co in Ox carts p 155 "Pioneer Women Western Reserve. Cop by J D.

YOUNG, JACOB, Fayette co, p 413

He is the same soldr as one filed new this vol 2 in Knox co. Rept by Kokosing chpt Mrs Ewalt chr. Miss Etta Kyle Youngstown repts one Jacob Young (Mahoning co) relative of Solomon came to Cornersburg abt 1850.

YOUNG, MORGAN, Delaware co, p 413

Pvt N Y Milit. Was b Oct 1752 Morris co N J. Pensd 1833; servd 9 mo. Res Delaware co Nov 19 1832 Berkshire twp. Res Morris co N J during Rev. Enl Spring of 1776. Aft Rev res abt 20 yrs in Morris co N J and then removd to Wyoming co (Pa ?); aft 15 yrs (abt 1816) he left that country and removd to Delaware co whr res in 1832. Ref S 4741 N J. Rept by State D A R.

ZANE, ELIZABETH, Belmont co, p 414

She was a sister of Ebenezer Zane. Livd for many yrs 2 mi above Bridgeport O. Heroine at siege of Fort Henry W Va 1782 whr she ran the gauntlet before the amazed Indians attacking, tied a tablecloth of powder around her waist, and fleet of foot, returned unharmed amid their volleys. She was b 1766 Westmoreland co Va; in 1786 mar (1) Ephraim McLaughlin; (2) —— Clark. Nancy (V 121 p 232 D A R Lin) and Mary (V 77 p 287 D A R Lin) were two of her chldr. She d at Martins Ferry O 1828 and suitable memorials have been erected to her memory. Ebenezer Zane mar Elizabeth McCulloch (McCullough) and it was his wf Elizabeth Zane who d 1814 ae 66 yrs. Ref Howes Hist Collections p 314; Belmont co Hist. Rept by Jane Dailey.

* Open for Research

www.ingramcontent.com/pod-product-compliance
Lightning Source LLC
Chambersburg PA
CBHW030233030426
42336CB00009B/85